THE CAMBRIDGE HISTORY OF
AMERICAN MUSIC

The Cambridge History of American Music celebrates the richness and diversity of America's musical life, in all its many manifestations. It is the first study of music in the United States to be written by a team of scholars: its twenty chapters have been contributed by nineteen authors, all experts in their chosen fields. American music is an intricate tapestry of many cultures, and the History reveals this wide array of influences from Native, European, African, Asian, and other sources. The History begins with a survey of the music of Native Americans and then explores the social, historical, and cultural events of musical life in the period until 1900. Other contributors examine the growth and influence of popular musics, including film and stage music, jazz, rock, and immigrant, folk, and regional musics. The volume also includes valuable chapters on twentieth-century art music, including the experimental, serial, and tonal traditions.

THE CAMBRIDGE HISTORY OF
MUSIC

The Cambridge History of Music comprises a new group of reference works concerned with significant strands of musical scholarship. The individual volumes are self-contained and include histories of music examined by century as well as the history of opera, music theory and American music. Each volume is written by a team of experts under a specialist editor and represents the latest musicological research.

THE CAMBRIDGE
HISTORY OF
AMERICAN
MUSIC

*

EDITED BY
DAVID NICHOLLS

CAMBRIDGE
UNIVERSITY PRESS

PUBLISHED BY THE PRESS SYNDICATE OF THE UNIVERSITY OF CAMBRIDGE
The Pitt Building, Trumpington Street, Cambridge CB2 1RP, United Kingdom

CAMBRIDGE UNIVERSITY PRESS
The Edinburgh Building, Cambridge CB2 2RU, UK   http://www.cup.cam.ac.uk
40 West 20th Street, New York, NY 10011–4211, USA   http://www.cup.org
10 Stamford Road, Oakleigh, Melbourne 3166, Australia

© Cambridge University Press 1998

First published 1998

Printed in the United Kingdom at the University Press, Cambridge

Typeset in Renard *(The Enschedé Font Foundry)* 9.5/13 pt, in QuarkXPress® [SE]

A catalogue record for this book is available from the British Library

ISBN 0 521 45429 8 hardback

Contents

PART TWO

Notes on contributors

STEPHEN BANFIELD, Elgar Professor of Music at the University of Birmingham, is author of *Sensibility and English Song* (1985), the award-winning *Sondheim's Broadway Musicals* (1993), and *Gerald Finzi: An English Composer* (1997). He is also editor of *Music in Britain: The Twentieth Century* (1995).

JONATHAN W. BERNARD is Professor of Music Theory in the School of Music at the University of Washington, Seattle. He is the author of *The Music of Edgard Varèse* (1987) and the editor of *Elliott Carter: Collected Essays and Lectures, 1937–1995* (1996).

PHILIP V. BOHLMAN is Associate Professor of Music and Jewish Studies at the University of Chicago. An ethnomusicologist, he has done fieldwork in the Middle East, Europe, and the United States. Author of *The Study of Folk Music in the Modern World* (1988), he is also coeditor (with Ronald Radano) of *Music and the Racial Imagination* (forthcoming).

WILLIAM BROOKS, composer and musicologist, teaches at the University of Illinois. His music and writings are interconnected, both frequently focusing on aspects of America's musical experience. Recent compositions include *Sweet Steel Suite* for steel band; among his recent writings is "John Cage and History," which appeared in *Perspectives of New Music* in 1993.

MICHAEL BROYLES is Professor of Music and American History at Penn State University. Author of *"Music of the Highest Class": Elitism and Populism in Antebellum Boston* (1992), he has recently turned his attention to the twentieth century, working on Ives and other American mavericks for a forthcoming book, *Mavericks and Other Traditions in American Music*.

DALE COCKRELL is the author of *Demons of Disorder: Early Blackface Minstrels and Their World* (1997), *Excelsior: Journals of the Hutchinson Family Singers, 1842–1846* (1989), other books, and numerous articles on nineteenth-century American popular music. He is Professor of Musicology and American and Southern Studies at Vanderbilt University.

NYM COOKE studied with Richard Crawford and lectures on American music history at the College of the Holy Cross in Worcester, Massachusetts. His edition of the music of American psalmodist Timothy Swan was published by A–R Editions as volume 6 in the series *Music of the United States of America*.

JACQUELINE COGDELL DJEDJE, Professor of Ethnomusicology at UCLA, has conducted fieldwork in West Africa and Jamaica, and among African Americans in the United States. She is author of several monographs, editor of a number of anthologies, has published in many scholarly journals, and is coeditor of *California Soul: Music of African Americans in California* (1998).

DAVID JOYNER is Associate Professor of Jazz Studies at the University of North Texas and is also active as a freelance pianist and singer. Author of *American Popular Music* (1993) and numerous articles, he is currently editing arrangements written for the Claude Thornhill Orchestra between 1941 and 1950 by Gil Evans and Gerry Mulligan.

KATE VAN WINKLE KELLER is executive director of The Sonneck Society for American Music. Author of bibliographies and studies of eighteenth-century popular music and social dance, she was coeditor of two projects supported by the National Endowment for the Humanities: *The National Tune Index: 18th-Century Secular Music* (1980) and *The Performing Arts in Colonial American Newspapers, 1690–1783* (1997).

JOHN KOEGEL is Assistant Professor of Music at the University of Missouri-Columbia. A specialist in Hispanic music of the Southwest and the music of Mexico, he has published articles on these topics in American, Mexican, and Spanish journals. He is currently writing a book about Mexican-American music in nineteenth-century California.

VICTORIA LINDSAY LEVINE is an Associate Professor at Colorado College, where she teaches ethnomusicology and Southwest studies. A specialist in Native American musical cultures, she has also conducted research on Latino musics in the United States and is an active performer of Balinese music.

JEFFREY MAGEE is Assistant Professor of Music at Indiana University. He has contributed articles to the *Journal of the American Musicological Society*, *American Music*, and *Lenox Avenue*. From 1993 to 1997, he served as Executive Editor of *Music of the United States of America* (*MUSA*).

DAVID NICHOLLS is Professor of Music at Keele University. Author of *American Experimental Music, 1890–1940* (1990) and of articles on a variety of topics – including Henry Cowell, the New York School, and transethnicism in

American radical music – he has also edited *The Whole World of Music: A Henry Cowell Symposium* (1997).

STEPHEN PELES is a composer and theorist with degrees from Princeton University, the University of Connecticut, and Rutgers University. His works have been performed in both Europe and America, and he has published in the areas of both tonal and post-tonal theory. An editor of *Perspectives of New Music*, he currently teaches at the University of Alabama.

KATHERINE K. PRESTON is Associate Professor of Music at the College of William and Mary in Williamsburg, Virginia. Specializing primarily in the history of music and musical culture in nineteenth-century America, she has published extensively on various aspects of this topic, focusing particularly on nineteenth-century American musical theatre, including opera performance history.

RONALD RADANO is Associate Professor of Music and Afro-American Studies at the University of Wisconsin at Madison. He is author of *New Musical Figurations: Anthony Braxton's Cultural Critique* (1993), and is currently pursuing a project on the idea of "black music" in American social history.

LARRY STARR is a Professor of Music History at the University of Washington, Seattle. Specializing in twentieth-century and American music, he is author of *A Union of Diversities: Style in the Music of Charles Ives* (1992) and coauthor (with Chris Waterman) of the forthcoming *Themes and Streams: A Journey through American Popular Music*.

ROBERT WALSER is Associate Professor of Musicology at UCLA. Author of *Running with the Devil: Power, Gender, and Madness in Heavy Metal Music* (1993), *Keeping Time: Readings in Jazz History* (1998), and of various articles on popular music topics, he is also editor of *American Music* and coeditor of Wesleyan's Music/Culture series.

Editor's preface

If there is a single feature which both characterizes and defines American music, it is diversity. Indeed, commentators and historians have increasingly recognized that, in America, almost uniquely among the world's nations, the many manifestations of music – from simple to complex, popular to recherché, concrete to abstract – are interdependent rather than independent, inclusive rather than exclusive. It is this interrelated diversity of musical experience which the *Cambridge History of American Music* (henceforth *CHAM*) seeks principally to celebrate.

CHAM has two other aims. The first – which has been achieved through a precise series of editorial checks and balances – is to represent the realities of America's music history as faithfully as possible. Thus (to employ H. Wiley Hitchcock's terms) the cultivated tradition is afforded significantly less prominence here than the various vernacular traditions. Also implicit throughout *CHAM* is the understanding that music in America has resulted not from the activities of a single culturally dominant group, but rather from the actions and interactions of a wide array of Native, European, African, Asian, and other peoples.

CHAM's second aim is to reflect the diversity of American music by studying it from a multiplicity of viewpoints. Thus no fewer than nineteen authors – all experts in their various fields – have contributed *CHAM*'s twenty chapters. Differing approaches have been adopted, different writing styles utilized, and diverging views expressed; the overall effect, I believe, is one of considerable freshness. One consequence of this multi-author approach is that each chapter is to some extent self-contained, telling its own story from its own perspective, and having its own bibliography and references. However, each chapter is also an integral part of the whole volume: where appropriate, readers are directed to other chapters, and the bibliography should be understood as a single, multi-section research tool rather than an assemblage of unrelated lists. Furthermore, one of my principal roles as *CHAM*'s editor has been to coordinate coverage by eliminating unnecessary overlaps and omissions between chapters, as far as possible. Of course, given the nature and scope of the volume, both inevitably occur to some extent: indeed, overlapping has been encouraged where a given topic seemed likely to benefit by being viewed from two or more perspectives. In the case of potential omissions, there have been numerous occasions during *CHAM*'s gestation when I have woken in a sweat, thinking "What about the Moravians?" (see chapter 4), "What about barbershop?" (see chapter 11), "What about the blues?" (see chapters 5, 11, and 14) and so on. The train-spotting fraternity will no doubt point to overlaps, omissions, and particular emphases with which they disagree; but overall, I believe that *CHAM* has achieved its goals. Readers may confidently consult individual chapters, groups of related chapters, or the whole volume, for a wealth of contemporary, informed, detailed, and in many cases provocative scholarship.

CHAM is arranged largely topically, with topics ordered mainly chronologically. One exception to this lies in the pair of themed overview chapters, 2 and 10, each of which looks forward as well as backward. A few general points: where they appear, octave-specific pitches are referred to via the Helmholtz system (i.e. C_1–B_1, C–B, c–b, c^1–b^1, etc., where c^1 = middle C). Octave-unspecific pitches simply use upper case (i.e. C, E♭, F♯). Tonalities use upper case for major (i.e. D major, D♭) and lower case for minor (i.e. b minor, c♯). References for quotations are via the author–date system; other bibliographical and discographic information (including published scores) has also been included where deemed appropriate by individual authors. Given the increasing availability and accessibility of scores, transcriptions, and especially recordings, relatively few actual music examples appear in *CHAM*, except where they are integral to the discussion. However, the text includes copious reference to the full range of musical experiences, from the individual to the collective, the fixed to the improvised, the recorded to the live, the planned to the spontaneous, and the enduring to the ephemeral.

Many of my coauthors would no doubt wish to express their thanks to those who have assisted them in their assignments; unfortunately, space prevents such a list appearing here. However, there are a number of individuals without whom the volume as a whole would have suffered. At the contracting stage, Richard Crawford, H. Wiley Hitchcock, and Judith McCullough all provided invaluable advice regarding possible authors. The soundness of their judgment is demonstrated in the chapters that follow. At CUP, Victoria Cooper (whose idea *CHAM* was) has been a constant (in both senses of that word) friend and adviser, while her assistant, Teresa Sheppard, has responded with infinite patience to a plethora of requests, both trivial and vital. During production, copy-editor Alan Finch, indexer Margaret Christie, and production controller Caroline Murray were all efficient and thorough. My wife, Tamar, and our children, Benjamin and Daisy, have given unquestioning support throughout *CHAM*'s gestation, as have our respective families. The same could be said of a fourth family – my colleagues at Keele – who have also been remarkably tolerant of requests for research support, financial and otherwise. Finally, especial thanks go to my coauthors, with whom it has been a privilege and a pleasure to work, and from whose contributions to this volume I have learned so much.

DAVID NICHOLLS
Keele University

· PART ONE ·

American Indian musics,
past and present

—

VICTORIA LINDSAY LEVINE

The history of American music begins with American Indians, who were the original inhabitants of North America. Their distant ancestors migrated from northeast Asia across the Bering land bridge and settled in the Americas some 15,000 years ago. Through time, Native Americans developed extraordinarily diverse lifeways as they adapted to a wide range of environments and climates. The first sustained contacts between Native Americans and Europeans began in the late fifteenth century, and by the early seventeenth century, Europeans had established permanent colonies in North America. Indian–White relations before 1800 were characterized by conflict over land, fraudulent treaties, and a steadily increasing imbalance of power. Native American social and economic conditions deteriorated during the nineteenth century, as the people were removed from their homelands, confined to reservations, and subjected to aggressive but unsuccessful acculturation programs. Misunderstanding and prejudice continued in the twentieth century, but Indian political activism since the 1960s resulted in legislation that supports tribal self-determination and religious freedom. Since the 1970s, Native Americans have experienced cultural renewal, and Indian identities remain strong and vibrant.

American Indians are the heirs to an enduring musical heritage that is as impressive in its modern richness and variety as in its historical depth and continuity. Each of the more than 200 tribes now in existence has its own historic musical culture, with unique repertories, styles, instruments, theories, and practices. American Indians also compose, perform, and listen to a wide spectrum of recently developed native musics, as well as European and American art, popular, and folk musics. Indeed, given the complexity of contemporary musical life, it is appropriate to ask what it is that makes American Indian music distinctively Indian. This chapter commences to answer that question through an introduction to Native American musics in both historical and contemporary perspectives. It begins with a survey of the historic musics found in different regions of Native North America, followed by a more detailed exploration of the musical culture of one particular Indian community and its efforts to preserve a traditional repertory. The third section considers historical dynamics in Native American music, including pantribalism, syncretism, new musics, and musical revitalization. The chapter concludes with a discussion of the unique contributions American Indians have made to the musical life of the United States.

A musical map of Native North America

In a global sense, American Indian musics are distinctive in their nearly exclusive emphasis on singing rather than instrumental music, in their unique approach to song texts (which tend to feature vocables or non-lexical syllables rather than words) and in their tangible connection to spirituality. Some indigenous systems of musical notation have been documented, but the vast majority of American Indian musics are preserved and transmitted through oral tradition.[1] Beyond these broad similarities, the many discrete tribal repertories in existence constitute a musical mosaic that eludes generalization. For this reason, scholars have developed a hypothetical map of Native North America that facilitates a concise survey of the musical styles, genres, and instruments found among American Indians (cf. Nettl 1954). The musical map is based on cultural and geographic relationships; each area on the map includes many separate, discrete tribes that are similar to one another in certain aspects of language, economy, social structure, material culture, and religious orientation. The musical map places the native peoples of the United States and Canada in six main areas: Eastern Woodlands, Plains, Great Basin, Southwest, Northwest Coast, and Arctic.

The Eastern Woodlands

The Eastern Woodlands area extends from the Atlantic Ocean to the Mississippi River, and from New Brunswick to the Gulf of Mexico. The tribes within this vast region may be divided into three musical subareas: the Northeast (e.g. Haudenosaunee-Iroquois, Wabanaki, Delaware), Southeast (e.g. Muskogee-Creek, Cherokee, Choctaw), and Western Great Lakes

---

1. The term musical notation is used loosely here to include any kind of formal mnemonic device for remembering song texts or the number and order of songs in a ceremony, including pictographs and notched sticks; for information on these kinds of systems in Native North America, see Collaer 1973, Densmore 1910, Dewdney 1975, Fenton 1950, Newcomb 1956, Rafinesque 1954, and Vetromile 1886.

region (e.g. Chippewa, Menominee, Potawatomi). The major language families of this area are Iroquoian, Algonkian, and Muskhogean. Today, Eastern Woodlands Indians perform traditional musics in many contexts, such as the seasonal thanksgiving ceremonies of the Iroquois Longhouse, the annual Green Corn ceremony of many southeastern tribes, private curing rituals, and folkloric demonstrations.

Eastern Woodlands singers generally use a moderately relaxed and open vocal style, emphasizing the middle and lower tessitura. In some northeastern styles, vocal pulsations are used to articulate phrase endings, while in the southeast, special vocal techniques such as rapid vibrato or yodeling may be used. Aspirated attacks and releases as well as vocal glides are common throughout this area. Most Eastern Woodlands song texts consist primarily of vocables (syllables that do not carry lexical meaning), although some lines of lexical text may be heard in communal dance songs, curing songs, and other genres. Some dance songs from this area are performed as solos or duets by one or two head singers, but most feature antiphony or call and response. The leader sings a short melodic phrase to which the dancers respond in unblended unison, the women doubling the men at the octave in some songs. Within Native North America, the use of antiphony is unique to the Eastern Woodlands.

Eastern Woodlands songs employ a variety of strophic, sectional, and iterative forms. The songs in strophic form often begin with an introduction, which may be performed as a solo by the head singer. Frequent metric changes within songs, syncopation, and *sforzandos* are rhythmic characteristics in this area. Various scale types are used in the Eastern Woodlands, although there is a predilection for anhemitonic scales with four, five, or six pitches. Communal dance songs from this area tend to employ melodic contours that descend or undulate with a descending inflection, usually with an ambitus of an octave or more. However, certain genres, such as medicine songs, feature a predominantly level melody with a narrow range and a scale of three or fewer pitches.

Many kinds of idiophones and drums are indigenous to the Eastern Woodlands. The most widespread idiophones in this area are container rattles, which are made of cow horn, tree bark, gourds, turtle shells, or coconut shells, depending upon the tribe and musical genre. Among some southeastern tribes, the head women dancers, called shell-shakers, wear leg rattles made of clusters of turtle shells, or more recently, evaporated milk cans. Water drums, double-headed hand drums, and cylinder drums accompany certain traditional styles from this area. As is the case throughout Indian America, drums are always played with a drumstick, rather than with the performer's hand. Other instruments from the Eastern Woodlands area include flageolets, flutes, and whistles, which are played as solo instruments.

The Plains

The Plains area reaches from the Mississippi River to the Rocky Mountains, and from south-central Canada to Texas, including tribes of the Northern Plains (e.g. Blackfoot, Cheyenne, Lakota), Southern Plains (e.g. Comanche, Kiowa, Osage), and Prairie (e.g. Winnebago, Prairie Potawatomi, Sauk and Fox). The predominant language families in this area include Algonkian, Siouan, and Caddoan. The primary context for the performance of Plains music today is the powwow; other contexts include communal religious ceremonies such as the Sun Dance, individual ceremonies such as medicine bundle rituals, social dance events, and personal prayer songs.

Plains singers employ a tense and nasal vocal quality, emphasizing the high range in the Northern Plains style and a somewhat lower range in the Southern Plains style. Singers from this area use heavy vocal pulsations on sustained tones, particularly at cadences and phrase endings, which may be further articulated by portamentos. Plains singers also perform extramusical vocalizations, such as stylized shouts or cries, to embellish dance songs. Plains song texts may be composed entirely of vocables, or may include some lines of lexical text framed by and interspersed with vocables. Songs from this area are performed in unblended monophony; in mixed ensembles, the women usually sing one octave higher than the men.

The musical structure most typical of the Plains area is a kind of strophic form known among music scholars as incomplete repetition form. This form originated in songs associated with men's ritual organizations, but it is now used extensively in powwow songs. In incomplete repetition form, the strophe contains two sections. The first section begins with a short solo, known as the lead or push-up, which is sung by the ensemble's leader. The other singers then repeat or vary the lead; this is called the second. The lead and second together constitute the first section of the strophe. The second section of the strophe, called the chorus, consists of two or more musical phrases sung in unison. The chorus is repeated once, completing the strophe. A strophe having two phrases in its chorus might be diagrammed as follows: AA′ BC BC. The strophe as a whole is repeated several times during the performance of a particular song. At the conclusion of the song, the final two phrases of the chorus may be reiterated as a coda; the singers call this the tail.

Plains songs in incomplete repetition form begin in the highest part of the singer's vocal range and descend by steps, cadencing on the lowest pitch at the end of the chorus. Scholars use the term terraced descent to describe this kind of cascading melodic contour. Songs of this type exceed an octave in range and tend to employ anhemitonic four- or five-note scales. A drum supports the underlying pulse of the song in steady duple beats, but the tempo of the drumbeat differs from the tempo of the song, which enhances the rhythmic complexity of the performance. At certain points in the song, the drummers alternate strongly accented beats with weak beats. These are called honor beats or heart beats; they are performed to show respect for the dancers or to honor the memory of a person invoked by the song text.

The most common musical instrument played throughout the Plains region is the single-headed frame drum, which resembles a large tambourine without jingles; this drum is played with a padded stick. A large bass drum, also played with padded sticks, accompanies powwow songs. Wind instruments from the Plains area include the end-blown flute, or flageolet, generally played as a solo instrument, and whistles made of metal or eagle bone, which are used in powwows as well as in certain ritual contexts. Container rattles made from gourds, or more recently, from aluminum salt shakers, as well as bells, tin jingles, and similar items sewn onto dancers' outfits, exemplify the kinds of idiophone used in Plains music.

The Great Basin

The Great Basin area stretches from the eastern slope of the Rocky Mountains to the Sierra Nevada and Cascade Range, and from the Fraser River to the Colorado River Basin; tribes from this area include the Ute, Paiute, and Shoshoni. Uto-Aztecan is the major language family of this region. Some contexts for the performance of Great Basin music include seasonal first-fruits ceremonies such as the Ute Bear Dance or the Paiute Round Dance, life-cycle rituals such as the Washo Girl's Puberty ceremony, shamanistic healing rituals, hand games, and storytelling.

In the Great Basin area, the preferred vocal quality is open and relaxed, emphasizing the middle part of the singer's range. Singers in this region do not employ vocal pulsation in traditional genres; instead, the singers ornament vocal lines through a range of special breathing techniques, such as aspirated attacks and releases. Communal dance songs in traditional genres are performed in moderately blended monophony and are unaccompanied, which is rare among Native North Americans. Another distinctive feature of music from this region is the structure and style of song lyrics. Songs performed in the context of storytelling involve unusually long, detailed lexical texts, while songs from seasonal ceremonials employ subtle imagery and an aesthetic sense that is comparable to haiku poetry. As in other American Indian musics, vocables may be interspersed within or between words, or may constitute the entire song text.

Music from the Great Basin typically features short melodies with a narrow range (smaller than an octave); scales with three, four, or five notes are common. Melodies tend to undulate, sometimes with a descending inflection. Most songs have a limited number of different rhythmic values, but singers perform barely perceptible rhythmic variations through the use of special breathing techniques. A variety of iterative and strophic forms are used in Great Basin music. Most seasonal Round Dance songs employ a form that scholars call paired phrase structure, which is unique to this area. In paired phrase structure, each phrase of melody and text is sung twice and alternates with one or two other phrases. A song of this type might be diagrammed as follows: AA BB CC AA BB CC, etc.

Compared to other areas of Indian America, relatively few instruments are used in historic genres of Great Basin music. The most distinctive instruments from this region, such as the musical bow, have been associated with shamanistic curing rituals. Shamans more commonly accompany curing ceremonies with whistles as well as different kinds of rattles, including container rattles made from gourds or rawhide and strung rattles made from deer dew claws suspended from sticks. Other idiophones from the Great Basin include striking sticks, used to accompany hand game songs, and notched rasps, played with an inverted basket resonator to accompany the Ute Bear Dance. Historically, the most common drum in this area was the shallow, single-headed hand drum. In the northeastern part of the region, where Plains influence is strong, the flageolet is played as a solo instrument and eagle bone whistles are used during the Sun Dance.

The Southwest

The Southwest area covers New Mexico, Arizona, and southern California. Two main musical subareas coexist in the Southwest: Pueblo (e.g. Hopi, Zuni, Rio Grande Pueblos) and Athabascan (Navajo and Apache). Most native languages spoken in this area derive from the Tewa, Tiwa,

Towa, Keresan, Uto-Aztecan, and Athabascan language families. Southwest Indians perform music in the context of communal agricultural ceremonies such as Hopi kachina dances, curing or life-cycle rituals such as Navajo Chantways or the Apache Girl's Puberty Ceremony, Catholic feast day observances among the Eastern Pueblos, tribal fairs, and informal domestic activities.

Pueblo singers cultivate an open, relaxed vocal quality, emphasizing the lower tessitura; ceremonial songs are performed by large choruses, singing in precisely blended monophony. Pueblo ceremonial songs have long, intricate poetic texts, framed by and interspersed with vocables. By contrast, Athabascan vocal style is tense, nasal, and exploits the singer's full vocal range. Athabascan singers embellish melodic lines with subtle vocal ornaments as well as with stylized shouts that are imbued with symbolic significance; group singing features unblended monophony. The structure and content of Athabascan song texts varies according to musical genre, but most songs combine vocables with lexical text.

Pueblo ceremonial songs are composed on a large scale and are systematically integrated with both choreography and sacred space. These songs tend to have five main sections, the overall plan of which may be diagrammed as AABBA. Each section contains a number of discrete musical and textual phrases, and is articulated by patterned pauses as well as by introductory and cadential formulas. Pueblo songs, which feature a moderate tempo, usually have a range of an octave or greater and employ several scale types; they are among the most rhythmically complex styles in Native North America. Athabascan songs usually employ strophic or elaborate sectional forms with complex phrase designs, involving interwoven melodic motifs. They tend to feature a relatively fast tempo, wide range, and impressive melodic variety.

The Southwest area has a rich assortment of musical instruments. Certain genres of Pueblo ceremonial songs are accompanied by a large, double-headed barrel drum, made from the hollowed trunk of a cottonwood tree and painted in bright colors. Pueblo container rattles may be made of gourds or tortoise shells, and commercial sleigh bells or tin tinklers sewn onto dance outfits add another layer of sound to performance. Athabascan musicians use several different kinds of drums, depending upon the performance context. One of the most distinctive Athabascan drums is the water drum, made of a clay or iron pot with a buckskin head; this is played with a stick bent into a hoop at the distal end. Athabascan musicians employ many idiophones, including basket drums (made of a shallow basket inverted on the ground and played with a drumstick made from yucca leaves), container rattles made of rawhide or gourd, and notched rasps. Bull-roarers and various kinds of whistles are used in both Pueblo and Athabascan rituals. Unique to the Southwest is the Apache fiddle, which has one or two strings and is made from a two-foot long hollow stalk of the century plant; the fiddle and bow strings are made of horsehair. The Apache fiddle is played as a solo instrument for entertainment.

The Northwest Coast

The Northwest Coast area extends from the panhandle of Alaska to northern California, but includes a narrow strip only about one hundred miles wide between the Pacific Ocean and the Cascade Range or coastal mountains of Canada. The indigenous peoples of this area include the Tlingit, Kwakiutl, Quileute, and many other groups. Some of the major language families of the Northwest Coast area are Salishan, Wakashan, Haida, and Chinookan. Northwest Coast musical performance contexts include ceremonies honoring ancestral spirits, gift-giving Potlatch feasts, seasonal ceremonies honoring game animals and fish, initiation rituals such as the Nootka Wolf Dance, shamanistic curing rituals, and regional dance festivals.

Northwest Coast singers are known for their dramatic, emotional performance style, and songs tend to rise in pitch over the course of performance. The preferred vocal quality in this area is moderately relaxed and open, and singers emphasize the lower vocal register. Singers from this area employ a variety of vocal ornaments, including turns, grace notes, and aspirated attacks and releases. Most songs are monophonic, but some examples of part singing have been recorded that appear to predate the influence of European music. In some Northwest Coast tribes, songs are learned and often performed in association with stories; these song texts emphasize vocables, using only a few words to evoke the full story. Among other tribes, song texts typically alternate a fully texted stanza with a vocable refrain.

Songs from the Northwest Coast area emphasize sectional and strophic forms with long, complex phrases. Most songs have a range of about an octave, and anhemitonic scales with four, five, or six notes are most common. Melodic lines tend to move by step in undulating shapes with a descending inflection. Rhythmic structures in Northwest Coast music are among the most complex in Native North America; meters tend to change frequently within a song, and the meter or tempo of the drumbeat may differ from that of the singers in certain genres. In many Northwest Coast songs, melodic rhythms derive from speech rhythms, producing a declamatory effect.

Northwest Coast music is perhaps best known for its spectacular carved and painted musical instruments. These include both strung and container rattles made of wood, horn, or shell in a great variety of forms. Container rattles from this area are usually carved to represent birds such as the hawk, kingfisher, grouse, crane, or raven. Raven rattles are especially numerous and significant; they symbolize Raven, the principal culture hero in Northwest Coast mythology. In the past, painted wooden box drums were played by Northwest Coast peoples in certain religious ceremonies. Many aerophones are indigenous to the Northwest Coast, including wooden whistles, flutes, horns, and reed instruments, which are unique to this area of Native North America.

The Arctic

The immense Arctic area includes the arctic region from Alaska to Greenland, most of Alaska except for the coastal areas, and much of Canada. The region is inhabited by many separate but related peoples, known collectively as Eskimos in Alaska and as Inuit in Canada. The predominant language family of the area is Eskimo-Aleut. Some of the contexts in which Arctic musics are performed include traditional games (Blanket Toss, string games, juggling games), religious festivals (such as the Messenger Feast and Bladder Festival), song contests, storytelling, shamanistic healing rituals, and all aspects of hunting, from launching a boat to harpooning a sea mammal.

The Arctic vocal style is moderately tense and nasal; group songs are monophonic, the women singing an octave higher than the men. Song texts consist of both vocables and lexical phrases. Arctic singers are known for their use of grace notes, vocal pulsations on sustained pitches, aspirated attacks and releases, and other melodic ornaments. Extended vocal techniques are a special feature of a genre known as vocal games, which are common throughout the Canadian Arctic. Vocal games involve the combination of intonation contours, rhythmic patterns, and vocal sounds either inspired or expirated (Nattiez 1983). They are performed by two people, usually women, singing separate motifs that are superimposed on one another in a rapid canon. Vocal games are heard in a variety of contexts and are intended primarily for entertainment, but they entail a competitive

element and performers are valued for their endurance, virtuosity, and
sound quality.

Songs from the Arctic area tend to be relatively brief but feature intricate strophic forms; each strophe contains a number of different phrases,
the endings of which are articulated by repeated notes. In some genres of
dance songs, the first strophe is sung quietly by a few members of the
chorus, accompanied by a soft drumbeat; the conclusion of the strophe is
marked by vigorous drumbeats, and the strophe is repeated in full voice by
the entire chorus. Arctic songs tend to employ a narrow range and emphasize tetratonic or pentatonic scales. Meter changes frequently within a
song and rhythmic patterns include syncopations, ties, and cross-rhythms.
In some genres, the meter or tempo of the vocal part differs from that of the
drum accompaniment, further increasing rhythmic complexity.

The two musical instruments native to the Arctic region are the tam-
bourine-like hand drum and the box drum. The hand drum, which is about
two feet in diameter, is held by a short wooden or bone handle; it is played
with a slender, flexible wooden stick. The box drum, which accompanies
the Messenger Feast and certain other ritual dances, is a rectangular
wooden box that is open at both ends and decorated with symbolic
designs. It is played while suspended from a tripod or ceiling pole. Few
rattles are indigenous to the Arctic area, but dancers usually wear or carry
gloves decorated with objects that rattle softly during performance.

*

The area approach has been controversial among scholars of Native American music, because it depends to a great extent on reductive generalities
and objectification. In reality, musico-cultural boundaries are fluid and
changeable; they cannot be constrained by artificially constructed maps.
The Native American musical map is therefore subject to continual revision and refinement, as new information becomes available. The map is
primarily useful as an introduction to historic American Indian musics,
but the music of each individual native community must then be
approached and appreciated on its own terms. To illustrate this point, the
following section contains a fuller exploration of the musical culture of
one particular Choctaw Indian community. The Choctaw originated in
the Southeastern United States. During the nineteenth century, the
United States government forced the Choctaw and other native Southeastern peoples to migrate from their homelands to the Indian Territory,
which is now the state of Oklahoma. Today, more than 25,000 Choctaw

people reside in Mississippi, Louisiana, and Oklahoma, as well as in other parts of the United States.

The musical culture of the Choctaw

Some sense of contemporary Choctaw musical practice may be gleaned from a description of a sing that took place on a winter evening in 1985. The members of the Choctaw-Chickasaw Heritage Committee of Ardmore, Oklahoma were congregating at a mobile home in a remote pasture some twenty miles from town. They had come to participate in a sing celebrating the birthday of their organization's chairman, who had founded the group about ten years earlier in order to revitalize Choctaw music. The singers visited and joked with one another in Choctaw and English as they settled into the seats that had been arranged in a circle around the living room. While the women admired a new grandchild, the men inspected a double-headed hand drum that had been completed a few days earlier. An elder, the group's principal song leader, began to beat the drum softly and the room grew quiet. He cleared his throat and cassette recorders were switched on. He sang the first phrase of a Jump Dance song; the men responded in unison, and the sing had begun. The song leader continued to sing Jump Dance songs for half an hour; he then initiated a series of Walk Dance songs, and the women began to join in on the choral responses. They sang Walk Dances for about an hour, and then took a break to enjoy birthday cake and other refreshments each family had contributed to the occasion. The singing resumed with a series of Drunk Dance songs, followed by War Dance songs. As midnight approached, they sang the Snake Dance song, marking the conclusion of the sing. The participants gathered their belongings, said their farewells, and headed for home.

The sing, an informal musical gathering at a private home, is one contemporary social context in which Choctaw people perform an important historic song repertory known as Social Dance music. Until the 1930s, this repertory was performed in a strikingly different social context: during a sacred festival known as the Ballgame. The Ballgame, from which lacrosse developed, existed in some form among virtually all tribes from the Eastern Woodlands and Great Lakes area. The game was played by two opposing teams; the players attempted to strike their own goal post with a ball, which could be thrown and carried only with special rackets. Performed in its full ritual context, the Ballgame was much more than a sport.

For the Choctaw, it was a complex ceremony that lasted four days and nights, combining shamanism, ritual purification, prayer, ballplay, oration, feasting, communal dance, and singing. The Choctaw performed the Ballgame to effect world renewal through the symbolic destruction and recreation of the cosmos. The Ballgame itself, played during the daytime, symbolized cosmic destruction and primordial chaos; the communal dances, performed throughout the night, symbolized resolution of conflict and recreation.

Four different musical genres were performed in the context of the Choctaw Ballgame, including shaman's songs and flute music, ballplayers' personal songs, songs to accompany the Ballplay Dance immediately before ballplay, and songs to accompany the communal dances throughout the night after ballplay. Of these four genres, only the songs that accompanied the night dances continue to be widely performed. The Choctaw have reinterpreted and recontextualized the night dances, which are now called Social Dances or Stomp Dances. The Social Dance repertory is rich and diverse, including at least fourteen different dances and more than ninety different songs. Both men and women perform the songs and dances, which move counterclockwise around a circle and include various formations and dance steps. In addition to the informal sings described above, the Choctaw also perform Social Dance songs at private dances held in school gymnasiums or at homes, as well as in public venues such as tribal fairs or demonstrations for educational, civic, and commercial groups.

While Choctaw musical performance contexts have changed dramatically during the course of the twentieth century, a study of musical transcriptions and sound recordings made between 1909 and 1985 reveals that the Social Dance repertory itself has changed very little in terms of style, shape, and content (Levine 1990). Choctaw singers perform Social Dance songs in a moderately relaxed, somewhat nasal voice, accompanied by a pair of striking sticks (Mississippi) or a double-headed hand drum (Oklahoma). Although some Social Dance songs are performed as a solo by the song leader, most involve call and response between the leader and the dancers. The women double the men's melodic line at the octave, except in Jump Dance songs, which are sung only by men (but which are danced by both men and women). Most Social Dance song texts consist entirely of vocables, although about one-fifth of these songs contain some lines of lexical text. Choctaw Social Dance songs generally employ anhemitonic scales with four to six notes; the melodies vary in ambitus from a fourth to a tenth. The meter changes frequently in most songs, and a variety of rhythmic patterns appear. Choctaw singers use vocal pulsations and *sforzandos* to accent the melodic line; aspirated attacks and releases are used to articulate melodic phrases. Social Dance songs conclude with a formulaic call of indefinite pitch.

The Choctaw Social Dance repertory features four different musical forms, each of which exhibits a cyclical approach to structure. Jump Dance songs, which generally last one minute or less, employ an iterative form with several brief motifs strung together in succession. Walk Dance songs last about five minutes and feature a sectional form with long, often asymmetrical melodic phrases. Some Drunk Dance, War Dance, and most animal dance songs use a verse and refrain form, in which the refrain may be repeated several times between each statement of the verse. Other Drunk Dance and War Dance songs employ a kind of strophic form that is common throughout the Southeastern tribes. These songs generally feature an introduction followed by a strophe; the strophe itself is repeated many times and constitutes the body of the song. The introduction may be sung as a solo by the song leader, or may be performed in call and response. The introduction is slow and often unmetered, in contrast with the quick, steady pulse of the strophe.

Prior to the 1930s, the night dance portion of the Choctaw Ballgame festival was divided into four main segments; each segment featured one particular category of music and dance, as well as variants on the standard dance style and related optional dances. Today, Choctaw singers classify the Social Dance repertory into four categories, reflecting the earlier structure of night dance events. These categories are Jump or Stomp Dances (*Tolobli Hihla*), Walk or Tick Dances (*Shotoni Hihla*), Drunk or Corn Dances (*Ishko Hihla*), and War or Drum Dances (*Shinka Boli Hihla*). Each main category includes many different songs, all identified by the generic title and used to accompany the same dance.

Each category of Social Dance music also includes additional songs bearing individual titles; these songs accompany a variant of the predominant dance or a related optional dance. Thus the Jump Dance category includes the Starting Dance and the Double-Header Dance (*Hihla Falama*), the Walk Dance category includes Stealing Partners (*Itomobli Hihla*), the Drunk Dance category includes the Wedding Dance (*Itau Waya Hihla*), and the War Dance category includes the Criss-Cross Dance (*Itiopatami Hihla*), the Parting Dance (*Itifalami Hihla*), and several animal dances. Night dance events concluded at sunrise with the performance of the Snake Dance (*Sinti Hihla*); Choctaw singers now usually end Social

Dance performances with the Snake Dance, which stands on its own musically and conceptually, constituting a fifth category.

This description of performance contexts, musical style, and repertory shape and content suggests that Social Dance songs embody the spiritual experience of renewal and recreation for the Choctaw people, despite the fact that they have recontextualized the songs and no longer perform them as part of a sacred ritual. Choctaw singers themselves confirm this interpretation through their accounts of the effect of a successful performance. They say that at dawn on the morning after a good sing, they can hear the voices of their ancestors singing and dancing at long abandoned dance grounds. The participants feel renewed in their identity as Choctaw and have reaffirmed their sense of community with one another, as well as with those who have gone before them.

The connection between Social Dance songs and spiritual experience is also manifest in Choctaw ideas about the origin, role, and meaning of music. The Choctaw attribute the origin of Social Dance music to *Shilumbish Chito*, their creator, who is said to have given the first people these songs and dances during their mythic migration. Thus for the Choctaw, Social Dance music was not a human invention; it came from an other-than-human source, and was a gift. Choctaw singers state that humans are incapable of composing new Social Dance songs; if a song from this repertory is forgotten, it can not be replaced by a new composition. Singers also assert that the Social Dance repertory has been maintained throughout Choctaw history without significant changes in style or content. Clearly, the Choctaw place a high value on musical preservation and stylistic continuity.

Insight into the role of Choctaw music may be gleaned from Choctaw legends, such as the story of the hunter who became a deer (Bushnell 1909, p. 32). In this story, a hunter kills a doe and soon after falls asleep near the carcass. At sunrise the next morning, the hunter is surprised to hear the doe ask him to go with her to her home. The hunter agrees to go, and the doe leads him through forests and over high mountains to a large cave under a rock. They enter the cave, where the hunter meets the king of the deer. Soon the hunter falls asleep, and while he sleeps, he is transformed into a deer. Many days pass, and the hunter's mother and all his friends think he has been killed. One day they find his bow and arrows hanging on a branch of the tree beneath which he had slept beside the body of the doe. Everyone gathers around the spot and begins to sing, when suddenly, they see a herd of deer bounding toward them through the forest. The deer circle the singers, and one large buck approaches them; the singers catch it, and when it speaks to them, they recognize the voice of the lost hunter. The singers restore the hunter to human form, killing him in the process. His body is then taken back to the village, where he is buried with proper ritual, including music and dance. The legend of the hunter who became a deer, along with other similar narratives, suggests that for the Choctaw, the most fundamental role of music is to summon a spiritual presence, to validate supernatural contact, and to mediate between the human and spiritual planes of existence.

The meaning of Choctaw music derives from its role as a method of communication between humans and spirit beings. Perhaps this is why the Choctaw do not rely upon lexical texts to convey meaning in their songs; while some songs do contain meaningful lyrics, most consist entirely of vocables. Instead, the Choctaw express meaning in their songs through the musical representation of important spiritual concepts. The most essential concept is that for the Choctaw, the sacred world is shaped in a circle, cross-cut by the four cardinal directions; the circle represents wholeness and continuity, while the number four represents balance and order. Choctaw musical forms, which are cyclical rather than linear, represent circularity. The number four tends to be incorporated into the phrase design of individual songs, as well as the structure of the performance as a whole. The symbolism expressed aurally in Choctaw music is reinforced visually by Choctaw dance; all of the dances move counterclockwise in a circle. Each separate component of the performance thus contributes to the meaning of the event.

Choctaw ideas about the origins, purpose, and meaning of music have a direct bearing on Choctaw musical processes, such as composition, preservation, and transmission of the repertory.[2] Although Choctaw singers state that it is impossible to compose a new Social Dance song, singers combine and vary fixed melodic materials in prescribed ways, so that no two renditions of one song are ever the same. In verse/refrain and strophic form songs, the song leader improvises variations on his call, while the dancers respond with fixed musical material. Iterative and sectional form songs operate differently; each individual song contains a stock of melodic motifs that serve as prototypes for separate musical sections. The song leader introduces a melodic motif, which becomes the dancers' response for the duration of that section. The leader then improvises

---

2. For additional information on music thought and process in other American Indian tribes, see Herzog 1938, Koranda 1980, La Vigna 1980, Merriam 1967, and Nettl 1955, 1989.

variations on that melodic motif during his calls. In addition to improvising variations, the song leader decides which, and how many, different sections to include in the song. This method of performance enables the song leader to demonstrate musical skill and knowledge of the repertory while expressing stylistic individuality. Although the number of different songs within each category is limited, every performance generates fresh interpretations, thereby sustaining musical interest.

Because of the repertory's sacred origins and purpose, the Choctaw place a high priority on preserving Social Dance music. The repertory has been maintained primarily through oral tradition and was not written or notated until the twentieth century. Prior to the 1930s, all members of a Choctaw community were expected to attend and participate in Ballgame festivals. Children learned the communal songs and dances through direct experience, participating in performances and imitating their elders. When the elders felt that a young man was ready, he would be asked to lead a set of dances. Members of the community showed their approval of a competent performance by joining the dance line behind the novice leader, and he would be invited to lead sets at subsequent night dance events.

The Choctaw have adopted new methods of musical preservation and transmission, since the Social Dance repertory has been recontextualized. Sound and video recordings have been produced by some Choctaw communities for teaching and preservation purposes. In addition, Choctaw singers have collaborated with educators and scholars to transcribe Social Dance songs in standard music notation. In Mississippi and Oklahoma, schools that serve Choctaw communities have added formal instruction in the Social Dance repertory to their music curricula at both the primary and secondary levels. Church-sponsored youth groups in some Choctaw communities also provide instruction in Social Dances. Despite the adoption of new teaching and learning methods, oral tradition – with its emphasis on direct experience through participation – remains an important means of preserving and transmitting Choctaw Social Dances.

Choctaw musical aesthetics, values, and concepts of talent further reflect cultural conceptions of musical origins, purpose, and meaning. In Choctaw music, the aesthetic ideal exhibits a subtle balance between repetition and variation. Finely detailed musical patterns are set into a repetitive, often symmetrical framework, and successions of musical motifs are layered in time, one after another. A good song leader is one who has a clear, strong voice that rings out distinctly against the dancers' response. In addition, the competent song leader must be able to remember dozens of songs and song prototypes, must have a thorough knowledge of the rules for combining musical motifs within a given song, and must have practical experience in improvising variations during actual performance.

Despite the changes that have occurred in the Social Dance repertory, it continues to play a central role in Choctaw life, especially as a powerful expression of ethnic identity. The Choctaw include other repertories under the rubric of traditional music as well, such as Christian hymns with Choctaw-language texts and "house dance music" or fiddle tunes that accompany country dances. These repertories originated during the nineteenth century, and since they combine European-American and native Choctaw musical elements, they represent syncretic styles. In addition to traditional repertories, Choctaw musicians perform musical repertories from other areas of Indian America, including the pantribal powwow and the Plains-style flute. The Choctaw also perform many non-Indian genres, from art music to rock and roll. Like the Choctaw, other American Indian communities also have a long history of maintaining and transforming their own tribal musics while simultaneously adapting and adopting the music of outsiders; this is discussed in the following section.

Historical dynamics
in American Indian music

Musics throughout Native North America have endured continual, albeit gradual, processes of change. People alter and adapt their musics in culturally patterned ways, which reflect their concepts and experience of history. Native American attitudes toward history and change are embedded in the sacred narratives and oral traditions of each tribe, which reveal that many Indians perceive time as operating through cyclical recurrence rather than linear chronology; thus change involves adoption, adaptation, and syncretism rather than displacement, radical innovation, or succession. These concepts have important implications for the methods Indians have developed to construct music history and to shape musical change. Native American processes of musical change include the adoption or adaptation of music performed by other peoples, the blending of indigenous and external idioms, and the revitalization and recontextualization of repertories that have become moribund or have been temporarily discontinued.

One of the most widespread methods American Indians have developed to facilitate the adoption and adaptation of another tribe's music is called pantribalism, panIndianism, or intertribalism. This involves the adoption by one tribe or community of a musical repertory indigenous to another tribe, in a process that helps to renegotiate ethnic boundaries while it perpetuates native beliefs, values, and aesthetic expression in changing social or geographic environments. There are many examples of pantribalism in the history of American Indian music; the most famous include the Ghost Dance, the Native American Church, and the powwow.

The Ghost Dance originated in 1889 through the vision of a Paiute prophet known as Wovoka or Jack Wilson; the ceremony was quickly disseminated among the peoples of the Great Basin and Plains areas. Wovoka taught that performance of the Ghost Dance would lead to the resurrection of deceased Indians and would restore bison to the plains and prairies, enabling Native Americans to rise against European Americans and expel them from the continent. The Ghost Dance was a communal ceremony that involved many people singing in unison, without instrumental accompaniment, while dancing in a circle. The wide appeal and rapid spread of the Ghost Dance may be understood in its historical context. Bison, on which the Plains Indians depended for their livelihood, were systematically slaughtered by mandate of the United States government beginning in 1870 and were nearly extinct within a decade. Plains and Great Basin peoples were fighting to maintain their traditional lifeways and to avoid confinement on reservations, but they were starving because of the loss of their primary food source. The Ghost Dance proffered renewal and return to a traditional way of life. The United States government banned the Ghost Dance in 1890, but the members of some Great Basin and Plains tribes continued to perform the ceremony privately and to follow its religious beliefs and practices well into the twentieth century. Many sound recordings of Ghost Dance music are available, some made by living proponents of the Ghost Dance religion as recently as 1980 (Vander 1988).

Ghost Dance songs reflect the general musical style of Great Basin peoples, among whom the ceremony began. Singers use a relaxed, open vocal quality and emphasize the middle tessitura. When sung by two or more people, Ghost Dance songs are performed in somewhat blended monophony. Because the Ghost Dance musical style derived from the seasonal Round Dance repertory, Ghost Dance songs feature paired phrase structure and maintain a moderate tempo. Most Ghost Dance melodies are short and have a relatively narrow range of an octave or less. Unlike many other Native American musical genres, Ghost Dance songs employ predominantly lexical texts that may be compared to haiku poetry in their imagery, ambiguity of meaning, and tightly compressed form (Vander 1988, p. 19).

Another major pantribal movement involves the Native American Church, which is based on a ritual practiced by the indigenous peoples of northern Mexico since pre-Columbian times. Native Mexicans introduced this ritual to the Apache by the eighteenth century, and the ritual expanded throughout Native North America during the nineteenth and twentieth centuries. Although not all tribes participate in the Native American Church, its practitioners are widespread and it is now recognized in the United States as a nationally organized religion. The religious ideology of the Native American Church combines elements of Christianity with indigenous beliefs and practices. Prayer meetings of the Native American Church take place in a tipi or other traditional dwelling; meetings begin in the early evening and continue through breakfast the next morning. The meetings include prayer, singing, ritual smoking, and the ingestion of peyote, a traditional medicine.

The songs associated with the Native American Church are known as peyote music. The style of this genre is easily recognizable among American Indian musics. Peyote songs are usually performed as solos; each participant in a meeting of the Native American Church has the opportunity to sing at least one set of four peyote songs, constituting a form of personal prayer. The singers employ a slightly tense and nasal vocal quality, and they perform the songs in a quiet, introspective manner. Peyote songs have a range of about an octave and employ a kind of strophic form; the strophe concludes with the vocable phrase "he ne yo we," which does not occur in any other Native American musical genre. The tempo of peyote songs is very fast, and they are accompanied by a rattle and a small water drum. Peyote song texts emphasize vocables, but some lines of lexical text are used.

The powwow is the most widespread and influential pantribal movement in the history of American Indian music. Powwows are multifaceted, multivalent celebrations performed by Indians throughout North America. They take place on rural reservations as well as in urban areas, and they occur virtually every weekend in Indian country. Participation at a given powwow may be limited to members of a local community, or may include visitors from one or more guest communities. The largest powwows, such as the annual Denver March Powwow, attract hundreds of participants and thousands of spectators, some of whom travel long distances to attend. The precise structure of each powwow varies, depending upon local traditions and ideology. During the summer months, powwows are usually held outdoors; dancers, singers, and their families camp together for the duration of the event near the dance arena. At other times of the year, powwows may take place indoors, at community centers, school gymnasiums, or sports arenas. Powwows vary in length from one to several days. They are held to honor a family member, to celebrate community heritage, to affirm and promote traditional values, or to raise money for charitable causes. Powwows are sponsored by families, tribes or communities, schools or student associations, and civic organizations.

The powwow is rooted in rituals performed during the nineteenth century by men's societies among the Prairie peoples, such as the Inloshka society of the Kansa, the Hethuska society of the Omaha and Ponca, and the Iruska society of the Pawnee. Men's societies performed ceremonies with music, dance, and feasting, in order to honor and tell the stories of the accomplishments of experienced warriors. By the 1860s, these rituals had been given to Northern Plains tribes, and they became known as the Grass Dance or Omaha Dance. The Grass Dance began to be performed in conjunction with other religious ceremonies, such as the Sun Dance. By the early twentieth century, the Grass Dance ceremony had blended elements from several ritual sources with newly created practices. At about the same time, European Americans began to use the term powwow to describe Indian gatherings; the word powwow comes from *pauau*, an Algonkian term for healers and curing rituals. By the 1950s, most Native Americans were using the word powwow in reference to the event that had gradually developed from the Grass Dance.

Two main styles of powwow are performed today, known as the Northern Plains and Southern Plains styles. They differ from one another in details of content, organization, terminology, dress, and choreography. Northern Plains powwows begin with a Grand Entry, or parade entrance of the participants into the dance circle, led by a color guard comprising Native American veterans of the United States armed forces. The color guard bears the American flag as well as tribal flags or other symbols of Indian identity. After all of the participants have entered the dance circle and the flags have been posted, a prayer is offered in an Indian language as well as in English, and everyone is formally welcomed by the organizing committee. The powwow's main program features the performance of the intertribal War Dance, which may also be known as the Grass Dance,

Omaha Dance, or Wolf Dance. Many dancers perform the War Dance simultaneously, each with his or her own individual choreography and unique outfit. Six main categories of dance and dress are recognized: Men's Traditional, Men's Grass Dance, Men's Fancy Dance, Women's Traditional, Women's Jingle Dress, and Women's Fancy Shawl. War Dances are interspersed with other dances, including social dances, exhibition dances, honor songs, and giveaways. Large powwows often include contest dances, during which participants in different categories compete for prizes and recognition.

Southern Plains powwows begin with a Gourd Dance session of two or more hours in duration. The Gourd Dance, which developed among the Southern Plains tribes during the 1940s, originated in rituals associated with warrior societies. After a meal break, the Southern Plains powwow follows a format similar to that of the Northern Plains, although the dance names and categories of dress differ somewhat. Following the powwow program, participants may change into everyday clothes and perform Forty-Nine Dances (a social dance genre) until dawn.

Powwow music developed primarily from Plains Indian musical styles. The dancers are accompanied by an ensemble called a drum, which includes three or more singers seated around a large bass drum. Each singer plays the drum with a single padded stick; the drumbeat supports the underlying pulse of the song in steady beats. At certain points in the song, the drummers may perform a series of accented strokes, known as heart beats or honor beats, in respect for the dancers. Powwow singers raised in Plains musical traditions perform the drumbeat slightly behind the melodic beat, creating a subtle rhythmic complexity that is maintained throughout the song. Powwow singers employ a nasal, very tense vocal quality with heavy pulsations on sustained notes and portamentos at phrase endings. War Dance songs tend to start high, and Northern singers may use falsetto at the beginning of the song. These songs usually feature terraced-descent melodic contours and employ the incomplete repetition form that is the hallmark of Plains musical style. The texts of most powwow songs emphasize vocables, which may frame some lines of lexical text. At urban powwows attended by people from many different tribes, social dance songs are often performed in English. Originally, powwow music was performed exclusively by men, but women began to join drum groups in many communities during the 1970s. The powwow is a dynamic, innovative artistic and spiritual medium that continues to evolve; new songs are composed each year, new styles of dress and dance appear, reflecting changes in the concept of personal and tribal identity, and the form and ideology of the event as a whole adapt to new settings and cultural objectives. The powwow is the only native performance event today in which men, women, and children of all ages, tribes, and socioeconomic backgrounds may join together to express and celebrate what they hold in common as American Indians.

In addition to pantribalism, Native Americans have adopted and adapted many styles, instruments, and concepts from non-Indian musical cultures. As early as the sixteenth century, Jesuit missionaries began teaching Catholic sacred music to members of the tribes with which they were in contact. During the seventeenth century, Indians began to be introduced to Christian hymns by Protestant missionaries, who translated hymn texts into Indian languages and taught these songs as part of the conversion process. Indians gradually began to adapt hymn tunes so that they more closely resembled indigenous musical styles, and supplemented the repertory with tunes and texts by their own native composers. A striking example of this occurred in the Indian Shaker Church of the Northwest Coast, which blended elements of Christian religion and hymnody with the Spirit Dance (Rhodes 1963, p. 10). Today, the members of many tribes regularly perform Indian hymns as a part of worship services as well as at informal domestic gatherings, and this repertory is considered to be traditional. Fiddle music represents another example of syncretism, as Native Americans have adopted and adapted European-American fiddle tunes and gradually made them their own. For example, fiddle bands originated among the Tohono O'odham of southern Arizona during the nineteenth century; today, O'odham fiddlers continue to perform their traditional repertory of polkas, schottisches, two-steps, and mazurkas.

A related phenomenon is the adoption of certain European-American musical concepts, including performance primarily for entertainment or commercial purposes. This practice may be traced to the nineteenth century, with the advent of Indian shows and living cultural exhibits at fairs and expositions. In recent decades, some tribes have adapted ritual musical styles to new, entirely secular contexts. For example, Navajo singers sometimes compose secular songs in the style of genres associated with the Enemyway ceremony. Secular Enemyway songs are performed at Tribal Fairs and other public events, often by women's ensembles, such as the Southern Maiden Singers, the Klagetoh Maiden Singers, and the Sweethearts of Navajoland. Women do not sing Enemyway songs in the traditional ritual context, and thus the development of secular contexts has created new performance opportunities for Navajo women.[3] A secular Enemyway dance song was composed and aired on the Navajo radio station to publicize the premier broadcast of the Superbowl in the Navajo language in 1996. Another example of the adaptation of indigenous genres to secular contexts is the American Indian Dance Theater, founded by Barbara Schwei and Hanay Geiogamah (Kiowa-Delaware) in 1987. This company presents highly professional staged versions of powwow dances as well as a range of tribal dances.

In addition to adopting some European-American musical concepts, Native Americans have inserted English words into certain genres of indigenous music at least since the 1920s (Rhodes 1963, p. 10). Many commercial recordings include examples of powwow Round Dance songs, such as Forty-Nine Dances or Rabbit Dances, which include English words; these texts are usually about love and are often humorous. English words have also been used in ritual songs among some tribes, but this is rare.

Many Native American composers and performers have adopted contemporary musical idioms, including jazz, rock and roll, country, folk-rock, gospel, reggae, rap, and hip hop. These musicians express a strong sense of Indian identity, but write music and lyrics directed at non-Indians as well as Indians. The best-known native singer-songwriter is Buffy Sainte-Marie (Cree) (born 1941), who blends native vocal qualities and instruments with various popular music idioms. Jazz fusion bands such as Jim Pepper's Powwow, as well as rock bands including Blackfoot Strikes, Redbone, and Xit, address the urban Indian experience and political consciousness. These performers create links to the past in their song texts, which often invoke historic leaders, incidents, or religious movements, as in the song *Wovoka* by Pat and Lolly Vegas of the band Redbone. Folk-rock performers such as Paul Ortega (Apache), Sharon Burch (Navajo), Joanne Shenandoah (Oneida), and Geraldine Barney (Navajo), tend to focus on themes from reservation life, often combining English lyrics with vocables and song texts in their native languages. The group Ulali, whose members are Cherokee-Tuscarora and Aztec-Maya, incorporates elements from traditional Eastern, Plains, and Mexican musics into blues, jazz, and gospel styles.

Native Americans have composed pieces in European-American sacred and art music idioms, using European notation, since the nineteenth century. The first published American Indian composer was Thomas

---

3. For further information on gender roles in American Indian musics, see Frisbie 1993, Giglio 1994, Hatton 1986, Keeling 1989, and Vander 1988.

Commuck (Narragansett) (1805–1855), who produced a hymnal for the Methodist Episcopal Church in 1845 (Stevenson 1982, p. 82). For this collection, Commuck wrote 120 hymn tunes, most of which he named after tribes or famous chiefs; the tunes were harmonized by Thomas Hastings (1784–1872). Some of the twentieth-century Indian composers who have worked in European art music idioms include Carl Fischer (Cherokee) (1912–1954), Jack Kilpatrick (Cherokee) (1915–1967), and Louis Ballard (Cherokee-Quapaw) (born 1931). Currently, the best-known American Indian composer working in such idioms is Brent Michael Davids (Mohican) (born 1959). Davids has received commissions from organizations such as the Joffrey Ballet, the Kronos Quartet, and the National Symphony Orchestra; his music has been performed in major cities throughout the world. Davids combines elements of traditional native musics with European-American compositional techniques, often incorporating native instruments or instruments of his own design into his works. His major compositions include *Moon of the Falling Leaves* (1991), *The Singing Woods* (1994), *Turtle People* (1995), *Native American Suite* (1995), and *Tukuhnikivatz* (1996).

One of the most eclectic young American Indian performing artists is Robert Mirabal (Taos Pueblo) (born 1966). Mirabal makes, performs on, and composes for the Plains flute, an instrument historically used for courting purposes by Plains and Prairie peoples, but which has been widely popularized in recent decades by musicians such as Carlos Nakai (Navajo-Ute). Although he is strongly rooted in American Indian idioms, Mirabal draws musical inspiration and uses many instruments from indigenous cultures around the world to express themes of cultural survival and revival. His recording *Warriors* (1991) includes a Plains flute rendition of the song *Summertime*, from George Gershwin's *Porgy and Bess*, as well as original compositions that exhibit the influence of jazz. In addition, the recording features several of Mirabal's works combining the Plains flute with Australian Aboriginal instruments such as the didjeridu, bull-roarer, and clapsticks. Mirabal has performed widely throughout the United States, Europe, and Japan, as a soloist, with symphony orchestras, and as a modern dance accompanist.

The revitalization and recontextualization of discontinued or moribund repertories has played a significant role in Native American music history. The revitalization process provides American Indian communities with a unique opportunity to reshape, redefine, and reinterpret historic performance traditions, not by simply modifying them on the basis of feasibility, but through the assertion of individual aesthetic sensibilities and choices. The understanding that a musical repertory may be discontinued for a time and later revitalized reflects Native American concepts of cyclical recurrence. At the same time, musical revitalization is articulatory in nature; it has to do with the way people use music to express ethnic identity, interpret their historical experience, and transcend social constraints. The revitalization and recontextualization of Choctaw Social Dance music was mentioned above (Levine 1990, 1993); many other musical revitalizations have occurred throughout Indian America, especially since the advent of the Indian Awareness movement in the 1970s.

The history of musical interaction and exchange between American Indians and European Americans may be traced to the earliest attempts explorers and missionaries made to describe, document, notate, and understand Native North American musics (Stevenson 1973a, 1973b). After more than five centuries, an immense and highly detailed body of information exists on American Indian music, including tens of thousands of sound recordings and musical transcriptions. Native Americans themselves have participated in the scholarly process, beginning with the collaborative research undertaken by Alice Fletcher and Francis La Flesche (Omaha) in the late nineteenth and early twentieth centuries (Fletcher and La Flesche 1992). As the twentieth century draws to a close, many scholars of Indian descent are active in teaching and studying American Indian musics at the primary, secondary, and university levels.

In addition to the work of American Indian scholars and educators, community-based musical research and preservation projects are being undertaken by many tribes, assisted in some cases through local, state, and federal agencies. An important resource for community-based research programs has been the Federal Cylinder Project, which was inaugurated in 1979 by the American Folklife Center at the Library of Congress. Through the Federal Cylinder Project, some 7,000 field recordings of Native American music and language, made by pioneers in anthropology and ethnomusicology, have been duplicated and disseminated to the peoples among whom the recordings were originally made.

The influence of American Indians on American music history

If the history of American Indian music has been intertwined with that of European Americans since the sixteenth century, American Indians have also exerted a profound influence on the development of American musical life. The ethnomusicologist Bruno Nettl has pointed out the prodigious contribution made by the study of Native American musics to the development of the field of ethnomusicology (Nettl 1986). Many of the most important figures in American music scholarship have worked with American Indian musics, including Alice Fletcher, Frances Densmore, George Herzog, Helen Roberts, David McAllester, Gertrude Kurath, Alan Merriam, and of course Nettl himself. Like American music scholars, American composers have been strongly influenced by native musics. Composers began to draw inspiration from American Indian musics in the late eighteenth century (Keillor 1995), but it was not until one hundred years later that they began to actually quote Indian melodies in their works, as is noted in more detail in chapter 9. One of the first to employ American Indian melodies was Edward MacDowell (1860–1908), who based his 1894 *Indian Suite*, Op. 48 on material published by Theodore Baker in the first scholarly treatise ever written on American Indian music (Baker 1882). Ironically, MacDowell based his third movement on a hymn tune by the Indian composer Thomas Commuck; Baker had published the tune without acknowledging its source (Stevenson 1982, pp. 82–83).

Composers such as MacDowell were influenced in part by the rapid growth of systematic research on Native American musics after 1880. However, they were also influenced by the drive to develop a nationalist American musical style based on indigenous sources. Following MacDowell, many American composers, known as "Indianists," wrote music based on Native American melodies. Most Indianist composers worked from transcriptions published by early ethnomusicologists, but some, such as Frederick Burton (1861–1909) and Thurlow Lieurance (1878–1963), carried out their own field research with American Indians to collect indigenous songs. Even John Philip Sousa (1854–1932) published harmonizations of American Indian melodies, some of which he himself had transcribed for the anthropologist James Mooney (Sousa 1977). The best-known Indianist composer was Arthur Farwell (1872–1952), who developed his own music printing business, the Wa-Wan Press, to publish the work of Indianists and other American composers (Culbertson 1992). The Indianist movement waned after the 1930s, but subsequent American composers have occasionally drawn inspiration from Native American music and culture. Some of these works include *Amerind Suite* (1939) by Henry Cowell (1897–1965), *Pocahontas* (1940) by Elliott Carter (born 1908), *Iroquois Dances* (1944) by Colin McPhee (1900–1964), *Cloud-*

Chamber Music (the eleventh of the *Intrusions* [1950]) and *The Bewitched* (1955) by Harry Partch (1901–1974), and *Koyaanisqatsi* (1983) by Philip Glass (born 1937).

American music educators at the turn of the twentieth century also wanted to foster the development of a national musical identity through the inclusion of American folk music in school song books. They considered Native American songs to come under the rubric of folk music, and therefore published Indian melodies in song anthologies. The melodies were often taken from scholarly sources, but were underlaid with lyrics in English and were harmonized in three or four parts or were provided with piano accompaniments. In some cases, music scholars themselves produced or contributed to collections of American Indian songs adapted and arranged for use in schools; sometimes they included elaborate directions for staging the songs as theatrical performances (Densmore 1921; Fletcher 1994). An offshoot of these collections was the development of illustrated instructional manuals for hobbyists of all ages who wanted to learn "authentic" Indian songs and dances (Buttree 1930; Evans and Evans 1931; Seton 1917). Such manuals were the mainstay of youth camp counselors and scout leaders from the 1930s through the 1950s. In reaction to the musical and cultural stereotypes perpetuated by the less sophisticated juvenilia, Native American composers and music educators have produced materials for classroom use since the 1970s (Ballard 1971; Black Bear and Theisz 1976; Toledo 1973). The better contemporary school music anthologies now draw Indian songs from the work of Indian composers, but some adaptations in the earlier style continue to appear.

Today, American Indians are active in all aspects of American musical life. They perform and compose in diverse idioms, from historic, pantribal, and syncretic musics to popular and art music styles. They are revitalizing and recontextualizing historic repertories to maintain and develop traditional culture. They have assumed leadership roles at all levels of music education, as well as of music scholarship. What makes American Indian music distinctively Indian, then, is its ability to survive in a context of change, to adopt in a context of exchange, and to adapt in a context of interaction. In all of these ways, American Indians have made – and continue to make – a unique contribution to the ongoing history of American music.

2

Music in America: an overview
(part 1)

WILLIAM BROOKS

Introduction

Deep in America's dreams, locked in a complex embrace, stand two mythic figures: the Pioneer (inventor, frontiersman, outlaw, tycoon) – naked, self-made, indebted to no-one, whose accomplishments dwarf his compatriots; and the Citizen – anonymous, unremarkable, but with the strength of thousands, shielded by the absolute equality of the polling booth. In their entanglements – sometimes cooperative, sometimes competitive – these figures act out the profound tension between two fundamental ideologies which drive America's politics and culture: individualism and egalitarianism.

On one hand America declares itself a land of freedom and opportunity, a country which guarantees each person's right to be different, to rise above the crowd, to become *un*common. On the other it declares all its citizens equal: no-one is privileged, no-one special; each is but a member of the common weal. The two declarations meet in America's most hackneyed phrases: "e pluribus unum" ["from many, one"]; "liberty [for each] and justice [for all]." They each claim a share of America's most fundamental laws, the egalitarian Constitution and the individualist Bill of Rights. And they confound each other in America's comic archetypes, from Brer Rabbit to Huck Finn to The Little Tramp.

The mythic reconciliation of these two ideologies has been situated physically on the frontier: there (the story goes) any Citizen can become a Pioneer, and in its wake Pioneers rediscover Citizenship. It has been economically situated in capitalism (rags to riches), and politically situated in democracy (my son, the president). Ideological reconciliation in cultural domains, however, has been more problematic; and the domain of art has been the most problematic of all. Great Artists (the story goes) have "genius"; in their presence the average Citizen is – in both senses – struck "dumb." Only a talented few become artists; it follows that (another story goes) all art is fundamentally "un-American," inconsistent with American values.

This chapter is an overview; it is my duty to simplify. I wish to claim that the most striking features of American art result from attempts to create an aesthetic domain in which American and artistic mythologies can be reconciled. Moreover, I would claim, music is the art most perfectly suited to this task. Music is at once personal and collective; it depends equally on invention and tradition; its performers range from acclaimed virtuosos to nameless choristers. It both levels and uplifts; to some it offers the comfort of anonymous hymns, to others the challenge of new-made experiments. Musicians produce not tangible products but ephemeral, profoundly useless experiences; and the social or aesthetic value of these, though generally acknowledged, cannot be easily quantified by markets, polls, or other egalitarian means. Rather, their values involve criteria which range from originality and inventiveness on one hand to universality and accessibility on the other.

Music, then, entails both individualist and egalitarian perspectives, and the problems faced by America's musicians parallel those faced by her body politic. Is the dichotomy between these two perspectives to be resolved? If so, how? What conceptual framework might make possible their constructive coexistence? What, after all, is music for (or by) the Pioneer? For (by) the Citizen? Can there be music for both? How can aesthetics be reconciled with capitalism? How can music be both original and popular? How can the elitism inherent in art be reconciled with egalitarianism?

I propose that there have been essentially six approaches to such questions. Three will be discussed below; the others are discussed in chapter 10. Though all are interconnected, and though each generates its own set of contradictions, these six approaches appear to me to be as useful as any in attempting to traverse the tangled terrain of American music; they can serve, in any case, to sketch a crude map which the remaining chapters of this book can elaborate and correct – or perhaps obliterate.

The first three approaches are linked by their relation to two other deeply problematic constituents of American culture: elitism and intellectualism. In theory, both individualism and egalitarianism preclude the creation of social classes: the former declares each person a class unto himself while the latter creates a single class to which all belong. In practice, however, where there are Pioneers there are followers; and where there are Citizens there are alliances. In both cases associations between individuals serve to distinguish segments of society from each other; and when one such segment is assigned an elevated status – economic or cultural, perceived or actual – an elite is created.

Associations of intellectuals are especially problematic. Many intellectuals seek to be associated with Pioneer thinking; that is, to form a vanguard (an elite). Others seek to champion Citizens; but their work sets them apart from the people for whom they would speak (again creating an elite). Either way, intellectuals constitute a class which claims a superior ability to understand, or at least to articulate; that they are a class is incompatible with individualism, and that they are superior is incompatible with egalitarianism. It would seem that only acts of self-effacement – isolation or anonymity – free an intellectual from this dilemma; all other stances appear to entail affirming one ideology at the expense of the other.

Not all musicians are intellectuals; but persons who write and speak about music are. The history of American music is in part the history of assertions about it, and many of these have indeed clustered around one of the poles of the American dialectic. One cluster asserts that music is indeed fundamentally elitist, that it can never be universal. Proponents of this position often argue that great music is necessarily created by great genius, and that it can only be apprehended fully by an elite cultural subgroup with special abilities and training. This position is (understandably) asserted almost exclusively by persons who believe (or wish to demonstrate) that they belong to this subgroup – that is, by intellectual conservatives. They choose to call their music *art* music, thus situating its value in a domain removed from commerce or utility; and I shall use this term also, despite the obvious dangers.

A second cluster asserts that music of real value must spring from or be embraced by common people – that is, it must be collectively owned, part of daily life. This assertion is made, but only implicitly, by the users of such music, the common people themselves; it is articulated by persons who have taken on a different role, becoming populists (if the discourse is polemical) or intellectual liberals (if it is scholarly). It is the latter who have chosen to call such music *folk* music, implying egalitarian anonymity even when the music's creator is known; again I shall use this term, though again there are considerable dangers.

Intellectuals in each camp recognize the existence of the other. They are, in fact, united in their desire to keep the two poles unentangled, to preserve the integrity of certain musical traditions; they differ in the traditions to which they are devoted. In this sense they are more like each other than like a third group which seeks to mediate the differences between the poles by promoting musical and social transformations. For this third group – intellectual reformers – the American vision requires that the two ideologies be reconciled, not that one emerge victorious; and the essential mechanism for this reconciliation has been education.

Historically, Americans have trusted to public education to mediate the tensions between intellectual elitism and social equality. Until relatively recently the mediation usually entailed attempts to convey to the general public the values and works cherished by intellectual conservatives. Thus music education, and musical reformers, sought primarily to increase the general understanding of art music: though (the argument went) the creation of great music was limited to gifted individuals (Pioneers), appreciation of and participation in such music could be made equally available to all (Citizens).

In a more recent counter-reform, however, educators have attempted the reverse: to convey to intellectual conservatives the values and works treasured by Citizens. In music, the sources of this effort go back at least to individuals like John Lomax and George Pullen Jackson; but the watershed occurred with Gilbert Chase, who asserted flatly that "[our folk-popular music] has been the most important phase of America's music" (Chase 1966a, p. xviii). Thereafter a wide range of scholars have sought, like Charles Hamm, to engage intellectuals in the practice and appreciation of non-art musics; or at the very least they have sought with Wiley Hitchcock to balance their accounts equally between "cultivated" and "vernacular" traditions.

As educators, then – and from a variety of perspectives – reformers and counter-reformers have sought to enlighten persons oriented to one type of music about the merits of another. In their writing and teaching, they have testified on behalf of art, folk, or some other music; but their testimony has been motivated not merely by enthusiasm, but by a desire to address America's ideological dilemma, to mediate between Pioneers and Citizens. They have served, in effect, as missionaries, using music as a tool for inducing a transformation, a change of mind by means of which (they hope) the tensions in their society can be understood and perhaps transcended. In their endeavors religion, art, and politics mingle in a distinctively American fashion which both derives from and acts upon the poles implicit in American culture.

At the boundaries, then, there stand art music and folk music; and between them, a rich and complex field of mediation, education, and

reform. It is to a survey of this terrain, and the journeys across it, that the
remainder of this chapter is dedicated.

Form and reform

Music in America, of course, long predates the colonies. Indian musics and
cultures, however, were initially far removed from the ideological tangle
described above; that did not take root until the newly discovered hemi-
sphere was invaded by a motley collection of European misfits ranging
from daredevils to utopians to gentleman farmers. And the earliest
responses to it were shaped by the earliest immigrants: the Tidewater
colonists and the Puritan settlers.

The gentry who colonized Virginia brought what they could of the
culture they left in England. In the New World, indeed, they rendered
even more extreme the stratification fundamental to that culture: holdings became plantations, servants became slaves. Preserving class distinctions, as they did, these colonists likewise preserved the distinction
between folk and art musics. On one hand were ballads, dance tunes, and
work songs; on the other were keyboard music, ensemble music, and
parlor songs. The former were primarily transmitted orally and were especially the purview of small farmers, indentured servants, and laborers of
various kinds; the latter were notated and were heard almost exclusively in
wealthy plantation households. The two did interact; colonists brought
with them such published hybrids as Playford's enormously popular
collections of dance tunes, and songs by composers like Arne and Shield
entered (or returned to) the oral tradition. But these interactions did not
manifest any fundamental dissatisfaction with the social structure or with
music's place in it. These colonists sought to *conserve* English culture, not
to change it.

In contrast, to the north was founded a *New* England: though the
surname remained, the child would be different. Nurtured by a New
World, delivered from a tyrannical fatherland, America's Puritans were
settlers on a mission – not merely to convert the heathen but to demonstrate to the Old World the power of the faith practiced in the New. They
were America's first reformers.

For the Puritans, music was a tool for social and spiritual change; and its
character, its place, its very existence had to be constantly tested against
this purpose. The Puritan mission was by no means hostile to secular
music; indeed, much of the music found in the southern colonies could be

found in New England as well. The difference lay in the extent to which the place and purpose of this music was debated.

Even more revealing were the debates about sacred music, which began as soon as the settlements were secure. The first volume published in the New World was the "Bay Psalm Book," the work of reformers seeking a collection of psalm texts which more closely suited Puritan views. The tunes for these texts were transmitted orally, in large part, since very few settlers could read music; and as time passed this repertory was transformed by common use, so that different congregations sang the same tune differently and individuals within congregations embellished each tune idiosyncratically.

These developments were noted with distress by musically literate clerics and by the preceptors who were attempting to maintain the notated versions of the tunes by "lining them out" for congregations. In effect, a conservative intellectual elite found itself struggling to preserve the melodies published by pioneer compilers (Ainsworth, Ravenscroft, Playford), while an egalitarian citizenry treated these melodies as communal property to be collectively used and transformed.

By the 1720s intellectuals found the situation intolerable, and a loose alliance of reformers proposed a solution: establish schools to teach congregations to read music. The reasoning was paradigmatic: education would reunite the culture by conveying to citizens a body of knowledge formerly limited to an elite. The knowledge in this case (music notation) was drawn from art music; it was used to literally re-form what had become a folk-singing tradition.

The outcome was also paradigmatic. On one hand, the reform was successful; the newly literate congregations returned to singing psalm tunes as notated, and the breach between the art and folk traditions was for the moment healed. On the other hand, the reform made it possible for the traditions to separate afresh, in a new domain. For citizens who could read music could also write music; and within a few decades a pioneering generation of "Yankee tunesmiths" had emerged, composing, compiling, and publishing their own psalm tunes and anthems.

Most of these tunesmiths were unschooled in composition (though excellently trained in music notation), and they devised their own solutions to problems of form, technique, and syntax. Once again an inherited practice was transformed by common use; composers of the new repertory diverged both from their English forebears and each other. In effect, a folk *composing* tradition evolved; and as before, the results distressed an intellectual elite which was well schooled in art music's theory and technique.

Again a reform movement arose, and again it funneled its energies into education. New pedagogical collections appeared in which the indigenous composers were largely supplanted by "approved" European "masters" such as Handel and Haydn. Works by the latter, however, were not presented in their original forms but rather arranged and simplified to suit the reformers' view of the public's abilities. They were supplemented by exercises, hymns, and secular pieces composed by the reformers themselves in an idiom designed to be both "correct" and easily comprehended. The result was a new body of music which was neither art nor folk, a music which both revered greatness and affirmed the importance of average citizens.

Individuals like Thomas Hastings introduced this new repertory first in singing schools and churches. Then, under the guidance of Lowell Mason, it became the basis for music education in Boston's public schools. The missionary character of reform efforts remained, though the emphasis shifted away from religious values and toward social ones: music was to be a tool for refining the taste and judgment of the body politic, for advancing civilized values in moral and aesthetic domains. And the reforms continued to mediate between elitism and egalitarianism; the public school music curriculum was intended, in effect, to elevate all the citizenry to a level of understanding formerly restricted to those with exceptional talent or means.

Mason's work was emulated throughout the nineteenth century in countless cities and towns. Moreover, the vocal repertory assembled by reformers was paralleled, less systematically, in instrumental tutors, method books, and collections. By 1850 the reformers had largely succeeded: in churches, schools, and informal institutions like village bands, Americans everywhere were learning to read, sing, play, and appreciate a repertory which was derived from art music but intended for all citizens equally. The repercussions were felt for over a century, as reform objectives continued to resonate in a wide range of America's musical activities.

Public music education continued to expand with the introduction first of instrumental instruction in public schools and later of music curricula in universities and colleges. The latter was given additional impetus by the development of large land-grant public universities after the Civil War; the egalitarian idealism of their charters was a happy match for the universal education desired by musical reformers. This expansion peaked as late as the 1950s, when advanced degrees in various specializations (composition, conducting, individual instruments) were established in many such institutions.

Music was also important to most nineteenth-century progressives. In labor unions, farm associations, settlement houses, and similar venues music was deemed vital to building community and advancing the collective good. Many progressive organizations were directed at immigrant populations, and progressive music thus overlapped and intermingled with transplanted European institutions like German *Männerchöre*; as time passed the whole was gradually transformed into such characteristic mid-twentieth-century institutions as community choruses and neighborhood music schools.

If (as reformers believed) music was a tool for social betterment, and if (as they hoped) the public could be made musically literate, then songs would be very useful tools for furthering specific political objectives. The extraordinary body of political music in nineteenth- and early-twentieth-century America is thus another extension of the reform movement. The Civil War produced the most lasting political repertory, but songs promoting the interlinked causes of temperance and suffrage more consistently adopt the moral tone of earlier musical reformers. Indeed, virtually every cause or platform of the nineteenth century – from the Greenback Party to Graham crackers – used music to rally its followers; and even after radio and television radically transformed the nature of campaigning, music remained a vital force in the Civil Rights and anti-war movements.

Finally, and perhaps most importantly, the extension of musical literacy to a large segment of the public helped transform the economic basis of music in America. Music publishing evolved in tandem with musical reform; indeed, among the first publishing magnates was Lowell Mason himself. In the second half of the nineteenth century printing became the primary medium for music's dissemination, and more music was bought for the home than was heard on the stage. This music formed a new genre – popular music – and though much of it was irrelevant (or even contrary) to the reformers' social purposes, a substantial part continued to maintain the link between cultured morality and ensemble singing. In any event, the industrialization of music by means of publishing was only made possible by the reformers' successes. Recording technology would eventually undo these successes and transform the musical economy again; but by then the very nature of reform would itself have changed.

Art music

Mason's work would have been impossible had there not been by 1820 a lively community of Americans already devoted to art music. Its precursors reach back to colonial amateurs, but America's concert life did not begin until the 1730s, when an economic upper class had begun to form in urban centers like Boston, Philadelphia, and Charleston. The programs, ticket prices, and venues of these early concerts all served to limit the audience to educated, wealthy persons; informal, exclusive clubs of subscribers led to the founding of private St. Cecilia and Philharmonic societies, which evolved in turn into the associations of wealthy patrons who financed the first professional orchestras in the 1830s.

The performers associated with all these early activities were primarily immigrant professionals who were largely untroubled by the elitist implications of their work. For the patrons, elitism was welcome; by associating with master musicians they could stand apart from (and in their view, above) the majority of citizens, who could neither afford nor (presumably) appreciate great music. If they suffered qualms, they soothed their democratic conscience in two ways: by sponsoring concerts intended to benefit the poor or other unfortunates; and by indirectly reducing the price of concert tickets for the general public, thus presumably contributing to reform objectives. For citizens thereby enabled to purchase a ticket, concert-going also served elitist ends, linking them by implication not only to musical greatness but also to the wealthy patrons in the dress circle.

The interlinking of art music, patronage, and elitism has continued unaltered to the present day; though its repertory differs (somewhat), the New York Philharmonic serves the same social function in 1997 as it did in 1847. The confusion of aesthetics with patronage has been constantly satirized, most notably in minstrelsy and its twentieth-century progeny; but it has had a profound effect on the course of art music. For the system only works when patrons have complete confidence in the greatness of the art they are supporting; the most unthinkable embarrassment (as the Marx Brothers knew well) is to patronize a fraud.

Art music patrons, then, required a *canon*, a list of works and composers of unassailable status, together with a means for assessing the qualifications of new works. A similar canon had already been established in Europe, not only by intellectuals but also by publishers and promoters; but the effects were heightened in America for two reasons. First, since patronage was at odds with important parts of America's ideology, patrons had to be especially cautious; their only defense against egalitarian attacks was to assert that artistic greatness was an absolute value which had been historically proven. Second, since art music in the New World served to separate its patrons from ordinary Americans, a canon that was literally alien (from the Old) was an advantage; European provenance became virtually a prerequisite for acceptance.

America's art music repertory was thus from the outset extraordinarily conservative. Almost without exception, new works were admitted only if they had been approved in Europe and were clearly distinguishable from popular or reform repertories. American arbiters of taste – initially European immigrants, later European-trained musicians and patrician critics – revised the canon only in ways which helped ensure its continuing alienation from the citizenry.

An early example can be found in the history of musical theatre. Until the 1820s America's theatres, unlike her concert halls, sought to offer entertainment for everyone, supplying boxes for the elite and a pit for the citizenry. When Italian opera was introduced, its European provenance was emphasized in appeals to the elite, but it was presented in English adaptations to attract the general public. In the 1830s, however, opera began to be presented in Italian in newly built opera houses funded in part by upper-class patrons. What had been a meeting-ground became a battlefield; a decade later opera had become an elite art, and a new musical theatre – minstrelsy – had been created for inhabitants of the pit. Among the mainstays of minstrel productions were operatic parodies.

As this process unfolded, important features of the Italian style were being absorbed into American popular song. This phenomenon peaked in the 1840s; precisely at that time, the American art music repertory began to shift toward Germany. Certainly a surge in German immigrants contributed to this, but clearly also Italian music had become too familiar to the citizenry to be useful in defining a social elite. A similar shift occurred in the early twentieth century, after Tin Pan Alley had largely replaced Italian elements with German ones: the art music canon was enlarged to encompass various national schools (French, Russian, middle European), and Italian opera was reestablished as an elite art.

The place and function of art music changed fundamentally – in Europe as in America – with the introduction of electronic broadcasting and recording in the 1920s. The reproducibility of music changed ways of thinking and hearing; it also meant that access to art music (in recorded form) was now available to virtually anyone. Technology accomplished instantaneously much of what reformers had sought for a century, and it thereby rendered obsolete the need for an intermediate reform repertory.

For patrons of art music, the reach of the new technology meant that the art music canon, by itself, was no longer sufficient to mark a cultural elite. Only recordings were widely available, however; live performances remained a useful indicator of class distinctions. But to maximize their effectiveness, the repertory at live concerts had to mirror the most widely distributed recorded repertory; the result, on both sides of the Atlantic, was to freeze the art music canon even further.

Art music composers, in America as in Europe, thus came to confront a difficult paradox. With the canon now in the hands of the citizenry, and with alienation from the citizenry a socially imposed condition for art music, it became necessary for art music composers to alienate themselves from the canon itself. There resulted a bevy of new names for twentieth-century compositions ("modern," "avant-garde," "new") and a multitude of composer-driven associations (notably in New York in the 1920s) which served not merely to promote members' works but also to distinguish them from the standard repertory.

Modern music's paradoxical relationship to the canon required a new set of arbiters for determining value. In America, especially, these were found among intellectuals, whose ideological position was similarly paradoxical; as the twentieth century unfolded composers were increasingly associated with universities, and their work was evaluated primarily by academic theorists and historians. Thus a composer like Roger Sessions has been validated as a central figure in American music primarily by virtue of his own position as a university teacher and by the status assigned him by collegial intellectuals.

Throughout its history, art music in the United States has been attacked by egalitarians, populists, and demagogues; in recent years, amplified by anti-intellectualism, the drumbeat has become especially deafening. Indeed, it is almost impossible to discuss art music's social position without appearing to invite (or even participate in) such attacks; the paradoxes of twentieth-century art music seem especially absurd. But all such attacks, and most social accounts, ignore the sizable and important collection of individuals – present throughout America's history – whose personal interest in and affection for art music has had little to do with elitism or social standing. These devotees have been baffled and sometimes enraged by the reduction of their devotion to a sociological footnote, and they have been enormously frustrated by the difficulty of articulating ideological alternatives.

A significant number of American performers have sought to decouple art music from patronage. For decades after opera passed out of popular culture, efforts were made to reintroduce English-language performances which would be more generally comprehensible. These efforts peaked toward the end of the nineteenth century in the touring companies of Emma Abbott, Clara Louise Kellogg, and others; but the controversy continued until quite recently, when a technological innovation ("surtitles") rendered it somewhat moot. Many (though certainly not all) touring virtuosos also sought to reach beyond the dress circle; Jenny Lind leavened her art music repertory with popular airs and acoustic stunts, and Ole Bull's appeal was so wide-ranging that his name entered American folklore as a metaphor for fiddling virtuosity.

Some orchestras were similarly motivated, at least in part, and made outreach a central part of their artistic missions. The quintessential American conductors, in this sense, are Theodore Thomas and Leonard Bernstein, both of whom were devoted and creative educators. Even John Philip Sousa described his purpose to be "to lift the unmusical mind to a still higher form of musical art" (quoted in Hamm 1983, p. 296). Sousa's programs, coupling popular novelties with transcriptions from the art music canon, make him close kin to Jenny Lind; and both are second cousins to many nineteenth-century reformers. Outreach and reform have been consistent allies, and the continuing importance of both is reflected in the recent history of public arts funding, with spending on education gradually displacing the funding of commissions, festivals, and the like.

America's art music composers have been less easily able to shape their work to egalitarian ends, though in their prose many have been either ideologically neutral or explicitly anti-elitist. They have responded to their dilemma with a variety of tactics. In the nineteenth century, composers like Fry and Bristow sought simply to place American and European art on a fair and equal footing. These advocates, however, never fully realized the extent to which European provenance was necessary to art music's social function; for America to possess an equal musical voice would be a danger, not a virtue, for upper-class patrons.

Accepting this necessity, other American composers attempted to become surrogate Europeans, turning to Europe for their education and writing music that left them stylistically indistinguishable from their colleagues overseas. The most notable group of such musicians formed the

Second New England School, but the practice extends back at least to William Mason and forward to the post-1945 international avant garde. Occupying a special position were Americanized Europeans like Varèse, Bloch, Weill, even Hindemith and Stravinsky; their importance to the canon was directly proportional to the extent to which America's elite continued to view them as foreigners.

Still other musicians assumed an extremist position within a European aesthetic, affirming by implication what many Europeans believed: that grandiosity and single-mindedness were central features of the American character. William Henry Fry's music employs the gestures of Italian opera with a relentless consistency that no Italian could have contemplated; Milton Babbitt takes to unequaled extremes the mannerism implicit in Webern's systematic serialism. After the Civil War, the monster concerts organized by Patrick Gilmore and others served in part to demonstrate the unchallengeable might of America's musical armies – bigger, broader, and (presumably) louder than any heretofore heard. The reiterative insistence of some minimalist music (especially the amplified works of Philip Glass) manifests a related extremism.

One other tactic could only evolve in the twentieth century, after composition had become fully alienated from the European canon. A small number of composers, working largely in isolation, accepted key principles of art music – especially a belief in composerly genius – but rejected the techniques and trappings which had become associated with it. Harry Partch is the best representative of these: undeniably an art music composer, he depended on benefactors throughout his life; but in aesthetic and technique his music rejected both the European tradition and the conventions of the concert hall.

There were also pioneers who situated themselves *within* the social and technical framework of art music, idiosyncratically reworking a European musical language to suit their own aesthetic or social visions. Among these are iconoclasts like Carl Ruggles and technicians like Wallingford Riegger; but also included are composers more directly concerned with the contradictions at the heart of American life. A nineteenth-century paradigm is Anthony Philip Heinrich; a twentieth-century paradigm, Elliott Carter. Both embellished received idioms – Classical harmony and modernist atonality – to produce musics of "strange ideal somersets and capriccios" (Heinrich's phrase, quoted in Hamm 1983, p. 213).

In Heinrich's case the elaboration is diachronic: his music wanders freely through America's collectively held landscapes *en route* to a destination that may little resemble the starting point. Using a fragmented syntax to express the unregulated, egalitarian opportunity of the frontier, Heinrich perfectly captured the interplay between culture and wilderness, Pioneer and Citizen characteristic of ante-bellum America. Elliott Carter's orientation, in contrast, is fundamentally *synchronic*; in Carter's work musical individuation persists in even the densest textures. Carter's rigorous structures mirror the intricacies of twentieth-century urban life; his pieces propose a future America in which an invisible order regulates the coexistence of individualism and equality.

Between Heinrich and Carter is situated the quintessential American Pioneer, Charles Ives. Ives is *the* central figure in America's art music not because he is unique but because so many threads cross in the warp and woof of his work. Ives, like Heinrich, composed landscape-narratives whose unpredictable paths are peopled with unexpected acquaintances; in their anarchic energy can be recognized rural America's nineteenth-century faith that on the frontier Pioneers and Citizens find common ground. But in Ives all this is retrospective. In his real life as a New Yorker, Ives was deeply concerned with creating unity in an increasingly scattered urban society – but without imposing a stifling conformity. Infused with the residue of the previous century's optimism, Ives built his musical models of a future America less systematically, less defensively, than Carter; but the complex layers of his music likewise propose a transcendental culture in which individuals are free to go their own way or to join hands, to insist or to accommodate.

Folk music

Among the shades who people Ives's landscapes is Lowell Mason, often embodied in the hymn *Bethany*. Ives quoted *Bethany*, however, in homage not to its author but to the millions of Americans who gave it voice, the citizens who through it found musical expression. Created not by a composer but by a community, this *Bethany* – the hymn Ives loved – was no longer art nor even reform music; it had become folk music.

Bethany's transformation is representative. American culture is constructed, often self-consciously, and much that it calls "folk" music has actually been appropriated from sources ranging from European dances to reform hymns to popular song. Such appropriations interact with more conventional folk repertories found in immigrant communities, with each subculture establishing a distinctive mix. Indeed, just as every American is

situated somewhere between Pioneer and Citizen, so each subculture situ-
ates itself between isolation and integration. On one hand, each seeks to
preserve its own music without change, to protect the purity of its inheritance. On the other, each seeks to enrich its tradition by absorbing alien
material whenever it appears useful.

Most subcultures, of course, move to and fro along this spectrum,
working though the dialectic between individualism (preservation) and
egalitarianism (appropriation) characteristic of American culture as a
whole. But all American folk musics occupy both poles in a certain sense.
All are necessarily removed – isolated – from art music and reform traditions: perhaps not ignorant of them (the literacy of some folk traditions is,
for example, a by-product of reform), but free of the reverence for genius
that both exhibit. And, lacking that reverence, all folk traditions are fundamentally egalitarian: all the music outside their tradition stands before
them on an equal footing.

A fine instance of all these workings can be found in the shape-note
traditions of the rural South. When the reform repertory supplanted the
music of the New England tunesmiths, the latter moved west and south
together with the singing-school tradition and the newly invented,
pedagogically motivated shape-notes. The whole came to rest in the rural
South, where it became a constructed folk music built upon a repertory
originally assembled by compilers like B. F. White and William Walker.
The first components of this repertory were threefold: New England
hymns and anthems which had survived the displacement; folk tunes
already known to the singers, harmonized in a distinctive polymelodic
style; and pieces resembling either of the preceding but newly composed
by the compiler or his associates.

Thus shape-note music's early history entailed both isolation (from
reform) and appropriation (of repertory). As time passed, shape-note
music became more defensively and self-consciously isolated; concurrently the repertory continued to expand, eventually incorporating even
reform works like *Bethany*. Shape-note music came to be defined by a performance practice more than by notated stylistic features; shape-note
singers sing *Bethany* without regard for its source, and it is this egalitarian
treatment which makes the diverse shape-note repertory a single "folk"
tradition.

The performance practice is itself a paradigm. The singers sit in a hollow
square, facing inward, with the leader in the center; persons not singing
may sit elsewhere to listen, but the music is in no way directed toward

them. Anyone may lead, and all the leaders take turns; thus although each song is supervised by a single individual, that individual is simply one among equals. Only the leader is positioned to hear all the parts in perfect balance, so that the leader's privilege is essentially that of an audience. Thus the usual fixed hierarchy (leader, performer, listener) becomes a floating one in which roles are conflated and opportunities exchanged. The vocal production is generally extremely loud and nasal; notes are connected with strong portamentos so that each is attended to individually but all are stressed equally.

Shape-note singing thus balances leader with ensemble, individual with community, element with totality. It models a utopian America; it also models its own subculture's attempt to balance self-protection with openness. In this regard it is typical of most American ethnic and sectarian musics; a few additional examples may suggest the range of possibilities.

Appalachian folk music both paralleled and interacted with the shape-note tradition. By the 1840s the Appalachian repertory, like shape-note music, had come to include works from three broad categories: traditional music brought from the British Isles; music from eighteenth- and early-nineteenth-century anthologies; and newly composed music which resembled the preceding. After the Civil War, Appalachia's cultural isolation both preserved and distorted this repertory, to which were added bits of mainstream America's musical jetsam – minstrel tunes, sentimental ballads, and topical novelties. By the 1920s, when Appalachian music suddenly acquired commercial importance, it was a jumble of widely disparate items unified essentially by consistencies in performance practice. The repertory of the Carter Family perfectly exemplifies both this egalitarian diversity and the defining importance of a distinct performance style.

More isolated still were non-English-speaking subcultures, but even these interacted distinctively with the larger culture. Cajun music evolved much like Appalachian, supplementing the settlers' repertory with songs appropriated from other traditions. But the appropriation was almost entirely in one direction; whereas Anglo-American folk music exerted a continuing influence on popular genres, Cajun music was essentially unknown until its discovery by recording companies and folk enthusiasts. The ensuing radical acculturation nearly destroyed the tradition; its distinctiveness became valued only in the 1960s, when authenticity itself became a commercial asset.

Secular Jewish-American music had quite a different history. Jewish immigrants of the late nineteenth and early twentieth centuries settled in

East Coast cities, and many quickly assumed leading roles in America's popular music industry. Thus a rich tradition of Yiddish music and theatre became immediately linked to American culture as a whole. More than most immigrants, urban Jews consciously chose the extent to which they would be assimilated or remain autonomous. Defining a relationship to the mainstream was a necessary undertaking for entertainers like Al Jolson and Irving Berlin; indeed, this was explicitly the subject of *The Jazz Singer*, to which both contributed.

Jewish-American identity was religious as well as cultural; throughout America's history religious groups, like subcultures, have positioned themselves somewhere between isolation and assimilation. The Shakers took their music in part from folksong and Pentecostal hymnody, but they created much of it themselves, recorded in notation largely incomprehensible to outsiders. Their self-conscious isolation helped to focus individual Shakers on direct revelations from God, which included both "gifts" of new songs and notational innovations. Shaker doctrine, indeed, asserted that revelation superseded tradition: a gift was more to be treasured than a learned melody. Individualism, then, characterized the relationship not only between Shaker communities and their secular environs but also between each believer and the community.

The Shakers, therefore, are situated very near an individualist extreme; other subgroups, often secular, created their music largely by appropriation. The folk music associated with labor unions, political parties, and social activism is replete with parodies of popular or traditional songs. In some cases, the act of appropriation was itself political; when Joe Hill made *In the Sweet Bye and Bye* into *The Preacher and the Slave* he sought to liberate not only workers but the song itself. In these traditions, even newly composed music was treated as if appropriated; Woody Guthrie's songs were to be used, not bought and sold. Even the mainstream culture has created "folk" songs out of appropriated (but usually apolitical) material; unattributed performances of *Happy Birthday to You*, for example, occur thousands of times daily.

All the subcultures mentioned above had at least some autonomy in defining their relationship to America as a whole; but two ethnicities – Indians and Africans – were given little choice. Indians were sometimes excluded, sometimes exterminated; Africans were included against their will. America's views about the extent to which members of these groups would be assimilated – that is, whether integration or separatism would prevail – have been a barometer for America's political climate. In progressive eras, such as the 1900s and 1960s, egalitarian opportunity has been viewed as more important than racial or ethnic identity. In conservative periods, such as the present, pluralism (currently "cultural diversity") has served to excuse economic and political exploitation as necessary to the preservation of distinct racial or ethnic identities.

Politically, African and Native Americans have both mirrored and resisted the swings between these poles; musically they have adopted somewhat different strategies. American Indians have been largely separated, by both prejudice and law, from the culture which now occupies their lands. Their influence on and adaptations of music by non-Indians have been subtle and restrained; and although forced displacements have produced some intra-tribal musical interactions, they have placed a high value on the maintenance of tradition.

African Americans, on the other hand, created from the outset a hybridized music by adapting imposed and appropriated elements from the mainstream to their own ends. Some elements of African music (the banjo, for instance) came with the slaves to colonial America; but most of their heritage was stripped away by owners who could not allow slaves to be regarded as humans. Nevertheless, by the Civil War African Americans had remade their music with a resourcefulness which owed as much to adaptive resistance to slavery as to their African roots.

Slaves encountered a wide variety of white musics, from Appalachian dances to reform hymnody to marches to sentimental songs. Some was imposed on them by well-meaning missionaries, some taught them by exploitative owners; but in all cases the received music was acted upon – sifted for items of particular value, transformed by African residues, intermingled with other materials. African Americans were never passive recipients of white culture; rather, they actively reworked it to suit their own lives. For over two hundred years they struggled not merely for equality but for individuality; they sought to be not invisible compatriots but distinct persons. They mirror with particular intensity the ideological tension at the heart of American culture; they are, in their situation if not their status, the quintessential Americans.

African American culture is profoundly utilitarian; materials at hand are redisposed to suit immediate purposes. For this reason it is especially difficult to separate the threads in African American traditions: a verse appropriated from a Protestant hymn might be transformed into a freedom refrain sung in call-and-response to a melody which derives from a field holler, with the whole reappearing later in a blues. Not uncommonly,

appropriations from white culture served political ends: plantation spirituals and hollers fused African idioms with scriptural texts to create a code
for underground communication; the music in black churches, partly
appropriated from white culture and therefore acceptable to it, became a
means for resisting oppression from that very culture.

Problems of lineage and appropriation are especially acute in secular
music, since African American creativity has repeatedly been looted by the
popular music industry, as a slave's handiwork might be taken and sold by
an owner. When this happens, African Americans have often turned away
from that which has been taken in order to create another new music. After
the banjo was popularized in minstrelsy, for example, it fell out of favor
among African Americans. The rhythms it had played were reassigned to
other instruments and merged with harmonies and forms appropriated
from Europe; ragtime and (arguably) jazz resulted. In the twentieth
century this process has become more self-conscious. Bebop was, among
other things, a critique of the white-dominated, monolithic jazz of the
1940s; part of that critique entailed composing new melodies to harmonies appropriated from popular music standards. More recently
African Americans have pioneered the use of sampling in hip hop and rap;
the appropriation of tracks from earlier recordings is in part a critique of
the exploitation intrinsic to the mainstream economy.

Bebop and rap were made both necessary and possible by the development of recording technology. The impact of this technology on all of
America's folk musics is incalculable: as soon as a folk music is made commercially available it becomes not only an economic commodity but also
an historical artifact. Externally imposed values grounded in profit, ownership, or authenticity begin to supplant the aesthetic and social values
intrinsic to the tradition. This process gathered enormous force in the
twentieth century, so that to most Americans "folk music" now describes
either a marketing or a scholarly niche. It was anticipated, however, by a
sea change in the reform tradition which occurred in the latter half of the
nineteenth century. That change, the relationship of popular music to
American ideology, and two interlinked affirmations of individualist
invention will be the subjects of chapter 10.

3

Secular music to 1800

KATE VAN WINKLE KELLER

WITH JOHN KOEGEL[1]

Throughout the world, music is used by the powerful to advance their personal or political agendas, by governments to achieve national objectives, by performers and tradesmen to earn a living, and by the people for entertainment and individual goals. Thus, the music played and heard in colonial America was defined by the distinct national cultures that held political power and whose people populated its land.

The first colonists arrived from and perpetuated a world in which the arts were divided. On one side were the cultivated arts of music and dance, enriched by centuries of patronage from the court and nobility. Settlers with ample means purchased instruments and music, hired professional instructors, and enjoyed playing or listening to new compositions of British and European artists. They performed the latest dances learned from their teachers or from books ordered from London, Paris, or Madrid, depending on trade connections at the time. In colonial societies that were anxious to appear as refined as those in the mother countries, capability in, or consumption of, the arts was a sign of gentility, affluence, and influence; it gave evidence of sufficient means to obtain appreciation, training, and leisure to practice necessary skills.

On the other side was the music of the people. The laboring, farming, and servant classes had little access to cultivated music. They did not understand it and they did not need it. Their long-lived ballads and dancing tunes were seldom consciously learned but rather absorbed from frequent hearing. They were an integral part of their community bond and identification. Those with little to spend amused themselves with familiar songs and free-form community dances to the music of their own voices, perhaps enhanced by the hum of a jew's harp or a homemade flute or fiddle.

During the Colonial period in America, class distinctions were blurred by new opportunities. Arriving in a place without established traditions,

---

1. I am grateful to John Koegel for writing the sections on the French and Spanish settlements in Canada, New Orleans, Florida, and the Southwest.

colonists set out to establish those they brought with them. In America, landed gentry, wealthy merchants, and political leaders assumed the role of the Old World courts in setting fashion. They banded together to promote and enjoy the arts of music and dance, trying to keep alive the distinctions in musical sophistication and social context of performance that excluded those with less privilege. Each group brought a distinctive repertory. Some sustained their traditions; some merged with others as power and fashion shifted. New music was written to suit new occasions. New audiences and opportunities emerged as the population grew larger and more diverse. Overarching the entire period is the phenomenon J. H. Plumb has called the "commercialization of leisure," the move of Western civilization to a market-based society (McKendrick 1982, pp. 265–285). Cary Carson has identified this further as a "consumer revolution" that preceded and enabled the Industrial Revolution (Carson 1994, p. 486). Carl Bridenbaugh observed that though urban culture was based largely upon wealth, it was also remarkably dependent upon the interchange and companionship of social living: "Those arts and amusements especially flourished which could be indulged gregariously, – dancing and dining, music and the theatre" (Bridenbaugh 1938, p. 464).

A democratizing of the arts in Europe and its colonies occurred during this period. It depended on a critical mass of population with the means, inclination, and free time to support such endeavors. As new groups of people rose in wealth and power, they demanded access to the cultivated arts as tokens of their new status. In turn, enterprising composers, arrangers, teachers, theatre managers, and other artists and businessmen developed ways to take advantage of the new demands and make those arts accessible to the new market.

Aiding this move was the development of inexpensive engraving techniques. In the sixteenth and early seventeenth centuries, art music of the courts and the cities of Europe was usually circulated in manuscript or in limited editions printed from moveable type. Copperplate hand-engraving techniques were used, but were more costly. With the introduction of the punch and pewter plates in about 1700, engraving gained ascendancy over typography. At about the same time, a new system of dance writing dependent on the new engraving techniques gave the public access to dances formerly available only through private lessons. Publishers flooded the market with method books for those who wished to learn to dance or play instruments without the expense of a master.

Mirroring these developments were changes in the repertory that made elite arts more acceptable to the new consumers. In social dance, the minuet and the country dance enjoyed enormous popularity because they were based on fairly simple figures with optional steps that could be more or less intricate depending upon the social setting and the skill of the dancers. Theatrical dancers performed fewer abstract bourrées and gigues and created character dances. Less highly regulated by government censors than spoken drama, opera became musical theatre with accessible music and contemporary plots.

Music itself changed. Renaissance compositions were linear; each voice was composed and each melodically important. In the Baroque era the emphasis shifted to a melody-based music for which a simple bass line provided the intended harmonic structure and conventions dictated the realization of the performance. This reduced the cost of printing scores and beginning around 1700 many collections of songs, opera excerpts, and instrumental music were printed in inexpensive editions in England, Amsterdam, Paris, and Madrid, and after colonial trade controls were lifted, in the United States in the 1790s.

Although the elite tried to retain a wall of privilege through adoption of ephemeral fad and fashion, the sheer size of the market serving the tastes of the new consumers made real control impossible. And though the changes occurred throughout the Western world, they were magnified in the American colonies where institutional power and control was less deeply rooted. A steady stream of immigrants brought new music and dance traditions. Some vanished; some found fertile community support and flourished. Some developed into new arts and new American musics.

The following discussion deals first with the various colonial areas in which secular music occurred prior to 1800, before moving on to the types of activities found generally throughout the colonies. Two points should be borne in mind. Firstly, information regarding the English-speaking East Coast colonies is in much greater supply than that relating to the French- and Spanish-speaking territories: thus this chapter inevitably focuses on East Coast activity. And secondly, particularly in the Southwest, secular musical activity was intertwined with sacred musical activity. Some information will be included that also relates to chapter 4 and – to a lesser extent – chapter 1.

Cultural settings

Boston

Initially, the New England colonies were bound to a religious ideal and their leaders held sway over private and public life. In the early days of settlement – that is, from the 1620s onward – and particularly during the tours of the charismatic revivalist preacher George Whitefield in the 1740s, there were public furors between local magistrates and overly enthusiastic dancers and musicians. They were the exception rather than the rule. The issue was usually inappropriate time and place rather than the activity itself.

The notion of Puritan hostility to all music is a myth. Many early citizens of New England welcomed music as a desirable recreation and dance as a useful physical and social skill. Barbara Lambert's study of household inventories from 1630 to 1730 reveals a vibrant interest in music. In the 1650s there were eighteen musical instruments along with one lot of nineteen jew's harps and the mention of a music teacher. However, the balance between perceived opportunity and civic control was very delicate. In 1678, a dancing master and his servant who played the fiddle attempted to move to Boston and were rejected for personal reasons, as were others in 1681 and 1685 (Lambert 1985, pp. 409–514, 943–954).

In 1713, perhaps because of increasing pressure from the residents, the selectmen finally allowed George Brownell (flourished 1703–1750) to open a public dancing school (*Boston News-Letter*, March 2). Two other dancing masters opened schools shortly thereafter. Beginning in the 1720s, many New England churches established singing schools, paying music teachers to instruct young people in reading, writing, and performing music. This surely encouraged participation in secular as well as sacred music.

The development of public concert life in Boston owed much to members of the Deblois family. Stephen Deblois (1699–1778) arrived from New York in 1728 with Governor Burnet, whose own interest in music was strong. In 1729 the earliest known public concert was presented "at the dancing school" (*Boston Gazette*, February 10). From the 1730s, the Deblois family and other Boston music teachers and performers organized many concerts, both public and private, giving them opportunities to showcase their own skills, and to gain financially from the public's interest in music as entertainment. In 1732 a dancing assembly was established at Peter Pelham's school.

In 1742 Peter Fanueil presented a fine building to the city and in 1754 the Deblois family opened Concert Hall. Many entrepreneurs in Boston organized events in these spaces, some reaching significant proportions, particularly after the British occupation forces arrived in 1768 with their professional bands. William Turner, David Propert, William Selby,

William Sampson Morgan, James Juhan, and Josiah Flagg all sponsored public and private performances in the years before the War of Independence (1775–1783). In the 1780s it was William Selby (?1738–1798) who dominated the concert scene. He held ambitious programs of vocal and instrumental music, many reflecting a newly fashionable mix of sacred and secular compositions in the concert hall.

In the 1790s as the ban on theatrical performances weakened, Boston came alive with entertainments and concerts. Charles Bulfinch was commissioned to design a new theatre that became the pride of the city. When it opened, even its bitterest opponent admitted that "the increase of publick amusements within a town becomes absolutely necessary with the increase of its inhabitants" (Lambert 1985, p. 853).

New York and Philadelphia

Unlike Boston, a culturally homogeneous world whose magistrates controlled permission to settle within its borders, New York City and Philadelphia welcomed anyone. The ethnic diversity of these cities was extreme. New York was a commercial enterprise from the beginning and as such attracted people from all over Western Europe. Founded by the Dutch West India Company, the first permanent settlement was on Manhattan Island (1626). Trade regulation led to conflict between Holland and England, and in 1664 Charles II of England granted his brother, the Duke of York, all the land from the Connecticut River to Delaware Bay, claiming earlier discovery. A fleet was sent to capture New Amsterdam, but the pragmatic Dutch leaders surrendered without a fight.

New York's full musical life has probably never been accurately reflected in the public media. The earliest concert on record, held in 1710 "at Mr. Broughtons," was probably a private affair (Benson 1963, p. 287). The governors usually marked significant events with well-reported processions, open-air music, and fireworks, but evening concerts and private balls were not publicized.

New York's public concert life may have begun in 1736 with an event organized by Charles Theodore Pachelbel (1690–1750), who had recently arrived from Boston. In 1752 the arrival of William Tuckey (1708–1781) marked a turning point in the musical life of the city. With other professionals, he organized subscription concerts and balls, and built a good choir at Trinity Church. Lewis Hallam's theatre company performed for six months in 1753 and 1754, and employed local artists, including Tuckey. William Charles Hulett (died 1785), who came with Hallam's company, stayed in New York to teach dancing, violin, German flute, and guitar and to organize many concerts. Other pre-war teachers were Charles Love, Alexander Dienval, James Leadbetter, David Propert, Hermann Zedwitz, and Nicholas Biferi.

Outdoor concerts were popular in the 1760s at pleasure gardens named Ranelagh and Vauxhall after their prototypes in London. It is interesting to note that in New York many pre-war concerts were organized by owners of the spaces rather than by individual musicians. In the 1770s, an "Harmonic Society" offered concerts, playing with professional musicians. In 1773, James Rivington (1724–1802) opened his well-stocked book and music shop. As New York filled with Loyalists, some 33,000 by the war's end, the city's musical and theatrical life flourished.

In the 1780s Hallam and John Henry reopened the theatre and regular public concert series were initiated in the 1790s by Henri Capron, James Hewitt, George Edward Saliment, Peter A. Van Hagen, John Christopher Moller, and the proprietor of a new Vauxhall Gardens, ice cream maker Joseph Delacroix. Private musical societies seem to have taken on a new life as well, a natural course in a social environment of such diversity.

Pennsylvania was founded in 1682 as a refuge for victims of religious persecution. An inland port, Philadelphia eventually became the largest city and cultural capital of the American colonies. Public music, dancing, and theatre had intermittent development, chiefly because of opposition from the Quakers. However, the citizens of Philadelphia certainly acquired and enjoyed musical and dancing skills privately. In 1710, a dancing master was mentioned in a private letter (Benson 1963, p. 213) and in 1730 Miss Ball offered to teach singing, dancing, and the spinet (*Pennsylvania Gazette*, March 13). It appears that the founders of the Philadelphia Assembly, which officially dates its existence from 1748, were already holding private events in 1740 when George Whitefield arrived. Whitefield's followers made much of his power to close the concert hall and the assembly room when, in fact, his visit occurred after the regular assembly series had ended. The concerts, a year-round subscription series, continued as usual (*Pennsylvania Gazette*, May 8).

In 1756, because of the urgent need to defend the colony against Indian raids, the pacifist Quakers finally relinquished their hold on government affairs. In 1757, John Palma was able to announce a concert open to the public. In 1759 Michael Hillegas opened a music store and James Bremner arrived in 1763, opened another music store, and organized concerts.

Public theatre in Philadelphia began with Kean and Murray's brief performances in 1749. Lewis Hallam brought his company in 1754 under stringent restrictions, and returned in 1759 to a building outside of the city's jurisdiction. It was within reach of the audience but not of the law against theatrical presentations. From 1767 until 1773 Douglass's company performed there for six-month seasons. It was not until 1791 that a theatre was allowed within the city limits, in response to the ultimate plea that men should be free to spend their time and money as they saw fit.

Maryland, Virginia, and the Carolinas

Music and dance in the southern colonies followed the same patterns as those in the north, filling the social and personal needs of the people. Distances were greater, settlements smaller, and plantations spread apart. But travel and correspondence brought the latest fashions, usually within the time span of a voyage or a post-rider's circuit.

Because Anglican and other Protestant sects and the Catholic church encouraged instrumental and vocal music in their liturgies, musical life in areas not under Quaker or Puritan control was much less constricted. Colonists were free to enjoy the arts as they pleased, and music and dance thrived in the free-market environment, unhindered by civic controls and spiritual threats. In fact, secular music edged out the sacred arts in the more hedonistic lives of the upper classes of the South.

Starting in the early seventeenth century, the fertile lands of Maryland, Virginia, and the Carolinas were settled in quite a different fashion from those of the Northeast. Rather than having port cities through which most settlers and goods were filtered, they were well served by navigable waterways and were colonized by proprietors whose policies encouraged the acquisition of large tracts of land. The first Chesapeake colonists were English adventurers who quickly established fortunes through the cultivation of tobacco. These entrepreneurs took on the life-style of English country gentlemen, managing burgeoning estates and shipping goods directly to London from their own docks. By 1700 the best land was taken up and the character of the laboring class had begun to change. As is discussed in chapter 5, for complex local and international reasons, black slaves were displacing white indentured servants at an accelerating pace, bringing a different kind of ethnic diversity to these lands (Bailyn 1986, pp. 101–102).

The few towns were small and served chiefly as government seats until after the War of Independence. These towns were the focus of cultural life several times a year when court and legislative sessions were held. With leisure and money to spend, visitors attended concerts, plays, balls and assemblies, shared songs and stories, and took new books of music and handwritten notes back home. While a small town might not support music and dance professionals most of the year, there was plenty of demand for them during these "seasons." Theatrical troupes and other professionals moved between towns like Baltimore and Annapolis, Maryland; Williamsburg and Norfolk, Virginia; and New Bern and Wilmington, North Carolina, for these busy periods. The hardiest entrepreneurs traveled like peddlers between plantations and smaller villages.

Charleston

The mainland colonies had many points of contact with the West Indies but none were as close as Charleston's. Wealthy residents in the British-held islands established concerts, assemblies, and theatres at a very early date. In 1682, a pamphlet described life in Jamaica's Spanish Town, listing horse races, dancing, music, and plays at a public theatre as evidence of the flourishing condition of the island. Charleston was established in 1670 by planters from Jamaica and Barbados and became a city of wealthy landowners and merchants, avid consumers of art, music, and the theatre.

Charleston's first newspaper appeared in January, 1732. Benefit concerts for John Salter and Henry Campbell were advertised almost immediately, implying that they had been active in the city long enough to merit public support. A subscription concert series was held the following season, so it is likely that such series were already in place. In 1734, Henry Holt (flourished 1734–1739) arrived, attracted from London by opportunities in the city. He was a professional dancer and had been a colleague of John Essex, choreographer at the Haymarket Theatre. It is likely that he was involved in the productions of *The Adventures of Harlequin and Scaramouch* and *Flora* in 1735, respectively the first pantomime ballet and first opera performed in the British colonies. In 1737 Charles Theodore Pachelbel arrived from New York to become organist at St. Philip's Church. He taught psalmody and instrumental music in town and on itinerant circuits, sponsored concerts, and played in the theatre. In 1737, Pachelbel arranged a public concert to celebrate St. Cecilia's Day, and thereafter an annual concert was given on November 22. Perhaps responding to population growth, this concert was made private in 1762 by the formation of the St. Cecilia Society, an exclusive and selective group. For many years, the Society sponsored four concerts a year and hired their musicians on generous multi-year contracts, effectively assuring their city of a permanent orchestra (Benson 1963, p. 150).

Later arrivals included Ferdinand Grunzweig, Edmund Larkin, Benjamin Yarnold, Peter Valton, George H. Hartley, and dancing master Thomas Pike (Benson 1963, pp. 132–168).

Québec and Louisiana

The French presence in North America began in Port Royal, Nova Scotia (1604) and Québec (1608). Through the efforts of explorers, fur traders, missionaries, and settlers, France eventually claimed a large portion of the continent, from Hudson's Bay to the Gulf of Mexico, even challenging Spanish authority in Texas and Florida. Records show that musical life in Québec and Montréal began early and was based on sacred and secular French models. The first organ was brought from Paris in 1664 by François Xavier de Laval, first bishop of Québec. The *Livre d'orgue de Montréal*, a large collection of anonymous pieces, was brought to Canada in 1724 by Jean Girard, organist of Montréal's parish church. Imported collections of motets have been preserved by the Université Laval. Other manuscript collections include dance music, instrumental music, and popular songs (Courville 1985; Keller 1981, pp. 115–116). The British assumed control of Canada in 1763, and *The Quebec Gazette* commenced in 1764, opening a window on musical activities with reports of balls, theatre, music lessons, and sale of musical wares (Bourassa-Trépanier and Poirier 1990).

New Orleans was first settled by French tradesmen and planters – and their slaves – in 1718. Lower Louisiana was a distant dependency of Québec and the Canadian city exerted an influence on musical life. Formal music education began in 1725 in a school founded by Raphaël de Luxembourg, superior of the Capuchin missions in Louisiana. This school lasted only six years but the Ursuline school established in 1727 flourished – the girls receiving the same sort of education as the students in Ursuline schools in Canada and France, including music instruction. The earliest music to survive in New Orleans is an important manuscript of French sacred music dated 1736, given to the Ursuline nuns in 1754 (Lemmon 1993, p. 490).

Pierre Fleurtel is the first musician known to have been associated with the parish church of St. Louis. He served as cantor, choirmaster, and school master from 1725. Other church musicians include François Saucier, Jean Louis, Claude de Borde, Hubert Sauvagin, and, during the Spanish period – 1762 to 1803 – Francisco Gonzáles, as well as organists Josepthe Martens and Vicente Llorca. During this period, a boys' choir was active at St. Louis Church, which became a cathedral in 1793.

In the last quarter of the century, French musical influence was still strongly felt alongside Spanish artistic customs. Concerts regularly preceded the numerous balls for which New Orleans became famous. Indeed, dancing is the best documented art in the early years of New Orleans's history. In May, 1789, ceremonies honoring the accession of Carlos IV to the Spanish throne included elaborate musical performances, two comedies, and a *sarao* or dancing party (Lemmon 1996). Several French operas were performed at the theatre that opened in 1792, including Grétry's *Sylvain*, Dezède's *Blaise et Babet*, and Dalayrac's *Renaud d'Ast*. Though the New Orleans opera companies toured the eastern seaboard after 1800, the city's most important professional and artistic links at this time lay with Paris, Italy, Havana, and sometimes Madrid and Mexico, rather than with other cities of the United States.

Florida

French Huguenot explorers established short-lived Fort Caroline in 1564, near present-day Jacksonville. On their arrival, they were greeted by a large band of Indian musicians playing on reed pipes. Among the French were a spinet player, a man who played violin and trumpet, horn and trumpet players, three drummers, and at least one fifer, musicians who played for entertainment as well as for military purposes. Similarly, when the Spaniard Pedro Menéndez de Avilés routed the French the next year and established the town of San Agustín, he brought instruments of both war and recreation. His staff included a harper, players on the psaltery and vihuela de arco, six good singers, and a dwarf who danced. With the surrender of Fort Caroline he acquired the French musicians and, presumably, their instruments.

When Sir Francis Drake attacked the Spanish at San Agustín in 1586, fifer Nicholas Bourguignon is said to have signaled to Drake that he was French by playing *The Prince of Orange's March*, a tune they both knew. With Bourguignon as their guide, the English landed their artillery and burned the settlement to the ground. Undaunted, the Spanish rebuilt the town which for many years served as the center of Spanish government in East Florida.

The Spanish also established many missions in Florida and parts of Georgia, in which liturgical music and spiritual songs were taught by the

Franciscan missionaries to Indians as part of the conversion process. Both chant and polyphony were heard in liturgical and para-liturgical contexts in the Florida missions relatively soon after first contact. Although few records have been found, it is clear that music flourished in the new colony. San Agustín had an organ early in the eighteenth century, and in 1760 the Spanish governor informed the King that his subjects enjoyed dancing parties, *musicales*, and theatrical performances.

The Southwest: California, Arizona, New Mexico, and Texas

Almost all contemporary documentation about musical life in these regions relates to music-making within the Spanish ecclesiastical and governmental systems. From the beginning of Spanish settlement in the late sixteenth century, music was used by the Franciscans and Jesuits as a tool in the conversion of indigenous peoples. As in Central Mexico from the early sixteenth century on, Indian musicians, taught by the missionaries, played in church services in many of the southwestern missions.

As early as the 1540s, the Spanish began to explore the Southwest. Among the men who accompanied Coronado on his early expedition was Juan de Padilla (died 1542), who reportedly taught European music to the Indians. The Spanish presence was established in New Mexico in 1598 and Santa Fe, the provincial capital, was founded in 1610. During the seventeenth century, Spanish Franciscans established a system of at least twenty-seven missions in New Mexico, most on the sites of pre-existent Indian pueblos. Franciscan missionary Cristóbal de Quiñones (died 1609), directed the building of the church at San Felipe, and taught the Indians to sing in church services. He was probably the first trained teacher of European music resident in the present-day United States and may also have installed an organ at San Felipe Pueblo. Another early teacher, Bernardo de Marta (died 1635), called a "great musician and organist of the skies" by his contemporaries, was sent to New Mexico about 1605. Fray Roque de Figuredo, missionary to the Zuni in the 1630s, was praised for having a fine voice, for being an expert in the performance of plainsong and polyphonic music, and for being a player of the organ, bassoon, and cornett. He and other musical Franciscans must have taught this music and these instruments to the Indian neophytes. Benavides, ecclesiastical visitor to the New Mexican missions, states in his official report of 1630 that European music was taught at schools in Pecos, Sandía, and Isleta Pueblos, and that bassoons, shawms, and trumpets were used in church services and to accompany polyphony. Seventeen church organs were known to be in New Mexico in the 1640s.

Inventories made in 1776 at the New Mexican missions verify the continued use of instruments in New Mexican churches: drums and trumpets at San Jerónimo de Taos, violins and guitars at Taos and at Santo Domingo and Jemez Pueblos. Violins and guitars commonly accompanied plainchant and possibly part singing. Reporting in 1761 about the lives of the Indian population at San Juan Capistrano Mission in San Antonio, Texas, the Franciscan missionary there wrote that most of the Indians "play some musical instrument, the guitar, the violin or the harp. All have good voices, and . . . on the feasts . . . a choir of four voices, soprano, alto, tenor, and bass, with musical accompaniment, sings so beautifully that it is a delight to hear it . . . Both men and women can sing and dance just as the Spaniards, and they do so, perhaps, even more beautifully and more gracefully" (Spell 1936, p. 9).

Though the musical accomplishments of the Franciscan order in Texas and New Mexico are indisputable, no actual music used in these missions has been found except for that in missals. However, significant collections of mission-era manuscripts used in Alta California have survived. These permit close examination of music and musical life in California's twenty-one Franciscan missions established between 1769 and 1823, from San Diego in the south to Sonoma in the north. Every California mission had a library, a collection of instruments, and offered an education in music and the manual and visual arts to Indian neophytes. European visitors to California missions frequently commented on the general excellence of Indian singers and instrumentalists. Inventories reveal that almost all of the European and folk instruments known in Mexico were also used in the California missions: organ, fortepiano, barrel organ, drums of different sizes and shapes, triangles, cymbals, bugle, trumpet, horn, flute, oboe, clarinet, violin, cello, and bass. Though guitars and harps are not mentioned in mission inventories, they were played by Indians as well as by Hispanic settlers.

Barrel organs brought previously unknown melodies to Alta California. Early visitors to California reported hearing such tunes as *La Marseillaise*, *Go to the Devil*, and *Lady Campbell's Reel* on these instruments (da Silva 1954, pp. 11, 21). On a visit to California in 1793, Captain George Vancouver presented his own barrel organ as a gift to Father Fermín de Lasuén, President of the California missions.

While Indian neophytes were initially taught to play on instruments by the Franciscan missionaries in California, New Mexico, and Texas, and by the Jesuits in Arizona, as they became proficient they undoubtedly took on some of the pedagogical duties themselves. Spanish Franciscan missionaries Narcisco Durán, Felipe Arroyo de la Cuesta, Florencio Ibañez, Estevan Tapis, and, above all others, Juan Sancho especially encouraged music-making in the California missions through their work as conductors, music teachers, performers, music copyists, and directors of musical scriptoria. The quality of the mission repertory in general, and the level of difficulty of three recently discovered concerted masses (two by eighteenth-century Mexico City chapel master Ignacio de Jerusalem) point to an advanced and well-developed musical life in the California missions (Russell 1993).

Although there were no large urban areas in the Southwest during the eighteenth century, towns, villages, settlements, and ranches all had resident instrumentalists, most frequently fiddlers, guitarists, and harpists. European musical instruments were important in the daily life of both the Indian and Hispanic communities, and were used in different contexts, sacred and secular. For instance, in some Indian communities, the violin was integrated into indigenous and mestizo-influenced rituals, ceremonies, dramatic representations, and dance events, most notably, the Matachines, still performed in New Mexico today.

The singing of folk and theatrical songs, either created by local singers or brought from Spain and Mexico, was the most common form of music-making in the Southwest. This music functioned almost entirely within oral tradition. Folksong genres cultivated in the Southwest include not only the lyric *canción* but also the traditional Spanish *romance*. Examples of the latter include *Delgadina*, *la dama y el pastor*, and *la esposa infiel*. Dance music, sung and played, was known everywhere: examples include indigenous dances such as *el sombrero blanco*, *el jarabe*, *la bamba*, and *la zorrita*. Music was always part of the Mexican shepherd plays given at Christmastime and played a significant part in passion plays, notably in the village of Tomé, New Mexico.

France and Spain, and later Mexico, claimed and selectively settled areas significantly larger than those of the British colonies. Russia, too, established a political, religious, and cultural presence in North America, a presence still felt in Alaska. Fort Ross, in Alta California, was its southernmost outpost. While more is known about musical life in British America, much information remains to be uncovered about the significant French,

Spanish, and Mexican musical activities during the eighteenth and nineteenth centuries.

Business and pleasure in the eastern colonies

Music and dance as a business

Although few East Coast entrepreneurs lived solely from the arts, music and dance provided business opportunities throughout the Colonial period. Shops specializing in musical wares were located in larger towns, and teachers were in demand everywhere. Music and dancing lessons were given in homes or in schools where both private and group lessons were offered. In rural areas and particularly the plantation areas of the South, enterprising dance teachers would set up tours, moving between locations to meet groups of youngsters for several days of instruction. In the north, such itinerants planned six- or eight-week sessions in successive towns, with classes two or three times a week, sufficient time to teach deportment and basic principles of the minuet and English country dance.

In addition to private lessons, early colonists used a popular English text, John Playford's *An Introduction to the Skill of Music*. Later students used tutors with basic instructions derived from works of Peter Prelleur and Francesco Geminiani. Although tutors for all instruments were easily available in Boston, in 1769 John Boyles attempted to reap some of the profit for himself. He published *An Abstract of Geminiani's Art of Playing on the Violin, and . . . instructions for playing in a true taste on the violin, German flute, violoncello, and the thorough bass on the harpsichord*. Perhaps in response to a similar market potential, Hall and Sellers published a tutor for the fife in 1776 in Philadelphia, and in 1778 H. B. Victor announced his own instruction books for the violin, flute, guitar, and harpsichord.

Edward Enstone (flourished 1713–1724) might be considered a typical European musician who emigrated to the American colonies. He arrived in 1715 from England, hired as organist for King's Chapel in Boston. To supplement his church income he opened a school as "Master of Music and Dancing," and the following year established a music store. His advertisement bears witness to his skills:

> This is to give notice that there is lately sent over from London a choice collection of musickal instruments, consisting of flaguelets, flutes, hautboys, bass-viols, violins, bows, strings, reeds for haut-boys, books of instructions for all these instruments, books of ruled paper. To be sold at

the dancing school of Mr. Enstone in Sudbury-Street near the Orange-Tree Boston. Note. Any person may have all instruments of musick mended, or virgenalls and spinnets strung and tuned at a reasonable rate, and likewise may be taught to play on any of these instruments above-mention'd; dancing taught by a true and easier method . . .

(Boston News-Letter, April 23, 1716)

Michael Hillegas began his mercantile career managing a tavern and music store in Philadelphia. In 1759 he advertised a harpsichord, violoncello, English and Italian violins, German [transverse] flutes imported from Italy, and an enormous assortment of music. James Rivington experimented with book and music shops in Philadelphia and Boston before settling in New York in 1773. Over the next ten years, he sold a wide variety of instruments, including bagpipes, barrel organs, bassoons, bugle horns, clavichords, clarinets, common flutes, drums, fifes, French horns, German flutes, guitars, harps, harpsichords, hautboys, hunting horns, organs, pastorales, pianos, spinets, tabors and pipes, trumpets, violins, violas, violoncellos, voice flutes, and Welsh harps (Anderson 1987, p. xv).

Pianos were used in America by 1770. David Propert offered a fortepiano for sale in New York on September 17 (New-York Mercury), and offered lessons and played in a concert in Boston in 1771 (Boston Gazette, January 7, February 25). John Sheybli announced that he made and repaired fortepianos in 1772 in New York (New-York Mercury, March 30), and in 1775, another German craftsman, John Behrent of Philadelphia, advertised that he had built an "extraordinary fine instrument by the name of Piano Forte" (Pennsylvania Packet, April 10).

Music for all these instruments was available directly from the publishers in Great Britain, from local shops, or from teachers. Public taste demanded the most up-to-date compositions, and shopkeepers usually advertised that they stocked "new" music. In 1764, Hillegas published a list of the over fifty – mostly contemporary – composers whose music he carried, among them Alberti, Albinoni, Boyce, Corelli, Handel, Hasse, Pepusch, Quantz, Domenico Scarlatti, Stamitz, Tartini, and Vivaldi (Pennsylvania Gazette, January 5). Gillian Anderson has analyzed all the musical items cited in Rivington's newspaper from 1773 through 1783 and identified many of the composers and works in his advertisements. Her list gives an excellent picture of the music heard in New York during this period. Anderson noted the amount of contemporary music sold; only twelve of the 170 composers cited in Rivington's advertisements were born before 1700. Library inventories like those of Cuthbert Ogle (Molnar

1963), Francis Hopkinson (Sonneck 1905), and Thomas Jefferson (Cripe 1974) as well as manuscript compilations of music by teachers and students give further insight into the repertories of individual Americans (Keller 1981).

By necessity, many musicians active in America were also composers. Most music circulated with a melody and figured bass line only; for dance music only the melody. Music had to be transposed for available instruments, harmonies realized, and inner parts developed before it could be played. In a period when new compositions were often transmitted in manuscript or from memory, a definitive composer's score was a rarity. Performers were expected to be able to improvise according to current practices and the conventions of thorough bass.

Occasionally, local composers supplied new works. A 1779 essay on "preserving liberty in a republic" recommended that "pieces of music should be composed . . . and performed on certain days, to commemorate remarkable events" (*New-Hampshire Gazette*, February 2). Commencements were often showcases for student works written and performed for the occasion. Often these were anthems or patriotic odes, but occasionally new organ preludes, marches, and instrumental interludes were a point of pride in public reports. Notices in colonial newspapers reported that compositions by Nicholas Biferi, Mr. Caze, John Gualdo, Francis Hopkinson, James Leadbetter, James Lyon, William Morgan, Philip Roth, Mr. Unison, Peter Valton, and Benjamin Yarnold were featured in specific concerts (Corry, Keller, and Keller 1997). While the bulk of the repertory was imported, these new pieces were part of the concert experience and gave composers a chance to display their creative capabilities to potential customers.

In the period before 1784, several teachers specifically advertised that they taught composition, among them Nicholas Biferi (New York, 1774), Mr. Fagan and Solomon Ballentine (Hartford, 1777), and Peter Van Hagen (Charleston, 1774). Among those offering their works for sale by subscription were Peter Valton (Charleston, 1768), Charles Leonard (Alexandria, 1770), John Gualdo (Philadelphia, 1770), H. B. Victor (Philadelphia, 1778), John Ross (Philadelphia, 1779), and William Selby (Boston, 1782).

The earliest extant body of secular music composed in America was that by several members of The Tuesday Club, a gentleman's club active in Annapolis from 1745 to 1756. It consisted of songs, odes, minuets, and other incidental music. The earliest surviving composition to have been written by a native-born American is the sentimental song, *My Days have been so Wondrous Free*, written in 1759 by Francis Hopkinson (1737–1791).

Music in private settings

The need for entertainment and the desire to acquire social graces meant widespread practice and performance of music in the home. Women were usually taught keyboard instruments and guitar, and learned to sing to their own playing. Men studied violin, German flute, and recorder and were expected to be able to carry a part in a catch or glee. In company, women might be asked to show off their skills by playing, singing, or dancing. George Washington's stepdaughter Nelly Custis wrote to a friend that they "have a large company of the *Honorable Congress* to dine with us, & I must not be so remiss [as] to go out in the evening as they *like to hear musick although* they do not know one note from another" (Britt 1984, p. 45). One of Nelly's favorite composers was Ignaz Pleyel (1757–1831). As Britt points out, although Pleyel's works now lie in the shadow of Mozart and Haydn, his music was much loved in his day. It could be enjoyed in a single hearing, it was cheerful, and perhaps most of all, it was easy to play, qualifications present in much of the music produced during the eighteenth century as composers met new consumers on their own terms.

Some people simply preferred other kinds of music. Fithian reported that two of his students had slipped off several times to dance and play music with the black servants, perhaps seeking relief from the structured dances and concert music in the parlor (Farish 1957, p. 62). Probably in search of the same pleasures, Thomas Jefferson's younger brother "used to come out among the black people, play the fiddle and dance half the night" (Cripe 1974, p. 13).

Men's clubs and other exclusive organizations became popular in the early 1700s in England, serving as business and social networks for their members. Similar clubs quickly sprang up in the colonies. Music, dance, and theatre were often an important part of their activities. The motto of Annapolis's Tuesday Club was "Fiddlers, Fools, and Farces," and in 1752, club members included five string players, two flutists, a keyboard performer, and possibly a bassoonist (Talley 1988, p. 13). Tuesday Club members not only performed for their own enjoyment, but probably provided the band for several professional theatrical productions. The Freemasons, strong supporters of music and theatre, had lodges in many American towns. They sponsored theatrical performances, commissioned music for lodge ceremonies, and hired musicians for processions, concerts, and balls.

Another type of club was the dancing assembly. Admission was controlled by the members who hired musicians, arranged for the hall and other amenities, and selected a manager from among their number. A function of social exclusivity, networking, and display of wealth and power, these clubs existed at various times in most urban centers and in many small towns as well.

Music in public places

Many professional musicians organized concerts and invited amateur musicians of the town to participate, thus showcasing their skills and their connections. Selection of what music to play depended entirely on the occasion and the participants. Outside, a military band played spirited British marches and familiar songs and dance tunes for all to hear. Private indoor concerts featured concertos, arias from operas or oratorios, instrumental duets, and overtures. Public concerts were more likely to include patriotic songs, pieces from the theatre, and works by the artists themselves.

As populations grew and more citizens acquired appreciation of the cultivated arts – or wanted to give the impression that they did – concerts were organized as commercial ventures. In this case anyone might buy a ticket, a reflection of the rise of the middle class as patrons of music. Depending on the tastes and level of sophistication of the expected audience, programs included more popular songs in English, and movements rather than whole works. An interesting mid-century "estimate of the manners and principles of the times" was printed in the *Pennsylvania Journal*. Although it was probably written for London readers, it reflects a changing artistic environment that must have rung true to the Philadelphia editor.

> This excess of effeminate delicacy has influenced every other entertainment; it has produced a low and unmanly taste in music. We do not go to concerts or operas to admire the composition, but the tricks of the performer, who is always most applauded when he runs through the compass of the throat, or traverses the finger board with the swiftest dexterity ...
>
> (August 4, 1757)

Andrew Adgate (1762–1793) gave American concerts a new richness, bringing together music from many strands of creative accomplishment.

In Philadelphia in May, 1786, Adgate programmed imported works of Aaron Williams and Handel, adding works by William Billings (1746–1800), a violin concerto by James Juhan (arrived in 1768, died 1797) and a flute concerto by William Brown (flourished 1783–1788), an anthem by William Tuckey and another by James Lyon (1735–1794). In 1787 he presented a fifty-piece orchestra and choir performing works by Arnold, Arne, Aaron Williams, Martini il Tedesco, Philip Phile (died 1793), Tuckey, Lyon, and Billings, ending with Handel's "Hallelujah Chorus," a program equally balanced between sacred and secular works written in Europe and in America.

In 1786 Alexander Reinagle (1756–1809) took charge of the City Concerts in Philadelphia, establishing himself as principal manager and featured performer on keyboard and violin. His superior abilities were recognized at once. He published his *Selection of . . . Favorite Scots Tunes with Variations* in 1787, an early example of music printed in America from punched plates. Working closely with John Aitken, he helped the engraver establish a successful business. Between 1787 and 1793, Aitken produced twenty-one publications, including nine by Reinagle and two of Reinagle's arrangements of songs by James Hook and Charles Dibdin.

Through his activities as composer, publisher, performer, and conductor, James Hewitt (1770–1827) was a major force in the concert and theatre life of New York and Boston from 1795 until 1820. His works include several of an old but newly popular genre, program music with descriptions of battles. *The Battle of Trenton*, a piano sonata, was published in 1797 and enjoyed considerable popularity.

A versatile performer, teacher, and composer, Benjamin Carr (1768–1831) contributed to the vocal repertory and to improvement of musical taste in Federal American life. But his most important work was as publisher and editor. With his brother and father, he established stores in Philadelphia, Baltimore, and New York. He imported the best vocal and instrumental music, but did not neglect local talent. The first issue of *The Gentleman's Amusement* (Philadelphia, 1793) included Philip Phile's *The President's March*, which was to become one of the most popular of all American patriotic tunes when Francis Hopkinson's son, Joseph wrote to it lyrics beginning "Hail! Columbia, happy land."

Music for military use was provided by two distinct groups of musicians: those whose duty it was to play the fife, drum, or trumpet for signals in camp and on the field, and a wind band, or *harmoniemusik*, hired by the officers to provide music for ceremonies and private recreation (Camus

1995, p. 6). The usual instrumentation of this group was paired oboes, clarinets, French horns, and bassoons. A number of British, French, and German bands served in America, and the officers of several American regiments maintained bands as well. Employed as independent contractors rather than soldiers, the bandsmen played important roles in the musical life of the cities they were stationed in. They performed in official ceremonies and outdoor events as well as participating in civilian musical activities in off hours.

Fifes, drums, and trumpets had provided music for the armies of Europe for centuries. In the seventeenth century the fife dropped out of use in the British army but was reintroduced during the Seven Years War (1756–1763). During the War of Independence, the British employed fifers in Grenadier companies only, with one or two drummers in all foot companies, bagpipers in Highland companies, and trumpeters in mounted troops. The Continental Army authorized one or two fifers and two drummers in every foot company, and trumpeters in mounted troops. This change from British practice implied that a higher importance was placed on the melodic instrument. Many American musicians served in the Continental Army. They had to learn the standard repertory needed to regulate troop life, but as they traveled, informal sharing of repertory resulted in a cross-fertilization of material across the colonies.

Most of the tunes played were of British origin: signals, marches, airs, and dance tunes (Camus 1989). While thirteen manuscripts made by known American fifers show interesting personal selections, they also describe a body of tunes all were expected to know, including *To Arms*, *The General*, *Rogue's March*, and so forth. The prevailing working repertory was that found in British fife tutors, with some specific additions. *White Cockade*, *Mrs. Baker's Hornpipe*, and James Oswald's *Flowers of Edinburgh* were widely popular. Rather than the standard tunes in the British books, *Lovely Nancy* and *Pretty Cupid* were used by American troops in retreat parades and Oswald's *Roslin Castle* as a dead march (Keller and Rabson 1980). One simple march melody became thoroughly associated with the American cause. Although its origins have yet to be determined, the tune of *Yankee Doodle* was played by British bands when they arrived in Boston in 1768. The title implies an insult and that is how it was first used. The melody was soon effectively used by the Americans as a counter-irritant. By 1775, it became a signature tune for the patriot cause.

Music was heard in public houses and taverns as well as on the parade ground. Some tavern keepers employed musicians as regular staff and many ran public dances and concerts at their establishments. Others sponsored horse races, and occasionally full-scale fairs, all to bolster business, of course. In Hanover County, Virginia, a forerunner of today's popular Scottish games was held in the 1730s. Among other races and competitions were several for fiddlers, singers, and dancers. In 1736, fiddle students of local music master John Langford were not permitted to compete, having, apparently, an unfair advantage (*Virginia Gazette*, November 26, 1736; October 7, 1737).

Tavern patrons often provided the music for themselves, particularly in times of political stress. In 1769, John Adams recorded that he and 350 other "Sons of Liberty" dined at a tavern in Dorchester, Massachusetts. After dinner someone sang John Dickinson's new *Liberty Song* and everyone joined in on the choruses (Lambert 1980, p. 105). Set to *Hearts of Oak*, a tune written by Englishman William Boyce, Dickinson's song was one of the very few secular pieces to be published with its music in colonial America.

Musical theatre

Of all the entertainments available to Americans, the theatre probably reached the widest segment of the population and encompassed the most musical forms. Entrance to the theatre was open to anyone who could afford a ticket; price structure and separate seating areas served to group the spectators appropriately.

Anxious for continued business, managers planned programs with broad appeal. The evening began with instrumental music – familiar popular marches and patriotic songs. An overture would follow, then a main piece, usually a tragedy, substantial comedy, or comic opera. Musical interludes, popular songs, and possibly a character dance would be performed within the play if appropriate, and usually between the acts and at intermissions. Then came a farce or shortened comedy, ballad opera, or perhaps a pantomime ballet featuring Harlequin with elaborate tricks and transformations. Epilogues and more songs followed the performance.

Before the War of Independence, music for these interludes might be chosen from English stage works like John Gay's popular *Beggar's Opera* (1728), Handel's operas and oratorios, and works of Henry Carey, John Frederick Lampe, and Charles Dibdin. Songs by such British composers as Richard Leveridge, Oswald, Boyce, Stevens, and Thomas Arne were among the favorites. Instrumental pieces were selected from the works of J. C. Bach, Hasse, Corelli, Stamitz, and other British and European composers. When Murray and Kean brought their troupe to New York in 1750–1752, they mounted *The Beggar's Opera* and between the acts included an oratorio sung by Mr. Kean, and three theatrical dances, *Harlequin Dance*, *Pierot* [sic] *Dance*, and *The Drunken Peasant* (*New-York Gazette or The Weekly Post Boy*, January 7, 1751). The dances were stock character-dance types; their choreographies depended entirely upon the skills of the artist performing them.

In the 1790s, as audiences demanded more patriotic numbers, several composers wrote overtures that included popular song tunes. In discussing Carr's *Federal Overture*, Irving Lowens remarked on the close interaction between music and politics in the 1790s, with the theatre serving as the catalyst (Lowens 1957, p. 1). Probably commissioned for the opening night of Hallam and Hodgkinson's season in 1794 and written with an eye keenly focused on the occasion and the audience's tastes, Carr's music quotes the consummately American *Yankee Doodle*, two French patriotic melodies, Phile's *The President's March*, and several other tunes. Similar trends were evident as early as 1757 when a group of students at the College of Philadelphia performed an adaptation of Arne's *Masque of Alfred* at a private gathering during the Christmas recess. Lyrics pertinent to the Philadelphia audience were added and the libretto was published in the *Pennsylvania Gazette* (January 20, 27; February 3, 10), so the impact went well beyond the audience gathered for its performance.

Many concerts and theatrical presentations were held on school and college campuses where they were generally uncriticized because they were considered educational. In New England these were usually performances of Addison's *Cato* or anthems; further south, secular themes prevailed. At the Princeton commencement in 1762, *The Military Glory of Great Britain*, a dramatic cantata consisting of alternating spoken lyrics and sung choruses, was performed. Probably written by James Lyon, it is the earliest-known original American musical composition intended for dramatic representation. An amateurish work, it is nonetheless a remarkable effort for a young theology student, and paved the way for his later accomplishments (Virga 1982, p. 279)

Theatre companies performed in British mainland colonies as early as 1716 when the first public theatre was built in Williamsburg, Virginia. The repertory was almost entirely English and was chosen from London playhouses rather than the Italian-style opera houses. Responding to a new audience potential, ballad opera had originated in England in the 1720s. Spoken dialogue, usually of a humorous and satirical nature, was amplified

by strophic lyrics set to pre-existing music, often tunes whose previous use
had relevance to the content of the new song. British pieces like *Damon and
Phillida*, *The Devil to Pay*, and *Flora* were perennial favorites in American
theatres until the 1770s, when newer forms, usually termed comic operas,
took their place. Comic operas differed from ballad operas in that they had
new music rather than known tunes with new lyrics. At first the new music
was eclectic. For *Love in a Village* (1762), for example, Arne selected music
by Handel, Boyce, Geminiani, and others, as well as his own. Other types
such as ballad-burlettas, pasticcios, and single composer comic operas had
all been performed in America by 1772 (Porter 1991, pp. 23–52).

With an ample supply of works from Great Britain, American dramatic
compositions were few and generally related to the political times. The
1757 adaptation of *Alfred* was cited above. In 1767 a Philadelphian writing
under the pseudonym of Andrew Barton wrote a comic opera, a sharp
satire on local personalities that was rehearsed but not performed. *The Dis-
appointment* was a clever pastiche using old and newly composed tunes.
Francis Hopkinson's *America Independent: or, The Temple of Minerva* (1781)
was an allegorical entertainment. Drawing on the technique of the pastiche but without spoken lines, Hopkinson created an all sung work using
borrowed music, chiefly by Jommelli, Handel, and Arne. In 1782 a similar
pastiche was written anonymously in New York. Called *The Blockheads; or,
Fortunate Contractor*, it includes solo airs, duets, and ensembles, and like
Hopkinson's work, reflected the patriotic sentiments of the time with its
use of allegorical figures such as Liberta, Amita, and Americana, but from a
loyalist's point of view (Virga 1982, pp. 255–261).

Later American theatre pieces include the opera *May Day in Town* (1787)
by Royal Tyler (1757–1826), a pastiche with music "compiled from the
most eminent masters." William Dunlap (1766–1839) created a popular
interlude, *Darby's Return* (1789), written specifically for actor Thomas
Wignell. Two other pieces were written with American audiences in mind,
but never performed. In 1789, Bostonian publisher Isaiah Thomas
released the one-act pastiche farce *The Better Sort* by William Hill Brown
(born 1767). His announcement described the play in terms that suggest
what an audience might best enjoy; it was

> an operatical, comical farce, containing eighteen new Federal songs, on
> love, friendship, courtship and marriage-matrimonial duets, and a Chevy
> Chacical dirge on the death of George IIId. Interspersed with much senti-
> ment, sound morality, and some general satire – forming in the whole, a
> fund of rational entertainment.

Peter Markoe (1752–1792) wrote *The Reconciliation* in 1790 in Philadelphia. He chose popular tunes from among traditional ballads, theatre music, and art songs written for the pleasure gardens of London.

Although little of their music survived, several pieces were significant milestones. Elihu Hubbard Smith's *Edwin and Angelina* (1791) with music by Victor Pelissier (*c*. 1754–*c*. 1820, principal composer for the New York and Philadelphia theatres), is the first opera that originated wholly in British North America – operas and ballets had been written and produced in Spanish colonies in Central and South America earlier in the century. The first theatrical work on an American subject was *Tammany; or The Indian Chief*; Anne Julia Hatton's highly political libretto was set by James Hewitt and performed in 1794. Another significant and popular piece was William Dunlap's *The Archers* (1796), with music by Carr. In 1794 William Francis directed the first serious ballet to be mounted in North America, *La Foret Noire*, with music by Alexander Reinagle and starring Madame Gardie, a brilliant dancer from Santo Domingo and Paris.

During the War of Independence, professional companies went into safe exile in Jamaica or Great Britain and amateur theatricals took their place. Both American and British officers presented performances for their garrisons in winter quarters. The orchestra of the Theatre Royal in New York in 1780 consisted of fourteen players from the regimental bands led by Hessian corporal Philip Pfeil, later Phile. As suggested earlier, this versatile musician and composer remained in America after the war and contributed considerably to musical life in Philadelphia.

As the war wound down, as early as June 1781 various small professional companies began performing again, occasionally with the assistance of French or American regimental bands. In 1784 Lewis Hallam brought his company to Philadelphia, signaling the revival of regular theatre. In the 1790s, as anti-theatre laws were gradually repealed, American musical theatre reached new levels of creativity and quality. Good theatres were built in New York, Philadelphia, Boston, and Charleston, and major companies took up residence in each. Off season, companies toured, carrying new music, dancing, and theatrical entertainment to smaller towns from New Hampshire to Georgia.

Each production provided employment and creative opportunities for local musicians, opportunities for arranging the vocal scores for available instruments, for composing new overtures, interludes, and dance numbers, and for performing as well. The major theatrical composers in the 1790s were immigrants from England, France, and Germany. Chief among these were Benjamin Carr, Gottlieb Graupner, James Hewitt, Alexander Reinagle, and Rayner Taylor. Carr, Graupner, and Hewitt are discussed further in chapter 8. Their works were no longer pastiches of rearranged material, but unified theatrical works on romantic themes composed in a new style, and now called musical dramas or comic operas.

Social dancing

To encourage attendance, managers often permitted the audience to dance after performances in the theatre or concert hall, taking advantage of the fact that the hall was open, lighted, and warm. Technically, anyone holding a ticket could come, but the level of performance and clothing of the participants made it clear who was and who was not welcome. Evidence suggests that professional dance musicians rather than concert musicians were hired. Public balls were also held by dancing masters as recitals for their students, to show off their abilities, or just to make money. Private balls were given by individuals or clubs for special occasions. Assemblies were usually a series of dances, sponsored by a group of citizens for their own pleasure or a teacher as a commercial venture. Most dances were managed by a master of the ceremonies who preserved order on the floor, ensured that proper precedence was observed, and relayed to the musicians the participants' selection of dances.

Dances usually opened with minuets for society leaders present, followed by English country dances for all and some informal reels for the young and energetic. Beginning in the 1770s, cotillions were also performed. The waltz was introduced into English ballrooms in the 1780s, was known in America in the 1790s, but was generally not performed in ballrooms until well after the turn of the century (see chapter 6).

While there are references to social dancing before 1720, there is little specific information about dance types used by British colonists before a diary entry by Virginia planter William Byrd. He described a party attended by the local dancing master at which the company danced the minuet, French dances, and English country dances (Benson 1963, p. 48).

Because of the invention of dance notation, the beginning of the eighteenth century was a watershed moment in dance. Before that time, educated dancers in Britain and Europe performed dances learned directly from dancing masters. Country dances were described in words and printed with their tunes in collections published by John Playford and others but solo, duo, and other group dances existed only in verbal descriptions in Italian and French dance manuals.

From 1700 to 1720, a number of duo and solo dances were created by French and English masters using a dramatically new presentational dance technique documented by a new notation system. For the first time, intricate dances were preserved in detail for future generations. These dances used a vocabulary of basic steps and combinations performed in a choreographed floor pattern to the music of sarabandes, courantes, gavottes, passepieds, bourrées, gigues, allemandes, minuets, and hornpipes. Only the rhythm of the music changed the essential nature of the dance.

The minuet emerged as the chief dance of ceremony and ritual. For a man and woman alone, it used a limited number of steps, and a specific floor pattern and sequence of figures. A symbol of precedence and power, opening minuets were performed at formal dance events by the most prominent couples. This ritual became standard practice from Moscow to Mexico City from 1700 through the end of the eighteenth century.

Both the minuet and the English country dance served the new consumers well. Ideally suited for adequate performance by dancers of varying skills and abilities, each offered a distinct structure that was fairly easy to learn. Like thorough-bass technique in music – by which fairly simple compositions could be realized in different ways by musicians of varying skills – these dances could be embroidered by their performers to suit their abilities and the occasion on which they were being danced.

English country dances involved many couples standing in a line, partner facing partner. Before 1690, Americans probably used familiar Renaissance steps. Once the new French technique was introduced, the basic step became a smooth *pas de bourrée*, with a half-coupé for setting and honors (Keller 1991a, pp. 14–20). Country dances were set to all kinds of music, from traditional ballad tunes to short marches by Handel. Rhythms ranged from slow courante and minuet tunes in 3/2 and 3/4 to fast hornpipes in 6/8 or 2/4.

In the 1680s, French masters developed a form of country dance called the *contredanse*. It was a complex non-progressive dance, usually for a fixed number of dancers. A variant, termed cotillion, was introduced into London ballrooms in the 1760s. It was promoted by dancing masters as a new dance which, not unintentionally, required far more schooling than the increasingly easier English country dances. A group of figures form the chorus of the dance, and before each repetition the dancers perform standard figures termed changes. Cotillions, direct ancestor of the American square dance, employed similar steps to those used in country dances, but often in more complex combinations.

Lower-class people enjoyed free-form jigs, hornpipes, and reels, dance types that did not necessarily need instruction and practice. Jigs and hornpipes were usually solos. The reel was an informal group dance for three or four people in a line, its roots in the older farandole. Passages of dancing in place alternate with traveling in a figure-eight pattern around each other.

Music of the people

In 1721, recent Harvard graduate Ebenezer Parkman owned a manuscript tune collection whose contents included psalm tunes, tunes from the 1706 edition of *The Dancing Master* – including *Cheshire Rounds*, *Lord Biron's Jigg*, and *Goddesses* – as well as Purcell's *Britons Strike Home* (from *Bonduca* of 1695) and a tune used in Handel's newly composed *Water Music*. More than 350 similar personal collections made in America before 1800 have been identified (Keller 1981). They contain everything from old ballads to new marches, from patriotic songs in local dialect and love songs in German to rather vulgar songs in plain English. These documents permit close inspection of actual repertory and it is here that we find glimpses of the music of ordinary people. Much was copied from printed sources, some was from memory, some was from the playing of others, and some newly composed.

Another place to find everyday music was in ballads printed on broadsides and in small booklets called garlands. In the 1640s, the Rev. Seaborn Cotton copied several of the most sentimental ballads imaginable into his daybook. In 1713, Puritan preacher Cotton Mather worried that "the minds and manners of many people . . . are much corrupted by foolish songs and ballads" that peddlers carried throughout the countryside (Lambert 1985, pp. 767–768). Favorite dancing tunes, songs, and ballads circulated in print and orally from generation to generation. Old ballads about kings and knights, love and death, or accidents and supernatural happenings lasted for many decades. New ballads criticizing contemporary personalities or describing local events were sung by street singers and printed in pamphlets, newspapers, and broadsides. These might be set to old tunes like *Chevy Chase* or *Children in the Wood*, recently composed marches, opera arias, or stage dance tunes by composers such as Purcell, Jeremiah Clark and Handel, or even to familiar psalm tunes. They had broad appeal to all classes.

As a teenager working for his printer brother, Benjamin Franklin wrote ballads on up-to-the-minute events, typeset them, and hawked them in the streets. They were a great success but Franklin's father was not pleased and discouraged his efforts as inappropriate to his station in life (Lambert

1980, p. 171). Throughout the eighteenth century in most Western cultures, the arts were haunted by class distinctions between those who practiced them professionally and sought patronage, and the patrons themselves who used them as recreation or display of status.

In 1715, young lawyer James Alexander landed in New York with memories of dances enjoyed with friends and fellow students in London. In 1730, he wrote out the figures for twenty-six English country dances to such old tunes as *Christ Church Bells* as well as dances named for historical events like *Marlborough's Victory* (Keller 1991b, pp. 353–369). Four years later in 1734, when local political affairs reached an impasse, two ballads highly critical of Governor William Cosby appeared. Probably written by Alexander or someone in his circle of friends, they were set to the widely known ballad tunes of *All You Fair Ladies Now On Land* and *Now, Now, You Tories All Shall Stoop* and published anonymously on a broadside by John Peter Zenger. Zenger was arrested and put in prison for "diverse, scandalous, virulent, false and seditious reflections." In the ensuing trial, the defense lawyer argued that to convict Zenger, the authorities had to prove that words of the songs were false. The jury agreed that this was not possible and Zenger was declared not guilty. Although the legal issues are not entirely clear, this has been called the first great victory for freedom of the press in English-speaking America. The lyrics were a foretaste of topical songs to be written by Americans that cultivated "the sensations of freedom" (Lambert 1980, p. 105). The power of such songs was recognized by the English author of "A General View of Liberty," reprinted in the *Boston Evening Post*, July 4, 1737: "A few ballad singers uncontroll'd, if their ditties be but tolerably droll and malicious, are sufficient to cause disaffection in a state, to raise disaffectation into a ferment, and that ferment into a rebellion."

*

Rapid growth, general prosperity, and continuous immigration produced considerable cultural mixing in the eighteenth century, but the power of fashion must not be underestimated. Although laborers from Ireland, craftsmen and merchants from Scotland and Switzerland, and musicians and dancers from Germany, France, Italy, Spain, and Mexico arrived, each bringing his or her own traditions, London continued to be the source of the majority of the public repertory in the eastern colonies. A steady stream of instruments, new music, and the latest dance books were unloaded onto colonial wharves. Passengers brought first-hand knowledge of the latest trends on the stage, the public ballroom, and the streets of the Old World. Some entrepreneurs traveled back to England and the Continent to gather the latest repertory or hire musicians and dancers for theatrical troupes. Most advertised that they used only the most fashionable new material with the latest techniques, in the style of the greatest masters of London, Dublin, and Paris.

James Alexander was a Scot living in a formerly Dutch-controlled town. But his tastes were guided by the leading citizens of his community, the English governor and his retinue. His Dutch-American wife may have sung old lullabies from the Low Countries to her children and James might have danced a wild Highland reel at home with his friends, but when they stepped together onto the ballroom floor in public, they chose the latest London fashion in dance. If Alexander wanted to make a political point in verse, he selected well-known English tunes for his songs.

Such was the power of the British-led consumer revolution. Music, theatre, and dance took on meaning beyond that of entertainment. Gentility went up for sale at the opening of the eighteenth century and the acquisition and display of status through the arts helped to create business and family dynasties. But by the end of the century a tidal wave of new consumers, new sources, and a new sense of the individual in his world had changed the tight control of the elite over public events. No longer was everything conducted with the "greatest order of decency" giving proof of the "good taste" of those in charge. Entertainment for its own sake was now accessible to the servants who had once been sent merely to hold seats for their masters. From their own seats in the theatre balcony they could demand that their favorite tunes be played. Change and opportunity was everywhere, and in the new Republic, the arts of music, dance, and theatre responded.

4

Sacred music to 1800

NYM COOKE

As with any music before the age of sound recording, what survives of pre-nineteenth-century American sacred music is that which was written down or published. This means, in the main, Anglo-American Protestant psalmody. Psalmody – the word here referring to musical settings not only of the Biblical psalms but also of hymn texts and Biblical prose – was an extraordinarily rich creative phenomenon in late-eighteenth-century America. The vast literature of this tradition and the high artistic quality of many of its compositions are substantially the reasons why a separate chapter on early American sacred music is found in the present volume.

It is important, however, to consider the tradition of Protestant psalmody within a larger context: that of music as an aspect of worship – or, more broadly stated, of sacred activity. Humans have used music in various ways to express, intensify, channel, or unblock their relationship to the divine. Music can bring a person closer to God or to the spiritual realm; it can also create and strengthen the bonds within a community of worshippers or spiritual seekers. In different ritual settings within different cultural traditions, religious music has worked in very different ways: intensifying consciousness or dissolving it; exciting the body and spirit or rendering them tranquil; reinforcing established social hierarchies or providing a temporary alternative.

Seen from these perspectives, Protestant worship music occupies a very particular place in a wide spectrum of traditions. Both German Protestantism and the mainstream of Anglo-American Protestantism have always been wary of departing from consciousness and rationality in worship. And they have rarely encouraged individual or personal religious experiences. Thus much Protestant music was neither created nor performed to encourage ecstatic, meditative, or non-conscious states: rather, it is music that serves to deliver text, within the context of an organized, written, and generally accepted theology. Sects within Protestantism that have encouraged movement, spontaneous utterance, improvisation, even trance in the worship service – such as the Freewill Baptists and Shakers of late-eighteenth-century New England – have always been marginalized minorities (Marini 1982).

Even the term "sacred music" cannot adequately represent the role of the sacred, or the role of music, in the lives of many Native American peoples, however. "Sacred music" suggests that there is a discrete realm that is sacred, and that it has its own music. Contrast this notion with the insistence of elders in the Yurok tribe (Northwest Coast) that "in ancient times, everything used to be religious" (Keeling 1992, p. 19). The Yurok and many other Indian cultures on this continent have found the sacred in what others might call the everyday. And they have frequently found it on their own, for Native American religious systems tend to be "extremely individualistic, allowing much room for personal vision and creativity" and to incorporate beliefs and practices that are "dazzling in their variety" (Keeling 1992, p. 5). This individualism is evident in the sources of much Native American music: visions or dreams. For example, the Arapaho, a Plains tribe, perform a Sun Dance ceremony centering on the individual warrior's search for a vision in which he will receive a guardian spirit; that guardian spirit may in turn teach the warrior a song or songs which he is to sing only when approaching death. And emotionally disturbed individuals among the Yuman tribes of the Southwest have traditionally secluded themselves in order to meditate and dream songs which have a restorative effect (Nettl 1973, pp. 160–163). How far back practices such as these date is not known; Bruno Nettl has observed that North American Indians "seem to have preserved earlier musical styles to a much greater degree" than their South American counterparts, and that in the United States music is "one of the few aspects of Indian life into which the white man has not penetrated" (Nettl 1973, pp. 159, 176).

It seems clear, at any rate, that for centuries most Native American groups have viewed musical composition, or transmission, as "a supernatural act" (Nettl 1973, p. 176), and that the most complex and charged songs of many tribes have originated and have been repeated in ceremonial contexts, as parts of rituals which have specific purposes. Ceremonial songs tend to be sung by solo vocalists or by groups in unison, with accompaniment by whistles, drums, and/or rattles; they tend to be longer and more complex than dance, war, love, narrative, or children's songs; and, like much other Native American music, their rhythmic and tonal relationships can only be approximated by Western musical notation. Because of the enormous variety of Indian musics, the lack of extensive written records for the early period, and the sensitive nature of the topic, it is inappropriate to make further generalizations here about Native American sacred music.

Easier to document and describe are early efforts to convert Native Americans to Christianity and to train them in Christian musical practices. In the 1560s the psalm singing of French Huguenots in what would become Florida was imitated by native peoples there; Spanish Catholic missionaries were teaching singing and instrumental music to Indians in the Southwest as early as the beginning of the seventeenth century; in 1745 at the Moravian settlement of Bethlehem, Pennsylvania the hymn *In dulci jubilo* was sung simultaneously in thirteen languages, including Mohawk and Mohican; and the Rev. Eleazar Wheelock instructed Native American youths in sight-reading and choral singing, among other subjects, in Lebanon, Connecticut in the mid-1700s. Several of Wheelock's students became missionaries themselves and taught psalmody to other young Indians; Wheelock's most famous pupil Rev. Samson Occom (a Montauk) published *A Choice Collection of Hymns and Spiritual Songs* in New London, Connecticut in 1774 (Chase 1966a, pp. 59, 61; Stevenson 1966, p. 3; Wilson and Keller 1979, pp. 60–62. See also chapters 1 and 2 of the present volume).

As is noted in chapter 5, similarly rich documentation is available for the conversion of African slaves to Christianity, and its attendant musical instruction. As early as 1693, in Boston, a servants' "Society of Negroes" was singing psalm tunes at its meetings (Southern 1983, p. 33). Just over a decade later the efforts of the Church of England's Society for the Propagation of the Gospel in Foreign Parts bore fruit at New York's Trinity Church, where in 1705 thirty black students learned to sing psalms in a catechizing school. Trinity continued to attract black servants to its singing schools over the next half-century, and in the 1760s and 1770s the Associates of Doctor Bray, a society allied with the aims of the SPG, taught psalmody to slaves in Philadelphia, New York, Newport, Rhode Island, and Williamsburg, Virginia (Southern 1983, pp. 38–39). Several ministers' descriptions of Protestant singing among blacks in late-eighteenth-century Virginia have survived, and almost all stress African Americans' musical skill and expressiveness.

But the dominant culture's religious and cultural imperialism often effaced African spiritual practices as surely as it did Indian, though hints of the former survive: a minister writes of "Heathenish rites" being performed at the burials of slaves in New York in 1712, while the records of the Superior Council of Louisiana mention a "service . . . sung in negro style and language" in the early 1740s (Epstein 1977, pp. 39, 40). And as late as 1811 a Russian visitor to the African Methodist Episcopal (AME) Church in Philadelphia observed that

> At the end of every psalm the entire congregation, men and women alike, sang verses in a loud, shrill monotone . . . When the preacher ceased reading, all turned toward the door, fell on their knees, bowed their heads to the ground and set up an agonizing, heart-rending moaning. Afterwards, the minister resumed the reading of the psalter . . . then all rose and began chanting psalms in chorus, the men and women alternating . . .
>
> (Quoted in Southern 1983, p. 78)

In this account and others cited earlier – the observers choosing words like "extatic," "torrent," "raptures," "agonizing," and "heart-rending" to describe what they heard – it is evident that the musical aspect of Christian worship among African Americans in eighteenth- and early-nineteenth-century America was at times spontaneous, kinetic, and emotionally charged. For black congregations, the acts of singing and vocalizing could take center stage in a worship service, occupying a place of equal importance to any religious text; the medium (music) was a crucial part of the Gospel message. This – despite the rationalistic, text-oriented nature of Puritan-descended Protestant worship – turned out to be very much the experience of young white choirs in New England churches at the end of the eighteenth century, as will be seen.

The presiding minister at the service described above was the AME Church's founder, Richard Allen (1760–1831), a major figure in the beginnings of the African American church. In 1801 Allen had compiled the first collection of hymn texts aimed specifically at a black American congregation. *A Collection of Spiritual Songs and Hymns Selected from Various Authors by Richard Allen, African Minister*, reissued later in the same year with a slightly variant title, is important (in Eileen Southern's words) as "an index to the hymns popular among black congregations . . . of the new nation" (Southern 1983, p. 75). While Allen may have written some of the hymn texts in his collection, he does not seem to have composed music. The first known black American composer, Newport Gardner (1746–1826), was like his white counterparts a product of the singing-school movement. Brought from Africa as a slave at age fourteen, Gardner likely studied with singing master Andrew Law in Newport, Rhode Island before purchasing his freedom (with lottery winnings) and opening his own very successful

singing school in Newport. Although he composed prolifically starting at
eighteen, and though the Biblical text of his "Promise Anthem" (with its
added lines addressing the "African race") has survived, none of his music
is known (Southern 1983, pp. 69–70).

While Native Americans and African Americans in the period before
1800 had sacred music traditions of undeniable richness, the religious
music of transplanted Europeans on these shores is much more extensively
documented. Europeans coming to the New World from early in the
seventeenth century onward brought with them a wide variety of religious
traditions. Although languages and liturgies varied between denominations, language and liturgy were themselves crucial to the musical practice
of all. Congregationalists, Anglicans, Presbyterians, Methodists, German
Protestants, Moravians, eventually Baptists and even Catholics all
included as a central component of their sacred music practice the
congregational singing of hymns or versified psalms; and for most of these
denominations, special rehearsed choral or instrumental music could be
found at prescribed points in the worship service. Established texts and
known tunes were essential to the worship music of these groups, while
non-verbal utterance, musical improvisation, individual spontaneity, and
liturgical flexibility were generally absent. Given the controlled, reason-
dominated, text-oriented norm for musical practice in these churches,
exceptions in early America stand out sharply: the anarchic "old way of
singing" described by New England ministers in the 1720s, the enthusiasm and spontaneity of the mid-century Great Awakening, the ecstatic
worship of "New Light" sects in the late 1700s.

The congregational singing of European-American religious denominations served an important function, however: knitting together the religious community. When "all the members of the congregation call out to
God together across the infinite" (Lomax 1968, p. 15; quoted in Britton,
Lowens, and Crawford 1990, p. 1), religious tradition and social ties alike
are reaffirmed. Congregational singing of the psalms had been mandated
for Protestant worshippers in the sixteenth century by French theologian
John Calvin, and Calvin's injunctions were followed faithfully by Anglicans, Pilgrims, Puritans, Presbyterians, and others coming to the North
American continent in the following one hundred years. The psalters of
these religious groups varied only slightly in title and contents: Thomas
Sternhold's and John Hopkins's *The Whole Booke of Psalmes* (1562 and many
later editions) was used by members of the Church of England, Henry

Ainsworth's *The Book of Psalmes: Englished both in Prose and Metre* (1612) by the separatist Pilgrims, *The Whole Booke of Psalmes faithfully Translated into English Metre* (1640 and many later editions; now known as the "Bay Psalm Book," the colonists' first published volume) by the Massachusetts Bay Puritans, and the Scottish psalter, *The Psalms of David in Meeter* (1650), by Presbyterian worshippers.

It is important to take special note of what H. Wiley Hitchcock has called "the richest and most sophisticated musical culture in colonial America" (Hitchcock 1988, p. 23) – that of the German-speaking Moravians in Bethlehem, Nazareth, and Lititz in Pennsylvania and Salem in North Carolina – and to acknowledge the sect's impressive accomplishments in musical composition, instrument building, and performance. But while the anthems and sacred songs of Moravian composers such as Jeremiah Dencke (1725–1795), Johannes Herbst (1735–1812), and Johann Friedrich Peter (1746–1813) – many of them with instrumental accompaniment – are undeniably impressive in quantity and quality, no less deniable is the insularity of their musical culture in the New World (pointed out by Hitchcock), and the derivative quality of the music itself.

Despite common devotional practices and texts, pre-nineteenth-century America's religious diversity only increased toward the end of the colonial era and into the new nation's first decades. But throughout this period, the changing musical values and practices of New England's Congregationalist churches dominated music-making, both within and beyond that denomination, involving thousands of people all along the East Coast as singing masters and scholars, proponents and opponents of musical reform, and – toward the end of the period – composers, publishers, and performers of new sacred music. Other religious groups – especially urban Episcopalians and rural Baptists – would make important contributions to the repertory and practice of sacred music in America, particularly as the century came to a close. While these contributions will be noticed here, the sacred music of Congregationalist New England plays by far the largest – and the most creative – part in the historical pageant. Singing schools were colonial America's first sites of musical learning; church choirs were its first common musical performing groups; singing masters were its first music instructors and, later, composers; and psalters with tune supplements were its first musical publications. And all these, while not exclusively Congregationalist, were most often found under Congregationalist auspices.

Change and resistance in Congregationalist
New England

The two most populous religious groups in colonial America – the adher-
ents to and dissenters from the Church of England – both changed their
musical practices in the course of the eighteenth century. New England
Pilgrims and Puritans at first steered clear of instrumental accompaniment
and professional singing leaders in their worship music, considering these
(along with harmony and counterpoint) to be "popish" excesses. Anglican
worshippers never had strictures against the use of instruments, though
at first practical considerations severely limited their introduction. By
the late 1700s in many urban Episcopalian churches, clerk-led psalmody
had given way to the singing of both psalms and hymns, with organ
accompaniment. But the change in the Congregationalist meeting houses
of New England had been a great deal more extensive. While at the end of
the century entire Congregationalist assemblies still rose to sing, it was
not unusual several times during the service for the congregation to sit
silently while a group of young men and women, seated together in the
"gallery" or balcony, stood to perform a four-voice tune or anthem – sometimes quite lengthy and florid, or containing a section of rapid-fire imitation – occasionally with the support of a bass viol or even of a small "gallery
orchestra." These youthful choristers (median age seventeen) were likely
the graduates of a local singing school, where they had learned the skills of
musical sight-reading, vocal production, and ensemble performance.
Much of the music they sang had been composed and published by local
artisans and tradesmen, no better versed in the musical art than they.

Clearly there was a sea change in the needs of Congregationalist worshippers in the course of the eighteenth century. And as these needs
changed, the role and form of that denomination's sacred music changed
with them. Psalmody, once a largely unconscious practice, became steadily
more conscious; once an encouragement to individual expression, it came
to depend upon communal coordination; once an activity done by all, it
eventually included performances presented by select groups of trained
musicians. In short, as Richard Crawford has pointed out, psalmody was
gradually transformed in Congregationalist New England meeting houses
from an aspect of religious ritual to a display of art (Crawford 1979a).

As eighteenth-century American worship music emerged from its
subservient role in religious ritual and started to play an assertive role as a

creative artistic activity, people reacted in different ways. To some, this change was only a further indication of declension from proper worship practice – an aesthetic mirror reflecting religious decline. For others, the change brought opportunities for self-expression – something given little support in this tradition, but always a human need. In fact, the entire process was shaped by something universal and very old: music's subversive, seductive power to distract people from a controlling institution's "business at hand." In the Puritan-founded Congregational church, that business was the direct, uncluttered worship of God.

The democracy inherent in Congregationalist worship meant not only that *every* worshipper sang God's praises (Calvin's recommendation, reinforced by such tracts as Boston minister John Cotton's 1647 *Singing of Psalmes a Gospel-Ordinance*) but that they did so without trained leadership. These circumstances – combined with the Puritan avoidance of instrumental accompaniment to psalm singing, a steady attrition of music books and of people who could decipher them (editions of the "Bay Psalm Book" from 1698 on, with their supplements of eleven or twelve monophonic tunes, did little to shore up musical literacy), and the practice of "lining out" the psalm (with a deacon or clerk reading each line of text before it was sung) – produced a style of congregational singing which sooner or later was bound to attract notice.

In the 1720s several Boston ministers began to protest, both from the pulpit and in print, the sound of the music in their churches. An essay by the Rev. Thomas Walter describes this sound:

> [Our psalm tunes] are now miserably tortured, and twisted, and quavered, in some Churches, into an horrid Medly of confused and disorderly Noises . . . Our Tunes are . . . left to the Mercy of every unskilful Throat to chop and alter, twist and change, according to their infinitely divers and no less odd Humours and Fancies . . . [Singing with rural congregations,] I have twice in one Note paused to take breath . . . I have observed in many Places, one Man is upon this Note, while another is a Note before him, which produces something so hideous and disorderly, as is beyond Expression bad . . . [M]uch time is taken up in shaking out these Turns and Quavers; and besides, no two men in the Congregation quaver alike, or together; which sounds in the Ears of a good Judge, like *Five Hundred* different Tunes roared out at the same time, whose perpetual interferings with one another, perplexed Jars, and unmeasured Periods, would make a Man wonder at the false Pleasure which they conceive . . .

(Walter 1721, pp. 2–5)

In these phrases are the main features of what became known as the "old way of singing": strongly independent individual lines, a lack of coordination between voices, considerable ornamentation, loud volume, extremely slow tempo, and scant regularity of rhythm.

Clearly, the old way of singing involved little or no use of written materials; this was an oral practice, orally transmitted. Surviving accounts leave little doubt that by the early eighteenth century lining out had become essential to remind congregations of the text and tune to be sung, that only four or five tunes were used in most parishes, and that even with this limited repertory individuals occasionally slipped from one tune into another before they had worked their way through a single stanza. (All these developments had occurred somewhat earlier in English parish churches, as Nicholas Temperley has shown; see Temperley 1979, chapter 4.) It is equally clear that the old way was a practice dear to the hearts of many, and that it would not be given up without a struggle. Straddling ritual and art – remaining faithful to Puritan Congregationalist worship practice while at the same time offering singers a chance for self-expression – it could be superseded only if its critics found a practice equally acceptable and alluring to offer in its place.

The Massachusetts Bay ministers hit upon that practice, with no inkling of how successful it would become, nor where it would lead. The original idea was simply to inculcate musical literacy among the people by teaching "regular singing" – singing by rule, or according to the way music was notated. This, the reformers reasoned, could not fail to improve congregational song. The Rev. Thomas Symmes of Bradford, Massachusetts outlined a plan of procedure in *The Reasonableness of, Regular Singing, or, Singing by Note* (1720):

> WOULD it not greatly tend to the promoting [*of*] *Singing Psalms*, if Singing Schools *were promoted?* . . . Where would be the *Difficulty*, or what the *Disadvantages*, if People that want *Skill* in *Singing*, would procure a *Skilfull Person* to *Instruct* them, and meet *Two* or *Three* Evenings in the Week, from *Five* or *Six* a Clock, to *Eight*, and spend the Time in Learning to Sing?
>
> (Symmes 1720, p. 20)

This is exactly what happened. There were precedents: Anglican religious societies of young men were studying regular singing in Maryland as early as 1699, a singing master is known to have taught in Virginia in 1710–1711, and psalmody instruction was advertised in Boston in 1714.

But the singing school really came into its own in New England in the half century following the reform of the early 1720s.

Colonial singing schools are documented in a wide variety of settings, from the Congregationalist parish of Windsor, Connecticut in 1727 to New York's Anglican Trinity Church in 1753 to a Boston schoolhouse in 1782 (taught by William Billings). Throughout the period they remained remarkably consistent in format and method. They tended to meet several evenings a week, as Rev. Symmes had suggested, and for a period of two or three months. Many were taught from printed or manuscript tunebooks that followed the "rudiments of vocal music" with actual tunes for practice. From the beginning they were an activity for youths – boys and girls aged eight to twenty-one, with the preponderance in their late teens – and they provided a much-needed opportunity for social intercourse. Before the Revolution, most singing masters were hired by local parishes, as when Lewis Edson, Sr. of Bridgewater, Massachusetts taught schools in next-door Halifax between 1769 and 1776; though the itinerancy of Connecticut River Valley singing master George Beale in the 1720s provides a striking early exception to this rule. But the itinerant singing master was largely a phenomenon of the late eighteenth century – as was the self-sponsored singing school, where a singing master set himself up in business by advertising for scholars.

Regular singing and singing schools, introduced to improve an aspect of religious ritual, ironically brought an invasion of art into New England's meeting houses. Striking innovations in themselves, they led to a series of further changes. Each new change took the churches further away from the first settlers' Calvinist ideal of general and unregulated participation in the music of worship. Thus for a time – particularly the last third of the century, when American composers of psalmody were becoming active – spontaneity, unselfconsciousness, and individual expression were at a low ebb in the singing of American sacred music.

A parish in eighteenth-century New England was a small democracy where church members voted on all questions, civil or ecclesiastical, that needed resolution. Many of these questions had to do with the music and texts for worship. Should regular singing be adopted by the parish? Who were to serve as choristers, or singing-leaders, and where were they to sit? Should the "New England version" of the psalms (the "Bay Psalm Book") be discarded in favor of Nicholas Brady and Nahum Tate's *A New Version of the Psalms of David*, or even *The Psalms of David, Imitated in the Language of the*

New-Testament by the Nonconformist theologian Isaac Watts? What tunes
were to be sung in the worship service? Should a singing school be set up?
Who was to be hired as singing master, what was his salary to be, and how
was he to be paid? Should the young people recently graduated from
singing school be allowed to sit together in the meeting house, in order
that they might more effectively lead the singing? Was the choir's petition
to sing one psalm in each service on the Sabbath to be granted? Was it time
to discontinue lining out the psalms? Should a bass viol be introduced to
accompany and support the singers? Discussions and decisions relating to
issues such as these are preserved in hundreds of New England town and
church histories published in the late nineteenth and twentieth centuries.
These accounts are notable for two things: the consistency from town to
town concerning what changed and when; and the degree of unhappiness
and even strife that each sacred music innovation caused.

   Once a congregation had adopted singing "by rule" in preference to the
"old way," a further innovation was usually accepted without much
difficulty: the appointment by the church of one or more men ("choristers") whose job it was to sound the starting pitch of a tune with voice or
pitch pipe and then to lead the singing. There are records of churches
choosing choristers from the 1730s through the 1770s; most choristers
seem to have been established citizens in their middle years. The chorister's duties were performed in the context of lining out, and were similar
to those of the parish clerk in the colonial Anglican church. A common
sequence of events would have the minister reading an entire versified
psalm, a deacon repeating the first line of text, the chorister sounding a
starting pitch and leading the singing of that line, the deacon reading the
next line, and so on. It is easy to see that reading and singing through a
psalm text in this manner – with Brady and Tate's versifications averaging
eleven four-line stanzas and Watts's averaging between eight and nine –
could still be a lengthy process, even when an attempt was made to follow
specified rhythmic values. Individual parishes are known to have resisted
the appointment of singing leaders, and objections were voiced to the choristers' beating time with their hands, to the use of pitch pipes, even to the
setting of any specific pitch at all. But opposition to these early changes
seems to have been neither particularly spirited nor sustained.

   By the mid-1700s the number of singing leaders had increased in many
parishes to three, six, or even eight men, and these individuals were being
permitted to sit together in the meeting house. Presumably they would
rise as a group to lead the congregation through a psalm at the appropriate

points in the service. At the same time, however, singing-school graduates were proliferating in many New England towns. These young people had learned skills that set them apart from their elders; they had tasted the pleasures of sight-reading music, of singing in parts, of regularly consociating with their peers. Not content to bolster the general singing from their families' pews, they began agitating for the right to sit together in the meeting house, and even occasionally to perform, as a separate group, the tunes and anthems they had learned. Their requests were opposed on various grounds, both social (one's seating in the meeting house directly reflected one's standing in the community) and religious (singing God's praises was held to be the duty of all, not the privilege of a few).

But perhaps it was felt that the young singers' diligence should not go unrewarded, for towns began to allow them to sit as a body: first in the "hind seats below," and later in the meeting house gallery, or balcony, which had formerly been the exclusive preserve of the indigent and of African Americans. And more and more churches voted to allot one psalm to the singers (to be sung in parts and not lined out) and one to the congregation. With these innovations the Congregationalist churches of New England, whose worship practice had traditionally been non-hierarchical and democratic, created a select body – the choir – and gave it special duties in the worship service. Boston's West Church designated "singers' seats" in 1754, and the town's First Church followed four years later; these early instances of *de facto* choir formation were followed by churches in Salem and Newbury, Massachusetts (1761); Greenland, New Hampshire (1762); Ipswich and Medford, Massachusetts (1763); and Beverly and Hamlet, Massachusetts (1764) – all towns on or near the coast. Seventeen New England churches are known to have taken this step by the end of the 1760s, and forty-eight by the end of the next decade (Crawford n.d., supplemented by the author's research).

Seating the singers together acknowledged their leadership role in the musical part of the service, and spelled the end of lining out. Indeed, many churches voted to seat the singers and to abolish lining out at the same time. The Worcester, Massachusetts church voted in August, 1779 "That the singers sit in the front seats in the front gallery" and "That said singers be requested to . . . carry on singing in public worship"; on the same occasion it was decided "That the mode of singing in the congregation here, be without reading the psalms, line by line, to be sung" (Lincoln 1837, pp. 178–179). The same source describes the subsequent tearful exit from the meeting house of "the aged and venerable Deacon Chamberlain," whose job it had been to read the lines of the psalm. Chamberlain was not alone in his distress. A survey of eighty-nine Massachusetts town histories found individuals in seventeen places – almost one-fifth of the total – leaving the meeting house or refusing to attend meeting because of musical innovations (Cooke 1993).

Sacred music publications and the
American composer

An irate letter written to the Portsmouth *New Hampshire Gazette* in January, 1764 introduces a new issue in the story of Congregational worship music – that of unfamiliar and inappropriate repertory being sung by the new church choirs:

> There are a set of Geniuses, who stick themselves up in a Gallery, and seem to think that they have a Priviledge of engrossing all the singing to themselves; and truely they take away a very effectual Method to secure this Priviledge, namely by singing such Tunes, as is impossible for the Congregation to join in. Whom they get to compose for them, or whether they compose for themselves, I will not pretend to determine; but, instead of those plain and easy Compositions which are essential to the Awful Solemnity of Church Music, away they get off, one after another, in a light, airy, jiggish Tune, better adapted to a Country Dance, than the awful Business of Chanting forth the Praises of the King of Kings.
>
> (Pichierri 1960, pp. 37-38)

The young people were not quite yet "composing for themselves," but the quantity and diversity of music available to them was rapidly increasing. The "light, airy, jiggish Tune[s]" they sang were taken from the publications of contemporary English country psalmodists such as John Arnold, William Knapp, Joseph Stephenson, and William Tans'ur (see below for more on these men and their music). When the American composer-compiler emerged in the 1770s and 1780s, two traditions had laid the groundwork for his efforts: the activities of these English psalmodists, and a history of American sacred music publication that stretched back more than three-quarters of a century.

By the Revolution's official end in 1783, forty publications containing sacred music (several in various editions) had been issued in America. Ranging from the ninth edition of the "Bay Psalm Book" (1698) with its supplement of thirteen tunes to Boston composer William Billings's *Peace an Anthem* (1783), these publications provide another measure of the transition from ritual to art that is being traced here. They also document the dominance of Congregationalism and of the Puritan/Congregational model of musical worship in this period. Although several early tunebook compilers were not Congregationalists (Thomas Johnston, Francis Hopkinson, and Daniel Bayley were Anglicans; James Lyon became a Presbyterian minister), only eight of the forty titles were aimed at non-Congregational worshippers (Reformed, Anglican, Baptist churches), and the earliest of these eight was not issued until 1752.

Sacred music was printed in early America as an adjunct to sacred texts. With the sole exception of Thomas Walter's *The Grounds and Rules of Musick Explained* (Boston, eight editions, 1721–1764) – a manual for instruction in "regular singing" – every American publication containing music issued before 1761 was either a collection of psalm or hymn texts with tunes interspersed or added in a group at the end, or a separately printed tune supplement designed to be bound or inserted into a text collection. Although it played an ancillary role to devotional texts, music made a strong showing in several of these early collections. The first edition of Walter's tunebook, for example, included among its twenty-four pieces eleven printed for the first time in the colonies. One of these, a simple three-voice, four-phrase composition titled *Southwel New Tune*, has not been traced to any earlier source and thus appears to be the first known piece of music composed in colonial America. A small tune supplement by John Tufts debuted in Boston in the same year that Walter's collection first appeared; Tufts's third edition of 1723 (the earliest we have), titled *An Introduction to the Art of Singing Psalm-Tunes*, offered thirty-four pieces, including nine not found in previous American publications. Among these nine, *100 Psalm Tune New* appears also to have been American-composed. Given this growth of the congregational repertory, it comes as no surprise that the church in Weston, Massachusetts, meeting on November 6, 1724, voted a list of fourteen tunes to be used in its worship services, with the requirement that "the Chorist[e]r do not Set any other publickly unless he has furth[e]r order fro[m] ye Church" (Weston 1901, p. 529). This concern to limit the number of tunes congregations should sing is typical of eastern Massachusetts churches in this period.

At the same time, however, singing-school graduates with new musical skills started to demand new music, and there was only so much available to them in imported English publications. It was only a matter of time before an enterprising singing master would try his own hand at composition. This is what James Lyon (1735–1794) seems to have done for his tunebook

Urania (Philadelphia, 1761; second edition 1767). The publication of *Urania* is a landmark in the history of colonial American sacred music. It was the first collection that aspired to fill the needs of congregations, of those who had only recently mastered the "rudiments of vocal music," and of experienced singers. As such, it represented a major step in the singing book's transformation from an accessory of ritual to a repository for art – a process that would lead eventually to such collections as William Billings's *The Psalm-Singer's Amusement* (1781), designed not so much for worship or instruction as for recreational use by trained choirs and experienced "singing societies" outside of the meeting house. *Urania* introduced sixty-nine pieces to the American-published tunebook repertory. Fifteen of these appear to be of American origin, including five probably by Lyon himself and three by William Tuckey (1708–1781), an immigrant Englishman active in the musical life of New York's Anglican Trinity Church (Temperley 1997, pp. 11–13). Further, *Urania* tapped a repertory hitherto unavailable in American musical publications: the "fuging tunes" and anthems composed or compiled by a talented new generation of English psalmodists: Abraham Adams, John Arnold, Caleb Ashworth, Uriah Davenport, Israel Holdroyd, William Knapp, William Tans'ur, Aaron Williams, and others. From these men's collections, almost all published between the 1730s and the 1760s, the first New England composers of psalmody would draw their models and inspiration (Billings 1977–1990, vol. 1, pp. xviii–xxviii, supplemented by the author's research).

The fuging tunes in mid-century English tunebooks proved especially inspirational to young American singing masters interested in composing. In this tradition, any musical setting of a psalm or hymn verse that involves, at some point, separate vocal entries and text overlap can be called a fuging tune. The most popular model in late-eighteenth-century America set the first two lines of a four-line stanza homophonically, then after a full or partial cadence brought the voices back in one at a time, closing with rough and rousing four-part counterpoint. English anthems published at the same time display a similar liveliness, frequently varying their texture and introducing contrapuntal sections. Fired by this material and by James Lyon's example, several American tunebook compilers of the mid- and late 1760s introduced large chunks of the contemporary British repertory in their publications; the most extensive example is Daniel Bayley's almost literal reprinting of two tunebooks by William Tans'ur and Aaron Williams under the title *The American Harmony* (1769 and later editions). At the same time, other American musicians followed the lead of Lyon and William Tuckey and started to compose their own material.

One who was composing in earnest by the late 1760s was a Boston tanner named William Billings (1746–1800). In 1770, aged twenty-four, Billings published *The New-England Psalm-Singer*, the first of his six tune-books. Every one of the 127 tunes and anthems in this collection was written by Billings, who moreover had "another Volume . . . consisting chiefly of Anthems, Fuges and Chorus's, of his own Composition" waiting in the wings (Billings 1977–1990, vol. 1, p. 4). Further, several of the pieces are of high quality; the anthem on the text "As the hart panteth after the water brooks," for example, is a work of considerable beauty and power. With its frontispiece engraved by Paul Revere, its many topical references, its settings of politically inspired texts, its lively prose introduction, and its torrent of homemade compositions that declare American musical independence and the presence of a new and sometimes inspired creative talent, *The New-England Psalm-Singer* is a remarkable document in the history of American music, and of America itself.

Billings evolved rapidly as a composer after his precocious debut. His second collection, *The Singing Master's Assistant* (1778), was aesthetically light-years beyond his first. While *The New-England Psalm-Singer* had included a large number of untexted psalm tunes, suggesting that it was partly intended for congregational singing, *The Singing Master's Assistant* was manifestly a book for choirs. It was fully texted; it contained eight anthems to the earlier book's four; and it offered pieces both topical (the anthem *Lamentation over Boston*, beginning "By the Rivers of Watertown we sat down and wept"; the patriotic hymn *Chester*, naming five British generals in its second stanza) and even prankish (the almost entirely dis-sonant *Jargon*). When one recalls the story of Worcester's aged Deacon Chamberlain tearfully exiting his meeting house because he was no longer permitted to line out the psalms, it is hard to credit that *The Singing Master's Assistant* had appeared in nearby Boston the previous year.

Billings's tunes and tunebooks provided an example to his musical New England contemporaries that was hard to resist. The Revolution limited tunebook publication, but large musical manuscripts dating from the mid-1770s by Daniel Read (1757–1836) of Attleborough and Abraham Wood (1752–1804) of Northboro, both in Massachusetts, make it clear that the composing of music was not severely affected. And in 1779 a new tunebook, *Select Harmony*, compiled by Andrew Law (1749–1821) of Cheshire, Connecticut, introduced pieces by nine previously unpublished

Americans – a sure sign that more and more singing masters were writing
their own tunes. With the Revolution's end, the floodgates were opened:
while in the first eighty-five years of American sacred music publication
(through Billings's *Peace an Anthem* of 1783) forty titles had appeared, in
the next seventeen years (the remainder of 1783 through 1799) well over
one hundred – introducing many hundreds of new American compositions – were published.

These publications were of various sorts. Some were collections
designed for the use of particular churches or religious denominations;
these tended to be non-Congregationalist (Protestant Episcopal,
Lutheran, Roman Catholic, German Reformed). Others, such as *The
Worcester Collection of Sacred Harmony* (eight editions, 1786–1803) and *The
Village Harmony* (seventeen editions, 1795–1821), were "greatest hits"
anthologies, oriented toward the largest possible sales. Others were single
pieces issued usually in relation to specific occasions, both sacred (*An
Anthem for Easter* by William Billings, 1787) and secular (Hans Gram's
Sonnet for the Fourteenth of October, 1793, "When were entombed the
remains of His Excellency John Hancock, Esq[.]"). Still others, including
the Uranian Society of Philadelphia's *Introductory Lessons* (1785), were
frankly pedagogical. Quite a few were gatherings of works by composers
active in a particular area and known to a particular compiler; *Federal
Harmony* (six editions, 1790–c. 1796) by Asahel Benham (1754–1803) is an
example. And finally there were all-original tunebooks, along the lines of
William Billings's, by such men as Daniel Read (*The American Singing Book*,
five editions, 1785–1796), Jacob French (1754–1817) (*The New American
Melody*, 1789), Samuel Holyoke (1762–1820) (*Harmonia Americana*, 1791),
and Supply Belcher (1751–1836) (*The Harmony of Maine*, 1794).

Late-eighteenth-century tunebooks contain much of the first music
composed in the United States of America – certainly much of that which,
because it was written down, has survived. Richard Crawford has suc-
cinctly characterized the specialness of psalmody: it was "a fully notated,
written practice whose creative roots r[a]n deepest in village and countryside and among the plain people who dwel[t] there, rather than in the more
sophisticated centers of civilization" (Crawford 1979b, p. 291). One might
add, as Crawford does elsewhere, a further special characteristic of
psalmody: it is polyphonic music, created (as both composers' writings
and manuscript drafts tell us) by the successive addition of vocal lines
rather than by the chordal harmonization of a melody. The tradition's
finest psalm tunes (homophonic strophic settings of single stanzas),

fuging tunes (described earlier), set pieces (through-composed settings of multiple verses of text), and anthems (through-composed settings of prose texts) are thus marked not only by the eloquent musical expression they bring to ideas and imagery in their texts but also by the strong, characterful lines they provide for all three or four vocal parts. This "folk counter-point" was an intriguing challenge to its largely untutored practitioners in the eighteenth century, and has proven intriguing to late-twentieth-century musicians as well.

The composers of psalmody were tradesmen, farmers, schoolteachers, merchants, and town officials who had in most cases no more musical education than a few months' study in a singing school. About 250 of them contributed tunes and anthems to American sacred music publications issued through 1810 (Britton, Lowens, and Crawford 1990, p. 10). Of these, only a tiny handful are known to have spent any portion of their life in a large city. Some of the most talented and original composers, such as Daniel Read in New Haven and Timothy Swan (1758–1842) in Suffield, Connecticut, also published tunebooks; others, such as Justin Morgan (1747–1798) in Randolph, Vermont and Lewis Edson, Sr. (1748–1820) in Lanesboro, Massachusetts, only had their music printed by others. While some of the best-documented psalmodists – Daniel Read and Oliver Holden (1765–1844), for example – produced first-rate tunes, there are also gems by virtual unknowns: *Hatfield* by [Thomas?] Baird, *Herald* by John Bushnell, and *Crucifixion* by one M. Kyes, for example, are as accomplished and powerful (or beautiful) as anything by William Billings. Example 4.1 shows another of these gems, the fuging tune *Blooming Vale* by a composer known only as J. P. Storm. Sung through once, even with a repeat of its fuging section, the piece is not likely to last longer than one minute; but Storm fills that minute as richly and satisfyingly as any composer working in any tonal tradition. The tenor melody is closely expressive of Isaac Watts's yearning words – starting to open up on "wings," expanding still further on the two "long remove"s, then quickening its motion again for the "restless things" that keep one tied down to the earth (that tying-down exemplified by the final descent of a tenth). Not only the tenor, but every vocal line is shapely and distinctive. The harmony stays close to tonic and dominant, though a touch of the relative major at measure 4 is felicitously recalled at measure 14. Rhythmically, the tune is a marvel of relaxed asymmetry: five-measure homophonic phrases (3 + 2; 2 + 3) bracket eight measures of polyphony which feature different-sized groups of three (a three-measure phrase in the tenor

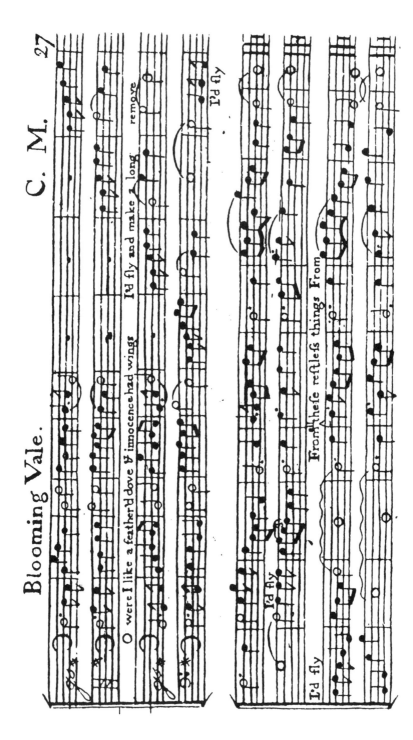

EXAMPLE 4.1 *Blooming Vale* (attributed to "Mr. Storm") in Lewis Edson, Jr.'s *The Social Harmonist*, 2nd edn. (New York, 1801). The clefs (from top down) are G, C, G, and F; the piece is in cut time; the melody is in the tenor voice; and the word "all" is inserted in the last line of text.

followed immediately by one of a measure and a half, overlapping with a measure-and-a-half phrase in the bass and followed immediately by similar phrases in treble and counter). Finally, the tune's rhythmic inter-lockings of voices, sensitivity to range, and extensive use of the lowered seventh degree add considerable charm.

With roughly 5,000 musical compositions by American psalmodists printed through 1810 (Crawford 1979b, p. 289), the measure of this reper-tory has yet to be taken; recent scholarly editions (Billings 1977–1990; Crawford 1984; Jenks 1995; Read 1995; Swan 1997) and an extensive series of anthologies (Kroeger 1995–) will facilitate this.

One further step away from ritual and toward art in the music of the Congregational worship service – the introduction of instruments other than the human voice – occurred toward the end of the eighteenth century. Anglican churches in the colonies had no prohibitions against instru-mental accompaniment, purchasing organs to accompany their singing as soon as funds were available. The King's Chapel in Boston had an organ by 1713 and the two other Anglican churches in that city had theirs by 1744; St. Philip's Church in Charleston, South Carolina and Christ Church in Philadelphia purchased organs in or around 1728; Trinity Church in Newport, Rhode Island had one by 1733, and Trinity Church in New York City by 1741; five Virginia churches installed organs between 1737 and 1767; and so it went. But New England's Congregational churches, as noted earlier, often had trouble admitting even the lowly pitch pipe. After that aid to singers was allowed, the next instrument introduced seems to have been the bass viol – also to support the singers, by doubling the bass line. Resistance to the "devil's fiddle" was particularly strong: in Roxbury, Massachusetts, "[o]ne old church member stood at the church door and showed his contempt . . . by making a sort of caterwauling noise, which he called 'mocking the banjo'" (Thwing 1908, p. 340). But in time the bass viol won a place in the church gallery, as did (in some locations) the violin, flute, clarinet, bassoon, and other instruments comprising what came to be called the "gallery orchestra." (There was no organ in a New England Congregational church until 1770, in Providence, Rhode Island; Barbara Owen documents only eleven Congregational church organs by 1800 [Owen 1985, pp. 681, 713].)

In time, too, it appears that choirs took over the entire musical portion of the worship service in most Congregational churches. With this step, the transformation from ritual to art – for most worshippers, from participation in a religious act to appreciation of a performance – was

complete. Music in rural New England meeting houses, as in urban Anglican churches, had become as much an object for contemplation as a means
for expressing sacred truths.

Emerging folk influence at the
turn of the century

While Congregationalist New England's emphasis on literacy and
notated, original compositions dominated American sacred music in the
second half of the eighteenth century, there persisted in the same decades a
second musical tradition marked by oral transmission and the use of folk
(or folk-like) melodies. This tradition was associated with evangelical
Christianity and particularly (as the century drew to a close) with the
Baptist denomination. The religious revivals of the early 1740s in New
England, sparked by the extemporaneous and emotionally charged
preaching of George Whitefield, brought a surge of enthusiasm for
spontaneous and emotional utterance in religious song. Paul Osterhout
points out that "The urge for individual expression, whether in prayer, in
general exhortation or in song, was a documented phenomenon of the
Great Awakening" (Osterhout 1978, p. 98). It seems likely that the singing
at many revival gatherings drew from the composed, notated repertory
discussed earlier. But Nicholas Temperley has found no source for three of
the tunes in a 1768 Baptist collection, *The Customs of Primitive Churches*, and
comments that "[t]wo of them . . . appear to be secular folk-songs, while
the third has the sound of a popular theatre tune" and that these pieces
"provide evidence, however indirect, that the music of the Great Awakening did indeed borrow popular tunes from secular sources" (Temperley
1995, p. 175).

Evidence that the music of the Second Great Awakening, which took
place in the opening years of the nineteenth century, drew upon such
sources is not at all indirect. Paul Echols has noted that at this time "[t]he
lack of hymnbooks and prevalent illiteracy [in the rural areas most touched
by this revival] encouraged the adoption of call-and-response patterns in
song," and that "[t]he presence of an oral tradition of folksong led naturally and immediately to the use of secular folk and popular tunes for hymn
singing" (Echols 1986, p. 447). A lack of hymn collections, musical illiteracy, and the availability of folksong were likely not the only causes of a
mode of religious singing in the early 1800s that seems to have been
marked by spontaneity, immediacy, emotionality, and the use of well-

known tunes. An equally likely cause is the rise of the Baptist and Universalist denominations in the last two decades of the 1700s. Even William Billings, as active as any in composing and publishing music for Congregational churches, felt the tug of these new religious currents: he was in North Yarmouth, Maine in 1780, when a religious revival partly spearheaded by Freewill Baptist proselytizers was cresting in that region (Cooke 1991), and more than half of the pieces in his tunebook *The Suffolk Harmony* (1786) set texts by James Relly, disciple of George Whitefield and the founder of the Universalist Church. Collections of folk hymn *texts* aimed at these denominations started to appear in this period; the first and most famous of these, Joshua Smith's *Divine Hymns or Spiritual Songs* (many editions from 1784 on), appears to have been designed for the use of rural Separatist Baptists (Klocko 1978, p. 127). In fact, in Paul Echols's words, "a body of backwoods hymnody had been circulating freely between North and South by the onset of the Second Great Awakening" (Echols 1986, p. 447). A central message of these hymns was the availability of God's grace to all. It was only fitting that this message should be sung to melodies known by all, or at least to tunes of a popular flavor.

The desire for melodies that were easily and generally accessible, combined with a need for rhythmically forceful music to accompany more enthusiastic, physical styles of worship, directed the attention of some tunebook musicians around 1800 to the rich repertories of dance tunes, marches, and ballad airs then current, both in print and in oral circulation. These melodies were adapted to religious texts and harmonized for three or four voices, producing the "folk hymn." Other composers imitated the melodic styles of these popular repertories, creating folk-like hymn settings. A tunebook that seems to include quite a substantial component of folk or folk-like hymns is *The United States' Sacred Harmony* (1799), printed at Boston for the compiler, Amos Pilsbury (1772–1812) of Charleston, South Carolina (Kroeger 1981). Several collections from the first years of the new century contain music that is strongly folk-flavored: Timothy Swan's *New England Harmony*, 1801 (see, for example, the tune *Claradon*), Abraham Maxim's *The Oriental Harmony*, 1802 (*Renovation*), and Oliver Holden's *The Charlestown Collection of Sacred Songs*, 1803 (*New-Union*) are examples. Swan and Maxim (1773–1829) lived in Suffield, Connecticut and Turner, Maine respectively – far from the coastal urban centers of cosmopolitan culture – when their tunebooks were published; Holden had for some time been affiliated with the Baptist church.

The importance of Joshua Smith's Baptist text collection *Divine Hymns*

Separation.

Lively.

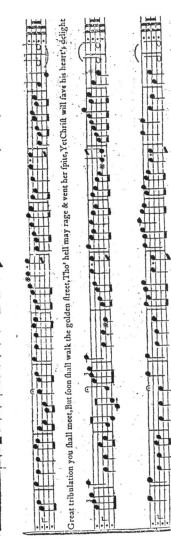

Come we that love the Lord indeed, Who are from sin and bondage freed ; Submit to all the ways of God; And walk this narrow, happy road

Great tribulation you shall meet, But soon shall walk the golden street, Tho' hell may rage & vent her spite, Yet Christ will save his heart's delight

3 The happy day will soon appear,
    When Gabriel's trumpet you shall hear,
    Sound thro' the earth, yea, down to hell,
    To call the nations great and small.

4 Behold the skies in burning flame,
    The trumpets louder still proclaim.
    The world must hear and know their doom,
    The separation now is come.

5 Behold the righteous marching home,
    And all the angels bid them come ;
    Whilst Christ the Judge their joy proclaims
    Here comes my saints, I own their names.

6 Ye everlasting doors fly wide,
    Make room for to receive my bride ;
    Ye harps of heav'n, come sound aloud,
    Here comes the purchase of my blood.

7 In grandeur see the royal lines,
    Whose glit'ring robes the sun outshines ;
    See saints and angels join in one,
    And march in splendour round the throne.

8 They stand in wonder and look on,
    And join in one eternal song ;
    Their great Redeemer to admire,
    While rapture sets their hearts on fire.

EXAMPLE 4.2 *Separation* (unattributed; secular melody, probably harmonized by Jeremiah Ingalls) in Ingalls's *The Christian Harmony;*
or, Songster's Companion (Exeter, New Hampshire, 1805). The piece is in cut time; the melody is in the middle voice.

or Spiritual Songs and of the Baptist denomination generally in the development of the new folk-influenced musical repertory is underscored by two similarly titled tunebooks which appeared in 1804 and 1805. Samuel Holyoke's *The Christian Harmonist* (1804), "designed for the use of the Baptist churches in the United States," announced on its title page that its tunes were adapted to all the text meters in, among others, "the collection of hymns by Mr. Joshua Smith." Holyoke may have "attempted to compose in the folk idiom," in the words of Irving Lowens (Lowens 1964, p. 142), but, never a gifted melodist, he had little success in producing tunes to match the freshness and spontaneity of Smith's texts. One who did, however, was Jeremiah Ingalls (1764–1838) of Newbury, Vermont, whose *The Christian Harmony* – setting more hymns from Smith's collection than from any other source – appeared the next year. In his tunebook Ingalls reprinted compositions by English and American psalmodists, and contributed some new music from his own pen. But for sixty pieces in the book he either borrowed secular melodies from a variety of traditions (both oral and written) or composed melodies in similar styles, and then set these to sacred texts, thereby creating some of the first known American *contrafacta*. *Separation* is reproduced from *The Christian Harmony* as example 4.2. It sets a text from Smith's *Divine Hymns* to a melody that in various forms is found as an Irish reel, *Johnny from Gandsey*; as a Scots ballad with a text beginning "Forever, Fortune, wilt thou prove / An unrelenting foe to love"; and as a tune for fife or German (transverse) flute, usually entitled *Logan Water* or *Logan[']s Wake* in late-eighteenth-century American music manuscripts. The various uses of the melody suggest a wide range of possible tempos. While singers would have to negotiate some rather daunting peaks and valleys in Ingalls's musical setting (further complicated by an obvious misprint – the melody's low B in the second full measure – and an awkward and questionable raised seventh degree at two points in the upper voice), and while Ingalls's probable source, the anonymous *Songster's Museum* (Northampton, Massachusetts, 1803), recommended a tempo of "very slow" for the ballad *Forever Fortune*, Ingalls's tempo indication here is "Lively." This suggests that he felt the tune more as a reel than as a dirge, and that walking the "golden street" of heaven, rather than the "great tribulation" met here below, was uppermost in his mind.

    David Klocko has rightly credited Ingalls as being "one of the first Americans to bring together in print the sacred and secular repertories and the written and oral traditions" (Ingalls 1981, p. vii). Klocko has also pointed out that *The Christian Harmony* "stands at a crossroads: it is one of the last New England tunebooks with indigenous American composi-tions, and it is one of the first collections of folk-hymns or spiritual folk-songs" (Klocko 1978, p. v). Its appearance is thus an appropriate point at which to break off this narrative, which is variously continued in chapters 6 and 8. Publications such as *The Christian Harmony* are a sure sign that by the opening years of the nineteenth century some Americans felt the need to democratize their sacred song – to make it available, once again, to those who were less musically literate, as it had been a century earlier. They did so now, of course, in a context that was immeasurably more secular.

5

African American music to 1900

JACQUELINE COGDELL DJEDJE

The history of African American music is fascinating because on the one hand very little disappears, but also nothing remains the same. The features that give African American music its unique character can be found in many of its genres and time periods. Differences only occur in the degree to which elements are emphasized. Although several of the features associated with black expressive forms can be found in the music of other cultures, the manner in which these elements are externalized and blended suggests that African American performance practices are derived from Africa (Wilson 1974). However, the type of music blacks created in the Americas, particularly before 1900, depended upon the extent of interaction and ethnic distribution among Africans, the demography and geographical location of black and white populations, the demands of the white masters, and the characteristics of the economy.

To appreciate fully the essence of the black music experience in the United States, a thorough understanding of its African roots is critical. While there have been several excellent studies that have examined *what* African Americans have created (see works by Southern and Epstein), few scholars have looked extensively at the roots, contextual factors, and demands which caused blacks to create their music. In addition, most overviews have not been successful in providing a clear and complete picture of the continent of Africa during the period when Africans were transported to the Americas. Not only have peoples on the African continent been presented as a homogeneous group, but the central focus has been on societies in West Africa. Africans were drawn from numerous ethnic and linguistic groups and different societies. While large numbers were transported from West Africa during the seventeenth and early eighteenth centuries, Central Africa was one of the primary sources for slaves from the mid-eighteenth to the early nineteenth centuries (Rawley 1981, pp. 17–18). Only when we are cognizant of regional differences will we be able to understand more clearly why and how black musical traditions evolved in various parts of the United States.

In many discussions of the African musical heritage, sources used to document the history date from periods other than those when Africans were transported to the Americas; nor are they presented in a systematic time frame so that comparisons in the development of the music are more clearly apparent. Sources from twentieth-century Africa (e.g. Nketia 1974; Waterman 1952) are sometimes used to make connections and validate practices that occurred during slavery and the pre-colonial era. This approach not only infers that African music is static, but it suggests that few changes have occurred in the development of music since pre-colonial times. Scholars who adhere to this way of thinking fail to realize that African cultures, like those in other parts of the world, are dynamic.

Another issue is the nature of contact between Europeans and Africans. Discussions of the origins and growth of African American societies in the New World have usually involved a model, implicit or explicit, of the ways in which encounters between Africans and Europeans occurred, and the consequences of these encounters. Usually, this model posits the existence of two "cultures," one African and one European. In order to think of an "African" culture coming into contact with a "European" culture, scholars have been compelled either to posit the existence of a generalized West African culture "heritage," which Africans of diverse background brought to a given colony, or to argue that the bulk of Africans in that area came from some particular cultural group (Mintz and Price 1976, p. 4). In addition, most arguments neglect to mention that Europeans were not a unified group. Each European power had a different agenda and philosophy about the institution of slavery which affected the treatment of Africans in both the Old and New Worlds. Related to this way of thinking is the inference that the interactions of African and European cultures helped to create a monolithic "African American" culture. Thus, the richness and diversity of all America's cultural traditions – African, European, African American, and Native American – are overlooked, avoided, or skewed in a misguided effort to show commonalities, similarities, and differences.

Of course, we may never know what really happened during the slave era for scholars still are unable to document with accuracy the number and names of specific African groups transported to the Americas. Therefore, we should not make broad generalizations. To assume that all Africans were somehow committed culturally to one or another path of development both evades the empirical question of what really happened and masks the central theoretical issue of how cultures change. We need to deal with questions as to which elements were transmitted, which lost, which modified, and by what processes traditions may be understood for what they are (Mintz and Price 1976, p. 9).

This chapter presents some of the music and traditions developed and performed by African Americans to 1900. In the first section, a discussion of African ethnic distribution, culture, and music history provides a framework for the examination of African influences in the Americas. The following three sections focus on African and African American music with attention given to context as well as intercultural contacts among groups. The history and unique features of black music raise several issues requiring more detailed knowledge of social history and anthropology than this chapter is able to explore. While discussion of such processes as maintenance and transformation, resilience and assimilation, syncretism and interculturalism as well as Africanization and Americanization is included to some extent, these issues are not discussed in depth nor do they serve as the primary focus. Also, little attention is given to the relationship of music to the social organization and stratification of blacks.

Africa

Areas in Africa most affected by the transatlantic trade include Senegambia (present-day Senegal and The Gambia); Sierra Leone (which extended along the coasts of present-day Guinea, Guinea-Bissau, and portions of Senegal and Sierra Leone); Windward Coast (mainly Liberia and present-day Côte d'Ivoire [Ivory Coast], but also portions of Sierra Leone);[1] Gold Coast (roughly the same as present-day Ghana); Bight of Benin (present-day Togo, Benin, and Nigeria); Bight of Biafra (from the Niger-Delta in Nigeria to Cape Lopez in present-day Gabon); and Central and Southeast Africa (Gabon down to the Orange River in Namibia as well as parts of Mozambique and Madagascar). Culturally, these regions can be divided into three broad areas: (1) Western Sudan, which includes Senegambia and portions of Sierra Leone; (2) West Africa, which can be divided into three sub-regions – the Bight of Biafra, the Bight of Benin and Gold Coast, the

1. In some studies, the Windward Coast includes Côte d'Ivoire, Liberia, and Sierra Leone. For the present discussion, Sierra Leone will be regarded as a bridge or area that includes features associated with both Senegambia and the Windward Coast. But see Paul E. Lovejoy 1982, pp. 493–494.

Windward Coast; and (3) Central and Southeast Africa (Curtin 1969, pp. 123–125; 127–128, 189; DjeDje 1998).

Western Sudan

The Western Sudan was home to a number of ethnic groups that established great empires and kingdoms (Ghana, Mali, and Songhai) prior to contact with Europeans in the fifteenth century. While several groups (Soninke, Sossu, Mandinka, Bambara, and Dyula) belong to the Mande language subfamily, others (Tukulor/Toucouleur, Fulbe, Wolof, Serer, and Jolla) speak a language that belongs to the West Atlantic linguistic subdivision. Excepting a few groups in the West Atlantic and Kwa language families, most Western Sudanese were centrally and hierarchically organized. These hierarchies ascribed social rank and specific roles to members of society according to their family heritage and craft specialization. Furthermore, prior to Sudanese contacts with Europeans, many groups had experience of both Islam and Arab culture.

The intercultural contacts and Arab influence that took place in Sudanic Africa early in history resulted in a number of similarities in the musical traditions of groups. In many Western Sudanic societies, musicians were craft specialists born into a family of musicians. As professionals who commanded a high degree of respect because of their attachment to royalty and other officialdom, musicians served as oral historians and verbal artists, acting as public speakers, interlocutors, and praisers. During times of conflicts with other nations, they accompanied warriors in battles to stimulate them to fight. It was not uncommon for musicians to travel as a family to visit patrons; the women sang while men played instruments and narrated stories. As an endogamous group who depended on the favor of others for their livelihood, musicians were also socially separated from others in society and sometimes held in low regard (Knight 1984).

Oral tradition indicates that the bala or balafon (xylophone) originated among the Sossu but was adopted by the Mandinka, who consider it to be their oldest instrument. It was normally constructed with as many as seventeen or nineteen keys tied to a low frame and played with a rubber-tipped beater in each hand. One of the first references to the balafon appears in 1353 in the writings of Ibn Battuta, an Arab traveler. Another instrument unique to the Western Sudan is the kora (harplute or bridge harp), which the Mandinka believe to be their youngest instrument. The first reference to the kora was made in 1799 by Mungo Park (Knight 1984, p. 69).

Because of influence from North Africa, plucked lutes (called bangelo, bangeo by European writers of the eighteenth century) and bowed lutes (fiddles) were also prominent in the Western Sudan, although a few varieties of plucked lutes are believed to be indigenous to Africa (Coolen 1984). Various types of drums (e.g. hourglass pressure, gourd, slit, and cylindrical), trumpets, and harps are other Western Sudanic instruments mentioned in the literature between the seventeenth and nineteenth centuries (Astley 1968; Epstein 1977, pp. 5–6; Hirschberg 1969; Knight 1984, p. 71). Richard Jobson, an English explorer who traveled in various parts of Senegambia between 1620 and 1621, is one of the first Europeans to provide detailed descriptions of contexts for music-making, musicians, and instruments such as the xylophone and lutes (Southern 1983a, pp. 6–22). Jean Baptiste Labat, whose publication on the physical environment and life of people in Senegambia appeared in 1728, also provides much information on music-making and recreational activities:

> The Women and Girls appeared first, divided into four Parties; having, at the Head of each, a *Guiriot*, or Female Musician, who sung some Verses relative to the Occasion, which the others answered in Chorus. In this Manner, they passed singing and dancing round a great Fire in the Centre of the Place, where the Chiefs and principal Men sat on Mats. Soon after appeared in another Squadron, all the young Men, divided, like the Women, into Companies, with Drums and Fiddles. They were in their best Dress, and armed as if for a Battle. They made their Procession round the Fire, and quitting this Dress and Weapons, began to wrestle singly with great Agility . . . This Exercise was followed by a Sort of Ball to their Violins, both Sexes showing their Skill in Dancing, which is their favourite Diversion, and of which they never tire.
>
> (Quoted in Astley 1968, p. 298)

West Africa

There is much more diversity and ethnic fragmentation among groups in West Africa. Although most speak languages that belong primarily to the Kwa or Benue Congo/Bantu linguistic subfamilies, linkages, contacts, and interactions were confined to small areas. Some societies developed highly organized nation-states, but most were not as large in scope as savannah empires. Others formed loosely organized confederacies that came together periodically for defense. Secret societies and age-grade associations served as important institutions. Most traditional religions acknowledged the belief in a supreme being, but it was the lesser deities and ancestor spirits that attracted worship and propitiation from people in the society (Mabogunje 1971, pp. 23–25). Although there was contact with groups who lived north in the savannah belt, the impact from Islam was slight and confined to small pockets.

IBO · Published in 1789, Olaudah Equiano's autobiography provides excellent details on music during the eighteenth century, the period when large numbers of Ibo were transported to the Americas. Similar to other parts of Africa, music was central to the lives of the Ibo people. At public gatherings to celebrate the triumph of a battle, music, dance, and songs would be heard. Performers would be divided by sex and age; married men and women would take on performance roles that were different from those performed by young men and maidens. Because each group depicted some aspect of real life or a recent event, there was always something new to perform. Two drum types (slit and gourd) have been documented for this period. Females were associated with the performance of the lamellophone (often referred to the "thumb piano" or "hand piano") and something "which resembles a guitar" (quoted in Southern 1983a, p. 12; Equiano 1969).

EDO · Except musical instruments, little is known about the music of the Edo people of ancient Benin. Archaeological findings (bronze plaques made by local artists) from the sixteenth century show that a variety of instruments were used. The idiophones include slit drums, percussion bells, clapper bells, and vessel rattles. Of the membranophones, there were hourglass drums and single-skin drums with cord and peg bracing. Among the chordophones, there was a pluriarc, an instrument found mainly in Central Africa and West Africa east of Côte d'Ivoire. Two main types of aerophones were made: end-blown flute and side-blown trumpet (Dark and Hill 1971, pp. 65–78).

YORUBALAND · Although little is known about music of the Yoruba kingdom of Oyo, information exists on Lagos, a neighboring Yoruba state, whose traditions are similar to that of the Oyo. According to Túnjí Vidal, music of Lagos's early period (1500–1700) was devoted to religious rituals and royalty. Musical characteristics included the use of cries and recited poetry, divisive rhythmic patterns, and simple bell accompaniment to drumming. Also, drum and aerophone signals were used to announce the passing of a spirit, the death of a respected leader or the imposition of curfew. During the middle period (1700–1860), not only did new forms (music and dance dramas), repertory, instrumental resources, and contexts (festivals) for music-making come into being, but divisive rhythms were replaced by additive rhythms and later combined to produce more complex polyrhythms. In vocal music, cries and incantations were replaced by chants and songs with drumming accompaniment and later combined with them (Vidal 1977, pp. 67, 72–74).

DAHOMEY · Among the Fon of ancient Dahomey, oral traditions document the names of kings who were responsible for the introduction of various orchestras and the names of the musicians who led orchestras. Music at the court was plentiful. Not only were there ceremonies to be performed, funeral rites to be celebrated, special agricultural and purificatory rites to be observed, but there were great festivals. Musicians validated the kingship. In song they extolled the might and majesty of the reigning monarch or recalled the lofty deeds of the royal ancestors. Royalty were given strong names or compared to powerful animals to show their courage. In addition to praising, musicians provided personal services for royalty. Music was performed before the king arose and periodically throughout the day (Nketia 1971, pp. 12–14). Although writers' comments about religious practices were negative, this information provides insight about the role of music in religion. One writer reports: "The kingdom of Ardra or Arder [Allada], whose inhabitants have lapsed into devil worship, borders on the Gold Coast. He (the devil) is consulted in all undertakings like an oracle; people bring him offerings on feast days and dance and jump to the rhythm of a wooden drum [slit drum]" (Hirschberg 1969, p. 8). Concerning religious worship among the Egun, William Smith, in 1726, stated: "The laity all go in a large body by night with drums beating and trumpets of elephants' teeth sounding in order to perform divine worship, and implore either a prosperous journey, fair weather, a good crop, or whatever else they want" (quoted in Vidal 1977, p. 68).

GOLD COAST · Most information from the Gold Coast concerns royal music of the Akan. According to Wilhelm Johann Müller, a minister from Harburg who traveled to the Gold Coast from 1661 to 1669, many courtiers, women, and servants were involved in the pageantry and performance of court music. Pieter de Marees, a Dutchman who traveled to the Gold Coast during the seventeenth century, indicates that women played cymbals and other types of instruments. In royal processions, male musicians (drummers and ivory horn blowers) walked in front of noble-men (Hirschberg 1969, pp. 6–7). In some Akan areas, the number of musicians attached to a king's court and the variety of musical instruments and ensembles reflected the king's greatness. The higher Asante chiefs were permitted drums and other instruments that junior chiefs could not keep. Short horns were reserved for chiefs, but only paramount chiefs could own ensembles of trumpets. Although the Asante kingdom gained musically (musicians, instruments, and new musical types) from territorial expansion during the eighteenth century, the Asante also influenced some areas. Features in the music of northern Ghana and traditions in ancient Dahomey demonstrate evidence of intensive contact with the Asante (Nketia 1971, pp. 17, 19).

Only a few sources make references to other ethnic groups and contexts for music-making in the Gold Coast. A surgeon from Philadelphia who visited the Gold Coast from 1749 to 1751 (for the purposes of trading in slaves) wrote in his diary on July 11, 1750: "Early this morning the King of the Fantees . . . sent his Canoe wth. 12 negroes for me . . . [and] from the Ship to the Shore I was attended with the Singing of them" (quoted in Epstein 1977, p. 69).

WINDWARD COAST · Information about music-making among groups in Liberia, Côte d'Ivoire, and Sierra Leone is minimal. Otto Friedrich von der Gröben, a German who traveled to Africa in 1682, states "At new moon the inhabitants of the Pepper Coast (= Liberia) sing, dance and play with a stick on a three foot high drum carved out of palmwood and covered with skin. In one hand they hold the drum stick, in the other a bell, and on the arms they have iron rings – all this together produces harmonic music in their opinion, and they dance until they collapse with fatigue" (Hirschberg 1969, p. 8). Three musical instruments in the area are believed to be of Sudanic origin: buru (an aerophone – the specific type is not known), koro (a flute), and tama, an hourglass pressure drum (Monts 1984).

Central and Southeast Africa

Because most people in this region speak languages that belong to the Benue-Congo/Bantu linguistic subfamily, scholars believe that the different ethnic groups have a common origin (Greenberg 1970). More than 2,000 years ago, Bantu speakers began to migrate from their original homeland in the Cameroon highlands southward and eastward across

Africa. As the indigenous peoples (Pygmy and Khoisan) were displaced, Bantu speakers either settled and established political institutions of their own or moved on to other areas. Prior to contact with Europeans in 1498, Bantu speakers who settled on the East coast had extensive interactions with Muslim Arab traders (Burke 1974, pp. 121, 126–127; Tracey 1948, p. 122). Kongo (a Central African kingdom) and Ngola (a small state south of Kongo) voluntarily established cultural exchanges and trade agreements with Portugal in the late fifteenth century. A Kongolese emissary went to Portugal and Portuguese missionaries, artisans, and explorers were invited to settle in Kongo. When the king of Kongo incorporated Christianity into his kingdom, a church was built in the Kongo capital and the king and royal family were baptized as Christians (Kubik 1980, p. 431; Vansina 1966, pp. 50, 125).

While no records have been found to document the early music history of Southeast Africa (Tracey 1980, p. 662), much documentation is available for Central Africa. Scholars believe that music from the fifteenth to seventeenth centuries was determined by two historical circumstances: the influence of the Kongo and Ngola states on musical practice in the form of court and military music with iron bells and drums; and the impact of Portuguese cultural influence. By the seventeenth century, sources indicate that musicians in the Kongo kingdom played on imported Portuguese military drums very skillfully. Around the same time, side-blown ivory trumpets used in church and court ceremonies were no longer performed horizontally, but were end-blown with wooden mouthpieces. However, musicians reverted to the side-blown types later, probably after the Portuguese were asked to leave (Kubik 1980, p. 432). In addition to bells, trumpets, and drums, much documentation exists for the marimba (xylophone), the nsambi (five-stringed pluriarc) and flute (Hirschberg 1969, p. 16). People of non-royal ancestry performed rattles and pipes, and similar instruments that were "harsher and ruder" in sound than those used by nobles. Lutes were played at weddings and other festive events (see Merriam 1980, p. 622, for a contemporary description), and it has been suggested that the English word banjo may be derived from the Bantu term mbanza, meaning stringed instrument (Vass 1979, p. 105). Andrew Battell, who, from 1590 to 1610, spent time as a hostage of the Jaga people in present-day Angola, indicates that funeral rites were important. The kin of a dead person would meet monthly and "sing doleful songs at his grave for the space of three days" (Merriam 1980, p. 622). Captain J. K. Tuckey, commander of an ill-fated expedition up the Congo River in 1816, states that singing was common; there were "songs on love, war, hunting, palm wine, and a variety of subjects" (quoted in Merriam 1980, p. 622).

America, 1600–1800

The transatlantic slave trade to 1700

The exportation of slaves from Africa varied and depended on supply and demand. During the fifteenth century, Africans were exported to Europe and the Americas primarily from a region stretching south of the Senegal River to the vicinity of present-day Sierra Leone, with only a scattering from other parts of West or Central Africa. Beginning in the mid-sixteenth century, the flow of trade changed and became more variable, shifting from a heavy dependence on Senegambia to an equally heavy dependence on Angola. In the seventeenth century, not only were the Dutch responsible for the first "parcel" of Africans to arrive in Jamestown, Virginia – in August, 1619 – but they brought the "sugar revolution" to the Caribbean and began the shift that was to make the West Indian islands the heart of the eighteenth-century South Atlantic System. England became a major importer of Africans into North America in the seventeenth century, but its source differed from that of other Europeans. The Gold and Windward Coasts accounted for 48 percent of English exports while the remaining were from Senegambia and Sierra Leone (12 percent), Angola (12 percent), present-day Benin (15.7 percent), and present-day Nigeria (6.7 percent). During the late seventeenth century, groups from Southeast Africa and Madagascar were imported into English colonies (Curtin 1969, pp. 96, 101–102, 117, 123–126; Higgins 1976, p. 118; Rawley 1981, pp. 279–281).

During the seventeenth century, the English transported most of their slave holdings to two Caribbean islands, Barbados and Jamaica (Curtin 1969, pp. 123–124). Enslaved Africans in the West Indies came to be known as "seasoned" slaves for they had been "broken in" and taught the ways of life in the New World. Because blacks greatly outnumbered whites, seasoning was important to Europeans: not only was it a means, although unsuccessful, to prevent uprising and escape, but as the years passed and "seasoned" slaves learned their duties, they performed them, albeit reluctantly. Africans were regarded as seasoned within three or four years and viewed by mainland planters as much more desirable than blacks imported directly from the African continent (Franklin and Moss 1994, pp. 43–49). The majority of Africans transported to North America during the seventeenth century, then, was from the West Indies, not Africa.

After the arrival of the first settlement in 1619, the African population in North America grew slowly (Wax 1973, p. 371). During the seventeenth and eighteenth centuries, North American colonies participating in the institution of slavery on a large scale were Virginia, South Carolina, and Georgia. Slavery was never really successful in the Middle colonies. The African population in New England also grew slowly. Despite some restrictions, Africans seemed to have been free to associate with each other and with peaceful Indians in northern areas. The houses of some free blacks became the rendezvous for recreational activities (Franklin and Moss 1994, pp. 65–67).

The social context of the African population in Virginia serves as a model for what occurred in other colonies in the South. Blacks constituted a small part of the population in Virginia, only about 3 percent of the people in 1650 and 15 percent in 1690. Most lived on small plantations of fewer than eleven blacks. Almost all slaves were immigrants, and most were from the West Indies. As blacks and whites worked together, blacks began to challenge white authority, and many whites treated blacks as they did white servants. Some blacks became and remained free. However, the social conditions for many blacks began to deteriorate during the 1660s when stringent racial laws were passed, though full-blown slave codes were not enacted until 1750 (Kulikoff 1986, pp. 319, 320). Because their numbers were small and different African groups were forced to interact with each other as a collective rather than as members of distinct communities, the situation in Virginia suggests that a multi-layered culture existed which had an interesting impact on music-making.

The Afro-Caribbean element in black music in North America to 1700

The major issues of the seventeenth century were the degree and manner in which Africans adopted elements from different European cultures while maintaining elements from their various homelands; and the extent that elements from the West Indies were reinterpreted in North America.[2] Because the number of Africans was small and they had close contact with whites, the adoption of elements from European cultures was substantial during the seventeenth century. Not only did slaves, particularly those in the New England colonies, sing psalms with whites in meeting houses, but

---

2. Focus will be placed on the activities of the English. While the English were not the first Europeans to transport slaves to North America, they were dominant in the development of the slave trade in North America.

Africans often performed for European dances. As early as the 1630s, some white northerners made efforts to introduce Christianity to blacks. Also, a few southern slave-owners allowed Africans to attend church with them, and some even invited ministers to the plantations to preach to slaves. Because many southern whites were not wholeheartedly following the Christian faith themselves and believed that conversion to Christianity meant the manumission of slaves, the number of southern slaves who became Christians and performed European religious music was minimal in comparison to what occurred in the North (Southern 1983a, pp. 37–38).

European holidays were important occasions for music-making for blacks and whites in the seventeenth century. In addition to celebrating with Europeans, blacks participated in their own events. Interestingly, elements from European and different African cultures were combined at such occasions. For example, on the King's Birthday, and at Christmas and Easter, Africans performed on drums, viols, fiddles, and the banjo (Southern 1983a, pp. 42–43).

It is doubtful that the performance of African music was totally abandoned. While extensive documentation exists on the degree and manner in which West Indian slaves maintained Africanisms, there is little evidence for North America; but because the slaves transported to North America were from the West Indies, scholars believe that similar practices took place in both areas (Epstein 1977, p. xvi). Many reports that contain information about music and the maintenance of Africanisms were written by European travelers who were on visits or briefly settled in the Americas. Morgan Godwyn, an English clergyman based in York County, Virginia, in 1665 describes dancing among slaves; Richard Ligon, resident in Barbados from the late 1640s through the early 1650s, discusses in some detail drum music, dancing, singing at funeral rites, and the construction of a xylophone; Sir Hans Sloane, a physician who accompanied the Duke of Albemarle to Jamaica in September, 1687, gives a detailed description of musical instruments used by Africans, including plucked lutes (antecedents to the banjo), drums, trumpets, the xylophone, rattles, and other idiophones (Epstein 1977, pp. 25–30).

Most scholars of African American music use the fiddle to show evidence of European influence and acculturation; basing their interpretations on comments by Europeans, scholars also marvel that Africans were able to learn how to perform the fiddle so quickly (Epstein 1977, p. 80). However, the use of the instrument among slaves actually reflects resilience and assimilation. Blacks did not merely adopt the fiddle because it was preferred by whites: rather, the popularity of the fiddle among white Americans allowed Africans the opportunity to maintain a tradition that was an important part of their culture prior to contact with Europeans. Evidence shows that prior to the arrival of Europeans, Senegambians who used the plucked lute also performed the fiddle. John Storm Roberts states: ". . . the enthusiasm with which New World blacks took to the fiddle, not only in Brazil but in the United States and Cuba as well, is surely related to the occurrence of fiddle-type instruments in parts of Africa" (Roberts 1972, p. 73). In addition, the manner in which the fiddle is combined in ensembles with percussive instruments also reflects an African aesthetic. Therefore, playing the fiddle in the Americas was more of a reinforcement of Africanisms which led to transformation and the development of new stylistic trends.

The African presence in North America in the eighteenth century

During the eighteenth and early nineteenth centuries, the percentage and origin of exports from Africa changed slightly. Roughly 59 percent of the Atlantic slave trade came from West Africa (including the Western Sudan) over the whole period 1701–1810, as against 41 percent from the Bantu-speaking portion of the continent. Also, the growth of trade proceeded quite differently in West and Central Africa. During the early part of the eighteenth century, West African exports increased. In the mid-century, exports from West and Central Africa reached a plateau of relative stability. The last burst of eighteenth-century slave trade came almost entirely from Central and Southeast Africa, which more than doubled its exports between the 1770s and 1780s (Curtin 1969, pp. 221–222).

While much of the literature suggests that a high premium was placed on slaves from the West Indies, this was not the case *throughout* the slave era in North America. By the early 1700s, imports directly from Africa became more common in southern colonies; slave-owners believed that Africans shipped from the West Indies and adjoining mainland colonies were either belligerent and unruly, behavior patterns that could be manifested in criminal activities, or were old, weak, and suffered from physical handicaps, which reduced the value of their labor (Wax 1973, pp. 374, 389).

As North American colonists became more directly involved in sending vessels to Africa and selling their cargoes in the plantation and island colonies, they became more cognizant of the differences in various African groups. It was at this point that slave buyers started to make requests for specific ethnic groups (Creel 1988, pp. 31–33; Curtin 1969, pp. 155–162; Wax 1973, pp. 389–393). South Carolina preferred above all to import Senegambians which meant principally Bambara and Mandinka from the interior of Sudanic Africa. As second choice, they took groups from the Gold Coast, but had a marked dislike for those from the Bight of Biafra. However, about 40 percent of all Africans imported into South Carolina in the eighteenth century originated from Angola. Although Virginia showed some preference for Senegambia and its hinterland, the aversion to Ibo and others from the Bight of Biafra is missing. Because the South Carolina slave market supplied many of the Africans for neighboring colonies, a bias toward Senegambia and Sierra Leone can be seen in Georgia, North Carolina, and Florida. Yet despite preferences, blacks taken to mainland colonies represented all sections of the West and Central African coasts (R. Hall 1990, pp. 99–102; Wax 1973, pp. 390, 396–399). Most slaves in the North were imported through the ports of Virginia and Maryland; thus, residents never developed a very acute sense of the differences between ethnic groups (Curtin 1969, pp. 155–158).

Again, the growth, ethnicity, and life of slaves in the Virginia-Maryland area are noteworthy. From 1700 to 1740, slave traders transported 54,000 blacks into this region, about 49,000 directly from Africa. About half the Africans who arrived in Virginia during the first half of the eighteenth century were from the Bight of Biafra (Ibos, Ibibios, Efkins, and Mokos), and another fifth were from Angola. As soon as Africans landed, many attempted to run away. Whenever they tried to establish an autonomous social life off the plantation, whites forced them to remain on plantations. Most new Africans spoke similar languages, had lived under the same climate, cultivated similar crops, and shared comparable kinship systems. When they arrived, many may have combined common threads in their cultures into new African American structures (Kulikoff 1986, pp. 320–322; 328–332). Occasionally conflicts arose between newly imported Africans and black natives primarily "because of differences in their respective experiences. Natives had not been herded into ships and sold into bondage. They were probably healthier than forced immigrants. Many of them were baptized Christians, and some became believers. To Africans, by contrast, Christianity was an alien creed, and they sometimes tried to maintain their own Islamic or African religions in opposition to it" (Kulikoff 1986, pp. 330–333).

Slavery in Louisiana was different from that in English colonies in several ways. Africans did not arrive in Louisiana until 1719, a century after the settlement of blacks in Virginia. Louisiana stopped importing slaves in the late 1700s, whereas other parts of North America continued into the late 1830s (Curtin 1969, p. 79). Also, Louisiana under French rule was not a prosperous slave plantation society that produced valuable exports. The French were more interested in the fur trade and military alliances with Indians rather than in taking over their land as was the case with the English. Although some groups from the Bight of Benin and Central Africa were imported, the majority of Louisiana imports in the early eighteenth century were Wolof and Bambara. This concentration of Africans, many of them from the same ethnic group, on relatively few estates facilitated the preservation and adaptation of African cultural patterns. In 1746, Louisiana's white population was estimated to be 3,200 and the black population 4,730 (G. Hall 1992, pp. 9, 10, 35, 40–43, 162).

By the time Spain took over in the 1760s, Louisiana was thoroughly Africanized. Also the colony prospered because Spain loosened trade restrictions to encourage population growth and economic development. Africans imported into Spanish Louisiana came primarily from Senegambia, the Bight of Benin, the Bight of Biafra, and Central Africa. Both Acadians (from Canada) and Canary Islanders arrived in the 1770s, while refugees from the Haitian Revolution of 1791 came in the late eighteenth century. Thus, the greatest strength of many white settlers of Louisiana was their openness and tolerance of peoples of other races and culture because whites needed them for survival. Intermarriages between Africans, Europeans, and Indians were common (G. Hall 1992, pp. 9, 14, 166–168).

In summary, the eighteenth century was the period when the largest and most diverse group of Africans entered North American colonies. Also, various groups dominated colonies at different points in history. Whereas traditions from one culture may have been prominent in early periods, features from another society may have become more dominant later as other Africans were imported into the area. But, in some ways, the complex formation of African American culture involved the concept of "hearth areas"; those who arrived earlier may have had as strong an impact as latecomers of more numerical strength (Creel 1988, p. 44).

The Africanization of music in North America during the eighteenth century

During the eighteenth century, African dancing, songs, festivals, instruments, rituals, and other musical activities were widely performed throughout the colonies. Instead of the disappearance of Africanisms, traditions associated with Africa were even more evident because the large number of Africans in North America resulted in a greater sense of self and community. While a lot of borrowing and sharing of ideas took place in an effort to bond together as a collective for survival, there were also tensions as different groups attempted to hold on to traditions from their home-land; some Africans began to create new forms of expressions. Not only did Africans comment on their own conditions through diaries and other writings, but colonialists and visitors often wrote about the music activities of slaves (Southern and Wright 1990).

Beginning in the late seventeenth and early eighteenth centuries, slave-owners had become much more active in trying to prohibit African musical practices because they feared rebellions. As early as 1695, Maryland passed laws restricting the gathering of slaves. After the 1739 Stono Rebellion in South Carolina, in which music and dancing had played an important part, slave-owners more strictly enforced the edicts regarding the performance of drums, horns, and other loud instruments. But, as Epstein (1977, pp. 52–59) explains, "Drums continued to be played, some secretly, some in the open" even into the nineteenth century.

Although the *kalinda*, a dance derived from Africa, had been documented as early as the mid-seventeenth century in the West Indies, reports of the dance in Louisiana do not occur until the mid-eighteenth and nine-teenth centuries (Epstein 1977, pp. 30, 33). Le Page du Pratz (1758) writes, "Nothing is more to be dreaded than to see the Negroes assemble together on Sundays, since under pretence of Calinda [*sic*], or the dance, they some-times get together to the number of three or four hundred, and make a kind of Sabbath, which it is always prudent to avoid; for it is in those tumultu-ous meetings that they . . . plot their rebellions" (quoted in Epstein, 1977, p. 32). The fact that this eighteenth-century writer suggests that the per-formance of *kalinda* had a double meaning is significant, for in many African contexts, individuals and social groups show their reactions to attitudes of hostility or cooperation and friendship held by others toward them through the choice of appropriate dance vocabulary or symbolic ges-tures (Nketia 1974, pp. 207–208).

Music-making was an integral aspect of the daily lives of enslaved Africans because it was used as a mechanism for survival. In addition to dancing, singing African war songs and participating in African funeral ceremonies were commonplace in some areas; social comment and work songs were also performed. Not only did slaves sing to assist physical labor and help to arouse and keep up their energy, but slave-owners required blacks to perform; whites believed that slaves were more productive when they sang. When work was not involved, some slave-owners still encouraged their slaves to sing and dance in an effort to raise their spirits (Epstein 1977, pp. 41, 64, 68–79). Indeed Courlander believes that in its choice of subject matter, its responsive form, its improvisation, its direct relation to work being done, and in the ties between sound and action, the work song bears a striking affinity to its counterpart in the African tradition. The literature contains many references to music associated with slave occupations, ranging from field labor to domestic chores such as flailing rice, grinding hominy, spinning, and making baskets (Courlander 1963, p. 90).

Because northern slave-owners did not feel threatened by the presence of Africans, there is more evidence of slaves participating in festivals in the North. 'Lection Day and Pinkster Day were two celebrations reminiscent of African and West Indian festivities. 'Lection Day, when blacks elected their own rulers in elaborate ceremonies, originated in Connecticut during the mid-eighteenth century and lasted in some New England towns to the mid-nineteenth century. The celebration normally began with an election parade: African leaders, mounted on horseback or marching on foot, would dress in their finest apparel and process with colors flying to the music of fifes, fiddles, clarionets, and drums. After the election ceremonies, there would be games, wrestling, jumping, singing, and dancing to the music of fiddles (Epstein 1977, p. 66; Southern 1983a, pp. 53–54). Reports from Newport, Rhode Island, in 1756, state: "Every voice in its highest key, in all the various languages of Africa, mixed with broken and ludicrous English, filled the air, accompanied with the music of fiddle, tambourine, banjo and drum . . ." (quoted in Southern 1983a, p. 54). Documentation of Pinkster Day celebrations in New York also dates back to the mid-eighteenth century. Interestingly, elements from several African areas are apparent in the description of this event: the king is believed to have been brought from Angola as a child; there is mention of the banjo, as well as drum types from West and Central Africa (Epstein 1977, p. 67; Southern 1983a, pp. 55–56).

As is also noted in chapter 4, greater efforts to introduce Christianity to Africans occurred during the eighteenth century. In northern colonies, the Society for the Propagation of the Gospel in Foreign Parts, the Associates of Doctor Bray, and the Moravians were all involved in religious instruction and the establishment of schools where blacks were taught academics as well as how to sing psalms and hymns correctly. A religious movement called the Great Awakening became widespread throughout the colonies during the 1730s. However, the movement was not successful in winning large numbers of African converts: language difficulties were a major obstacle and the slaves' preference for their own gods was another (Epstein 1977, p. 101). Also, many southern slave-owners were reluctant to allow Africans to convert; not only would there be no justification for enslaving them, but whites thought blacks were incapable of being converted and were wary of them congregating in large numbers (Lovell 1972, pp. 147–154; Southern 1983a, pp. 38–40). The few blacks who did convert during the eighteenth century found it necessary to establish independent religious groups so they could not only worship in their own way, but also avoid conflicts with whites (Raboteau 1978, pp. 212–219). In his 1785 narrative, John Marrant, an ex-slave author born in New York, states that on a visit to South Carolina he observed that slaves held secret prayer meetings in the woods after midnight to avoid persecution from slave-holders (Southern and Wright 1990, p. 7).

Several Baptist groups in Georgia were organized during the late eighteenth century. George Leile, the slave of a Baptist deacon, preached to slaves in Georgia and South Carolina before he left for Jamaica in the 1780s. The first permanent congregation was the First African Baptist Church in Savannah, Georgia, founded in 1788 by Andrew Bryan. Blacks who worshipped with Methodists left white churches because of discrimination. As early as 1787, blacks in Baltimore organized as an autonomous group, separate from whites. But the group that had the most dramatic impact on black religion was the Free African Society and one of its leaders, Richard Allen (1760–1831), who established the African Methodist Episcopal (AME) Church in 1794 and later became its first bishop.

While little is documented about the type of music used by Christian groups during these early years, reports indicate that the worship was African in character. John Leland, in discussing religious services of slaves in Virginia during the late eighteenth century, notes that they are "more noisy in time of preaching . . . more subject to bodily exercise . . . than are whites" (quoted in Southern and Wright 1990, p. 6). In his travel diary of a journey in 1793 through Massachusetts, Connecticut, Pennsylvania, and Virginia, Hezekiah Prince describes black services as "wild, and at times almost raving . . ." (quoted in Southern and Wright 1990, p. 7).

In eighteenth-century literature, traditions from a variety of African groups are apparent, but evidence of influence from Central Africa is prominent. Many of the instruments, music compositions, and place names use the term "Congo" – e.g. Congo drum, Congo jig, and Congo Square/Place Congo (Epstein 1977, pp. 39, 67, 94, 124; Congo Square is discussed below). It is not known if "Congo" was used in a generic sense to Africa as a continent or whether it specified peoples from Central Africa. But slaves from Angola were identified as the leaders of the Stono Rebellion; during Pinkster festivities in New York, the king was referred to as someone from Angola; and the terms *bamboula, kalinda, juba*, marimba, and mbanza (string instrument) as well as other words are believed to be of Bantu origin (Southern 1983a, pp. 55–56, 58; Vass 1979).

Not only did the different African groups maintain their own individual musical practices, they also created a common musical tradition that was a fusion of elements from various parts of Europe and Africa. Although blacks selectively borrowed European elements, the music they created was not always understood or respected by whites because it had been fused with African features. For example, when blacks performed hymns, whites believed the music was a corruption of European melodies when in essence blacks had created their own song forms. Through the process of Africanization, the music was no longer African or European. It is difficult to document with any accuracy how and when a new common style of music – one that can be referred to as African American – came into being. In most cases, African music coexisted with syncretic/Creole music (Epstein 1977, pp. 77–87). Evidence of syncretisms can be found in the late eighteenth century, but syncretic music also probably existed in the seventeenth century.

America, 1800–1900

Black movement toward independence in the nineteenth century

Migration westward greatly influenced the institution of slavery during the nineteenth century. By 1830, there were more than two million slaves in the United States. The South Atlantic states, from Delaware to Florida, were ahead in numbers, with 1,300,000. But as more whites moved into the cotton kingdom of the Gulf and south central states, the geographical distribution of blacks changed, causing domestic trade to become a major economic activity. Some slaves in the upper south were shipped to the Gulf states via the Atlantic Ocean, while others were sent over land. To maintain a substantial supply, slave breeding and hiring were common; also families were often separated from each other. While many blacks were taken involuntarily into the south central states where slavery was deeply entrenched, a number of African Americans voluntarily moved into the north central states and western territories, where presumably slavery would not exist. By 1830, there were more than 16,000 blacks in Ohio, Indiana, Illinois, and Michigan (Franklin and Moss 1994, pp. 112–119). When California was admitted into the union in 1850, the United States census listed the black population at 962. Whereas about twelve lived in Los Angeles, approximately 464 of San Francisco's total population were African American (Mason and Anderson 1969; Bunch 1988, p. 11).

In 1850, the slave population of the United States had grown to 3,953,760 of whom 400,000 lived in towns and cities. A small number in urban areas were involved in non-agricultural pursuits, which left approximately 2.8 million to do the work on the farms and plantations. The large plantation always had at least two distinct groups of workers, the house servants and the field hands. The two times at which slaves could look forward to recreation and relaxation were the summer lay-by and Christmas. Also, weddings, anniversaries, and the like, whether for whites or blacks, were other opportunities for merrymaking. Some planters even gave dances for their slaves. In spite of these activities, the desire for personal freedom as well as intellectual, and economic self-sufficiency were urgent. While some blacks were philosophical about their situation and escaped through ritual and song, others engaged in elaborate programs of sabotage, ran away, or conspired to revolt (Franklin and Moss 1994, pp. 127, 134, 144–145). The movement toward independence can be seen in their efforts to create separate social and religious institutions and to elevate themselves intellectually before and after the Civil War.

At the beginning of the 1800s and even earlier in Louisiana, free blacks grew in number and influence as slavery ended in northern states and was excluded from western territories. Harriet Beecher Stowe's *Uncle Tom's Cabin* (1852) raised the question about the morality of slavery. Not only did a number of slave-owners, struck with guilt, begin to free their slaves, but enterprising slaves amassed enough capital to purchase their freedom and that of their loved ones. Because greater opportunity for economic advancement could be found in cities, free blacks tended to be urban where their pleasure came from visiting, singing, or attending meetings and organizations to which they belonged. Many enjoyed dances given by various societies and benevolent organizations. Also, religious services offered opportunities for social intercourse as well as spiritual uplift. As the opportunities to secure an education widened, some attended black institutions of higher learning, and a few were admitted to predominantly white colleges and universities (Franklin and Moss 1994, pp. 148–164, 193).

The Americanization of African music in the nineteenth century

While the desire for freedom and movement toward independence had always been close to the hearts and minds of Africans in the Americas, the way in which it was manifested in the expressive arts during the nineteenth century was similar to, but also different from, what had occurred in earlier years. On the one hand, Africanisms continued to be strongly pervasive: the songs, dances, and instruments used in performances hearkened back to seventeenth- and eighteenth-century practices. On the other hand, uniquely African American expressive forms were created and developed within all aspects of life. As slaves borrowed from whites and drew on the values and beliefs their ancestors had brought from various parts of Africa, they created musical traditions not only significantly different from those of European Americans but also distinct from those of ethnic groups in Africa. Also, assimilation was apparent in that the influence of European culture was so dominant that elements from Africa appeared to be nonexistent. Therefore, by the mid-nineteenth century, the Americanization of African music was well under way (Levine 1978, p. 135). While certain traditions can only be documented from the memories of ex-slaves,[3] some writers actually reported on what they experienced and observed.

The music and dance of some blacks in the nineteenth century displayed a distinctly African character. John Canoe (or Conny, Kuner, Connu), a festival believed to have been brought from Jamaica or perhaps Africa, was celebrated before the Civil War at Christmastime in sections of North Carolina and Virginia. The costumes, instruments, and organization of the festival were similar to those held in West and Central Africa. African music and dancing in New Orleans's Place Congo on Sundays, a tradition that began in the late eighteenth century, continued through the early nineteenth century (Epstein 1977, pp. 131–136; Estes 1990; Southern 1983a, pp. 136–138). At Place Congo, various groups would assemble in

---

3. Ex-slaves' narratives collected by the Works Progress Administration include information about instruments, dances, types of songs, song texts and titles, contexts, attitudes and behavior of blacks and whites, as well as other comments about music-making (see Rawick 1977–1979; Southern and Wright 1990, pp. 208–226).

sections, dance, and sing songs to the accompaniment of their own musical instruments. The most detailed account comes from the diary and sketches (1818–1820) of Benjamin Henry Latrobe, who not only provides information about the size of the crowd, the dimension of the individual rings of performers, and the placement of musicians in the center of each circle, but also discusses the music, the instruments used, and the performance role of women and men. James R. Creecy's description, based on observations from a visit to New Orleans which began in October 1834, also gives details about what took place at Congo Square:

> Groups of fifties and hundreds may be seen in different sections of the square, with banjos, tom-toms, violins, jaw-bones, triangles, and various other instruments from which harsh or dulcet sounds may be extracted; and a variety, indeed, of queer, grotesque, fantastic, strange, and merry dancers are to be seen . . . most fancifully dressed, with fringes, ribbons, little bells, and shells and balls, jingling and flirting about the performers legs and arms, who sing a second or counter to the music most sweetly; for all Africans have melody in their souls; and in all their movements . . . the most perfect time is kept, making the beats with the feet, heads, or hands, or all, as correctly as a well-regulated metronome!
>
> (Quoted in Epstein 1977, p. 134)

Work and recreational activities on plantations included elements that suggested the maintenance of Africanisms; but musicians also created music that was a blending of cultures. When groups of slaves were transported to markets and other plantations, they were often organized into coffles and expected to sing and play musical instruments as they moved from one destination to the other. Interestingly, fiddlers were often used to lead slave coffles (Epstein 1977, pp. 148–149). Farm or plantation work gave rise to harvesting, corn-shucking, and fireside game songs. The corn shucking was a time of song and gaiety because slaves from surrounding communities were invited to participate. Interestingly, both blacks and whites considered corn-shucking songs to be music of the devil because of slaves' behavior and activities that took place at these events. On another level, the corn shucking event meant something different to black participants and white observers. To white onlookers, the event was entertainment verging on the spectacular; to slaves, it was an opportunity to celebrate together – a time of mutual participation in working, eating, and dancing. Because the social conditions of African Americans did not drastically change after slavery officially ended, many continued in the pre-Emancipation occupations. Thus, the context for the performance of work songs from the late 1860s through 1900 was similar to that of former years (Epstein 1977, pp. 161–162; Southern and Wright 1990, pp. 70–71).

There are few pre-Civil War sources that include references to the cry, call, whoop or field holler, even though some investigators believe this music evolved during slavery (Ramsey 1960). Epstein (1977, p. 182) believes that "perhaps the people who heard them then did not know how to describe them, or possibly they did not consider them worth mentioning." However, Hinson (1978) suggests that field hollers "developed primarily after the Civil War, when black farmers were able to work alone on land they owned or sharecropped rather than in the work crews of the plantations." One of the first descriptions of the call is found in writings of Frederick Law Olmstead, a journalist/landscape architect who traveled in the South between 1853 and 1854 and was awakened one evening around midnight by the sounds from a black loading gang (Olmstead 1976, pp. 140–141). In other early sources, descriptions refer to the sound that slaves made while working in the fields on plantations and farms or those who worked with animals (Southern and Wright 1990, pp. 49, 134). Cries and hollers were important because they provided a counterpart to work songs, but ranged beyond a direct concern with labor to a concern with the most personal expressions of life's travail. As such, they created a piercing history of the impact of hardship and sorrow on black people (Genovese 1974, p. 324).

Like the field holler, blues was a highly personalized music. While early examples of the blues existed in the last half of the nineteenth century and possibly before Emancipation, it was not until the twentieth century that it became one of the dominant forms of African American music. The blues is an excellent example of the Americanization of African music because it reflects a major degree of acculturation to the individualized ethos of the larger society – an ethos that was alien to Africans who were transported to North America and which remained one of the chief sources of difference between black and white Americans throughout the nineteenth century (Levine 1978, p. 221; see further discussion of blues in chapters 11 and 14 of the present volume).

Dance music continued to be an important genre in African American culture during the nineteenth century, and blacks provided much of the music for dancing because whites looked upon it as a demeaning occupation (Jerde 1990, p. 19). In many instances, the music and dance tended to be different at black and white events. "The slaves were proud of their dancing prowess and considered the 'measured, listless and snail-like steps' of white society cotillions inferior to their own lively reels and jigs. All contemporary accounts of slave dancing emphasize its vigor and vitality" (Southern 1983a, p. 178). Thus, knowing several musical traditions was critical for African American musicians, for in addition to providing accompaniment for African dances, they performed music for European dances. It was not unusual in the nineteenth century for black and white musicians to play together; as a result, black jigs, breakdowns, reels, and rags became part of the white musical tradition while tunes from southern white music, many tracing back to the British Isles, entered the repertory of black songsters (Hinson 1978). After Emancipation, the African American dance tradition did not drastically change primarily because, as indicated above, the socio-cultural environment of many blacks remained the same. In rural areas, particularly regions where a sparse population of blacks closely interacted with whites, string band music continued to be a favorite among both groups, and frequently black musicians were the major performers.

In spite of organized attempts by various religious groups, slave conversion to Christianity was not complete by the early nineteenth century for many whites continued to be indifferent and opposed religious instruction to slaves. Some slave-holders tolerated and even encouraged the use of African traditions; contrarily some African traditions continued even though they were not encouraged. Vodou, a religion that was re-interpreted in Haiti from West and Central African religious practices before it was transported to the United States, was prominent among slaves in Louisiana and pockets of Georgia, Florida, and Missouri (Southern 1983a, pp. 138–139). Not only was the music and dance African in character, but the veneration of African deities was an important part of vodou. In addition to the resilience of African religious practices, there were numerous instances of the reinventing of religious traditions. Combining European and various African religious traditions, many blacks created a distinctive African American religious experience, one that offered a basis for collective identity and an avenue of psychic resistance to oppression. Because the use of music was central to the creation of an identity that was distinctly African, church leaders found it difficult to keep Africanisms from creeping into religious services.

Much of the religious activity developed concurrently in different parts of the country. As various black groups in the South and North established black congregations and independent black denominations, many African Americans continued to worship with whites on plantations and in city churches. At the same time, religious revival movements were attended by both blacks and whites. All this activity gave rise to a complex of religious musical forms (hymn, camp meeting song, spiritual, and shout), wherein blacks in different ways fused elements from European and African cultures.

The movement toward independence and the assertion of an African identity in religion can be seen in the efforts of Richard Allen. Not only did Africans continue to perform hymns written by Europeans; African American ministers compiled hymnbooks specifically for the black community that included original creations by blacks and borrowings from white hymnists. In 1801, Allen published the first hymnal for a black congregation. *A Collection of Spiritual Songs and Hymns, Selected from Various Authors by Richard Allen, African Minister* was printed by John Ormrod and contained fifty-four classic and folk hymn texts without tunes. Later in 1801, a second edition of the hymnbook was printed by T. L. Plowman. This contained sixty-four hymn texts, some incorporating modifications of the texts of the original edition. The importance of Allen's publications arises from the fact that he published his own hymnal instead of using the official Methodist hymnal. In addition to its position in music history as the first anthology of hymns collected for a black congregation, it was also the first to employ the so-called wandering refrains; it was the first to include songs of the oral tradition; and it is a document that reflects the musical taste of early nineteenth-century black Protestants (Southern 1983a, pp. 75–79). Although the authors of hymns are not indicated, most were written by Europeans (Charles Wesley, Isaac Watts, John Newton), and one was by Allen himself. After the two editions were published in 1801, subsequent hymnbooks by the AME Church appeared in 1818, 1837, 1876, 1892, and 1898. The 1898 edition is important: not only was it the first to include music; it also contained several hymns written by black authors and composers. While other black churches periodically published hymnals (e.g. *Union African Hymn Book*, 1822, and *Hymns for the Use of the African Methodist Episcopal Zion Church in America*, 1838), the AME is the only church that regularly produced hymnbooks throughout the nineteenth century (Spencer 1990).

Called the Second Awakening, the revival movement dominated the religious life of the new frontier communities. Blacks and whites of different Protestant denominations held religious services in a forest or woods, worshipping in large tents and living in small tents. The historic first camp meeting was held in Logan County, Kentucky, in July 1800 and drew thousands of participants (Southern 1983a, p. 82). As more whites converted to Christianity during these revivals, "they were soon convinced that religion for the slaves was not only morally correct, but financially profitable as well" (Epstein 1977, p. 111). Yet few slave-holders approved of black preachers because of fear of their role as potential leaders of revolts and uprisings, although it was not uncommon for blacks to preach at inter-racial camp meeting services. By the 1820s, however, camp meetings under black leadership were common in northern cities, and attended by blacks and whites (Epstein 1977, pp. 194–195; Southern 1983a, p. 83).

Music-making was integral to camp meeting worship. Not only did blacks sing during the service, but they continued singing in their private quarters long after "the whites had retired to their tents for the night . . ." (Southern 1983a, p. 84). Many scholars believe the songs that blacks performed in these contexts gave rise to the African American spiritual. The comments of white Methodist minister John F. Watson provide vivid evidence of the use of Africanisms as well as the influence of black culture on white performance practice:

> . . . the coloured people get together, and sing for hours together, short scraps of disjointed affirmations, pledges, or prayers, lengthened out with long repetition *choruses*. These are all sung in the merry chorus-manner of the southern harvest field or husking-frolic method, of the slave blacks; and also very greatly like the Indian dances. With every word so sung, they have a sinking of one or other leg of the body alternately; producing an audible sound of the feet at every step, and as manifest as the steps of actual negro dancing in Virginia, &c. If some, in the meantime sit, they strike the sounds alternately on each thigh . . . the example has already visibly affected the religious manners of some whites.
>
> (Quoted in Southern 1983b, pp. 63–64)

Because most attendees were not able to read, hymnbooks were rarely used in worship. Instead, everyone sang from memory. "Song leaders added choruses and refrains to the official hymns so that the people could join in with singing. They introduced new songs with repetitive phrases and catchy tunes" (Southern 1983a, p. 85). These new camp meeting songs, called "spiritual songs" (later referred to as "folk" spirituals) as distinguished from hymns and psalms, were composed on the spot. The distinctive features of the songs "were the chorus and/or refrain, the popular tune or folksong-style melody, and the rough and irregular couplets that made up the texts which often referred to everyday experiences as well as scriptural concepts. The choruses were freely added to any of the standard hymns and eventually there developed a body of these 'wandering verses,' which became immensely popular with camp-meeting congregations" (Southern 1983a, pp. 85–86).

Not only did the slave maintain an African sensibility through religious worship; the Christian church became a locus to blend and perform traditions that included features from different African and European cultures. Blacks created expressive forms wherein they could worship their god in the way that they preferred. As Southern explains, "Nowhere in the history of the black experience in the United States was the clash of culture – the African versus the European – more obvious than in the differing attitudes taken toward ritual dancing and spirit possession" (Southern 1983a, p. 170). For example, there was strong disapproval of the holy dance or shout, probably because it was in the "same tradition as the eighteenth-century 'jubilees' and Pinkster dances, the Place Congo dancing in New Orleans, the circle dances at camp meetings, and the 'Methodist praying bands'" (Southern 1983a, p. 170). In spite of the protests from whites, the shout continued to be performed in different parts of the South primarily because it provided blacks an opportunity for collective cooperation and an expression of identity. The shout was an act of protest, a medium through which slaves "transformed into actual participants in historic actions: Joshua's army marching around the walls of Jericho, the children of Israel following Moses out of Egypt" (Levine 1978, p. 38; also see Allen, Garrison, and Ware 1983, pp. 156–157). Spirituals were important not only because they provided hope, faith, and a sense of community; they were sometimes used for revolt and escape (Levine 1978, p. 33).

After Emancipation, many of the religious traditions continued but were transformed. Similar to what occurred with work and dance songs, blacks used the same music in institutions of worship because their lifestyle had not drastically changed. The so-called "folk" spiritual continued to be performed as it had been during slavery. In urban areas, it became the foundation for the gospel song which evolved during the early twentieth century with composers like Charles Albert Tindley (1851–1933) and Thomas Dorsey (1899–1993). The lively foot-stomping music was improvisatory in character with lots of embellishments and physical involvement of its participants.

The "concert" spiritual also evolved from the "folk" spiritual, but the performance took on a different character. Arranged by mainly black composers trained in European art music, concert spirituals were performed in four-part harmony by mixed ensembles. Like other musical forms that had been created by African Americans, elements from African and European cultures were fused. Although the delivery called for a European vocal quality, call and response, off-beat phrasing, complex rhythms, and melodic variation could be heard in spiritual performances (see Southern 1983a and Lovell 1972 for further discussion). The Jubilee Singers of Fisk University were the first group to introduce and perform concert spiritu- als outside a religious context. Because of the Jubilee Singers' success in raising money for their school, other black colleges and professional groups organized similar vocal ensembles (Southern 1983a, p. 228).

The rise in urbanism and the size of the free black population resulted in greater opportunities for the professional black musician. While profes- sional musicians had existed in earlier years, their performances were limited to activity on slave plantations: many performed for whites and blacks or were hired out by their slave-owner. But the nineteenth century brought new contexts for music-making, as many blacks became free and made decisions about their lives as musicians. While some went into popular entertainment, others specialized in art music. Both traditions coexisted and some performers were active in both settings.

During the nineteenth century, minstrelsy – which is discussed primar- ily in chapter 7 – was the most popular form of theatrical entertainment in the United States. While the tradition was not created by blacks, African American culture served as the source material; but it had to be filtered through whites before it received recognition and acceptance in the wider world (Southern 1983a, pp. 89–93). Black involvement in minstrelsy began in the 1820s: at least two performers were influential during the early years, although neither blackened his face. In New Orleans, there was Signor Cornmeali (died 1842) or Mr. Cornmeal (his real name is unknown) who first attracted attention as a street vendor who sang minstrel songs. Cornmeali is believed to have influenced white minstrels George Nichols and Thomas Dartmouth Rice (1808–1860), furnishing songs and pro- viding ideas for acts. John "Picayune" Butler (died 1864), who played banjo on street corners of New Orleans as early as the 1820s, became famous along the Mississippi River for his banjo skills. His best-known song was *Picayune Butler is Going Away*. William Henry Lane (1825–1852), known as Master Juba, was the only black entertainer to tour with the early major minstrel groups. He began his career as a dancer in the Five Points district of New York City. Later he joined Charley White's Serenaders as a tambourine player and banjoist and toured with Richard Pell's Ethiopian

Serenaders in England. Because of his talents and accomplishments, not only was he an idol of the entertainment world, but he was a link between the white world and authentic black source materials (Southern 1983a, p. 95).

After the Civil War, several black troupes came into existence. The first permanent black minstrel troupe to be formed was the Georgia Minstrels, organized by white entrepreneur W. H. Lee in 1865, who used fifteen ex-slaves from Macon, Georgia. Later, the group was managed by Sam Hague, also white, who added more men, changed the group's name to Sam Hague's Slave Troupe of Georgia Minstrels and took the troupe to England where he settled. Charles "Barney" Hicks (1840–1902), in Indianapolis, Indiana, was the first black to organize a minstrel troupe and managed other groups. Although members of the group did not come from Georgia, his troupe was also called the Georgia Minstrels, probably because Hicks had heard of the success of Hague's Georgia Minstrels and decided the name might bring good luck to his group; or perhaps he remembered the popularity among blacks of an old folksong, *Sold Off to George*. Hicks's group became world renowned, touring in Germany and Great Britain. Lew Johnson (1840–1910) was regarded as the most successful black manager of the period; he organized his first group in 1869 in St. Louis, Missouri. Once Hicks and Johnson had entered the field a number of other blacks followed (Southern 1983a, pp. 229–230).

The theatrical world became a major source of income for black entertainers during the latter part of the nineteenth century (Southern 1983a, pp. 233–234). Although the field was large, only a few received acclaim. The biggest stars were James Bland and Sam Lucas. James Bland (1854–1911), who was known as "The World's Greatest Minstrel Man" and "The Idol of the Music Halls," attended high school in Washington, D.C., and enrolled at Howard University as a pre-law student. But his first love was entertainment. He taught himself to play banjo and began performing at private social entertainments. In 1875, he left home to become a professional minstrel and toured with a number of groups. Bland wrote hundreds of songs, some of which became themes for important events and celebrations in American life. His *Carry Me Back to Old Virginny* became the state song for Virginia. The inclusion of elements associated with African music were often used in his material and he usually portrayed blacks in a dignified way. The fact that he did not conform to the musical tastes of the times may have been the reason that his career went into decline later in the 1890s.

Samuel Lucas (born Samuel Milady; 1840–1916) was a self-taught musician. Not only was he successful in performing in minstrel troupes in his
early career, but he toured with plays and concert companies, vaudeville
companies, and musical comedies. Unlike Bland, Lucas easily adapted to
performances on both the popular and concert stage. While his early career
was spent in performing with minstrel shows, he later performed in
Broadway musicals written by Bob Cole and the Johnson Brothers (J.
Rosamond and James Weldon) in the early 1900s. He also starred in the
film version of *Uncle Tom's Cabin*. Because of his talents, he was known as
the "Grand Old Man of the Stage" and "Dean of the Theatrical World." In
addition, he toured with his own concert company and wrote his own
songs, many of which were published. Other noted minstrel performers
of the late nineteenth century include William "Billy" Kersands
(1842–1915), who made worldwide tours with his own troupes; Wallace
King (1840–1903), known for his singing talents; Horace Weston
(1825–1890), a noted banjoist; and Gussie Davis (1863–1899), one of the
few black songwriters of minstrel songs to succeed in Tin Pan Alley.

Most free, middle-class African Americans of the nineteenth century
lived in much the same way, regardless of their location. Almost every
parlor contained a piano; young ladies were expected to exhibit skill in
piano playing, singing and painting, as well as in the traditional literary
and culinary arts. Like their white fellow citizens, middle-class blacks
filled their houses with stuffed furniture and bric-a-brac and their cultural
life with musical soirées and parlor parties. The kind of music cultivated in
the homes of middle-class blacks was the trite and rather superficial music
favored by white society during the same time period (Southern 1983a,
pp. 100–101). Middle-class blacks often attended balls and dances organized by civic organizations. Dancing schools were available to those who
were able to afford their services, and many enjoyed the entertainment of
traveling minstrel performers and circus musicians (Bailey 1985, pp.
3–12).

Much of the musical and social activity in the black community during
this period centered around the church, which saw enormous growth
during the nineteenth century. Not only did churches provide schools
where children could acquire a basic education, singing lessons for amateurs were available and some churches even sponsored concerts and lectures on sacred music. By the mid-nineteenth century, Sacred Music
Concerts were less popular than Grand Concerts of secular music and
Musical Soirées (Southern 1983a, pp. 104–106). Music in the theatre also

became prominent. Philadelphia was the center for the concert world, while New York with the African Grove Theater took the lead for black theatre. Several types of dramatic entertainment were performed: tragedies, ballets, or operas, with songs and dances interspersed among these events.

As middle-class African Americans in the larger public world changed their status and position in society, those in music pursued careers in European art music. "The rise of the black prima donna in the years between 1820 and 1920 was one of the manifestations of the ever-changing profile of black society throughout the country" (Jordan 1988, p. 35). Among these prima donnas were Elizabeth Taylor Greenfield (1824–1876), born a slave in Natchez, Mississippi, but raised in Philadelphia by her adopted Quaker family. After her debut in 1851, singing before the Buffalo Musical Association, she was able to establish her reputation as an artist. She toured for several years in London and the United Sates before she organized and directed an opera troupe in Philadelphia. Many other black singers and instrumentalists achieved success during the period (High 1988, p. 117; Jordan 1988, p. 35).

One of the most celebrated musicians of the nineteenth century was Frank Johnson (1792–1844) who is considered to be one of the greatest bandleaders of all time. Southern (1983a, p. 107) states that he was a man of many firsts: "first to win wide acclaim in the nation and in England; first to publish sheet music (as early as 1818); first to develop a 'school' of black musicians; first to give formal band concerts; first to tour widely in the nation; first to appear in integrated concerts with white musicians; first (of blacks or whites) to take a musical ensemble abroad to perform in Europe and the first to introduce the promenade concert to the United States." Johnson's ensembles were noted for their unique instrumentation: his early military bands consisted of woodwinds, a French horn, a serpent, cymbals, bells, triangles, and drums. However, when he performed at dances, his band members substituted string instruments for winds, which made their sound change from that of a military band to a quadrille band. Most bands played for balls and assemblies, dancing schools and concerts, and were in residence at fashionable resorts during the summer. In addition to Johnson's groups, there were bands in other major urban areas, including New York, Boston, and New Orleans. Bands also flourished among blacks who migrated to the Gulf states and western territories (Bailey 1988, p. 177; Stoddard 1982, pp. 118–127).

Black composers were not as active as performers during the nineteenth century. Of the few from the Philadephia school, Frank Johnson was most prolific as a composer and arranger: "his output of more than 200 compositions included cotillions, ballads, patriotic songs, arrangements of operatic airs, and even minstrel songs" (Southern 1983a, p. 112). Representative composers in other cities include Henry F. Williams (1813–1903) of Boston; Joseph William Postlewaite (1837–1889) of St. Louis, Missouri; the Lambert family of New Orleans: the brothers Sydney (born 1838) and Charles-Lucien (born 1828 or 1829) were gifted pianist-composers who studied and published works in Paris. Sydney remained in Paris, while Charles-Lucien settled in Brazil. Lucien-Leon-Guillaume (born 1858), son of Charles-Lucien, wrote a greater variety of compositions than his father, including a ballet, symphonic poems, a piano concerto, a work for organ and orchestra, and a Requiem (Sullivan 1988, pp. 59–60). Instead of emphasizing African elements or themes in their works, most composers wrote music in the styles of the time and employed conventional forms (Sears 1988, pp. 135–136).

*

Historically, interculturalism has been an important aspect of African and African American music and culture. Prior to contact with Europeans, ethnic groups in Africa regularly interacted with each other through trade, migration, and warfare, which resulted in the borrowing and integration of new traditions into their own. Therefore, it was common for them to create syncretic musical forms and use similar instruments in variant ways. Upon arrival in the New World, Africans used different strategies to survive. While many maintained African practices, others selectively fused musical features from contrasting parts of Africa and Europe. Tensions sometimes arose between blacks and whites when the resilience of African elements conflicted with European performance practices. In spite of opposition, however, Africanisms prevailed as can be heard in various styles of African American sacred and secular music. The coexistence of distinct musical traditions and cultures allowed blacks to be flexible and creative because the aesthetics of music-making in different contexts and among various groups were not always identical. By no means was the music ever a monolithic entity. Through the constant negotiation of different ideologies, African Americans created a rich, diverse musical tradition that has served as the roots and foundation for all types of music in the United States.

6

Immigrant, folk, and regional musics
in the nineteenth century

―――

MICHAEL BROYLES

As the United States expanded in the nineteenth century its population increased dramatically. Much of that increase came from immigration, which was spurred by severe economic and political problems in parts of Europe. The overwhelming majority of immigrants to America still came from Europe in the nineteenth century, primarily from Germany, Ireland, and Great Britain. Only slightly fewer came from Scandinavia. On the West Coast there was considerable immigration from China. After 1880 Italian immigration began to rise, but the large waves of Italian, Russian, and Austro-Hungarian immigrants arrived only after 1900 (Thernstrom 1980, passim).

In this chapter I will discuss the kinds of music that the principal immigrant groups brought with them and the role immigrant musicians played in nineteenth-century American culture. I will not limit the discussion to new immigrants, however; I will also discuss the principal types of folk music that immigrants arriving before 1800 planted on American soil.

The subject matter presents immediate methodological problems, as much of the musical activity of immigrant groups was in the folk tradition. It was spontaneous and oral, leaving few documents. And though many of the traditions persisted into the twentieth century, they were not static. Thus to determine what nineteenth- as opposed to twentieth-century practice was can be elusive. In some areas documentation does exist. Collections of dances for the violin or flute almost certainly reflect folk practice, as do instrumental tutors, a particularly valuable source. Because of the tutors and many instrumental collections, we know more about nineteenth-century folk dance music than folksongs of several important ethnic groups. This is particularly true regarding the Anglo-Celtic tradition. It was, without question, alive and well in America in the nineteenth century, but most of our knowledge about it comes from either before or after this time. Collectors and other scholars have documented its continuing presence well into the twentieth century, as well as the age of its repertory, much of which predates the nineteenth century. Yet what happened in the middle is less clear.

Nineteenth-century folksong practice can be inferred to an extent from several indirect sources. Contemporary comments add detail about what was played or sung, in what circumstances, and in some cases how. Collections of broadside ballads and songsters from the nineteenth century exist. But only a very few contain music, and many do not even indicate the tune used. Most contain only text. Rural hymnody provides further clues about the Anglo-Celtic tradition. Hymns, in themselves an extremely important part of American musical culture in the nineteenth century, were transmitted via printed music, even in rural areas. They may be viewed two ways: as a musical type in itself, extremely important in much of the country; and as a broader record of folk practice. Hymnodists of all stripes throughout the nineteenth century saw music as a bridge to the people. Music with which the congregation could identify, music that had immediate emotional impact, was all-important. It is no surprise that such music would be close to the folk style, particularly in a rural community. That it was written down is of immense value to later scholars.

Although I will not focus on popular music *per se*, the lines between folk and commercial music were too blurred in the nineteenth century for the distinction to have much meaning. Singers such as Henry Russell (1812–1900) frequently sang folksongs in concerts, and commercial composers such as Stephen Foster (1826–1864) saw their pieces enter the folk repertory. The songs of Thomas Moore (1779–1852) were adaptations of folksongs. All are discussed in chapter 7. The distinction between folk and popular is even more nebulous in instrumental music, which in the vernacular meant by-and-large dance music. When an Irish fiddler for instance joined a minstrel show and continued to play the same jigs and reels that he had learned in the more informal setting of folk culture, where is the line to be drawn?

Music from the British Isles[1]

Although British immigration to America remained strong in the nineteenth century, more immigrants came from Ireland than any other country. Irish influence, however, went far beyond ethnic enclaves. The

---

1 Welsh immigration is discussed in the later section on "Other immigrant groups."

Irish impact on American vernacular music rivals that of the Germans in art music.

Irish immigration needs to be divided into two periods. Most Irish immigrants arriving before 1820 were Scotch Irish, or Ulster Scots, as they were usually called. Ulster Scots came from families who had immigrated to Northern Ireland from the Scottish lowlands as part of the British government attempt to impose order on Ireland, and they maintained many Anglo-Scottish traditions, including religion. Approximately two-thirds were Presbyterian. In the early Federal period many were skilled workers and artisans rather than unskilled laborers or rural workers, thus of a higher status than either those that came during the Colonial Era or those that followed. Many Scotch Irish settled in the southern Appalachian mountains and developed a musical culture that remained relatively isolated and consequently unchanged until well into the twentieth century.

Catholic Irish began to arrive in the United States in large numbers only in the 1830s. Irish immigration showed a five-fold increase in the 1830s over the previous decade, and peaked in the 1850s, with nearly 1 million immigrants. That number compares with 54,000 in the 1820s (Thernstrom 1980, p. 528) and approximately 75,000 in the twenty years following the end of the Revolutionary War in 1783. Irish immigration continued strong throughout the remainder of the nineteenth century, although as other immigrant groups swelled, it went down from 46 to 10 percent as a total percentage of arrivals.

Equally important to American music was the type of immigrant that arrived. Ireland had been the breadbasket of Europe during the Napoleonic Wars. The precipitous drop in the price of grain that followed the peace affected primarily the rural laboring class. The hardship caused by the potato failures of the 1830s and 1840s was likewise confined almost completely to rural workers. The nineteenth-century Irish immigration was overwhelmingly a rural, peasant event. This meant that the music that came was in European terms essentially peasant music.

In Ireland the harp was the instrument of the aristocratic tradition. But the collapse of the Gaelic aristocracy in the eighteenth century had wiped out the harp tradition. The fiddle, the flute, and the uilleann or union pipe, a bagpipe, were considered peasant instruments. With a few exceptions, Irish piping never caught on in America, possibly because the fiddle was cheaper and more easily transportable by an immigrant in dire poverty. The flute in America had its own associations. It was the instrumental choice of gentlemen, and the fife was the prime military instrument. The fiddle, however, was already popular throughout America as a dance instrument, and more than any other instrument it became associated with Irish music in nineteenth-century America (McCullough 1974, p. 179; O'Neill 1973, p. 359).

In Ireland the traditional musician held a position comparable to a lower-level tradesman in a rural community. He, and it almost always was he, was itinerant, in a society in which wealth and status were measured by land. Irish musicians in America were respected in the Irish community as upholders of Irish tradition, and found a market in the larger community as performers in ballrooms, music halls, and minstrel shows. Some became well-known, and some were sufficiently successful to become entrepreneurs. Patrick Fitzpatrick, a uilleann piper who was twenty-one when he arrived in New York, was able to build Celtic Hall in New York City eleven years later (McCullough 1974, pp. 180–182).

The traditional Irish musician was able to move into the commercial music world so easily because Irish music was already popular. It had been established in America well before the nineteenth century, not only through Irish immigrants, but also because it had been thoroughly absorbed into British culture by the early 1800s. The United States, at the time still a cultural colony of Great Britain, followed British practice. Most printed music available in the United States was either imported directly or pirated from England, and the theatre in particular was dominated by British managers and performers in the early nineteenth century. Irish ballads were regularly sung in Federal America, and Irish songs and dances appeared in many collections of instrumental and vocal music beginning in the eighteenth century. Irish characters and Irish farces were a staple of the theatre for decades before Harrigan and Hart's "Mulligan Guard" series, which began in 1871, and much of the dance music of the minstrel show had Irish origins (Nathan 1962, pp. 159–170). And even where the repertory of the theatre, music hall, and minstrel show was not Irish, much of it was close enough in style and content to allow Irish musicians a smooth transition into the American music world.

Irish song was extremely popular in early-nineteenth-century America. It began to appear in collections in Europe in the 1770s and 1780s, but Thomas Moore's *Irish Melodies* established the vogue of the Irish song. Originally published in Dublin and London in 1807, songs from the collection began to appear in the United States by 1811. Many of Moore's songs, such as *Tis the Last Rose of Summer* and *Believe Me, If All These Endearing Young*

Charms, remained in print throughout the nineteenth century, rivaling Stephen Foster's as cornerstones of American popular culture (Hamm 1979, pp. 43–46).

The origins of the music to Moore's and similar collections is not entirely clear. They are based on folksongs, but how old were the sources? Edward Bunting, who had assembled a collection of Irish songs in 1796, claimed that the melodies were ancient; Moore himself believed that they were modern, not older than the eighteenth century. They were probably mixed, some older than others, but they almost certainly represent an oral tradition, although it should be stressed that Moore often altered the melodies to suit his purpose. Thus his songs, extremely close to the folk tradition, are not folksongs in one sense (Hamm 1979, pp. 44–55). But in another sense they are; Moore only did in print what many folksingers do orally: modify the melody to suit his purpose or taste.

No type of folksong was more esteemed in the early nineteenth century than Scottish. Respect for Scottish song dates from late-eighteenth-century England, where its cause was taken up by many serious musicians. When Haydn visited London in the 1790s he was persuaded by publishers to arrange Scottish songs; Beethoven likewise did the same, although from a greater distance. In both England and America articles on national music extolled Scottish music as superior to all others.

In spite of such praise Scottish song did not have the lasting impact in America that Irish song did, although a handful, such as *Auld Lange Syne* or *Coming Through the Rye* entered the folk arena. Scottish immigration was not comparable to Irish, and the most popular collection of Scots songs, Robert Burns's *Scots Musical Museum*, was almost too ethnic to enjoy wide popularity. It was in the Scottish dialect, and the topics, more varied than Moore's which stressed nostalgia, often had to do with specifically Scottish events. Furthermore *Scots Musical Museum* was not marketed in either England or America to nearly the extent that Moore's *Irish Melodies* was.

Printed distribution of songs in nineteenth-century America took several forms: sheet music, songsters, and broadsides. Sheet music, consisting of a complete musical setting of the song, usually for voice and piano, was the most authoritative and the most respected. It was aimed at the musically literate, and belongs more to the history of popular music than folk music. It is discussed in chapter 7. Songs and ballads closer to the folk tradition were distributed more often by broadsides, single sheets of paper sold on the street. The broadside tradition goes back to sixteenth-century England and flourished in colonial America, with printers in the major cities turning them out by the thousands (Laws 1957, p. 45; see also chapter 3). Songsters or song books were collections of songs, ranging from bound volumes of two or three hundred pages, to unbound pamphlets of sixty to seventy pages. Judging from their popularity in the nineteenth century, they supplanted the broadside as the most common method of song distribution (Laws 1957, pp. 47–48).

Broadsides tended to celebrate news or sensational events, although the event could be local or personal. Songsters were often what their name implied, collections of songs, sometimes from the current theatre, such as *The Songster's New Pocket Companion* (Boston, 1821) sometimes with an ethnic or sentimental theme, such as *Tony Pastor's Irish Comic Songster*, *The Love and Sentimental Songster*, or *Songs of Old Ireland*, all published in New York in the 1860s.

Broadsides and songsters have one trait in common that separates them from sheet music: they practically never contain any music. Only occasionally is there an indication of the tune to be used. In such cases the tune is often a traditional one, illustrating further the thin line between folk and popular. When a currently popular song was reproduced there would of course be little need to designate the tune. The broadsides and songsters thus tell us little about the music of the time other than that traditional tunes from the British Isles were still current, and that they continued to serve as a musical vehicle for new song texts.

Isaiah Thomas (1749–1831), who assembled a collection of broadsides printed in Boston in the early nineteenth century, confirms that they were aimed at the working class or the people. He bound them up "to show what articles of this kind are in vogue with the Vulgar at this time, 1814" (Broyles 1992, p. 18). Few other contemporary collections of broadsides or songsters exist, although several libraries have gathered extensive holdings in the twentieth century. These include Harvard, Yale, and Brown University libraries, the New York and Providence Public Libraries, and recently the Center for Popular Music at Middle Tennessee State University (Laws 1957, p. 46). These recent collections, however, leave open many questions of provenance, as broadsides and to a lesser extent songsters were frequently published with no indication of place and date. Both types of material need further scholarly examination.

It is hard to overestimate the importance of Anglo-Celtic instrumental music in nineteenth-century America. It found its way throughout American culture via the fiddle, no other instrument being more important or more ubiquitous at this time. It was found in both urban and rural areas, in all geographic regions. The fiddle was sufficiently respected that several politicians campaigned with it. In 1878, for instance, "Fiddling Bob" Taylor of Tennessee, a decided underdog, won a seat in the Congress in large measure because of his fiddling. He was later elected Governor and then Senator (O'Neill 1973, p. 361). Even as late as 1994 the fiddle helped reelect Robert Byrd of West Virginia.

The fiddle was the favored instrument for dances. Dancing masters themselves often carried one. In rural areas a single fiddler frequently provided music for dances. In more urban areas dances would have a band, a term that in the nineteenth century meant practically any combination of two or more instrumentalists. Bands often consisted of two or three fiddlers and occasionally one or two other instruments, such as flute, clarinet, or banjo. The combinations depended more on who was available than aesthetic choice. The sound, however, favored the treble, with little emphasis on bass or depth of harmony. These impromptu groups are ancestors of the string bands that were later to have a significant impact on the development of country music.

Although Irish and Scottish fiddling traditions differ considerably in performance practice, there are many areas of overlap. Many of the same dances and the same tunes are found in both. Furthermore, immigration patterns blurred the distinction for many. Only later in the century when large numbers of immigrants began to arrive from Ireland did the Northern Irish, who had ties to Scotland, seek to distance themselves from the Catholic Irish. But since the instrumental music of the two groups was so similar, it is difficult to distinguish between them before 1830.

Social dancing had long been a favorite pastime in all geographic areas of America, even New England, and in all levels of society. Although many traditional dances continued, as was noted in chapter 3, dancing underwent something of a revolution at the end of the eighteenth century. The traditional Anglo-Celtic fiddle repertory dates mostly from that time, and by the early nineteenth century, some dances, such as the minuet, had lost favor. Country dancing had become sufficiently popular in England to be considered the British national dance, but most important, new dances began to arrive from central Europe.

The three most common dances in America at the beginning of the nineteenth century were the reel, the jig, and the hornpipe. Most of these developed in the eighteenth century, although some had older roots. Since British immigration was high at this time and America was at least culturally still a British province, importation of British dances is no surprise.

Defining traditional dances according to musical characteristics is at best an imprecise art. Meter, tempo, accent, flow, and phrase structure can be specified, but there are always many exceptions, and different writers have different meanings for the same term. Not infrequently the same dance tune will be identified as a completely different dance in different collections. *Hull's Victory* for instance, most commonly identified as a hornpipe, has also been labeled a reel and a contra dance. This does not even address the problem of tune families, in which similar tunes appear as different dances, possibly as variants on an original tune. The most famous example would be the basic tune variously known as the jig, *The Campbells are Coming*, *Miss McLeod's Reel*, and *The White Cockade*. The last of these titles has been identified at different times as a jig, a reel, a polka, a march, and a country dance. And how a piece is played can affect what it is. A strathspey for instance might have begun as a reel, to be transformed by the performance style. O'Neill recorded many hornpipes that had enough triplets to assume the qualities of a jig, though in some cases he may have been attempting a literal transcription of a performer's elaborations. Thus the following definitions are given only to describe what is most common or typical for the specific dance.

Almost all traditional dances are in a binary structure, AABB. The B section may be a variant of the A; most frequently it begins with different material before returning to material similar to the A section at least by the close. Jigs and reels are generally considered the older of the traditional dances, with strathspeys and hornpipes somewhat more recent. Some writers have suggested that this is apparent in their titles. Reels and to an extent jigs tend to have more elaborate titles, whereas hornpipes and strathspeys are often named for a person or a place. According to this line of reasoning, hornpipes and strathspeys have not yet had time to come loose from their origins (Stewart 1995). Beyond such general observations, which are by no means certain, little can be determined by most titles. The association of titles and tunes is at best loose. One tune can have many titles, and the same title can be used in different places for very different tunes. Samuel Bayard summarized this situation: "Any traditional player could give any tune he knew any title he wished, at any time" (Bayard 1982, p. 5).

Jigs are typically in fast compound meter. Most nineteenth-century collections notate jigs in 6/8, with two eight-measure strains, although there are many exceptions to both meter and phrase structure. There are several types of jigs – single jig, double jig, slip jig, hop jig, and sand jig –

and the meanings of the terms themselves are not always clear. A double jig differs from a single jig according to the rhythmic pattern used: in a single jig the ♩♪ pattern prevails, and in a double jig, the ♪♪♪ pattern (Stewart 1995). Breathnach adds that the double jig is so named because of the doubling of the basic "batter" dance step in each measure, to create a pattern in which the floor is struck three times per beat corresponding to the prevailing rhythm (Breathnach 1971, p. 46).

The terms slip jig and hop jig are used interchangeably; both refer to a dance in 9/8, the term coming from the dance step, which consists of "light hopping, tripping, and sliding actions" (Breathnach 1971, p. 47). The terms sand jig and plantation jig refer to tunes from a minstrel show, the former term derived from the practice of spreading sand on the floor to facilitate dancing (Stewart 1995).

Reels are in fast duple time, 2/4, 4/4, and 2/2 all being used in nineteenth-century collections. Regardless of meter, reels have relatively even accents in the measure, little variation in note values, and brief cadences that often fall on the second half of the measure. Together this creates the effect of relatively continuous running motion. Hornpipes are similar to reels but are generally a little slower and, more characteristic, have a more pronounced accent on the first and third beats as well as a stronger cadence. Hornpipes typically cadence with three quarter notes beginning on the bar line. Arpeggiated melodic ideas are also typical, particularly eighth-note motifs – for instance g^1–d^2–b^1–d^2 – that stress the downbeats.

The hornpipe was a favorite theatrical dance of the late eighteenth and early nineteenth centuries, but it was not the only type of traditional dance to be found in the theatre. Many minstrel show tunes were derived from jigs, reels, and hornpipes, all of which were common in minstrel shows, the fiddle being the backbone of the band (Nathan 1962, pp. 159–213). Beyond their use in minstrel shows, three of the best fiddle tunes still in the repertory illustrate the close connection between vernacular dance, fiddle-folk music and the theatre in the nineteenth century: *Durang's Hornpipe*, *Speed the Plough*, and *Arkansas Traveler*.

Durang's Hornpipe has the clearest connection with the theatre because we know specifically its origins. John Durang was an actor and dancer in America in the late eighteenth century. According to his autobiography, the hornpipe that bears his name was composed specifically for his use in the theatre by a Mr. Hoffmaster, "a German dwarf," in 1785. Durang gives the music in his autobiography, establishing presumably the original and authoritative version of the tune, and further comments on how quickly it spread, observing that "I have since heard it play'd the other side of the Blue Mountains as well as in the cities" (Downer 1966, p. 22). Durang's account of course leaves open that Hoffmaster himself may have drawn on an older tune.

The origin of *Arkansas Traveler* is itself a folk tale. It is attributed to Colonel Sandford C. Faulkner around 1840. According to the story Faulkner came across a mountain fiddler who repeatedly played the first half of the song. Requests for food, drink, lodging, and directions were summarily and humorously dismissed by the fiddler until Faulkner took the fiddle and played the second part of the tune, which the native did not know. The native then could not have been more generous toward Faulkner. The dialogue made its way into the theatre, and became a relatively common nineteenth-century routine. Its best-known appearance was in Edward Spencer's play *Kit, the Arkansas Traveler*, which appeared in several American cities in the 1870s and 1880s.

Speed the Plough was a play by the British playwright Thomas Morton. It appeared at Covent Garden in 1800 and was performed frequently on the American stage in the early nineteenth century. There is no direct testimony connecting the play with the music, but circumstantial evidence is compelling. Act II ends with a dance, in which the principal character, Sir Abel, after watching hesitatingly, "seizes a fiddle and plays 'till the curtain drops." Was it the tune *Speed the Plough*? According to *British Musical Biography* and repeated by O'Neill, the tune was composed in 1799 by John Moorehead, an Irish violinist at the Covent Garden Theatre between 1798 and 1804 (O'Neill 1973, p. 367).

Several new dances appeared in the nineteenth century, supplementing or in some cases replacing older ones. The first to arrive was the waltz, which was little known in American before 1800. It slowly gained a foothold in the first decade of the nineteenth century, to become the rage after about 1815. At the time considered a bacchanalian couples dance, the waltz was danced in rapid triple meter, with a continuous turning motion, as the couple orbited each other as they circled the room. It was the first modern ballroom dance, in which the couple remained in physical contact and did not interact with others as in the country dance or quadrille. Between 1815 and 1825 the waltz established itself as the most popular dance in America. Its unrivaled popularity lasted until the mid-1840s, when the polka arrived. By then the waltz was considered "antiquated" (Ferrero 1859, p. 72), and the polka, if anything, created a greater sensation than the waltz.

Whereas the waltz always had an Old World flavor, the polka was more in tune with nineteenth-century America, in spite of its central-European origins. A vigorous two-step dance, the polka, along with the galop, the schottisch, and march, form a large rhythmic cycle extending through the lifetime of John Philip Sousa (1854–1932) and leading into ragtime. Ferrero noted that the polka also represented an even greater freedom than the waltz had, "allowing the performers to turn in any direction which their fancies suggest." Ferrero also observed that its fast, lively character, appealed to those dancers who "favor the 'age of progress'" (Ferrero 1859, p. 148). For that reason it was favored over the schottisch, a similar duple meter dance that arrived at approximately the same time, but which was slower. The strathspey, a Scottish dance originally synonymous with the reel but gradually being differentiated from the reel as it became slower, had the same fate as the schottisch. Except among Scottish immigrants, the strathspey never became popular in America. The polka fit right in with the prevalent upbeat, militaristic rhythms of nineteenth-century America.

In spite of the new fads, however, neither the waltz nor the older dances went away. The waltz found a place in popular vocal music, and by the end of the century the waltz-song dominated the genre. As an old-fashioned but loved nostalgic dance with hints of an older European culture, the waltz evoked feelings easily transformed by the song writers of Union Square and Tin Pan Alley into the prevailing sentimentality of the day. The quadrille and country dance lost favor in the cities and among the fashionable but in rural areas they persisted, as did the fiddle. In some rural areas, such as Appalachia, tradition remained exceptionally strong, as early twentieth-century folklorists discovered. Cecil Sharp concluded that the *Running Set* he found in Kentucky was the earliest known form of the English country dance, predating even the first printed description by John Playford in 1651 (Sharp 1917).

Music from Germany

Germans immigrated to America prior to the nineteenth century largely for religious reasons, with most immigrants being Anabaptists fleeing intolerance or persecution. Like the Pilgrims, Anabaptist groups such as the Moravians in Pennsylvania tended to form relatively insular communities. Their musical activity was varied but usually quite high. In the nineteenth century economic problems following the Napoleonic Wars led to further German immigration and the greater disbursement of Germans throughout the country. Political unrest and repression, particularly after the revolts of 1848, further swelled the number of German immigrants, until in the second half of the century German immigration rivaled that of Ireland.

Because of the various reasons for immigration, Germans immigrants were a heterogeneous group. Germany itself was a patchwork of small states. Artisans, farmers, laborers, and highly educated professionals arrived. And trained musicians, particularly instrumentalists, immigrated from Germany in sufficient numbers to have a major impact on American music. This was mostly on art music, however, and is therefore discussed in chapter 8.

The distinction between art and folk music is particularly elusive in one of the most important musical traditions of the German communities, the singing society, or *Männerchor*. The *Männerchöre* were men's singing societies, although women were sometimes invited to participate so the mixed choral repertory could be sung. Women were virtually never given membership in the organizations, however. The repertory ranged from German folksongs to more extended works of art music composers. Most *Männerchöre* emphasized lighter, traditional music, often nostalgic songs, but in some cities, such as New York and Philadelphia, *Männerchöre* presented art music concerts that in quality and seriousness of repertory matched those offered by any other organization.

Two of the earliest and largest societies were the Philadelphia *Männerchor*, founded in 1835 and the Baltimore *Liederkranz*, founded in 1836 or 1837; *Der Deutsche Gesangverein* of Cincinnati was founded in 1838, followed by *Die Deutsche Liedertafel* in the same city in 1844 and the New York *Liederkranz* in 1847. By 1850 German singing societies existed in Boston, Charleston, Buffalo, Pittsburgh, Cleveland, Milwaukee, and Louisville. Others followed soon in St. Louis, Madison, Indiana, Columbus, Ohio, and Saginaw, Michigan. By the late nineteenth century virtually every German community of any size had at least one such society, and many large cities had several. The founding dates of *Männerchöre* correlate closely to German immigration which, high throughout the second half of the nineteenth century, was particularly strong in the 1850s and 1880s.

Singing societies had both a musical and a social function. Membership included actives, who actually participated in the music, and passives, who joined for the social aspects. The inclusion of passives was important as their dues helped support the organization. Most societies had several activities per year, and some distinguished between "Musical Evening Entertainments" and concerts, as the *Frohsinn* of New Orleans did. The concerts were more formal occasions, consisting mostly of art music, often with orchestra. The Musical Evening Entertainment or Family Evening consisted of lighter music and often included a musical farce. Such evenings frequently ended with a dance (Morrow 1989, pp. 7–9).

Individual societies quickly organized into larger confederations. In 1849 Fritz Volkmar, the founder of the *Liederkranz* of Cincinnati, invited all of the singing societies in the United States to a Sängerfest (singing festival) in Cincinnati. Only those organizations close by accepted, but the following year the *Männerchöre* of Philadelphia issued a similar invitation to those groups in the East. From those original festivals two organizations were formed, the Nordamerikanischer Sängerbund in the West and the Allgemeiner Deutscher Sängerbund von Nordamerika in the East. To indicate their priority the western group changed their name to the Erster Deutscher Sängerbund von Nordamerika, and the eastern one later changed to the Nordöstlicher Sängerbund von Nordamerika.

The festivals were primarily competitions between the different singing groups, interspersed with guest soloists and massed singing where all the choruses joined together. There were several classes of prizes, the most highly esteemed in the nineteenth century being the "Kaiserpreis," a silver statuette of a Minnesänger given by the German Emperor. The competition itself resembled those of the Meistersinger of the fifteenth and sixteenth centuries. Some of the larger competitions drew from 15,000 to 20,000 listeners (Faust 1909, pp. 274–275).

Besides providing a sense of community for German immigrants, the *Männerchöre* contributed much to the musical life of an area. This is particularly true in the Midwest, where many German immigrants settled. In smaller towns and cities other formal musical activities were practically nonexistent, and the concerts the *Männerchöre* presented were often the only organized music in a community. And as German immigrants integrated into the community the *Männerchöre* were frequently the seedbed of other musical organizations.

Even in eastern cities with other established musical organizations the *Männerchöre*'s contributions were historically important. The *Männerchöre* were usually led by professional musicians, some of whom, such as Leopold Damrosch, Frank Van der Stucken, and Hans Balatka had prominent careers in several areas of American music. Important premieres, such as the first American performance of Wagner's *Tannhäuser* came from a *Männerchor*, the Arion society of New York (Snyder 1991, pp. 7–8).

Many *Männerchöre* constructed their own Sängerfest Halls. In either the late nineteenth or early twentieth century elaborate halls were built in Cleveland, Baltimore and Philadelphia. The Philadelphia Hall, the latest of the above, built in 1912, was 265 by 408 feet and would hold over 19,000 persons. Many other less grand and less permanent structures were built. After the Sängerfest the halls would be available for a variety of uses by the community (Snyder 1991, pp. 202–212).

Other immigrant groups

Because of their sheer numbers and widespread geographical distribution, immigrants from Germany and from the larger constituent parts of the British Isles had the most widespread influence on American music. Other immigrant groups had a more regional impact, but within those regions played an important role. Welsh immigrants, who began to arrive in the 1830s and whose numbers increased considerably after the Civil War, established large settlements in central Pennsylvania and Ohio. The principal musical tradition they brought was the eisteddfod, a great gathering in which competitors vie for prizes. Established in the Middle Ages, these originally included music and literature, especially poetry. More recently in Wales they have involved music, prose, poetry, and arts and crafts.

Eisteddfods may have appeared as early as the 1830s in America although the first documented ones date from the 1850s. Most were small local events, held in churches or other community halls, as they were in Wales. Interest in the eisteddfod in the Welsh-American community was undoubtedly heightened by the first large national gathering at Llangollen in North Wales in 1858, which eventually led to the founding of the Welsh National Eisteddfod Association in 1880 (Hartmann 1967, p. 143).

In America eisteddfods were primarily musical events (Hartmann 1967, pp. 139, 146), the choral competitions, which usually featured art music compositions, being particularly important. In some ways these competitions were comparable to the German Sängerfest. The largest eisteddfod held in America in the nineteenth century occurred at the Chicago World's Columbian Exposition of 1893. Exposure at the Exposition made many Americans aware of the performance level within the Welsh tradition, which was quite high. And though eisteddfods continue today, with the gradual acculturation of Welsh Americans and the consequent abandonment of the Welsh language, they have become essentially choral festivals (Hartmann 1967, pp. 148–149).

Although Scandinavian immigrants did not rival those from Ireland or Germany in total numbers, between 1865 and 1900 a significant percentage of the Scandinavian population immigrated to America. Adolph Benson estimated that close to a quarter of the working population of Sweden came to America during that time, literally threatening to depopulate the old country. Norwegian immigration was almost as high, with Danish and Finnish being considerably less. Most of the reasons for Scandinavian immigration were economic. In particular the availability of land in America, the encouragement of both state governments and private landholders, including the railroads, to have farm land developed, and the proven ability of Scandinavian immigrants to turn virgin land into prosperous farms, combined to create a situation beneficial to both the new immigrants and vested interests in America. This combination also affected the geographical dispersal of Scandinavian immigrants, who settled mostly in the upper Midwest (Benson and Hedin 1950, pp. 159–160).

The immigration patterns created predominately Scandinavian communities, which continued the same musical practices found in Europe. In the Swedish communities, sacred music, while specifically Swedish, had many similarities to that of other rural churches in America. It consisted of unaccompanied hymn singing, led by a precenter. Reports of each member going his or her way when the tune was sung, of inordinate dragging of the tune, and of efforts to reform the "peculiar noise," through regular classes that taught singing by note and the introduction of instruments, reinforce Nicholas Temperley's observation, that the "old way of singing," unaccompanied congregational singing, leads almost invariably to the same results (Nelson 1963, pp. 53–55). At the very least, the issue confronting the Swedish communities of the Midwest as well as the solutions parallel closely the problem New England Congregationalists faced in the early eighteenth century.

Folk music in the Southwest had close ties to the music of Mexico. Although direct evidence is scarce, the musical culture of nineteenth-century Texas in particular owed a significant debt to that of Monterey, with which it was closely linked in commerce and trade. Ironically this connection strengthened non-Hispanic European music roots in Texas, because Monterey itself was heavily Europeanized. Italian opera was popular there, as were many European dances, such as the waltz, polka, schottisch, and *redowa*, as well as the traditional Spanish *habenera*.

Mexican influence on southwestern American music is most apparent in instrumental ensembles. String ensembles, or *orquestas típicas*, were common by the early twentieth century. They almost certainly existed much earlier. Strings were used early in Mexico for religious music, and the violin was the backbone of nineteenth-century theatre and salon music in Monterey. Most of the ensembles in the Southwest in the nineteenth century were probably *ad hoc*, based on available resources, but mostly derived from the *orquestas típicas* until at least the 1930s, when the influence of American swing bands became more apparent (Peña 1985, p. 31).

The accordion was introduced into the Southwest after 1850 and seems to have been common at dances and weddings by the 1890s. Although this point is not entirely clear, it probably came from German immigrants who began to settle in northern Mexico and in parts of Texas itself as early as the 1830s. By the 1850s towns such as Galveston had large German populations (Fornell and Fornell 1957, p. 29). Inexpensive, easy to learn, and capable of accompaniment, the accordion became the traditional instrument of Tejanas working-class culture. For dances or other events requiring music, it was easier to hire an accordion player than an entire orchestra. The accordion was often coupled with a drum, the *tambora de rancho* and possibly a guitar, to form a rudimentary ensemble (Peña 1985, pp. 35–38).

The most prominent types of Spanish vocal music throughout the Southwest in the nineteenth century were the *romance* and the *corrido*; both are narrative ballads. The *romance* is the older of the two; of Spanish origin, it deals with a tragic or heroic topic, usually involving persons of high station from a distant time or foreign land. The *corrido* flourished specifically in the nineteenth century; it recounts real, usually local events in considerable detail. The hero was typically a common man or someone of lowly birth (Robb 1954, p. 2). The *corrido* was almost always sung by a male, often accompanied on a guitar, in a deadpan style, and both the text and the singing style were meant to celebrate frontier values of bravery, resilience, and an in-your-face aggressiveness (Roberts 1979, p. 25). The earliest documented *corrido*, *La Batalla de los Tulares*, from 1824, recounts an Indian uprising against the Spanish in Santa Barbara, California. As with instrumental music, the affinity between Hispanic and Anglo culture is apparent in the *corrido*, which shares many characteristics with Anglo-Western ballads. According to Roberts the cowboy ballads *The Texas Rangers* and *Buffalo Skinners* are "mirror-image corrido(s)" (Roberts 1979, p. 26).

One of the most important musical melting-pots in America was New

Orleans, its French past unique within the continental United States. A particularly strong musical folk culture developed in the area around New Orleans with the forced importation of the Acadian French from Canada in the mid-eighteenth century. The Acadians were the predecessors of the Cajuns, the term itself being a derivative of Acadian. In the early nineteenth century the Acadians fiercely resisted assimilation, and lived with some acrimony with the English settlers who eventually became dominant by dint of sheer numbers. But by the 1870s Acadian culture had undergone considerable intermingling with the English culture, particularly through marriage among the English and the Acadian elite. Even more destructive to Acadian culture was the Anglo tendency to lump all non-English inhabitants of Louisiana, including both the Creoles and the foreign French elite, together as Cajuns. By the end of the nineteenth century the term Cajun designated a synthetic culture, whose main characteristic was the use of the French language, but which could otherwise be quite heterogeneous. But because most wealthy Acadians had assimilated into English culture, the term also became associated with the French-speaking Louisianans of the rural working class.

Dancing to this day continues to be an important part of Cajun culture. In the early nineteenth century the *bals de maison* or house dances, were one of the most important social events among Acadians. In some places they would be held weekly, the privilege of hosting rotating from house to house. Participation was almost universal, as invitations, delivered in colorful ways, were general; that is, the entire population would be invited. Dances, which often lasted until four or five in the morning, consisted of cotillions and round dances, with music in the early years typically being by two or sometimes three fiddlers (Brasseaux 1992, pp. 28–29).

The fiddle probably came to Louisiana with the Acadians, although the first mention of one is in a succession record of 1780. Sometime in the second half of the nineteenth century the button accordion was introduced, probably through German immigrants who settled in Louisiana after the Civil War (Ancelet 1984 p. 23; Lyon 1980, p. 15). The accordion became the favored instrument, relegating the violin to a supportive role; it was loud, and it was brash, expressive of "the frontier character of Cajun culture" (Ancelet 1984, p. 23). At the end of the century pioneering accordionists, such as the Creole musician Amédé Ardoin, introduced more syncopation and a blues quality into Cajun music.

There were significant numbers of Chinese immigrants in the West by the 1850s. Except for a few who arrived in the gold rush days, most were laborers from the Kuangtong province employed in the construction of the railroads. They lived mostly in all-male "Chinatowns," and they drew Cantonese opera troupes from Canton and Hong Kong. Cantonese opera flourished throughout the nineteenth century, San Francisco at one time supporting four theatres. Many of the troupes were large, and they often performed for mixed audiences; in 1852 for instance the Tong Hook Company, consisting of 123 performers plus a Chinese orchestra, appeared at the American Theatre in San Francisco (Lengyel 1939, p. 175).

The Cantonese opera tradition began to wane at the end of the nineteenth century. Anti-Chinese sentiment, evidenced in a number of American ballads (Lengyel 1939, pp. 140–145) and in law by the Exclusion Acts of the 1880s, forced Cantonese opera out of the principal theatres, and the San Francisco earthquake of 1906 delivered the coup-de-grâce when it destroyed most of the surviving Chinese theatres. Chinese music, which never disappeared, was performed thereafter mostly in private and strictly within the Chinese community.

Rural hymnody

At the beginning of the nineteenth century two very different events occurred, which would largely determine the course of rural or folk hymnody for the rest of the century. In August, 1801, some ten to twenty thousand people gathered at Cane Ridge, Kentucky. They came from Kentucky, Tennessee, and even the Ohio Territory, pitched tents and settled in for a camp meeting, a week-long orgy of ecstatic religious revivalism. Contemporaries describe emotionally charged preaching, mass singing, thousands of conversions, and hundreds being overtaken with deliriums of leaping, jerking, and writhing on the ground. A gathering of this magnitude, in a thinly populated frontier wilderness, in itself was unprecedented. Sparked by the fervor of the evangelical preachers, intensified by the sheer size and spectacle of the assemblage, conditions were favorable for an emotional explosion. Years of living on the edge of civilization, in relative isolation, in constant danger, and in perpetual struggle against hostile elements, erupted into a sudden and unprecedented emotional catharsis.

Camp meetings had occurred before – for instance that held a year earlier, in Logan County, Kentucky, as noted in chapter 5 – but not of the magnitude of Cane Ridge. The events of 1801 became a symbol, a sort of benchmark, for the movement. The camp meeting, which may be defined as a mass, extended, outdoor, emotionally charged revival, quickly spread to the East and North until by 1805 it could be found from Georgia to Massachusetts.

Meanwhile, in Philadelphia, William Little and William Smith introduced a new tunebook, *The Easy Instructor*. It was copyrighted 1802, but it probably first appeared in 1798 (Jackson 1933, p. 25). In this tunebook they pioneered a new type of notation, based on four differently shaped notes – a diamond, a right-angle triangle, a circle, and a square – corresponding respectively to the syllables, mi–fa–sol–la. They referred to them as the "four singing syllables." In this scheme mi–fa always represented the half-step. Thus a major scale would be fa–sol–mi–fa–sol–la–mi–fa. The use of shapes for syllables, even the tetrachordal breakdown of the scale into four syllables, was not new, although Smith and Little thought it was. Certainly few in America were familiar with some of the early precedents, which go back to Thomas Morley's *A Plaine and Easie Introduction to Practicall Musicke* (London, 1597) and John Playford's *An Introduction to the Skill of Musick* (7th edn., London, 1674) (Taddie 1996, p. 43).

The idea of the "four singing syllables" quickly caught on. Almost immediately and probably independently Andrew Law (1749–1821) attempted to obtain a patent for his own shape-note method, similar except that it abandoned the staff altogether (Crawford 1968, pp. 158–233). The combination of syllables for note-heads with otherwise traditional notation won out, however, and Law's scheme went nowhere. Little and Smith's approach received a big boost when John Wyeth (1770–1858) adopted it for his two collections, *Repository of Sacred Music* (Harrisburg, 1810), and *Repository of Sacred Music, Part Second* (Harrisburg, 1813). These were by far the most successful of the early shape-note tunebooks. They were followed soon by Ananias Davisson's *Kentucky Harmony* (1815).

Although hymnbooks containing only text were used to some extent in the early camp meetings, most of what was sung was strictly oral. In some cases lining out continued. A special type of revival hymn quickly developed, however. It resembled Anglo-American folksong, the melodies themselves often taken from the folk repository. The well-known folk hymn *Wondrous Love*, for instance, uses the tune from the ballad *Captain Kidd* (Eskew 1971, p. 149). There was much text repetition in camp meeting hymns, either through a verse-refrain pattern, or through a verse repetition in which one or two words would be changed. Such hymns could be committed to memory quickly and effortlessly, making lining out unnecessary. As a consequence revival singing, like most other aspects of the revival, had a spontaneous quality to it (Cobb 1978, pp. 79–80).

With Wyeth's *Repository, Part Second* the fasola – as four-syllable shape-note singing was called – and the folk streams merge. Many of the tunes have a folk quality, and are found in later collections of folk hymns, such as those of George Pullen Jackson and Annabel Morris Buchanan (Buchanan 1938; Jackson 1933, 1937, 1939; Stevenson 1966, p. 88). The harmoniza-tions also have a strong folk character. After about 1825, shape-note tune-books (tunebooks employing the four-syllable system) appear mostly in the rural South and Midwest. The most important of the later tunebooks were the *Missouri Harmony* by Allen D. Carden (St. Louis, 1820), the *South-ern Harmony and Musical Companion* by William Walker (Spartensburg, South Carolina, 1835), which purportedly sold 600,000 copies, the *Social Harp* by John Gordon McCurry (Philadelphia, 1855), and the most influential of all, *The Sacred Harp*, by B. F. White and E. B. King (Philadel-phia, 1844). *The Sacred Harp* has lent its name to a style of singing still prac-ticed, and the tunebook itself continues to be reprinted. (A full list of tunebooks can be found in Perrin 1968, pp. 210–213, and Jackson 1933, p. 25.)

Shape-note tunebooks met with less success in the Northeast due to the dominant influence of reform hymnists, such as Thomas Hastings (1784–1872) and Lowell Mason (1792–1872). The reform hymnists, mostly Congregationalist or Presbyterian, attempted to write in a more "scientific" style (their term), following European common-practice rules of harmony and voice-leading. Yet often their tunes, in themselves, were not all that different; for example both Hastings's *Toplady* ("Rock of Ages") and Mason's *Bethany* ("Nearer My God to Thee") became favorites across the evangelical spectrum.

Shape-note tunebooks were mostly in three parts, with a distinctive contrapuntal-harmonic style. Later on four parts become more common. The tunes tend to be rhythmic and lively, and there is no instrumental accompaniment. Open sounds and parallel fourths, fifths, and octaves abound. The melody is usually in the tenor, and each voice is a line unto itself, suggesting a compositional approach based on contrapuntal layer-ing rather than simultaneous, harmonic working out. For that reason W. M. Cooper could add a fourth voice to the three-voice compositions in *The Sacred Harp* without fundamentally changing their nature (Cobb 1978, p. 91). Charles Seeger, the first scholar to describe the style of these hymns, noted their similarity to the thirteenth-century conductus, and wondered if they might represent an old folk tradition, extant for centuries, but which only occasionally surfaces in printed form. Regardless of their origins, they represent a musical style quite different from the common-practice harmonization of more mainstream or – to use the nineteenth-century term – "scientific" hymnody.

In the second half of the nineteenth century another type of religious song, the gospel song, appeared. Two musicians, Philip P. Bliss (1838–1876) and Ira D. Sankey (1840–1908), working closely with the evangelist Dwight L. Moody (1837–1899), gave shape to the genre. Moody was the most successful evangelist in the second half of the nineteenth century. In 1869 Bliss, active in music education, sang in some of Moody's services. Bliss's singing convinced Moody of the value of song in revivalism. The next year Bliss, by then associated with the John Church Publishing Company, began to issue several collections of sacred songs, the most important being *Gospel Songs* in 1873.

Shortly after Moody encountered Bliss he met Ira D. Sankey, a YMCA worker, soloist and song leader, and invited him to become a member of his revival team (Sankey 1906, pp. 5–6). To fill a need for published hymns on an evangelical visit to England in 1872, Sankey published *Sacred Songs and Solos*. This collection continued to grow with each edition, until by 1903 it contained 1,200 songs (Reynolds 1963, pp. 105–106).

Upon returning to America Sankey and Bliss agreed to merge their efforts into a joint publication. The result was *Gospel Hymns and Sacred Songs* (New York and Cincinnati, 1875). Subsequent compilations, *Gospel Hymns (Nos. 2–6)*, followed between 1876 and 1891, culminating in *Gospel Hymns, Complete*, in 1894. The final edition contained 794 songs. These collections totally dominated the market and defined the gospel song in the nineteenth century.

The term gospel song comes from Bliss's original title. Gospel song melodies, derived from improvisatory folk style, are often close to the popular secular idiom. Although in later gospel practice they are frequently accompanied, in the manner of popular song, with oom-pah accompaniment, sometimes with the same instruments found in corresponding secular music, making them all but indistinguishable from popular music, Bliss and Sankey set them in standard SATB four-part accompaniment, with the melody in the soprano. The harmonies, however, are very simple, using mostly primary chords in root position. Whereas each voice in shape-note practice is a line, in gospel practice melody prevails with the other voices providing strictly harmonic support. This is particularly true of the bass, which often remains static on one of the primary chord roots until it moves by a fourth or fifth. Occasional chromaticism appears, but almost always as passing or neighbor notes.

The prevailing texture is frequently altered in two ways: first with sustained notes in the upper voices while the bass has a (moving) line; second the bass is given some rhythmic counterpoint, either in dialogue with the upper voices or by delaying or anticipating rhythmically the beginnings of phrases.

Even though the gospel song has strong folk roots, it is completely separate from the shape-note tradition. The contrapuntal approach, the use of open sounds, the absence of instruments and the placement of the melody in the tenor distinguish the shape-note hymn from the gospel song, although gospel songs can be sung *a capella*. Both types are related to camp meeting hymnody at least indirectly, in that each emphasizes rhythmic, lively tunes, with folk-like qualities. The gospel song, however, does have strong, specific roots in the revival tradition. It may be traced back to Asahel Nettleton's *Village Hymns* of 1824, and even more directly to Joshua Leavitt's *Christian Lyre* of 1831 (Reynolds 1963, p. 92). Except that many of Leavitt's hymns are in two rather than four parts, many are virtually indistinguishable from those of Bliss and Sankey. They are similar in tone, subject matter, and both melodic and harmonic style. And the difference between a two-part and a four-part arrangement was not as great as might be thought: at least in Leavitt's time, hymns were often performed in two parts (bass and treble), even though four parts might be written out (Broyles 1992, pp. 82–83).

Both Nettleton and Leavitt were active in the revival movement in upstate New York led by Charles Finney. Finney was the most successful revivalist before Moody, and revivals were so common at the time in western New York that the area became known as the "burned-over district." Leavitt made clear his intention, "to supply the revival need with somewhat lighter and more songlike hymns with rippling rhythms and sometimes 'choruses'" (Reynolds 1963, p. 92).

*

In a country as varied as the United States it would be impossible to discuss all the types of folk music that immigrants brought with them or which developed in particular regions or among particular ethnic groups. I have not even tried. I have only attempted to mention briefly those that had the greatest overall impact on American culture, a situation related closely to the demographics, to the sheer number of arrivals of each group. At least one important group of immigrants, however, those brought involuntarily from Africa, I have not discussed at all. As has already been shown, theirs is a story – and hence a chapter – in itself.

7

Nineteenth-century popular music

—

DALE COCKRELL

At heart, this is a chapter about the early development of what musicologist Richard Crawford calls the music of "accessibility," a music which seeks "most of all to find and please audiences and to increase their size" (Crawford 1993, pp. 86–88). To judge by events and developments in the nineteenth century, popular music pleased its audience by speaking directly to its needs and wishes. This chapter, then, will attempt likewise to discover and analyze audience and its concerns, in the belief that such a method leads most directly to understanding. By concentrating on reception and audience, instead of production (i.e. the performers, composers, and publishers), one hopes with Walt Whitman to find Americans – his mechanics, carpenters, masons, boatmen, shoemakers, hatters, woodcutters, ploughboys, mothers, wives, girls, young fellows – again "Singing, with open mouths, their strong melodious songs," all "singing what belongs to [them], to none else" (from *I Hear America Singing*, 1860).

*

The range of popular music available to nineteenth-century Americans followed from developing notions of public and private spheres. Until this period, "privacy" in Western society was something unique to the few, generally those of exceptional wealth or special status. Most white Americans and their cousin Europeans of the previous centuries lived in a public world, where the individual's primary role was the sustenance of the community. Accordingly, the music of this earlier period was almost always for public venues, whether theatres, churches, streets, or byways, for audiences that were often in some way participants as well. Communities sanctioned, varied, and sustained folk ballads; operas were social occasions; church music served to unite a congregation and bind it through ritual. Much of the popular music of the nineteenth century developed from older musical traditions based in the public sphere, principally theatre music (which includes a rich variety of forms and types), band music, music for

[158]

dancing, even some church music. These were the original musics of accessibility, for they had long been readily available to listeners; sometimes a ticket was required, but more often just simple presence. This music generally required no special form of media for its popularity, for its life revolved around live performance and an involved, often adoring, audience.

The music for the private space was different altogether, virtually an invention of the nineteenth century and heavily redolent with that century's values. The private space was a concept made possible by the development of the nuclear family, one ideally situated in the haven of the family – the home. It followed from the establishment of rigid lines that defined function within the family unit: the husband was the breadwinner and undisputed authority, the wife nurtured (i.e. birthed, nursed, cooked, kept house), and the children obeyed (cleaned their rooms, did their chores and schoolwork). The husband's world was the rough-and-tumble public world of business, commerce, and industry; women and children lived in the shielded, secure private world of domesticity. The noise, excess, unrestrained emotionalism, and showy professionalism of much public music was thought inappropriate for such a new sphere, and a form of popular music came about, one that treasured reserve and sentiment, was without ostentation, and could be performed by the competent amateur. Significantly, it required media for its dissemination, specifically printing, or sheet music. By setting up a kind of closed loop – printed media, which needed a marketplace, which needed a middle class, which needed a home sphere, which needed printed media . . . – this music reinforced and was in turn buttressed by the very values it espoused. At the century's end, it was America's most important form of popular music, at least economically, and would have much to say about the shape of popular music in the twentieth century.

Popular music in the public sphere

The most public of nineteenth-century American spaces was the street. In early century, at least, it was a noisy place, but one filled with much music-making. Here, ballads were hawked and sung, parades of all sorts wended their carnival ways, vendors bellowed signature calls, bands marched, and mummers mummed. Scholars are just beginning to recreate, understand, and appreciate what must have been a constant creative cacophony, an omnipresent part of early American urban life, for much of it has been lost to lore and memory. America's streets by the 1830s were also places of conflict, often violent and sometimes deadly, between an old world view of the world, one that treasured cacophony and disorder, and a new, with values that stressed the importance of order. The new won out, of course, supported by newly established police departments and merchants and businessmen who believed that public thoroughfares should reflect the moderation and decorum of what was in their view the streets' primary purpose, expediting commerce. With this victory, traditions belonging to common people, which were often ancient, had to accommodate themselves to a brave new world, or suffer imminent demise. Two musical institutions adapted well: bands, which fed off life in the streets, and theatres, which brought life in from the streets.

Bands

The written record probably does not extend far enough back to capture the beginning of the European street music tradition. Since the Middle Ages, there have been accounts of more-or-less organized bands of street musicians, often associated with festivities (such as carnival and Mardi Gras) or civic celebrations; or associated with military campaigns and maneuvers. The military had long used sounded signals to direct troops in battle, which insured a supply of "musicians" among the ranks who, in addition to their practical value, also provided entertainment for and raised the morale of soldiers. Perhaps it was only natural that music for the military and music for the streets would meld during the eighteenth century, as Europeans and Americans of lower ranks volunteered for or were conscripted into huge armies to fight in massive campaigns (Napoleonic, Revolutionary, or otherwise). Benjamin Franklin, with characteristic prescience, seemed to have recognized this when he, as commander of a militia regiment, ordered musicians "in Ranks" to precede his soldiers through the streets of Philadelphia in 1756 (Camus 1986, p. 127). Undoubtedly his musicians helped foster a festive, celebratory public spirit among the citizens, infecting the troops, which was of course precisely the intention.

After the War of Independence, musicians discharged from military bands formed the cores around which civilian bands grew. These civilian bands were commonly associated, often by name, with cities and towns of some size at the beginning of the nineteenth century. From this modest beginning, the band movement grew to immodest proportions. At first, cities maintained an alliance with a pre-existent band, which was often made up of professional musicians. Eventually, towns as small as two hundred persons managed to support a volunteer or, perhaps, semi-pro-fessional band. They were eventually to be found in every state and terri-tory, in every region (Hazen and Hazen 1987, p. 5). By mid-century, there were perhaps 3,000 bands nationally, and 60,000 bandmembers.

The period after the Civil War saw the heyday of professional bands, often headed by energetic and flamboyant showmen like Patrick S. Gilmore (1829–1892). The most important of these, though, was John Philip Sousa (1854–1932). His rise to national prominence came as the conductor of the prestigious United States Marine Band. In 1892 he estab-lished his own professional civilian band, although it retained many mili-tary aspects (such as uniforms and a regimented performance style). His ensemble of some fifty players toured throughout the United States and Europe well into the twentieth century, to the general approbation of mil-lions of fans who loved the lush, rich symphonic band sound and the finely crafted, infectious marches of Sousa himself.

But full-time professional bands were the great exception. At century's end, there were more than ten thousand bands, only a bare handful profes-sional, touring ensembles; the great majority were bands composed of local citizens, strongly associated with place. The importance of a band for community identity was evident to a writer in 1878: "A town without its brass band is as much in need of sympathy as a church without a choir. The spirit of a place is recognized in its band" (quoted in Camus 1986, p. 133).

Much of a typical town band's repertory consisted of an eclectic mix of arrangements of music taken from European and American sources: sym-phonies, overtures, and operatic arias, adaptations of popular songs, dances, and hymns, and, at century's end, Sousa's marches. Programming was for the many. Bands provided music for dances, parades, picnics, and other important social occasions, as well as just for entertainment on a summer's Sunday afternoon. They also allowed access to public spaces for many who were otherwise denied it: there were, for example, children's bands, women's band, and even bands whose members were Native Ameri-cans (Hazen and Hazen 1987, pp. 52ff.). Nor did the appeal for and mem-bership in bands stop at racial barriers, for one of the very first professional bands, that directed by Philadelphian Frank Johnson (1792–1844) which flourished from the 1820s through the 1840s, was all-black and played for many all-white audiences. The Civil War found many African American regimental bands in the Union Army, and black bandsmen after the Civil War in New Orleans laid the groundwork for jazz. And at century's end even all-white bands, like Sousa's, were playing heavily syncopated arrangements for white audiences, in anticipation, we now see, of the wide acceptance of dynamically syncopated musics in the twentieth century.

No American music had a firmer basis in the musical tastes and dispositions of more Americans than nineteenth-century band music. If ever there were a music truly democratic in its appeal it was this. No one could easily escape the far-reaching sounds of a brass band, and there is no evidence that anyone – adult, child, woman, man, rich, poor, black, or white – wanted to. This music of the streets was truly music for all the people in those streets.

Theatre music

Right off the public thoroughfares, with its doors flung open to all, was the theatre to which citizens could gain access by a simple exchange of relatively small coin. As was noted in chapter 3, without question the most important forms of public music-making occurred here, whether for the elite "upper tens" or for the most common of the "common sorts."

OPERA, OPERETTA, AND MUSICAL COMEDY · In the early years of the century, America's business and professional people, from shopkeepers to lawyers to manufacturers to accountants, controlled the public space, as they also controlled the theatre. What went on in those theatres was "popular" in the sense that there was no implied opposition to "art music" (as in today's formulation of those terms), and in that it was appreciated by many. In New Orleans, where French culture dominated, *opéra comique* was imported directly from Paris for the pleasure of many of its citizens. Most of the rest of the United States too looked to Europe, but to England instead of France. American urban stages resounded with the latest comic operas from London, or with works by American composers based on ones premiered in England. These were relatively simple affairs descended from the ballad opera tradition, in English, but of a more "refined" tone and tenor. Plots typically involved "the use of disguises and mistaken identities, romances foiled by misunderstanding, confrontations between villains and heroes, plot twists based on social position or custom, [and] complications based on human foibles and frailties" (Porter 1991, pp. 32–33). The music was somewhat more complex than that found in ballad operas, and was usually the product of a single composer. In a society that was elevating respect for the individual and that individual's prerogatives, the cultural work done by early-nineteenth-century comic operas was a perfect reflection.

Later in the century tastes shifted toward Italian opera. The Italian operas of Mozart had never fallen out of wide favor. Lorenzo Da Ponte (1749–1838), librettist for *Don Giovanni* and *The Marriage of Figaro*, emigrated to the United States in 1805 and campaigned thereafter with success to keep Italian opera before the American public. The event that made Italian opera widely popular, though, took place in 1825, when a troupe of European opera singers, headed by Manuel García, visited North America to great acclaim. After him, a steady stream of European (mainly English) troupes toured the country, spreading a love for opera (sung in English) throughout many parts of the social spectrum. The arias audiences heard – from operas by Mozart, Rossini, Donizetti, Bellini, and later, Verdi and Wagner – became enormously popular, essentially setting a new musical standard. Let one example serve. *Una voce poco fa*, an aria from Rossini's *The Barber of Seville*, is exemplary of bel canto style in its sheer tunefulness. Its exquisite melody is built through the repetition of short graceful phrases, which culminates in an extended and elegantly contoured melody with a prominent climax on a high note toward the close; harmonies are clearly implied and adhere to common tonal practices; rhythm is the engine that drive's the whole ahead, with a persistent emphasis on the downbeat; accompaniments generally feature arpeggiation. When arias like this one received a new English text, in this case with the title *Once a King there Chanced to Be*, it was bought and performed widely, to judge from the large number of extant pieces of sheet music. *Una voce*, now *Once a King*, was popular music, perhaps not fully for the masses, but certainly for the many.

Italian opera style was widely influential, and it affected and changed the mainstream of popular music in significant ways. Composers in England imitated (and generally simplified) aspects of it, and their works enjoyed success in the United States. Arias from Italian-inflected English operas, such as *I Dreamt that I Dwelt in Marble Halls* from *The Bohemian Girl* by Michael William Balfe, were widely disseminated in the United States as sheet music suitable for performance by amateurs. The pattern was set, and much of the rest of the century found Italian opera, or one of its derivatives, in fashion among some sector of American music lovers.

The performance of opera (especially that in a foreign language, usually Italian) by mid-century, and especially after the Civil War, became more and more the private province of the upper classes. (By 1840 a New Orleans opera house was advertising that its boxes could be locked, thus excluding those not of the private circle of friends and family.) Personalities, stars, and extravagance (of character and of production) all enforced the notion that this experience was elevated, no longer of the common people. A fuller discussion of nineteenth-century opera in the United States can be found in chapters 8 and 9.

Musical comedy came about in part to fill the void left by the appropriation of opera by the upper classes. *The Black Crook*, of 1866, is generally considered the first in the line. Set to a play by Charles M. Barras that followed loosely the Faust myth, the show featured melodrama, ballet, music, awe-inspiring special effects, and simmering eroticism, altogether dazzling. Producers were quick to mount similar shows as the public swarmed to see *The Black Crook* (importantly among them the popular and influential *Evangeline; Or, The Belle of Acadie*, by E. E. Rice). The genre was intentionally set off from "lower" forms of musical theatre (such as blackface minstrelsy) by using plots drawn from "serious" literature and by employing the idioms of art music, although simplified. Seen in this light, the greatly popular operettas by Jacques Offenbach, the comic collaborations of W. S. Gilbert and Arthur Sullivan, and the turn-of-the-century light operas by Rudolf Friml, Victor Herbert, Gustave A. Kerker, Franz Lehar, Sigmund Romberg, and Johann Strauss were from the same line and were attractive to the same white, urban, middle-class audience. For the most part, this was professional, public entertainment not easily transplanted into the private, amateur musical sphere. Almost none of the songs heard in these productions (with the notable exception of a few by Victor Herbert) made their way into American parlors.

But *The Black Crook* also spawned a line of more popular and accessible musical theatre, something much closer to what we would today call musical comedy. Theatregoers came to demand a plot that was compelling and logical, yet contained characters and situations that were somewhat true-to-life. Energy and excitement should approach that generated in more popularly based genres like minstrelsy and vaudeville. It was the music, though, that was the show's driving force and primary reason for being. Audiences insisted on some stylistic coherence, but more important was that it be accessible and lively. *A Trip to Chinatown*, from 1890, was the trendsetter. The plot was ordinary, but the music (and dance, too) entranced. This *was* music that translated well to the Victorian home, and *After the Ball* by Charles K. Harris (1865/7–1930) sold a claimed 5 million copies of sheet music, much of that on the basis of its wide exposure in traveling productions of *Chinatown*. The fuller development of musical comedy, though, awaited George M. Cohan (1878–1942) and the twentieth century; it is discussed in chapter 12.

BLACKFACE MINSTRELSY · The decade of the 1820s was an especially tumultuous one in American social history, as urban areas grew and industrialization geared up the engine for change. Cities like New York drew great numbers of working-class people from both Europe and rural areas of the United States. Ethnic and religious lines were drawn sharply and severely. Unfortunately for many, the American dream became a day-to-day struggle, with shelter, decent food, potable drink, and sanitation all life-or-death issues. An important result of such conditions was that an (unspoken) urban hierarchy was codified. According to this, it was manifestly better to be from the city than the country; it was better to be a landowner than not; it was better to be rich than poor; better to be Protestant than Catholic; English than Irish; white than black; freedman than slave. The northern, urban American stage vicariously played out these human realities by giving voice to those people with little more than the wherewithal to buy a cheap ticket to the gallery. For example, Edwin Forrest (1806–1872), the greatest American actor of the period, made heroes of white working-class folk, which was a social vindication, if only fantasized, of his most loyal fans, the so-called "gallery gods." Under such conditions and for such an audience was blackface minstrelsy born.

European common people had long utilized blackface in their public theatricals. Mummers, morris dancers, carnival figures, and many others featured characters in blackface, the most basic form of masquerade for those with pale faces, a mask that surely signaled "other-ness." Common Europeans, who became common Americans, knew these traditions and understood them to signify a means of expressing social concern (with working conditions, with disintegration of community, with the need for a successful harvest, and so on) by giving ritual voice to the blackfaced one, who could thus speak about the inside from the perspective of the outsider. With the denial of full and easy access to American streets by civic authorities and the repression of traditional means of voicing social issue came the need to seek alternate means and venues. The theatres – cheap, open to the public, bendable to the whims and concerns of the audience – served such a need. So blackface moved indoors, and came to be called minstrelsy.

Thomas Dartmouth Rice (1808–1860) was the first blackface comic to borrow manifestly from the folk tradition. A professional actor in circuses and traveling shows, he developed, performed, and made famous the blackface character Jim Crow, probably first in 1830. Unlike the blackface in many European folk theatricals, Jim Crow was a representation of an African American, a fact that would have been perfectly obvious to white

American audiences given the character's shabby clothing, "grotesque" dancing, and, of course, blackface. The text to the song *Jim Crow* also shows the influence of black American culture. The famous refrain – "Turn about an' wheel about an' do jis so, / An' ebery time I turn about I jump Jim Crow" – is written in a dialect that appears to be similar to that then spoken by many African Americans. The fact that a disjointed, "illogical," non-narrative is employed throughout the song also suggests something of traditional African storytelling structures.

> I wip de lion ob de west,
>   I eat de Allegator;
> I put more water in my mouf,
>   Den boil ten load ob tator.
> De Nigs in de Orleans,
>   Dey tink demselves so fine;
> But Nigs in ole Virginny,
>   Be so black dey shine.

Even the music perhaps owes something to black cultural traditions, since it might have been derived from a "corn song" like those heard at corn-shucking rituals.

The range of blackface entertainment was measurably broadened in 1834 when George Washington Dixon (1801–1861) sang *Zip Coon* for approving New York audiences. If Jim Crow established the stereotype of southern plantation slave, with his ragamuffin motley, his exaggerated physical characteristics (woolly hair, grotesquely large feet, big lips), and his utter lack of urban sophistication, Zip Coon was his polar opposite. Zip was a northern freedman, a so-called darky dandy from the city who dressed in high hat, yellow waistcoat, light-colored breeches, and fashionable swallowtail coat; he carried a watch, wore jewelry, and twirled a pince-nez (implying not only high fashion, but literacy as well). Yet in keeping with the long tradition of blackface comedy, Zip Coon was not quite right. His arms, for one thing, were much too long and awkward; sheet music covers show us a figure grossly disproportioned, and too much kinky hair spills from under his hat. He never quite manages to get the cadence of "proper" speech either: "Ole Zip Coon he is a larned skolar, / Sings possum up a gum tree an coony in a holler." He was altogether wrong, ultimately a figure of ridicule and laughter. He tried to reach for a social rung beyond his reach and the resulting fall and crash was greeted joyously by those in the audience.

Manifestly, one cannot ignore minstrelsy as an important marker of race relations. Issues of slavery and race were crucial parts of the Jacksonian period's public discourse, and blackface minstrelsy engaged them in significant ways. There can be no doubt that black people were misrepresented and viciously stereotyped on the stage, nor that whites took pleasure in a spectacle that, to some extent at least, reflected back to them their own perceived racial superiority. On the dark side of minstrelsy, the white person gained voice at the expense of the black.

But to stop there and declare, as many have, that "Jim Crow" or "Zip Coon" is simply a demeaning portrayal of a black man is to ignore the ambiguous, even paradoxical nature of burlesque (which minstrelsy is, at base) and to miss the complex constitutions of common audiences. At worst, one simply misses the whole point. Those lower-class white Americans who made up the house knew the society of African Americans through daily contact. Although fights were common, and there was sometimes hatred in the air, so too were marriages, friendships, joint music-making, and shared values and traditions. And many (perhaps most) early blackface minstrel songs, including *Jim Crow*, contained textual elements that can only be interpreted as antislavery in tone and spirit, as there is evidence too that Rice, Dixon, and perhaps others of the early blackface performers were antislavery in their politics. Burlesques were aimed by white performers and audiences not always *at* African Americans, but often *through* the blackface mask to the rich and powerful, the common oppressors of common Americans. *Zip Coon* satirizes the pretentious upper class at least as much as lower-class blacks. Significantly (and frequently overlooked), it was often the music that confirmed for the audience that they were in the presence of burlesque. *Jim Crow*, for example, is an awkward tune artificially made over into a jig; it is disjointed, "illogical," even noisy; it is appropriate for dancing, but only when grace is not a requirement. It is, in other words, all that the music of the powerful was not. That common audiences could take great pleasure from what some might (and did) call noise, that the song could prompt public displays of high spirits (as it did), suggests that *Jim Crow* was the music of hope for joy and pleasure, a music that offered relief from a world grown grim and gray with oppression and despair.

In the early years blackface minstrels danced, played fiddles or banjos, sang songs, and told jokes generally as solo performers or duo acts. They were usually members of a larger troupe of actors and musicians, who together presented a great variety of theatrical fare during a typical entertainment. The singing families (discussed below) demonstrated that a quartet of accomplished and flexible performers could carry a whole show, and divide the evening's proceeds among themselves, instead of receiving a (barely) subsistence weekly salary. In January, 1843 four minstrel performers emulated this format by banding together, calling themselves the Virginia Minstrels (a burlesque twist on the name of one of the most popular singing families), and presenting a whole show of blackface entertainment. By March of that year, they had further refined their programs to attract – again like the singing families – middle-class audiences interested in "representations," in this case of African Americans. With the appeal to a new audience came music that was less "noisy" than the early blackface favorites, songs that were more melodic (and less dance-based), with clearly implied harmonies, and more "logical" musical structures. Their innovations were so significant that within weeks other groups were modeling themselves after the Virginia Minstrels. By the year's end, dozens of these minstrel troupes were traveling throughout the United States and even England, with names like Ethiopian Serenaders, Buckley's New Orleans Serenaders, Kentucky Minstrels, White's Minstrels; and 1844 brought the most famous of them all, E. P. Christy's Minstrels.

A format was soon in place that would govern blackface minstrelsy for decades to come. In the new minstrel show all performers were in blackface, and attempted to impersonate black Americans. Typically, there were four to six blackfaced performers, who usually arrayed themselves in a line, with "Mr. Bones" (who played a rhythm block-like instrument often fashioned from the rib bones of an animal) on one end and "Mr. Tambo" (who played the tambourine) on the other; "Mr. Johnson" (the "Interlocutor"), who served as a foil for the comic antics of Bones and Tambo, was framed in the center of the semi-circle "line." The minstrel show contained a wide variety of entertainment, including dancing, singing, playing (usually fiddles and banjos, plus the rhythm instruments), jokes, stump speeches, and skits. The program was presented in two parts, with the first section focusing on the urban dandy stereotype, and the second representing slaves on a southern plantation. The mix was breathtaking. It seemed to have everything: comedy, music, dance, and the hilarious blackface mask. Further, the audience was being accustomed to seeing blackface as representation, instead of real enough, as had formerly been the case. And minstrelsy more and more proved a convenient purveyor of social and political attitudes as racism permeated white society, arguably from the top down. White Americans filled the theatres for this new entertainment and established it as the most popular form of musical theatre in nineteenth-century America.

Most of early minstrelsy music was like *Zip Coon* (today generally known as *Turkey in the Straw*) in that it was a part of the then-developing fiddle-tune tradition, which is discussed in chapter 6. Songs featured limited melodic ranges and were supported by basic harmonic progressions. Befitting dance music – as this was – there was a great deal of repetition. But by about 1840, minstrel songs were more often consciously "composed" than collectively "made" by some anonymous folk, and were frequently alloyed with other song traditions, significantly that of romantic love. Results often proved humorous to audiences because of resulting incongruities. By way of example, *Miss Lucy Long*, published in 1842 by one of the (soon-to-be) Virginia Minstrels, may have been the most-performed song of the early minstrel show stage (Winans 1984, p. 81). The text places the "beloved" in rather degrading situations, thoroughly consistent with the representations of slave-life known to northern whites. Still, there is amorous intrigue of a sort, and the singer in fact asks Lucy to marry him. But, lest this get too close to "real" romantic love:

> If she makes a scolding wife,
> As sure as she was born,
> I'll tote her down to Georgia,
> And trade her off for corn.
> Oh take your time Miss Lucy,
> Take your time Miss Lucy Long.

An innovation here is the couplet at the end of the verse, which is repeated throughout like a refrain and serves thus to unify the song. Perhaps more importantly, though, the refrain provides the song with a musical focus, for the repeated words direct attention to the music-making, which is here at the highest level in the whole song.

The coming of the minstrel show in the 1840s and 1850s changed significantly the business of minstrelsy. As it became bigger and immensely more popular, the more it required the machinery of sophisticated stage production: logistical support, publicity, professional management. And as this happened, the managers (who might or might not have been performers as well) simplified the structure of the entertainment and its message, in order to appeal to larger audiences. Gone was the carnivalesque helter-skelter of the early years, replete with ambiguity of meaning. In its place was a show with a well-defined structure and a clearly articulated set of values. Another section was added to the show – the middle in what became a tripartite form – called the olio, which featured a miscellany of blackface songs and burlesque skits on some of the day's popular entertainments, with operas and singing families primary among them. Here so-called "nigger wench" roles were developed in which, most grotesquely, white men portrayed black women, managing to disparage both race and gender in a single stroke – all to the immense satisfaction of the audience. The first section diverged significantly from its "darky dandy" roots. It came to consist of songs of gentility, of domesticity, family, pets, loved ones – a "concert" obviously designed to delight middle-class audiences. There was often no dialect here, and some troupes advertised that the musicians were "citizens" instead of "Ethiopians," that is, without blackface. The third and final section remained the heart of minstrelsy though, with its extended, large-scale plantation scenes. Everything was capped by the "walkaround" finale, in which the whole troupe paraded, danced, sang, played, and joked at once, in some kind of grotesque apotheosis borne aloft by sensory overload. Surely the most famous of these was *I Wish I Was in Dixie's Land* (today, *Dixie*) by Dan Emmett (1815–1904), first produced in 1859.

The ante-bellum minstrel show sharpened the lines in the ongoing public discourse on matters of race and gender. It was manifestly about degrading African Americans in favor of white Americans; and men were always elevated over women. In these ways, and others less explicit, the minstrel show was a powerful vehicle for affirming the values of the powerful, who formed a significant part of the audience by this time. Yet it was not unambiguously that, for the merchants of entertainment seemed not to have fully understood that their "product" was different from other manufactures, for it could never be completely consumed. In fact entertainment (and music) has always served to some extent to disrupt the status quo; most fundamentally, people seek entertainment because their lives are colored by varying degrees of dullness, boredom, sadness, insecurity, or some other such negative. To be entertained by national anxieties, such as race and gender, holds out, somewhat paradoxically, the possibility of undoing those very things, and a reordering of them.

The music that provides the richest example of the transgressing possibilities inherent in minstrelsy issued from the pen of the day's most important American composer, Stephen Collins Foster (1826–1864). Born and reared in Pittsburgh, a young Foster performed in amateur blackface minstrelsy. He also composed songs for the medium, among the first of

EXAMPLE 7.1 Stephen Foster, *Oh! Lemuel*, chorus melody.

which was *Oh! Susanna*, published in 1847 although not under his own name. It is typical of early minstrel songs in its non-narrative, irrational lyrics, and in its dance-tune based melody. Its use of syncopation does set it off somewhat, and suggests why it achieved such immense worldwide popularity. The fame he garnered from this song and others of the period encouraged Foster to attempt (and succeed at) what no other American had achieved – status as a professional composer of popular songs.

Against a social and political backdrop in which racism and slavery were hotly debated, Foster's minstrel songs trace a remarkable line. *Susanna* was nearly all idiom and convention, with few indications that the composer (who was also his own lyricist in this and many others of his songs) was aware of any political or social message conveyed by the song. *Oh! Lemuel*, from 1850, was out of the same mold. It featured dialect and painted pictures of slaves with unattractive physical features; blacks were represented as simple-minded lovers of dancing and music-making. Their songs were, to gather from *Lemuel*, highly repetitive, of limited range, and supported by rudimentary harmonies. Only the rhythms were of vital interest, with their liberal and effective use of syncopation (see example 7.1). This song reflected back to white audiences their views of blacks and slavery, and reaffirmed them. In sum, the song suggested that slaves were stupid, lazy, overwrought, musical, and given to sexual debauchery, wild dancing, and endless partying. In other words, life on the ole plantation (given conditions in the urban, industrial cities of the Northeast, where the biggest audiences were found) actually sounded pretty good.

Old Folks at Home, published the following year, became Foster's most-popular song. Like *Lemuel* the text is in dialect, and it depicts happy slaves on a southern plantation. Its deviation from the convention is significant, though, for the song's protagonist has real feelings, in spite of being a slave.

He is full of nostalgic longing for past happy days, for his mother, and for his childhood home. These kinds of sentiments were held by many in the audience, and they were asked by this song to project their own feelings onto those of a slave. In the process, the slave was somewhat humanized. The music reinforced the process, for, although still not complex, Foster composed a song about a slave that is of a type with a multitude of sentimental, melancholic, parlor songs of nostalgic longing. The slave sang about issues and in such a way that Foster suggested that the line that joined black with white – common humanity – was stronger than the line that divided. *Old Folks at Home* is a song of discourse, rich in transgressive possibilities.

Massa's in de Cold Ground (published in 1852) is a further development on the issues introduced in *Old Folks*. It too is in dialect and sets slaves on a southern plantation. The people are still helpless, childlike, and find comfort in their music, and "Ole Massa" is part convention – fatherly, kindly, and good. But the song, sung from the perspective of the slave, is about deep, seemingly real affection for a dead father figure. It is closely allied in both text and music with a genre of "deceased loved one" songs then popular in the private sphere, many of which were written by Foster himself (*Gentle Annie* being a prime example). These are songs of deep sentiments, full of poignant loss. Significantly, of course, such feelings were not traditionally associated with slaves. But by dragging white private emotions into the brash public world of minstrelsy, Foster further strengthened the underlying message, which was that slaves in many fundamental ways were much like those whites then sitting in the audience, and that real human beings were being denied basic human rights.

My Old Kentucky Home, Good Night (1853) makes utterly clear Foster's intention. There is no dialect to start with, for Foster came about this time to condemn it as fundamentally degrading. The narrative is of a family in happy times, into which comes tragic disruption and death. In this way, it is like many such stories told, read, and sung in middle-class parlors of the period. The music too is melancholic and filled with limpid, bittersweet melodic contours. But the chilling reason for the disruption and the melancholia is that the central father figure is missing from the family hearth because he has been sold downriver: *this family is a family of slaves!* No mourning period wrapped in a comfortable middle-class life awaits them; only backbreaking labor, then the final release of death. *My Old Kentucky Home* followed directly on the heels of *Uncle Tom's Cabin*, the widely read novel by Harriet Beecher Stowe of 1852. The themes are quite similar, as is the polemic – the abolition of slavery. In fact, Foster intended the parallel, for he originally titled his song *Old Uncle Tom, Good Night*. Once again, though, it is the music that ultimately convinces the listener of the lyric. Foster never wrote a more deeply searing melody. The chorus, which in his hands came to be the musical focus of the song, is especially compelling, with its powerful and dramatic commencement on the verb most descriptive of the song's message: "Weep!" *My Old Kentucky Home* was Stephen Foster's strongest statement to that point on the issue of slavery, articulated clearly, and proclaimed in a vastly popular public forum to precisely the audience most concerned with issues of race and its representation. Much more than artifice, evidently this was Foster speaking of his own commitment to radical change.

Under the leadership of Stephen Foster, the issue of slavery was engaged by minstrelsy during the years leading up to the Civil War, although often with some ambivalence and reluctance. After Emancipation and an unprecedented shedding of blood, the consciences of white (largely northern) Americans seem to have been washed clean. And with no Foster – who had died in 1864 – to set the agenda, minstrelsy quickly reverted to earlier modes of representation. Two important songwriters demonstrate this. Will S. Hays (1837–1907), a Kentuckian, wrote one of the most popular songs of the period in his *The Little Old Log Cabin in the Lane* (1871). The lyrics included:

> Dar was a happy time to me, 'twas many years ago,
> When de darkies used to gather round de door,
> When dey used to dance an' sing at night, I played de ole banjo,
> But alas, I cannot play it any more.

This song, which borrows from the pathos associated with songs of nostalgia, is a paean to the happy days of slavery! And to show that Hays's southern heritage was not necessarily the primary factor in his perspective, compare his verse with that of Charles A. White (1829–1892), a Bostonian, who wrote in his popular *The Old Home Ain't What It Used To Be* of 1874:

> Oh, the old home ain't what it used to be,
> The Banjo and fiddle has gone,
> And no more you hear the darkies singing,
> Among the sugar cane and corn.
> Now the old man would rather lived and died,
> In the home where his children were born,
> But when freedom came to the colored man,
> He left the cotton field and corn.

> No, the old home ain't what it used to be,
> The change makes me sad and forlorn,
> For no more we hear the darkies singing,
> Among the sugar cane and corn.

The well-formed, musically memorable choruses to both of these songs date them as post-War. In narrative, though, these, and many others like them, could have been written in the 1840s, as if Stephen Foster and the 1850s had never been.

Minstrelsy's "Golden Era" extended through the 1870s. The shows got larger and larger, with thirty or more performers appearing together eventually. The move toward the "gigantic" show was a marketing ploy, a response to the many different types and varieties of stage entertainment that developed after the Civil War. Other theatrical strategies included the staging of all-female minstrel shows and, most significantly, blackface minstrelsy by black Americans, which is discussed more fully in chapter 5. It had been integral to the concept of early minstrelsy that white males masqueraded as blacks, to underscore the notion of "the mask" and what it meant to common people and their culture. But with the meaning of the mask obscured by the commercial development of the show and diluted by new audiences who did not share the same traditions, the original reason for blackface changed. And with that – and the novelty marketing angle – came the possibility that blacks themselves could be minstrels. The first important troupe of black minstrels, established in 1865, was called the Georgia Minstrels, who (strange as it may seem to us now) made famous *The Little Old Log Cabin in the Lane*. The best-known of the black minstrels was James Bland (1854–1911), born and reared a freedman in the North. He did not challenge minstrelsy's conventions; in fact his famous *Carry Me Back to Old Virginny* (1878) includes the lines:

> Massa and missis have long gone before me,
> Soon we will meet on that bright and golden shore,
> There we'll be happy and free from all sorrow,
> There's where we'll meet and we'll never part no more.

Emancipation (and death) might have split slave and master, but heaven would reunite them, presumably in some form of utopian enslavement! This is not to say that Bland condoned such a message, for he manifestly did not. With other African American minstrels he was generally unhappy over the derogatory representations he was compelled to fashion of his own race.

By the 1890s, though, African Americans on the American popular stage had become such a force that the development of musical theatre by and for blacks was possible. Like so much theatre of the nineteenth century, its germinal source was the minstrel show. In fact, the first important black production, *The Octoroon* (in 1895), was shaped like and only slightly more cohesive than a typical minstrel show. *Clorindy, The Origin of the Cakewalk* by Will Marion Cook (1869–1944) and *A Trip to Coontown* by Bob Cole (1863–1911) (the first musical written, directed, and performed by black artists) were both loosely joined, vaudeville-like productions. One notices from the titles that the subject matter, again like the minstrel shows, was ersatz African American culture. The music was more varied than that found in white musical theatre, primarily because black musicals expanded the range to include the new highly syncopated songs of the time, called "coon songs."

One other important new branch of the musical theatre was born out of the minstrel show. In 1865 the doors first opened to the New York City Opera House of Tony Pastor (1837–1908) and this ushered in the age of vaudeville. Like the post-bellum minstrel show it consisted of a range of entertainments, yet the point of reference was not race but ethnicity and urbanism. In 1871, Ned Harrigan (1844–1911), from the Irish neighborhoods of New York City and formerly a blackface minstrel, collaborated with Tony Hart (1855–1891) to develop further this new genre. Their "Mulligan Guard" skits featured many of the cultures then making up urban America, a reflection of their urban, working-class audience. The songs, usually by David Braham (1834–1905), were prototypical for the time, but emphasized the chorus and added a dash of brassy energy, suitable for a public, staged form of music. Harrigan, Hart, and Braham recognized that the American landscape was by then as much urban as rural, and their shows and songs were among the first to reflect this new truth.

The concert hall

Public and private musical lives met most frequently in the concert halls. There Americans ventured forth with their neighbors to enjoy the day's most noteworthy, compelling, topical, dynamic, or exciting popular music. The music did not stop with its concert performance, for as sheet music publishers had learned by the 1840s music popular on the concert stage (and in the theatre), if quickly made available as sheet music, would be purchased for private enjoyment in the home. This led, eventually, to an industry geared primarily toward the home market, which responded by consuming staggering volumes of sheet music, and generating commensu-rate profits. The publication of popular music shaped the genre in ways so different from that found uniquely in the public sphere that I will treat it independently below. At mid-century, though, many public and private concerns were shared, and performers and audiences reflected such. Not so much a time of contestation, it was still a time of dialogue.

Concerts had long been a part of American musical life. By many mea-sures, songs for the eighteenth-century American pleasure gardens fit the description for popular songs. Yet, to return to where we began here, *accessibility* to the pleasure gardens was limited, by economic means pri-marily but effectively by race and class as well. The early nineteenth century continued the trend, with concerts that were mainly for the upper reaches of society, and music simpler than art music, but based on it never-theless.

Arguably, concert music for the many began not with music-making, but with lecture-giving. The great lyceum movement of the early nine-teenth century brought knowledge and information to all kinds of Ameri-cans, big city and small, rich and poor. Generally, learned men (Ralph Waldo Emerson was a favorite) would travel a circuit delivering learned, informative, and entertaining public discourses on subjects of wide inter-est. Audiences paid handsomely for an opportunity to hear such a speaker. By the 1830s performers were emulating the success of the lyceum speak-ers by giving entertaining, engaging, and meaningful concerts for which they too received the gate receipts, often in gratifying amounts. The pivotal figure in this, and several subsequent and related developments, was Henry Russell (1812–1900).

Russell was a European cosmopolitan who could communicate with backwoods America. Born Jewish in provincial England, he was trained musically in London and Italy. Around 1835, he moved to Canada, then on shortly to Rochester, New York. Russell's innovation was to allay the sus-picions that many Americans held of the theatre by giving concerts with popular songs (usually composed by himself) that had some didactic quality, were morally uplifting, and were generally entertaining. A single concert might touch upon political history (*Charter Oak*), poverty and social responsibility (*A Christmas Carol*), emigration (*The Emigrant's Fare-well*), gambling (*The Gambler's Wife*), the ill-treatment of Indians (*The Indian Hunter*), westward migration (*A Life in the West*), marriage (*Not Married Yet?*), insane asylums (*The Maniac*), and temperance (*The 'Total Society*). To leaven the fare he included melodramatic or heroic songs that often featured histrionic display (*Land Ho!*, *A Life on the Ocean Wave*, *Ship on Fire*, *A Leap for Life*). Russell's concerts affirmed middle-class social values, such as respect for family (*The Old Arm Chair*), God and motherhood (*My Mother's Bible*), and nostalgic regard for the past (*Woodman, Spare that Tree*). Musically, many of his songs owed a great deal to the Italian opera style. Crowd-pleasers like *The Maniac* were dramatic and grand, like opera, with heightened moments of suspense.

Henry Russell had a special, perhaps unique, understanding of the American audience of the time. He worked up close to them, listened to them, and was one of the very few performers who composed his own songs, obviously designed specially for them. His charismatic qualities then carried the evening, leaving a hunger for more.

SINGING FAMILIES · Some of that was fed by a group of singers from the European Tyrol, the Rainer Family who came to the United States in 1839 and toured throughout the East until 1843. Their songs too were morally uplifting and spoke in their name and in their music of the importance of family, home, and domesticity. Their music was simpler than Russell's, derived largely from the four-part European glee, a tradition similar to one known to many Americans since the days of the eighteenth-century singing schools.

The Rainers' success produced a rage for groups of "singing families," one that has not entirely died even today. By far the most successful of them was the Hutchinson Family Singers, initially and most influentially a quartet of three brothers and a sister. Within a short time, beginning in the summer of 1842, they went from unrecognized to, by the end of 1843, probably the best-known and most-influential popular musicians in the nation. Millions heard them sing in the United States and Great Britain by the end of the decade; they were the toasts of "respectable" (i.e. middle-class), music-loving society everywhere. Their early songs were glees and ballads, like the Rainers'. Soon though, they wedded the insights of Henry Russell to the musical concepts of the Rainers, and began to compose their own songs, which generally meant to set new topical verses to old tunes, after a time-honored tradition found in much folk and church music. Among their "new" songs was that which became their signature song – *The Old Granite State*. Set to an old hymn tune, it introduced the singers, their histories, and proclaimed their views on a range of matters, political, social, and artistic.

Audiences came out by the thousands to hear extraordinary performances of the Hutchinsons' simple songs. Accounts of their singing are legion and unanimous in effusive praise. In part, reviewers loved their close, "sweet" blend, which the Hutchinsons had borrowed from a sound ideal then prevalent in New England church music. They sang in an open-throated, non-constricted style ("natural" some called it) that was new for the day; their sense of pitch was extraordinary; the texts were cleanly artic-ulated. Their songs were simple in melody, rhythm, harmony, and form, and were thoroughly accessible. Their stage manner was comfortable and casual. Altogether, these were performers and performances that respect-able audiences everywhere loved deeply, not from curiosity for some exotic other-ness (such as was the case with minstrelsy), but because this was fine music made by good and decent neighborly family folk. Their values and those of the audience were shared in many regards, especially when it came to directness of expression, respect for simple values, and the centrality of home and family. And beyond that was patriotism, for the Hutchinsons were among the first to herald that their music was by Americans, specially for Americans. Typically all the songs on their programs touched on Amer-ican values, hopes, and ideals in some form.

Like Henry Russell, the Hutchinsons combined entertainment with their audience's insatiable commitment to knowledge and its acquisition. At the heart of their concerts were the social issues of the day: temperance, women's rights, communal living, dress reform, food reform, medical reform, and, most explosively, abolitionism. They took stances in favor of these issues in their lives and on the stage, alienating some no doubt, but convincing others through the sheer dynamic force of their commitment. The Hutchinsons lived in a time of transition, from when understanding was public and communal, where the world was interpreted by authorities (usually religious), to a modern age that centered the private rights and responsibilities of the individual and privileged scientific endeavor, where knowledge was non-canonic and change was possible, even desirable. Their songs addressed the period's complex and exciting relationship with understanding, and drove home the belief that popular music should both reflect and shape the day's political, social, and cultural discourse.

Music of the private sphere

Music for private spaces has been found in Western culture since the late Renaissance. But the idea that private music could also be widely popular was largely a phenomenon of the nineteenth century. That "private" and "popular" are seemingly contradictory only points up the ambiguity and paradox that has come to characterize the nineteenth century (indeed, "Romanticism" is built on it) and the confusion that society had toward the roles of its citizens. It was, after all, the first century that held that captains of industry, politicians, and other powerful, emphatically public men, were at base private individuals.

The *Irish Melodies* of Thomas Moore (1779–1852), published in seven volumes beginning in 1808, were the first popular songs that achieved important status in the private world. They were "melodies" written by an Irish poet about his beloved homeland (although he chose to live in England all his adult life), generally employing a wistful, nostalgic tone, about a past that, ironically, no-one really wanted to reclaim. The beauty of the music (generally borrowed traditional folksongs set in arrangement by leading musicians of the day) overrode any confusion of purpose in the texts, though, and established a standard for songs of the home in both the British Isles and the United States. Featuring melodies that were pentatonic (or functionally pentatonic), of gracefully etched contours produced by generally conjunct motion with a characteristic leap to a climactic note, this style has come to signify much of that which is associated with the home and the private sphere: sentimentalism, nostalgia, femininity, leisure, emotionalism, and, one might argue, a certain confusion about place and purpose.

John Hill Hewitt (1801–1890) was the first American songwriter to develop a style of popular music intended for the private sphere. He combined characteristics of Moore's songs with those of the English pleasure-garden style. The narratives are simple and direct; the music is usually in the major key, with diatonic melodies; the rhythms are square-cut, predictable. Hewitt's most successful effort in this vein was *The Minstrel's Return'd from the War*, published in 1825. This song told a compelling story relevant to the experiences of many Americans who knew the sacrifices of those who fought in the War of Independence and the War of 1812. In it, a musician-soldier goes once again to war, to protect his family and his nation against outside aggression. Musically, the song was not complicated, and easy enough for modest talents. Stylistically, it is of a type that came to characterize songs for the parlor, the room in the nineteenth-century middle-class home that most signified the private sphere. An eight-measure introduction for the keyboard (piano, at this time) establishes the key, meter, and mood; the song's melody is revealed in the verse, of a shape somewhat like those found in the *Irish Melodies*; phrases are

regular and complementary; only three harmonies are employed throughout: the tonic, subdominant, and dominant. In addition to being a fine and
important musician, Hewitt was also a businessman; his father had been a
leading musician and music publisher of the generation before. Like all
successful businessmen, Hewitt learned his patrons (or audience in this
case) and gave them what they wanted. He kept his product up-to-date by
constantly reinvigorating it with new ideas and by incorporating new stylistic developments. And as middle-class Americans came more and more to
venerate the family as the cornerstone social unit, Hewitt was there with
music expressing that point of view. There is no more important American
songwriter for establishing the style most appropriate for the private
sphere.

The 1830s and 1840s saw important contributions to home music from
performer-songwriters like Henry Russell and the Hutchinson Family.
But these, and most other songwriters of that time, were performers first
and composers second. Publishers solicited their songs for the home sheet
music market primarily because of reputations gained in concert halls;
sheet music covers regularly trumpeted the names of performers associated with the songs in much larger print than that accorded the songwriters.

By the 1850s, though, a single name, that of a composer alone, stands
above all else. It is hard to overstate Stephen Foster's importance for the
development of parlor music, as it is hard to do so for his minstrel music.
He was one of the first to realize that music for the private sphere was
inherently more profitable than that for the public, over which copyright
laws of the time offered little protection to those not the performers of
their own songs. Perhaps as a result of his insight, he wrote many more
songs for the home than he did for the minstrel show. Many of these were
modeled after the *Irish Melodies*. (In fact, early in his career Foster sometimes used the pseudonym "Milton Moore," combining the names of two
beloved poets.) Favorites like *Sweetly she Sleeps, my Alice Fair*, *Comrades, Fill
no Glass for Me*, *Gentle Annie*, and *Jeanie with the Light Brown Hair* all have
romantic, melancholic, often nostalgic texts that sometimes border on the
morose. The melodies are usually functionally pentatonic, or are derived
from Italian opera styles, which themselves are stylistically similar to
Moore's melodies (and vice versa, of course). The well-known *Beautiful
Dreamer* would be perfectly appropriate in a period opera. And Foster's
Wilt Thou Be Gone, Love?, a setting of the balcony scene from *Romeo and
Juliet*, is shaped much like an operatic *scena*. But whether the music was

Irish or Italian, the audience was American, and Foster seemed to know instinctively that American popular songs were most successful when they were synthesized from musical and textual materials at hand, already known and loved by the audience. Knitting everything together into an undeniable whole was a remarkable feel for melody, something of the order of what is sometimes called genius. In all likelihood, the songs of Stephen Foster were and are the most-loved, world-over, of any composer from any time and place.

If Foster fully established the genre of parlor song, it was the Civil War that consolidated it. No event is more significant in the social and political history of the United States. It is not surprising then, that the country's culture would reflect so starkly emotions generated and heightened by that cataclysmic conflict. The nation was a singing nation then, and song was the vessel into which many Americans poured their greatest hopes and fears. These were, furthermore, songs for the home – the theatres found the scale of the war unmanageable – where private citizens grappled with the horrors of a nation divided violently against itself.

There are three major categories of Civil War songs. Musically, they all share certain general characteristics: attention-grabbing, repetitious melodic germs, supported by straightforward harmonic schemes, a verse-chorus format, with the chorus carrying the primary melodic material, and march-like rhythms spiced with moderate amounts of syncopation. The first group, not surprisingly, consists of patriotic songs. Two stand above all others in the manner in which they expressed regional loyalties. *The Battle Hymn of the Republic*, set to a text by Julia Ward Howe (1819–1910) and a tune by William Steffe, is just what it purported to be – a rousing "battle hymn" that led the righteous in their crusade against those unfavored by God. *Dixie*, attributed to Ohioan Dan Emmett, was originally an exuberant walkaround for a minstrel show finale. The South appropriated it presumably for its flag-waving, foot-stomping expressions of joy in place. Honorable mention must surely go to *The Battle Cry of Freedom* by Unionist George F. Root (1820–1895) and *The Bonnie Blue Flag* by southerner Harry Macarthy (1834–1888).

Songs about soldiering form the second group. Many of these provided comic relief of a sort by commenting on military food (*Goober Peas*, *The Old Army Bean*). Others were deadly serious and helped those at home deal with the conditions endured by their soldiering fathers, brothers, and sons. Root's *Tramp! Tramp! Tramp!*, or the Prisoner's Hope was about being a prisoner-of-war, and supposedly sold 100,000 copies. *Tenting on the Old Camp*

Ground by Walter Kittredge (1834–1905) spoke of the side of war that was not glory, but suffering, pain, misery, and death. Ultimately, it spoke of hope – a hope for peace. Even the defining reality of soldiering was confronted in song. John Hill Hewitt's *All Quiet Along the Potomac Tonight* is about a lonely, frightened, innocent sentry, far from home, who dies from a single gunshot in the still of the night. The official report ignores his ultimate sacrifice: "Not an officer lost! Only one of the men . . . All quiet along the Potomac tonight." These lines are sung to a bitterly bland, even ironic, piece of brilliant melody-making. *The Drummer Boy of Shiloh* by Will S. Hays spoke of the cruel death of an innocent child. Central to the effect, though, were the child's last thoughts: of home, of family, of God, all affirmations of important middle-class values. Other songs were expressions of love, and many tended to idealize womanhood (*Aura Lea, Lorena*), establishing a standard that would prevail for decades after the War.

The third group consisted of songs for the domestic front. Composers and publishers on both sides of the conflict composed and printed songs for home consumption. There were differences in styles and perspectives, though. Southern songs tended more toward abstract idealization, set in a kind of pastoral paradise, and musically were throwbacks to earlier styles, such as that of the pleasure garden. Northern songs were more cosmopolitan in outlook and preached an urban sophistication, although they were still anchored in middle-class values like reverence for privacy, individualism, family, paternalism, marriage, homelife, and Christianity. Of the latter, Root's *Just Before the Battle Mother* reassured those at home that the boys in the field thought first of them. *Weeping Sad and Lonely* by Henry Tucker (1826–1882) carried the sheet music dedication: "Inscribed to sorrowing hearts at Home," and gave those at home a sense of shared loss and affirmed the value of their enterprise, which was to preserve the hearth flame for the ultimate return of the triumphant warriors.

With northern victory came the ascendance of northern values and styles over southern. After 1865, popular music was understood to be of northern origin and aspect. In the South, one might find important developments in white sacred or folk music and in African American music generally, but not in popular music. The South would wait until 1955 and the era of rock and roll before again claiming a major role in the story of American popular music.

Popular music entered something of a "classical era" in the period after the Civil War. A standard song-form was arrived at: a keyboard introduction prepared the principal melodic idea; the verse was sixteen measures

long, with four complementary melodic phrases; the lyrics were organized into two to four verses; the song climaxed in a four-part vocal
chorus; and it was closed off with a short keyboard postlude. One songwriter of the generation after Foster stands above the rest: Henry Clay
Work (1832-1884). His war period songs earned him his first fame.
Kingdom Coming and *Marching through Georgia* were each immensely
popular. But *Grandfather's Clock* (of 1875) was likely his most popular,
with perhaps 800,000 copies sold. Musically, the song was prototypical.
Textually, it tells the story of a man's life and affirms the value of hard
work, materialism, timeliness, and, predictably, family, home, and religious values. Other important and popular songs were *Whispering Hope* by
Alice Hawthorne (pseud. for Septimus Winner, 1827-1902), Henry
Tucker's *Sweet Genevieve*, *Silver Threads Among the Gold* by H. P. Danks
(1834-1903), and *I'll Take You Home Again, Kathleen* by Thomas P. West-
endorf (1848-1923).

The 1880s found popular song little different stylistically from that of
the 1870s. The biggest change was in the development of the industry.
Through the 1870s publishers and dealers offered a wide range of styles
and genres. A publisher like Oliver Ditson of Boston sold songs, piano
pieces, arrangements, sonatas, opera scores, instrumental and vocal
instructors, and so on. But the firms of Thomas B. Harms (established in
1881) and M. Witmark & Sons (1885) published only popular songs. Able
now to concentrate their attention on a single, highly profitable publishing niche, publishers like these developed great efficiencies of production
and marketing, and as a result, popular music became a very big business
indeed.

Just how big (and how profitable) it remained for the 1890s to discover.
Charles K. Harris's *After the Ball* first received wide attention when it was
interpolated into *A Trip to Chinatown* in 1892. One of many waltz-songs of
the period, it is a sentimental narrative about mistaken identity and a life
without marriage, for that period and the audience one of the most tragic
of consequences. Although finely crafted, it hardly seems that it exceptionally deserved to sell as many as 5 million copies, perhaps making it the most
popular song of the period. Harris shrewdly declined to sell the rights to an
established publisher, choosing rather to publish and distribute it himself.
This one song made him a wealthy man, as all the unshared profits flowed
into his coffers. His publishing house, which not surprisingly featured
songs by Harris (*Just Behind the Times*, 1896, *Hello Central, Give Me Heaven*
of 1901; each sold perhaps a million copies), located in New York City,

helped establish that city as the heart of popular music publishing and set the industry standard. Only one other songwriter of the period – Paul Dresser (1857–1906) – approached his entrepreneurial skills; and Dresser's songwriting abilities might well have exceeded his. Although Dresser's best-known songs were kin in many ways with the sentimental ballads of the Civil War period, *On the Banks of the Wabash* and *My Gal Sal* featured more complex "modern" harmonies and greater attention to the chorus. A whole "cycle" of Dresser's song (such as *Just Tell Them that You Saw Me* and *She Went to the City*) dealt with problems special to urbanism.

As the private sphere became more institutionalized in American life, its relationship with the public sphere became weaker. Home and work assumed ever more separate identities. Musically, the parlor cut its connection to the music of the concert hall and theatre; and instead of the theatre or concert hall introducing Americans to their favorite music, music teachers – who were necessarily located in population centers – became the conduit. The privacy of the studio, which functioned in many ways like the parlor, insured the insularity of the style. While forms and genres proliferated on America's stage, propelled by the forces of pluralism as a surge of immigration further enriched the ethnic and racial mix that was America, music of the private sphere became whiter, more middle-class, and more homogeneous. As a result of middle-class economic clout, publishers and composers directed ever more of their attention to the parlor and the studio; by 1870 about 250,000 pieces of music were available for sale in the United States, most for consumption in the private sphere.

The social context influenced too the rise of the piano in American musical life. Publishers had long assumed a place for the keyboard in song production, but mainly as rudimentary accompaniment; the emphasis was clearly on the voice. But as private studio teachers proliferated, especially after the Civil War, so likewise did solo pianists. American piano manufacturers did their parts as well, and by the 1870s they set the world standard for both total output and quality. Therefore, music in quantity was needed for those who played their parlor pianos. One can practically trace the capabilities of parlor pianists through this literature alone. In mid-century, relatively easy-to-play dances – waltzes, polkas, mazurkas, schottisches – were in favor, as were variations on well-known songs. Soon, though, quasi-virtuosic pieces began to appear in great number, often with provocative titles like *The Last Hope* and *The Banjo* both by Louis Moreau Gottschalk (1829–1869). By century's end, millions of amateurs, generally women, were playing in their parlors quite capably a wide range of piano literature, and conceiving of it as popular music for the piano.

*

With the triumph of the parlor piano, lines drawn between sets of seeming polarities are completed – such as, from the public to the private, the voice and the instrument, technology and human experience. But in all these, as in many other such dialectical pairings, the ends should more appropriately be drawn up, into a circle, for while this is a story about the American veneration for the marketplace, where music became a commodity that was subjected to a sophisticated process in the hopes of widescale consumption, hence profit (arguably the world's first music with such an intention), the quasi-industrial product seemed then (and seems yet today) to lie near a primal point where human beings found identity, community, meaning, and happiness. By so doing, somewhat ironically, the popular music of nineteenth-century America can and often does mark for the cultural historian those gripping moments when social or intellectual pretensions were dropped in favor of visceral joy and pleasure, thus (unintentionally?) revealing baseline human (and historical) truths and values, moments in musical lives when fun should be taken with profound seriousness.

8

Art music from 1800 to 1860

KATHERINE K. PRESTON

In 1780, John Adams wrote home from Paris to his wife Abigail:

> I could fill volumes with descriptions of temples and palaces, paintings, sculpture, tapestry, porcelain, etc., if I could have the time, but I could not do this without neglecting my duty. My duty is to study the science of government that my sons may have the liberty to study mathematics and science. My sons ought to study geography, navigation, commerce, and agriculture in order to give their children a right to study philosophy, painting, poetry, music, architecture, sculpture, tapestry, and porcelain.
>
> (Quoted in Mueller 1951, p. 17)

Adams's prescience – at least concerning music – was remarkably accurate: it was not until the mid-1840s, when his grandson Charles Francis Adams was a young adult, that musical culture in America came of age. Music, of course, had been an important part of American life during the Colonial and early Federal periods. But the 1840s marked the United States's emergence as a true music-supporting nation, equipped with the infrastructure necessary for the performing arts. With that development, musical culture could only grow, as it did throughout the 1850s.

Because the American musical environment changed so significantly after the mid-1840s, this chapter is divided into two parts. The first half introduces the situation at the dawn of the century and explores the foundation-building endeavors of the 1810s through the mid-1840s; the second covers the context and circumstances of musical activity in the mid-1840s and 1850s. The period from 1800 to 1860 was crucial for American music history; during those decades Americans laid the foundation for the subsequent cultivation of music in their country. For that reason alone, the first half of the century deserves close scrutiny.

The foundations

The beginning of the century

Written secular music in early-nineteenth-century America was European music. As was noted in chapter 3, colonial Americans had always looked to England, Spain, or France for cultural inspiration, and this orientation continued well into the nineteenth century. This artistic reliance is clearly reflected in the fact that around 1800, almost all of the well known, active, secular composers and performers were immigrants.[1] The vast majority were British, including George K. Jackson, James Hewitt, Rayner Taylor, Alexander Reinagle, Benjamin Carr, and Charles Gilfert; a few others – like Gottlieb Graupner and Victor Pelissier – were from Germany and France. Most of these individuals (and others) had arrived in the United States in the mid-1790s. This sizable influx of skilled European musicians just prior to the dawn of the century obviously would have considerable impact on American musical development.

Immigrant musicians brought European music with them; once established, they set up music businesses: firms to import and sell European compositions and instruments; music publishing houses; establishments to manufacture instruments. Musical cultivation in the early Republic, in fact, was first and foremost a business, and in a manner that differed significantly from that in Europe. European musicians, of course, were learning to deal with changing conditions, for at the start of the nineteenth century the box-office system of patronage was beginning to compete with the traditional court- and church-based systems. In America, however, there had never been aristocratic courts or a powerful state-supported church to sustain music; rather, music had always been a commercial endeavor, and professional musicians had to find or create music-related jobs. As a result, American musicians were jacks-of-all-musical-trades: they held steady jobs in the theatre or as church organists; established music businesses; organized concerts and acted as impresarios; founded performing societies and organizations; taught; composed. A brief examination of the careers of three such musician-immigrants – Benjamin Carr, Gottlieb Graupner, and James Hewitt – should suffice as examples.

1. There were also, of course, many native-born Americans active as composers, but mostly of sacred music. William Billings, Timothy Swan, Daniel Read, and other composers of the First New England School are discussed in chapter 4.

Benjamin Carr (1768–1831) immigrated from London in 1793 and for almost forty years had his fingers in various musical pies. He appeared as an actor and singer with the Old American Company in New York in the 1790s; was organist at several churches in Philadelphia; managed, organized, or performed in concerts; helped to found the Musical Fund Society; established an important American music publishing firm; taught; and wrote many compositions, including sacred pieces, piano compositions, songs, and operas and incidental music for many plays.

Gottlieb Graupner (1767–1836) of Hanover immigrated from London in 1795. He moved from Canada to Charleston and performed in the city's theatre orchestra. In 1797 he and his wife, the actress-singer Catherine Comerford Graupner (c. 1769/1772–1821), settled in Boston, where both worked in the theatre. Graupner eventually became one of the most important music businessmen in Boston as an instrument seller and music publisher. He also taught various instruments, served as leader of the Boston Philoharmonic Society (1809–1824), and helped to found the Boston Handel and Haydn Society. He composed songs, instrumental works, and pedagogical compositions. Catherine Graupner was also an important Boston musician; in addition to her theatrical work, she sang in oratorios, benefit concerts, and for the Handel and Haydn Society.

James Hewitt (1770–1827) arrived in 1792, and until 1808 was the musical director and conductor of the New York Park Theatre orchestra; he also organized many concerts. From 1811 until 1816 he had similar theatre duties in Boston, where he was also a church organist, composer, teacher, and publisher. In the 1820s Hewitt traveled between Boston and New York, and also toured the South. He was a publisher, a teacher, and a composer. His best-known compositions, such as *The Battle of Trenton*, are for the piano. Four of James and Eliza Hewitt's six children enjoyed musical careers: their eldest son, John Hill (1801–1890), became a successful composer of musical-dramatic works and songs (he was later known as "the bard of the Confederacy"); James Lang (1803–1853) and George Washington (1811–1893) became a music publisher and a teacher/composer, respectively; Sophia (1799–1845), an accomplished performer and teacher, was one of the few professional women musicians active in America during the period. She later toured New England with her husband, the violinist Louis Ostinelli.

I single out these three not because they were extraordinary, but because their musical infrastructure-creating activities were so typical. As the musical directors of theatres, organizers of concerts series, teachers, and musical businessmen, these immigrants were the most visible, powerful, and active members of the secular musical profession in America during the early decades of the century.

And what of American-born musicians? If we had to rely on the historical record for names, we would have to conclude that there were precious few. But historical invisibility, as we have learned from African American and women's studies, does not necessarily mean nonexistence. And there were, in fact, countless anonymous American-born performers active at the beginning of the century. They were the rank-and-file musicians: the members of bands, theatre orchestras, and singing societies; the amateur and professional performers in subscription concerts, church choirs, and benefits. They were, in effect, the nucleus of American musical life.

The extent of Americans' musical activity is suggested by a brief examination of some of the musical organizations that sprang up during this period. The urge to establish such ensembles had commenced in the mid-eighteenth century; by the early nineteenth it was a fairly persistent impulse. For example, between 1800 and 1825 in the Boston area alone there were numerous independent musical organizations, including the Franklin, Lock Hospital, Norfolk, Essex, and Massachusetts musical societies; the Handel and Haydn, St. Cecilia, and Lockhart Singing societies; the Boston Musical Association. This list, of course, does not include church musical societies or choirs (Broyles 1991, p. 138). Nor were musical associations limited to large cities like Boston. In 1807 an Apollian Society was formed in Pittsburgh; in 1809 Providence residents founded the Psallonian Society; in 1814 a Handel Society of Maine appeared in Portland. Although many of these organizations were ephemeral, others were long-lived. Many ensembles included both amateur and professional performers, for the transition to fully professional ensembles (mostly instrumental groups) occurred gradually during the nineteenth century. The most common instrumental ensembles (either professional or amateur) of the period were woodwind bands.

Americans were also prodigious consumers of music. They attended theatrical performances, where they saw entertaining plays full of diverting music. They went to concerts that included such works as traditional Irish or Scottish songs, themes and variations or battle pieces for the fortepiano, operatic arias translated into English, and overtures or movements from symphonies by Haydn, Pleyel, or J. C. Bach. They danced to bands and heard these ensembles in parades and concerts. They played chamber music in their homes. They heard and sang music in church, and attended and performed in concerts by the amateur organizations mentioned above. Americans also – with increasingly regularity – purchased sheet music arrangements of operatic arias, traditional tunes, popular ballads, theatre songs, and piano pieces, and performed this music. The goal of all this activity was amusement and entertainment, which introduces a crucial point: all music – with the possible exception of most sacred music – was first and foremost entertainment.

Romanticism

That music was amusing, diverting, and entertaining during this period is an extremely important concept. Also crucial is a realization that the clearcut categorical differences so dear to us today (distinctions of classical/art *versus* popular/vernacular and – to a lesser extent – of sacred *versus* secular musics) do not work well when applied to this historical period.

During this period all music (excepting sacred) was entertaining; all music (including sacred) was functional. No music (again possibly excepting sacred) bore the implications generally associated today with art or "classical" music: as morally uplifting, superior to "popular" music, and somewhat exclusive. All of these implications – which eventually became associated with a particular repertory – were outgrowths of German Romanticism, the nineteenth-century philosophical movement. Of course, neither Europeans nor Americans of the period lumped all musics together into one large indistinguishable heap. They passed judgment on musical works: some were clearly superior and were considered durable and long-lasting (although, of course, most music was newly or recently composed); other compositions were obviously ephemeral. It was performance venues rather than compositions *per se* that were viewed as hierarchical: one type of activity might be considered more "high class" than another, but the evaluation was of the music's *function*, not its inherent quality.

To use as one example a piece that today is considered inherently "classical": a symphony movement by Haydn. This work could be performed by an orchestra at, say, a Philadelphia subscription concert attended by the town's social elite. This venue would be regarded as "high class," because a concert to which admission was purchased by subscription was, by definition, exclusive. The same composition, however, as arranged for piano four-hands, could be played rather bumptiously on a parlor piano at a party or after dinner – performance contexts that are neither exclusive nor "high class." That the latter performance was of a transcription is also significant, for the commonplace modification of compositions during this period suggests clearly that the works themselves had not yet acquired the sacrosanct status of "artwork," another Romantic period concept.

This all started to change during the early nineteenth century. Some music began to be regarded as "art" and some composers as "artists," the latter idea a manifestation of the cult of genius, another Romantic notion. These new perceptions of music and musicians contrast markedly with the traditional view of music as craft and musicians as craftsmen. Of course these changes involving music were only a small part of the huge social and cultural transformations that were occurring in the first half of the nine-teenth century, for this was a period of tremendous social, cultural, and technological change; a time of political revolutions, of the expansion of industry and technology, and of massive urbanization. The philosophical or cultural shifts that occurred did so as result of myriad interconnected factors, and even a cursory examination of them is too involved for our pur-poses. Suffice it to say, however, that the nature and function of music began to undergo significant and long-lasting changes during this period, and that it became possible to regard different kinds of music as "art" or "non-art," as edifying and morally uplifting or "merely" entertaining; this theme is further elaborated in chapter 9. For the time being, however, the crucial word is "began." For although we will return to this topic, it is important to emphasize here that the shift took place gradually and affected only some music-lovers. The vast majority of Americans contin-ued to regard music as an entertaining, diverting, and pleasing pastime throughout the ante-bellum period.

The 1820s and 1830s

During the second, third, and fourth decades of the nineteenth century, the United States grew significantly in both population and landmass. Nine states were added to the Union, which almost doubled the landmass occupied by the twenty-six states; population increased by over 30 percent in each decade from 1800 to 1830. The frontier was pushed ever westward, the economy grew, and so did the transportation system. By the mid-1820s all major cities in the northern and eastern states were connected by turn-pikes and surfaced roads. There was a canal-building boom in the 1820s (the Erie Canal opened in 1825) and some railroads began operations in the 1830s. Transportation by steamboat proliferated on Lakes Ontario and Erie and on the major rivers; it also became significantly cheaper during the period. The cost of passage from New Orleans to Louisville, for example, decreased by nearly 50 percent between 1825 ($50) and the 1830s ($25–30), and the cost of travel between Cincinnati and Pittsburgh dropped from $12 in 1825 to $5 in the 1840s (Morris 1976, p. 602). Cities like Pittsburgh, Cincinnati, Louisville, and St. Louis became transportation hubs for the shipment of raw materials to the coasts for export. A direct consequence of the expanding transportation network was an explosion in the size of established coastal cities: between 1800 and 1830 the population of New York grew from 60,000 to 202,500; Philadelphia went from 70,000 to 167,300; Boston from 25,000 to 61,400; Baltimore from 26,500 to 80,600; New Orleans from 8,000 (1803) to 46,300.

This urban growth resulted in a real proliferation of musical activities. More and larger cities meant more theatres and halls where concerts could be held; an improved transportation network allowed easier access to American towns and cities for traveling performers. Furthermore, there was concomitant growth in the middle class – that socioeconomic group most likely to attend performances, purchase sheet music, buy instruments from the ever-growing numbers of American instrument builders, or hire musicians to teach their sons and (in particular) their daughters.

American women became an increasingly important part of the music-supporting public. The numbers of women who were music students, purchasers of music and instruments, or members of audiences or performing ensembles, grew steadily, especially as music became ever more integrated with the social meaning of femininity (Tick 1983, p. 7). The changing role of the family in a progressively industrialized and urbanized America contributed to this phenomenon: the role of women was gradually more relegated to the home and to the family circle. Music, which in the eighteenth century had been an accomplishment for upper-class women, was now considered an appropriate home-related activity and a suitable pastime for middle-class females (Tick 1983, pp. 21–31). Starting in the 1830s, in fact, private girls' schools – where many young American women were educated – were the major employers of music teachers in the United States (Tick 1983, p. 33). During this same period, ladies' magazines, many of which were chock-full of both sheet music and information about music, proliferated. Both fueled an already-burgeoning female interest in music's cultivation and support (Miller 1994, pp. 156–166); the importance of this development during the second half of the century is discussed in chapter 9.

Performing organizations continued to materialize in the 1820s and 1830s all over the country. A few of the many include the Philadelphia

Musical Fund Society (1820), the Sacred Music Society in New York City (1823), the Philharmonic Society of New Orleans (1824), the New York Choral Society (1824), the Handel and Haydn (1828) and Mozart Musical societies (1832) of Portland, Maine, the *Männerchor* and the *Junger Männerchor* in Philadelphia (both 1835), the Portland Sacred Music Society (1836), the Philharmonic Orchestra of St. Louis and the St. Louis Musical Fund Society (both 1838), the Negro Philharmonic Society of New Orleans (late 1830s), the Richmond (Virginia) Sacred Music Society (1830s), and the St. Louis Sacred Music Society (1840). A list in *The Euterpiad* of the numerous performances that occurred during one week in May 1821 suggests that organized musical activity was widespread:

> A concert of sacred music by the Beethoven Society at Portland (Me.), a grand concert at Augusta (Ga.), a select oratorio at Providence by the Psallonian Society, a grand concert of music by the Philadelphia Musical Fund, the grand oratorio the "Creation" by the Harmonic Society of Baltimore, a performance of sacred music by the New-Hampshire Musical Society at Hanover, in Boston an instrumental and vocal concert for the benefit of Mr. Ostinelli, and a public oratorio by the Handel and Haydn Society.
>
> (Quoted in Ritter 1890, p. 145)

Ritter dismissed the significance of various "musical entertainments . . . given by local musical societies" as "only of local importance, exercising little influence outside the city limits" (Ritter 1890, p. 134). Music historians today, however, believe that history is a sum of many parts and welcome such information (incomplete as it is) as evidence of a thriving and growing musical culture in the United States.

Musical immigrants and visitors

Musical immigrants continued to arrive in the States during this period, and they either quickly became associated with established ensembles or launched their own. Britain continued to contribute incoming musicians, but the complexion of the American musical landscape was gradually becoming more cosmopolitan, including more French-, Italian-, and (especially) German-speaking performers, teachers, composers, and conductors. The clear connection between immigrants and organized musical activity can be demonstrated by mere mention of some of the more prominent newcomers and their relationships to American performing organizations: Charles Zuener arrived from Germany in the 1820s and promptly became associated with the Boston Handel and Haydn Society. George Loder, an English conductor and composer (arrived 1836) and

Henry Christian Timm, a German pianist (arrived 1835), would both be founding members of the New York Philharmonic Society (1842). Eugène-Prosper Prévost, from France, was conductor of the orchestra at the Théâtre d'Orléans from 1838 to 1859. Leopold Meignen, also French, became conductor of the Philadelphia Musical Fund Society. The German conductor William Robyn settled in St. Louis in 1837 and was associated with the Philharmonic Society, the Brass Band, and the Polyhymnia Orchestra there. Charles Balmer, another German (arrived 1836), also settled in St. Louis, where he worked with the Sacred Music and Oratorio societies and founded a music publishing firm.

In the 1810s the stream of immigrant musicians was greatly augmented by itinerant European virtuosos. The first wave of performers to visit America consisted of singers. Among the earliest were Charles Incledon and Thomas Philipps, both British singers who arrived in 1817 to perform in operas (in local theatres) and in concerts. They were followed in the 1820s by a host of mostly-British vocal stars, who performed on the theatrical circuit. The most important were the soprano Elizabeth Austin, who performed in America from 1827 to 1835, and Joseph and Mary Anne Paton Wood, from Covent Garden and the Italian Opera (London), who delighted Americans from 1833 to 1836 and again in the early 1840s. These singers both acquainted American audiences with Italian melody and opened the floodgates to other stars of opera in English: in the late 1830s Jane Shirreff, John Wilson, and Anne and Edward Seguin all arrived in the States and created their own furors. Meanwhile, Americans also heard opera in French and Italian. In 1825 the Spanish tenor Manuel García and his family (including his daughter, later known as Maria Malibran), visited New York for a year and performed the country's first operas in Italian. Two years later John Davis's French Opera Company of New Orleans made the first of six annual pilgrimages to the north, performing French operas on the East Coast. Other short-lived Italian companies were formed, performed widely, and disbanded in the 1830s; the Havana Opera Company first visited New Orleans in 1837.

Opera and operatic music had a pronounced effect on American musical culture. One contemporary commentator claimed in 1847 that Austin and the Woods had "made the citizens of these United States [fall] in love with music" (quoted in Preston 1993a, p. 19). Staged operas, of course, easily fit into an American theatrical world that already included comic and ballad operas, pantomimes, and melodramas. But the introduction of Italian melody itself – in concert and on the stage – was electrifying. Americans became infatuated, and developed an almost-insatiable demand for it: in mounted operas, concerts (in Italian or English), and in instrumental arrangements of "gems from the operas." Eventually Americans would laugh at operatic burlesques by blackface minstrels, dance quadrilles to arrangements of opera tunes, perform operatic airs in their parlors, and sing Italianate melodies by composers like Stephen Foster (1826–1864) and Henry Russell (1812–1900). The visiting singers, however, introduced more than operatic music to Americans: they also introduced higher performance standards. And as audiences were exposed to performers of increasingly high caliber, their levels of expectation increased; this, in turn, meant that managers had to engage better performers. This pattern of increased levels of expectation, introduced in the 1820s and 1830s, would continue throughout the ante-bellum period, especially with the arrival in subsequent decades of additional European vocal and instrumental virtuosos.

American composers and performers

Home-grown American performers began to appear during the late 1810s and early 1820s. The first such soloists were bandsmen, which is perfectly understandable since bands continued to be the most popular and ubiquitous of instrumental ensembles. One of the first such virtuosos was the keyed bugle player Edward Kendall (1808–1861), a native of Providence. Kendall performed in Boston in the Tremont Theatre orchestra and the Brigade Band; in 1835 he formed the Boston Brass Band, one of the earliest and most popular ensembles of the phenomenally successful nineteenth-century American brass band movement. Another important American performer associated with bands – and also a keyed-bugle player – was Frank Johnson (1792–1844), who is discussed in chapter 5.

The most prominent American composer of this period was Anthony Philip Heinrich (1781–1861). Although born in Bohemia, he is generally regarded as an American composer because he became a professional musician only after his immigration. Heinrich was in Philadelphia in 1817 when he learned that his business had collapsed in Europe. He had always liked music, but his decision to embark on a musical career in America is rather astonishing. A firm believer in the Romantic view of art as self-expression, Heinrich was completely undaunted by his own lack of formal training, and headed West, searching for solitude in the wilds of nature. By 1818 he was living in a Kentucky log cabin, teaching himself the rudiments of composition; he emerged to publish *The Dawning of Music in Kentucky, or,*

The Pleasures of Harmony in the Solitudes of Nature (1820), a quirky collection of forty-six vocal and instrumental compositions. This work was quickly followed by *The Western Minstrel* (1820) and *The Sylviad, or, Minstrelsy of Nature in the Wilds of North America* (two volumes, 1823, 1825–1826).

A prodigious composer, Heinrich was well known in the United States; some critics referred to him (rather grandiosely) as the "Beethoven of America." He once claimed as his goal the creation of an indigenous American style of instrumental and vocal composition. His music is eccentric, often complex and ornate, and sometimes coarse and unpolished. The piano works are highly embellished and full of difficult and unidiomatic passages, chromaticisms, and unconventional harmonies. The music is rarely developmental; rather, it is often intuitive, additive, and sectional (he preferred theme and variations and dance forms). In some ways, however, Heinrich's compositional style also foreshadows techniques adopted by twentieth-century composers. For example, *The Banjo* (from the *Barbecue Divertimento* for piano), an evocative recreation of an improvising banjoist, is essentially a stream-of-consciousness composition. Heinrich was also fond of quotation, both of his own work and of popular and patriotic tunes; like Charles Ives (1874–1954), he often used this technique for programmatic purposes.

A quintessential Romantic, Heinrich regarded nature as the wellspring of artistic creativity. His programmatic compositions (descriptive pieces, autobiographical songs, short piano works, and symphonies) are also aesthetically attuned to the avant-garde style of Romantic composition. All of his large orchestral works are programmatic, and they reflect his love of the American wilderness (*The War of the Elements and the Thundering of Niagara* [before 1845]), interest in animals (*The Ornithological Combat of Kings, or the Condor of the Andes and the Eagle of the Cordilleras* [1847]), and fascination with American Indians (*Pushmataha, a Venerable Chief of a Western Tribe of Indians* [1831]). As one of the first prolific composers of orchestral music in America, Heinrich experienced great difficulty having his works performed. During this period most orchestral concerts were given by pick-up ensembles assembled for the occasion, and most of Heinrich's orchestral performances were by such ensembles, organized and paid for by the composer. Heinrich made several extended visits back to Europe, where his work was known and performed, but he considered himself an American. He was regarded with affection by the American musical press, which attempted to drum up financial support for him during his final, impoverished years in New York.

Singing societies and sacred music

Next to bands, singing societies were by far the most popular American performing organizations in the 1820s and 1830s. To a great extent, these societies filled the same social need that singing schools had satisfied in the eighteenth century. This interest in amateur vocal performance, of course, was not peculiarly American: choral societies were similarly ubiquitous in nineteenth-century England, and somewhat later a proliferation of German singing societies on both sides of the Atlantic embodied a similar response to the same need.

Although singing societies should fall under the rubric "sacred" (rather than "art") music, it is important to mention them here. First, many sacred music societies consciously endorsed a particular European repertory consisting of works by those composers increasingly regarded as "geniuses" by German Romantics. By doing so, American sacred music societies, in effect, acted as agents for German Romanticism. Second, some societies (like the Boston Handel and Haydn Society) had an important role in the second major reform of American sacred music, which resulted in endorsement (for different reasons) of a similar European repertory.

Many American sacred music societies overtly promoted European choral music by certain composers. The New-York Choral Society, for example, worked on behalf of "classical sacred music" (Ritter 1890, p. 136) and the Providence Psallonian Society championed music by the "best and most approved European masters" (identified by Hamm as Handel, Haydn, Mozart, and Beethoven) (Hamm 1983, p. 161). The powerful Boston Handel and Haydn Society was dedicated to "cultivating and improving a correct taste in the performance of Sacred Music"; it also wished to "introduce into more general practice the works of Handel, Haydn and other eminent composers" (quoted in Broyles 1992, p. 145). The confluence of these two repertories (the "sacred" and what we call the "classical") might not be obvious today, but to members of sacred music societies the connections were clear: compositions from both repertories were weighty, serious, and morally uplifting.

The nexus between singing societies and sacred music reform is most obvious with the Boston Handel and Haydn Society. In 1822 the Society published *The Boston Handel and Haydn Society Collection of Church Music*, an anthology of hymn texts set to melodies by "eminent" European composers; it was compiled by Lowell Mason (1792–1872), an American educator, composer, and conductor. Mason was the most powerful leader in this second wave of sacred music reform; others were Thomas Hastings (1784–1872) and William Bradbury (1816–1868). Their efforts were directed at the music of the previous generation of reformers, the singing masters and composers of the First New England School (who are discussed in chapter 4). The goal was to improve congregational singing, which the reformers believed had again degenerated into "a scandalous mockery of psalmody, led by a barrel organ or an incompetent professor" (Perkins and Dwight 1883–1893, p. 26). Not only were the fuging tunes, anthems, and hymns of Billings, Read, Swan, and other singing master/composers (in the opinion of the reformers) full of improper harmonies, incorrect voice-leadings, and the like, but they encouraged entirely too much inappropriate individual improvisation by members of the congregation, who could be heard

> singing flat with a nasal twang, straining the voice to an unnatural pitch, introducing continual drawls and tasteless ornaments, trilling on each syllable, running a third above the written note; and thus, by a sort of triplet, assimilating the time to a Scotch reel, etc. etc.
> (Perkins and Dwight 1883–1893, p. 26)

The reference to dance music is important, for many of the reformers considered the joy and energy of American fuging tunes to be completely inappropriate for sacred music. Sacred music, they believed, should have no secular implications; furthermore, it should be serious and – above all – morally uplifting.

The reformers replaced the corrupting music of the tunesmiths with more appropriate hymns: dignified texts set to melodies with absolutely no secular implications (either from previous lyrics or through "inappropriate" tempos or meters) and written in a "scientifically" correct manner. Mason, Bradbury, and Hastings, in their quest for such melodies, turned to European tunes, and the Handel and Haydn Society (of which Mason served as president from 1827 to 1832) wholeheartedly supported these efforts. As a result, the *Collection of Church Music* is full of tunes by Haydn, Handel, Mozart, and Beethoven (it also includes melodies by a cohort of lesser European composers). It is interesting but certainly not coincidental that in their quest for serious, superior, and morally uplifting compositions the reformers turned to works by those composers increasingly being viewed as "artists" by the Romantics.

The efforts of American sacred music societies, sacred music reformers, and the proselytizers for German Romanticism would eventually bear fruit. For the time being, however, only a minority of American music-lovers were altering their conceptions of the nature of music. To most Americans, music continued to be primarily entertainment, with little appreciable difference (beyond personal taste and utilitarian function) between its various categories. But the seeds were being sown, and the ideas would inevitably have an impact on the cultivation of music in the United States – especially when, in the late 1840s and 1850s, the new ideas they contained would be endorsed by those conservative German immigrant musicians who came to dominate American musical life.

Building the structure

The infrastructure necessary to support cultural life in America reached a critical mass by the mid-1840s, as represented, to a certain extent, by sheer population increase. In 1830 the population of the United States was almost 13 million; by 1860 it was 31 million, an almost-240 percent increase. Population growth was boosted, of course, by a phenomenal immigration rate: apart from the involuntary immigration associated with the slave trade (see chapter 5), many voluntary immigrants fled poor economic conditions or political and social upheaval; a vast majority were from Ireland and Germany (see chapter 6). The influx of German immigrants in particular dramatically affected the cultivation of music in this country, for among them were hordes of professional musicians, most of whom believed implicitly in the superiority of their musical heritage.

Compounding the increase in population was accelerating urbanization. In the United States, as in rest of the western world, the relentless force of industrialization meant that cities could sustain larger numbers of people. Several of the larger American cities illustrate this growth: between 1830 and 1860 New York's population quintupled (to over 1 million), Boston and New Orleans both nearly quadrupled in size (to 177,840 and 168,675, respectively), and Philadelphia and Baltimore tripled (to 565,529 and 212,418). The transportation network continued to expand, spreading ever westward; from 1840 to 1860, an additional 28,000 miles were added to the country's railroad system, mostly connecting the Midwest with the East Coast (Morris 1976, p. 610). Modes of transportation between Europe and the United States had also improved considerably. By 1845, there were fifty-two transatlantic packets operating thrice weekly from New York, and by the late 1840s the average crossing time from Liverpool to New York had decreased to thirty-three days. Travel time diminished significantly after 1847, with the establishment of the first steamship service between New York and Liverpool (Morris 1976, pp. 609, 705). The improved transatlantic travel conditions had a major impact not only on potential immigrants, but also on European performing musicians, who began to show up in the United States in droves.

Immigrants and virtuosos

Virtuoso instrumentalists began to arrive in the States in significant numbers in the early 1840s: they included the violinists Alexandre-Joseph Artôt, Ole Bull, Henri Vieuxtemps, and Camillo Sivori; pianists Leopold de Meyer and Henri Herz; and the double-bassist Giovanni Bottesini. All of these instrumentalists had traveled and performed extensively in Europe prior to casting their musical bread upon American waters; all of them toured widely in the United States, performing both on the well-trammeled concert and theatrical circuits of the East Coast and in smaller cities and towns located in the interior. In essence, the American tours by these virtuosos were extensions and continuations of their European ventures: by the late 1840s, America was the most distant but nevertheless a regular concert-circuit option. Operatic impresarios working out of Milan and Rome maintained regular contact with singers and managers in New York, and instrumentalists who toured the European continent increasingly regarded a trip to America as normal. By the 1840s itinerant performers – instrumentalists as well as singers – were touring widely all over the eastern half of America in an area that stretched west to the Mississippi River. By the end of that decade, musicians also traveled by boat (and by land across Panama) to California, whose population was exploding as a result of the gold rush. Itinerant musicians performed in theatres and halls in San Francisco, Sacramento, and Los Angeles as well as in towns and camps in the mining fields.

Tours by Bull, de Meyer, and Herz are good examples of the extent of American audiences' exposure to virtuoso musicians. Ole Bull (1810–1880), one of the finest violinists of the nineteenth century, traveled over 100,000 miles and gave more than 200 concerts during his first tour (1843–1845). Pianist Leopold de Meyer gave some eighty-five concerts in twenty-six cities between October, 1845 and May, 1847; Henri Herz, who quickly followed, gave close to 200 concerts in fifty cities during 1846–1849. The range of the two pianists' itineraries was typical of that of many virtuosos: in 1845 de Meyer toured in an area bounded by Montreal to the north, New Orleans and Mobile to the south, and St. Louis to the west; Herz duplicated that basic range the following year, but filled in the intervening spaces more completely by performing in such tiny towns as Alton, Missouri; Maysville, Kentucky; St. Francisville, Louisiana; Utica, New York; and New Bedford, Massachusetts (Lott 1986, pp. 75–76, 243).

In the mid-1840s Americans also became acquainted with itinerant European chamber ensembles. Among the first such groups to arrive in the United States was the Steyermarkische (Styrian) Company, an ensemble of nineteen performers that made its American debut in 1846 in Boston, performing overtures, potpourris, light dance music, and solos (Lawrence 1988, p. 545). In 1848 three additional ensembles arrived: the Germania Musical Society (October), the thirty-two-member ensemble of Hungarian composer and conductor Joseph Gungl (early November), and the Saxonia Band, an ensemble of twenty-four from Dresden (late November). In New York, all of these ensembles performed overtures and incidental music by Mozart, Auber, Rossini, and Donizetti, potpourris, dance compositions, and works by Mendelssohn: a repertory that is (to modern eyes) "mixed." All of the ensembles also toured in the United States.

The Germanians, the most influential of the four ensembles, consisted of twenty-five musicians from Berlin; they came to America to "further in the hearts of this politically free people the love of the fine art of music" (Johnson 1953, p. 75). The ensemble gave some 900 concerts all over the United States and Canada during its six years of activity (1848–1854). Their impact was significant, especially outside of New York City (Hart 1973, p. 7). In addition to the musical fare mentioned above, the Germanians also performed much of the Austro-German orchestral repertory (including works by Haydn, Mozart, Beethoven, Mendelssohn, Liszt, and the young Wagner); by introducing it as "fine art," the Society overtly reinforced the message that many Americans were now hearing about this repertory. The ensemble also, however, toured widely with many of the favorite virtuosos who visited the United States (including Jenny Lind, Henriette Sontag, Bull, Camilla Urso, and Alfred Jaëll), and as a consequence attracted large popular audiences. Their high performance standards (both technical and interpretive) were a revelation to American musicians and audiences alike. Equally important, when the ensemble disbanded in 1854, many of its members elected to remain in the States, where they pursued careers as performers, teachers, and organizers of concert series.

Growing numbers of opera companies and singers also visited during these decades. By the 1840s, English opera had become firmly established in the United States as a popular musical and theatrical form. The dominant performers were the immigrants Anne (1814–1888) and Edward (1809–1852) Seguin and their Seguin Opera Company, a troupe that was both wildly popular and enormously successful throughout the 1840s. They – like other English troupes – performed repertory that included works by British composers (Wallace, Balfe, Rooke) as well as translations of operas by composers who were French (Auber, Adam), German (von Weber), and Italian (Bellini, Donizetti, Mercadante, and Rossini). In addition, various incarnations of the Havana Opera Company visited occasionally during the 1840s (performing in New Orleans, Pittsburgh, Cincinnati, and on the East Coast), and numerous New York-based Italian companies imported from Europe appeared and performed a repertory of works by Rossini, Bellini, Donizetti, and – increasingly – Verdi before disbanding. The overall picture of operatic activity in the 1840s and 1850s is one of growth: larger and more polished companies (both English and Italian), more extensive itineraries and repertories, and more troupes. Furthermore, many of these singers – like members of the Germania orchestra – remained after the completion of their companies' tours. They settled in American cities, where their presence as teachers and performers would have a lasting impact on American musical culture in the post-bellum period. By the early 1850s, in fact, there were enough Italian singers living in New York to make possible the formation of locally based Italian opera companies. Because of this development, impresarios such as Bernard Ullmann (who arrived in America in the early 1840s), Max Maretzek (1847), the pianist-impresario Maurice Strakosch (1848), and Max Strakosch (who joined his brother in 1853), could circumvent the logistical and financial difficulties inherent in recruiting an entire company from abroad and were now free to concentrate recruiting efforts (and funds) on big-name stars. This meant that impresarios could engage higher-caliber performers, which contributed to the established trend: heightened audience expectations and subsequent engagement of even more highly skilled musicians.

This unprecedented amount of musical activity by visiting European artists in the late 1840s – and their financial and artistic success – set the stage for similar and even more frenetic levels of activity in the 1850s, when Americans witnessed performances by some of the most important European musicians. In the realm of piano performance, for example, de Meyer and Herz were followed in the early 1850s by the French pianist Alfred Jaëll and in 1856 by Sigismund Thalberg, Franz Liszt's most formidable competitor and one of the greatest piano virtuosos of the nineteenth century; he made three separate tours of the United States. Violinists Bull (who toured widely in America between 1852 and 1857) and Vieuxtemps (who returned in 1857–1858) were joined in the 1850s by Hungarian Eduard Reményi and French prodigy Camilla Urso. The list of stellar opera singers who appeared in various companies in the States during the period includes some of the most outstanding vocalists of Europe: Marietta Alboni, Henriette Sontag, Teresa Parodi, Giovanni Mateo Mario, Giulia Grisi, Lorenzo Salvi, and many others. In addition to performing with opera companies, many of these singers also organized concert troupes, often in conjunction with various of the instrumental virtuosos, and toured widely. The repertories of such troupes consisted of a mixed bag: original compositions by instrumental virtuosos; piano or violin works by composers such as Chopin, Viotti, Beethoven, Mendelssohn, and Kreutzer; operatic arias and ensembles; Scottish tunes and popular ballads (Bishop's *Home, Sweet Home* was ubiquitous); and sometimes chamber works and movements from symphonies.

An important visiting orchestra of the mid-1850s was the ensemble of the French conductor Louis Antoine Jullien (1812–1860), who arrived in New York in 1853 with twenty-seven instrumentalists (to whom he added some sixty local performers). Jullien's wildly successful "Monster Concerts for the Masses" consisted of dances, overtures, and symphonies by such composers as Mendelssohn, Mozart, and Beethoven (he also frequently programmed works by American composers). A flamboyant conductor, he was dismissed by many as too theatrical and gimmicky. His influence on American musical culture, however, was pronounced, both on audiences (the orchestra made a six-month tour of the United States) and on the American performers who played under him. Many of his instrumentalists, furthermore, remained in the United States after he returned to France in 1854.

The best-known and most widely bruited European performer to appear in the United States during this period was the Swedish soprano Jenny Lind (1820–1887), who visited from September 1850 through May 1852. Her American tour was initiated by P. T. Barnum; the portion that he managed (September 1850 through June 1851) was spectacularly successful, due in large part to his astonishing promotional and managerial skills and to his remarkable ability to manipulate American audiences. The

relentless publicity that Barnum concocted attracted to Lind's performances many Americans who had never before attended concerts, and
many of these auditors were astounded by her artistry. Furthermore, the
extent to which Lind's name and celebrity were successfully used for commercial purposes (to sell all sorts of mercantile goods) revolutionized
American managerial methods.

Opera companies, concert troupes, and virtuosos toured widely all over
America during the 1850s, performing regularly almost everywhere an
audience could be assembled. By this time both opera troupes and concert
companies were touring extensively in the same area covered in the 1840s
by de Meyer and Herz; increasing numbers of troupes and individuals,
however, also made the trek across Panama to perform in California (primarily in San Francisco), often prior to heading south to Mexico, to
Central and South America, and to Australia. Opera companies, in particular, were welcomed in San Francisco, where Tom Maguire operated a
theatre to which he recruited opera troupes from the East (Preston 1993b).
Performances by these itinerant companies were not at all limited to large
– or even medium-sized – cities: residents of villages and hamlets (especially if conveniently located between two larger towns) could also attend
concerts. Nor was this performance culture yet upper class: although the
idea that certain types of music were serious and morally uplifting was
developing, most concerts by touring musicians during this period (like
most concerts in Europe) continued to be marked by variety – of genres, of
performing forces, and of repertory. Furthermore, although it is clear that
during this period Italian opera was starting to be regarded as an aristocratic pastime, this development (which had nothing to do with the evolving "classical" repertory) was extremely limited even in the late 1850s, for
most Americans continued to think of opera as part of the popular theatre.
In general, the vast majority of Americans continued to be attracted to concerts for their entertainment value: as Barnum, Lind, and dozens of other
virtuosos demonstrated, celebrity (especially foreign celebrity) was a
potent and attractive aspect of performance culture during this period.

The growing German influence

The many visiting performers who remained in the 1840s and 1850s
became part of an increasingly cosmopolitan American musical community, now dominated by Italian as well as English singers, by French and
German as well as English and American instrumentalists. German musicians, in particular, were a conspicuous presence, and this growing hege-

mony is one of the most significant facets of American musical life of the time.

Mere mention of some of the most prominent German immigrants illustrates clearly how much they dominated American musical life during the 1850s. Two of the many former Germanians who settled were particularly influential: Carl Zerrahn (1826–1909) was the conductor of the Boston Handel and Haydn Society for forty-two years; Carl Bergmann (1821–1876) settled in New York, directed the *Männergesangverein Arion*, played cello in the Mason-Thomas chamber ensemble, conducted the Philharmonic Society from 1855 to 1876, and championed the music of (mostly) German composers. The Germanians, of course, were just a drop in the bucket. A short list of some of the multitudes of German- or Austrian-trained performers, conductors, composers, concert organizers, and teachers who immigrated in the middle and late 1840s includes Theodore Eisfeld (1816–1882), a composer and co-conductor with Bergmann of the Philharmonic Society; cellist Wulf Fries (1825–1902), a founder of the Mendelssohn Quintette Club (Boston) and member of the Musical Fund Society; Hans Balatka (1825–1899), conductor, composer, and important figure in musical development in Milwaukee; and Theodore Thomas (1835–1905), member of the New York Philharmonic and one of the most influential American conductors during the second half of the century. Many other immigrant musicians of other nationalities also encouraged the cultivation of the now-dominant Austro-German repertory.

The German domination of American performing organizations can be demonstrated clearly by the early history of New York's orchestra. The Philharmonic Symphony Society of New-York (the modern New York Philharmonic Orchestra) was founded in 1842 by a group of musicians that included Ureli C. Hill (American), Henry C. Timm (German), Anthony Reiff (German), and Charles Edward Horn (English). The twenty-two Germans among the orchestra's fifty-three founding members already demonstrate a strong Teutonic presence. A decade later the presence had became overwhelming: in 1855, fifty-three of the orchestra's sixty-seven musicians were Germans. Furthermore, although during its first decade the ensemble worked under various conductors (two Americans, two Frenchmen, one Englishman, one Austro-Bohemian, and four Germans), this changed when Theodore Eisfeld became the first full-time conductor in 1852: for the rest of the century the orchestra's conductors were all German nationals (Shanet 1975, p. 109).

Domination of the orchestra's repertory by Austro-German music is

equally obvious – and of more serious consequence to American composers, whose works the ensemble essentially refused to perform. As instrumental musicians and Germans, the immigrant members of the orchestra
unquestionably endorsed the Romantic notion that instrumental music
(in particular symphonic compositions) represented the apex of musical
expression. As Europeans, they also were unified in their support of the
Austro-German repertory: from the very beginning of its existence, the
orchestra performed a large percentage of compositions by "geniuses" like
Beethoven, Mendelssohn, Mozart, and Haydn. (It also performed works
by forgotten European composers, a clear indication of Euro-centrism
[Shanet 1975, p. 110].) Where the musicians apparently parted company
with Romanticism, however, was in a lack of support for modern music:
the Philharmonic's repertory plainly indicates a preference for absolute
music, to the neglect of more progressive and avant-garde abstract or programmatic works, whether American or European (Hamm 1983, p. 214).
This preference for the more rational music of a bygone era might have
been a natural reaction by musicians who were in essence political and
social refugees. It is telling, however, that this conservatism seems to have
been shared by the orchestras of Western Europe, for the repertorial idiosyncrasies of the Philharmonic Symphony Society of New-York were
remarkably consistent with those of orchestras "back home."[2] The end
result was that the (mostly programmatic) works by American composers
were not heard by American audiences; whether this was because the
music was not absolute or because the composers were not European is
irrelevant. The German domination of orchestral music in America had
become a *fait accompli* by the 1850s.

    The audiences of the Philharmonic Symphony Society represent a
minuscule fraction of the American concert-going public. Most Americans
patronized concerts by singers, instrumental virtuosos, or bands, and
these repertories continued to be eclectic and varied. But thousands of
Americans participated in singing societies and other thousands attended
their concerts, and the repertories of these organizations increasingly mirrored those of the orchestras, for they, too were controlled by Germans.
The conservative choral and orchestral repertories mutually reinforced the

---

2. The conservative musical taste of German immigrant musicians, particularly of those associated with New York's Philharmonic Symphony Society, is regularly mentioned in histories of
American music. A common inference is that this conservatism was a peculiarly American phenomenon. An examination of the repertories performed by major European orchestras of the time,
however, suggests that the Philharmonic Society's repertory was anything but unusual. For further information, see Sachs 1991, Weber 1986, and Mahling 1991.

promotion of European art music compositions. Not coincidentally, this repertory was very similar to that simultaneously being promoted by the sacred music reformers.

Still further reinforcement came from the editors of growing numbers of American music periodicals (such as *The World of Music*, *The Boston Musical Gazette*, and, especially, *Dwight's Journal of Music*), many of whom had likewise become convinced of the superiority of German music (in general) and absolute instrumental music (in particular) (Crawford 1993, p. 288). John Sullivan Dwight (1813–1893) was an especially resolute disciple of this growing German instrumental hegemony; the goal of his journal during its nearly thirty-year run (1852–1881) was to educate Americans about the superiority of this music. Dwight's overt (and covert) bias was toward the music of Beethoven, Mozart, and Handel; he disdained operatic music (especially by Italian composers) despite its popularity among American audiences, and resisted "modern" music, including Wagner's. Dwight's journal was one of the longest-lived of the period, but its peak circulation was only 1,500; it was hardly the only influential music periodical of the time. Henry Cood Watson and Nathaniel Parker Willis, to name just two others, were likewise influential as music journalists, both serving as critics for various newspapers and music periodicals in New York City. They (and other music critics and editors) shared some of Dwight's biases about the function of music in general; they all viewed themselves as educators and molders of American musical tastes.[3] Because the goals of these musical journalists coincided nicely with the conservative repertories being promoted by the choral groups, orchestras, and sacred music societies, the idea that an older, "classical" repertory was somehow different from and superior to other musics gained momentum. And although the vast majority of American concert-goers paid little attention to it, this concept, which took root during the ante-bellum period, would have a profound impact on American musical life in the second half of the century.

American performers and composers

A natural by-product of the maturation of musical culture in America was the emergence of American-born composers and performers. Some of these musicians peacefully coexisted with the increasingly dominant Germans and others worked in musical spheres not particularly affected by

3. For an enlightening discussion of the important role of New York music critics in the formation of musical tastes in the 1840s and 1850s, see Lawrence 1988 and 1995.

them. Yet another group resisted the German domination and bitterly protested what it regarded as the usurpation of American musical life by musical carpetbaggers.

Ureli Corelli Hill (1802–1875) and William Mason (1829–1908) are examples of the first category. Hill was one of the first American musicians to make the musical pedagogical pilgrimage to Germany (where he studied violin); thousands would do likewise later in the century. Before and after his sojourn in Europe, he worked with New York ensembles that were increasingly Germanic, including the Sacred Music Society and the Philharmonic Society; he also organized the first chamber music concert series in New York, which featured "classical productions for stringed instruments" (Lawrence 1988, p. 221). Mason, a pianist, teacher, and composer, also seems not to have chafed under the German domination of New York musical life. The son of Lowell Mason, he benefited from impeccable German training in Leipzig and Weimar. Although he concertized in America (with Thalberg) and in Europe, he disliked the nomadic lifestyle and settled down to compose and teach (endorsing, of course, the Austro-German repertory of his training). Mason also established (with Theodore Thomas) the Mason and Thomas Chamber Music Soirées, to help introduce to Americans chamber music by Schubert, Schumann, Brahms, and others.

The American musicians who worked outside the German sphere were of two types: singers, whose musical world was dominated by Italians, and virtuosos. Among the former were Virginia Whiting, a Boston soprano who appeared in the early 1850s with Max Maretzek's Astor Place Opera House Company, and Elisa Biscaccianti (1824–1896), daughter of Sophia Hewitt and Louis Ostinelli, who enjoyed some success as an operatic soprano during the 1850s. Clara Louise Kellogg (1842–1916), a soprano who had a major impact on opera performance in the second half of the century, commenced her nearly thirty-year career in New York in 1861. Of the virtuosos, by far the most important was the first home-grown American virtuoso, the New Orleans native Louis Moreau Gottschalk (1829–1869).

Gottschalk is today considered one of the most important nineteenth-century American composers and performers. He was sent off to Paris in 1841 for advanced tutelage on the piano and remained there, performing, studying, and composing, until 1850. He began his career as a touring virtuoso in 1851 and subsequently became a musical idol in Spain. Gottschalk's style of performing was compared favorably with that of

Frédéric Chopin; the young American, in fact, heard Chopin play in private salons and adopted in large measure the Polish composer's bel canto style of phrasing, his legato touch, and his revolutionary approach to pedaling (Starr 1995, p. 52). He returned to the States in 1853, but success was much more elusive at home than it had been in Europe: a native-born performer (even one whose mother tongue was French) did not have the same kind of *éclat* with American audiences as did foreign-born virtuosos. Gottschalk toured the United States widely until 1857, then again from 1862 until 1865, maintaining brutal schedules. The remainder of his time (and the last four years of his life) he spent in Central and South America and the West Indies.

Gottschalk wrote songs, orchestral works, and operas (mostly lost), but he was first and foremost a composer of piano music. His works run the gamut from virtuosic and brilliant dance-inspired character pieces and operatic transcriptions to sentimental parlor songs-without-words (including *The Last Hope, méditation religieuse* and *Morte!! (She is Dead)*). Most enduring, however, are his "Creole" compositions: piano character pieces that feature quotations of Creole and Haitian folk tunes, a heavy sprinkling of "signature chords" (diminished sevenths and augmented sixths), and exhilarating Afro-Caribbean syncopations (Starr 1995, p. 75). *Bamboula, danse des nègres* (Op. 2, 1847?) and *Le bananier, chanson nègre* (Op. 5, 1848) are perfect examples of this style. To Europeans infatuated with the strange and the unfamiliar (another tenet of Romanticism), these "Creole" compositions were eye-opening and deliciously exotic; in Paris, Gottschalk was hailed as the first musical spokesman of the New World. Gottschalk continued throughout his career to write compositions that are evocative of the "exotic" places he visited: he wrote Spanish-inspired music in Spain (*Canto del gitano*) and Cuban-inspired music in Havana (*Grand caprice cubain de bravura, Souvenir de la Havane*); in honor of his native country he composed works like *Le banjo* and *Union, paraphrase de concert* (incorporating *The Star-Spangled Banner, Yankee Doodle,* and *Hail Columbia*).

The protestors

The Teutonic bias of performing ensembles became more obvious in the 1850s when more American composers began to produce large-scale works (symphonies, operas, oratorios), only to discover that although there were plenty of American ensembles that performed such works, few (if any) were interested in their compositions. The problem was not just with societies like New York's Sacred Music or Philharmonic, or Boston's Handel & Haydn, or Philadelphia's Musical Fund: now there were hundreds of similarly named ensembles with similar repertorial bents in cities as geographically diverse as Cincinnati, Milwaukee, St. Louis, Pittsburgh, and Baltimore – and in the myriad tiny towns in between. But although the Philharmonic Society was hardly alone in its promotion of German music, its practices came under increasing scrutiny by New York musicians, who believed that the country's most prominent permanent orchestra should at least occasionally program compositions by American composers. That the orchestra had dramatically failed to do so was obvious: of the seventy-four different "grand instrumental pieces, such as Overtures and Symphonies" performed by the Philharmonic Society from 1842 through 1854, only one – George Bristow's *Concert Overture* (in E♭) – was American (Shanet 1975, p. 113).

Some American composers protested by establishing rival performing ensembles. Jerome Hopkins (1836–1898), a Vermont-born composer of orchestral works, operas, songs, and piano compositions, became a champion of American composers, helping to establish in 1856 the short-lived New-York American-Music Association, an ensemble devoted to the performance of "native" compositions. Charles Hommann (*c.* 1800–*c.* 1862), a Philadelphia composer of overtures, at least one symphony, and chamber works, also lent his support to this venture, as did Louis Gottschalk, William Mason, George Bristow (1825–1898), and William Henry Fry (1813–1864) (Lawrence 1995, pp. 750–756). The last two were the most productive native-born composers of orchestral music in the United States during the 1850s; they were also the most vociferous American music champions and the ones who chafed most at German domination.

Fry and Bristow both lived in New York during the 1850s. Fry, born in Philadelphia and the son of a publisher, was a composer, lecturer, and music critic in Philadelphia and New York (where he worked for the *Tribune*). Bristow, whose father was an English theatre musician, was a Brooklyn native who enjoyed a lengthy and successful musical career: as a violinist in the Philharmonic Society for thirty-six years (1843–1879), the director of the Mendelssohn and the New York Harmonic societies, a music teacher in New York public schools, and an organist and choir director for several New York churches. Both composers wrote large-scale works and both looked to America for thematic inspiration and to Europe for harmonic language and musical forms.

Fry devoted his compositional energies primarily to opera and to programmatic symphonic works. The derivative nature of his compositions might seem to contradict his American music flag-waving, but to Fry the two were not mutually exclusive. His attitude toward opera is illustrative: he fervently believed that it was possible to wed English (American) words to Italian melody. He ridiculed the standard style of adapting Italian opera for the American stage as a "wretched, vulgar plan of speaking and singing by turns" and believed that it was possible to make "the English language [into] the medium for the grand, serious, or comic opera" (quoted in Chase 1987, p. 305). In 1840 Fry and his older brother Joseph Reese demonstrated what he had in mind by skillfully translating Bellini's *Norma* into English with very little alteration of the music. Fry wrote three of his own operas, all to English librettos crafted or adapted by his brother. He regarded his middle work, *Leonora*, as an *American* triumph: "As England denies the possibility of having a grand opera written originally in our tongue," he wrote, "it was the business of America to prove the possibility – and I did so" (Upton 1954, p. 128). Despite the fact that *Leonora* was soundly criticized as too Italianate, it was certainly the first completely sung opera by an American mounted in the United States, of which Fry was not too modest to boast. Fry also wrote overtures, large choral compositions, numerous chamber works (including seven extant quartets), songs, and orchestral compositions. The latter, which include *Niagara* (1854), *The Dying Soldier* (Dramatic Symphony) (n.d.), *A Day in the Country* (1853), and *Santa Claus: Christmas Symphony* (1853) are programmatic; the last piece has an extensive written program. Although Jullien's orchestra performed a number of these works, their programmatic nature made them aesthetically and ideologically unpalatable to the German musicians who dominated the Philharmonic Society.

Bristow was also a prolific composer, again of works heavily influenced by European harmonic language and musical forms. He wrote three operas (one unfinished), four symphonies (between 1848 and 1872), many sacred and secular choral works, songs, keyboard compositions, and other orchestral and chamber music. His early works – in particular the chamber compositions from the 1840s – are clearly classical in orientation. Works from the 1850s were influenced by the composers whose compositions he most frequently performed or heard in New York: Beethoven and Mendelssohn were the inspiration for his chamber, orchestral, and choral works; for his piano compositions (*Grand duo . . . sur. . La fille du regiment*, 1845; *Life on the Ocean Wave*, 1852) he looked to the repertories of virtuoso pianists, opera companies, and ballad-singers like Henry Russell.

Bristow's programmatic inspiration, however, was primarily his native land. His first opera, *Rip van Winkle* (1852–1855), was based on the Washington Irving tale; he also penned overtures entitled *Columbus* (1861) and *Jibbenainosay* (1889), the cantatas *The Pioneer: A Grand Cantata* (1872) and *The Great Republic, Ode to the American Union* (1880), piano compositions like *Souvenir de Mount Vernon* (1861), and a late *Niagara Symphony* (1893), scored for vocal soloists, chorus, and orchestra.

Bristow's success as a performer, teacher, and conductor suggests that he blended into the German-dominated musical world of New York more easily than did the prickly Fry. The two composers teamed up, however, for a high-profile journalistic fight in 1854 with the Philharmonic Society on behalf of American composers. The brawl, which Gilbert Chase called "one of the most extraordinary public correspondences in the annals of American music" (Chase 1987, p. 313), clearly established the battle lines: American composers *versus* those who controlled American performing ensembles. The fight, which lasted four months, resolved nothing; the extent of the German hegemony, in fact, grew during the second half of the century. But it does serve as a clear-cut delimiter of the extent to which German taste had infiltrated American performing ensembles by mid-century. It also illustrates clearly that some American musicians unquestionably understood the consequences of that infiltration, and were willing to resist it.

*

The first half of the nineteenth century was a crucial period in the development of American musical culture. It was also a time of dramatic and far-reaching cultural and social change in the new American Republic. Furthermore, fundamental changes that occurred in Western European music-making during this period – the development of the virtuoso cult, the increasing influence of the growing middle class as musical patrons, the impact of industrialization, and – most important – the far-reaching effects of German Romanticism – all had a profound impact on the development of American musical culture.

Two basic concepts are worth reiterating: that early-nineteenth-century westerners (Americans and Europeans alike) regarded music in a manner fundamentally different from how we think of it today, and that over the six decades covered in this chapter, this different way of looking at and thinking about music started to change significantly, in ways that still affect us today. Apart from (but, of course, entangled with) these shifts in the musical paradigm are the other significant developments in contemporary American musical life: the spread of a musical infrastructure; the explosive growth of the middle class; the increasing importance of music in the homes of Americans and (in particular) in the lives of American women; the proliferation of American amateur and professional performing organizations; the "invasion" by itinerant European virtuosos; the rise of American-born composers and performers; and – finally – the overwhelming domination, by mid-century, of American musical life by German musician-immigrants. All of these factors, and others, were important features in the stew that was American musical life during this fascinating period.

Musical life in America during the first half of the nineteenth century was varied, changing, widespread, and flourishing. Musical cultivation occurred all over the country, in areas both urban and rural; music itself was not clearly divided into "art" or "popular," but rested somewhere between the two poles. By the middle of the century, however, it is clear that concert music was an undeniable and vital part of American culture; it would become even more so in the ensuing years. The stage was now well prepared for the important developments of the second half of the century.

9

Art music from 1860 to 1920

MICHAEL BROYLES

"Art music, what is that?" Music lovers and many others in the second half of the nineteenth century were confronted with a new idea, a choice and an obligation. Some music, art music, had acquired a special status, and whatever one thought, there were things one was *supposed* to think about it. Earlier it had been much simpler: music was either utilitarian or fun. As utilitarian it had a function, be it in church, a militia ceremony, or a public commemoration, but the event dictated its role and except for the musicians, there was nothing to ponder. Music for music's sake, that was just a diversion, enjoyable, entertaining.

A lot of earlier nineteenth-century music had of course been serious, in either perception or intent. Church music composers sought to enhance the dignity and decorum of the worship experience in their hymns and anthems; Henry Russell's songs moved the population to tears; and vocal groups such as the Hutchinsons stirred, inspired, and outraged the population with their moral and political topics. But only in the second half of the century did the notion spread generally through society that certain types of music were fundamentally different. This music, the argument went, had the capacity to do more than entertain; it inspired and elevated. Even though it might be instrumental and abstract, it spoke to the ethical side of humanity. Even though it might be secular, it was sacred, in an intangible way. It was moral, it was good, it was good for you. Such music was called art music.

Today, when a symphony orchestra conductor can appear on stage in a black leather vest and sleeveless T-shirt designed purposely to show off his biceps, and lead a rock group, a subset of the orchestra, called the Dogs of Desire (*Wall Street Journal* January 7, 1996), or a rock drummer can admit he knows nothing about opera and then receive a commission to compose a grand opera for a major metropolitan company (Broyles 1992, pp. 3–4), or a rock-pop-megastar can write an oratorio that is performed on several continents, the distinction between art and other kinds of music seems almost irrelevant, another reminder of the confusion, uncertainty and at the same time breathtaking potential that exists in our current artistic world. Yet as we grope toward an uncertain musical future, the residue of that distinction is still much with us, shaping our perceptions and our reactions to music and musical events.

In this chapter I use the above nineteenth-century definition of art music partly to delimit and give shape to the topic, but more importantly because the nineteenth-century concept of art music has affected every aspect of our musical world. As already suggested in chapter 8, its original delineation was a major turning point in American musical life. The spread and acceptance of the idea of music as art was the most important musical development in America in the second half of the nineteenth century.

It should be noted, however, that even in the late nineteenth century the distinctions were not always clear. In practice art music encompassed a good deal more than music specifically designed to be moral and in an intangible way sacred, and some art music composers would have been astounded to discover their works so characterized. In addition some music blurred into a vaguely defined middleground, a type of music that emulated art music in some ways but in others assumed a more popular or commercial character. Much piano music of the late nineteenth century, for instance, fell into that category. Everyone played MacDowell's short piano pieces, but MacDowell was the most respected composer of the day, an artist *par excellence*. Nevertheless the above definition of art music became the benchmark, the fundamental test, whether hidden or overt, that went far toward determining a composition's or a composer's status.

From this orientation a hierarchy quickly developed. A handful of composers were canonized, their works given a special place and status. A pantheon coalesced. The idea had come from Europe where artistic canons were common by the 1840s, but it found its own special resonance in America through a group of Boston writers led by John S. Dwight (1813–1893). Dwight and others argued as early as the 1840s for a musical hierarchy with Handel, Haydn, Mozart, and Beethoven at the pinnacle. Especially Beethoven. These composers retained their status, if not always their popularity, for the rest of the century. The real question, around which much activity and debate about art music in the nineteenth century revolved, was who else belonged.

The importance of musical institutions

Once the pantheon was in place, institutions were needed to nurture and support it. The nature of the institutions did much to determine the nature of the music. And herein lay the foundation of American musical culture. Although there were precedents (see chapter 8), the types of institutions and patterns of individual patronage that support art music to this day were defined largely in the second half of the nineteenth century. They are the key to understanding the world of American art music for the past 150 years.

Maintenance of art music in America involved four types of activities: first, musical organizations, orchestras, opera companies, or chamber ensembles had to be formed. Second, they needed places to play, theatres and concert halls. Third, individuals willing to provide both resources and leadership were essential; many were women. And fourth, the public itself needed to be educated about art music, what it was and why it should be patronized.

Institutions capable of nurturing and promoting art music, convincing the public of its value, and making it accessible nationwide, had to be consistent with American society. Some were unique to the United States; most had European counterparts. Fundamental American beliefs about art and society, however, demanded solutions that had no exact European equivalents. America was no absolutist state where a soprano would squelch a cadenza in her throat if the sovereign stood up. Nor was a significant percentage of the gross national product available to a governor or president to indulge personal predilections toward opera or symphony: state patronage, prevalent in Europe, was out of the question in America. Americans had to find a mix of private and civic support that was both worthy of the new reverence for art and consistent with cherished principles of democracy. And this was no theoretical question seen only by later historians. Many musicians and patrons were keenly and consciously aware of the problem and the opposing, at times contradictory viewpoints.

In the first half of the nineteenth century musicians themselves formed organizations to present concerts for their own individual or collective benefit. The Philo-Harmonic Society of Boston, the Musical Fund Society of Philadelphia and the New York Philharmonic Society fit that category. The earlier ones often began as collaborations with amateurs, when amateurs and professionals still performed together. Sometimes interested amateurs would go it alone, presenting their own performances, with occasional professional help, as had been the norm in the eighteenth century: in this, the St. Cecilia Society of Charleston, South Carolina, and the Tuesday Club of Annapolis, Maryland, were typical. In the nineteenth century many amateur organizations such as the Harvard Musical Association of Boston or the Italian Opera Association of New York also sponsored professional performances.

In the second half of the nineteenth century professional musicians came much more to depend on outsiders to organize musical activity. As audiences grew, as expenses mounted, and as art music became more prestigious, musical sponsorship became both a higher-stakes financial gamble and an attraction for those with wealth. Bold entrepreneurs, seeking to capitalize on the new demand, built larger halls and had to fill them. Personal managers took charge of virtuosos' touring arrangements, which had become more complex as the nation expanded. Yet amateur sponsorship remained important. Women's clubs in particular took on new patronage roles, negotiating with professional managers who came increasingly to depend on them as their leadership role in the community increased. Economic leaders of towns and cities were eager for the prestige the new culture awarded. Support for art music thus took on a complex mix of private, philanthropic, civic and entrepreneurial activities. The next sections will examine that in more detail.

America on the move

In the second half of the century, art music went from being nowhere, an oxymoron to most Americans, to being everywhere. Once the notion caught on, art music could be found in every state, city, territory, or even mining town. Far from being an urban phenomenon limited to a few cultural centers or large eastern cities, by the end of the century art music had become a familiar if not common aspect of American life throughout the country. As the frontier pushed westward, it was never far behind. The story of art music in nineteenth-century America is the story of a restless, expansive, hungry nation fed by equally restless artists and entrepreneurs eager to satisfy needs dimly perceived but keenly felt. It is about America on the move.

True, most American composers did congregate in a few large cities, and musical life was certainly richer there, if for no other reason than simple mathematics: a more concentrated population meant a larger potential audience. The emergence of American compositional schools, however, was only one aspect of a much broader nineteenth-century musical culture. Composers themselves had little impact on the American musical landscape until near the close of the century. And to limit a description of art music to urban areas would seriously distort the American musical situation. The most important musical development in America through the 1890s was the spread of a culture of art music throughout the country, first through touring virtuosos and ensembles, and then through local organizations, many of which grew directly from the activities of touring artists.

And how extensive touring was. Technology, specifically the railroad, made it possible. In 1865 there were 35,083 miles of track in the United States. By 1897 that had increased to 243,013. The rapid building of an elaborate rail system did more to further art music in America than any other single development. The railroad was especially crucial in the West. Distances between population centers were far greater, and the vastness of the land was difficult to conceptualize. That vastness, however, worked to the advantage of both musician and audience. As America expanded, many musicians, particularly European virtuosos, became fascinated with America and sought to travel extensively throughout it. This desire was not, of course, entirely free of profit motives. Towns in the West were relatively isolated and essentially culturally starved. Thus a traveling artist, even a second-rate one, could almost always expect a welcome reception.

A vast land of natural wonders and virgin audiences! That presented an opportunity irresistible to many virtuosos, both American and European. As discussed in chapter 8, a few pioneering Europeans such as Ole Bull and Henri Vieuxtemps made forays in the 1840s. Vieuxtemps returned twice, in 1857 with Thalberg and in 1870 with Christine Nilsson. Bull became so fascinated with America that he even attempted to found a Norwegian colony in Pennsylvania. He later married an American and for a time resided in Boston.

The event that made clear, however, the potential America held for the virtuoso, was the 1850 to 1852 tour of Jenny Lind, the Swedish soprano; much of that success was due to her sponsor, P. T. Barnum. Lind gave ninety-three concerts that altogether grossed $712,000, at a time when an accumulated wealth of $100,000 placed one among the very rich.

Because of Lind's success Barnum became the most famous musical impresario in American history; he was not the first nor were his techniques unique. As the railroad opened up the American countryside, impresarios – mostly European – moved in quickly to exploit the possibilities. The most successful at mid-century were the Strakosch brothers, Max Maretzek, and Bernard Ullmann. All were active through the 1880s. Other impresarios had a regional but no less important impact: Tom Maguire dominated musical presentations throughout California and Nevada.

The first American-born virtuoso to take full advantage of the new possibilities of a touring artist was Louis Moreau Gottschalk (1829–1869). From 1853 until his death Gottschalk toured continually, taking breaks only when sheer exhaustion forced him to. He not only toured the continental United States but later the Caribbean and South America. His touring in the United States reached a peak during the Civil War. From 1862 to 1865 Gottschalk traveled throughout America, giving an estimated 900 or more concerts (precise numbers are impossible to determine). By the summer of 1862 he had, according to his own accounts, given 109 concerts in 120 days; by September, 1863, he had logged an estimated 95,000 miles on the railroads. He literally lived in railroad cars for days at a time, frequently giving two concerts a day. He even attempted three concerts in three different cities on the same day. By his own admission he became an automaton and ended up wrecking his health (Starr 1995, pp. 331, 346). His efforts, however, did much to open America to art music.

Prior to the 1870s individuals seldom toured alone. Even Gottschalk had a retinue, usually a small troupe of opera singers, to provide variety to his concerts. Touring instrumental ensembles date from at least the late 1840s, when the Germania Musical Society traveled extensively.

Probably the most extraordinary touring feat in the nineteenth century was the series of trips the Theodore Thomas Orchestra took in the 1870s and 1880s. Unlike most virtuosos, Thomas (1835–1905) traveled with a full orchestra of from forty to sixty musicians. He refused to compromise in personnel, repertory, or according to his own claims, performance level. On some of the programs he proclaimed "This is the only organization which, when traveling, gives their Concerts with the same number of artists and in the same style of perfection as in New York, Boston, Philadelphia, &c" (Thomas, Newberry Library Collection).

A typical Thomas tour was undertaken in the fall of 1873. In fifty-one days between September 29 and November 18 he gave forty-eight concerts in the following cities: Troy, Syracuse, Utica, Rochester, and Buffalo, New York; Toronto; Chicago, Jacksonville, and Springfield, Illinois; Milwaukee, Wisconsin; Bloomington and Terre Haute, Indiana; St. Louis, Missouri; Louisville, Kentucky; Cincinnati, Dayton, Toledo, and Cleveland,

Ohio; Detroit, Michigan; Pittsburgh, Harrisburg, and Philadelphia, Pennsylvania; Washington, D.C.; and Newark, New Jersey. His 1874 tour was even more extensive. In addition to many of the same cities as in 1873 he added Kalamazoo and Grand Rapids, Missouri; Zainsville, Ohio; Wheeling, West Virginia; Erie, Albany, and Poughkeepsie, New York; Northampton, New Bedford, Gardner, Cambridgeport, Pittsfield, and Fitchburg, Massachusetts; Providence, Rhode Island; Baltimore, Maryland; Hudson, Jersey City, Paterson, Meriden, and Hoboken, New Jersey; Winsted, Manchester, Bridgeport, and Easton, Connecticut; Norristown, Scranton, and Wilkes Barre, Pennsylvania (Thomas, Newberry Library Collection).

The 1873 and 1874 tours were not Thomas's first, last, or biggest. He began touring in 1869 and continued until 1888. His most geographically extensive tour occurred in 1883. Beginning in Baltimore, Thomas cut a wide swath through the middle of the country – Pennsylvania, New York, Ohio, Kentucky, Tennessee, Missouri, Iowa, Minnesota – to arrive in San Francisco. After seven concerts in San Francisco, he then backtracked through the West – Utah, Colorado, Kansas, Missouri, Nebraska, Iowa, and Illinois. George P. Upton, the editor of Thomas's autobiography, dubbed the tour Thomas's "march to the sea" (Upton 1905, p. 93).

Thomas would not get rich playing in small towns. Expenses for his 1883 tour ran $1,500 per day; other tours could not have been much less. Clearly Zainesville, Ohio, or Poughkeepsie, New York, could not produce sufficient revenues to even approach these kinds of outlays, much less turn a profit, although sizable audiences in the larger cities could offset the losses in the smaller ones. In addition the psychological difficulties of keeping forty plus musicians on the road were formidable. But the tours did allow Thomas to keep his orchestra together, and they did bring the sound of a disciplined orchestra to many listeners who had undoubtedly never heard such before.

I give a detailed list of cities for Thomas's 1873 and 1874 tours to demonstrate an important point: just how decentralized art music was in America. The dynamic, restless nature of American society, as well as the freewheeling financial situation for artists, motivated many to travel extensively, with an energy that is almost unimaginable today. For whatever reasons, the American public was hungry for art music, and in cities and towns throughout the continent they found artists eager to satiate their wants, and equally important, entrepreneurial concert managers eager to establish new markets.

Thomas was surprised to discover a hunger for a heavier repertory in unexpected places. Residents of St. Joseph, Michigan, and Burlington, Indiana, telegraphed Thomas asking him to substitute Beethoven symphonies for some of the lighter pieces scheduled. According to Charles Locke, who helped arrange the tour, "Wagner's music was received better than any other, and the musical culture showed throughout the West by the enthusiastic reception of the best classical music was a surprise to Mr. Thomas and the whole company. It was a discriminating interest that was shown, and not an interest worked up because it is 'the thing' to admire classical music" (Petteys 1992, p. 174).

Local newspaper accounts of the Thomas visits confirm that such tours did much to stimulate local musical activity. The San Francisco *Morning Call* expressed the hope that a local school of music might result from the interest Thomas's orchestra generated. The Memphis *Daily Appeal* commented that "nothing that Memphis has ever done will be so productive as this of desirable and lasting results." The Kansas City *Daily Times* thought the festival might act as a "local musical awakening." Those involved with the tour saw their role as evangelical. Frank King, business manager, commented that those concerts in which local choruses assisted "educate them up to a higher standard of musical composition" (Petteys 1992, p. 173).

Virtuoso pianists, both American and European, were especially prominent on the touring circuits. With the piano becoming a fixture in many homes, interest in it was high. With the railroad a pianist could travel with his instrument. And the pianist could of course do it all alone. At first he brought other musicians, but as the century progressed solo recitals became more and more common. Sigismund Thalberg's visit in 1856, close on the heels of Jenny Lind, demonstrated to Americans what a first-rate artist could do on the piano. Gottschalk and William Mason (1829–1908), native-born Americans, were not far behind, soon followed by the European giants Anton Rubinstein and Hans von Bülow. In tours of 1870 to 1873 Theodore Thomas took with him three women pianists, Anna Mahlig, Alice Topp, and Marie Krebs. Although the piano had become a familiar instrument by 1870, hearing it with orchestra was still a new experience for most Americans. In the 1880s Anna Essipoff, Teresa Carreño, Julie Rivé-King, Rafael Jossefy, William H. Sherwood, and Louis Mass toured throughout the country. The 1890s saw the arrival of Ignace Paderewski and Vladimir de Pachmann.

Nothing better illustrates the crystallization of the idea of art music than the dramatic changes that the programs of the traveling piano

virtuosos underwent in the two decades between Thalberg and Ruben-
stein. Thalberg, considered the great rival to Liszt, played mostly his own
pieces, usually virtuoso elaborations on Italian opera tunes. He would
intersperse these with Irish and Scotch songs and almost always *Home,
Sweet Home*. By 1875 Julie Rivé-King could play a program consisting of a
late Beethoven sonata, a Schubert sonata, the Schumann *Symphonic Etudes*,
Mendelssohn's *Rondo Capriccioso*, a Chopin Rondo, a Beethoven symphonic transcription, and the lightest piece on the program, Raff's *Grand
Waltz de Concert*. Yet not even that compares with an 1873 Rubinstein New
York concert, in which he played the last five sonatas of Beethoven
(Matthews 1889, pp. 113–118). No audience would have stood, or sat, for
that twenty years earlier.

In the second half of the nineteenth century traveling opera companies
presented opera, often grand opera, throughout the country, in towns far
removed from the eastern seaboard. Although no single operatic troupe
traveled as extensively for as many years as Thomas's orchestra, and none
could match the schedule of a Gottschalk, the logistics of opera presentation made their efforts even more challenging. The tours demanded
considerable resourcefulness and imaginative improvisational skills to
succeed at all. Early in the century singers traveled in small troupes augmented by local musicians along the way. The Havana Opera Company did
arrive in 1847 with a contingent of seventy-three (Preston 1993, p. 131).
This was especially large by contemporary standards, but they limited
their performances to major East Coast cities. By the late nineteenth
century opera production had become even more lavish, and some traveling companies tried to take it all on the road. The most ambitious was the
American Opera Company, founded by Jeanette Thurber in New York in
1885. She had strange ideas for the 1880s – that opera should be accessible,
in English, at reasonable prices, that American singers should be hired, and
that the production values and ensemble, including orchestra, chorus, and
ballet, should take precedence over the star system. To that end she hired
the ubiquitous Theodore Thomas.

After a successful season in New York the company began their first
tour. They triumphed in Boston. Things began to unravel the following
spring, however, as touring became more extensive, finally reaching from
coast to coast. For even in the gilded age, a retinue of 300, with 4,000 costumes, scenery, and props to match proved too much to manage. By 1887
the company was bankrupt.

Many new western cities such as San Francisco had opera companies almost from their founding. Opera meant many things to nineteenth-century Americans, but at some level it was a mass, popular idiom. Operatic arias were among the most popular tunes of the time. A city such as San Francisco took to Verdi with an enthusiasm reserved today for blockbuster movies.

But opera also had a special aura. Tom Maguire, who built a theatrical empire in California, was an illiterate, brawling owner of a gambling hall and saloon. For him opera was bad business; Maguire quickly discovered he could make much more money running a saloon than an opera house. Opera, however, was his passion, and he was willing to bankrupt himself, which he did several times, in order to indulge that passion. Altogether he built twelve opera houses in California in addition to arranging performances in many others (Martin 1993, p. 111); and his cousin John Maguire built two opera houses in Montana, claiming the second, in Butte, to be the West's "finest opera house outside of San Francisco" (Davis 1970, p. 11).

Key to the definition of opera was its relation to theatre. In the early nineteenth century the theatre was a popular but somewhat unsavory place. Opera was by and large associated with theatre. As such it was considered neither elite nor high art. It never fully shed that association in the nineteenth century, but as early as 1825 attempts were made to disassociate opera from theatre, mainly as a class separating means. Opera became an upper-class social event precisely correspondent to the process of disassociation of opera from theatre, which gained momentum throughout the nineteenth century. The creation of separate opera houses and the presentation of opera in foreign languages were the most visible symbols of this change.

The most famous opera house in the United States today, the Metropolitan Opera in New York, had its origins in an internecine tiff among the socially elite, between the old rich and the new very rich. The old rich controlled the New York Academy of Music, the principal opera house in New York in the 1870s. When William H. Vanderbilt, heir to a fortune close to $100 million, applied for a box and was rejected, that was it. In 1880 a group of *nouveaux riches*, including some of the most powerful families in America, formed the Metropolitan Opera Company. By 1883 they had a new $1.7 million building, and a hot competition between the two opera houses opened up. The Met won easily, and the Academy folded in 1886.

All was not well at the Met, however. The first season ran a large deficit. In response the conductor Walter Damrosch offered to put on an entirely

German season. This was accepted, and Wagner became the centerpiece, supported by Italian, French, and other German operas, all sung in German. German immigrants, who had before heard Wagner mainly in the Bowery, flocked to the Met, swelling receipts. The *nouveaux riches* still had their boxes, but for seven seasons the Metropolitan Opera House was essentially the musical home of middle-class German immigrants. In 1891 the box holders prevailed, Italian opera returned, and the Met became what it still is today, the symbol of operatic high culture in America (Horowitz 1994, p. 172).

Just how important opera was to nineteenth-century America is vividly demonstrated in the building boom in "opera houses" that occurred after the Civil War. By 1889 there were 1,848 opera houses in America. Many were concentrated in the Midwest, states that had flourished only after mid-century. Curiously, in 1889 Iowa had more opera houses than any other state in the country, with 157, followed by New York with 154, Illinois with 149, and Kansas with 135 (Jeffrey 1889).

This does not mean that the houses were built for opera, or even that opera ever played in them, however. The term "Opera House" became a favorite late-nineteenth-century title for any kind of auditorium. Most were theatres. The size, elaborateness, and purpose of these structures differed greatly. They ranged from the massive and ornate Metropolitan Opera House, which seated 3,615 or the Grand Opera House of San Francisco, with a stage 100 feet by 122 feet, to Yerger's Opera House in Keosaqua, Iowa, that had a stage 16 feet by 18 feet and seated 250. Relatively opulent houses, however, appeared in unusual places, such as Butte, Montana, mentioned above; Virginia City, Nevada; or the mining town of Leadville, Colorado (Davis 1970, pp. 11–13). Presentations in opera houses ranged from theatrical productions to trained animals, knife throwers, and sporting events (Glenn and Poole 1993, p. 72).

The term opera house became popular because of the ingrained prejudice against theatre that still existed in America. More to the point, however, the opera house euphemism could exist because opera was redefined in the second half of the nineteenth century. It became a musical rather than a theatrical medium. It was reconceived as abstract high art music rather than as the violent, unscrupled, Machievellian drama that it was. For that reason opera in a foreign language was preferable; whether in the original or in a translation into German didn't matter. The language barrier distanced the audience from the drama, and in essence made opera respectable.

TABLE 9.1 *Major symphony orchestras established before 1920 still in existence, 1996*

Orchestra	Date founded	Source of backing	Principal persons and organizations involved
New York Philharmonic	1842	Cooperative society, musicians	Ureli Corelli Hill
Symphony Society of New York*	1878	Private benefactors	Walter Damrosch
Boston Symphony Orchestra	1881	Individual	Henry Lee Higginson
Chicago Symphony Orchestra	1891	50 Private benefactors	Charles Norman Fay
Cincinnati Symphony Orchestra	1895	Private benefactors	Ladies Musical Club
Philadelphia Orchestra	1900	120 Private benefactors	Musical Fund Society
Minneapolis Symphony Orchestra	1903	Private benefactors	Emil Oberhoffer, Elbert L. Carpenter
St. Louis Symphony Orchestra	1907	Private benefactors	St. Louis Choral Society
San Francisco Symphony Orchestra	1911	Private benefactors	Musical Association of San Francisco
Houston Symphony Orchestra	1912	Private funds	Ima Hogg
Baltimore Symphony Orchestra	1914	Municipal grant	
Cleveland Orchestra	1918	Private benefactors	Adella Prentiss Hughes
Detroit Symphony Orchestra	1919	Private benefactors	
Philharmonic Society of Los Angeles	1919	Individual	William Andrews Clark

*Merged with the New York Philharmonic in 1928

If opera had to struggle because of its theatrical associations, the symphony orchestra had no such problem. In the second half of the nineteenth century the symphony orchestra became the very symbol of art music, an institution that universally garnered civic pride even if its supporters were not always versed, knowledgeable, or even interested in its music. The growth of art music in nineteenth-century America correlates closely with the establishment and spread of symphony orchestras.

Almost all of the major symphony orchestras in the United States today were founded between 1860 and 1920. Only the New York Philharmonic predates the Civil War, the Philharmonic Society being established in 1842. As discussed in chapter 8, some eastern cities, such as Boston and Philadelphia had orchestras and similar organizations earlier in the century, but they did not survive as such. Table 9.1 indicates the founding of some of the major orchestras. Table 9.2, which lists the founding dates of other orchestras, indicates the geographical spread of the symphony orchestra into many medium-size towns and cities throughout the United States.

Decentralization is apparent in many of the major institutions whose origins date from the nineteenth century. Some institutions were founded

TABLE 9.2 *Other cities with symphony orchestras established before 1920*

Orchestra	Date founded
Columbus (OH) Orchestra	1886
Boise (ID) "Boise Orchestra"	1887
Buffalo Orchestra	1887
Salt Lake Symphony Orchestra	1888
New Haven Symphony Orchestra	1894
Portland (OR) Symphony Orchestra	1896
Dallas Symphony Orchestra	1900
Honolulu Symphony Society	1903
Seattle Symphony Orchestra	1903
St. Paul Orchestra	1905
Philharmonic Society of New Orleans	1906
Wilmington (DE) Orchestra	1906
Memphis Symphony Orchestra	1909
Austin Symphony	1911
Sacramento Symphony and Oratorio Society	1911
Denver Philharmonic Orchestra	1912
Kansas City Symphony Orchestra	1912
Spokane Orchestra	1915

by wealthy Americans, who saw them as their personal fiefdoms. Henry Lee Higginson established the Boston Symphony Orchestra in one stroke in 1881, putting up a guarantee of $1 million to cover expenses and deficits. And Higginson controlled all aspects of its operation until 1917, managing it in great detail. Other institutions such as the Metropolitan Opera, were founded by groups of wealthy individuals, for their own benefit, in that sense emulating European academies. Others were founded by speculators as money-making ventures, including some founded by musicians themselves. Still others, such as the Chicago Symphony Orchestra, originated as an act of civic pride. The Cleveland Symphony and the Houston Symphony have similar origins. In such cases, however, virtually all of the resources came from private money, from wealthy individuals acting out of a sense of community.

In Chicago the orchestra may have been private but it had a quasi-public character, and its conductor Theodore Thomas, who was already known nationwide, was a public figure in the minds of all but the city's accountants. A pattern such as Chicago's is as close to government sponsorship as existed in the nineteenth century. Only in 1914, when the city of Baltimore put up $8,000 to establish a symphony orchestra, did municipalities contribute directly to musical institutions. And the idea of federal or even state support for the arts would wait until even later in the twentieth century.

A new breed of women

The railroad and the touring virtuoso, as restless as America itself at this time, make up the supply side of the equation explaining the unprecedented growth of art music in the United States. But what about demand? What was going on in all these towns and cities the virtuosos visited? Why the sudden interest in art music?

Of many factors one stands out: a new breed of women and the organizations they formed. Nothing was more integral to late-nineteenth-century musical developments than music clubs. Contemporary writers called them "the most potent force" in American music (Whitesitt 1986–1990, p. 663). Sometimes they were a branch of a larger organization and sometimes they were independent. With exclusively female membership, however, they were organized and run by women.

Practically every town of any size had a music club, and some demanded very high levels of musical ability from their members. A violinist wishing to join the Women's Music Club of Columbus, Ohio, had to play in audition a Romantic concerto, a sonata, a concert piece by Wieniawski, Vieuxtemps, or Sarasate, and at least one piece from the "modern school," all from memory (Whitesitt 1986–1990, p. 667). The President of the Women's Philharmonic Society of New York from 1903 through 1912 was Amy Fay (1844–1928), pupil of Taussig, Kullack, and Liszt, a virtuoso in her own right. Her memoirs, *Music Study in Germany*, had interested many young women in studying music.

Most clubs distinguished between active members (those who performed in club recitals and concerts) and associate members (who did not). Associate members became more important as the century progressed and the activities of the clubs expanded. Although most clubs originated simply as places for women musicians to make music, by the 1890s they were more often than not the principal music organization of the town or city. The women who ran these clubs took their civic duties seriously, and the clubs began to sponsor many types of public concerts, including those of touring virtuosos. Their activities often led to the founding of other musical institutions, including in some cases symphony orchestras.

Leaders of the music clubs exerted enormous influence on the musical life of a community, and many women remembered for their patronage had a musical club as their base.

The women's musical club movement was a post-Civil War phenomenon. The Rossini Club of Portland, Maine, was reportedly the oldest club, founded in 1871. By the end of the century some 300 clubs existed, according to *Etude* magazine; the largest was the Schubert Club of St. Paul, Minnesota, with 431 members. Growth continued into the twentieth century: associate membership in the Columbus, Ohio, Women's Music Club reached 3,500 in 1907, making it the largest in the world (Whitesitt 1989, pp. 176, 161).

By the 1890s the movement had become national. In 1893 the first National Convention of Women's Musical Clubs was held at the Chicago World's Columbian Exposition, organized by Mrs. Theodore Thomas. This led to the founding of the National Federation of Musical Clubs in 1898 by Florence Sutro.

Comments from the early twentieth century indicate just how important women's clubs were to a community. In 1904 the *New York Sun* editorialized that "Without this guarantee and the influence [of the club members] many small towns would never hear the well known artists . . . All over the country these clubs have done a wonderful missionary work in bringing to people of the smaller cities the best of the virtuosos." *The Musician* commented in 1911 that "the clubs are almost everything to the music of America" (Whitesitt 1989, p. 177).

Nineteenth-century attitudes, rooted in the notion of separate spheres for men and women, put music mostly in women's sphere. Many girls and young women received musical training, most often in piano and voice, but by the late nineteenth century on the full range of instruments. Thus the Los Angeles club could maintain a full symphony orchestra, composed entirely of members. With careers outside the home generally discouraged, voluntary community and charitable organizations gave women an entree into the public sphere. A music club not only allowed women with musical training an opportunity to perform but to work for the good of the community.

Throughout the country men saw the activities of their wives or daughters as a valuable but innocent and dilettantish pursuit of the arts ideal that the doctrine of separate spheres bequeathed to women. Comments from the late nineteenth and early twentieth century regarding the musical clubs were couched in this idealism: "Man wins the kingdom home, while woman guards its sacred precincts." "Music for women is one of the spiritual lights of the modern world, without which our civilization cannot endure" (Whitesitt 1989, pp. 161, 176).

Unbeknownst to many men, however, a quiet revolution was occurring. Women in the clubs were moving far beyond the idealism these statements assumed. They were becoming able, indeed, shrewd business practitioners. The activities of the clubs provided women one of the few opportunities to stand toe to toe with men in the overwhelmingly male world of business. No arena gave women a broader or more powerful platform in the public sphere than they found in music entrepreneurship. And for many women the music club was only a beginning. Many went on to manage and run a variety of musical activities and organizations, in many cases as amateurs, but often as professionals.

For by the early twentieth century, music clubs had become a powerful economic force, handling an estimated three-fourths of concert engagements outside the large cities (Whitesitt 1989, p. 162). Men in the business end of the musical world knew what was happening. John C. Freund commented in 1915 that the hold New York managers had was giving way to local managers, including "many women of ability and responsibility." And in 1909 "J. B.", writing in *Musical America*, observed that "many musical bodies owe much of their success to the capable business qualities and unflagging devotion to art [women] demonstrated" (Whitesitt 1991, p. 175). "C. A." writing in *Musical America* in 1910 acknowledged that women concert managers had "an executive ability equal in its results with that of the majority of successful business men" (Whitesitt 1991, p. 163).

Robert Grau described in 1914 just how important women were in the music business. He observed that in many cities, in which from three to six impresarios were active, the majority were women. And many smaller towns would have no musical activities at all were it not for women managers. He estimated that 90 percent of the contracts in small to medium towns were signed by women. One result, according to Grau, was that the number of cities capable of hosting grand opera since 1900 increased from approximately 25 to over 300 (Grau 1914, p. 13).

Some cities had the women's music club to thank directly for performing space. The St. Cecilia Club of Grand Rapids, Missouri, under the leadership of Mrs. Charles B. Kelsey, President of the National Federation of Music Clubs, and Ella May Smith, its first President, managed to erect its own building. They pulled it off through a combination of fund raising and shrewd real estate entrepreneurship. Consisting of an auditorium, ball room, and reading room, the building hosted a variety of concerts and was described by a contemporary writer as "one of the finest of the kind in the country" (C. A. 1910, p. 3).

The Seidl Society of New York was typical of many music clubs. In May, 1889, it was organized under the leadership of Laura Langford "for securing to its members and to the public increased musical culture and of promoting musical interest among women particularly" (Horowitz 1994, p. 191). Its immediate goal was to provide a means for women to attend Anton Seidl's summer concerts at Brighton Beach, which often featured Wagner's music. Many women found Wagner's erotic message and powerful heroines intensely attractive in the emotionally restricted Victorian environment. But attending the Brighton Beach concert presented serious practical problems. In the 1890s a proper woman did not just go from New York to Brighton Beach unescorted. Langford arranged a package, including special railroad cars, for members and friends to attend, thus allowing women the opportunity for an outing without the problem of securing male escorts.

Langford soon branched out. In the summer of 1889 the Seidl Society began to sponsor trips for thousands of working girls, children, and orphans to attend Coney Island and the concerts without cost. Beginning in 1890 she organized primarily Wagner concerts at the Brooklyn Academy of Music, with Seidl conducting. In these activities she was, as Joseph Horowitz put it, "all business," adroitly handling daily problems and crises, standing "unquestionably on equal footing in Seidl's world of art and artists" (Horowitz 1994, pp. 236–237). While not working on behalf of Wagner she wrote romantic biographies, including the massive *The Mothers of Great Men and Women, and Some Wives of Great Men* (New York, 1883). In it she deplored the fate of the wives of public men who were "left behind" and "doomed to slavery of the most repulsive kind during perhaps the best years of life" (Horowitz 1994, p. 236). Langford not only chafed at her culture's restrictions but sought to do something about them.

Horowitz saw in the efforts of women such as Langford a type of protofeminism, an apt characterization clearly not unique to New York. In many ways Langford's story occurred over and over nationwide. It was a wedge driven time and again into the restrictive Victorian monolith. Pushing for equal rights, denied full entree into the public sphere, women took one part of it, the music world, and demonstrated an acumen and entrepreneurship that was probably a surprise to all but those men in the music business whose own success depended on them. Both the musical life of America and many individual communities were richer for these efforts.

A successful club president negotiated contracts for artists, arranged concert halls, goaded the community – often business men who would rather sit in hot oil than attend a concert – into buying sufficient tickets to support the endeavor, and carried on her back the financial success of the presentations. She was by any measurement an impresario. It was only a small, almost infinitesimal, step to independent impresario. Several women made the transition, using their club experience as the foundation for an independent career. The best-known was Adella Prentiss Hughes (1869–1950), a charter member of the Cleveland Fortnightly Musical Club and a pianist of considerable talent. Spurred on by the many guest orchestras she brought to Cleveland, Clevelanders founded the Musical Arts Association in 1915, the parent organization of the Cleveland Orchestra. Hughes was at the center of it. She convinced wealthy citizens to back the Association, she secured Nikolai Sokoloff as conductor in 1918, a coup in itself, and when the orchestra was formed, she served as manager for fifteen years (A. P. Hughes 1947, pp. 246–262).

Powerful women entrepreneurs operated in the largest cities, as witness the impact women had on the musical life of New York City alone. In addition to Laura Langford, Mrs. George Sheldon essentially saved the New York Philharmonic Society in 1909. Organized as a cooperative society, with financial responsibility and benefits in the hands of Actual (in contrast to Honorary) Members, by 1908 it was in a financial crisis. Mrs. Sheldon led a drive to reorganize it into a corporation and was instrumental in securing financial backing to insure its future. A. Lenalie, meanwhile, took over management of the People's Symphony Orchestra and Auxiliary Club of New York in 1906, when it was in serious difficulty. In two years she increased membership from 400 to 8,500 (which guaranteed an audience base of at least 1,700), expanded performances to include four orchestral concerts at Carnegie Hall and six chamber concerts at Cooper Union, and established fifteen-cent tickets at Carnegie Hall so those otherwise financially unable could hear orchestral music (J. B. 1909, p. 6).

Many important musical educational institutions were founded by women. Musical ability was considered an important accomplishment in young women of the nineteenth century, and for those with talent and a genuine interest in music a conservatory was an acceptable, indeed a proper place for higher education. Clara Baur founded the Cincinnati

Conservatory of Music in 1867; for many years it was the premier educational institution west of the Alleghenies, and one of the most important in the nation. Jeanette Thurber founded the National Conservatory of Music in New York in 1885; it remained operational until about 1930. Thurber made her mark on American musical history when she convinced Dvořák to come for a two-year residency there. As we will see his presence was an important milestone in the evolution of American music. Harriet Gibbs Marshall founded the Washington, D. C. Conservatory of Music in 1903; and in 1924, Mary Louise Curtis Bok founded the Curtis Institute in Philadelphia.

Although most women patrons worked through organizations such as clubs, a few supported the arts independently. Isabella Stewart Gardner of Boston, as eccentric as she was wealthy, befriended both artists and musicians. Active in support of the Boston Symphony Orchestra, she underwrote other concerts as well, assisted musicians with contracts, and provided instruments for their use. Her home featured a large collection of paintings and a concert hall capable of holding a symphony orchestra and 300 listeners. It has since become the Gardner Museum (Locke 1994, p. 804), although the concert hall no longer exists.

Monster concerts

Another important creator of interest in art music in America were monster concerts and festivals. These were usually multi-day events that involved orchestras with players numbering in the hundreds, and choruses that sometimes reached several thousand. They came to America with a long European history, which goes back to at least eighteenth-century England. The Handel Commemoration of 1784, if not the first, became the prototype in the English-speaking world. Held in Westminster Abbey it featured an orchestra of 250 and a chorus of 274. In revolutionary France mass celebrations of music, born of an idealism that sought to connect music with the people, employed huge orchestras and choruses in outdoor fêtes. Romantic composers such as Berlioz continued this tradition.

Monster concerts had first come to America in the mid-1850s under the leadership of Louis Antoine Jullien (1812–1860), who had already honed his skills in Paris and London. No detail of showmanship escaped Jullien. His concerts were visual as well as musical spectacles, and he conducted Beethoven with a jeweled baton and white gloves brought to him on silver tray. Crude as it was, the gesture made a point to the audience: this music was different, to be approached reverentially. Jullien's own showmanship thus reinforced the message of a musical hierarchy.

Jullien stayed in America only briefly. Patrick S. Gilmore (1820–1892) who picked up the flame Jullien had lit, immigrated permanently from Ireland, via England and Canada. Arriving in Boston at age nineteen, he founded the Boston Brigade Band in 1859. In 1864 Gilmore had his first opportunity to organize a monster concert, in New Orleans, to celebrate the inauguration of Michael Hahn as Governor. Gilmore assembled a chorus of 5,000 adults and children, a band of 500 pieces, and a large fife and drum corp. All of this was augmented by church bells and artillery. The final piece, *Hail Columbia*, concluded with thirty-six canon (Davis 1980, p. 1).

Gilmore organized another monster concert for the Peace Jubilee in Boston, June 15–17, 1869. It was twice the size of his New Orleans adventure: a chorus of 10,000 and an orchestra of 1,000, with Ole Bull as concert master. A special coliseum holding 50,000 was built in St. James Park. The repertory was mixed: patriotic songs and hymns, selections from a Mozart mass, overtures by Rossini, and pieces by John Knowles Paine and Dudley Buck. Verdi's "Anvil Chorus" had 100 local firemen in uniform, including helmets, playing the anvils. The old conservative musical elements of Boston were aghast. The Handel and Haydn Society refused to participate, and John S. Dwight purposely stayed aloof during its planning, although he did attend. (Poor Dwight. He later wrote at great length about it in his journal, and even though he was appalled, he could not help but be grudgingly moved.)

The jubilee was so successful that Gilmore determined to outdo himself three years later, with the World Peace Jubilee. Again he doubled the numbers: a chorus of 20,000, an orchestra of 2,000, a coliseum seating 100,000. He secured military bands and virtuosos from Europe. Most important he brought Johann Strauss the younger, whose presence proved an attraction unparalleled in American music.

The jubilee was too much. The chorus of 20,000, necessitating 100 assistant conductors was unwieldy. Strauss took one look at the situation and observed, correctly, that any sort of polished performance was out of the question. The crowds, probably still satiated from 1869, did not appear. It was a financial disaster and would not be repeated, at least on that magnitude. Yet the idea continued, only elsewhere.

The monster festival soon spread to New York. There Walter Damrosch and Theodore Thomas were engaged in a fierce struggle for musical

hegemony: Thomas the established star *versus* Damrosch the upstart new-
comer trying to break in. Thomas made it clear how he felt about challenges. On meeting Damrosch he reportedly said, "I hear, Doctor
Damrosch, that you are a very fine musician, but I want to tell you one
thing: whoever crosses my path I crush" (Damrosch 1923, p. 22). Damrosch founded the Oratorio Society of New York in 1873, and as an extension, the New York Symphony Society in 1878. Still, Thomas's hold on the
city seemed unbreakable, even though he took a two-year hiatus in Cincinnati, from 1878 to 1880. In May, 1881 Damrosch launched his heavy
artillery, a monster music festival. It lasted a week, with a chorus and
orchestra numbering 1,500, and an organ moved bodily into the Seventh
Regiment Armory building from St. Vincent's Church. Damrosch featured Beethoven's Ninth Symphony, Anton Rubinstein's *Tower of Babel*,
Handel's *Messiah*, and Berlioz's Requiem. The Berlioz Requiem in particular created a sensation, and a packed audience of 10,000 was claimed for
every performance (Damrosch 1923, pp. 32–33).

Thomas soon retaliated. Within days of Damrosch's festival he
announced his own for 1882 in the same armory building. Thus New
Yorkers were to be presented with the spectacle of dueling monster music
festivals. Thomas had already created monster festivals in Cincinnati and
Philadelphia, but even the Philadelphia Centennial Festival, with an
orchestra of 150, a chorus of 1,000, a march especially composed for the
occasion by Wagner, and with President Grant and many other national
leaders present, was small potatoes to what he envisioned. Thomas essentially doubled Damrosch's forces – geometric increases seemed to be the
order of the day for these events – with an orchestra of 300 and a chorus of
3,000. He also had broader plans; it would be a tri-city festival, presented
in New York, Cincinnati, and Chicago respectively. With each presentation momentum built, as audiences, receiving newspaper reports from the
other cities, eagerly anticipated his arrival. It was a technique worthy of
Barnum. And Thomas, true to his reputation, did not compromise on
repertory. The programs were long and heavy, featuring among other
works, the first complete performance of Bach's *St. Matthew Passion* in
America.

Monster festivals, part serious music and part hoopla, extravaganza, and
P. T. Barnum showmanship, nevertheless did much to interest Americans
in art music, however vaguely that term was understood. Thomas saw in
the festivals an opportunity to evangelize for better music: "You see, we
must place the great masters before the people at these festivals in the very

best way, or our work goes for naught." Thomas also recognized how well the festivals caught the tone of the times. "Everything is bigger here," and America, with an "ambitious driving purpose which compels us to extend our efforts," "expects bigger, greater, more impressive [concerts] than its predecessors" (quotations from Schabas 1989, p. 115).

All in all monster concerts were important in shaping musical culture in nineteenth-century America. The *Chicago Interocean* acknowledged that Thomas, with his festival, "continues to discipline Chicago successfully in the growth of taste," and connected art music directly with morality: the festival contributed to "public knowledge [of music] and indirectly, public morals" (Schabas 1989, pp. 119–120). Not all festivals had such lofty goals, but all had a major impact. The very presence of Johann Strauss in Boston was in itself cause for much publicity. The concerts attracted the curious and the thrill-seekers, but many went away supporters. Whatever their musical value, and that was hotly debated in the nineteenth century, monster festivals built audiences for art music.

Composers

As was noted in chapter 8, only a handful of American composers wrote art music before the Civil War: among the most prominent were Anthony Heinrich (1781–1861), Henry Fry (1813–1864), and George Bristow (1825–1898). These composers had begun to develop a rudimentary American style. It consisted of a balance of light and heavy elements, and was derived partly from Italian opera, partly from Mendelssohn's more descriptive instrumental works. But this direction was cut short by two changes in the American musical world. The first was the clearer distinction between art music and other types, and with it new expectations about what art music should be. The second was a much closer connection to Germany. Many German musicians immigrated to the United States after 1848, and many Americans went to Germany to study. Together these developments brought a new sense of calling: music of a higher purpose, and music of a new seriousness.

American composers had three agendas or challenges in the second half of the nineteenth century, which unfolded more or less consecutively. The first was acceptance. Throughout the nineteenth century the American public continued to assume that if a composer was American, he was inferior. A European education solved this issue in the short term. Beyond intrinsic benefits to a composer, European study provided a stamp of approval to a public very unsure about the art. It legitimized American musicians. The second challenge facing the composer was opportunity. Americans could learn their craft in Europe, they could be sanctioned by names such as Liszt, Berlioz, Chopin, or Thalberg, but that did little good if their compositions could not be heard.

The third challenge was identity. Only after American composers had gained the requisite craft, had secured a pedigree, and found at least a potential audience, was the call for a uniquely American musical art heeded seriously. A few composers had sensed this issue from the beginning. In the first half of the century, Heinrich and Fry approached it in radically different ways. For Gottschalk at mid-century it seemed moot. More than any other composer of his time he blended art and his native vernacular in a natural, unforced way. He remained, however, acutely sensitive to criticism that some considered his pieces vulgar. But for approximately twenty years after the Civil War American composers were more intent in proving their mettle than establishing a national independence. Beginning in the 1880s, however, calls for an American music were heard with increasing frequency.

Compositional activity in the second half of the nineteenth century was much more geographically concentrated than other musical activities. Much of it centered in Boston, and historians have used the term Second New England School to delineate the group of composers who worked in the Boston area, distinguishing them from the First New England School of eighteenth-century singing-school tunebook composers.

Who comprised the Second New England School? This is not entirely clear. A core group of composers lived and worked in Boston, had similar but not identical musical philosophies, and exerted mutual influence, often meeting to critique each other's works. The most important were John Knowles Paine (1839–1906), Arthur Foote (1853–1937), George Whitefield Chadwick (1854–1931), and Amy Cheney Beach (1867–1944). A number of other composers had New England connections but either worked elsewhere much of their career or had a sufficiently different aesthetic orientation to place them outside the New England School itself. These included Dudley Buck (1839–1909), Charles Martin Loeffler (1861–1935), Edward MacDowell (1861–1908), George Whiting (1861–1944), Horatio Parker (1863–1919), Arthur Farwell (1872–1951), Daniel Gregory Mason (1873–1953), and Charles Tomlinson Griffes (1884–1920). Horatio Parker falls outside the core group only because opportunity took him to New Haven, Connecticut, in 1894, although he maintained professional connections with Boston until 1902 (Crawford 1996, p. 531).

Except for Amy Beach, whose career took a different path because she was female, the core group was associated with Boston educational institutions: John Knowles Paine taught at Harvard and George Chadwick at the New England Conservatory; Foote mostly taught privately but after 1921 was at the New England Conservatory; he spent the year 1911–1912 as lecturer and Acting Chairman of the Music Department at the University of California at Berkeley. Parker left Boston in 1894 to assume a professorship at Yale University.

John Knowles Paine (1839–1906) was the acknowledged leader of the New England school, partly because he was approximately a generation older than the others and partly because he was appointed the first Professor of Music at Harvard. Earlier writers referred to him as not "'A Patriarch' but 'The Patriarch' of American Music," and the "veritable Dean" of the "academic" composers (Howe 1939, p. 257; R. Hughes 1900, p. 146). Paine's works are usually considered very competent although conservative, a charge not altogether accurate as we will see. Paine, himself, was much aware that he would be judged according to the classical pantheon, and like other art music composers, by what he could do in the larger forms. His principal historical importance, however, is the impact he had on other composers.

Unlike most of his contemporaries Paine's principal influence was not Mozart, Beethoven, or early Romantic composers, but J. S. Bach. This put him somewhat at odds with prevailing aesthetic expectations. Primarily an organist, Paine studied with the German Bach devotee August Haupt, and was probably the first American to master the organ literature of Bach. In spite of his reputation as an organist and in spite of holding important organ posts throughout his life, however, Paine composed few organ works. A fair fraction of those he did compose were variations on well-known tunes, comparable to what the piano virtuosos were doing. But there was little place for the organ music of Bach in the Romantic canon. Had Paine lived a little later and come to know the French organ school of Franck and Widor, his compositional output might have been quite different.

Paine's most important compositions are two symphonies and two large choral works. His first major choral work, a Mass in D, was written in 1865 and premiered in Germany. In 1872 he completed his oratorio *St. Peter.* It brought him much closer to both Bach and American audiences.

No major musical genre had deeper roots in American soil. Oratorio societies, an outgrowth of the singing-school movement, had been performing large oratorios since the beginning of the nineteenth century. Critics hailed *St. Peter* as a landmark, "without doubt the most important musical work yet produced in this country," and "the first direct proof we have had of the existence of creative musical genius in this country" (Matthews 1873, p. 116, quoted in Smither forthcoming, pp. 31, 33). The Bachian influence is apparent in its serious tone, incorporation of chorales, and polyphonic choruses.

Paine composed his First Symphony in 1876, and the Second, entitled *Im Fruhling*, in 1879. Both pieces refute the charge that Paine was a competent but somewhat dull composer or that he was ultraconservative. He may have been a dull lecturer, as Chadwick intimated, but the symphonies themselves are passionate Romantic works. The First, in c minor, has a Romantic fire that elicits comparisons with both Beethoven's Fifth and Brahms's First. The latter comparison is particularly telling because Brahms and Paine completed their works simultaneously. Neither could have known the other's. The Second was probably influenced not only by Schumann but also Raff, who completed a similar work in 1878. Paine's titles for individual movements closely parallel Raff's.

Both symphonies were well received. At the premiere of the Second ladies waved handkerchiefs, men shouted, and the reserved John S. Dwight reportedly stood on his seat opening and closing his umbrella to show his enthusiasm. Paine was compared favorably to Mendelssohn and Schumann. The musical *cognoscente* of Boston clearly wanted a first-rate composer in their midst. Chadwick later said that Paine's two symphonies more than any other works interested American composers in that genre.

Paine's greatest long-term legacy may have been in defining a role for the composer. His success in establishing music at Harvard inaugurated a trend that was to affect American musical composition into the late twentieth century: the association of the composer with academia (see in particular chapter 18). This freed the composer from the marketplace, allowing him and later her to write, for a limited and erudite audience, works that need not have broad appeal or impact. It also constricted the composer. Endemic to the prime argument that secured music in academia, that it should be studied as literature, was the notion of a canon of great masterpieces worthy of such status. This placed a particular obligation on the academic composer, to write in that tradition. It provided a standard against which his work would be measured, and he knew it. It also fostered an innate conservatism, as the past as model and exemplar was always visible. Finally this approach led to considerable theorizing about music, not only by scholars studying works of the past, but by composers themselves to explain and justify their music.

The most original and creative nineteenth-century New England composer was George Whitefield Chadwick (1854–1931). In many ways his career is quintessentially academic: study in Europe with Reinecke, Jadassohn, and Rheinberger, organist and teacher in Boston, a major force at the New England Conservatory, author of an influential text on harmony, and finally successor to Edward MacDowell as the musical member in the Academy of Arts and Letters. Chadwick's work at the New England Conservatory is particularly important. Appointed director in 1897 he remolded it from essentially an advanced finishing school for singers and pianists to a full-fledged conservatory on European lines. It remains today one of the most important educational institutions for music in the United States.

As a composer Chadwick was anything but stuffy. His study in Europe, which did not commence until he was twenty-three, already indicates a sense of purpose and individualism. After succeeding spectacularly at the conservatory in Leipzig – his Second String Quartet and his *Rip van Winkle Overture* receiving enthusiastic performances and praise – Chadwick decided to study in Munich. On the way he fell in with a group of painters, known as the Duveneck Boys, after their leader, and accompanied them on a sojourn to France. Short-lived, the experience probably opened up to Chadwick possibilities of color and softened the Teutonic bent of his European education (Yellin 1990, pp. 36–37).

Chadwick was at his best in the major instrumental genres, in particular orchestral music and the string quartet. He wrote five string quartets, which establish him as a major Romantic chamber music composer. The best known was the Fourth, first performed in 1896. Chadwick's individuality is most apparent in the character of his melodies, and this quartet is a particularly good example. Many of the themes, although not pentatonic, have a pentatonic bent. Gapped notes, particularly in scalar passages, are typical. The tunes resemble Anglo-Celtic folk music. Although Chadwick himself was of Irish descent, the Celtic presence is less a commentary on his ancestral heritage than on the prevalence of such music in nineteenth-century America. As was pointed out in chapter 6, Anglo-Celtic music was common in American dance music, the fiddle remaining a ubiquitous instrument throughout the nineteenth century, and Irish ballad had a major impact on popular song, from the early importation of Thomas Moore's ballads through Stephen Foster and later Tin Pan Alley.

The quartet owes a debt to Dvořák's "American" Quartet, although how much is unclear. Chadwick undoubtedly knew Dvořák's quartet, which was premiered on January 1, 1894 in Boston by the Kneisel Quartet, for whom both Chadwick's Third and Fourth Quartets were written. Chadwick, however, had begun to incorporate the Anglo-Celtic folk idiom into his music long before Dvořák arrived in America. He was fully aware of what he was doing. He claimed to have used an Irish tune, *Shoot the Pipe*, in the scherzo of his First String Quartet. Other movements of this and other instrumental works have similar if less obvious folk qualities.

Chadwick was fundamentally a late Romantic composer. His incorporation of vernacular elements and an Irish piquancy into his music was uniquely refreshing at the time, even though some critics had difficulty accepting the humor. The folkish elements coexisted with characteristics typical of the nineteenth century: longer, more complex phrases, heavier, relatively chromatic harmony, and cyclic form. The last of these, typical of Dvořák, was too common in late Romanticism to be attributed directly to Dvořák. Particularly striking in Chadwick's music were his varied textures. This is noticeable in both the Second Symphony, where the trio of the scherzo and the principal theme of the first movement have a similar drone-like pedal built on the open fifth F–C, and in the fourth movement of the Fourth String Quartet, which opens with a unison variant of a theme from the first movement.

One other melodic feature appears so frequently in Chadwick's music that it is almost a signature: a sudden chromatic turn near the end of his folk-like melodies. It usually involves one particular scale degree, and most often was a lowered tone. In the opening themes of both the first and last movement of the Fourth Quartet an F♮ suddenly appears, the only chromaticism in an otherwise diatonic environment.

Chadwick's first major success was his *Rip van Winkle Overture*, written when a student in Leipzig. Throughout his career Chadwick continued to write orchestral music, and was more respected as an orchestral composer than in any other genre. Orchestral music played to one of his greatest strengths, a sense of instrumental color and imagery. He wrote three symphonies, all before 1895. After that he focused on orchestral works with programmatic connections: overtures, symphonic poems, and suites. His most popular, *Symphonic Sketches*, Suite for Orchestra, written between

1895 and 1904, consists of four works that may be played separately. They share many traits with the earlier symphonies and string quartets, but their individuality is even more striking. Nowhere is Chadwick's sense of color more vibrant. That summer of 1879 may have had a lasting impact on Chadwick.

If Chadwick was the most original composer of the New England school, Amy Cheney Beach (1867–1944) was the most talented. A virtuoso pianist, her gender determined her career. After a spectacular initial success, including a debut in Boston when she was fifteen and an appearance with the Boston Symphony Orchestra when she was seventeen, she married in 1885 and drastically reduced her performing activities. As the wife of a prominent surgeon, musical activities were all right in the home but not in public, unless it was for a good cause. Thus for twenty-five years Beach continued to compose, but limited her public appearances to one or two annual charitable events. Only after her husband's death in 1910 did she once again resume an active concert career.

Beach wrote a handful of large works and many smaller piano pieces and songs. In several of the major genres, she composed only one work: a Mass, a symphony, a piano concerto, a violin sonata, and a piano quintet. But each shows a remarkable mastery of the idiom. Her Mass, written in 1890, first attracted the public to her. The piano concerto and *Gaelic Symphony* became her best-known larger compositions. The symphony, composed in 1894–1896, was first performed in 1896. It is one of the largest works to come from the Second New England School. In it Beach combines the use of folk melodies, a late Romantic sound, chromatic harmonies, and a surprisingly mature sense of overall structure, given that this was her first symphonic composition. The symphony contrasts two expansive, passionate outer movements with two more lyrical and haunting middle movements, which quote Gaelic themes in their entirety. The second movement, the dance equivalent, is entitled *Alla Siciliana*. In both movements Beach breaks the melancholy lyricism with contrasting sections, a middle *perpetuum mobile* in the second, and two development sections in the third.

Adrienne Fried Block has pointed out parallels between Beach's symphony and Dvořák's "New World" Symphony. These include key, the use of pentatonic folk themes in a late Romantic harmonic environment, and prominence of the oboe and English horn in the slow movements (Block 1990b, p. 269). Whatever the extent of Dvořák's influence, however, Beach's choice of subject matter had less to do with a conscious nationalism than a fascination with old Gaelic tunes. In that sense she is closer to Chadwick than Dvořák.

Beach's *Gaelic Symphony* disproves many clichés about late-nineteenth-century American music. The first is that European training was essential for a composer. The second is that a derivative work could not be important. Beach's symphony, like her violin sonata and piano concerto, sound reminiscent of Brahms and Dvořák (for the sonata throw in a little Grieg and a touch of Franck). But Beach is still a strong, compelling voice. This is all the more remarkable since these were her first efforts in the genres; but all too sadly her only efforts.

The final point is the issue of gender as a factor in composition. There is no question that gender played a major part in Beach's career, as she chose to subordinate her musical activities to being a wife. The role of gender in her compositions, however, is another issue. In Beach's lifetime many critics openly doubted that a woman could successfully compose in the large instrumental forms. Unable to deny Beach's success, these writers then faulted her works for being too masculine. In fact it is difficult to hear them as a different type of statement from what a male composer of major talent would make. They are convincing within the same framework that we judge Brahms or Dvořák. If the interpreter considers that a masculine framework, then they are masculine. More important, however, they demonstrate that writing extended Romantic compositions had little to do with being born male or female.

Another side to Amy Beach is seen in her songs. She and her Boston compatriot Margaret Ruthven Lang (1867–1972) were two of the most successful art song composers of the early twentieth century. Beach's *Three Songs on Poems of Robert Browning* and her song *Ecstasy*, on her own text, were the most popular. *Ecstasy*, written for voice, piano, and violin reportedly received over 1,000 performances (Block 1983, p. 49).

Lang, who was active in Boston between 1887 and 1916, composed orchestral and choral music as well as songs. Her *Dramatic Overture* was the first work composed by a woman to be played by the Boston Symphony Orchestra, and her overture *Witichis* had three performances at the 1893 World's Columbian Exposition in Chicago. Most of her recognition, however, came as a song composer. Altogether she wrote over 150 songs. Both she and Beach proved to be highly sensitive to text, mood, and nuance.

At the turn of the century Edward MacDowell (1861–1908) was the best-known and most respected composer in America. His career spanned both Europe and America, and he was the first American since Gottschalk to receive wide recognition in Europe. Rupert Hughes, writing in 1900, left no doubt about MacDowell's position: "an almost unanimous vote would grant him rank as the greatest of American composers, while not a few ballots would indicate him as the best of living music writers" (R. Hughes 1900, pp. 34–35). MacDowell's reputation suffered along with other composers as part of the early-twentieth-century reaction against Romanticism, but has since returned, if not fully to the level that Hughes placed it. In retrospect MacDowell was an important composer, but not of the stature that Hughes suggested.

MacDowell, who showed extraordinary talent as a pianist in New York City where he grew up, followed the usual path to Europe, but with some unusual detours. When he was fifteen he went to Paris with his mother and soon won a scholarship at the Paris Conservatory. He also showed enough talent in painting that he was offered free instruction from the painter Carolus Duran at the Ecole des Beaux Arts and briefly considered a career in art. He chose music, and struck out for Germany, eventually to study with Raff and become a protégé of Liszt, who encouraged his composition. MacDowell's proclivity for painting and his association with Liszt determined his direction as a composer. Except for two piano concertos and four piano sonatas, vehicles for his own virtuosity, MacDowell eschewed the classical forms. His was the music of the future, the symphonic poem, the suite, and programmatic sketches.

MacDowell's best music is his piano music, which falls into the two extremes of Romanticism, the large or grandiose, and the miniature. Among his large works, the four piano sonatas, all the products of his maturity, are significant contributions to an important Romantic genre. Each sonata has a subtitle, and the last three have more specific programmatic references. The First, entitled *Sonata Tragica*, was composed in memory of his teacher Joachim Raff. In its tone and massive textures it conveys what Lawrence Gilman called the "strikingly orchestral character of his thought," even though, like his other sonatas, it is thoroughly pianistic (Gilman 1908, p. 150).

Each of MacDowell's last three sonatas is associated with a Nordic or Gaelic legend. MacDowell was not a nationalist, but like Chadwick his music has a Gaelic quality. Gilman labeled him flatly a Celtic composer (Gilman 1908, p. 1). MacDowell leans more toward the Scottish than Irish, the most obvious feature being his use of Scotch-snap rhythms. MacDowell's music also bears a stylistic similarity to Grieg's, to whom he

dedicated both the Third and Fourth Sonatas. The Third Sonata has been
called the "Norse", although MacDowell did not so entitle it. He did
include at the top of the score a poetic reference to Nordic legend. Even
this sonata, however, is as much Gaelic as Nordic. MacDowell may have
been partly drawn to the Gaelic element in Grieg, for both had Scottish
great-grandfathers.

MacDowell's Gaelic heritage is most obvious in his Second and Fourth
Piano Sonatas, the *Sonata Eroica* and the *Keltic*. The Second is based on the
Arthurian legend, and even though MacDowell acknowledged that each
movement represented some particular aspect of the legend, he insisted
that it was not strictly programmatic. The *Keltic Sonata* is based on the Irish
legends contained in the Cycle of the Red Branch (Gilman 1908, p. 156).

No group of pieces by an art music composer was better known in the
early twentieth century than MacDowell's character pieces for piano. The
best appeared as individual numbers in four suites, *Woodland Sketches*, *Sea
Pieces*, *Fireside Tales*, and *New England Idyls*. The appeal of these pieces was
partly their accessibility; many were easily playable by amateurs when the
piano was still at the center of many homes. More important, however,
MacDowell was able to evoke strongly and directly both place, usually
nature, and mood. Unlike Debussy, he never went beyond Romantic
harmony and melodic gesture, but his sense of color, focus, and economy
of means was extraordinary. These works suggest another connection to
Grieg, who was also a master of short, lyrical, evocative piano pieces.

In the last twenty years of the nineteenth century approximately 5,000
Americans departed for Mecca-am-Rhine, for Germany, to become musicians. The Leipzig Conservatory alone admitted 455 American students in
the 1890s (Bomberger 1991). One young American musician, however,
Charles Ives (1874–1954), had something else in mind. No European
education for him, although he was an extraordinary pianist and organist.
If we can believe Ives he was more interested in baseball than music. He
had his eye on Yale, not for music, but as the springboard for a business
career. By chance he arrived at Yale the same year as Horatio Parker, and
although he complained about Parker's conservatism as Beethoven did
about Haydn's, he did study music with Parker and benefit from the
association. Indeed, Ives's works from the period through 1905, including
the first two symphonies and a number of songs, are to a considerable
degree rooted in and indebted to the European Romantic language of
Parker and his colleagues, as well as the broader European traditions of
Brahms, Dvořák, and Tchaikovsky.

Having graduated from Yale, Ives moved to New York and evolved a dual life. Professionally he eventually became a partner in the most successful life insurance agency in New York. His creative accomplishments in insurance rival those in music. However, after a lukewarm public reception for his cantata, *The Celestial Country* (performed in 1902), which may have been a trial run for a musical career, and a few unsuccessful attempts to interest professional musicians in his music, he retreated, to compose in isolation. At this time, Ives's music rapidly moved away from the Romantic norms of the Second New England School, as Ives embraced a widening palette of new compositional ideas. With no record of performance or publication to guide the historian, controversy surrounds exactly what Ives wrote when, but I believe his own recollections are neither entirely disingenuous nor inaccurate. Even if we give him no benefit of doubt, however, in a fifteen year period, from roughly 1905 until 1921, he composed what must rank as one of the most original and extraordinary oeuvres in the history of not just American but Western music.[1]

Ives's principal instrumental compositions include four numbered symphonies and a number of other major orchestral works, several pieces for theatre orchestra, three piano sonatas, four violin sonatas, two string quartets, and one piano trio. He also composed many smaller piano pieces and studies. His most important vocal compositions are his approximately 150 songs, and a large quantity of choral music. Most of the choral music is early, written before 1902, when he was active as a church organist. His songs span his entire career and embrace a wide variety of styles. They range in length from the approximately thirty-second *1, 2, 3* to the dramatic five-minute setting of *General William Booth Enters into Heaven*, generally considered Ives's greatest song. They vary in style from relatively straightforward almost vernacular pieces to highly experimental settings that embrace all of Ives's advanced musical devices. His use of programmatic allusion and quotation is extensive, the extramusical meaning of both clearer than in his instrumental music because of the text. Ives's songs both display the entire range of his imagination and establish him as the outstanding composer of art song in the history of American music.

Many of Ives's songs and instrumental pieces have close ties, one often being based on the other. Parts of *The Fourth of July*, for instance, are based on the song, *Old Home Day*; *The Housatonic at Stockbridge*, originally

1. The "standard" datings of Ives's works are given in *AmeriGrove*; Gayle Sherwood and J. Peter Burkholder are reexamining this issue, with some preliminary findings, based on handwritings, manuscript paper, and other evidence, reported in Burkholder 1995, passim.

composed for orchestra in 1908, was arranged as a song, with text by Robert Underwood Johnson, in 1921; and *In the Cage* was written both as a song and as a movement from a set for theatrical orchestra around 1906. There are many other examples of this type of crossover in Ives's music.

Ives experimented with polytonality, extreme dissonance and chromaticism, tone clusters, atonality, and unusual sound combinations at least concurrently with if not before these devices were common in Europe. Rhythmically he was ahead of everyone. Metrical changes abound; lengthy unmetered passages are common; layers of different meters pile on top of one another. And through it all are passages of extraordinary rhythmic complexity; even the most flexible metrical patterns could not contain Ives's rhythmic subtlety.

Structurally Ives was equally innovative. He drew heavily on the American vernacular, integrating songs, hymns, band pieces, and fiddle tunes into his musical vision in a way no previous American composer had done. He built up textures through layering, often creating the effect of several simultaneous and marginally connected musical events. He moved away from traditional musical structures, at a time most American composers adhered doggedly to classical forms, to develop new methods of musical organization.

Most of Ives's music is associative if not programmatic. Ives recorded the past, his own past, and the world around him. At times this can result in relatively literal renderings, such as the final rocket and explosion of *The Fourth of July*, or the description of a *Yale-Princeton Football Game*, where even the referee's whistle is easily identifiable. At other times, his associations are more abstract. Influenced particularly by transcendentalism, Ives addressed deep philosophical questions in his music. In *The Unanswered Question*, one of the earliest of his mature works, the solo trumpet ponders, in Ives own description, "The Perennial Question of Existence." The Fourth Symphony, considered his greatest completed work, probes the same issues: according to Henry Bellaman's 1927 program notes, written almost certainly in consultation with Ives, the symphony asks "the searching questions of What? and Why? which the spirit of man asks of life." Each movement then projects a different answer (Kirkpatrick 1965, p. viii).

No one familiar with American folk and popular music can miss the way in which vernacular tunes pop in and out of Ives's pieces, tantalizing the listener with a snippet here, a fragment there, a phrase that seems to go awry, as it suddenly veers off in some unusual direction, another phrase that gets buried under layers of competing material. The tunes seem to be everywhere, with no rhyme or reason to their appearances. And their presence differs from other twentieth-century composers who used vernacular in a studied, almost self-conscious way. Ives's borrowings seem spontaneous and natural, a fundamental part of Ives's own musical language.

Their appearance, however, is anything but random. Vernacular tunes in Ives's compositions almost always have a structural or a programmatic purpose. Sometimes the programmatic nature is apparent, as in *Decoration Day* (the holiday now known as Memorial Day) in which Ives quotes several Civil War songs, *Taps*, and the hymn *Bethany* ("Nearer My God to Thee"). In many other cases, indeed in most cases, the programmatic purpose is much less obvious, in fact debatable. The three movements of Ives's Second Violin Sonata demonstrate how much of the absolute-programmatic spectrum Ives covers, and how difficult it is to pin him down to any one band.

The presence of fiddle tunes in the second movement comes as no surprise. Ives entitled it *In the Barn*, and in tone and spirit as well as tune source it suggests a nineteenth-century barn dance. It is clearly programmatic. The title of the first movement, *Autumn*, is for program hunters a red herring. The title derives from the hymn tune *Autumn*, which Ives used as the basis for the movement. There is no overt reference to a season. The final movement is entitled *The Revival*. It is also based on one principal hymn tune, *Nettleton*. The programmatic nature of this movement is ambiguous. The hymn itself suggests a depiction of a revival meeting, but how precisely? I have heard a concert violinist describe it in relatively literal programmatic terms, associating the opening Largo with the people assembling, the tune with the revival meeting itself, which reaches a peak of frenzy with the tune stated relatively completely in *fortissimo* quadruple stops in the upper register of the violin, and the brief closing tag, on a surprising F♮, with the crowd dispersing after the meeting with a final echo of the tune ringing in their heads.

Such an interpretation makes perfect sense and is entirely consistent with what we know Ives wanted to do in other pieces. Yet there is no confirming evidence that this is what he had in mind here. Another interpretation, also compelling, is that the first and third movements are about the tunes themselves, as the title of the first movement itself suggests. This interpretation is also supported by another aspect of Ives's music, his use of vernacular tunes for structural purposes.

J. Peter Burkholder has recently described a type of structure common in Ives, cumulative setting (Burkholder 1995, pp. 137–267). It is not entirely unique to Ives, but Ives is the only major composer to explore it consistently and thoroughly. A cumulative setting is based on one principal tune, with other possible countermelodies. The tune is heard first in fragments or in an altered or distorted version and only gradually emerges, to appear relatively complete near the end of the movement, usually as the climactic event. Cumulative setting can be likened to sonata form in reverse, in which the development precedes the statement. The first and third movements of the Second Violin Sonata are clear and straightforward examples of cumulative setting.

Ives's exploration of cumulative setting is intimately linked to his use of vernacular tunes. For the recognition of a tune, at first dimly and then more and more clearly until it bursts forth triumphantly and unadorned, is an important psychological aspect of the dynamics of the form. Ives almost always chose well-known tunes for cumulative setting. But even today, when many listeners do not have the background in nineteenth-century American culture to recognize specific tunes, their stylistic properties are sufficiently distinct within Ives's musical fabric that cumulative setting retains its impact.

A listener hearing Ives's music for the first time is often struck with its density and complexity. Multiple layers of activity may invoke multiple meanings, some programmatic, some structural, some arresting because of the sheer sound. This is particularly apparent in his orchestral music, where he exploits fully the sonoric richness of the medium, and nowhere is it more apparent than in his Fourth Symphony. In the first movement a chorus sings, unison until the last few measures, the hymn "Watchman, Tell Us of the Night," within a particularly thick and sumptuous orchestral texture. The second movement contains some of the most complex music written in the twentieth century. At one point Ives divides the orchestra into two clashing ensembles (1965 score, p. 26), reminiscent of his accounts of hearing two marching bands as a youth in Danbury; at other times he will have as many as four layers of overlapping rhythms, most independent of the bar line (p. 31); and at one point all of the following rhythms occur simultaneously: eighth-note sextuplets, eighth-note quadruplets followed by eighth-note sextuplets within a half-note duplet, and half-note triplets in 3/2; quarter-note quintuplets, sixteenth-note quintuplets, half-note triplets, against four quarter-notes in 4/4; and quarter-note duplets and eighth-note triplets in 6/4 (p. 77). Within this rhythmic free-for-all, one hears fragments of at least two dozen tunes. The entire movement has as a programmatic base Hawthorne's story *The*

Celestial Railroad, a parody on Bunyan's *Pilgrim's Progress*. Ives uses this material in two other works: a piano piece called *The Celestial Railroad*, and the second movement of the "Concord" Sonata. Each time he reworked it, adding further layers and other material.

But not all of Ives's music is noisy and rambunctious. Some of his most effective moments occur in quiet passages, where Ives seems to suspend time to create music of quiescent allusion. These contemplative moments often use what Robert Morgan calls "spatial techniques," devices that undermine tonal and rhythmic drive to allow the listener to focus on the immediate, on the music occurring there. Paradoxically such music often bears programmatic reference to both a particular time and a particular place. *The Housatonic at Stockbridge* especially has this character; and significantly it had a specific programmatic allusion, a walk Charles and Harmony took along the Housatonic River in 1908, the year they were married. But like many Ives "place pieces," the program is less introspective than descriptive (Cooney 1996, p. 276).

In 1921, as his compositional career was coming to a close, Ives attempted to familiarize the public with his music. He assembled at his own expense three remarkable publications: *114 Songs*, a selection of most of his songs, dating from his college days at Yale in the 1890s to ones just completed; the massive Second Piano Sonata (*Concord, Mass., 1840–60*), which attempts to evoke the spirit of the principal writers of Concord in the mid-nineteenth century; and *Essays Before a Sonata*, a prose exposition of his philosophy, particularly in reference to what the "Concord" Sonata is all about. In both the Sonata and the *Essays* the influence of transcendentalism is strong. The reception of these publications was luke-warm at first, but gradually Ives's music began to be known. By 1930 a younger generation of avant-garde composers, notably Henry Cowell (1897–1965), looked upon Ives as a pioneer and almost a father figure in new American music. From that point on his reputation and recognition grew.

Nationalism

How could an American composer be American? This question was heard on and off throughout the nineteenth century. Before the Civil War two foreign born musicians who made America an adopted home addressed it in different ways. The Bohemian-born Anthony Heinrich discovered his compositional talent in a log cabin in Kentucky in 1817 and never let anyone forget that. He composed many programmatic pieces on American subjects and proudly proclaimed himself to be an American composer. In the 1850s Norwegian Ole Bull took over the Academy of Music in New York and established a prize for "the best original grand opera by an American composer, upon a strictly American subject" (Howard 1931, p. 200). Unfortunately the Academy folded before the prize could be bestowed. Bull himself never forgot his heritage, even though his association with America was extensive and deep.

In the 1880s musicians became more assertive about American creativity. In 1885 Calixa Lavalle presented a piano recital of all-American music before the Music Teacher's National Association. It was a risky venture, but it succeeded. The association then began to present annual orchestral concerts of American composers. Frederick Grant Gleason, describing the event, expressed hope that "the time is at hand when the native artist or composer will be granted equal rights with his brother from over the sea." Gleason blamed the situation squarely on "musicians of foreign birth (who) look with scorn and disdain upon the efforts of every native American" (Gleason 1887, pp. 261, 273).

By the 1890s isolated nationalistic cries had become a homophonic chorus. Two events in 1893 brought the subject of American national music to a head. The first was Dvořák's challenge to American musicians to compose pieces emblematic of their country; the second was the Chicago World's Columbian Exposition. Much has been written about Dvořák's primary example to American musicians, the Symphony *From the New World*. Did Dvořák really know what he was doing in both his choice of material and its realization? That is, was it primarily American or Czech? I will not address that issue; in regard to later developments of American music, it matters little. Dvořák, it should be noted, also composed several other pieces similarly designed, the F major String Quartet Op. 96, and the E♭ major Quintet Op. 92. Some musicians of the time resented Dvořák's hubris in telling American composers how to write American music. Besides, some rightfully claimed, this was already on their mind. In addition, Dvořák was not quite in touch with the way things worked in America; make music a line item in the national budget and the problem would be solved, he argued (Mussulman 1971, p. 117). Nevertheless his charge served as a wake-up call, spurring much consideration of the topic, and much compositional activity.

The immediate problem nationalistic-oriented composers faced was source material. British folk sources, from ballads to fiddle tunes, had become part of the fabric of American life. And they were the rightful heritage of most American composers of the time. With a few exceptions, however, they were either ignored, or considered European. As late as 1890 Frédéric Louis Ritter could state outright that America had no "people's-song," by which he meant folk music (Ritter 1890, p. 420). The Chicago World's Columbian Exposition of 1893, however, suggested otherwise.

The Exposition contained a number of ethnic villages from around the world – Celtic, Teutonic, Islamic, Asian, African, and American Indian. The entire fair was a paean to nineteenth-century progress and social Darwinism. The White City glorified European white male culture. The ethnic villages were arranged on a "sliding scale of humanity" (Block 1990a, pp. 143–144), with the Europeans at one end and the African and American Indian at the other. Nevertheless Native American music became the hit of the show. The concept of the noble savage, prevalent in Western literature and thought until Americans encountered the reality of the Plains Indians in the 1850s, was revived. Suddenly many American composers become fascinated with Indian music.

African American music as a nationalistic source was essentially rejected. The guilt and stigma of slavery and the tensions of reconstruction were still too much on people's minds. And although many European elements had been absorbed, African American music was still fundamentally African. American Indian music was just as foreign to European immigrants, but it had an exotic appeal of its own, it was native in the deepest sense, and it did not remind the white elites of their less than glorious racial past.

Native American music was also safe. By the 1890s the frontier was closed, the Indian wars were over, and Indians had been contained in reservations. The distance between Native and white American culture was sufficiently great that it posed no threat. And the reservations system had a practical bonus for ethnologists interested in Native American music. The Indians were all in one place, easily identifiable. It was almost as if the government in its wisdom had assembled a ready-made lab for scholars. The logistics of study were much simplified.

Two books in particular spurred interest in American Indian music. The first was Theodore Baker's dissertation *Uber die Musik der nordamerikanischen Wilden*, published in Leipzig in 1882; MacDowell used it as the musical source for his *Indian Suite*. As noted in chapter 1, the second was Alice Fletcher's *A Study of Omaha Indian Music*, published in 1893, concurrent with the Chicago Exposition. Fletcher worked directly with the Omaha Indians from 1883, and had begun to make wax cylinder recordings as early as 1890. Other scattered publications of Indian music appeared at this time, including B. I. Gilman's study of Zuni melodies.

By 1900 an "Indianist" movement was in full swing. The leader of the movement was Arthur Farwell (1872–1951), a young composer recently returned from European study. He had seen at Bayreuth what Wagner had done with Teutonic legends, and shortly after he returned to Boston in 1899 he encountered Fletcher's book, which inspired his *American Indian Melodies* (Culbertson 1987, p. 158). When he found no publishers interested in this and other similar pieces, he established his own press. From 1901 to 1912 the Wa-Wan Press periodically issued compositions by American composers, many based on Native American music, and all adhering to Farwell's broader principles, to provide an outlet, free of commercial limitations, for music that reflected the American democratic spirit. That the press, begun with little capital and no outside funding, lasted as long as it did, is tribute to Farwell's ingenuity and tenacity.

Other composers associated with the Indianist movement were Henry Franklin Belknap Gilbert (1868–1928), who used Indian, African American, Creole, and Celtic sources, Carlos Troyer (1837–1920), Harvey Worthington Loomis (1865–1930), Edgar Stillman Kelley (1857–1944), and Charles Wakefield Cadman (1881–1946). All except Cadman were published in the Wa-Wan Press. Cadman, however, had the most mainstream success. His song based on an Indian melody, *From the Land of the Sky-Blue Water*, became a popular hit, and his opera *Shanewis*, one of two on Indian themes, was produced at the Metropolitan Opera in New York in 1918. His other Indian opera was *The Sunset Trail*.

The use of Indian themes in American music at this time went far beyond the work of Farwell and the Wa-Wan Press. Their presence was not only part of a broader search for nationalistic identity but spilled into the exotic stream of Romanticism. MacDowell is the best example of this tendency. His 1894 *Indian Suite* is less a nationalistic expression than an attempt to incorporate unusual or exotic materials into a late-nineteenth-century European harmonic idiom. The Indian material provides an exotic color that becomes the springboard for typical Romantic symphonic development.

Although MacDowell was supportive of an American music, he explicitly rejected the use of folksong as a nationalistic device. To him nationalism meant the association of specifically musical characteristics with ethnic or geographical areas, and he claimed that "true folksong has but few marked national traits." He classed folksongs into six types, based on rhythmic and intervalic features: Oriental, which included Hindu, Moorish, Siamese, Gypsy; Russian and Northern European; Swiss and Scotch; Spanish and Portuguese; Arab and North American Indian; and German. He further stated that the Arab and North American Indian type was a subset of the Oriental. In essence MacDowell distinguished between different European musics and considered the rest of the world "oriental" (MacDowell 1912, pp. 141–57).

MacDowell represents one end of the cultural spectrum: the user in search of exotic material, or according to Crawford, musical nationalism as a means to create his own personal expression (Crawford 1996, p. 558). Farwell, Cadman, and other Indianist composers attempted to get closer to the material itself. Some did field work among the American Indians, attempting to absorb the spirit of the music as well as its technical features. Farwell respected the identity of the Indian melodies. Rather than using them as a springboard for large-scale sonata structures, he allowed the material itself to determine the limits of the piece. Thus his *American Indian Melodies* consists of short piano pieces, with little or no classical-style development.

Yet in spite of Farwell's and others' attempts to come to terms with Native American culture, the result was more an appropriation than an indigenous setting. Even composers such as Farwell grafted Indian songs onto a conservative, nineteenth-century harmonic idiom. The result was still European. Cadman's title for one piece, *Idealized Indian Themes*, suggests he was aware of this dichotomy. In the end the Indianist movement, although it did bring the music of Native Americans into public awareness, did not establish an extended or viable compositional school. And it did not solve the problem of American nationalism. The Indianist movement began to fade during the 1920s, as Americans woke up to another uniquely American idiom, jazz (see chapter 17).

*

In 1915 Edgard Varèse (1883–1965) arrived in America, a bonafide radical, an avant-garde, modernist composer. He had seen the revolution in painting in Europe, he had heard the music of Stravinsky and Schoenberg, he had read the symbolist poets. He was distressed at what he found in America. The principal American composers, George Whitefield Chadwick, Daniel Gregory Mason, Arthur Foote, and Amy Beach were still writing nineteenth-century music. Some of it was very good, but it was conservative. German Romanticism reigned. Ives he knew nothing about; but neither did anyone else.

Modernism had arrived in the visual arts. Alfred Stieglitz's gallery had become a hotbed of modernist activity. The Armory Show of 1913 had created a sensation far greater than expected; and Dadaists appeared that same year. In music only Leo Ornstein (1894–) was writing what Varèse considered contemporary music, and Ornstein, as it turned out, soon withdrew from public life. Worst of all there seemed no young generation pushing for new and radical ideas.

Varèse indeed arrived at a time of consolidation in American music. The gains since the Civil War had been immense, and art music continued to spread. New orchestras were being founded every year, and large new works continued to be written. Even interest in opera was growing with the spread of the new medium, the phonograph. Opera singers were ideal for acoustic recording; they could generate the needed volume without the challenging problems of balance a larger ensemble created.

New technology, the radio, the electronic phonograph, jazz, popular music, modernism, and new currents from France, would soon appear, changing the face of American music for ever. But except for the sudden infusion of jazz into the American mainstream through the first recordings of the Original Dixieland Jazz Band in 1918, no-one in 1920 could have imagined what was coming. The American art music world of 1920 to most seemed only a bigger and better version of what it had been in 1900.

· PART TWO ·

10

Music in America: an overview
(part 2)

WILLIAM BROOKS

In chapter 2, I discussed three aspects of the interaction between individualism and egalitarianism which characterizes American music as well as her politics and society: elitist art and egalitarian folk musics, which in some respects mark the poles of a spectrum, and the mediational role of musical reformers. The present chapter explores three other aspects: a counter-reform, the popular music industry, and the interlinked techniques of improvisation and experiment. I begin by returning to the reformers.

Counter-reform

The reformers sought to elevate America's tastes by presenting artistic values in a musical language suited to ordinary citizens. They were most successful in cities, where their ideas both supported and rested on a rich concert life. The links between art music, reform, and patronage thereby grew steadily stronger, so that by the 1870s many reformers had effectively become upper-class conservatives.

By that time, however, America was becoming more self-critical about its social and economic polarities. The aesthetics of working-class citizens seemed less important than their economic position, and values derived from European art music seemed far removed from the affection citizens granted their folk and popular musics. Though reform methods still served to promote musical literacy and performance, they became increasingly irrelevant to the reformers' original, broader objectives: mediation, reconciliation, acculturation. A counter-reform was needed.

This, like its predecessor, was grounded in religion – in particular, the unending succession of religious revivals that swept across nineteenth-century rural America. The music sung at these ranged from traditional psalms to remnants of the New England repertory to, eventually, reform hymns by Mason and his brethren. But regardless of the music's source,

the performances were anarchic and ecstatic; each of thousands of cele-
brants could inflect any phrase individually, moved by a personal epiphany.
As in New England a century before, a notated repertory was transformed
into a folk performance tradition; and as before, a new repertory by a new
generation of composers eventually resulted.

These composers, however, built upon the reformers' successes. They
could assume that revival congregations would generally be musically literate; hence they could disseminate their work in notated form without necessarily linking it to singing schools. They also knew that literacy had made
possible a sheet music industry which shaped its products for maximum
popularity, and they hoped to redirect toward ecstatic salvation the
affection and pleasure these products evoked. The result was a new missionary music: the gospel hymn. The reforming urge remained, but its focus was
reversed: the staid artfulness of the inherited repertory was to be transformed by an infusion of energy from folk and popular musical traditions.

Like previous reforms, revivalism and the music it engendered sought to
mediate America's ideological polarities both socially and technically.
Egalitarian masses flocked to hear charismatic individuals preach; a single
authority (the Bible) was given a multitude of sectarian readings. Tub-
thumping rhythms ensured ensemble, while simple harmonies invited
extemporization; call-and-response patterns modeled a balance between
leaders and followers.

In important ways, however, the counter-reform was the converse of its
predecessor. Its crusades were focused not on artless villagers but sin-laden
urbanites. Its message was disseminated not through schools and churches
but through popular media: journalism, publishing, and eventually broadcasting. And its music sought not to propagate the values of high culture
but to sweep them aside, to overpower intellectual elitism with the sheer
energy and abundance of a redirected popular culture.

Education and scholarship underwent a similar counter-reform somewhat later; but unlike a century before, this depended less on religion than
on a new technology. In the early twentieth century, broadcasting and
recording began to make music universally available in an acoustic, rather
than notated, form. Suddenly musical literacy was no longer a precondition
for music's reproduction; and with the introduction of long-playing discs,
transistor-based sound equipment, and cassette tapes, the cultural shift
was completed. By the 1960s virtually all young Americans were learning
nearly all their music – popular, folk, or art – from recordings, not scores.

All music thereby became part of a new aural tradition, and the focus of music education shifted toward listening and away from theory and performance. In effect, values previously associated with folk music or the music industry – familiarity, utility, popularity – began to be applied universally. Both nineteenth- and twentieth-century educators sought to mediate between citizens and an elite; but whereas the former taught music notation so that popular taste could be shaped to approach high art, the latter taught by means of recordings so that art music could be approached as if it were popular.

Recordings also made possible a new kind of scholarship. Notation had enabled a particular piece to be replicated at will, so that analysis, criticism, and theory could be brought to bear. Recordings enabled the replication of non-notated performances; suddenly the scholarly study of folk and popular musics became practical – so practical that by the 1950s a new discipline, ethnomusicology, had been formed to encompass much such work. But ethnomusicology entailed important departures from nineteenth-century art music scholarship; in particular, it generally rejected both the analysis of individual works in themselves and respect for composerly genius. It was a small step to another counter-reform, in which ethnomusicological methods were applied to other domains. The "new musicology" of the 1980s and 1990s offers one example; a more pointed instance, in the present context, is the increasing legitimacy granted scholarly studies of American music.

Art music itself underwent a related reorientation. By the end of the nineteenth century, a significant number of composers had begun incorporating folk and popular musics into their works. Earlier aesthetic assumptions were inverted: rather than improving a people's music by imposing elitist values and techniques, the counter-reform composers hoped to revitalize an elitist art by injecting national or populist values and materials.

Although this reorientation occurred throughout the West (it was a European, Antonín Dvořák, who famously argued the point in the United States), its application was especially problematic in America. European nationalists worked in relatively homogeneous cultures with long-standing indigenous folk traditions; but America was a salmagundi of uncounted immigrant groups. Moreover, many American folk traditions were being continuously transformed by appropriations from others; worse, most had become inextricably entangled with America's popular music industry. On what tradition could a composer base a truly *American* music? Or were all traditions equally serviceable?

In their replies, American composers distributed themselves along a spectrum much like that occupied by folk traditions (see chapter 2): from individualism (regionalism) to egalitarianism (eclecticism), linked by appropriation. One large group, reaching back at least to Louis Moreau Gottschalk, focused on the musics through which their own sensitivities were formed. Some, like Virgil Thomson, embraced a variety of sources from a particular geographic region; others, like William Grant Still, drew on ethnic traditions which had evolved nationwide. An important sub-group turned to jazz and popular music. Composers from John Alden Carpenter to Gunther Schuller sought to invigorate art music with vernacular rhythms and gestures; others, from George Gershwin to Anthony Braxton, applied forms or techniques from art music to essentially vernacular idioms. Still others, like Leonard Bernstein, drew on both vernacular and ethnic streams, sometimes in the same work.

Yet another subgroup, in America as Europe, grounded art music's reform in art music itself. As the twentieth century unfolded, art music composers became so alienated from the received canon that historical art music was as removed from their own work as were popular or folk traditions. Composers like Lucas Foss and George Rochberg began to re-present in their own work the historical art music on which they had been raised. By the 1990s, in works of John Adams and others, music had joined other post-modern arts in taking its own history for its subject matter.

All these composers, though drawing on very different sources, sought to re-form their art around a music which was part of their personal heritage. In this sense their music parallels that of folk traditions which tend toward isolation and preservation. But appropriation (acculturation) had its analogue too, in composers who drew on musics which were largely foreign to them.

Dozens of European Americans, led initially by Arthur Farwell, rebuilt their art around materials taken from Native American or African American folk traditions. For other composers, the Anglo-American mainstream was equally distant; Aaron Copland's scores from the 1930s and 1940s – probably the best known of all "Americanist" compositions – generally utilize idioms and references which had little or no bearing on Copland's formative years. Other composers reached even further afield, and in so doing allied themselves with the emerging discipline of ethnomusicology. Colin McPhee and Lou Harrison turned to Indonesia; La Monte Young and Terry Riley, to the Indian subcontinent. Mixed-repertory performers like Jenny Lind and John Philip Sousa, who sought to educate vernacular audiences about art music values, gradually gave way to ensembles like the Kronos Quartet, who sought to educate art music audiences about a variety of ethnic traditions. Intuitive polyglots like George Crumb combined ethnic, vernacular, and historical sources into a highly idiosyncratic personal idiom.

Like many American folk musicians, ethno-composers enlarged their own art music tradition by acts of appropriation. But few shared the radical egalitarianism that lay at the heart of folk appropriations. Many, in fact, were essentially elitist, attempting both to reform their own alienated tradition and to demonstrate that the music of a different culture possessed analogous high-art values. Others, entranced by the "simplicity" or "purity" of folk traditions, implicitly reaffirmed the distinction – and the relative positions – of "high" and "low" art.

Some, however, were more profoundly eclectic, arguing for a non-hierarchic field of possibilities which would include art music itself. For individuals like Charles Seeger, Henry Cowell, and Charles Ives, the friction between an elitist art and an egalitarian ideology would be substantially reduced if art music were recognized as simply one musical path among many. Composerly greatness – pioneering accomplishments in art music – could be reconciled with democratic citizenship if a composer grounded his work in the musicality inherent in everyone: "eclecticism," Ives wrote, "is part of [a composer's] duty" (Ives 1961, p. 79). The precise source was irrelevant (it could even be art music itself); Ives required only that "local color, national color, any color, [be] a true pigment of the universal color" (p. 81).

Such unprejudiced eclecticism collapses the polarity between art and the vernacular into a universal, non-hierarchical domain. In this sense it runs counter not only to previous reforms but to the missionary qualities of reform itself. Since all musics stand on an equal footing, none can be used to "improve" another; what is reformed, rather, is the presumption that improvement is needed. The American eclectics propose a transcendent alternative in which individual genius and egalitarianism are mutually supportive; the conflict between Pioneer and Citizen is transformed into cooperation.

Popular music

Even the eclectics, however (possibly excepting Ives), found equality easier to accept for folk and art traditions than for popular music. In the

former, at least, values like beauty or utility were deemed independent of
economic worth; in the latter, musical and market values were thoroughly
entangled. For popular music, as I shall use the term, is by definition evaluated primarily by its economic success – in America, by its success in what
is described as a free market. In American ideology, free markets mediate
economically between Pioneer and Citizen: the value of each Pioneer creation is established by the price assigned it by Citizen purchasers. In theory,
every creation has an equal chance at collective approval, and the collective
judgment is made without prejudice; individualism and egalitarianism
achieve a symbiotic balance. In practice, "free" markets are never unregulated: at times equality is enforced at the risk of damping initiative; at other
times individualism is encouraged at the risk of monopoly.

Music both fits and resists this model. In all but wholly participatory
traditions, music performed by individuals is heard (purchased) by a body
of listeners; in this sense, theatres and concert halls mimic markets. Strictly
speaking, however, a live performance never recurs; it cannot be resold,
and approval of it is expressed only in the purchase of another, different
performance. Marketers (whether of orchestras, Broadway shows, or rock
stars) exploit this contradiction, implying paradoxically that successive
performances of the same production are both identical and unique.

Only when music can be widely disseminated in reproducible form does
it become fully compatible with free-market ideology. In America this
occurred when musical literacy became sufficiently widespread to make
the mass production of sheet music economically viable. Thus, although
early reformers initially promoted literacy to mediate between folk and art
music traditions, they indirectly fathered an altogether different music,
one which bypassed entirely the values associated with either tradition.
With the advent of recording, the new genre, with its monovalent measure
of success, became the most universally accepted mechanism for reconcil-
ing art with America's ideology.

Rather than attempting to mediate concepts like aesthetics, elitism, and
community, the popular music industry acts as a broker between music-
makers and music-users. It addresses the American dilemma by asserting,
on the one hand, that each piece of music is created (owned) by a gifted
individual or team of individuals, and by requiring, on the other, that each
piece be approved (purchased) by a significant number of ordinary citizens. Both these conditions are vital to its function. The industry cannot
be radically egalitarian; it must insist that good music is produced only by
extraordinary people, for if it granted musical creativity to all citizens

equally it could offer no rationale for the purchase of its products. Nor can it, as a whole, be explicitly elitist; to declare that only certain citizens are aesthetically qualified to be consumers would violate both the ideology and the practice of a free market.

The industry has never been, however, a monolith; like other musics in America, its components have situated themselves in a field defined by the same sort of spectra that characterize America's social and political domains. For producers of popular music, these spectra are translated into what are, in effect, marketing strategies. At one extreme producers seek to draw into a single audience individuals from a variety of subcultures – an egalitarian strategy which appeals to the citizenry's desire for shared, fundamental values. At the other, producers create products intended for a specific subculture, or even to create a subculture – an individualist strategy which appeals to each citizen's desire to be different.

In practice most popular music occupies an intermediary position, aimed at a distinct market but receptive to crossover success. In times when America's integrationist impulse is ascendant – between, say, 1955 and 1963 – the number of crossover hits increases and the boundaries between markets are blurred; in pluralist eras, such as the 1980s, marketing categories proliferate and products are narrowly targeted. At all times, however, both strategies are viable; their persistence is perhaps best exemplified by the different stances adopted by top-forty and country music producers toward the subcultures defined by purchasers' ages. The former, especially since 1955, have promoted music as a cultural marker by which each new generation can distinguish itself from its elders; new top-forty music is therefore constantly differentiated from the old, with a major change declared every few years, as a new generation defines itself. Country music, on the other hand, is essentially conservative; because it aims to integrate old and young into a single audience it changes gradually, avoiding disjunctions that might create a generational split in its market.

These different strategies are illustrative of an even broader dichotomy – that between synchronic and diachronic popularity, between "hits" and "standards." Much popular music aspires to be both immediately successful and long-lasting, of course, but a significant portion is marketed with either obsolescence or endurance primarily in mind. Songs associated with dance crazes (Do the Bird), for example, are intended to lose favor quickly so that new ones can be marketed in their stead. Successful show tunes (Old Man River), on the other hand, are usually meant to persist in a variety of performances and revivals over many years.

Music which is popular over an extremely long span of time often comes to occupy an intermediate position between commercial music and art or folk traditions. Certain art music works have come to function much like very long-lived commercial products, either because of inherent qualities like compactness and adaptability ("Air on the G String") or because of unique cultural associations (the *William Tell Overture*). There has resulted a distinct "pops" repertory – a peculiar mix of classical music, show tunes, film scores, and popular song – which claims both aesthetic and economic virtue. Conversely, some long-lived commercial products have become situated somewhere between popular and folk music. When copyright expires, incentives to promote a work are greatly diminished; its continuing popularity thereafter (which often depends on oral transmission rather than commercial transactions) signals the kind of egalitarian, non-commercial approval which is usually reserved for music from a folk tradition. Many nineteenth-century songs (*Little Brown Jug*, for instance) have acquired this patina; but the best illustration is provided by Stephen Foster, who is taken to be, simultaneously, the voice of the folk ("America's Troubadour" [Howard 1953]), a canny writer of commercially successful songs, and a creative artist of great genius. That none of these descriptions alone suffices is precisely the point; Foster's ambiguous position is both a justification and a consequence of America's musical and ideological dialectic.

Diachronic popularity requires creators of popular music always to position themselves with respect to the received "standards" or "classics" of their time. These change constantly, to a far greater degree than for art music; thus alienation is less pervasive in twentieth-century commercial music than in art music. But it remains a potent force whenever a group of citizens or artists believes the received repertory reinforces the status of a cultural or economic elite. The creation of a new, notably different music provides the disenfranchised group with an emblem marking a rejection of the status quo; the music both reflects and shapes the individualist impulse which underlies social change. This phenomenon has occurred irregularly among European- and Anglo-Americans, from the minstrelsy of Jacksonian democracy to the folk-rock of the 1960s; among black Americans, forcibly alienated from mainstream culture, it has recurred generation after generation, from blues to bebop, jive to rap.

Such striking disjunctions have attracted much commentary; but most popular music continues, rather than rejects, the received repertory. Every new song, of course, differs in some way from those which are already popular; commonly, however, the differences are slight, so that an identified market is retained, with one or more of the previously popular items replaced by the new one. When the differences are more substantial, they usually signal the presence of one of the two strategies described earlier: splitting an existing market to create subgroups whose identity depends on the purchasing of new products; or combining portions of different audiences to create a new, potentially larger market. These two approaches have engendered two tactics which typically mediate between change and continuity in popular music: the promotion of individual artists and the transformation of style by means of appropriation.

The former long predates the modern music industry; sheet music from the 1700s already proclaimed on its covers "as sung by —," and early American impresarios associated their seasons with star performers. When sheet music became a product in its own right, rather than a mere echo of the theatre, the focus of promotion shifted to composers; Stephen Foster is again an early paradigm, with composer-performer Henry Russell a noteworthy, hybrid precursor. By the Civil War sheet music companies had begun to cultivate distinct stables of songwriters, a process which culminated in turn-of-the-century Tin Pan Alley.

Thereafter performers became increasingly important. Popular music was increasingly disseminated by means of recordings, rather than sheet music, and promoters consequently focused on the acoustic event (the performance) rather than on a notated abstraction (the score). By the 1950s the marketing focus was so concentrated that most purchasers were wholly unaware of the composers of the hits sung by their favorite performers. Intermediate between these two eras were the big bands of the 1930s and 1940s, whose leaders were composers of (at least) idiosyncratic arrangements but were also performers whose primary products were recordings. Since the 1960s the distinction has increasingly been lost; except in country music, most performers are now their own composers and vice versa.

The focus of popular music promotion thus shifted gradually from performers in the early nineteenth century to composers in the early twentieth and back to performers (or performer-composers) after World War II. But the objective was always the same: to carve from an unreliable general audience a smaller, secure group of fans who could be counted upon to purchase each of their idol's new products.

The marketing of individual artists reinforces individualist tendencies in American culture: by proclaiming the irreplaceable genius of a particular composer or performer, it encourages devotees of this genius to distinguish themselves from (and sometimes contend with) devotees of different individuals. Indeed, there often results an elitism akin to that associated with art music; contending enclaves of consumers deliberately disregard economic measures in order to argue the merits of their favorites on artistic grounds. In recent years some such enclaves have even come to constitute a separate marketing category, "alternative" rock.

In practice, of course, individual composers or performers rarely offer a significant alternative. Their innovations are meant to attract devotees from their competitors or from a well-defined market, not to question the structure or function of markets themselves. Even when an individual (James Brown, for instance) is sufficiently inventive to precipitate an entire substyle, the consequences are essentially reductionist and divisive, continuing the status quo. More radical change results only when a different tactic is employed, often without conscious planning: the creation of a single, more universal audience by the conflation of enclaves previously devoted to wholly different musics or performers. This process depends not on innovation but on appropriation.

Most popular music is derivative, of course, in that each marketable item appropriates much of its content from a pool of received material. Moreover, popular artists develop consistent styles by, in effect, appropriating from themselves; and within genres, they imitate their rivals in attempts to capture fans. But when appropriation alters the orientation of an entire audience, it has a more profound effect: a new, rather unpredictable market is created, with the possibility that a sea change in popular music's structure and style will follow.

I have previously discussed appropriation in folk and art music traditions, where the identity of the appropriated material is generally acknowledged openly. For art musicians vernacular material usually critiques the elitism of their own tradition, while for folk musicians appropriation openly confirms their essential egalitarianism. In popular music, however, appropriation is often masked, at least initially; the audience reorientation which it seeks to precipitate would be defeated were listeners to recognize the source, with all its concomitant associations.

In its most limited form, then, appropriation results simply in a "cover," re-presenting in a form palatable to certain listeners a song or performance which would not be acceptable in its original version. Were that all, a cover would simply be a mechanism for creating new products; but commonly at least part of the targeted audience eventually becomes reconciled (or even devoted) to the original. Thus Pat Boone's *Tutti Frutti* was not merely a clean-cut, restrained rendition of Little Richard's woolly, exuberant recording; it also, indirectly, encouraged at least some of its consumers to purchase Little Richard's version itself. Covers thus serve in a sense as mediators, functioning economically the way the reform repertory did socially: they shape a new market by introducing purchasers to values they had previously rejected.

When covers draw repeatedly from particular peripheral styles, aspects of those styles eventually surface, unmasked, in the mainstream. In the decade 1945–1955, for example, dozens of hillbilly (country music) hits were covered by mainstream performers like Jo Stafford and Patti Page. Other artists, like Tennessee Ernie Ford, masked their country roots in mainstream recordings which were in effect their own covers; still others, like Frankie Laine, built careers by hiding urban origins behind Western facades. African American music was appropriated similarly: white performers ranging from the Weavers to Johnnie Ray adapted widely different elements from it; black performers like the Inkspots and Nat King Cole masked parts of it to create mainstream hits. As the decade passed, elements from the appropriated styles surfaced more and more explicitly, gradually reorienting mainstream markets toward the periphery and the periphery toward the mainstream. The process culminated in seminal recordings (many of them still covers) by Elvis Presley and others, which fused both markets and styles into a new social and musical genre: rock and roll. Almost immediately, of course, the new market began to fragment, in ways already described; but the fractures were new ones, and the course of both style and industry had been irrevocably transformed.

Similar developments had occurred at least twice before: in the 1830s and 1840s, when aspects of African American and lower-class white musics gradually penetrated a European-based song style, culminating in the music of Stephen Foster and the maturation of America's sheet music industry; and in the 1910s and 1920s, when aspects of African American jazz not only transformed the mainstream style but fostered the industry's shift from sheet music to recordings. In all three cases the appropriated ("covered") materials were taken in large part from African American music – a measure not only of the unrelenting marginalization and exploitation of black culture but also of its extraordinary vitality. In response, African Americans usually discarded the appropriated style, replacing it with a newly adapted one which in some way critiqued the exploitative mainstream; this was in turn appropriated, and the cycle continued.

Processes of assimilation and appropriation have been greatly accelerated by music technology. Recordings freed "covers" from the constraints
of notation; they also decoupled venues for production and reception, so
that in a sense a performance is appropriated every time a recording is
played. Recent developments in sampling technology, especially as applied
in hip hop and rap, have made recordings themselves subject to appropriation and challenged the very notion of ownership. (Again African Americans have been the primary innovators.) The internet may have even more
radical consequences: in cyberspace itself there is nothing to be owned,
and so marketing must focus on access, not products. Audiences and
genres then become self-selecting, so that economic mediation between
individualism and egalitarianism becomes far more fluid and unpredictable. Some form of that mediation, however, will remain fundamental to
the working of America's popular music industry.

Improvisation and experiment

New technologies commonly engender new skills unrelated to conventional schooling: hip hop virtuosity is not learned in conservatories. In this
sense, much recent popular music is linked to the final path which I wish to
trace through America's musical terrain – a path marked by individuals
who apparently deny that music-making requires formal training, conventional skills, or even talent. Some have worked primarily in performance,
as musical *improvisers*; others have focused on composition and musical
experiment. These domains are often entangled (in, for example, the music
of Charles Mingus or Anthony Braxton); but even when separate, they can
together be distinguished from other strands of America's music.

For all the paths thus far discussed, from reform to popular music, are
implicitly affiliational: that is, they ask individuals – composers, performers, listeners – to ally themselves with others, to situate their work in a
context of mutual support. In this sense (and this sense only) their fundamental orientation is collective and egalitarian. Improvisation and experiment, on the other hand, are fundamentally individualist; they require
that each creative act be independent, and they permit (or even encourage)
artists to imagine themselves isolated. Both improvisation and experiment
reach back at least to colonial America; but both acquired new importance
with the advent of recordings and are therefore often associated with the
twentieth century.

Improvisation might be said to occur any time an individual spontaneously embellishes or transforms received material. In American culture, however, it is useful to distinguish between embellishments which seek only to realize the intentions implicit in the received material and those which impose an added layer of intention which is the performer's alone. In the former case one speaks of interpretation; in the latter, of improvisation.

Improvisation requires individual inventiveness, but it also has egalitarian implications: the added layer of intention places performers on a more equal footing with composers. Improvisation thus flourishes where veneration for composers is diminished; it also flourishes where tools are needed to protest imbalances in an allegedly egalitarian society. In America both these conditions exist; especially in America's folk traditions, particularly of oppressed minorities (African Americans, for instance), improvisation has been absolutely central.

An improvisation is usually assumed to be unique not only to a performer but to an occasion; that is, an improviser is expected to embellish a work differently in each performance. When this is not the case, one might speak of a performer's "version" of a work, rather than an improvisation; but the boundaries are often unclear: a version may crystallize from successive improvisations, and an improvisation may be assembled from fragments which are reused in successive performances. Moreover, differing versions often function socially exactly like differing improvisations. Thus, in the seventeenth century, when hymn singers developed idiosyncratic renditions of the received repertory, it was the variations between performers, not between successive performances, that so exercised literate musicians.

It is assumed an improvisation will never recur; but a recorded improvisation *does* recur, as often as a listener wants. Recordings convert improvisation into composition: each recording becomes a piece in its own right, on which the entire evaluative apparatus associated with art music can be brought to bear, so that certain recordings can be judged especially artful, selected artists declared to be geniuses, particular performances cited as paradigmatic masterpieces. Around recorded improvisations there has thus coalesced an elitist subculture not unlike that associated with art music, and performers in improvising traditions – notably jazz – have confronted some of the same difficulties faced by art music composers. Certain recordings have come to constitute a core repertory, creating a canon which functions much like the art music canon and toward which each new generation of improvisers must take some sort of stance, respectful or otherwise.

The situation is further complicated because recorded improvisations, unlike art music, are often also commercial products. Folk improvisers are members of a subculture; recordings convert that subculture into a market and its improvisers into producers whose products are subjected to the strategies and measures associated with popular music. In particular, improvisers are asked to succeed, paradoxically, both in continuing the tradition (that is, creating re-productions which will maintain or broaden existing markets) and in distinguishing themselves *from* it (that is, creating an individual style around which a reliable submarket can be formed).

However, because improvisation is often situated in economically marginal subcultures, the recording industry is especially motivated to produce "covers" which will appeal to audiences with greater purchasing power but who stand outside the tradition itself. Jazz – a primarily African American tradition in a racist culture – was therefore disproportionately represented either by white performers whose music, no matter how skilled, was derivative (The Original Dixieland Jazz Band, Paul Whiteman, Benny Goodman, the Dorseys) or by African Americans willing in effect to cover their own music, either by masking themselves with white stereotypes (Louis Armstrong, Cab Calloway) or by masking their work with white musicians (Fletcher Henderson, Don Redman).

Musicians in improvising traditions – especially African Americans – thus faced an extraordinarily complex situation in the twentieth century. Before the advent of recordings the individualism intrinsic to improvisation was mediated by the ephemeral nature of performance and the egalitarian nature of folk traditions. Recordings upset this balance, setting improvisers competitively against not only each other but also all previous recordings (including their own). Recordings also thrust communitarian, non-commercial music into the mainstream, free-market music industry, which reshaped audiences and products for maximum profit.

The results were unprecedented and paradoxical. Some musicians – notably Duke Ellington – sought to reconcile the conflicts intrinsic to their changing situation, to create a music which was abundant enough and large enough to absorb and transform the disparate cultural pressures to which it was subjected. Thus Ellington orchestrated individuals, not instruments, so that his band (far more than most) was a community shaped by distinct, improvising voices; he alternately exploited and challenged the technical implications of recordings; and he took racial and stylistic stereotypes – covers – to be the very subject of his music.

Paradoxically, the great integrators of jazz (Ellington, Coltrane, Mingus, and others) were all extraordinary individuals – pioneers, even geniuses in the art music sense. Quite different responses were provided by groups of musicians who were acutely aware that recordings had come to serve either as an improvisational canon (art music) or objects of trade (popular music); their music critiqued both of these functions while inevitably being subsumed into them. Their responses ranged from revisionist (the New Orleans revival) to radical (free jazz); nearly always they arose first in non-commercial venues from small communities of players which may have included astonishing virtuosos (Charlie Parker, for instance) but did not depend on the leadership of a particular individual. Commonly the structure of the response was itself a comment on social or musical circumstances; thus the stereotypical form of a bop performance (unison head, solos by each player, unison close) asserts both the equality and individuality of the performers – a comment on not only the radical inequality of the Depression but also the commercial anonymity of big bands.

Similar developments can be traced in other improvisatory genres: the blues, of course, but also country music, where the emergence and subsequent history of bluegrass closely parallels that of post-big-band jazz. However, it was in jazz that the social and aesthetic conflicts were sharpest. If, as many have claimed, jazz is the quintessential American music – as blacks are the quintessential Americans – it is because its history so directly manifests, in so many ways, the dialectical tensions at the heart of America's culture. Since the 1950s rock and roll has largely supplanted jazz, in the public view, but rock differs in crucial respects: it is explicitly commercial; it is more racially integrated; it is created specifically for recordings; and it quickly became truly international. As a result, even at its most "alternative," rock has rarely achieved the self-aware complexities of jazz, and its artists have almost never found themselves alienated from their own tradition to the extent that jazz artists have.

Indeed, in their post-war alienation jazz improvisers resemble not folk or commercial musicians but composers of art music, and devotees of jazz have also often been devotees of the contemporary arts. Musicians in both domains must somehow distinguish themselves from a received canon of works even though those works constitute the very tradition in which they were trained. They also stand in a tangential and paradoxical relation to popular music and to values associated with economic success. And, like all American musicians, they must find a way to reconcile individual creativity with good citizenship.

The latter invites a more narrow parallel: between improvisers and what have been called "experimental" composers. Innovative improvisers, it is argued, are largely self-taught; formal instruction may grant technical facility, but at the cost of converting a creative endeavor into a commercial one, sacrificing "soul" for success. Experimental composers make an analogous claim: although a formal musical education is usually presumed beneficial to the composition of art music, under some circumstances training is not necessary and may even be a liability. Experimental composition, in this view, entails the invention and application of a system, a collection of premises; each piece of music explores the implications of a particular system, and the value of the process (the experiment) transcends that of the outcome (the piece).

But if composition requires invention rather than talent or training, then anyone – quite literally – can be a composer; all citizens stand on an exactly equal footing, unbiased by education or social standing. Complementarily, each newly invented music distinguishes its creator from all others; each experiment, regardless of its outcome, carries traces of a single person's unique way of thinking. Experimental music thus empowers the Citizenry in the domain of art music exactly the way American democracy empowers them socially: it assigns equal value to each citizen, gives each a right to self-description, and places primary value on the integrity of a process, not an outcome.

Experimental music is generally thought to be a twentieth-century phenomenon, with John Cage alternately serving as progenitor and apotheosis. But there are ample precedents in America's past. William Billings, speaking for a generation of tunesmiths, declared that "every Composer should be his own Carver" (quoted in Chase 1966, p. 31), an assertion which gave him liberty to experiment widely with form and technique and served further as a premise embraced by nearly all the later shape-note composers and compilers. A more ambivalent precursor was Charles Ives. Dozens of Ives's pieces explore newly invented methods for composing music; but Ives was also highly critical of music grounded only on such methods, finding them "a weak substitute for inspiration" which could be applied by "any high-school student" (Kirkpatrick 1960, pp. 126–127). This is, of course, precisely the point: experimental music is necessarily radically egalitarian. And for Ives egalitarianism was both ideal and inadequate; although he envisioned a day "when every man while digging his potatoes will breathe his own epics, his own symphonies . . ." (Ives 1961, p. 128), he also venerated "genius" (p. 91) as manifested in "men like Bach and Beethoven" (p. 73).

Ives was, of course, an improviser as well as an experimentalist; indeed it may be in his work that these two approaches meet most closely. His objections to experimental methods have more to do with spontaneity and purpose than with the methods themselves: musical "substance," Ives writes, "comes from somewhere near the soul" (Ives 1961, 77; an improviser's phrase, surely), and systematic experiments are necessarily highly calculated, reminiscent of what Ives called "manner." When such experiments were incorporated into larger works – when methods served ideas larger than themselves – Ives was more comfortable; but experimentalism's egalitarian implications are quickly negated in such a larger, artful context.

Most experimentalists followed Ives in this regard, employing their inventions primarily in more explicitly artful works. Henry Cowell and Ruth Crawford, for example, invented and explored compositional methods which, in their theoretical transparency, were potentially applicable by "any high-school student"; but in nearly all their music these methods were deployed in support of a relatively conventional, somewhat elitist aesthetic. For other composers (Harry Partch, Henry Brant, Conlon Nancarrow), the invention of new methods was only one tool among many used to shape a highly refined art; though such composers are often described as experimentalists because of their self-reliance and inventiveness, they stand well apart from experimentalism's social and aesthetic implications.

Those implications were addressed much more directly by a later generation. The so-called "minimalists" – notably Steve Reich – began in the 1960s with works of such reiterative simplicity that they seemed to require no compositional activity whatsoever beyond the presentation of an initial premise. Closely allied were others who could be called "conceptualists" (Pauline Oliveros, Alvin Lucier, the Fluxus group); their works, though less repetitive, were similarly uninflected. For all these composers both the processes and the performances stood well apart from art music; each piece explored a premise which could have been proposed by anyone, and the performance techniques required had to be newly learned even by trained musicians. But like their predecessors, most minimalists and conceptualists eventually moved away from radical egalitarianism. Many of the latter – notably Oliveros – began creating large-scale structured improvisations, while the "post-minimalists" applied techniques like repetition and pulse to quite conventional aesthetic ends.

The composer who most consistently resisted assimilation into art music's mainstream was John Cage, the paradigmatic experimentalist and arguably the art musician who most self-consciously addressed America's social and political contradictions. Although Cage at first followed in the steps of his mentor, Henry Cowell, inventing methods and instruments which he applied in artful works like *Sonatas and Interludes*, his adoption of chance techniques led him irrevocably back to radical experimentalism. Chance techniques were unmistakably egalitarian; over the last fifty years of his life Cage constantly faced the objection that, as he himself phrased it, "if this is what music is, I could write it as well as you" (Cage 1961, p. 17). To which he invariably replied affirmatively: yes, chance operations require only discipline, not talent or training. But chance techniques also invite individualism; because they set no limitations on materials or form, every piece is uniquely invented, and no two applications – no two compositions – are ever the same.

Chance techniques thus apparently intercede between individualism and egalitarianism, making moot the conflict between them. Moreover, a score produced by chance techniques is both entirely unique and merely one of many possible outcomes; it is thus both irreplaceable and of no particular value, making moot the assignment of value to unique objects which has historically characterized the fine arts. Further, when chance techniques are incorporated into the score itself, each performance of the work is both unique and one among many equals; it too becomes both valuable and valueless, making moot the assignment of value to reproducible objects which has historically characterized the commercial arts. In these domains and others, by simultaneously affirming both poles of the American dialectic, chance techniques call into question previous attempts to mediate between them.

But in a larger sense the intercession of chance techniques (and to some extent of experimentalism in general) is not necessarily welcome. The dance, the struggle, the embrace between Pioneer and Citizen is not meant to end by separating the two figures; the conflicts intrinsic to American culture are not to end in a draw, any more than in a victory. It is the dance itself, in its constantly shifting gravities and balances, that animates American culture. To redefine music so that it can no longer be stressed by the pull between individualism and egalitarianism is to bypass tension in favor of tranquillity, to flatten into utopia the rugged resistance of America's tangled terrain. It is in the persistence of the dance that America endures; that so many responses, rhythms, gestures, have been engendered – only a few of which have been traced in these overview chapters –

speaks not only of the dance's irreducibility but of America's deep desire that it continue.

Envoi

On the cusp of the twenty-first century a book devoted to the history of American music is both anachronistic and timely, and for the same reason: that there is now a global culture is ever more certain, as is the hope of most Americans that that culture will be modeled on their own. Even at their least imperial, Americans seek to balance equality and individuality in phrasing their global visions: "To us and all those who hate us," Cage wrote, "that the U.S.A. may become just another part of the world, no more, no less" (Cage 1967, p. [v]). And at their most imperial Americans insist not only on their core ideology but on a specific mechanism for mediating its contradictions: the free market, which – left to itself – converts all creation into commodities, all art into industry.

But the world contains other visions and other forces – spiritual, ecological, moral, and more – and most of these are grounded in beliefs far removed from America's central preoccupations. A truer extension of American ideology would ask that these multiple, individual visions somehow coexist as equals even though some may deny the very notion of equality. Such a recursive, paradoxical demand is impossible to countenance in domains like government, economics, or science; it can be expressed well only in the domain of art, and arguably best of all in that of music. If America's musical progeny have a place in the next millennium, it is here, demanding that Difference, by describing itself, close the sphere without bounding its contents. In addressing that task the manifold interactions of America's musical forebears will be both suggestive and deceiving.

11

Immigrant, folk, and regional musics in the twentieth century

PHILIP V. BOHLMAN

Prologue – "Americana" at century's end

With little fanfare and without anyone really taking notice, a new type of music appeared during the early months of 1997 in the bins of record shops, the announcements of CD catalogues, and on radio folk-music shows: "Americana." From the beginning it was hard to determine what Americana was, or rather, what it embraced. Americana surely embraced folk music, and, indeed, many singer-songwriters were quick to use the term to refer to the music they created and performed. Singer-songwriters are on the whole politically liberal, which by extension suggests that Americana does not have the more conservative overtones it might otherwise possess. The music of this "Americana," moreover, is eclectic, multicultural, and multiracial; its styles embrace ethnic diversity, and its repertories self-consciously reflect racial diversity, notably the blues. Americana, so it seems at first glance, offers something to everyone. It's a music that provides aesthetic and ideological identity to each individual and to a limitless range of cultural and political issues. If stylistic borders are blurred in Americana, the ability to use music to cross social and class borders is nonetheless crucial to the cultural agenda of those who perform and consume it, those who transfer its sense of engagement with America to their own lives.

Americana is taking shape as the twentieth century is coming to a close. Not only is it a product of a particular moment in American history, but it is a music that describes and ascribes the changing American identities that mark that moment. Through its wanton embrace of folk, ethnic, racial, regional, and class distinctions Americana lays claim to multiculturalism and postmodernism, that is to the aesthetic ideologies of inclusivity that characterized many sectors of American society in the post-Civil Rights and post-Vietnam era of the 1970s and 1980s. With its political agendas Americana strives to memorialize the folk-music revivals of the 1950s and

1960s, and before that of the 1930s. With its stylistic mixtures of African American music from the rural South, labor songs from the industrialized Midwest and Northeast, and Chicano and Latino influences from the Southwest and West, Americana embodies an historical landscape of intersecting regions. Americana is the music of difference, and it bears witness to the fact that it has been music in the United States that has provided one of the most powerful means of inscribing difference on American history itself.

The historical potential represented by Americana notwithstanding, the present chapter perforce grapples with one of the most pervasive contradictions in American music historiography: the paradox of this chapter is that the musics and musical practices I consider here are usually considered nonhistorical, if not ahistorical, the musics of Americans without larger histories of their own. To the extent that the musics of this chapter exhibit historical processes at all, those processes are seen as bounding the music and its makers. According to music historiographical myth, folk music belongs to a closed community, and it is musically cohesive only within the strictures of oral tradition. Immigrant music is bounded by the components of the "immigrant experience," whose pastness music preserves as long as it can, a couple of generations at the most. The boundedness of regional music is obvious; in addition to geographical boundaries, however, cultural, political, and ethnic boundaries accrue to regions through regional music. The more boundaries pile upon immigrant, folk, and regional musics, the greater the cause for celebrating their atavism and their position outside American music history.

In this chapter, conceived within the larger context of a history of American music, I endeavor to restore immigrant, folk, and regional musics to history. There are compelling theoretical and empirical reasons to do just that. The different musical practices that the chapter includes have historically entered into complex interactions, and from these have emerged historical processes. Different styles, genres, and repertories overlap – indeed, they enter into particularly contested interrelations – and these unleash the "music histories of difference" that so powerfully characterize immigrant, folk, and regional musics in the twentieth century. The musics examined in this chapter spill over into other chapters, and it is important for the reader to recognize the implications of this. Ethnic music often displays religious functions, and it appears on the popular stage (Slobin 1993) or even in contemporary art music (Nicholls 1996). Race and region are rarely separable, and this is obvious from the ways in which regional labels define the blues and are seldom absent when the patterns of jazz history are traced. The interconnectedness of immigrant, folk, and ethnic musics to the entire fabric of American music history notwithstanding, the discussions here do not cross chapter boundaries and interlope upon those elsewhere in the book. There is, however, an integrity to the ways in which the chapter and its musics draw our attention to borders – historical, cultural, and musical borders – while crossing and blurring them.

This chapter concerns itself with musics that express difference, and they are musics that represent the ways in which Americans use music to strengthen their group and community identities, that is, the ways in which they use affiliational patterns to articulate selfness. Many labels and rubrics commonly refer to the musics treated in the chapter: folk music, popular music, vernacular music, traditional music, music in oral tradition, and people's music. The labels are themselves important because they participate in the historical processes of identifying and expressing difference.

Although the chapter seeks to include twentieth-century musics of difference, it also stresses the patterns of continuity more than those of discontinuity. The emphasis, therefore, falls primarily on the ways in which distinctive musical repertories and practices serve as means of connecting different groups and communities to American history. The chapter employs diverse forms and materials of documentation for a social history because the concern here is not to describe isolated objects, such as ethnic musical instruments, but rather to show the ways in which the musical evidence serves constantly to interpret and reinterpret history.

The chapter, moreover, deliberately avoids any sense of atavism, that is of musical practices from the past or from remote places. The immigrant musics here are not limited to surviving an immigrant generation, and the folk musics are not bound to oral traditions struggling against escalating industrialization. Quite the contrary, this is a chapter in which musical practices allow us better to understand the changing fabric of American history in the twentieth century, indeed, at the end of our own century. Hence, I examine here a series of "new" transformations and developments: the "new immigration," the "new ethnicity," the "new regional landscapes," both in the USA and globally (Appadurai 1996, pp. 27–47, and Slobin 1993), and even "new folk musics," such as Americana. In the twentieth-century history of musics of difference there are, too, new forms of racism and ethnic prejudice, and the musics examined in this chapter reveal much about the ways in which the musics of difference map these on the American musical landscape. These more troubling components of musical difference are not peripheral, but rather central to any American music history.

The following three major sections in this chapter represent the three major components constituting the chapter's subject matter: immigrant (section I), folk (section II), and regional (section III) musics. Immigrant music connects to American concerns for "Origins." Folk music expresses complex issues of "Identity." Regional music differs according to the ways in which Americans construct their "Senses of place." The "American music histories" that the fourth major section traces symbolize the underlying role of history in the chapter and in the entire book. Each of the following three sections, moreover, unfolds according to three historical processes that are at once specific to certain musics and musical practices and essential to the ways in which differences connect to provide an impetus to American music history. Punctuating these processes in the section are distinctive "Performative moments" and representative cases of "Historical processes," that contribute empirical and theoretical substance for a twentieth-century history of musics of difference.

I. Origins – immigrant and ethnic musics

Fundamental to the ways in which Americans understand and express difference in their vernacular musics is a fascination – even an obsession – with origins. The origins of immigrant musics are elsewhere, beyond the shores of the United States and prior to the American phase of the music's history. Folk music, in different ways, is a music that connects people to origins, to an original moment of music-making. Regional music, too, expresses some aspect of the place that originally shaped it and that provides it with its original contexts. Twentieth-century vocabularies embracing the persistence of difference in American culture are filled with metaphors for origins. The concern for "roots" and "African elements in music" are but two of the most obvious concepts in this vocabulary. The defining qualities of the concern for origins would seem to make it very simple, but that is hardly the case. The concern for origins also generates particularly American ideas about authenticity in American musics, and it plays a crucial role in spawning the plurality of histories that distinguish the American musics in this chapter. It is precisely because the origins of immigrant, folk, and regional musics are so nebulous and so difficult to establish that they provide so many different processes of cultural and historical change.

Immigration and immigrant musics

At the end of the twentieth century the flow of immigrants to the United States continues unabated. There is no evidence to justify any claim that the United States does not remain a land of immigrants, nor is there any evidence to suggest that it has ceased being a land filled with immigrant musics. The linguistic, cultural, and national groups constituting late-twentieth-century immigration differ in many ways from those in the Colonial Era or during the 1880s and 1890s, but the political and human motivations for immigration to the United States remain remarkably the same (cf. chapters 3 and 6). Political refugees continue to seek protection in America; the economically disadvantaged seek new futures for their families in America; the prospects of religious and ideological freedom, whether imaginary or not, attract hundreds of thousands of immigrants each year.

One does not have to search far to realize that immigrant musics are everywhere. Immigrant musics dominate the airwaves of the urban landscape. It would be difficult, for example, to take a taxi in any large American city without experiencing an immigrant music on the radio, Pakistani or Nigerian music in Chicago, or Haitian or Ukrainian in Baltimore. The sources for the music differ, but the driver is not wanting for an abundant supply of cassettes or available radio stations; ask the driver where you can hear such musics live, and she or he will have no trouble providing you with a list of addresses; if you want to pursue the matter further, the driver will surely take you to a club or a concert that very evening.

This example of the taxi as a site for immigrant musics may at first seem jarring, but why, we must ask ourselves, is it substantially different from immigrant musics at any other moment in American history? The taxi driver has at her or his disposal repertories and practices that originated elsewhere; in the late twentieth century the countries of origin are different from earlier moments, but the need to remember and represent them musically has diminished not the least. The postmodern venues for immigrant music may also be different from those of an earlier historical moment, but the motivations for using music to strengthen the social cohesion of the group – its self-identification as a collective of immigrants – are very similar: immigrants use music when they eat and drink together, when they dance together, and when they pray or worship together.

The identities of immigrant communities and immigrant musics powerfully represent origins. As a result of twentieth-century recording technologies immigrant musics may even themselves be a simulacrum for cultural or national origins. There are immigrant musics, moreover, that physically connect immigrants to their origins. Mexican immigrants throughout the United States, for example, share the sacred repertories associated with the Virgin of Guadalupe, and they sing from these repertories not only in their homes and churches, but on the massive pilgrimages to Guadalupe in Mexico in which Mexican Americans participate. Immigrant musics ensure that origins will be remembered and reinscribed in countless American music histories.

Ethnicity and ethnic musics

Ethnic musics emerge in the historical stages that follow immigration. In ethnic music the sense of maintaining or representing immigrant origins is replaced by strategies of adaptation to the new American culture. Ethnic musics, therefore, become more "American," providing individuals with cultural connections to their ethnic group in the United States, rather than to the culture, region, or nation of which they were a part prior to immigration. Ethnic groups are distinguishable because, even at the broadest level, they bear witness to the mixture of cultures. Categories such as "Jewish-American" describe ethnic groups, rather than, say, "Orthodox-Lithuanian-Yiddish-Dialect-Speaking-Jews-from-Belarus." If this point seems exaggerated, it becomes necessary only to consider the ways in which the fastest growing *ethnic* populations of the late twentieth century have become Asian Americans and Hispanic Americans, both cases in which processes of ethnic adaptation immediately greet immigrants.

Origins become more symbolic than palpable in ethnic music, but they have no less potential to ascribe identity. In the transition from immigrant to ethnic music, one of the first markers of origins to disappear is language. Shared song repertories emerge as dialect differences retreat. Usually within a single generation, English songs supplant non-English, and most ethnic communities accept this change, if with some reluctance, for ethnic music, far more than immigrant music, helps to keep those born in America in the community. Language transition in music is an internal ethnic change, but ethnicity also results from external change, in other words, from the use of music to cross the borders between ethnic groups. Religious and instrumental practices provide obvious strategies of ethnic negotiation. Larger religious affiliations, such as Buddhism in West Coast

Asian-American communities, create new possibilities for mixing musical practices. Ethnic bands admit musicians and instruments from other traditions so that their sounds will become modern and so that their potential ethnic audiences will multiply.

In a multicultural society ethnic music is the predominant form of folk music. Each ethnic group or affiliation has its own folk music, and many recognize that other groups and affiliations have their own folk music. Ethnic music is folk music in the United States because it remains participatory on several essential levels. Religious ethnic music provides the basis for communal worship; ethnic instrumental music is played at dances. Ethnic music, moreover, is often not the music with which one is born or even with which one was raised; on the contrary, individuals learn ethnic music, and even those crossing ethnic borders – marrying into a group, for instance – are able to strengthen their group affiliation by participating in ethnic music. It may well be because of the extensive industrialization of modern American urban centers and because of the extensive disjuncture resulting from postmodern social instabilities that ethnic music continues to provide significant forms of social and group cohesion at the end of the twentieth century. Ethnic music connects the individual to her group, but beyond that to the history of that group as it establishes its place in the United States.

PERFORMATIVE MOMENT – POLKA DANCE · Origins converge, dissolve, and reformulate themselves at a polka dance. In twentieth-century America polka has developed both specific and general meanings, and these are expressed fully by the musicians and dancers who perform polkas at thousands of community halls, fraternal lodges, or taverns throughout the United States each weekend. Specifically, the polka is a dance form, derived from military practices, especially the march, which developed into regional and national forms in Central and Eastern Europe, notably in the Czech lands, and then took root and spread with the settlement of immigrants from those areas in the United States. Generally, polka is an American folk music. It still flourishes in areas settled by European ethnic groups, and its prominence in such areas as the Upper Midwest, the industrialized Great Lake states, and the Northeast has given this area, stretching from North Dakota to New York, the name, "Polka Belt" (Pietsch 1994). For many Americans who consciously maintain ethnic affiliations, polka music is simply "our music" (see Greene 1992, and Keil, Keil, and Blau 1992).

Polka crosses ethnic boundaries, and its capacity to mix and negotiate group affiliations makes it one of the most pervasive musics of postethnic America. Native Americans of the Southwest, for example, use polka, called "Chicken Scratch Music," as their most common social dance form. In Texas polka musically connects Mexican Americans to European ethnic groups, among them the large German and Czech communities. The connectiveness – the *conjunto* – that polka produces in Texas stems from multiple origins, and its history constantly mixes styles and instruments. In the northern Polka Belt itself musical practices weave the traditions of one ethnic group with those of another, not eliminating distinctive ethnic sounds, but rather remixing them to respond to a changing musical landscape. It is hard not to distinguish the Chicago sound from the Cleveland sound, but the reasons for the distinctiveness derive from complex ethnic histories (Polish and Czech in Chicago, Slovenian in Cleveland), equally complex music histories (contrasting wind and accordion practices in the two cities), and quite different genealogies of musicians (e.g. Walter Jagiello and Eddie Blazoncsyk in Chicago, and Frankie Yankovich in Cleveland).

On the dance floor polka music plays out these distinctive ethnic American histories. The instruments in a band connect one to Central European histories (e.g. with a dominating low-brass sound) or Eastern European histories (e.g. certain clarinet and sax combinations signal Czech traditions, and button-box accordions locate the sound at the Austrian-Hungarian border, or in the Balkans). There are songs at the polka dance, whose significance is also ethnically charged. By and large, the lyrics are in English, but singers know only too well that certain verses must be sung in Polish, Spanish, or Slovenian in order to heighten the group's sense of ethnic affiliation. As an American music polka not only responds to the transformations in ethnic history: polka inscribes and multiplies ethnic distinctiveness.

Postethnic America and its music

In postethnic America musical identities multiply as individuals are able to create new groups and communities by choosing selectively from different origins, blurring and combining origins, and determining for themselves which affiliations serve their cultural needs most effectively. David A. Hollinger has argued forcefully for a theory of postethnic America that locates it historically in the late twentieth century, at a moment when models of cultural pluralism and multiculturalism – both of which accept a

multitude of ethnic and racial groups, but treat them as highly independent units that together form a cultural mosaic – no longer adequately
address the extensive processes of mixing (Hollinger 1995). Key to the
concept of postethnicity is *choice*, in fact, choice that results from a multitude of alternatives. Historically significant to postethnicity is the reality
that ethnic and racial mixing has been extensive during the twentieth
century, and therefore each individual has the options to choose which elements in the mix, which sets of origins, will determine her affiliations.

The processes of affiliation and mixing that characterize postethnic
America are abundantly evident in its immigrant, folk, and regional
musics. Music, furthermore, might well be used by social historians as evidence for the affiliational processes that have created postethnic America.
In the subsection on the early blues that follows it becomes apparent that
many musics associated historically with racial distinctions have transgressed those distinctions. The experiences represented by musics of black
Americans bear witness to African American interaction with other ethnic
and racial groups. The patterns of interaction themselves have created
mixtures that remap regions – zydeco in Louisiana, the urban blues on the
South Side of Chicago – and provide a rich range of affiliational choices for
immigrant and ethnic Americans.

From the many possible musical practices that illustrate postethnic
America, I should like to choose one that has received remarkably little
attention, arguably because its forms of postethnic mixture do not fit the
earlier models and agendas of cultural pluralism and multiculturalism: the
Asian-American instrumental ensemble. Asian-American orchestras have
proliferated in the second part of the twentieth century, taking quite
different paths, which in turn have spawned endless possibilities for affiliational choices. At one extreme are Japanese-American taiko (drum and
percussion) ensembles. Taiko ensembles allow members to connect
themselves to Japaneseness, but in fact they make conscious choices about
which Japaneseness, that is, which generation after immigration or which
temple or religious group in an urban center; Chicago's largest taiko
ensemble, for example, is Buddhist, and it consciously includes several
generations.

Japanese-American members predominate in taiko ensembles, but in
Javanese gamelan ensembles (primarily constituted of gongs and other
idiophones) in the United States, Indonesian musicians – much less,
Javanese or Central Javanese – are at best a minority. In any American
gamelan there are many members who have joined the ranks as a means of

exercising their interest in ethnic musics, perhaps through college and university training programs. Gamelans demonstrate a further capacity to attract members with Asian-American ancestries that do not necessarily include Indonesia. In particular, Thai and Filipino Americans often play in gamelans. When one joins an Asian-American instrumental ensemble, one makes many choices about identities, and, moreover, each individual has choices to make that are unlike anyone else's. In postethnic America music offers an incredible range of ways to choose and then express one's ethnic and cultural identities, and this freedom is surely one of the most compelling markers of postethnic music's Americanness.

HISTORICAL PROCESSES – ROOTS OF THE BLUES · Origin myths surround the blues, and it is in these origin myths that we recognize some of the most fundamental issues of identity in American music. The origin myths of the blues concern three primary issues of identity and history: (1) where and when the *real blues* had their origins; (2) the identity of the blues as opposed to other American vernacular and folk musics; and (3) how the blues traveled from their points of origins to where they established new roots and assumed new identities. These are no small issues, and the debates that the origin myths of the blues spin off are among the most important in twentieth-century American cultural history (see, for example, Baker 1984). It is emblematic of the profound significance of an American concern with the origin myths surrounding the blues that every discussion or extensive history of the blues cannot begin without staking out a position on just what the blues are and where they began (cf. Work 1940 and Courlander 1963).

If there is any common element in debates about the roots of the blues it is that they came into being as an expression of African American experience, in particular those experiences that came to affect African Americans around the turn of the century (see chapter 5). Early chroniclers and collectors of the blues insisted on their folk quality, particularly their connection to the rural South and the transformation of the Southern economy from slavery to small-scale agricultural production. The blues emerged from the failure of this transformation, which in turn led to a breakdown in the socioeconomic life of southern blacks. The moment of crisis produced by this transformation took place between *c.* 1890 and 1914, depending on the region in which one searches and on what type of music one is ontologically connecting to the blues. When I refer to these debates as origin myths, I do so for specifically historical reasons, for one of the powers of myth is that it marks transition into history. If there has been any American music associated primarily with the twentieth century, it is the blues (Bastin 1986, pp. 3–10).

Questions of region plague discussions about the origins and dissemination of the blues. Different regions – the Southeast, the Southwest, the Mississippi Delta – lay claim to their own blues histories. The prehistory in each region, moreover, is distinctive, with jug bands in the Southeast, and the group processes of work songs taken up by prison chain gangs in the Southwest. Both ethnicity and religion also map the origins of the blues on different regions. The musicians who brought the blues into being, too, have achieved mythical status. Blues historians recognize the crystallization of early blues styles in the 1920s recordings of Blind Blake and Robert Johnson, who, despite the paucity of information we possess about their lives, symbolize genealogies originating in the Southeast and the Southwest. The crucial genealogical question has become the transferal of human musical resources from the South to the North, and this question has in turn generated a new ontological question, or rather complicated the original ontological question about whether the blues really constitute an African American folk music. As the blues traveled North, there was a concomitant urbanization, so mid-century myths claim, and new regionalisms emerged, for example, the South, West, and North Sides of Chicago.

Religious transformations of the blues complicated this question even more, particularly Thomas A. Dorsey's seminal role in establishing a place for the performative power of blues music in the hymn texts of mainline American Protestantism (Harris 1992). Equally as sweeping was the transformation of American evangelical gospel traditions as a whole, which have responded in kind to the improvisation that Dorsey's blues compositions introduced to the hymns of white Americans. At the end of the twentieth century the histories of the blues are no less complex than at the turn of the past century. The questions of regional, racial, and ethnic identity are all the more crucial, indeed, precisely because American histories do not easily disentangle questions of origins that underlie the complex musical identities narrated by musics such as the blues.

II. Identity – folk musics

Music gives voice to difference, affording individuals, small groups, communities, and regions the opportunity to choose and cultivate those musics that create and express the identities that are most meaningful to them. In this section devoted to identity, I turn to those musics that Americans use to construct their identities. In the broadest sense, these are the folk musics of the United States. American folk musics, it must be stressed from the beginning, are inclusive rather than exclusive, they actively participate in the construction of new identities rather than serving as traces of past identities, and they cross the boundaries of genre, social and ethnic group, and class. Americans sing folksongs in order to express something about the ways they make choices about the groups to which they belong. These groups, however, may be of vastly different types, as the theoretical and empirical examples in the present section, as well as the entire chapter, illustrate. The use of folk music to ascribe difference is of singular significance in twentieth-century American history, for it brings us closer to the root causes for the predominance and proliferation of difference in American music itself.

Folk music

Folk music is the music of individual, group, and local identities. In the United States many factors come to bear upon each of these identities, and it is therefore necessary to speak about the plurality of objects – repertories, styles, instruments, etc. – that constitute American folk musics, but also the plurality of processes whereby Americans establish and affirm their affiliational identities. There are folk musics that affirm connections to places of origin, and there are folk musics that articulate the path along which the individuals in a highly mobile society travel in order to make decisions about shifting their primary affiliations. There are, therefore, folk musics based on ethnicity, on occupation, on religion, and on politics. In the twentieth century Americans have increasingly been able to choose the folk musics with which they most closely wish to identify themselves. The issues of identity embedded in folksong are, therefore, reflexive.

American historians frequently place considerable emphasis on the role of individuals in community-building, and American concepts of folk music similarly recognize the ways in which individuals contribute musically to their communities. Folk singers and instrumentalists, therefore, are often portrayed as extraordinary individuals (see Abrahams 1970 and Glassie et al. 1970). Edward Ives, in particular, has examined the ways in which individual musicians both symbolize larger historical narratives and embody more localized, community narratives (e.g. Ives 1978). The eponymous quality of folk music traditions further provides a means of narrating more extensive music histories in the twentieth century. The folk revival of the 1950s and 1960s, for example, most often takes shape as a history of individuals, beginning with Leadbelly, and John and Alan Lomax, increasing impetus through the efforts of Pete and Mike Seeger, and diffusing into contradictory rock styles through musical and ideological transformations wrought by Joan Baez and Bob Dylan. In the collectivities that constitute the folk in the United States, individuals rarely fail to stand out because of their extraordinary contributions to folk music.

Folk music undergirds group cohesion, and therefore folk music repertories often serve as texts for the historical processes that motivate the formation and dissolution of groups. In the late nineteenth century and in the early twentieth century, specific song repertories with identifiably coherent themes characterized certain occupational groups. In the coastal regions of the Northeast and Middle Atlantic states, largely English folksong repertories represented maritime occupations. The sea shanties of the East spread westward with the maritime industries of the Great Lakes and of the river networks connected to the Mississippi River, and quickly new texts and folk music styles shaped folksong repertories of these regions. In wooded areas, lumbering songs often replaced maritime songs, not least because of the frequency of syncretic themes (e.g. transporting felled lumber downstream on rivers gave rise to songs about river disasters). Folksongs also accrued around the occupations of cowboys in the American West and around the sweatshops and garment factories in the East, where Eastern European Jewish immigrants used Yiddish song traditions to translate forms of European economic repression into those of the United States.

Folk music blurs the borders between occupational identities and social, political, and ideological identities. During the Depression of the 1930s and during World War II, occupational folk music underwent a radical transformation, reemerging in the late 1940s as a politicized music of the American Left (see Greenway 1953; Denisoff 1973). Historically, folk music passed from group formations in the early twentieth century to a new public sphere in the second half of the century. Several historical processes expedited this transformation: in the 1950s, revival, not least the folk revival whose power derived primarily from folk music (Cantwell 1996), and in the 1960s, resistance, especially that engendered by folk music in the Civil Rights Movement and then later in the decade in the protest against the Vietnam War. Folk music's historical narratives, therefore, form around many different social collectives, but folk music also serves to connect those collectives to the larger narratives of American history.

Religion and religious music

One of the most distinctive features of the American cultural landscape is the plurality of religious experiences. The American religious experience has historically taken just about every shape possible. Individuals and cults localize religion; ethnic groups translate religious orthodoxy into cultural diversity; some religious groups create new possibilities for racial and social understanding, while others endeavor to shut down the dialogue of difference at all costs. Religion provides Americans with ways of being diverse, and it is one of the most American of all forms of choosing and constructing identities. In the powerful diversity of the American religious experience music occupies a central presence (see Bohlman and Blumhofer forthcoming).

The diversity of American religious musics is almost never beyond earshot. Visit the dozen or so churches in a midwestern small town on a Sunday morning, and you'll hear at least as many musical repertories. Take part in prayer on the Sabbath at several neighborhood synagogues in New York City or Atlanta, and you'll not only participate in different styles of cantillation, but the cantors will regale you with music from every corner of the Jewish Diaspora, past and present. Muslim prayer services on Friday in Chicago provide one with a choice from Bosnian genres in the city's oldest Muslim community to those performed by Pakistanis and African Americans, the city's newest Muslim communities. There are American religious musics that have survived in remarkable isolation; the Amish are perhaps the best-known group to place rigid restrictions on its members, but there are more recently arrived groups marking religious isolation with musical practices, such as the German-speaking Mennonites (see Klassen 1990) and the Russian-speaking Molokans (see Mazo forthcoming).

American religious identities are not only – indeed, not primarily – isolationist. The freedom to cross borders between denominations is great, even when the conditions for joining a new religious community are extraordinarily demanding. American religious musics provide a fundamental means for expediting the crossing of religious borders. In mainline Protestantism, hymnals and hymnbooks have always taken account of changing ethnic and social memberships. In proselytizing evangelism music provides one of the most attractive ways of winning converts and spreading to new communities, and to do this evangelical musics have effectively responded to as many diverse identities as possible. Historically, American musical styles as diverse as the shape-note singing of the nineteenth century (see chapter 6) and the syncretic fusions of blues and gospel in the hymns of black evangelicals in the twentieth century (Harris 1992) have both responded to the patterns of mobility in American society and affected these patterns in such ways that new forms of religious identity alter the American musical landscape.

PERFORMATIVE MOMENT – THE GOSPEL REVIVAL MEETING · Music fills the air at the revival meeting – gospel music, from a vast array of repertories, performed by quartets and choirs, accompanied by thumping pianos and jazz bands. Gospel, from both black and white traditions, arose from the revivals that followed westward and southern expansion immediately after the War of Independence, and revival provides no lesser context for gospel music two centuries later. American religious revival is all about expanding into the public sphere, about molding new identities through religion, so it is hardly surprising that revival meetings take place in a central park of the city or during inclement weather at a convention center. If the revival reaches out into the public sphere with all possible means at its disposal, it ultimately draws the crowds into its world of American evangelical identity: the world of gospel music.

For the first-time visitor to the revival meeting it is not a specific identity but rather the mixture of identities that is most striking. The revival consciously and publicly blurs racial boundaries. Depending on the city or the neighborhood, African Americans may or may not dominate the crowd, but the presence of African Americans in the music-making of the revival is unmistakable. Black and white gospel traditions began both separately and together, which is to say, their early histories were segregated, but there was musical exchange between the two from the beginning (Raichelson 1975). White hymn forms may have been borrowed to serve as the basis for black contexts, especially before the Civil War, but the performance practice of all gospel is undeniably the product of complex African American musical influences (Heilbut 1985).

Musical exchange is fully evident at the revival meeting. One context for exchange lies in the musical resources available to the public, that is, to the assembled congregation. Many clasp their own hymnals, well-worn compilations, which, despite other differences, contain roughly the same canon of settings by Ira D. Sankey, Philip Bliss, or Fanny Crosby (Blumhofer forthcoming), and gospel hymns by Thomas A. Dorsey and Lucie Campbell. The genealogy of great gospel composers is no less significant to the congregation than the tradition of evangelists leading up to any given revival (see Burnim 1983; Jackson 1979). In the history of gospel, as well as in church and revival performances of gospel, preachers and musicians may well exchange positions on occasion. The hymnals provide the core of a written tradition, but the stage band and the choir establish the performative conditions necessary for improvisation.

The interplay of gospel canons and genealogies notwithstanding, it would be a mistake to imagine that sameness and stability pervade gospel music. Gospel music responds to social change, if indeed with a conservative message; gospel breaks the boundaries of racial separation, if indeed many of its practitioners, especially in white evangelical churches, are unlikely to cross racial barriers outside their religious experiences. The musical exchange that takes place between gospel repertories draws our attention to critical historical moments and geographical settings. The influence of southern blues on northern gospel hymns in the 1920s, for example, expands our historical understanding of the Great Migration of southern blacks to the urban North enormously. The African American gospel-quartet style, moreover, spilled over into white popular musics, transforming them from the late nineteenth century to the mid-twentieth century (Lornell 1988). The gospel music of the revival meeting may initially provide a new public space for diverse religious and racial identities, but it quickly spreads beyond even this space, changing the ways religious identity reshapes American music history.

Popular music – popular identities

The distinctions between folk music and popular music have always been blurry, and they are especially so in twentieth-century America. Their other differences notwithstanding, folk and popular music do participate in different processes of constructing and expressing identity; because they share musical turf, they encourage extensive exchange of musical and cultural resources. In this subsection I concern myself primarily with ethnic popular music, that is, with popular genres that allow ethnic groups to respond to changing conditions of affiliation and identity. We have already encountered the most common ethnic popular music in areas with extensive Central and East-Central European ethnic groups, the polka. On one hand, the polka is a folk music in many communities, and many young musicians learn to play it, just as practically anyone can express themselves on the dance floor. Since the 1920s, polka musicians have been able to make recordings, with local and regional labels at their disposal, but above all ethnic labels served the needs of polka musicians until the 1940s and 1950s. At a mass level, it was Lawrence Welk who was most responsible for polka's transformation to a real popular music. Welk's Saturday night television show of the 1950s and 1960s portrayed polka and ethnic music of the Upper Midwest – Welk was from North Dakota, and he cultivated his German accent just enough so that few missed the ethnic message that he meant to convey – as a popular music for all Americans of a certain generation. Polka thus provides a means of performing one's identity as an ethnic American, not specifically as a Polish or German American. By the final decade of the twentieth century, polka's popularity had become so firmly established that a category was created for it in the annual Grammy Awards.

Mediation plays an important role in the exchange across generic and socioeconomic borders between folk and ethnic popular music, and the reader will want to turn to chapter 13 for a more extensive discussion of the commercialization of American music. In the present chapter, however, it is also important to recognize that folk and ethnic popular musics have depended on complex processes of mediation that may also be different from those affecting other popular musics. In the early years of the recording industry in the United States, for example, major labels found it profitable to produce recordings directed at specific ethnic groups (see McCulloh 1983). Richard K. Spottswood has documented the history of ethnic recording with painstaking detail, and his monumental study of the recordings produced for the mosaic of ethnic consumers is standard reading for anyone interested in American music (Spottswood 1990). Other forms of mediation also participated in the popularization of ethnic music. There were music publishers that produced and disseminated arrangements of ethnic dance music, such as Vitak-Elsnik in Chicago. Fan magazines (e.g. *The Polka News*) and regional and national conventions promulgate forms of popularity that fulfill the needs of consumers for the hallmarks of American popular culture, the "Concertina Hall of Fame" in Wisconsin, for instance, the Valhalla for great accordion players.

Whereas these popular musics blur immigrant and ethnic identities, they by no means eliminate them. Quite the contrary, ethnic popular musics provide new possibilities for altering and reformulating ethnic identities. An ethnic popular song by Frankie Yankovich, such as his cover of *Rosamunde*, *Beer-Barrel Polka*, might contain snippets of text in three or four languages, but most important of all is that those who listen to Yankovich's many recordings find a common musical ground in America for their ethnic differences to coexist (Pietsch 1994).

HISTORICAL PROCESSES – ALTERITY · More often than not, studies of musical identity stress conditions of sameness: folk music is a common cultural good, something that the folk share just as they share in its making and transmission. Early concepts of identity in the United States, especially those addressing immigrant, ethnic, and religious identity, also stressed sameness. The concepts of cultural pluralism, formulated by Horace Kallen early in the twentieth century (see Kallen 1956), and of multiculturalism, formulated by scholars in ethnic and cultural studies at the end of the century, present models of identity cohering about a recognizable core. Music had the power not just to symbolize that core but also to represent its quintessence, its capacity to offer a cultural vocabulary shared by all in the group.

I conclude this section on identity by turning to a very different condition of musical identity in the United States: alterity. I suggest, moreover, that it is alterity and the ways music can complement and express its historical processes that have made the musics of difference – the musics addressed in this chapter – so significant in American music history. Alterity is an historical process that employs music to distinguish identities of selfness in a cultural context of multiple others. At issue is not simply that alterity separates Self from Other, but rather that it creates new ways for different individuals and groups to interact with each other. The musical ramifications of alterity are clear, if also very complex, in gospel music. Gospel has historically provided a musical context for racial alterity; African Americans and white Americans, coming from different musical traditions, make music together. Gospel does not erase racial alterity, but it does recontextualize it; gospel forms a field of alternative identities.

Alterity is very much at issue as new forms of individual and group identity emerge in postethnic America at the end of the twentieth century. Alterity provides a means of constructing new folk musics and making them meaningful as means of expressing and celebrating difference. At mid-century, it was this capacity to construct new folk musics that empowered the Folk Revival to address issues of racial inequality and ideological prejudice against the politics of the working class (Cantwell 1996). In the 1970s and 1980s it was again folk music that empowered women to transform local activities to a nationwide movement in support of gender equality. "Women's music," whether in neighborhood coffee houses, on specialized recording labels, or at the annual National Women's Music Festival in Michigan, has taken shape historically not because of its sameness, but rather because of the complex differences it can articulate. In the 1990s musics that gave meaning in smaller groups (e.g. in gay discos – see Currid 1995) to differences in sexual orientation also spilled across social borders to exert their presence in the public sphere, notably in the annual Gay and Lesbian Pride parades that take place in virtually every American city (cf. the essays in Case, Brett, and Foster 1995). At century's end music has lost none of its power to represent the issues of identity that are so essential to Americans' notions of their selfness and their differences.

III. Senses of place – regional musics

American vernacular musics rarely hide their associations with place. Immigrant musics announce their origins, ethnic musics bear witness to geographical transformations, and folk musics of all kinds narrate journeys across the American musical landscape. The images of place in American vernacular musics do not just represent the nodes and arteries of a musical landscape, but rather they are imbued with agency, processes of participating in and making history. The early blues, therefore, accompanied singers moving across the Mississippi Delta or from the rural towns in the South to the industrialized urban neighborhoods of the North. The "Highway 61" of the blues song with the same name was and is a very real place, the major thoroughfare running parallel to the Mississippi River. The agency of the sense of place in American music may well be one of the most persistent processes constituting the Americanization of music. In the United States, the narrative settings for Child ballads shift from European courts to small towns in the South or Midwest. Some genres attach their images to localized senses of place (e.g. barbershop quartets, discussed below), while others interact with the conditions of geographical and physical displacement (e.g. rap and hip hop, discussed in chapters 10 and 13). It is the sense of place in America that undergirds the nation's many different kinds of regional music.

Displacement and diaspora

Americans have historically interpreted region through music that expresses senses of arrival and departure. Individual and group histories include processes of identity formation that narrate how it is that the group formed after departing from one place and arriving at another. That place is not separate from displacement is obvious in the American penchant to hyphenate identities, the hyphen marking the disjuncture of displacement itself, as in Greek-American or Mexican-American. The disappearance of the hyphen sometimes marks a new stage in the historical process of displacement, for example, in "Cajun music," the traditional music of French-speaking – which is to say, French- and English-speaking, and sometimes Spanish-speaking – residents of Louisiana, whose cultural history begins with displacement from France to "Acadia" in Canada, and from there to Louisiana through yet another displacement. Cajun music, then, embodies the sense of displacement essential to Cajun identity in a particular region (Ancelet 1984). Not only do vocal repertories maintain regional dialects of French, but genre, form, and dance are distinct from other musics of the Mississippi Delta region. Musically, they narrate connections to Canada and beyond to France, but at the same moment they draw attention to the ways in which those connections have been severed.

There is no single form of displacement, nor is there any single, or even predominant, motivation for displacement. Diaspora, for example, includes many of the conditions of displacement, but the culture of diaspora produces distinctive forms of regionalism. Diaspora spawns various ways of imagining that displacement can be sutured, if not repaired, and music is one of the agents that represent possibilities for repair. Paul Gilroy has suggestively proposed the geographical metaphor of the "Black Atlantic," a space of ongoing cultural exchanges between Africa and the various regions of the African diaspora along the coasts of the Atlantic Ocean (Gilroy 1993). Even as it has variously been applied to African American musics, diaspora depends on extremely nuanced relations between music and region. Within the African diaspora there are places of isolation, literally, that is, "islands" where black music has or had presumably resisted change, such as the Georgia Sea Islands off the coast of the American Southeast. The folk culture and the folk music of the Georgia Sea Islands, because of the presence of African elements, remains historically connected to the place of diasporic origins. Other musics of the African diaspora in the United States narrate the irreparable forms of displacement, that is, the impossibility or even danger of affirming regional connections. The texts of the early blues at the beginning of the century evoke regional landscapes disrupted by crossroads and railroad

lines; the texts of rap and hip hop at century's end represent the disruption of the black spaces of postmodernity with even more trenchant
lyrics.

Regional musics in the United States frequently voice the tensions that
are inherent in historical processes of displacement and diaspora. Country
music, an emblem of the rural South, expresses various forms of fear that
social connections that create southern regionalism will disintegrate: the
collapse of the nuclear family, the social fabric of evangelical Protestantism, and the poverty that drives the working class from the South.
Country music, with its representations of disintegrating regionalism, is
counterpoised to the bounded isolation of folk musics in the southern
highlands, notably in the Appalachian Mountains (Malone 1979). Regionalism in southern folk music, at least in the national imagination, has come
to depend on the displacement of being "cut-off," of surviving in the
remote regions of the mountains (Whisnant 1983). The essential question
that these different notions of region in the South pose is not whether one
extreme or the other is more credible, but rather just how southern musics
define and allow Americans to imagine the South in such different ways.
The South as a region must include country music and Appalachian folk
music, as well as the blues, Cajun music, and the work songs of the Georgia
Sea Islands. It is in the ways these different musics express displacement
that they provide a complex model of an American region.

Regionalism and American mobility

Two dimensions characterize regionalism on the American cultural landscape: boundedness and mobility. The first dimension privileges stasis and
the longevity of certain population groups. The culture of the region – and
for our purposes, the music culture – sustains very little change, and when
change does occur, there are adjustments to the regional culture to stem it.
The music of a bounded region demonstrates patterns of unity, and the distinctions between stylistic elements that belong to a region and those that
do not are presumably self-evident, particularly to the residents of the
region. The bounded dimension of regionalism dominates the music histories of certain American regions, notably the South and New England.
The role of region itself in the music histories of these areas is, therefore, of
considerable importance in understanding the nature of their musics.

In this subsection I turn my attention primarily to the second dimension of regionalism – mobility – and I do so because mobility has played an
enormous role in determining the ontologies of regional musics and in

constructing regional music histories. Indeed, I should argue that one of the ways in which American music history is most unlike European music history is the overwhelming presence of mobility in changing American regional cultures. Perhaps the strongest evidence for the role of mobility is the inability of geographical boundaries to contain regional musics. The Polka Belt crosses numerous regions; Tex-Mex musics belie regional boundaries; the blues connect regions in the course of extensive migrations from South to North. In the twentieth century Americans have become even more mobile, and in consequence the ethnic and socioeconomic makeup of regions are constantly in flux. It is hardly surprising, therefore, that regional musics have come to represent the incessant mobility of American modernism.

From the many American musics that might illustrate mobility, I turn briefly to one that, at first glance, seems an unlikely candidate because of its imagery of stasis: barbershop quartets. In highly symbolic ways, barbershop quartets seem to be the ultimate symbols of places that change very little. The tight, four-part, unaccompanied harmony performed usually by male quartets celebrates the close groups that form in small towns and on street corners, "around the lamppost," as one of the earliest images expressed it. Barbershop melodies occupy narrow ranges, usually within an octave, and because the melody falls to the "lead tenor," the lower of the two upper voices, the sense of boundedness is even greater (Spaeth 1940). The barbershop quartet movement – and it is by no means accidental that it is referred to as a movement – began as a context in which traveling salesmen gathered together and performed. The singers were, therefore, literally "on the road," moving across the face of the Midwest from Tulsa to Ohio.

The images of home and security grew from distinctive forms of mobility. Gage Averill suggests that barbershop music is a phenomenon of ongoing revival, musically and historically (Averill forthcoming). Barbershop music revives earlier styles in American history, especially black male quartets and nineteenth-century minstrel shows, but transforms them for the cultural needs of twentieth-century, usually white, Americans. Barbershop music culture is ceaselessly on the road, with local groups gathering at contests of the male Society for the Preservation and Encouragement of Barber Shop Quartet Singing in America (SPEBSQSA) and the female Sweet Adelines. Dependent on small-group affiliations, barbershop quartets give meaning to regional and national histories no less dependent on extensive mobility.

PERFORMATIVE MOMENT – AMERICA ON PARADE · There is no more intensified moment for the musical performance of American senses of place than the parade. Every parade, whatever its location and circumstances, juxtaposes numerous ways of expressing what place means to Americans. The two most obvious ways in which the parade uses music to reconfigure American notions of regionalism derive from the geography of the parade route itself and the place from which the participating bands or floats come. The juxtaposition of these two regional dimensions alone collapses several forms of displacement. Perhaps most important, the parade connects the musicians and the places they represent to America.

Ethnic parades have historically provided one of the most significant forms of performing ethnic identity in the American public sphere. The ethnic parade, celebrating "independence days" for immigrant communities (e.g. Mexican Americans in mid-September) or "the contribution to America" for communities of long-standing residence (e.g. Irish Americans on St. Patrick's Day), muster enormous musical resources that take over a specific urban region (also small-town streets and athletic fields throughout the nation) and ascribe to those regions a specific identity. Some ethnic parades take place in ethnic neighborhoods. The musicians who perform in the ethnic neighborhood parade, however, may come from throughout a much larger region. The German bands from the Midwest that perform in the German-American Day Parade in Chicago's Lincoln Square neighborhood symbolically redefine the urban region as German, connecting it to the extensive German heritage of the Midwest, especially in nearby Wisconsin. Ethnic parades also occupy a central region of a city, that is, a complex of streets that lend themselves to repeated ethnic remappings. Dearborn Street, which runs through the Chicago Loop, its geographical core, will support several ethnic parades each weekend through much of the summer and fall.

The wash of sounds that an ethnic parade creates mixes and remixes identities, but it does so within certain types of regional boundaries. Musically, the parade is a simulacrum for the ways in which American musics map and remap American regions. The musical landscape of the parade is at once real, indeed identifiable on a city map, and imaginary, constantly assuming new meaning because of the different perspectives with which the music is perceived. American composers – Charles Ives is the most obvious case (e.g. *Three Places in New England*) – have recognized the ways in which parades and other public performances determine the shape of the American musical landscape. Music, whether police bagpipe bands wearing kilts or a small-town high-school marching band wearing *Lederhosen*, provides the agency that gives meaning to an American region. In a culture of extensive displacements the music of parades provides the vehicle of return to the regions that most powerfully shape American senses of place.

Globalism and transnationalism

If one visits a pub in a village on the west coast of Ireland to hear folk music in a session, the chances are that the musicians have learned their repertory from Frances O'Neill's publications of Irish folk tunes and dances, collected and published in Chicago during the early decades of the twentieth century (O'Neill 1903, 1913). If one travels into the Tatra Mountains of southern Poland to hear one of the much-touted folk festivals in the heartland of Polish folk culture – the center for movements driven by revival and espousing authenticity – many in the new generation of Polish musicians who turn to early recording sources for their authentic sound, will be playing versions learned from ethnic recordings made in Polish immigrant communities of the American Midwest in the 1920s. These recordings were brought back to Poland, where the "Podhale sound" would absorb recognizable traces of the "Chicago Highland sound" (Cooley forthcoming). If one visits the cities and villages of Africa, wherever Protestant missionaries have preached the gospel and enjoined the congregations to sing gospel music, it will not be difficult to hear strains from Sankey or Dorsey hymns woven into indigenous styles of vocal music, especially the choral styles that had influenced American gospel music from its beginnings.

Such cases of globalism and transnationalism in American music were well under way in the first decades of the twentieth century, and in some ways they are phenomena of the twentieth century. O'Neill's transcriptions and collections circulated in Ireland because of the increased affordability of publishing and distribution. The Polish immigrants in the Midwest turned to the technologies of ethnic recording like many other immigrant groups. Polish music is only one case among many, in which the "first recordings" were made in American immigrant communities, even decades before the first recordings in the "old country" (see McCulloh 1983). In one extreme case, the recordings made of German-speaking immigrants from Romania (Siebenbürgen and Banat Germans) provide the only aural documentation of their musical traditions, which were dispersed and destroyed in World War II. The gospel hymns of Africa, too, owe their prominence to the technologies of mass-production and distribution of hymnals, as well, though to a lesser degree, to the portability of pump organs. In South Africa, especially, gospel quartets toured extensively and sometimes remained there, profoundly influencing both sacred and secular choral repertories (Erlmann 1991).

The globalism and transnationalism demonstrated by American musics are therefore not only the products of the explosion of American popular music and recording technologies at century's end. Globalism was present at the turn of the last century, and it has persisted throughout this century. The many forms of globalism, moreover, intersect particularly well with the music histories we have witnessed in the present chapter. This may not be surprising, for we have repeatedly seen the ways in which the musics of difference respond to – even embody – the mobility that is so characteristic of immigration, ethnicity, and region. Global musical change and exchange have, moreover, responded to historical moments and processes throughout the twentieth century.

Many of the new immigrant, folk, and postethnic musics at century's end are themselves fundamentally global products. Asian Americans on the West Coast make extensive use of karaoke, even mapping the immigrant landscapes of their Los Angeles or San Francisco neighborhoods with bars and clubs where young Asian Americans may come to reproduce Asian musics through karaoke technologies. The musical border culture of the American Southwest continues to demonstrate extreme transnationalism, which we witness even in the label "Tex-Mex," given to many of the musical styles of the region. As Mexican-American ethnic communities at century's end grow in northern cities, the musical narration of conflicts along the international borders spreads throughout the United States. It becomes increasingly evident that the processes of musical exchange that globalism and transnationalism unleash move in both directions simultaneously. In the folk-music sessions at Irish-American bars in Chicago suburbs, musicians play tunes collected by Francis O'Neill, but borne to the United States in the violin cases of new immigrants; the Polish-American dance troupes at Chicago's "Highland Hall" depend on the constant influx of immigrant musicians who have learned their Chicago Polish repertory in Poland; in countless black "storefront churches" throughout Chicago, every effort is being made to make gospel singing as African as possible.

HISTORICAL PROCESSES – TERRITORIAL TRANSGRESSIONS · In the United States an accordion is rarely just an accordion. Accordions connect music to place, and they influence significantly the way music reflects the sense of place. Accordions in one region differ from those in another, sometimes because they originated in a different place prior to immigration, more often because they have participated extensively in the musical remapping of the region. As American musical instruments, accordions are inseparable from the diverse music histories with which the sense of place is constructed and communicated. Accordion styles may bound the styles and repertories of an American region, or they may accelerate the historical processes that cause regions to change and territorial transgressions to take place.

Region is especially evident in the structure and material nature of the accordion when it arrives in the United States as an immigrant instrument. In the old country each type of accordion needed to be responsive to localized musical styles, and their names confirmed the extent to which they were responsive. To respond to a localized style meant, for example, that the accordion's tuning had to fit local repertories, and that it had to be compatible with the instrumental ensembles of the region. Button-box accordions are diatonic and therefore limited to diatonic melodies and restricted modulations, such as those in Central Europe. Button-box accordions, for example, predominate in Alpine repertories, where musical style reflects the distinctive regional influences of history, social structure, and dialect. To make the point explicit, the yodeling characteristic of Alpine singing lends itself to representation on the button box. There is, however, no single Alpine accordion. In southern Austria, the most common form of button box is the "Steirische," literally an accordion from Styria. This button box, however, has myriad local and individual forms, some which distinguish nearby Slovenian musics, and others that have dominated Austrian immigrant practices, notably the "Grazer," literally an accordion from Graz, which is the capital city of the province of Styria. The differences in accordion style and structure are significant, and they become more so in American dance music. The button box of Slovenian-influenced dance in western Pennsylvania is very different from the button box of Austrian-influenced dance in eastern Pennsylvania.

There are three very general theories that explain the historical processes underlying the accordion's territorial transgressions in American music. Indigenous perspectives (i.e. those maintained within an ethnic group) privilege the accordion's adaptability and its ability to respond to a

wide range of musical demands in the changing cultural contexts of the
United States. It can function as a solo instrument, even at a dance, or it can
take its place in almost any ensemble, large or small. The second theory, in
contrast, takes the material structure of accordions as evidence of a capacity to survive just about any cultural threat accordions must face. In E.
Annie Proulx's novel, *Accordion Crimes* (1996), a single Sicilian button box
travels from hand to hand, ethnic music to ethnic music, throughout the
twentieth century, the same instrument giving voice to an enormous range
of American lives and, above all, tragedies. From a third perspective we can
see that both the flexibility and inflexibility of the accordion empower its
territorial transgressions. Accordions may have an individual quality –
they are often handmade – and they may influence mass culture – there are
large manufacturers, such as the Hohner company of Germany (Wagner
1993). Individual immigrants may bring their instruments with them, but
so too are there cases of mass-produced instruments targeted for sale in a
particular region, such as Cajun Louisiana (Ancelet 1984) and the Tex-Mex
border musics. Even when mass produced, the accordion becomes an icon
of the individual musicians – Lawrence Welk in the Dakotas, Frankie
Yankovich in Cleveland, or Alphonse Ardoin in Louisiana – who draw and
redraw the regional maps of American music.

IV. American history – American music histories

The American musics of difference have generated a multitude of American music histories, which in turn reveal a complex web of historical processes in twentieth-century music history. In this section I concentrate on
the historical processes in order to suggest some models for rethinking just
what it means to claim that twentieth-century America embodies a multitude of music histories. The few accounts of American music that recognize musics of difference usually employ vague models, based on plurality:
just as there is a mainstream American music history, there are also individual ethnic music histories (Italian-American, Hispanic-American, etc.),
which together constitute an historical mosaic. If one begins with the
musics of difference themselves and then looks more carefully and critically at the vastly different historical processes that influence the ways in
which Americans express identity and form affiliations, models of plurality become woefully inadequate. The American music histories of the
twentieth century are not simply mosaic pieces, but rather they arise from

the ways in which music participates in historical processes that empower Americans to make aesthetic and religious choices, ethnic and political choices, and choices about the ways in which music connects them to or distances them from the places in which they live.

Preservation (stasis)

The power of music to preserve the past is one of the most prevalent processes in the historical reproduction of difference. The capacity of music to undergird the memory of the past is one of its most persistent narrative qualities. There are ethnic and religious groups that make extensive use of music to remember the past, with each performance or ritual connecting the group to its origins. The hymn-singing traditions of the Amish and Hutterites, for example, consciously retain a repertory and style these German-speaking Protestant sects believe stems from the sixteenth and seventeenth centuries. The core of the past is never abandoned, and when new narratives – either as new songs or as new verses appended to old hymns, some of them hundreds of verses in length – enter the historical tradition of the Amish or Hutterites, it is to preserve new layers, rather than to supplant the distant past with a more recent past (Bachmann-Geiser and Bachmann 1988). Such sects offer an extreme case, which recent scholarship has tended to dismiss as extraordinary and uncharacteristic, arguing instead that stasis is only hypothetically possible. If we regard preservation as an historical process rather than as the result of history that fails to change, it demonstrates quite a different importance for the musics we have examined in this chapter, and, by extension, for most of the musics in the present book. In sacred music, language strengthens the imperative to preserve; Muslim and Jewish prayer and liturgy, for example, preserve religious identity through the use of Arabic and Hebrew texts, even though the Arabic and Hebrew of those texts are not vernacular languages in the United States. The messages of nostalgia that many regional repertories convey may preserve only an idealized past, but preservation has no less presence. Preservation, therefore, is rarely isolated as an historical process, for it spills over to influence other historical processes.

Assimilation and acculturation (change)

In the scholarship devoted to American ethnic music, change is usually counterpoised against preservation. At the end of the twentieth century, in large part due to modern scholarship in folklore and ethnomusicology, there are few who doubt that change occurs, if for no other reason than the resources necessary for the preservation of an old-country style diminish, and pressure from the mainstream is too overwhelming to resist. Such generalized studies of change are rarely helpful, for they are so generalized as to assume that the path to assimilation offers no detours and no possibilities for retracing historical steps. If one looks beyond the generalizations, however, it becomes apparent that change does not simply happen, but it, too, is the result of decisions by musicians and the communities they represent. There is, then, a difference between assimilation – unbraked change – and acculturation – change created through active, decision-making processes. As two different forms of change, assimilation and acculturation also enter into a dynamic tension, and it is in this tension that the historical processes of change become differentiated from each other. Because of the tension, there may be ethnic dance bands that consciously assimilate styles from other groups or from the ethnic mainstream in order to stimulate interest in the acculturative distinctiveness of ethnic style. Successful dance musicians, in fact, turn to the mainstream not to adapt to it, but rather to tap its receptacle of differences, thereby expanding their capacity to create and redirect change. Through creative engagement with change, such dance musicians prevent any single form from overwhelming others.

Dynamic between center and periphery

The dynamic between center and periphery generates some of the most diverse and historically significant processes of American music history. In this chapter, we should understand center and periphery as both geographically real and temporally metaphorical. The importance of origins in the maintenance of immigrant musics, it follows, results from metaphorical notions of centeredness. Preservation and change rely on trajectories toward or away from stylistic centers. It is in the study of regional musics that the dynamic between center and periphery most literally maps and remaps the American regional landscape. Musics of certain regions, such as the South, cohere to centers; musics of other regions, such as the Texas-Mexico border, undergo the multiple influences of border crossing, hence demonstrating the conditions of a periphery. The ethnic map of American musics, too, places some musics closer to the mainstream, while treating others as marginal. Many historical processes are unleashed through the dynamic between center and periphery. Urbanization, for example, occurs when the musics of disparate rural areas undergo the musical influences from the urban center. Gospel styles form along the faultlines between "mainline" churches and splinter denominations. The regional mobility, upon which the blues or barbershop music depends, forms geographies out of nodes and arteries, with musicians frequently opting to move from the peripheries as close to the center as possible. Perhaps most characteristic of all when we view the fundamental mobility enabled by the American musical landscape are the ways in which center and periphery may be interchangeable at times. The ethnic parade, formed from bands at the peripheries, redefines the center of the city, if for one highly symbolic moment in history.

Revival and festivalization

Most Americans use their musics of difference to express a variety of identities, not just distinctive religious or regional identities that may be unrelated to each other, but various combinations of ethnicity and group affiliations. Just how are such choices possible in a modern world, with its incessant demands on professional and personal lives? The historical processes of revival and festivalization offer one set of answers to that question. Revivals enter American music history most notably through religious movements, and as both this chapter and chapter 6 have shown, musical diversity is often one of the most significant results of revival movements, not to mention revival meetings themselves. Secular music, too, lends itself to revival, so much so that one approach to writing a history of folk music in the United States would be to analyze successive revivals. Revivals, like musical change, do not just happen, and it is therefore necessary to look beyond the cyclicity that usual notions of revival imply and to ask more nuanced questions about the reasons that revivals take place (see the essays in Rosenberg 1993). The Folk Revival of the 1950s and 1960s resulted from crucial issues of political and racial freedom (Cantwell 1996). The bluegrass revival of the 1960s and 1970s provided a response to the commercialization of a regional music by shoring up an idealized regional core. Festivals represent an even more extreme site for the historical processes of revival by condensing them to a set of highly symbolic performances at a specific place and time. Festivals are at once the product of displacement and a means of suturing disjuncture, for they depend on further historical processes that connect one festival to the next.

Technologies of musical reproduction

Immigrant, folk, and regional musics in the United States benefit from enormously complex technologies that both maintain and transform them. The technologies we have seen throughout this chapter, moreover, are not bounded by simple reproductive capability; in other words, we have not primarily been concerned with "recorded music" or "print technologies," or for that matter with "oral traditions" with a specialized dependence on technology. The technologies influencing the histories of American musics of difference more frequently form because of the need to strengthen and diversify historical processes. The *Ausbund* hymnbook of the Amish, published since the sixteenth century, which is to say, still published in eastern Pennsylvania, makes it possible to perform preservation at each Sunday's worship service. Ethnic and race records take technological innovation as a starting point, but direct it toward the collection and dissemination of immigrant repertories. The ethnic recording early in the twentieth century preserved immigrant sounds, but its technologies also made it necessary for musicians to respond to the conditions of the recording, for example, the restriction of most records prior to the 1940s to cuts no longer than three minutes. Radio and television technologies both define and diversify regional musics, and no regional music in the United States demonstrates this more extensively than southern music, which has been broadcast beyond the South since the earliest years of American radio, in the 1920s. Revival is remarkably dependent on the technologies that make it possible to study what are imagined to be authentic versions. Performers of the Jewish instrumental traditions known as klezmer, for example, have stimulated a revival of Jewish-American music by deliberately learning pre-Holocaust repertories from "old recordings." For the Klezmer Revival, technology has made it possible to cross one of the most tragic historical fissures of the twentieth century.

Americanization

I conclude this overview of historical processes with Americanization not to suggest a dissolution in the hyphen of ethnic or racial difference, but rather to draw our attention to the ways in which Americanization is also an historical process that leads to the construction of new conditions of difference. These are the historical processes that lead musicians to imagine new categories, such as "Americana." Far from bringing about an homogenization of American culture, Americanization provides means of surviving the melting pot and entering into postethnic America. Americanization results from the dynamic tension evident in the extraordinary ways ethnic communities compete for turf on an urban regional landscape. When one community organizes a festival or parade, it is only a matter of a few years before many other groups muster the forces necessary to lay their claim to the festival and parade seasons. The diversifying functions of Americanization are also clear in the ways denominationalism pervades the music of the American religious experience. Just as American Lutherans sing from hymnals that still reveal a diversity essential to their immigrant origins in various parts of Central and Northern Europe, so too do American Baptists rely on gospel traditions that reflect a surfeit of regional and racial differences. At the end of the twentieth century, the historical processes that Americanization embodies assure that difference is no less significant in the nation's immigrant, folk, and regional musics than it was at the beginning of the century. These are not the musics of other times and other places, gradually fading from modernity. They are the musics that give voice to difference in postethnic America.

Epilogue – Chicago's Von Steuben Day parade at century's end

After a summer of countless neighborhood festivals and major music festivals (Blues, Gospel, Latino, etc.) in Grant Park, fall provides Chicago's ethnic groups one final period of sustained good weather to perform their identities and affiliations on the city's streets and stages. Fall is a transitional season in the ethnic year, connecting seasons of exceptional heat and cold. Whereas ethnic and folk musics find their way to local, outdoor venues in the summer, and they retreat to ethnic churches, fraternal lodges, and neighborhoods in the winter, fall is the season in which postethnic musical experiences fill the urban landscape. Fall is the season in which music powerfully provides the possibilities for celebrating differences.

On the third weekend in September, ethnic parades take over the thoroughfare designated for that purpose, Dearborn Street. On the same weekend, Chicago's Celtic Fest takes place in Grant Park, in fact joining the city's grand festival tradition for the first time in 1997, despite the historical presence of Celtic musics of all kinds in Chicago for well over a century. On Saturday afternoon, two Hispanic parades pass down the street, first a parade celebrating "Central America" and then the parade in honor of "Mexican Independence Day." Officially, the two parades recognize two different histories of ethnic difference in Chicago. Ironically, though the Central-American communities distinguish themselves from the Mexican-American community, the city's largest Spanish-speaking community, they prefer to join together as a group of immigrants with different nationalities and languages. Musically, there is little difference, for many bands finish one parade, only to return to the beginning of the parade route to play again.

For many bands, in fact, the Mexican-American parade is the last of three. The first parade of the day celebrates "Von Steuben Day," named for General Friedrich Wilhelm von Steuben, a Prussian officer who trained American soldiers in the War of Independence. For an ethnic symbol, von Steuben would seem like a bit of a stretch – the United States is not wanting for important German Americans – but the historical reason for choosing von Steuben is obvious: he connects the parade not just to America but to American history at a point of origins.

From the diverse bands, some sporting *Lederhosen*, others *Fasching* costumes, many playing varieties of German folk music and polka repertories, one captures the attention of everyone along Dearborn more than any other: the Whitney Young Drum Corps, with its banners proclaiming the school's celebrating German-American Day, and its uniforms constituted of T-shirts and shorts in gold, red, and black, the colors of the German flag. The drum corps consists entirely of African Americans, and the music the high-school musicians play is an extremely disciplined genre juxtaposing diverse African American styles. More than other styles, hip hop predominates, and the musicians and dancers have fitted it marvelously to the street, enhancing both its transitional qualities and its ability to provide momentary stages that capture the attention of the crowd.

It's a stunning musical performance. We might wonder at first whether something does not quite fit, whether it's just a juxtaposition of differences born of random circumstances. Marching bands, after all, survive by playing in parades. I should like to close this chapter, however, by suggesting that the performance of the Whitney Young Drum Corps in the Von Steuben Day Parade symbolizes the musics and historical processes that this chapter has examined not because it is exceptional but because it is unexceptional. It is unexceptional, moreover, in the 1990s, when this ethnic parade integrates musical differences into public moments in which ethnic and racial difference come together. If we take the opportunity to experience these musical differences, we shall come all the closer to understanding how the musics of difference trenchantly narrate American music history.

12

Popular song and popular music on stage and film

STEPHEN BANFIELD

Anatomy

It is a perfect, warm spring day in Denver, Colorado. The tops of the city buildings trace sharp edges against the infinite, cloudless blue of the sky, and boulevards speed across the plains until stopped by the glittering snow-peaks of the Continental Divide. I take the bus from downtown to Cherry Creek. There, at the huge shopping mall, a more all-American crowd you could not find – healthy, young, handsome, casual, and easy in their clothes and with their bodies. Heady with purchase, pizza, and wine, I modulate into an epiphany of recognition that the American dream has somehow survived the latter-day depredations of media, technology, politics, and environment after all and, on a day like this, can suddenly glow with the splendor of all its old tangibility. A wave of satisfaction sweeps over me, and I find myself humming *The Trolley Song*.

It is, perhaps, rather touching that the desiccated soul of a musicologist can yet respond to the blandishments of sentiment, wit, association, and presentation that Tin Pan Alley forever traded in: for it is obvious that *The Trolley Song* still fits the experience. (The song, from the musical film *Meet Me in St. Louis* [1944] was written by Hugh Martin [born 1914] and Ralph Blane [1914–1995] and presumably "routined" and orchestrated by Roger Edens [1905–1970] and Conrad Salinger [?1900–1962].) The "ideal motion" of a ride to the consumer's paradise in the suburbs remains, even if for shops rather than Louisiana Purchase Exposition stands and on a bus rather than a trolley. So does the spiritual distance from the constraints of New York. And still there is the holy feast of corporation power, ambition, personal vision, fashion, innocence, and sheer beauty represented both by the film's narrative and by its corollary, the production number with its great song, its great star (Judy Garland), and its overall aesthetics of opulence (Osolsobě 1981, p. 2) erected by the brilliant yet unpraised army of designers, directors, producers, costumiers, trolley-builders, cameramen,

and musicians, from the arranger and orchestrator – we do not even know
who wrote what – who forged a score with the voice-leading finesse and
yearning of Rachmaninov and the gestural precision of Ravel, to the
instrumentalists who played it with unrecapturable slickness. The
moment they created returns, fifty or sixty years later, to tell me that all
manner of thing can still be well, still "OK by me in America."

At such a moment, to one susceptible to its workings (and the question
of who still is, who ever was, susceptible is vast), Tin Pan Alley is no more
dead than Elvis to a rock fan, and the livelier apprehension is to wonder
how the two deities will cohabit in the twenty-first century. Can either
assume the role of representing the omni-American experience (Murray
1970)? The case for Tin Pan Alley is strong, but for all that it has gloried in a
local habitation and a name it is not an easy entity to define and, for a
unified musical product of specific substance, dimensions, and characteristics, singularly lacks identification and anatomy. What was it that arose
some time before 1900 and, like Latin after the Renaissance, lost linguistic
authority to the rock revolution in and after the 1950s?

It certainly starts with the length and breadth of song, which is its
modulor, as was the human body to Le Corbusier. This means "quadratic"
melody built up of multiples of two-, four-, eight-measure units, cali-
brated by musical cadence and verbal rhyme and affording the standard
thirty-two-measure span, generally in an AABA or ABAC pattern, the
former more common. Already we can begin to see where other forms of
vernacular music lie beyond this particular horizon. Cadences within a
quadratic build-up will be balanced and contrasted, which implies, for
melody and harmony, structural tonality rather than modality and ostinato. The twelve measures of the blues are not strictly quadratic. And the
placing of rhyme, according to or offset from the ballad norm (of four-beat
lines of verse) that is the poetic corollary to quadratic melody, will cast the
discourse epigrammatically, be its mode one of sentimentality or of wit
(corresponding very roughly to the two basic types of Tin Pan Alley song,
ballad and novelty) – a prescription that would not apply to a good deal of
blues-, rock-, and folk-oriented song. (For the understanding of poetic
meter according to the co-ordinates of musical beats rather than the quantities of prosodic feet, see Attridge 1982, pp. 76–122. For further distinctions between song types, see Tawa 1990, pp. 162–197, borrowing from
Wickes 1916; Hamm 1994, pp. xxviii–xlvi; and Goldberg 1930, pp.
211–216.) Most of what surrounds this modulor is clothing or accretion,
largely a matter of presentation by way of introduction, repetition, varia-

tion and embellishment. Once the thirty-two measure chorus has become the norm (which gradually happens during the early decades of the twentieth century) the verse is introductory trimming. Contrast and conflict of material within the musical unit generally play no part in the point of the thing, therefore, and the lengths to which a structure based on consecutive choruses of the same melody can be taken are an important measure of Tin Pan Alley's later achievement, though the role played by the *release* in this continuum (the B section in an AABA structure) needs to be properly understood. Conversely, the concept of *refrain*, the moment at which word and note become indivisible, is vital.

The refrain idea, and the conditions of rhyme and cadence within quadratic forms, should have (but on the whole have not) alerted commentators to the dangers of treating lyrics and music separately when trying to account for the workings of what we can equally well call the Tin Pan Alley song, the golden-age American popular ballad (Forte 1995), or the musical theatre and musical film number. For those workings rely on a songwriting craft – in many ways a traditional one – that might be simply termed "dittying" and that has some very specific features and effects, regardless of whether or not one person writes both words and tune. This amounts to the *melopoetic* dimension of our product (Banfield 1996), and it is the first level of its identity and the one hitherto least investigated. In the case of an unlettered songwriter such as Irving Berlin (1888–1989) it may even be considered the only level for which the author was responsible, though there is still plenty to admire within it.

The other three levels of such a product's identity are those of *presentation*. Level two is best called *arrangement* and has three aspects. The first would be absolutely integral were we dealing with art music – and may still be in this genre, depending on the songwriter – for it includes its harmony and its accompaniment figure, vamp, or rhythmic setting. Insofar as these can sharply define the character of a song, dance, or march, they are essential to it, but one of the crucial evolutionary traits of the Tin Pan Alley song was how, particularly after World War I, it learnt to survive wholesale changes of character that varying presentations began to force upon it. Songs became "standards," perceived as the same item whether crooned or belted, sung, or played, highlighted as a dramatic performance in the theatre or heard as foil, accompaniment, or background to some other function in film or in the ballroom. (Jazz both completed and reversed the process of stripping away and re-clothing a number with presentational layers insofar as it eventually learnt to do without the melody and words and just left the harmony and the title. See Larson 1993.) The second aspect of arrangement is the coloring of a song by instrumentation, a facet invisible to the eye from the piano-oriented sheet music (to which guitar and ukelele symbols began to be added – and at first explained in a footnote – around 1930) but crucial to the ear in anything other than parlor performance. It is also an art which is largely beyond the province of the composer, whether by skill or circumstance: on the one hand, very few musical theatre composers have had the time or the ability to orchestrate their own songs (Victor Herbert [1859–1924] and Kurt Weill [1900–1950] were thoroughgoing exceptions, Leonard Bernstein [1918–1990] a partial one); on the other, the traditional Tin Pan Alley songwriter sent his ditty out into the world straight from the office as published sheet music and was largely uninvolved with its performance once it had been successfully "plugged," literally sold to someone – a performer or producer – who mattered. Arrangement as instrumentation feeds back into the rhythmic setting when instruments such as the banjo, guitar, percussion, and string bass highlight and give texture or layering to particular pulses, a factor crucial to the identity of a song or instrumental number when it accompanies or represents a social dance. The third aspect of arranging entails secondary composition – or even primary composition in the case of an amanuensis such as Berlin's Helmy Kresa and others, who had to fix the harmonies of a song by writing them down, though Berlin was careful to approve them (see Bergreen 1990 passim, especially pp. 476–477). Voice-leading is developed, harmonies are varied or altered, countermelodies and characterful "fills" between the vocal phrases are added, and choruses, whether or not with additional matter interspersed, are strung out into a *routine*. Broadway, and even more Hollywood, developed this craft into the apotheosis of the Tin Pan Alley genre, never more radiantly than in *The Trolley Song*.

Complementing these variables are those of the third level in the Tin Pan Alley product's anatomy, that of *performance*. A singer's style and persona can fix or transform a song's generic identity and fulfill its quality or specific gravity. (After World War I the same could begin to be said of a band's entertainment persona, and occasionally a pianist's.) It is crucial to know if a song was written with, say, a "coon shouter" in mind, for it may make little sense or become irretrievably dead when performed otherwise, whether or not this involves departure from the strictly notated details; paradoxically, however, performing styles such as the one just mentioned become inaccessible to later audiences and performers, so a song that is to survive *has* to change its identity according to who is singing it, when and where (see Hamm 1994, pp. xlvi–xlix; 1995, pp. 370–380).

Finally, there is the level of *production*. As stated above, the early and to a lesser extent later Tin Pan Alley product might be minted simply as sheet music, regardless therefore of this level except insofar as the illustrated cover affected its identity (see Hamm 1994, pp. xxiii–xxiv on covers). Two enduring agents, the stage and the new technological media, did the rest. Producers and their values on the stage would include, for instance, how a song was incorporated into a comedy or vaudeville act (in which case its production level was fused with its performance level), or how it featured in a musical drama. Broadway's musical theatre has used the Tin Pan Alley modulor as a basic dramatic vehicle – the equivalent of an operatic character's singing an aria as the representation of his or her emotion or moment of action or apprehension; but it is crucial to recognize that it also uses it, and Hollywood for a long time used it almost exclusively, as a dramatic *object*. That is, characters on screen only burst into song or dance *diegetically*, when they knew they were singing or dancing because it was singers and dancers that the plot was depicting. This was the backstage or show musical, in effect.

It is beyond the scope of this chapter to discuss how song and dance can exploit levels and ambiguities of diegetic production. But the opposite phenomenon – how a composer partakes of the production level by exercising the authorial function of dramatic commentary and interpretation – is very much a part of the exercise, for it is what accounts for the recurrent tendency of popular music of this sort to aspire to the condition of opera or symphony. It also defines the role of the composer in narrative film, where the modulor may be abandoned altogether and just the commentary and its devices retained – though this is an old technique, taken over from circus, melodrama and vaudeville accompaniment. On the stage or in the musical film the modulor remains the score's basis, and how a song or dance is placed within a suite, contrasting succession, or aggregation of musical numbers is a function of the composer's narrative authority. How and when it is reprised or recalled; how motifs span and interconnect and interpret numbers; how underscoring, recitative, instrumental links, transitions and, above all perhaps, personal styles and pastiches create a narrative viewpoint – all these can amount to considerable creative pretension even while the modulor is never lost sight of, however distorted or overlaid as well as surrounded and multiplied it may become. A composer such as Stephen Sondheim (born 1930) can still rely on the basic Tin Pan

Alley product through all his ambition for the musical theatre as an expressive medium. At the same time this level of production can be the province of the director, the scriptwriter or the choreographer in the studio or theatre. Furthermore, it can overtake a song in the singular when a recording is popularized on the radio and becomes a hit or a long-running signature tune. Or this production function can be its origin, as when Tin Pan Alley-style modules were (are?) especially written as television programme theme tunes or even as advertising jingles.

What, then, does the classic American popular song or instrumental number need to guarantee its identity and do its job? We have already mentioned the quadratic co-ordinates. Added to these are the absolute requirement of a harmonic and tonal accompaniment with firm bass line, nearly always instrumental and establishing a homogeneous rhythmic pattern and texture very often indicative of a dance type. Indeed, throughout the Tin Pan Alley period the oompah-oompah (OPOP) and oom-pah-pah (OPP) accompaniment figures of the nineteenth-century polka and waltz respectively remain standard, though their character and disposition undergo far-reaching transformations, largely to do with being slowed down and smoothed out. Shorthand for these figures, which indicates a single or octave bass note followed by a chord higher in the texture, may be further refined, as when the root of the chord in the bass is followed by its fifth (OPoP) or third (OPoP), or the "pah" is a single note (Opop), or it or the "oom" is omitted (OP-, a French waltz; OP-P, a beguine). Harmonic rhythm sometimes permits a change of chord within an OPoP unit but rarely or never within an OPP one (though the pattern may be suspended for a chromatic progression) and frequently is slower still. It makes little structural difference whether OPoP is notated in 2/4, 4/4 or cut time or OPPoPP in 3/4, 6/4 or 6/8, though the cavalry-march (or two-step) O-Po-P figure needs six pulses (normally in 6/8) to form a unit and would rarely have a change of harmony within it, and the change from one meter to another within and between songs and indeed periods carries implications of tempo and character, however difficult to pin down. The harmony itself is highly tonal, with much use of tertiary and secondary dominants, for instance III–VI–II–V–I, mostly with sevenths or (as the period progresses) higher-power additional notes, far less commonly with minor thirds (iii–vi–ii etc.) or in minor tonalities until a particular point in the early 1930s. Voice-leading is by and large smooth and firm, with the added notes offering considerable scope for chromaticism; harmonic allure is therefore a significant factor, taking the tonal language of Tin Pan Alley roughly as far as Rachmaninov. Later inroads include occasional titillations by parallel fourths and triads (especially in fills), though still largely within the cycle-of-fifths framework, and a certain amount of jazz coding (blue notes and chord substitutions); and especially in the theatre there had always been the exotic "Other" on hand, signified by drone basses, pavan rhythms, non-tonal melodic arabesques, pentatonic collections, or whatever. Modernism and primitivism beyond these belong largely to the world of narrative film music rather than that of the modulor.

The melopoetic formula is strictly accentual and almost entirely syllabic except when coloratura is used in operetta – the syllabic norm being another obvious indication of the boundary between Tin Pan Alley and folk or rock styles, which use moaning or whining techniques, nasal distortion of vowels, closed-eye withdrawal and so forth rather than the Alley's direct if often camp address. Indeed, Tin Pan Alley's melopoetic rhetoric is essentially that of speech exchange, its pacing, clarity and grammatical completion being enhanced by the wit of meter and rhyme. Its vocabulary tends increasingly away from the poetic and toward the smart as well as the colloquial as the genre develops, and dialect, especially black dialect, prevalent in the coon song of the earlier period (see chapter 14), gradually loses its appeal (see Furia 1990). Concurrently, title and motif phrases in words and music, separately or (as a refrain) together, become increasingly important, and melodic phrases shorter and shorter, away from the patter continuity of Offenbach's "couplets" to an often hymn-like smoothness of a few notes per phrase, including long ones, interspersed with cheeky instrumental fills often by way of call-and-response. (Or the melody itself may carry such contrast between the serious and the comic, the high and the low.) Leaving half or more of each quadratic span unsung probably originated partly in blues phraseology, partly in cabaret techniques (and limitations) of singing and acting. Melodic lines tend toward the archetypal, cadences being particularly formulaic, and apart from strong and increasing use of pentatonics and fanfare structures show little conflict with Schenkerian models of structural line. (See, accordingly, the two pioneer models for popular song analysis of this cast, Forte and Gilbert, both 1995, and note that another Schenkerian, Maury Yeston, composes musicals.)

What none of the foregoing explains is how the vernacular number achieves its appeal. This is not the quite same thing as asking what makes a popular hit, and one may be inclined to agree with Northrop Frye (1957, p. 4) that there need be no relationship between a work of art's popularity and its quality, either direct or inverse. It is more a question of codifying its ear-catching mechanisms, and although these are notably diverse – not just between composers, markets, and periods but within, say, one musical theatre score – they all need to provide some quality and dependable quantity of *allure*, to fasten on a word used earlier. Or to quote one of the songs themselves, *You Gotta Get a Gimmick*. This song was actually written for *Gypsy* (1959) in order for its protagonist to explain and indeed exemplify the great shift in popular taste that the arrival of the gimmick seems to have implied, for one shares Goldberg's puzzlement about how (for instance) an 1890s waltz song, that "sermon – in 3/4 time – upon the sanctity of the nuptial promise" (1930, pp. 136–137; see also Mooney 1954), can have become so emotionally inaccessible to us. Something changed massively around the turn of the century to render popular song as "keepsake" nostalgia obsolete and song with some kind of fashion-index street value more and more an exciting commodity. It probably had to do with the closing of the American frontier, for this must have changed people's emotional relations radically. Before, it was common enough to depart young from the bosom of a family and community knowing that one would never see those friends and relatives again: memory could never be supplemented with reunion – at least, not this side of the grave. In such circumstances possessions, including songs, had an utterly different value (one that symbolized the past and separation) from their new guise in settled, money-making surroundings, where they came to represent leisure, purchasing power, and the day-by-day social interchange of fashion and entertainment. Both could be uplifting, but in very different ways.

On the whole, however, one can still isolate and respond to the agent of captivation. It may lie largely in the words and the density of their projection of stage character or caricature through dialect, attitude, predicament, or whatever; many "novelty" songs rely thus on humor and need no particular weight of musical coinage beyond, say, a frenetic, syncopated ragtime pulse or a tripping dotted rhythm: these are just enough to float the energy of the verbal persona. Or the gimmick may be a kind of musical "hook," to use the word the latter-day music business understands – not necessarily a catchy refrain, title phrase or persistent motif (though these are all standard) but perhaps just a musical idea that can be heard to fulfill itself, cleverly or obviously, almost as if it were a mathematical series – which is what makes a jingle. Berlin's *A Couple of Swells*, as an example, uses the proposition of a bugle call at the opening of the verse – an idea left over from World War I songs and college quodlibets – and in letting it run its course the songwriter finds himself with a non-quadratic melody (of seven measures before the vamp returns) and a triple rhyme on his hands, very much a jingle rather than part of a song. The allure resides both in the jingle and in furnishing it, a catchy but undiscursive snippet, with regular harmonic unfolding, the witty tension between the two (no doubt worked out by the arranger, even if subconsciously grasped by Berlin himself) arising from the fact that the fanfare is all on the tonic and thus gives rise to a delicious ii9–V13 progression on the second rhyme. Following from this, perhaps, is also an explanation for the apotheosis of the arrangement: one era's generic sufficiency – take the waltz song again, or the bugle-call melody on its own – can become the next generation's background material for a new layer of allure. Ragging or jazzing up a song – the history of taste shown in the making when this is applied to *Can't Help Lovin' Dat Man* as a crucial part of the plot of *Show Boat* (1927) – is the most obvious example, but the use and re-use of the song *Singin' in the Rain* by Nacio Herb Brown (1896–1964) is a good case in point. It was the hit of two musical films, *The Hollywood Revue of 1929* and, a generation later with Gene Kelly, *Singin' in the Rain* (1952), but Edens's chic, riff-like fill, in its latter incarnation – constantly dancing rings round its harmonic progressions as in *A Couple of Swells* – is what immortalizes the number.

In general a popular number needs to be sure of its allure in one of the four basic spheres: verbal, rhythmic, melodic/harmonic, or arrangement. (Whether one should add a fifth, that of the performer, is a moot point. Can a crooner, for instance, make a success of a song with no positive qualities at all? It sometimes seems so.)

Verbal allure includes patter, comic dialect, rousing rhetoric or cynicism (as with George M. Cohan [1878–1942] and with Berlin's army songs), and the use of chic references – ones that make the audience feel smart when they understand them – in later lyrics (for instance, those of Lorenz Hart [1895–1943], Cole Porter [1891–1964] and Sondheim) stemming from *vers de societé*, as Furia (1990, pp. 6–7) has shown, a technique especially to the fore in "list" songs. Rhythmic allure is most standardized at first in the triple-time waltz songs and compound-time march songs – stemming from John Philip Sousa (1854–1932) – in which the equal-note flow, gallop, or jog-trot of dactylic meter tends to be self-sustaining in terms of momentum, regardless of the content. In the wake of the various ragtime crazes this function is taken over not so much by syncopation as by cross-rhythm, or rather by a mixture of the two. The chorus of *Any Old Night* exemplifies this. An early hit by Jerome Kern (1885–1945) when used in the London production of *Tonight's the Night* (1915) (though it was written with Otto Motzan for *Nobody Home* in New York), it has lyrics (by Schuyler Greene and Harry B. Smith) that are dactylic:

/x x /   xx / x x /
Any old night is a wonderful night
x x   /   x x / x x /
If you're there with a wonderful girl,

But instead of being set, Sousa-wise, in an equal-note 6/8 or with the pattering, quantitative insouciance of the French *rataplan* (of which Kern is fond enough for other purposes), they emerge in a mixture of triple-time cross rhythm (the *x* phrases) and syncopation (*y* phrases) over a 2/4 OPoP frame:

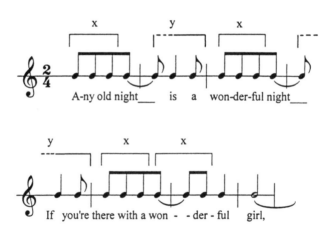

This, particularly the initial triple-time unit giving rise to a premature second main beat, is the standard indication of the fox trot lilt, and it survives, like the dance itself, until the 1950s, and beyond in some stage contexts. A well-placed "lilt" can achieve marvels in setting the character of a song, not necessarily right at the start: in *The Lady Is a Tramp* (composed by Richard Rodgers [1902–1979] for *Babes in Arms* [1937], with words by Hart) it comes in the second line of "I get too hungry / For dinner at eight." It is worth noting that the "slow-quick-quick-slow-(slow etc.)" steps of the fox trot and its faster cousin the quickstep also involve a three-beat pattern against a duple musical metre, though generally in counterpoint rather than in unison with the melody's cross-rhythm. As for the other dances of the 1910s, 1920s, 1930s and 1940s, their essence might be musically codifiable in a single rhythmic sign – such as with the tango and Charleston – but more broadly it was subsumed into two fundamental models of rhythmic allure, jazz and Latin American, the former sweeping all before it after World War I, the latter beginning around 1930, more or less with *The Peanut Vendor*, a rumba song of 1931. As John Storm Roberts has pointed out (1979, p. 220), the identifying sound or "beat" of a dance number is not simply a matter of "'rhythms' that can be tapped with a pencil, but combinations of rhythmic pulse, melodic phrases, speed, song form, and so on." One can add that with jazz and Latin American numbers the whole idea and persona of the *band* is what matters, and that when a band in the 1920s or 1930s takes over a Tin Pan Alley song the first thing it tends to do is substitute patterns and pulses of its own for the OPoP accompaniment, their corporate kinesis constituting the allure.

Melodic/harmonic allure is less easy to pinpoint. For all that Steven Gilbert and Allen Forte can explain the well-made song in terms of the standard fundamental lines and harmonic structures of Western tonality (to which Gilbert [1995, p. 8] adds the breathtaking corollary, "Nobody dislikes a Gershwin tune"), it tends to be just those unexpected or foregrounded details that do not show up or sit comfortably on a reductive graph that give a song its value. A single, well-placed blue note can do the trick, as in the second measure of *Bess, You Is My Woman Now* from *Porgy and Bess* (though see Starr 1986 for its possible structural implications). So can a single melody note or two- or three-note motif placed with finesse and offering some kind of emotional flux between the logical (which is also the routine) and the rebellious, poles to be steered between rather than visited. Octave or arpeggio shapes embedded in the stepwise fundamental line of a melody often achieve this function, for example in the opening of the chorus of the 1933 song *It's Only a Paper Moon* by Harold Arlen (1905–1986), and this is especially true at cadences where the line's doom is most difficult to escape or where harping on the dominant (fifth) degree of the melodic scale is concerned. So does, say, the inexact sequence outlined by the downward seventh in the second "they didn't believe me" iteration from the chorus of Kern's 1914 song of that title written for *The Girl from Utah*. Comparable to this breaking of sequence and on a broader scale, a well-judged *release* is just that, frequently a breaking of register, broadening of rhythm, and flight of harmony (or a modulation), such as provides the perfect foil to Rodgers's favorite repeated-note motifs in *The Surrey with the Fringe on Top* from *Oklahoma!*. Rodgers always provides harmonic allure for his repeated notes by anchoring sententious chord changes and voice-leading to them, whether or not they are dominant pedals and very much as we have seen with Berlin's *A Couple of Swells*, and it is always the way a melodic feature sits on the harmony that gives the former manifest value rather than just potential, as anyone who has had to harmonize a melody knows. This is how Broadway – rather more than the other Tin Pan Alley outlets – learnt the trick of *seductive* melody: much as with rhythmic cross-accentuation, its wit and power lay in the ever bolder lie of melodic dissonance on ever-simple harmonies. In musical terms, this constituted much the same casual efficacy in the handling of language as was developing in "book" dialogue (the prose libretto) and lyrics. The difference between an Offenbach OPoP melody and a Lehár one frequently resides in the number of appoggiaturas, *échappés*, and unresolved Viennese sixths – the amount of moral license, as it were – the latter permits himself, and the smoother the melody the more liberties it tends to take with its harmonic anchorage. Herbert learnt how to purvey this kind of charm or potency, as did many of the great Broadway and Hollywood songwriters such as Jule Styne (1905–1994) and Harry Warren (1893–1981). A potent example from Styne, relatively late in the presupposed life-span of the genre, would be the opening of the chorus of *Everything's Coming Up Roses* from *Gypsy*. The long, stressed third note of each three-note phrase is the sixth degree of the scale, consonant only at the first, harmonically parenthetic, statement and not even then once the chord changes (from ii7 to V, when it becomes the ninth). After that it becomes an added (Viennese) sixth before settling on the fifth degree of the scale, itself complemented sequentially, with still bolder dissonant placing, by the third degree over chord IV, forming a major seventh.

The allure of arrangement includes rhythmic, harmonic, and melodic features but resides in the clothing these represent – or, indeed, in the removal of it, for one only has to think of a standard big band striptease number to appreciate what levels of excitement those interjectory, end-of-phrase brass fills can achieve, along with modulation by semitone or third for the next chorus, the use of "stop-time" interludes and "strut" codas, with hammering triplets and silent beats measured between them, and so on. The musical equivalents for the "bump and grind" repertory of gestures were one successor to the more balletic, essentially French tradition that sustains not just operetta style but the tripping lightness of many a musical comedy number right through Kern, Berlin, and Rodgers and Hammerstein, where the turn of a flounce-skirted ankle and the wave of a hand or a fan were titivation enough. Light dotted rhythms and daintily linking triplet eighth-notes accompanied these, as in the sequence of numbers that forms the opening scene of *Show Boat* and (to take a period pastiche) in *All I Want Is a Room Somewhere* from *My Fair Lady* (1956). It can all be traced back, seemingly, to the German-born British theatre composer William Meyer Lutz (1829–1903) and his *Pas de Quatre* (1888), just as the chordal woodwind chatter that mimics verbal manners of the period can be heard in French nineteenth-century ballet scores. But perhaps the American music industry's greatest contribution to the survival and appeal of the thirty-two-measure modulor lies in its sanctification by smoothness. Those tenor-line long-note appoggiaturas and suspensions, analog to the gliding ballroom step that sustained the fox trot for thirty years and called "footballs" by the pit cellists who have continually to play them, counterpoise an almost chorale-like serenity to the go-getting energy of stage or screen character or chorus and add the ingredient of transcendence. This binding element began to appear in scores in the 1920s – curiously at the same time as early dance band textures tended to render Tin Pan Alley songs uniformly choppy with their PPPP strum over a heavy O-o- bass – and, as has already been suggested, was also felt in the increasing use of long or held notes in melodic motifs. The Broadway or Hollywood arranger's art extended these explorations of line and mass to all manner of expert orchestral voice-leading. Salinger's and Edens's cradling of Judy Garland's "trio" section melody in *The Trolley Song* could scarcely be beaten for skillful, loving gloss of core material and for long-line expression.

Finally, it must be repeated that in the Tin Pan Alley tradition, the refrain concept is at more of a premium than any of these other factors taken singly. For the thirty-two-measure modulor I use the term *chorus* rather than *refrain*, reserving the latter for those nodal points where verbal and musical motifs come together – which indeed happens in a thirty-two-measure chorus on the larger level. Often it is a matter of verbal title and musical head-motif and of keeping the two slightly at a slant rather than predictably reinforcing each other. There is not space here to analyze the dimension of wit that refrain techniques can and must achieve, but the reader may be pointed to one example. Kern's *I'm Old Fashioned* (1942, from the film *You Were Never Lovelier*), a near perfect song in its richness of voice-leading, sequential teasing, rhythmic poise, and many other features, also shows great skill in the aesthetic balancing of its (verbal) title phrase with the gently syncopated melodic motif that is that phrase's musical setting, though at first the prospects seem clumsy. The point is that the two coincide far less than the title's rhetorical statement would have us expect. As a love song, the number's goal is to reach the assurance that "you're old fashioned" too. The fact that the chorus's opening musical proposition is immediately repeated in an expanding melodic sequel, and the knowledge that there is no rhyme available for "old fashioned," would predicate the goal's arrival all too soon, were it not for the way in which Kern and lyricist Johnny Mercer (1909–1976) manage to keep the whole thing going, matching musical phrases and words, rhymes and cadences, in a rich flux of ambiguity and irregularity until the very end before once letting these particular words and notes come together to resolve the proposition (and then it is in the broader phrasing of "As long as you agree to stay[,] old fashioned with me," and with the sole fulfillment of an upper dominant as the high note of the motif on the word "stay," giving the only octave leap after all those fourths, sixths, and a seventh). All of which is merely to make a long-winded explanation of the patent job of any popular song; but as it takes a great deal of craft, even genius, to do that job, the explanation will never be as simple as the effect.

History

Three men plucked mainstream American vernacular song out of the functional anonymity that was, by and large (and with exceptions such as Stephen Foster), all that its nineteenth-century street and stage status required of it, and conducted it into the hall of memory to which style holds the key: John Philip Sousa, George M. Cohan, and Victor Herbert. (This is to pass over the operettas of Reginald De Koven [1859–1920] and musical comedies of Gustave Kerker [1857–1923], as well as the popular ballads, waltz songs, plus many other types, of such early Alley denizens as Paul Dresser [1857–1906], Charles Harris [1867–1930] – he of *After the Ball* [1892] – and Harry von Tilzer [1872–1946]. But it cannot be helped; their world was sepia, now faded beyond emotional reconstruction.) It needs to be remembered that what Sousa achieved in instrumental terms he also achieved with words and on stage, for many of his marches originated as numbers in his operettas. Encountering *El Capitan* in its original guise as a song in the 1896 operetta of the same title, one appreciates how his particular manner of plain and jaunty speaking in notes – tripping and prancing fast ones, emphatic, confident and straight-to-the-point slow ones – could begin to seem like a real American vernacular, their accent and cadence as laconic and lively as the wit and wisdom of Mark Twain, even without the words that solve the melopoetic equation. (An example: the dotted-quarter consequent of the main march tune after the dominant and double bar is sung to "Behold El Capitan; / Gaze on his misanthropic stare, / Notice his penetrating glare.") Cohan appropriated such brashness – in *El Capitan* it is that of a weak governor who learns courage through decep-tion, not unlike the transformation of the anti-hero in *The Music Man* by Meredith Willson (1902–1984) sixty-one years later – and applied it to his own personality, dramatizing himself as the Yankee go-getter in his invet-erate role as performer and producer as well as creator (words and music) of such stage songs as *Give My Regards to Broadway* and *The Yankee Doodle Boy* from *Little Johnny Jones* (1904), and the World War I patriotic number *Over There* (1917). Nowhere are his impatience with deadening gentility and his persuasive eye for the main chance more strikingly demonstrated than on an archive compilation of original musical stage recordings from the turn of the century (*Music from the New York Stage*, vol. 1). After endless maudlin Irish ballads, with their sobbing, Italianate tenor delivery, we suddenly hear Cohan shouting at us, to an irresistible military two-step:

> I want to hear a Yankee Doodle tune,
> Played by a military band

This is the man of money calling the tune of taste in America's gilded age (the song dates from 1903), even if, like most American musical theatre songs until well after World War I, the stylistic mold is borrowed from Europe (in this case, one suspects, from *I Want to Be a Military Man* in *Florodora* by the British composer Paul Rubens [1875–1917], a show that played, celebratedly, in New York from 1900 to 1902). Herbert, Irish by birth, German by training, was not incapable of such verve: hear him conduct *The Irish Have a Great Day To-Night* (from *Eileen*, 1917) on that same collection of recordings (volume 4). But he offset it with the cultural aspiration that has sustained and ultimately defeated many an American (and European) theatre composer after him: that the musical show wants to be an opera when it grows up. He certainly knew how to handle the French and Viennese musical manners of his generation, and could write as sumptuous a waltz as Lehár – there is more than one in *Naughty Marietta* (1910) – but the future of taste (and of his royalties) surely lay more in a "novelty" march number such as his *March of the Toys* from *Babes in Toyland*

(1903), with its repertory of circus pantomime, than in the delicate perfume of Marietta's eighteenth-century gavottes and minuets with their lace-and-ribbon orchestration.

Yet the next generation's musical theatre manners never stopped prizing the charm, poise, and chic that sooner or later will lead to France and its three centuries of their perfection. This is surely the case with Jerome Kern, who alongside Irving Berlin – the one the gentleman crafts-man, the other the shrewd artisan – saw the American popular song right through its golden age.

Both Kern and Berlin were Jewish, as have been most of the major cre-ative practitioners in musical theatre and film in America subsequently (see Pessen 1985). This is a simple yet hitherto largely unexplained fact, though Adorno surely grasped it when he pointed to the close connection of late-nineteenth-century popular song and operetta with "the economic sphere of distribution – more specifically, with the garment business" (Paddison 1993, p. 204). If the majority genre of Broadway and Hollywood music is effectively a Jewish-American art form, how important to its development was Yiddish theatre (on which see Irene Heskes in Root 1984, pp. 73–87)? This was one of a number of minority genres which at the turn of the century cohabited before being forced by changing circum-stances to seek separate lodgings, marry, or perish. (Viewing it this way, one could say that black musical theatre survived and sometimes flour-ished, largely segregated, while Irish and eventually English and German were subsumed. But the issue is complex – see Hamm 1997, pp. 217–223.)

The landlord was the theatre impresario (and later the film mogul). The Hammerstein family and Charles Frohman (1860–1915) exemplify the role, the latter helping us understand Kern's emergence from and relation to fellow lodgers, who were at first transatlantic, in that Frohman's model of musical theatre was to produce London (British) shows in New York as well and set young practitioners such as Kern to work in either city (see Lamb 1986). In other words, the type of song and show Kern cut his teeth on and, because of his ambition, in due course developed was initially cos-mopolitan or specifically Anglo-American. It became solely American only after Frohman's death on the Lusitania, with which an individual World War I casualty became a generic one.

Kern had early hits with his interpolations into British shows on both sides of the Atlantic (*How'd You Like to Spoon with Me?* in *The Earl and the Girl*, 1905) and little by little broadened his style as his composer's brief grew. He above all others was responsible for the eventual self-sufficiency of the thirty-two-measure modulor, as he discovered how to slow down a chorus's harmonic rhythm, thereby strengthening its structure so that it could eventually rely on a single midway pivot on the dominant (or other related key such as the mediant in *They Didn't Believe Me*, the *locus classicus* of this discovery). As always with music in the commercial sphere, it was not an independent breakthrough: social dance, with its new-found ballroom suavity epitomized by Vernon and Irene Castle, led the way or followed suit, as did song lyrics. Whichever discipline got there first, a question tantalizing to the researcher, the upshot is that Herbert Reynolds's words in *They Didn't Believe Me* accomplish something congruent with Kern's melodic span: a persuasive, intimate argument that manages to get from flattery to marriage in a single sentence tied up with a crucial rhyme ("see" / "me") and the all-important, rhetorically crafty title phrase.

Kern's ambitions were therefore lyrical, as his culture was genteel, and he was susceptible to the operatic siren. Berlin was not, with his raw immigrant's background: he was born in Russia, had started as a saloon and cafe singer and, like any good journalist turned newspaper magnate, knew exactly how to represent, echo, and mold the people's voice. No-one ever judged comedy in music – which is, indeed, musical comedy – better than Berlin, or brought it to wider appeal. The diffuse and ancillary role of the songwriter in his period suited him, and his writing experience in shows for the forces in two world wars, in Broadway revue (which he also produced, at his own theatre, the Music Box), in Hollywood musical films, and in honest old-fashioned printed ballads would eventually stand him in good stead in *Annie Get Your Gun* (1946). He was the natural successor to Cohan, a wholly vernacular phenomenon, adaptably equipped and content to go wherever the whiff of show business, both the show and the business, was the strongest.

By comparison, the times were somewhat against Kern, and one might say the same about his immediate successor, George Gershwin (1898–1937), for both had above all a musician's gift that needed to find and develop its fullest authority but could not, quite, in the commercial world. Kern's lyrical charm did find repeated outlet in the Princess (Theatre) shows, often identified (and always wrongly punctuated) as the first real American musical comedies, namely *Nobody Home* and *Very Good Eddie* (both 1915), *Leave It to Jane* and *Oh, Boy!* (both 1917), and *Oh, Lady! Lady!!* (1918); they were capped by *Sally* (1920). But dramatically they only reached the point of elegant or homely romance within the leisured, salon (i.e., moneyed) comedy of manners, which with a comic admixture of crime and farce was the shows' parish boundary. The worlds in conflict were solely those of youth and age, smartness and innocence, business and pleasure, beauty and money, frequently represented by transatlantic contrasts (American wealth *versus* English class) as in the comic formulas of P. G. Wodehouse (1881–1975), who with his Albion-born colleague Guy Bolton (1884–1979) wrote the lyrics and librettos. Genuinely tender though it might be, love was baby-talk, exemplified by Gershwin's *Someone to Watch over Me* (words by Ira Gershwin [1896–1983]) from *Oh, Kay!* (1926), a show still wholly within this tradition, as is Cole Porter's *Anything Goes* (1934). This was the fairy tale musical *tout court*, one of the three types identified on film by Rick Altman (1987; the other two are the show musical and the folk musical). Most of Gershwin's best-known songs serviced now forgotten shows of this type, including *Lady, Be Good!* (1924) and *Funny Face* (1927).

Set in and celebrating the present, this phase of musical comedy was developed by Kern and Gershwin but immortalized by Vincent Youmans (1898–1946), whose *No, No, Nanette* (1925; lyrics by Irving Caesar and Otto Harbach) is its one canonical survival, probably because it makes explicit the dance-band frivolity of the era by casting every single number of the vocal score in duple quickstep meter and banishing waltz and 6/8 march, symbols of an older world, to short sections in the second-act finale (though a waltz, even more pointedly, is recast as a fox trot between the verse and chorus of one number). Poetic sensibility is reserved for the verses (still essential, and often exquisite), since the feet, not the head, rule the heart in the choruses, each of which relies for its catchiness on fox trot cross-rhythm or a riff, as in *Tea for Two* and *I Want to Be Happy*. In the 1920s such catchiness was beginning to be most fully exploited when a theatre song crossed half-way over the footlights into the dance hall and became a band "standard" (whether or not this treatment is considered jazz), which two period recordings of *I Want to Be Happy* conveniently demonstrate. Its 1925 performance in the original London production is slow and plodding, with string- and harp-based orchestra, an operetta soprano with faultless English enunciation and trained breath control, and a male comedian dandy who cannot really sing. The Ipana Troubadours recording of 1929, half as fast again, follows jazz formulas. There are four thirty-two-measure AABA choruses, the song's verse features only once, and the crooning American voice relies on amplification for its suave intimacy. (Amplification was at this period, and remained until the 1950s, largely incompatible with acting on stage; thus a clear distinction between dramatic theatre singing and band, cabaret, or film singing was of necessity long maintained.) Saxophone solo, jazz fills (including blue notes), brass chording and rhythms precisely syncopated and swung far beyond any ragtime legacy tell us that instrumental characterization, interaction, and infectious energy are everything.

The implication of such contrasting treatments is that until the end of the 1920s dance-band cover versions of theatre songs or domestic ballads could still be regarded as parodies or burlesques of "straight," if popular, material – almost as knockabout comedy acts where the antics of some early bands, not to mention the dancers, were concerned. Kern, for one, so objected to the leveling treatment of the dance bands that he legally protected one of his scores, *Sitting Pretty* (1924), from it (see McGlinn 1990, pp. 12–13). But as the stars of shows themselves began to record dance-band versions of their songs, such artifacts rapidly became central and standard to everyone's musical experience in their ubiquity, enormously fueled as it was by radio and electrical recording, mainstream developments where the second half of the decade was concerned. To a certain extent the generic transformability itself was the point, a cardinal fact of popular musical life, as our anatomy of the Tin Pan Alley product has already suggested; but there were also integrating forces at work on style and genre from the 1930s, though it took until the end of World War II for them to become fully realized.

Hollywood provided one of them, and in many ways Kern and Hammerstein's Broadway musical *Show Boat* is more a foretaste of what the sound film might be expected to attempt with popular music than the theatrical breakthrough it is always taken to be, for it spawned no immediate stage progeny and remains an eccentric, unbalanced score, however powerful. Its epic dimension, necessitated by its taking, unlike previous musicals, a historical novel and a forty-year time period respectively as its source and subject matter, boils down musically to a superior silent-film technique of motivic underscoring. However, on top of the show musical's diegetic numbers occasioned by the story (some of which, notably *After the Ball*, were borrowed rather than composed) and the fairy tale musical's love songs occasioned by the inherited musical comedy genre (such as *Make-Believe* and *Why Do I Love You?*), the authors added the folk element, not quite so central to Ferber's novel, of African American singing, most strikingly the spiritual *Ol' Man River* but also the blues number *Can't Help Lovin' Dat Man* and the crucial offstage voicing of Julie's heartbreaking theme.

Blues inflections and burlesque numbers paced according to a blues throb had been present in commercial popular song and therefore on the commercial stage for some while. Kern utilized something of the latter in *Katy-Did* from *Very Good Eddie*, an early proto-striptease number, and in *The Magic Melody* (1915) introduced the blues chord IV7 which, to Carl Engel, thereby sounded "the opening chorus of an epoch" (Gammond 1991, p. 291). Gershwin's early songs still treat the blues idiom as a novelty style for speciality numbers; and then suddenly, starting with *Somebody Loves Me* from *George White's Scandals of 1924*, his regular structures learn momentary yet wholesale enrichment from a single blues inflection. But the most important step toward what we might think of as a center to the musical experience whose span this chapter is attempting to define came when Gershwin went beyond Kern and integrated not just the blues idiom but the dance-band viewpoint into the whole musical world of a stage show. Here, surely, *Girl Crazy* (1930) rather than *Show Boat* is the seminal work. There were two simple, practical ramifications of this new stance in *Girl Crazy*: saxophones in the orchestra pit and a Broadway belter on the stage. The belter, vocal successor to coon shouters such as May Irwin, was Ethel Merman, making her metropolitan debut singing *I Got Rhythm*; the saxophone writing was courtesy of Robert Russell Bennett (1894–1981), whose Broadway orchestrations underpinned the developing practice of several generations of composers, performers, and producers. The instrumentalists were an entire dance band hired for the occasion, an augmented Red Nichols line-up including Benny Goodman, Glenn Miller, Tommy Dorsey, Gene Krupa, and Jack Teagarden. With them swing entered musical comedy.

Merman and Nichols's players were white, but a black idea propelled them and must long have caught Gershwin's eye and ear as embodied not, in this context, in concert jazz but in the 1920s Broadway renaissance of black musical theatre. This genre had enjoyed considerable success around the turn of the century with a cavalcade of top professional performers ranging from song-and-dance comedians (Bert Williams and George Walker) to opera singers. Composers included Will Marion Cook (1869–1944), best known for his work with Williams and Walker, particularly the musical *In Dahomey* (1903), and the team of Bob Cole (1868–1911) and J. Rosamond Johnson (1873–1954), who wrote shows including *The Shoo-Fly Regiment* (1906) and songs such as *Under the Bamboo Tree* (1902). A lean period for black musicals around World War I was triumphantly countered with the success of *Shuffle Along* (1921). Its songs, composed by

Eubie Blake (1883–1983) and Noble Sissle (1889–1975) and including the robust *I'm Just Wild About Harry*, were irresistible; and as with *Girl Crazy* a decade later, its performing talent was prodigious: Blake and William Grant Still (as oboist) were in the pit, Josephine Baker, Florence Mills, and Paul Robeson on the stage. Descriptions of the elements that appealed most in *Shuffle Along* and the black shows that soon followed make it clear that they set a new agenda for the whole of Broadway: soft shoe and tap dancing; radiant chorus and solo singing; demonic dance (including the Charleston); and above all, the viewpoint of a "folk show in which no concessions were made to . . . theater clichés. [*Shuffle Along*] was funny (and sometimes sentimental), fast-moving, and . . . put an indelible stamp upon the development of American musical theater" (Southern 1983, pp. 428–429).

Nevertheless, things being what they were, white appropriation of these elements was inevitable, which is where *Girl Crazy* comes in, historically definitive not least because in this show the Gershwins also succeeded in broadening the folk element into an integral layer of white myth in the shape of the Wild West: *The Lonesome Cowboy*, musically a conventional two-step but with a new seductiveness of inner line and outer sparkle, already shows the hallmark of the Rodgers and Hammerstein style as found in *Kansas City* from *Oklahoma!* Perhaps not until *Annie Get Your Gun* did all these elements come together again, into the defining moment of the American musical, "merry and very loud," as *Girl Crazy* was also remembered (Kreuger 1990, p. 22).

There are, however, various reasons why the contexts for the American popular ballad remained multifarious and unfocused at the very time when it was reaching its expressive culmination. Not all popular song was aimed at theatre or film in the first place, and *Stardust* (1929) by Hoagy Carmichael (1899–1981), a Midwest songwriter-pianist on the fringes of jazz, seems virtually to do away with the modulor in its (dis)embodiment of the crooner's improvisatory balladry. Conversely, one might say that the surer the artifact itself became, the more convertible was its currency, which is consistent with our theory of the modulor. Rodgers and Hart epitomize this, for their exquisitely distilled songs, unlike those of Rodgers and Hammerstein but often like those of Gershwin and Porter, are never quite remembered as belonging to a particular show, none of which in any case became fully canonical. Their casual, sophisticated, often rueful gloss on romance and, still more, on its masks renders songs such as *There's a Small Hotel*, *It's Got to Be Love*, *My Funny Valentine*, *Bewitched*, and

I Could Write a Book (the first two from *On Your Toes* [1936], the third from *Babes in Arms*, the remainder from *Pal Joey* [1940]) a melopoetic experience indissociable from the intimacy of the nightclub or revue singer (who is indeed the subject of *Pal Joey*). One hears them sung to, or indeed by, oneself, not by or to characters in a story. Stretched and kneaded by crooning and jazz techniques, such songs – along with many of Porter's with their witty *double entendres* and Latin American eroticism (*Let's Do It*, from *Paris* [1928]; *Night and Day*, from *Gay Divorce* [1932]) and Gershwin's because of their enticing harmonic structures and melodic hooks – became the archetypal, almost anonymous vehicles for the great vocal entertainers of the mid-twentieth century, above all Frank Sinatra and Ella Fitzgerald.

Beyond Gershwin, Rodgers and Hart, and Porter, the number of songwriters' names more readily associated with the fame of singers than that of films or stage shows spreads into a broad hinterland encompassing the work of DeSylva, Brown and Henderson, Walter Donaldson and Gus Kahn, Livingston and Evans, Harold Arlen, Sammy Fain, Vernon Duke, and Jimmy McHugh, whose products have in many cases passed more or less into folk status. It can even come as a shock to learn details. Lyricists Buddy DeSylva (1895–1950) and Lew Brown (1893–1958) and composer Ray Henderson (1896–1970) worked as a trio for only six years; Henderson's *Don't Bring Lulu* (1925) and *Bye, Bye, Blackbird* (1926) were sheet music hits, but other songs, including *Black Bottom* and *You're the Cream in My Coffee*, came from Broadway shows, the former from *George White's Scandals of 1926*, the latter from *Hold Everything* (1928). DeSylva also composed (*If You Knew Susie*, from *Big Boy*, 1925). Kahn (1886–1941) wrote lyrics to the music of Donaldson (1893–1947), their hits including *Makin' Whoopee* (for Eddie Cantor on Broadway in *Whoopee* [1928]) and *Yes, Sir, That's My Baby* (1925). The later partnership of Jay Livingston and Ray Evans (both born 1915; Evans seems to have been the lyricist) produced title songs for post-war films, *Que Será, Será* (*The Man Who Knew Too Much*, 1956) and *Buttons and Bows* (*The Paleface*, 1948) being forever inseparable from images of Doris Day and Bob Hope. Fain (1902–1989) was also linked with Day, for he wrote the score for the film musical *Calamity Jane* (1953), including the song *Secret Love*, though as early as 1937 he had written *I'll Be Seeing You* for *Right This Way* on Broadway. He also wrote songs for some of the Disney cartoons. McHugh (1894–1969) worked with lyricist Dorothy Fields (1904–1974), mostly in Hollywood, though two Broadway hit songs, *I Can't Give You Anything but Love* (*Blackbirds of 1928*) and *On the Sunny Side of the Street* (*Lew Leslie's International Revue*, 1930), predated this. Much of Arlen's material, like that of Carmichael, went straight into the jazz repertory, for before he turned to Broadway and Hollywood he was writing songs such as *Stormy Weather* (1933) for Cotton Club revues, perhaps more typical of him than his later songs for the film *The Wizard of Oz* (1939), one of which, *Over the Rainbow*, has nevertheless become a singers' and jazz instrumentalists' standard. The traffic between Tin Pan Alley and jazz was occasionally two-way, for Thomas "Fats" Waller (1904–1943) wrote for stage and screen and like Carmichael actually featured in films. Arlen wrote further for black performers in the stage show *House of Flowers* (1954) and with a song added for the film version of *Cabin in the Sky* (1943), whose Broadway score (1940) had been by Vernon Duke (1903–1969) and included *Taking a Chance on Love*. Two of Duke's biggest hits, *April in Paris* and *Autumn in New York*, came from ephemeral Broadway revues, *Walk a Little Faster* (1932) and *Thumbs Up!* (1935): like many of the other titles mentioned in this paragraph, the songs were built to survive, the shows were not.

Gershwin's ambitions were for scores, not just songs, yet he aimed at no single kind of musical drama except insofar as *Porgy and Bess* (1935), an all-sung folk opera, was by far his largest work and most ambitious musical structure, one which in many ways solved the technical challenges (including orchestration) he had begun to set himself in *Rhapsody in Blue* (see chapter 17). At the same time a vein of operatic burlesque, curiously harking back to Gilbert and Sullivan (especially in the use of the chorus and recitative) even while it conveyed up-to-date political satire, ran alongside his modern folk and romantic outlets in *Strike Up the Band* (1927, second version 1930), *Of Thee I Sing* (1931, Pulitzer Prize) and *Let 'Em Eat Cake* (1933). There was no future for this kind of show after Marc Blitzstein (1905–1964) replaced bourgeois affection with angry agitprop in *The Cradle Will Rock* (1937), though Sondheim and his librettist John Weidman salvaged something of both approaches in *Pacific Overtures* (1976) and *Assassins* (1991) and Blitzstein himself eventually moved on (see Shout 1985).

The Depression and subsequent New Deal lay behind *The Cradle Will Rock*, and linked with the effects of both in the early to mid-1930s was the lure of Hollywood as the sound film and in particular the musical film developed. Until after World War II and the advent of long-distance passenger flights it was impossible to traverse the 3,000 miles between New York and California on a commuting basis, and careers and creative continuity were fractured as some of the best talent began to spread itself too thinly under quite different systems. Hollywood drew Kern, Berlin, Rodgers, Hart, Hammerstein, Gershwin, and many others to its untrustworthy bosom at various times in the 1930s, playing Scylla to the Charybdis of Broadway where any kind of artistic stability was concerned.

The seven popular songs sung by Al Jolson (1886-1950) and others in *The Jazz Singer* (1927) made that not the first sound film but the first film musical. From this shaky but indicative beginning – Jolson was after all the pre-eminent entertainer of the time – the early Hollywood musical film developed, faltered and recovered within the short space of the years 1929-1933 (see Bradley 1996, p. ix), but in so doing equally quickly created its own canon whose types and generic contrasts were closely related while somewhat tangential to those of Broadway. (As an example of the differences, a Broadway show might have ten to twenty musical numbers; many musical films have only four or five.) Two of these types can be singled out: the Busby Berkeley spectacular and the romantic operetta.

Operetta was an obvious genre for Hollywood, whose romantic (as opposed to comic) silent film stars had been perforce melodramatic or flirtatious, and it came in two guises, boudoir and Ruritanian. Boudoir operetta, more or less the invention of director Ernst Lubitsch, gave superlative results in at least two films, both from 1932, starring Maurice Chevalier and Jeanette MacDonald: *Love Me Tonight*, its score by Rodgers and Hart, and *One Hour with You*, with songs by Richard Whiting (1891-1938) and lyricist Leo Robin. (Whiting was already famous for *Till We Meet Again* [1918]; a later hit was *Too Marvellous for Words*, written with Mercer [1937].) Ruritanian operetta had flourished on the Broadway stage throughout the 1920s, *The Student Prince* (1924) by Sigmund Romberg (1887-1951) being the longest-running show of the decade; *The Desert Song* (1926) and *The New Moon* (1928), also by Romberg, and *Rose-Marie* (1924) and *The Vagabond King* (1925) by Rudolf Friml (1879-1972) were also highly successful. Built more around scores than around stars, they have also remained to this day in the repertory of amateurs, only one facet of Ruritanian operetta's curious afterlife as a genre. It was old-fashioned long before the 1930s; nevertheless, Kern and Hammerstein's *Music in the Air*, full of *Gemütlichkeit* in a German setting, came as late as 1932, the film versions of several of the Friml and Romberg shows and other operettas still later (1935-1940), starring the operatic MacDonald and Nelson Eddy. Nor have the European fairy tale settings and costumes of many of the full-length musical cartoon films of Walt Disney failed to perpetuate features of the genre, including soprano warbling (especially in *Snow White and the*

Seven Dwarfs, 1937 – compare Sondheim's Rapunzel in *Into the Woods*, 1987) and hearty male choruses – see *Heigh-Ho*, the dwarfs' work song from *Snow White*, whose first-rate musical numbers were by Frank Churchill (1901–1942), composer of the scores for *Dumbo* (1941) and *Bambi* (1942), and of *Who's Afraid of the Big Bad Wolf?* from *The Three Little Pigs* (1933). Indeed, *The Mob Song* scene from Disney's *Beauty and the Beast* (1991) can only have been a conscious parody of *Stout-Hearted Men* as seen and heard in the film version of *New Moon* (1940). *Gaston* from the same expertly crafted score (music by Alan Menken, lyrics by Howard Ashman) is scarcely less of a tribute to the *Drinking Song* in *The Student Prince*, as is *Belle* to countless marketplace openings from light operas for the stage, whither the genre has astonishingly returned with Disney's Broadway version of *Beauty and the Beast* (1994). Musical numbers in other Disney films have owed more to pop and jazz than to the modulor-based song considered in this chapter, this being true up to a point of Ashman and Menken's score for *Aladdin* (1992) and the music by Robert B. and Richard M. Sherman (born 1925 and 1928) for *The Jungle Book* (1967). But other music by the Sherman brothers is very much in the Tin Pan Alley tradition, including their scores for the (largely) non-cartoon *Mary Poppins* (1964) and the non-Disney *Chitty Chitty Bang Bang* (1968).

The Hollywood musical spectacular took the principle of the modulor perhaps to its farthest extreme in virtuoso production numbers. Their chief musical architect was Harry Warren, working with lyricist Al Dubin, for he composed the songs for the films and routines of Busby Berkeley. In truth, though, precious little architecture was required of the composer, for his job on each song was to supply a standard AABA modulor that could be indefinitely extended and routined by arranger, orchestrator, choreographer, and director. Warren was a supremely good songwriter and provided the harmonic strength and melodic smoothness required for what was by and large a swing product and process, though the orchestra in the films was as much string- as brass-based and other idioms were sometimes given the treatment (as in the curiously old-fashioned *Shadow Waltz* from *Gold Diggers of 1933*). *Keep Young and Beautiful* from *Roman Scandals* (1933) is typical. A thirty-two-measure AABA song multiply extended into a visually outrageous, and characteristically risqué, production number, it is mapped out along the lines of dance-band choruses, of which there are eleven, sometimes consecutive, sometimes punctuated by short interludes or breaks, and sometimes omitting the second A section. The first two choruses are instrumental, underscoring diegetic action and dialogue, and are interspersed first with an instrumental verse and then a different, twelve-measure, *parlando* vocal one, so that when the number's protagonist, Eddie Cantor, enters with the title lyrics it is like the vocal chorus, typically the third, of a dance-band hit. Solo and close-harmony chorus girls and Cantor sing various eight-measure sections in later choruses, which are thus musically "choreographed" in blocks like the camerawork, action, and design, and choruses four to eight are almost entirely instrumental, dance breaks in effect, with band sections highlighted, themselves chorusing, in the swing tradition. Cantor sings the final chorus, merely a dissolving A section, sealing the daring burlesque with Dubin's lyrics: "Oh death, where is thy sting? / I don't care, 'cos I've seen everything." The Hays Code censors seem to have been sleeping where such numbers were concerned; yet Berkeley stressed the Depression in his 1933 films, for Cantor is in an extended dream sequence in *Roman Scandals*; *We're in the Money* is tantalizingly broken off in *Gold Diggers of 1933*; and Warren had a genius, perhaps unique in this period, for world-weary, minor-key songs that owe as much to Jewish folk styles as to the blues. The title song in *42nd Street* (1933) is sleazy beyond its years, looking ahead to the imagined New York of Frank Loesser and director/choreographer Bob Fosse; *Remember My Forgotten Man* in *Gold Diggers of 1933* is built by the production team into an immensely powerful anthem to the white inter-war dispossessed. Each provides its film's final tableau, which was where Berkeley (or his director) tended to place the musical center of gravity, not only by analogy with the climactic sequence of an evening of spectacular stage revue but, for all his surreal camerawork, taking repeated pains to remind the audience with his backstage (and often auditorium) voyeurism that they are watching a show musical. He transferred the "follies" and "scandals" of Florenz Ziegfeld and George White to the screen, though White himself, who produced a stage show most years from 1919 to 1939, included (and appeared in) some Hollywood versions, simply adding the backstage element – a story about a show and its stars in the making – to his usual formula. The *Ziegfeld Follies* ran annually with few breaks from 1907 until their creator's death in 1932, and indeed beyond; at their height they were the closest thing to a national institutional home for the American popular song, and though they never transferred directly to Hollywood, Ziegfeld did attempt an assault on the cinema with *Glorifying the American Girl* (1929), featuring the first crooner, Rudy Vallee. Once again Sondheim provided a deconstructive footnote to a genre's place in American history with *Follies* (1971), as indeed he had previously done for intimate revue with *Company* (1970).

Some of the greatest American popular songs were written after the decline of spectacular revue, for musical films that had nothing to do with contemporary Broadway. We have already encountered *The Trolley Song* and *Over the Rainbow*; Berlin's *White Christmas*, the title song of the 1954 film and first heard in *Holiday Inn* (1942) sung by the arch-crooner Bing Crosby, is another, but it shows Hollywood still relying on the show musical's pretexts, as did most of the other films featuring Fred Astaire – gentleman counterpart to the street kid Gene Kelly. More and more, however, it relied instead for its musical appeal on stage history (including "biopics," such as *Words and Music* [1948], about Rodgers and Hart) or on the making of film versions of stage shows, themselves increasingly set in the past as their scores began to gather up a cornucopia of historical styles and treatments of the modulor which was by now looking to an attenuated future. Thus *A Couple of Swells*, coming from *Easter Parade* (1948) and featuring Astaire and Garland in a well-nigh perfect musical comedy routine, depicts a putative vaudeville song-and-dance act from 1912. *The Band Wagon* (1953) takes a Broadway revue score of 1931 by Arthur Schwartz (1900–1984) and lyricist Howard Dietz, plus its star, Astaire, and makes them both subject and object, adding the reflexive song *That's Entertainment*. One of the finest of all musical films, *An American in Paris* (1951), is like a biopic with the subject absent, for it uses only music by the deceased Gershwin.

Gershwin had written "symphonic" (as opposed to "modulor") music that could be adapted for the screen, as it was in this film, but by and large the Tin Pan Alley songwriters had no hand in this other kind of film music. In *Roman Scandals*, for example, the seven-minute *Keep Young and Beautiful* routine is shortly followed by the film's culminatory chariot chase. This is of roughly equal length and wholly accompanied by orchestral music that was written not by Warren, who lacked the training for it, but by Alfred Newman (1900–1970), one of Hollywood's quite separate breed of composer. These were men paid to write largely romantic background and title music and tending to come, like Newman, from an apprenticeship or earlier career in theatre or classical concert conducting, arranging, orchestrating, even opera composing or concert pianism, often in Europe (thus reaching California as later and more direct immigrants than most of the songwriters). The tools of their trade were not the modulor at all, but Wagnerian motivic symbolism, symphonic development and concerto rhetoric, because the last thing they could afford to do was lay out a musical idea that would take thirty-two measures to unfold: instead they had to match split-second screen timings with single gestures and musical cells capable of instantaneous emotional connotation and infinite extension and compression. When they did write a sweeping title tune such as the 1939 *Gone with the Wind* theme – by Max Steiner (1888–1971) – it rubbed off on the musical theatre by providing a new, more subliminally emotional motivic basis for popular song – compare that theme with Rodgers's *Bali Ha'i* in *South Pacific*. But their work and craft as a whole are beyond the scope of this chapter, though the two types of composer and assignment did sometimes come together in one person, as with David Raksin (born 1912), up to a point with Franz Waxman (1906–1967) in a comedy score such as that for *The Philadelphia Story* (1940), and for a later generation when a different kind of musical authority might be required, as in the black jazz and arrangement work of Quincy Jones (born 1933). The remaining names in the romantic pantheon can only be catalogued: Erich Korngold (1897–1957), Dimitri Tiomkin (1894–1979), Roy Webb (1888–1982), Miklós Rózsa (1907–1995), Bernard Herrmann (1911–1975), and, latterly, Elmer Bernstein (born 1922) and John Williams (born 1932), the last three impressively cornering the market in everything from horror, thrillers, and comedy to the family-oriented adventure epics of Steven Spielberg.

Two further aspects of music in films must be mentioned. One is the potent currency of popular song borrowed rather than written for film, often used as a diegetic adjunct as with Herman Hupfeld's 1931 song *As Time Goes By* in *Casablanca* (1942). The other is the impossibility of drawing a firm line between musical and non-musical films. The Marx Brothers' films parody vaudeville and operetta numbers and could be excluded from the musical genre by stance but not by material.

Also merely acknowledged rather than discussed must be the rather more germane secondary life of popular song on the small screen. The composer of television background music has been a different species again from the film composer, but programme signature tunes and even advertising jingles, already current in radio, enjoyed a slick, comfortable, and, in retrospect, rather hoary liaison with the modulor between the 1950s and 1970s, by which time Tin Pan Alley's innocence was altogether too crass for anything except children's programmes; everything else, when not ethnically denotative (folk, country, soul), tended toward the quasi-symphonic (and quasi-modernist) or rock. This last product has been magnificently analyzed, in the guise of the *Kojak* theme, by Philip Tagg (1979).

Its more Tin Pan Alley-oriented precursor has not, but should be. Two examples must suffice for mention. The Flintstones theme, *Meet the Flintstones* (1960), is a well-loved, melopoetically regular thirty-six-measure song module (i.e. thirty-two measures plus standard four-measure extension) written, like those for their other cartoon productions such as *Top Cat*, by Hoyt Curtin, Joseph Barbera, and William Hanna and scored up with all the instrumental finery of late swing. Equally overflowing with frantic percussion, a Rice Krispies commercial, *Snap, Crackle, Pop*, inhabits a cozier, jauntier world of 1950s novelty song and light music, though one well along the road toward "mickey-mousing," that pantomimic middle way between the jazzier trappings of Tin Pan Alley arrangement (especially well developed in the Tom and Jerry cartoons) and the kind of film underscoring described earlier. An all too cursory sampling of television commercials largely from this period suggests that they approached the modulor with caution. They could not afford the leisure of thirty-two-measure unfolding, a *release* had to be avoided (your desire for the product must not be satisfied), and shorter strophic associations of campfire togetherness and concomitant memorability were exploited in the jingle – one eight-measure vocal chorus each for the snap, the crackle, and the pop, followed by one of instrumental pantomime, with the product name tagged on as a two-measure strophic extension. Curiously, some of the Coca and Pepsi Cola themes seem closer than this to Tin Pan Alley traditions. Research in this field (see Huron 1989, Isacoff 1986, and Karmen 1989) needs consolidating.

Concert light music, a majority popular genre throughout the 1950s, must also be mentioned here. Its dean, Leroy Anderson (1908–1975), was in some respects successor to the Gershwin of *An American in Paris* and knew exactly how to infuse an essentially European melodic and orchestral sensibility with elements of Americana, including luscious filling and vamping and the odd melodic syncopation, blues inflection, or swing break. His *Sleigh Ride* (1950) – to which words were later added – would be described as a rondo rather than an embodiment of the thirty-two-measure modulor, but it amounts structurally to much the same thing prior to the C section, because his B section functions as a release, though at double the normal length. Anderson also wrote a fine musical, *Goldilocks* (1958 – see Briggs 1985), but guaranteed its neglect in that it was not about the three bears or for children.

The American stage musical's defining moment came around the mid-1940s in two forms: the folky, "sincere" Rodgers and Hammerstein musical play, and the more carnivalesque musical comedy traceable through *Girl Crazy* and *Annie Get Your Gun* to *Finian's Rainbow* of 1947 (music by Burton Lane [1912–1997]) and beyond. The shows of Rodgers and Oscar Hammerstein II (1895–1960) are with precious few exceptions the earliest American musicals whose librettos as well as scores have remained in the repertory (see Block 1993). Whether as cause or effect, this is not unconnected with their adaptability for the cinema, and all five of the team's unqualified successes became major films. To give the Broadway dates first, the Hollywood second, these were *Oklahoma!* (1943/1955), *Carousel* (1945/1956), *South Pacific* (1949/1958), *The King and I* (1951/1956), and *The Sound of Music* (1959/1965). Hammerstein's mixture of a sense of history, idealistically liberal politics, romantic sentiment, and colloquial family humor came at exactly the right moment in American culture, the moment of national largesse both in and following the war years: for it spoke in song and script more broadly and authoritatively than American musical comedy had ever yet done and more inspiringly than American opera – whither to some extent it was still headed (see *Soliloquy* and the bench scene preceding *If I Loved You* in *Carousel*) – could ever hope to do. Nevertheless, Hammerstein's greatest strength was in dramatizing the resolution, or at least the emotional understanding, of community conflict in those areas for which imperialist America (or in one case Britain) had successfully acted out its responsibilities or sustained its stewardship and whose voice (for which read style) it had therefore appropriated and sanctified. These include the frontier (*Oklahoma!*), the industrial and immigrant working classes (*Carousel*, *Flower Drum Song*), the Far East (*South Pacific* and *The King and I*), the fascist threat before World War II and domestic readjustment after it (*The Sound of Music*, *Pipe Dream*), and modern middle-class affluence (*Allegro*). It is less easy to imagine Hammerstein entering the contemporaneous domain of the *film noir*, for instance by dealing with the Cold War or any comparable area in which melodramatic conflict was bound to spell defeat, not victory. In a sense, his pupil Sondheim's *Sweeney Todd* (1979) would become that hitherto unwritten musical theatre melodrama of darkness. Something comparable might be said of Rodgers. He broadened his style remarkably for this, his second career, if one compares it with that of his songs written with Hart; but this always involved resolving differences with the authority of harmonic lubrication, never, unlike Sondheim, pursuing a relentless line to motor conclusions. To take one practical example, he found simple ways in his melodic writing of combining romantic lyricism with the colloquialism of unlettered speech, by juxtaposing contrasting phrases or periods based respectively on shapely long-note motifs and pattering repeated notes. Using a release to accomplish this in *The Surrey with the Fringe on Top* has already been mentioned; doing it within a shorter space of eight measures can be seen in *Mister Snow* (*Carousel*), between verse and chorus in *Happy Talk* (*South Pacific*). His harmonic genius, underneath the repeated notes or releasing a melodic consequent, was correspondingly hymnic, reassuring and uplifting, though great tonal moments such as the third and fourth measures of the chorus of *If I Loved You* are supplemented by epiphanic modal touches as in *You'll Never Walk Alone* from *Carousel* – see the flatward passage at the words "At the end of the storm is a golden sky / And the sweet silver song of a lark."

These distinctions within the mature American musical should not be overstressed, for, thanks above all to the work of Gershwin and Berlin, its fount of mode, style, and genre was by this time broad, inclusive and versatile enough – and its lyrics, dialogue (increasingly cinematic), and plot and staging mechanisms tight enough – that the types easily blur and admit of successes beyond them or even *sui generis*. Hence Kurt Weill's second musical theatre career, the American one, starting with *Johnny Johnson* (1936) and continuing with a sheaf of works all heterodox in some way or another (not unlike Sondheim a generation later, though for different reasons). *Lady in the Dark* (1941, lyrics by Ira Gershwin) is perhaps the best of them, a musical about psychoanalysis that uses the modulor span in an original, structural way, for it movingly reveals a complete, beautifully simple, song (*My Ship*, whose opening phrase has been haunting the heroine) only at the end of the show when her history and motivations are at last fully revealed to her; elsewhere the musical production numbers are her dream sequences. Hence also Porter's *Kiss Me, Kate* (1948), a twentieth-century American musical about putting on a twentieth-century American musical about a group of Italian strolling players (period unclear) putting on a musical about a pseudo-sixteenth-century musical about Shakespeare's play *The Taming of the Shrew*. (Another layer was added for the 1953 film.)

The diegetic labyrinth apart, there was a celebratory unselfconsciousness in shows of *Kiss Me, Kate*'s period that flourished throughout the 1950s – for instance, in *Guys and Dolls* (1950) by Frank Loesser (1910–1969) – and culminated in *Gypsy*. This was because in this classic period Broadway hoofing, belting, crooning, and wisecracking continued to cover all song presentation with a sheen, comparable to that coming from the orchestra pit, as both swing and classical elements of orchestration, harmony, and arrangement became ever more integrated. Sondheim himself has never lost that sheen, and the music and lyrics of all his shows honor its overall achievement through continued use and distillation rather than parody or even simple pastiche of it. Because of the underlying melopoetic language, this is as true of *Passion* (1994) – a work in which, continuing a process begun in *Sunday in the Park with George* (1984), virtually every "showbiz" element of popular musical theatre has been stripped away – as it is of *Merrily We Roll Along* (1981). Here, conversely, the modulor is injected with new life through conscious deconstruction – as when, for instance, the release of one song turns up as the chorus A section of another, or one song's verse becomes another's release.

A number of practitioners and teams apart from Sondheim kept the torch of the classic American popular song aflame against encroaching odds. Alan Jay Lerner (1918–1986) and Frederick Loewe (1901–1988) set a theatre record with *My Fair Lady* which, like *Kiss Me, Kate*, has transferred to the operetta stages of Central Europe in repertory easily enough because of the solidity and security of the nineteenth-century German styles underlying the musical gloss. (One notices these qualities particularly in Loewe, trained as a concert pianist, for his voice-leading and textures are those of the piano *morceau*.) Lerner's romanticism was more that of the well-educated, rich American, but both partners traded in heritage and history in their "stylishly old-fashioned" material (Gammond 1991, p. 340) for *Brigadoon* (1947), *Paint Your Wagon* (1951), the film *Gigi* (1958), and *Camelot* (1960). Of these, only *Paint Your Wagon* had an American setting, and although Lerner critically articulated American themes with other partners (most notably Weill in *Love Life* [1948]), and thus bears some relation to Hammerstein (see Citron 1995), individual love and the battle of the sexes always takes precedence over folk values in his work – hardly surprising for a man who was divorced seven times. Jule Styne's offerings included *Gentlemen Prefer Blondes* (1949), *Bells Are Ringing* (1956), and *Funny Girl* (1964) as well as *Gypsy*. Composer/lyricist Jerry Herman (born 1933), master of the show-stopping number, invested it with new levels of celebratory camp in such songs as the title numbers from *Hello, Dolly!* (1964) and *Mame* (1966) and *I Am What I Am* from *La Cage aux Folles* (1983). Cy Coleman (born 1929), closest to Sondheim in being able to use his harmonic musicianship as the critical basis for a wide variety of dramatic aims, has worked partly in television and with lyricist Carolyn Leigh but most notably with Dorothy Fields to produce the stage musical *Sweet Charity* (1966). He followed it up with *On the Twentieth Century* (1978), *Barnum* (1980), and *City of Angels* (1989), to the words of various lyricists and book writers including the team of Adolf Green (born 1915) and Betty Comden (born 1917), who had also partnered Leonard Bernstein for *On the Town* (1944) and *Wonderful Town* (1953). Charles Strouse (born 1928) is best known for *Bye Bye Birdie* (1960) and *Annie* (1977). Richard Adler (born 1921), with lyricist Jerry Ross, composed two durable Broadway scores – *The Pajama Game* (1954) and *Damn Yankees* (1955) – Mitch Leigh (born 1928) one, *Man of La Mancha* (1965). Following the inter-war songwriting contribution of Kay Swift (1907–1993) and despite the uncircumscribed success of a few female lyricists, only two women composers made much of an impact: Carol Hall wrote *The Best Little Whorehouse in Texas* (1978), Mary Rodgers (born 1932), daughter of Richard, *Once Upon a Mattress* (1959).

What, then, about the encroaching odds? ASCAP's loss of constituency, to BMI and the minority styles (such as country) it could newly represent, through the 1940–1941 radio boycott has been seen as the beginning of the end for Tin Pan Alley's stylistic hegemony (Hamm 1986, p. 601). On the stage, playing for lower stakes than the increasingly risky Broadway represented a generic dissipation evidenced in *The Fantasticks* (1960) by Harvey Schmidt (born 1929), which ran continuously in Greenwich Village for over thirty years on a ticket of modest but somehow inconsequential minstrelsy. Conversely, the so-called concept musical was a potential pitfall at the ambitious end of things, with material kept increasingly at arm's length as content and form, matter and manner, fused in a Broadway version of alienation techniques sometimes inspiring more admiration (or even discomfort) than entertainment and love. In particular, two composers have worked with two lyricists largely on this front, John Kander (born 1927) with Fred Ebb (born 1932), Jerry Bock (born 1928) with Sheldon Harnick (born 1924). The first team's pre-eminent achievements are *Cabaret* (1966), *Chicago* (1975), and *Kiss of the Spider Woman* (1990); the second's *Fiddler on the Roof* (1964) and *She Loves Me* (1963), though this last was a curiously old-fashioned, almost Edwardian musical comedy, at least in its trappings. *A Chorus Line* (1975), composed by Marvin Hamlisch (born 1944) with lyrics by Edward Kleban, managed to marry a concept musical format with the emotional engagement of intimate revue, but at the price of a certain obsolescence.

On the other hand, the operatic siren continued to sound, luring Loesser uncertainly into its clutches with *The Most Happy Fella* (1956). A simultaneous crossover from the opposite side proved more indicative, however, and it may be no accident that Bernstein passed through the musical theatre but did not devote a professional life to it. His *West Side Story* (1957, with Sondheim lyrics) was amplified at a time when many or even most Broadway shows still were not, and required of its cast an unprecedentedly youthful agility of dance, song, and delivery: the old certainties, including the rule of the modulor, were being discarded as other song and stage mythologies began to be built up. The law of the microphone quickly led to – or reflected – a new aesthetic law of stance and voice, based more on black and folk melopoetic traditions of performance than on the structural quadratics of Tin Pan Alley, and whose yardstick therefore was a measure of soulfulness essentially independent of rhyme, harmonic span, and motivic development. Still securely anchored to a song vamp in *Something's Coming* (though with a new generation's sophistication of Latin American rhythm) and to the well-established crossover with jazz in *Cool* (though here in a kind of "third stream"), the new presentational voice nevertheless rapidly detached itself from these traditions. It cemented its alliance with the rock ostinato, the backbeat, and modal or reverse harmonic argument; around 1960 the hit song finally parted company from narrative drama altogether, exchanging that ancient tradition for the equally (or more) ancient minstrel one newly embodied in the stage persona of the rock group. *Godspell* (1971) by Stephen Schwartz (born 1948) typifies the rock musical that emerged from this shift.

Bernstein had set a new agenda for the musical theatre composer as early as *On the Town*. This was premised on New Deal nationalism, in that Copland, with such works as *Appalachian Spring*, had shown how modernist ballet could be musically rugged yet populist in spirit and popular in appeal; its fidgety energy, ultimately Stravinskian in origin, contrasted strongly with the complacency of swing, getting rid of the gloss and setting a new dance pace and presentational imperative when imported into the musical theatre and film. Quirky, vibrant, aggressive, or surrealist dance and dream ballet sequences began to propel considerable stretches of musicals, including *Oklahoma!*, *Carousel*, *West Side Story*, and Sondheim's *Anyone Can Whistle* (1964); and where the work of choreographer/director Jerome Robbins was concerned – he directed *West Side Story* and many other shows – there was simply no professional difference between ballet and musical. The same was true of Bernstein's musical language, a consideration extending for him to film music as well, as a comparison of his New York music in *On the Town*, *West Side Story*, the ballet *Fancy Free* (1944), and the film score *On the Waterfront* (1954) readily shows.

But in squaring this circle with words, rather than just with instrumental music and action, the texture of wit in the spoken comedy of manners – upon and in the interstices of which the modulor had sat for all those decades – was left behind altogether. There remained some degree of accommodation between pop delivery and Tin Pan Alley, and this was perhaps best exploited by Burt Bacharach (born 1928), working with lyricist Hal David largely in the studio and on film (*Raindrops Keep Falling on My Head* from *Butch Cassidy and the Sundance Kid*, 1969) but occasionally in the musical theatre (*Promises, Promises*, 1968). By and large, however, the rock alliance outlined above took over, and a new, all-sung form of melodrama – indeed another attempt by the musical to become opera – arose. Curiously, it took firmest hold in Britain, with the songs of Andrew Lloyd Webber (born 1948) and, stemming from them and from other pop reach-me-downs, with the international "megamusical" phenomenon of the 1980s exemplified by *Les Misérables*, *Miss Saigon*, and *Chess* (the first two basically French in origin, the third Swedish, coming from members of the pop group Abba). Together with the continuing currency of rock itself, these products, through which only the occasional shreds and tatters of the American popular song can be glimpsed, have all but eclipsed other models of anglophone popular song around the world. And the dwindling American harvest of stage and screen songwriting of the past two decades is comparably oriented, including the *Marvin Trilogy* of William Finn (born 1952) – *In Trousers* (1978), *March of the Falsettos* (1981), and *Falsettoland* (1990) – and *Rent* (1996) by Jonathan Larson (1960–1996), a highly acclaimed rock-, drug-, homelessness-, and AIDS-oriented reworking of the *La Bohème* scenario. *Rent* might be thought to indicate decisively enough that the American popular ballad has long ceased to be equal to the stageable emotions of modern life; yet the intimate "yuppie revue" musicals of the 1980s, of which the Finn shows are examples, include the work of composer David Shire (born 1937) and lyricist Richard Maltby. Maltby co-wrote *Miss Saigon*, but working with Shire on a very different front he has produced a portfolio of outstanding, diamond-hard songs to which the Tin Pan Alley tradition remains in all respects central. With Sondheim still at work, and with Maltby and Shire's *Baby* (1983) and *Closer Than Ever* (1989) still ringing in ears that can hear, perhaps reports, like this one, of the death of the modulor have been exaggerated. Age has certainly

transformed it in response to *The March of Time*, to take the title and a
sample of the lyrics of one of the *Closer Than Ever* numbers –

> I wasn't ready to have in-laws.
> I wasn't set for things to pall.
> Or sex that's once a week . . .
> (I'd kill for once a week!)
> Or sex that isn't safe at all.

– but as these words are sung in the show to a classic military two-step,
albeit one with post-rock modal touches, it would seem that Maltby and
Shire are still firmly in the business of giving George M. Cohan his Yankee
Doodle tune.

13

The rock and roll era

ROBERT WALSER

This chapter traces the complex results of a paradigm shift: around the middle of the twentieth century, commercially mediated working-class and rural musics disrupted the dominance of Tin Pan Alley popular song. Records became more important than sheet music, and oral traditions grew ever more audible and less local. The music industry resisted these changes, which rewarded "untrained" performers and songwriters, upstart record companies, and eccentric disc jockeys more than the composers, arrangers, copyists, crooners, and studio orchestras of the reigning commercial system. But by 1952 the value of record sales exceeded that of sheet music, and the handful of major record companies saw their share of the popular music market drop from 78 percent in 1955 to 34 percent in 1959, even while that market tripled in size during those few years. Never before had the sentiments and critiques of working-class music been so accessible and persuasive to other groups. Previously separate audiences found new affinities as mass culture offered them fresh pleasures and identities. Music that had expressed the world views of primarily marginal groups brought its styles and sensibilities to the center stage of American life.

From the early days of the recording business, genre categories served to separate artists and audiences along racial lines, implying that "race records" and "hillbilly," for example, came from mutually exclusive sources. But demographic shifts encouraged cultural mixtures throughout the twentieth century: not only generational changes, but perhaps more importantly, the mass movements of people from the country to the cities. Mass mediation accelerated the interactions in which all musical traditions participate: radio and records supplemented the influences that grew out of regional proximity or common experience. This chapter surveys the popular mass-mediated styles that developed out of common roots in the music of working-class and rural black and white Americans.

"Rock and roll" first appeared in print in a 1946 issue of *Billboard*, which used it to describe a record by Joe Liggins and his Honeydrippers, a Los Angeles rhythm and blues band. It had long been a common slang term, however, in blues lyrics and among those who listened to the blues, as a synonym for sexual intercourse; blues-related musics have always retained connections with the pleasures of dancing, community, and sexuality. "Rock" has often been used as a general term for all styles of post-1955 popular music, and it became the preferred name in the last half of the 1960s for a music scene dominated by white musicians like the Beatles and Bob Dylan. But "rock and roll," though frequently used in a narrow sense to refer to music of 1955–1959, has persisted as a looser term able to embrace many styles. Inclusively defined, rock and roll has been the primary vehicle for the global dominance of African American music in the last half of the twentieth century.

Country music – called "hillbilly" until World War II – is often treated as a pure outgrowth of Anglo-American folksong, but it is actually as multicultural as any music, incorporating the fiddle from Europe, the banjo from Africa, the guitar from Spain, the mandolin from Italy, the yodeling of the Swiss musical families who toured the United States in the nineteenth century, and the Hawaiian steel guitar, which resonated with the bottleneck playing of the Delta blues. Many "traditional" hillbilly songs were actually written by professional songwriters for northern audiences before they entered the oral tradition; like their blues-playing counterparts, hillbilly musicians learned songs and styles from records and radio. Many white and black musicians were also shaped by religious repertories held in common.

Much of the music that has been called rock and roll or country shares certain musical characteristics: amplified electric instruments, especially guitars; a focus on solo singers (less often, groups); forms and techniques borrowed from the blues, including "blue" (bent) notes and song structures that use or vary the classic twelve-bar blues form (three four-measure phrases in the harmonic scheme I-I-I-I, IV-IV-I-I, V-IV-I-I); and a strong rhythmic drive in 4/4 time, usually emphasized by bass and drums (although 3/4 waltzes have remained popular in country music). These features clearly differentiate this music from that of the Tin Pan Alley system, but the new paradigm included many disparate features, such as a wide range of singing styles. Elvis Presley's crooned ballads, such as *Love Me Tender* (1956), were accepted by his fans as part of rock and roll. Bob Dylan's *Nashville Skyline* (1969) was regarded as a part of the rock world, even though it sounded like straight country. When the pedal steel guitar

entered country music in the early 1950s, it helped create a new and distinctive "traditional" sound; but when drums had been introduced a few
years earlier, they connected country more closely to swing and blues.

If there is any sonic basis for distinguishing these post-war styles, it
would seem to be the use of the electric guitar. But not even all rock and roll
privileged the guitar: Little Richard and Jerry Lee Lewis both kept the
piano dominant in their recordings, yet their rhythmic energy and singing
styles made them part of rock and roll. Most "girl group" recordings of the
early 1960s didn't feature the guitar prominently, yet their drumming
marked them as belonging to the same universe. Although rock and roll
was perceived in the 1950s as a radical break with previous styles of
popular music, it appropriated a variety of other styles and never ceased to
develop them: pop vocal harmony, Tin Pan Alley song formats, boogie-
woogie grooves, the crooning style of Bing Crosby and Frank Sinatra, the
ecstatic shouts and harmonizing of gospel, hillbilly yelping, the cries and
moans of the blues.

While labels such as "country" or "rock" may be difficult to define precisely in terms of musical style, they have been more clearly deployed by
the music industry as marketing categories. Industry-defined genres such
as rock and roll, or rhythm and blues, have always been marketed to
different publics with separate and unequal production and promotion
budgets. Even today, these genres are defined less by musical differences
than by the race of the performers and the presumed audiences. For the
most part, black artists have had to demonstrate success in the black
market before gaining access to the mainstream, a policy which has
encouraged the segregation of American popular music and limited the
opportunities of black artists. Musically, the flow has always gone both
ways, although the primary innovations have more often come from the
black side. Country music, though heavily influenced by black musical
styles, has included very few black performers. Rock and roll, though primarily the creation of black Americans, has seen its rewards claimed disproportionately by white artists and the white businessmen who have
controlled the music industry.

From the beginning, rock and roll was not only a musical discourse and a
marketing category: it was also an ideological construct. Historians typically stress the generational aspects of rock and roll, but because many
people found the music powerful, it intersected with many kinds of social
claims to power. Rock and roll, rock, country rock, rockabilly, hard rock,
folk rock, art rock, acid rock, progressive rock, punk rock, alternative rock,

heavy metal (rock): all of these have been associated primarily with white male performers and, to a lesser extent, similar audiences. Soul, pop, disco, rhythm and blues, dance music, doowop, rap, funk, and the blues were separated from this rock family less because of how they sounded than because of who made those sounds: black, female, or gay artists. Counter-examples such as the Black Rock Coalition or "women rockers" simply prove the point: theirs have been attempts to lay claims to the social power of rock from outside its ideological boundaries.

All of these styles are electric, mass-mediated, amplified, commercially recorded and distributed, and all of them spring from the same sources in African American blues, gospel, and jazz, and working-class white country music. But genre distinctions merit careful consideration because of the interests they reflect and the implications they carry: an MTV vice-president once shrugged off charges that the channel's early programming policies were racist by arguing that black artists simply didn't make rock and roll; by definition, their music was disco, or rhythm and blues, and thus unsuitable for MTV's playlists. Genre labels affect and reflect the ability of popular music to participate in maintaining or modifying social categories such as race and gender.

Before rock and roll

Rock and roll didn't come out of nowhere, though to many people who were unfamiliar with black and white working-class music, it seemed to. The characteristic rocking rhythms of rock and roll can be heard as early as certain country blues recordings of the late 1920s. Moreover, hillbilly music of the same period displays the straight eighth-note driving rhythms that would later merge with the jump blues to create rock and roll's fundamental groove. The boogie-woogie pianists of the late 1930s and early 1940s – especially Pete Johnson, Albert Ammons, Meade "Lux" Lewis, and Camille Howard – popularized a driving left hand ostinato figure that would eventually become the most important rhythmic figure of rock and roll guitar.

Kansas City orchestral jazz bands were crucial forerunners of rock and roll from the 1920s, especially the Count Basie bands of the 1930s. Basie (1904–1984) used both Tin Pan Alley thirty-two-measure songs and blues forms as frameworks for innovative soloists such as Lester Young, and call-and-response interplay among the various sections of the band. His band helped establish the instrumentation of the smaller combos that would largely replace the big bands after World War II: saxes, drums, bass, piano, and sometimes trumpet.

The first commercial hillbilly record was made in 1922 and the Grand Ole Opry began its broadcasts three years later. Both events were part of the communications revolution of the 1920s, which both preserved older styles and made them available to be blended with other regional and nationally disseminated music. Later in the decade, the Carter Family established one pole of country music's long-standing dialectic, drawing on British ballads and American sentimental and gospel songs to glorify home and family. Country music's first star pulled in the opposite direction: Jimmie Rodgers (1897–1933) combined the sounds of blues, folk music, jazz, Hawaiian music, and yodeling as he embodied the carefree, rambling man. From around 1934, Gene Autry and other "singing cowboys" put the "western" into "country-western."

Country music expanded during the thirties, as radio spread the music and more songwriters met the demand for new songs. Southeastern bands tended to absorb more jazz and boogie-woogie influences, anticipating the fusion of rockabilly, while southwestern bands emphasized fiddling and dancing. Radio and records taught Milton Brown and Bob Wills (1905–1975) what they needed to invent "Western swing," a mixture of fiddle tunes, jazz, the duo harmonies of mariachi music, and the blues; some of Wills's 1940s recordings come close to the beat and chord progressions of rock and roll. Demographic shifts caused by World War II accelerated the interactions of white and black music, as over a million African Americans moved north and west during the war years, and many northern soldiers discovered new musical experiences as they trained at southern military bases.

Technological advances and business clashes decentralized the popular music industry in the 1940s. In 1940, when ASCAP (the American Society of Composers, Authors, and Publishers, founded in 1914) raised its licensing fees for radio broadcasts of recordings, resistance among broadcasters led to the formation of a rival organization, BMI (Broadcast Music, Inc.). To build up its roster of performers and composers, BMI turned to folk, rhythm and blues, country, and Latin performers, providing greater exposure for music that had been marginalized by ASCAP. A similar challenge to the dominance of Tin Pan Alley and Broadway resulted from the AFM (American Federation of Musicians) recording ban of 1942–1943, which protested the replacement of live music with "canned" – the playing of records over the radio. The ban had the unintended effect of spurring the rise of vocalists and vocal groups, since the strike covered only "musicians" – not singers. While the major record labels dominated country music during the 1940s, they ignored African American music, and more than 100 independent labels sprang up to record blues and other styles. German magnetic tape technology spread after the war, enabling these small companies to record economically and to develop new recording techniques.

Jump blues had its biggest home on Central Avenue in Los Angeles during the boomtime of World War II, where Johnny Otis (born 1921), a drummer, vibraphonist, bandleader, radio DJ, and entrepreneur of Greek ethnicity, became "black by persuasion" and a major figure on the burgeoning LA scene. Otis, like many other rhythm and blues artists, had played with big bands but found it impossible to find bookings for large groups after the war. The honking sax solos of the jump blues bands would provide an important model for the guitar solos of rock and roll – perhaps even more important than the harmonica and guitar solos of post-war urban blues. For while the electric blues of Muddy Waters and John Lee Hooker was an important stream of African American music, record sales of such music were tiny compared to those of the jump blues bands and the vocal harmony groups. Urban blues musicians shaped the rock and roll of the 1950s less directly than that of the 1960s, when they were revived and widely imitated.

Perhaps the most successful jump blues performer was band leader and saxophonist Louis Jordan (1908–1975), who combined the riff style of Count Basie's band with boogie-woogie rhythms and a comic manner. Jordan based his music on the swinging rhythms and twelve-bar blues of previous black music, but some aspects of his style also drew upon the music of rural working-class whites: if Jordan's saxophone style came out of jazz and the blues, his vocal style owed more to country music. Jordan's synthesis of blues and country traditions had the effect of moving black and white working-class musics closer together. His music drew upon pre-existing musical sources, but historical changes made it possible for Jordan to succeed in reaching a mass audience where other black artists had failed: in addition to the cultural mixtures and social changes of the post-war period, the growth of the mass media helped to create common frames of reference across racial lines. White country music had preserved a pre-industrial world view parallel to that conserved by the blues, and the historical interactions between these musics helped lay the foundation for Louis Jordan's accomplishments and other fusions of the

1940s. The blues became rhythm and blues (a category used by *Billboard* from 1949 to 1969), country music led to rockabilly, and the two helped to transform American culture when their interaction produced a new genre – rock and roll.

The 1950s

Louis Jordan's fusion was not a fluke, and many other black musicians succeeded with similar music. Wynonie Harris's *Good Rockin' Tonight* (1948) was only one of many "rockin'" songs that celebrated sexual desire with rhythmic energy and slyly overt lyrics. Like Jackie Brenston's *Rocket 88* (1951) and Big Joe Turner's *Shake, Rattle, and Roll* (1954), the heavy backbeats, boogie bass lines, blues progressions, and ecstatic energy of such songs established rock and roll conventions. Singers such as Ray Charles (born 1930) and Little Richard (born 1935) brought the fervent cries of gospel music into rhythm and blues – Charles most explicitly (and, for some, controversially) in 1954, when he transformed the gospel song *I've Got a Savior* into *I Got a Woman*.

Mid-1950s hits by Fats Domino (born 1928) and Little Richard, such as the latter's frenetic *Tutti Frutti* (1955), still included the honking tenor sax solos of the jump blues bands, but even in the early 1950s such bands were shifting the focus away from horns and onto the electric guitar. T-Bone Walker (1920–1975) is often called the inventor of the electric blues guitar; one of the first blues musicians to use the instrument (in the 1940s), he developed some of the guitar licks that Chuck Berry would later use to found rock and roll guitar playing. Walker also established some influential rock and roll performance practices through his stage routines (which included doing splits and playing the guitar behind his head), his guitar style (which featured fluid single-line solos and bent string riffs), and the mildly distorted sound he used by the early 1950s.

Mergers with white working-class music continued. Hank Williams (1923–1953) attacked the artificial walls dividing white and black music; he had learned to sing from a black street singer, and his up-tempo songs were another influence on early rock and roll. Howlin' Wolf developed his trademark howl by imitating the yodels he heard on Jimmie Rodgers's records. Ray Charles was attracted to country music because of the ways that electric and pedal steel guitar players imitated the sounds of the human voice; he would later have his only number one hit album with *Modern Sounds in Country and Western Music, Vol. 1* (1962). Bull Moose

Jackson's rhythm and blues hit *Why Don't You Haul Off and Love Me* (1949) copied the original version recorded three months earlier by country singer Wayne Raney. Fats Domino became famous as another black pioneer of rock and roll – outselling all other 1950s rock and roll stars except Elvis Presley – but his black producer Dave Bartholomew remembers that "we all thought of him as a country and western singer" (Broven 1974, p. 32). White singer Johnnie Ray found in black music a way of reflecting upon and coping with experiences of rejection, one that made more sense of his own lived experience than did other kinds of music; Ray was so adept a student of black culture that he found himself marketed on race labels to black audiences until his success enabled him to cross over to the white audiences targeted by the pop charts. The white songwriting team of Jerry Leiber (born 1933) and Mike Stoller (born 1933) transcended categories by writing many hits for black and Chicano rhythm and blues artists.

Rhythm and blues, although it was marketed by record companies and radio stations to black audiences, increasingly crossed over to white radio listeners and record buyers in the late 1940s. By 1952, Los Angeles's Dolphin Record Store was selling over 40 percent of its rhythm and blues records to white customers; a few years earlier, its clientele had been almost exclusively black. Among the most popular groups were black vocal quartets and quintets who blended the new rhythmic feel with the techniques of gospel quartets and vocal groups of the 1940s like the Ink Spots and the Mills Brothers. The smooth harmonies and romantic ballads of the Coasters, the Drifters, the Orioles, and the Platters drew heavily on Tin Pan Alley precedents as well. Beginning around 1954, such vocal groups began featuring the nonsense syllables and onomatopoeic imitations of instrumental sounds that earned them the label "doowop. " Many of these groups were named after types of birds and models of cars, and most were "one-hit wonders" who vanished after one great song. White groups like the Crew-Cuts, and Danny and the Juniors, exemplified similar street-corner adaptations of gospel and Tin Pan Alley models. In 1955, the Platters's *The Great Pretender* crossed over from rhythm and blues to hit number one on the pop charts; overall, black rhythm and blues record sales increased 200 percent over the previous year. If the increasing popularity of white cover versions would indicate ambivalence about black culture among many Americans, the success of crossovers was a clear sign that black music was attracting a multiracial audience.

The birth of rock and roll is often dated to June 1955, when *Rock Around the Clock* by Bill Haley and His Comets grabbed the number one slot on *Billboard*'s "Best Sellers" chart. Though he had mostly performed country music himself, Haley (1925–1981) admired Big Joe Turner, Louis Jordan, and other black musicians, and at the end of his performances in the early 1950s he would sometimes perform a "special" set, inflecting rhythm and blues songs with his country-based style. In 1951, he recorded a cover of Jackie Brenston's *Rocket 88* and between 1954 and 1956 his formula resulted in seventeen best-selling records. Haley's decision to change the name of his band in 1952 from "Bill Haley and the Saddlemen" to "Bill Haley and His Comets" marked his reconception of the group. The inclusion of Haley's *Rock Around the Clock* in the 1955 film *Blackboard Jungle* helped sell seventeen million copies of the single and made that song a symbol of teenage rebellion and desire. But while his song made clear the commercial potential of a new musical fusion, Haley's sound was hardly innovative, and many historians prefer to found the history of rock and roll in rhythm and blues records such as Wynonie Harris's *Good Rockin' Tonight* or Jackie Brenston's *Rocket 88*.

Others place the birth of rock and roll in the early 1950s, when white teenagers started dancing to rhythm and blues, a lineage which suggests that the genre was defined less by musical differences than by social significance. Black and white audiences were not just listening to the same music; they were listening together. White radio DJ Alan Freed (1922–1965) had spun "blues and rhythm" records in 1951 for a predominantly black Cleveland audience, but over the next few years white teenagers increasingly tuned in to such radio programs. While parents, police, and government authorities could and did strive to maintain racial boundaries in night clubs, juke boxes, dance halls, and record stores, it was impossible to segregate the airwaves. Freed called his program a "rock 'n' roll session," and he began referring to the music itself as "rock 'n' roll" in 1954. The new name not only proclaimed important shifts in American music but also served to disguise the cultural miscegenation that occurred when whites listened to rhythm and blues.

Early rock and roll is usually tied to demographic and economic changes that enabled the emergence of "teenagers," a social group whose sense of identity was bound up with their age. Post-war prosperity and the growth of higher education extended young people's dependence on their parents but enabled them to begin seeking out alternatives to the dominant conventions governing sex, love, gender, race, and class. Yet rock and roll was not simply a music of adolescents, as its origins in adult working-class musics and its subsequent history prove: Chuck Berry and Bill Haley were both over thirty when they had their biggest hits. The popularity of rock and roll came about, as George Lipsitz puts it, because "the working-class understanding of the world that was embodied in rock and roll's lyrics, functions, and forms gained credibility with large numbers of people." Rock and roll "elevates the world of play over the world of work, and carves away a limited sphere of autonomy in an increasingly regimented world." The music "expressed the same critique of work, hierarchy, and exploitation" as did the many strikes and demonstrations of the post-war years (Lipsitz 1994a, pp. 327–328).

For the most part, black rock and roll musicians of the 1950s were rhythm and blues artists who found themselves included in the popular enthusiasm for rock and roll. Fats Domino came to be considered a rock and roll musician even though he simply kept playing the New Orleans rhythm and blues he had always played. Ruth Brown (born 1928) was a successful jazz and rhythm and blues singer before she became the first woman to be called a rock and roll singer. In contrast, most white rock and roll musicians came from southern country music backgrounds. Some of the white musicians whose adaptation of black styles became known as "rockabilly," such as Jerry Lee Lewis, Carl Perkins, and Elvis Presley, had learned from black musicians while young, benefiting from the fact that black and white cultures were mixing in ways that had not been possible before. Other country musicians, such as Buddy Holly and Bill Haley, picked up the feel of jump blues but kept their own instrumentation, emphasizing guitars rather than piano and sax. As Ed Ward points out, the very idea of rock and roll "was a way of saying that Fats Domino had more in common with Bill Haley than he did with Wynonie Harris, that Elvis Presley had more in common with Ray Charles than he did with Ernest Tubb" (Ward, Stokes, and Tucker 1986, p. 97).

The music of Chuck Berry (born 1926) came from the same sources as Haley's – the blues, country, and Louis Jordan – and Berry would probably have been classified as a country singer had he not been black. Berry's first record was his 1955 version of *Ida Red*, a tune that Bob Wills and other country musicians had recorded; Berry changed the name to *Maybellene* in order to secure publishing royalties, and his recording became one of the best-selling records of the year. A string of rock and roll hits followed, celebrating youth, mobility, play, and the new genre itself, as in *Rock and Roll Music* (1957), *Roll Over, Beethoven* (1956), and *Johnny B. Goode* (1958), all of which defended rock and roll against automatic dismissal and celebrated the community that had formed around it. Berry's trademark double-string licks made him one of the most influential guitar players of the century.

As the 1950s passed, the beat of rock and roll became heavier as many musicians adopted the electric bass. But if anything clearly distinguishes rock and roll from rhythm and blues, it is the change from swung to straight eighth-notes, as the rhythmic feel of jazz and boogie-woogie gave way to the even division of the beat found in much country and western music (and some country blues). Chuck Berry's recording of *Rock and Roll Music* is fascinating in this respect, in that half of the band seems to be swinging the beat while the other half, including Berry, plays straight eighths.

Berry's commercial success was far exceeded by that of an equally charismatic – but white – performer, Elvis Presley (1935–1977), a Memphis truck driver who turned to music as a means of escape from a life of low-paying jobs. Presley had learned to sing in church, at revival meetings, and from the country and blues singers he heard on the radio; like many white rural southerners of the time, he imitated black urban trends, dyeing his hair black and adopting the "cat" style. His first recordings were made by Sam Phillips, a man who had repeatedly boasted that he would make a fortune if he could find a white singer who sounded black. Their first session in 1954 produced a cover version of Arthur "Big Boy" Crudup's *That's All Right*, with Bill Monroe's *Blue Moon of Kentucky* on the flip side; thus, Presley's debut record had a white interpretation of a black song on one side, and a black-influenced version of a white song on the other.

When he became the most successful performer of rock and roll, Elvis Presley's musical talents – as well as the sexiness, freedom, and power with which many fans identified – were properly rewarded. But as has happened so often throughout the history of American popular music, black musicians saw white people profit disproportionately from their culture. Fans bought Presley's versions of *That's All Right* and *Hound Dog* (1956) instead of the original versions of those songs by black artists. Moreover, many black songwriters such as Arthur Crudup never received any royalties for the songs that made Elvis famous. Yet Presley's success undercut the naturalness of racially based genre categories. In 1956, his recording of *Hound Dog* and *Don't Be Cruel* reached number one not only on the *Billboard* pop chart, but also on the rhythm and blues and country-western charts. *Billboard* had assumed that there were three discrete audiences for American popular music. But as Charles Hamm has pointed out, at this moment "one strain of popular music cut across racial, social, and geographic lines in a way not seen in the USA since the days of Stephen Foster" (Hamm 1986, pp. 62–63).

Although his debt to African American music was tremendous, Presley also brought into rock and roll many elements of country styles. His lead guitar player, Scotty Moore, mixed T-Bone Walker's influence with a long tradition of country lead playing while Elvis strummed a rhythm part on the acoustic guitar, as had long been done in country bands. Presley's recording of *That's All Right* is wholly country except for his bluesy vocal – and the fact that it's a cover of a rhythm and blues song. The rhythmic feel of this tune, especially, was changed from Crudup's strong backbeats to a country emphasis on beats one and three. After Elvis, country music was split into rockabilly – singers who followed Presley's lead, like Eddie Cochran, Jerry Lee Lewis, Carl Perkins, Gene Vincent, the Everly Brothers, Buddy Holly, and, for a time, Johnny Cash – and straight country, following the example of Hank Williams.

The post-war years were a booming time for country music, as live performance burgeoned, particularly in California, and recording was increasingly centralized in Nashville. The era's biggest star was "The Tennessee Plowboy," Eddy Arnold (born 1918), whose smooth crooning anticipated later country pop. Ernest Tubb, "The Texas Troubadour," achieved nearly comparable success with his fusion of southeastern and southwestern styles. Roy Acuff (1903–1992) became known as "The King of Country Music" not only through his performances and recordings, but because of his accomplishments as a songwriter and publisher, with his partner Fred Rose. The main country style of the 1950s was "honky tonk," which had its roots in the 1930s, when the repeal of prohibition allowed the music to move into bars. Honky tonk was beer joint music, strongly working class in its orientation and with little of the pastoral sentiments of other country styles. Sung by the agile-voiced Lefty Frizzell, or Webb Pierce, who introduced the pedal steel guitar to country music in 1953, such songs described the isolation and loneliness of displaced rural men, openly expressing a man's view of work, family, love, drinking, adultery, and divorce. Kitty Wells (born 1919) emerged as country's first female star; with hits like *It Wasn't God Who Made Honky Tonk Angels* (1952) – an "answer song" to Hank Thompson's *Wild Side of Life* (1952) – she addressed the popular topics of drinking and cheating with performances of wholesomeness and dignity, foreshadowing the self-assertion of later female singers.

Hank Williams's weary, vulnerable, and honest-sounding voice made him one of the most influential musicians of his time, despite his brief life. He virtually defined country music for millions of people, yet his music reflects a blending of many influences and his songs were covered by Tin Pan Alley singers. Guitarist Chet Atkins became the driving force behind the creation of the country-pop "Nashville sound," which was intended to preserve the feel and lyrical themes of previous country music while appealing to a wider audience. Jim Reeves, Eddy Arnold, and many others recorded in this style, while singers such as George Jones and Ray Price stuck to "hard country." Bluegrass, a virtuosic style featuring acoustic instruments, had been developed by Bill Monroe in the 1940s but drew larger audiences in the late 1950s, along with the urban folk revival.

Vocal groups also continued to be popular in the late 1950s, especially the Platters, and romantic ballads based on the chord progression I–VI–IV–V proliferated among black and white groups alike. The Five Satins's *In the Still of the Night* (1956) was one of the first, and hundreds followed, including more than a few recycled Tin Pan Alley tunes such as *Blue Moon*, recorded in 1961 by the Marcels. In 1956, Chess released an album of music from the film *Rock, Rock, Rock*, with recordings by Chuck Berry and two doowop groups, the Moonglows and the Flamingos. The album's liner notes firmly placed the vocal groups' music at the center of rock and roll, attributing the latter's success to its variety, freshness, and absorption of many influences.

Throughout the second half of the 1950s, rock and roll was often criticized by those who attempted to link it to juvenile delinquency, asocial behavior, sexual promiscuity, racial conflicts, and deafness. Anti-rock demonstrations and posters were common across the country; performers were banned from some communities, even beaten up in others. Historians have often trivialized the controversy by characterizing it as a generational conflict involving "exasperating teenagers"; in fact, much of the hysteria was provoked by the spectacle of white youth moved by and moving like black musicians. The music not only encouraged racial integration, but many fans found in another culture things that were lacking in their own. Rock and roll triggered a crisis in cultural authority as new ideals of community, ways of moving the body, forms of sexual display, and models of racial and sexual ambiguity reached a large white audience.

The impact of rock and roll was felt simultaneously with that of the Supreme Court's decision in *Brown* v. *Board of Education* (1954) to overturn the doctrine of "separate but equal." Racists attacked rock and roll because of the mingling of black and white people it implied and achieved, and because of what they saw as black music's power to corrupt through vulgar and animalistic rhythms. To be sure, rock's outrageousness made many people uneasy, not least because of how gender categories that were previously thought stable and natural were shown to be fluid. Little Richard, for example, liked to boast: "This is Little Richard, King of the Blues, and the Queen, too"; yet he maintained a pose of flamboyance and craziness partly in order to make his ambiguous sexuality seem harmless. The popularity of Elvis Presley was similarly founded on his transgressive position with respect to racial and sexual boundaries. The transgressors were all male, however: women were idealized or demonized in lyrics, yet rock and roll all but eliminated female musicians from the pop charts. Attacks on rock and roll were founded partly in racism and partly on an accurate assessment of the music's power to legitimate alternative constructions of gender and sexuality.

By the late 1950s, governmental and private censorship had destroyed the network of radio stations, record labels, and urban dance halls that had nurtured rhythm and blues. The largest corporations regained control from the independent record labels and concentrated their efforts on promoting white singers, including "teen idols" such as Paul Anka, Frankie Avalon, and Fabian. White cover versions of hits by black musicians, such as Pat Boone's covers of Little Richard's records, often outsold the originals; it seems that many Americans wanted black music without the black people in it. Such recordings displayed little familiarity with or aptitude for African American musical traditions, but it is not that they were simply "watered down," as is often charged. It is more accurate to say that they articulated different priorities and cultural values: they defused many of rock and roll's challenges; they moved popular music back toward Tin Pan Alley models and sensibilities; they presented a more passive, patriarchal, and repressed sense of the body at the same time that they reflected the pervasiveness of white racism and the effectiveness of monopoly marketing.

Prompted by the controversies over rock and roll, Congress conducted hearings from 1959 to 1961 on the practice of "payola," whereby record companies paid radio disc jockeys to play certain records (variations included inviting DJs to claim songwriting credit, and thus royalties, in exchange for airplay). Payola was not illegal – similar practices had been common fifty years earlier in the system of Tin Pan Alley – but the investigation was lent urgency by widespread moralistic denunciations of rock and roll. The hearings seemed to endorse the conspiracy theory that rock and roll music was so bad that payola was the only way to account for its popularity: DJs played it only because they were paid to do so; fans listened only because there was nothing else available. The investigation's outcome was capricious, as witch hunts tend to be: Alan Freed, probably because of his championing of inter-racial concerts, was denounced by the committee and driven out of the music business, while Dick Clark, whose network of music business interests was far more extensive, slipped through the inquiry unscathed.

By the end of the decade, many of rock and roll's greatest performers had dropped out of sight and the very survival of the music seemed in doubt to many people. Little Richard quit rock and roll in 1957 (temporarily, as it turned out) to become a preacher. In 1958, Elvis was drafted into the Army, and Jerry Lee Lewis found his career derailed by the scandal over his marriage to his thirteen-year-old third cousin. The following year, Buddy Holly and promising Mexican-American singer Ritchie Valens died in a plane crash while on tour, and Chuck Berry's career was disrupted by a racist arrest for transporting a minor across state lines, for which he was made to serve two years in prison. Despite these setbacks, however, rock and roll had already set crucial precedents, and not only musical ones: many assumptions and behaviors relating to race and sexuality had become naturalized within American culture.

The 1960s

Many people remember the 1960s as the decade of Woodstock, the Summer of Love, the British Invasion, and psychedelia. But all historical perspectives are partial: the five best-selling artists of the decade were Elvis Presley, Brenda Lee, Connie Francis, Ray Charles, and the Beatles, and the single most popular song of the sixties was Percy Faith's instrumental *Theme from a Summer Place* (1960). Similarly, many historians have characterized the early 1960s as a bleak lull between the fall of rock and roll and the arrival of the Beatles. Accounts of these years bemoan the rise of the teen idols' "schlock rock" and Dick Clark's "American Bandstand" television show, as the songwriting of Neil Sedaka, Carole King, and other writers at New York's Brill Building moved popular music back toward Tin Pan Alley production methods and sensibilities. Yet 42 percent of the best-selling singles of 1962 were by black artists. This was a period of great vitality that included the revival of doowop, the emergence of Motown and the girl groups, the beginnings of Memphis and Chicago soul, and the development of James Brown as a major artist. The perception of 1959 to 1963 as rock's dark ages was developed after the Beatles helped create rock criticism in their own image.

Berry Gordy's Motown label, based in Detroit, created the perfect music for the early phase of the civil rights struggle: sensuous but elegant gospel-influenced black pop. With singers including Diana Ross and the Supremes, Marvin Gaye (1939–1984), Smokey Robinson and the Miracles, the Temptations, the Four Tops, and Stevie Wonder, performing material by the songwriting and production team of Brian Holland, Lamont Dozier, and Eddie Holland, Motown became the largest black-owned corporation in the United States. Later in the decade, the southern soul of artists like Solomon Burke, Otis Redding, Wilson Pickett, and Aretha Franklin (born 1942) fit the times: rawer, less produced, more militant in affect. Franklin's *Respect* (1967) made demands that resonated with both racial and gendered injustices at a time when "Black is Beautiful" and "Black Power" were becoming slogans. Soul music's equivalent to Motown was Stax Records in Memphis, where the fusions of gospel vocals and rhythm and blues instrumentals achieved by Ray Charles and Sam Cooke crossed over to the pop charts in 1965 with Wilson Pickett's *In the Midnight Hour* and James Brown's *Papa's Got a Brand New Bag*. The latter record, with its static harmonies but dynamic polyrhythms and percussiveness, is the founding document of funk, as well as the dance music and hip hop that would later spring from it. Brown (born 1928) went on to chart half again as many singles as did the Beatles. White-owned Stax employed black and white musicians and sold mostly to black audiences, while wholly-black Motown sold most of its records to white audiences.

The Shirelles's *Will You Love Me Tomorrow?* (1961) was one of the first "girl group" hits, and many others followed as the Crystals, the Angels, the Ronnettes, and the Shangri-Las sang romantically about boyfriends and other topics having to do with young womanhood. Phil Spector (born 1940) was the leading producer of such vocal groups, but more than that, he set important precedents by fusing the energy of rhythm and blues with professionally composed songs and his "wall of sound" studio techniques, which layered many separately recorded instrumental tracks. The girl group message wasn't monolithic masochism, however, as Leslie Gore (born 1946) showed with the three top five hits she had within a year with increasingly assertive songs: *It's My Party* ("and I'll cry if I want to"), *Judy's*

Turn to Cry, and the explicitly feminist *You Don't Own Me*. At the same time, the Beach Boys were becoming vastly popular by mixing the vocal style of doowop with more energetic instrumental accompaniment, advanced studio techniques, and a mythological celebration of surfing in particular and middle-class white California culture in general, as in *Surfin' Safari* (1962), and *Surfin' USA* (1963). Continuities with earlier rock and roll are clear; the latter song "borrowed" so much from Chuck Berry's *Sweet Little Sixteen* (1958) that a lawsuit ensued.

Country music survived the challenge of rock and roll, but it was permanently marked by the encounter; most obviously, the use of drums and electrified instruments became nearly universal during the 1960s. That decade also saw the worldwide dissemination of country music, with considerable credit for this due to the radio broadcasts of the Armed Forces Network. From its founding in 1957, the Country Music Association aggressively promoted the country music industry, and Nashville emerged as a major center for music production. In 1969, three country music television shows moved to network programming, reflecting both the broader popular appeal and greater commercial potential of a genre that openly celebrated working-class perspectives and ideals. Traditionalists such as Buck Owens (born 1929), Merle Haggard (born 1937), and Johnny Cash (born 1932) were successful, but so were singer-songwriters like Willie Nelson (born 1933) and Kris Kristofferson, who crossed over to pop and rock audiences. A new generation of female stars addressed formerly taboo topics in newly assertive ways, as with *Don't Come Home A'Drinkin' (With Lovin' On Your Mind)* (1967) by Loretta Lynn (born 1935) and *D-I-V-O-R-C-E* (1968) by Tammy Wynette (1942–1998). Most people came to associate country music with conservative political positions, however, including pro-war and anti-youth attitudes. As Bill Malone described this moment, "For the first time in its commercial history, country music became equated with establishment values – a strange position indeed for a music once dismissed as hillbilly and the product of a region that had always stood apart from the rest of American life" (Malone 1990, p. 18).

As the decade progressed, rock music became increasingly identified with movements for social change around the world. Protest singers of the early 1960s, such as Bob Dylan, Joan Baez, Phil Ochs, and Tom Paxton, greatly affected subsequent rock lyrics both in political content and poetic aspirations. They set musical and lyrical precedents for the singer-songwriter boom of the late 1960s, which moved women back into the spotlight for the first time since the girl groups: Joni Mitchell, Judy Collins, and

Carole King were among the most successful, along with Paul Simon (born 1941), sometimes partnered with Art Garfunkel.

Bob Dylan (born 1941) personalized folksongs, reconnected rock and country, and performed complex lyrics in his rough, nasal voice, becoming perhaps the most influential American musician of the decade. Initially a disciple of Woody Guthrie, Dylan wrote lyrics that included social criticism and dry humor; these were endlessly analyzed, and the singer-songwriters who followed him tended to favor poetic language, self-absorption, ironic distance, and music which largely abandoned the energy of rock and roll. Dylan inspired many of the founders of folk-rock and later country rock, such as the Byrds, Buffalo Springfield, the Flying Burrito Brothers, and the Eagles.

Rock and roll had reached England almost immediately by means of recordings and tours, and young British musicians, many of whom were devoted fans of African American blues artists, soon formed bands of their own. The Beatles were the first British group to achieve great popularity in the United States, charting *I Want to Hold Your Hand* and five other number one singles in 1964, their first year of American distribution. The Beatles had started out as the Quarrymen, a working-class skiffle band from Liverpool, performing covers of Little Richard and Chuck Berry until the management skills of Brian Epstein and the songwriting skills of John Lennon (1940–1980) and Paul McCartney (born 1942) helped make them the biggest musical success since Elvis. Lennon and McCartney composed a seemingly inexhaustible supply of catchy but complex songs with unusual harmonies and forms; their light-hearted sexuality, wit, and ballads were a throwback to Tin Pan Alley or music hall days, but much of their music also displayed the musical edge of the early rock and rollers and the political edge of Dylan, their colleague as spokesmen for the emerging counterculture. The Beatles's androgynous haircuts violated gender norms, prompting both criticism and imitation. They were among the first popular groups to write their own material (outside of country music, where the practice had already existed) and their success naturalized this fusion of performance and composition, which had usually belonged to separate specialists.

Other bands of the "British Invasion" included Herman's Hermits, the Rolling Stones, the Yardbirds, the Kinks, the Who, the Animals, Manfred Mann, the Dave Clark Five, and Gerry and the Pacemakers. These groups were heard as a resuscitation of the energy of early rock and roll, which had temporarily been supplanted by other styles. In 1963, not a single British record had reached the Top Ten in America, but in the following year, almost a third of the Top Ten hits were by British bands. Some of them, particularly the Beatles and the Rolling Stones, openly acknowledged their debts to black musicians. The Stones had formed as a cover band devoted to the music of Chuck Berry, Little Walter, and Muddy Waters, gradually introducing their own compositions based on those models. They adopted a working-class image that disguised their art school backgrounds, in contrast to the Beatles, whose clean-cut presentation effaced their working-class origins. As producer Quincy Jones has commented: "They were students of American music – much more than American musicians were" (Solt 1995). But along with the British Invasion came a precipitous drop in the number of black artists on the charts, which had been growing steadily.

In the mid-1960s the San Francisco Bay area emerged as the center of a youth counter-culture that rejected many of the values and behaviors of middle-class white adults. This development reflected the fact that the growth and increasing diversity of college campuses made them an important site of activism and debate. The challenges to dominant values that resulted were, however, also related to other contemporary events, such as civil rights struggles and rebellions against colonial repressions throughout the world. The alternative values of many residents of the San Francisco area encouraged the development of psychedelic or acid rock. California bands such as the Grateful Dead – whose eclectic, experimental, and communal approach won them a devoted fan base through thirty years – the Jefferson Airplane, Country Joe and the Fish, Moby Grape, and the Byrds increased the amplification and improvisation of their music and added light shows to their concerts; the Jefferson Airplane's Grace Slick became a psychedelic sex symbol.

Genre categories – always more useful to the music industry and critics than to artists and audiences – began to seem less clear-cut and more arbitrary in the 1960s, along with other barriers and categories that separated individuals and groups. Rock audiences embraced the urban folk revival, the Indian sitar playing of Ravi Shankar, and the jazz fusion of Miles Davis (who opened concerts for the Grateful Dead and the Steve Miller Band), as well as Eastern religions. For the counterculture, overcoming collective divisions depended on freeing up personal thinking, knowing, and feeling. Drug experiences challenged the naturalness of social and even perceptual conventions; at the same time, musicians as different as the Grateful Dead, the Beatles, Bob Dylan, and James Brown demonstrated that they had fans and musical influences in common. The counter-culture emphasized not only personal expansion of awareness and options, but also collective experimentation with free living and free loving (enabled by recent advances in contraception). Non-competitiveness and harmony were symbolized in 1967 by the "Summer of Love" and the first large rock festival, the Monterey Pop Festival. However, men and women were not equally freed by the sexual revolution; moreover, the place of women in popular culture shrank as their presence on the singles charts declined from 32 percent in 1963 to only 6 percent in 1969.

The Beatles encountered psychedelic rock while touring the United States, and by 1966 their music showed its influence in the form of more obscure lyrics, references to drugs, and innovative timbres and textures. Their producer George Martin was, like Phil Spector, an imaginative and skilled user of early multitrack recording. Martin's classical training enabled him to suggest many of the peculiar sounds that appeared on the Beatles's albums, such as the piccolo trumpet (a modern instrument now associated with Baroque music), classical string quartets, odd metric and phrase patterns, and orchestral accompaniments. With *Sgt. Pepper's Lonely Hearts Club Band* (1967), one of the first and most influential "concept albums" of interrelated songs, the Beatles kicked off an era of self-conscious experimentation with the instrumentation and stylistic features of art and non-Western musics. Requiring over 900 hours of studio time to construct, and unperformable in a live setting, *Sgt. Pepper* confirmed the recording studio as a place of musical creation rather than documentation.

The Moody Blues collaborated with the London Festival Orchestra for *Days of Future Passed* in 1968, and groups as different as Yes, the Kinks, the Who, and Emerson, Lake and Palmer composed classically influenced rock songs, rock concertos, and rock operas. Deep Purple, later to be recognized as one of the founding bands of heavy metal, began to develop in that direction only after guitarist Ritchie Blackmore grew dissatisfied with fusions such as keyboardist Jon Lord's ambitious *Concerto for Group and Orchestra* (1969) and reoriented the band. Emerson, Lake and Palmer's neoclassical extravaganzas, such as their rendering of Mussorgsky's *Pictures at an Exhibition* (1972), were constructed as elevations of public taste and expressions of advanced musicianship, in opposition to what Keith Emerson saw as the degraded level of ordinary popular music. Bands like Rush, Pink Floyd, and Yes continued this style of complex, often self-consciously elitist music; labeled "progressive" rock, it also displayed an emphatic turning away from African American influences. Many rock fans and critics were flattered by the artistic pretensions of such music, regarding its adoption of classical devices and values as an evolutionary improvement, and art rock came to be very influential in shaping the canons of rock criticism and justifying serious study of the music.

Yet an anti-elitist sense of community and equality was more typical of rock culture, with large festivals such as Woodstock (1969) demonstrating and affirming cultural unity. In 1965, Bob Dylan made the transition from folk musician to rock star by using a rock band on his album *Bringing It All Back Home*, but some of his fans never forgave him for playing an electric guitar during his appearance at the Newport Folk Festival; to them, electric instruments exemplified commercial rock and roll, and Dylan's actions signaled a betrayal of their ideals of folk authenticity (for some reason, microphones and electric amplification didn't have the same connotations). Even the early folk and folk-rock singers of the decade, such as the Kingston Trio, Joan Baez, Pete Seeger, and the trio Peter, Paul and Mary, had often projected a sense of superiority to what they saw as the compromised, commercial culture of rock and roll.

The construction of a rock aesthetic owed much to the professional rock critics who emerged in the middle of the 1960s, especially Jon Landau, Lester Bangs, Greil Marcus, Dave Marsh, and Robert Christgau, the last three of whom were still active and influential in the 1990s. *Hit Parader* was the first important forum for American rock criticism, followed by *Rolling Stone*, *Crawdaddy*, *Creem*, and many others. In contrast to the industry-oriented reporting of the trade magazines – *Billboard*, *Cash Box*, *Record World* – these critics offered analyses and consumer guides, provided defenses of rock which often argued for its status as art, and created influential myths about and interpretations of rock's meanings, which were frequently thought to revolve around youth, rebellion, and fun. This was only part of the story: as some of these critics (particularly Marsh) have since admitted, that version of rock and roll's significance was produced by marginalizing all but white male musicians. Moreover, despite common perceptions of rock's rebelliousness, much of the music's power actually came from its ability to prefigure or temporarily create a society worth fitting into.

The main models for the British and American musicians who created the hard rock style of the 1960s were the songs, vocal styles, and guitar playing of country blues artists of the 1920s and 1930s. Often these sources were not acknowledged, as when the last cut of Led Zeppelin's second album copied Sonny Boy Williamson's recording of Willie Dixon's *Bring It On Home*, and Robert Plant and Jimmy Page claimed songwriting credit and royalties without even bothering to change the title. The reworkings of African American country and urban blues artists by blues scholar Eric Clapton (born 1945) made him the inspiration for a whole generation of British blues/rock bands and helped lay the musical groundwork for hard rock and heavy metal, especially through his playing on Cream's *Wheels of Fire* (1968). Other crucial precedents for the rock music of subsequent decades were set by the power chords and intensity of the Who, and the dark posturings of the Doors.

Demographics and style changes have always played an important part in shaping the music industry. In 1964, seventeen-year-olds became the largest age cohort in the United States, and by the early 1970s, the various styles of rock and roll accounted for nearly 80 percent of recorded music. Since the hard rock and heavy metal of the late 1960s and early 1970s was rarely played on the radio, the ascendance of bands who (like Led Zeppelin) rarely released singles contributed to the increasing importance of albums. Hard rock seemed to sound especially good in cars – or it fit well with the freedom, power, and mobility the car enabled – so it stimulated cassette tape sales as well (after 1963). Because they too brought mobility as well as privacy, transistor radios became increasingly popular during the decade.

Rock differed from earlier rock and roll in several ways, even though a loose conglomeration of styles was regarded by fans as making up rock. Most obviously, rock relied more completely on amplification, and even deliberate electronic distortion, which made guitars sound more powerful. Even though the blues and Tin Pan Alley forms were still important models in the 1960s and 1970s, many rock songs were more elastic in form, sometimes including lengthy improvisations, facilitated by the increasing displacement of the 45 rpm single by the more capacious $33^1/_3$ rpm album. Rock instrumentation expanded, with greater usage by many bands of keyboards – electric pianos, organs, and later synthesizers – to enlarge the timbral palette. The early 1960s saw the widespread adoption of the solid body electric guitar, initially by instrumental groups like the Ventures, and in the late 1960s Jimi Hendrix (1942–1970) revolutionized that instrument by exploiting the wild noisiness of feedback and distortion with unprecedented virtuosity. (Who else could have turned the national anthem into a protest song, as Hendrix did at Woodstock in 1969?) According to Brian Eno, Hendrix was "the first properly electronic composer" (Steinberg 1995).

Many musicians of the late 1960s creatively mixed musical codes, staking out explicitly political positions and making available other sorts of equally consequential identities. In one of the decade's most popular singles, *People Got to Be Free* (1968), the Rascals, a white group from New York, used the musical techniques of black gospel and the southern soul sounds of Stax to animate anti-racist lyrics that promoted peace and harmony. Barry McGuire warned that America was on the *Eve of Destruction* (1965), using Dylan-influenced vocals and a military-style snare drum to deliver a pessimistic critique of the contradictions and cruelties of the times. In *White Rabbit* (1967), the Jefferson Airplane used a similar snare drum and a flamenco-derived half-step progression to create a feeling of suspension with growing intensity, dramatizing lyrics that invoked the imagery of *Alice in Wonderland* to glorify drugged transcendence. A different kind of transgression was achieved by Janis Joplin, whose raspy, bluesy voice articulated claims to power and intensity of experience that directly challenged dominant ideas about feminine attitudes and behaviors, whatever the subject of her lyrics. In *A Whiter Shade of Pale* (1967), Procul Harum combined a harmonic progression adapted from J. S. Bach with vocals derived from soul models such as Otis Redding, relying upon what musicologist Richard Middleton called a "congruence of codes" but producing new signification, whereby the counterculture could see itself as "'sensuously spiritual' (Bach mediated by soul singing) [and] 'immanently oppositional' *vis-à-vis* bourgeois culture (rock made baroque)" (Middleton 1990, p. 31).

Such fusions demonstrate how popular music can offer messages, experiences, and identities that are no less powerful for being nuanced and even contradictory. The Who's *My Generation* (1965) angrily dismissed the future with its lyrics, even as its music created a present that many listeners found attractive, credible, and energetic; it performed perseverance in the face of doubt and disorientation, just as did the impassioned vocals and startlingly adventurous harmonic progressions of the Four Tops in *Reach Out I'll Be There* (1966). Songs about romance are often dismissed by critics as trivial, but records such as Marvin Gaye's *I Heard It Through the Grapevine* (1968) provide complex, conflicted, even epic reminders that for most people, few topics are more important than human relationships. In *Everyday People* (1968), Sly and the Family Stone celebrated difference, diversity, and the potential of music to heal rifts among races and classes; in this doubly integrated band, men and women, black and white, created literal harmony. The popular music of the 1960s exemplifies Christopher Small's argument that music "is no mere entertainment, but a vital tool in the building and the maintenance of identity. It is a weapon for the

imagination in bringing to being, at least for the duration of a performance, a society which is richer and less coercive than that which today we
know in reality, where individual and community enhance and complement, rather than oppose, each other" (Small 1987, p. 463).

The 1970s

In the 1970s, rock and roll grew from the music of a counter-culture to the
music of virtually the entire culture. There were now Chuck Berry fans
who were in their thirties, and by the late 1980s, it would not be uncommon to find two generations of heavy metal fans living in the same house.
At the same time, the music industry expanded throughout the decade –
doubling in size between 1973 and 1978 – and it increasingly relied on
genre labels and strict radio formats to make marketing more efficient,
helping to fragment the rock community of the previous decade. The
specialized formats had the effect of resegregating radio, undoing the
genre-blurring of the 1960s, although a few groups, such as Fleetwood
Mac, Peter Frampton, Elton John, and, among black musicians, Stevie
Wonder and Al Green, managed to appeal across formats to a broad audience. Along with performers from the 1960s who continued to be successful, black audiences had the Jackson 5 and the soft soul sound of
Philadelphia International Records. But the "album-oriented rock" FM
radio format redefined "rock" more narrowly than before: by definition,
blacks and women didn't play it; Led Zeppelin, Journey, Rush, Styx, REO
Speedwagon, and Kansas did.

Social protest in popular music continued in the early 1970s: Crosby,
Stills, Nash and Young wrote *Ohio* (1970) to cry out against the killing of
four college students by the National Guard. Motown had its biggest-
selling album with Marvin Gaye's *What's Going On*, the first concept album
unified by themes of socioeconomic critique. Civil rights themes declined,
however, and performers like Barry Manilow pushed popular music back
toward Tin Pan Alley musical models and lyrical sensibilities. The Carpenters, John Denver, Harry Chapin, Olivia Newton-John, and Abba (from
Sweden) were other 1970s soft pop singles artists. *Tapestry* (1971), by
Carole King (born 1942) set a new record for album sales and helped establish the introspective singer-songwriter style of the 1970s, with artists
including Paul Simon, James Taylor, Neil Young, Billy Joel, Jackson
Browne, and Cat Stevens continuing this personal style. Fleetwood Mac, a
blues-oriented band at first, also reflected these influences as they culti-

vated an adult rock audience with catchy, well-crafted albums, such as *Rumours* (1977). Bruce Springsteen (born 1949) brought together many strands of rock and roll history in a compelling new fusion; his albums of the 1970s and 1980s, especially *Born to Run* (1975) and *Born in the U.S.A.* (1984) offered lyrics that were grounded in working-class dreams and tensions, set to a sound that was both orchestrally grand and passionately hard-edged. Another blues-derived fusion of the time was the music of Carlos Santana, who succeeded with a combination of guitar virtuosity and Latin percussion that reflected his bifocal ethnic perspective.

Helen Reddy scored a surprise hit in 1972, when *I Am Woman* achieved huge sales while earning respect as a feminist anthem. Women negotiated the tension between strength and difference: all-women rock bands such as Fanny or the Runaways harnessed rock and roll's energy and rebellion, while Cris Williamson, Meg Christian, and other folk-based "women's music" artists who were associated with Olivia Records were more separatist, addressing women's concerns with gentle acoustic music, nurturing voices that expressed something different from the rock and pop mainstream. It was during the 1970s that the dominant patriarchal ideals started to unravel in the face of feminist activism, leading toward a time when women wouldn't have to choose between being feminine and being powerful. From the 1970s to the 1990s, Bonnie Raitt's worldly voice and exquisite slide guitar playing made that argument.

Southern rock bands, such as ZZ Top, the Allman Brothers Band, Lynyrd Skynyrd, and the Marshall Tucker Band, fused blues and country influences with a boisterous assertion of regional pride; unlike some rock stars, the Allman Brothers scrupulously credited the black bluesmen whose songs and styles they absorbed. The country rock fusion flourished as Bob Dylan lent it greater respectability among rock audiences; prominent groups included the Byrds, the Eagles, and the Nitty Gritty Dirt Band. Songs that dealt with the lives and dreams of working people were popular, and Conway Twitty (1933–1993), Merle Haggard (born 1937), Loretta Lynn (born 1935), and Dolly Parton (born 1946) emerged as the decade's most successful country singers, along with Charley Pride (born 1938), the only African American ever to become a star in the genre. Songs about modern gender relationships were common, but all of these singers came from poor or working-class backgrounds, and many of their lyrics dealt with the struggles of working people for survival and dignity. The development of "progressive" or outlaw country, exemplified by Willie Nelson (born 1933), Waylon Jennings, and Jessi Colter, and based in

Austin, Texas, created a new bridge between country music and youth audiences. Collaborating, Nelson and Jennings had a number one hit with *Mammas Don't Let Your Babies Grow Up to Be Cowboys* (1978).

Depending on your point of view, Miles Davis (1926–1991) either killed jazz or made it relevant to a large audience again with *Bitches Brew* (1969), an electric jazz-rock fusion that made it to number 35 on the pop charts. Bands such as Weather Report, Chicago, and Blood, Sweat and Tears filled the resulting jazz-rock market niche, usually with more weight on the rock side, although Steely Dan found popular success with complex jazzy harmonies. Reggae was imported from Jamaica but never became as popular in the United States as in England: Bob Marley (1945–1981) – whose passionate, socially observant songs of determination and faith made him the first black international superstar and arguably the first modern exemplar of "world music" – was the only major figure to succeed in America, although others did well by picking up on reggae's influence, particularly the new wave band the Police at the end of the decade.

By this time, amplification of all instruments, with volume and timbre controlled by a central mixing board, had become the normal practice in all styles of rock and roll. Refinements of multitrack recording made it possible for Stevie Wonder (born 1950), John Fogerty, and later, Prince (born 1958), to play most or all of the instruments and sing multiple vocal parts on their albums. Wonder's *Living for the City* (1973) was an extended meditation on urbanization, migration, and racism, set to celebratory, gospel-driven music.

Although heavy metal had important precedents in late 1960s hard rock, the genre's founding documents appeared in 1970: Led Zeppelin's *Led Zeppelin II*, with mysticism and passionate vocals by Robert Plant; Black Sabbath's *Paranoid*, with occult references and Ozzy Osbourne's paranoid whine; and Deep Purple's *Deep Purple in Rock*, with its appropriations of harmonies and riffs from eighteenth-century classical music. Bands such as Judas Priest, AC/DC, Aerosmith, Blue Öyster Cult, and Grand Funk Railroad confirmed a set of conventions, developing a distorted electric guitar sound, heavy drums and bass, and powerful vocals that helped make metal sound louder than any other style.

Many heavy metal bands explored occult and mythological ideas in their lyrics, a practice derived from Black Sabbath and, earlier, blues singers such as Robert Johnson and Howlin' Wolf. Nearly all metal bands developed increasingly elaborate and spectacular stage shows to accompany their huge sounds. Heavy metal rarely received any radio airplay – the most notable exception being Led Zeppelin's *Stairway to Heaven*, which became the most requested song in the history of radio – but bands were able to depend on the concert attendance and album purchases of a loyal audience of mostly white and male fans in their teens and twenties. As a genre, heavy metal's greatest popularity would come in the 1980s, yet attendance at Led Zeppelin's concert tour of 1973 broke the record previously held by the Beatles, and Kiss was the most successful band of the decade, charting thirteen platinum albums in ten years with virtually no airplay. Along with Alice Cooper and others, Kiss explored "glam" spectacularity and androgyny with a heavy metal sound (androgynes flourished outside of metal as well, in the glitter or glam rock of Marc Bolan, Roxy Music, and especially David Bowie). Heavy metal emphasized drums and, especially, the electric guitar, as virtuosic solo instruments. In 1978, his band's debut album made Eddie Van Halen (born 1957) the most influential guitarist since Hendrix and shaped the course of the music's resurgence in the 1980s.

In the late 1970s, popular music was dominated by disco. As had been the case with rock and roll, most of the early disco recordings were by black artists who were initially ignored by the music industry. Disco developed in dialogue with funk, the name claimed by George Clinton (born 1941), Sly Stone, and Earth, Wind and Fire, as they psychedelicized and technologized James Brown's rhythmic innovations. Clinton's techno-funk, as Cornel West put it, Africanized and technologized African American popular music, articulating "black middle-class anxieties toward yet fascination with U. S. 'hi-tech' capitalist society; black working-class frustration of marginal inclusion within and ineffective protest against this society, and black underclass self-destructive dispositions owing to outright exclusion from this society" (West 1988, pp. 182–183).

American disco also reflected the influences of salsa, the soft soul sounds from Philadelphia International (the O'Jays, Harold Melvin and the Blue Notes) and, later, the synthesizer-dominated beat of Eurodisco. Like funk, disco was a music of the dance floor, created by musicians at the fringe of the rock industry. Disco disc jockeys in New York and San Francisco developed special techniques for mixing and cutting among records using two turntables, building and releasing tension to sustain dancing pleasure indefinitely. Artists such as KC and the Sunshine Band, Sylvester, and Donna Summer (born 1948) celebrated the non-teleological joys of sex, dance, and community. Some songs, such as the international hit by

Cameroonian artist Manu Dibango, *Soul Makossa* (1973), avoided conventional verse-chorus forms in favor of sustained grooves with accretionary structures and limited improvisation.

Initially, disco musicians and audiences alike belonged to marginalized communities: women, gays, blacks, and Latinos. Songs such as the Trammps's *Disco Inferno* merged gospel ecstasy, sedimented memory of social protest (as in the chorus lyrics "Burn, Baby, Burn"), and sexual excitement for a dancing community. Barry White (born 1944) surrounded his languid, sexy, growl with an opulent string orchestra and Los Angeles's best studio musicians. The Village People managed to sell eighteen million albums without most of their audience having noticed that they built their image and their most successful lyrics (*Y.M.C.A.*, *Macho Man*, *In the Navy*, all 1978–1979) on gay stereotypes. In the mid 1970s, disco crossed over from a gay and black urban audience to the mainstream. As usual, a white, straight, male group eventually attracted the largest audience: in the case of disco, that group was the Bee Gees, made up of three brothers named Gibb from Australia. When their soundtrack for the movie *Saturday Night Fever* (1977) became the biggest-selling rock album in history – foreshadowing greater synergy between movies and songs in subsequent decades – radio stations began converting to a disco format, and by 1979, there were at least 200 all-disco stations broadcasting in the United States.

With the possible exceptions of heavy metal and rap, disco was probably the most despised genre in the history of American popular music. Some of this reaction can be traced to hatred of the original constituency of disco – that is, to racism and homophobia (as in the extensive "Disco Sucks" campaign). Also, disco became in large measure a producer's art, created in the studio, which led performing musicians to lead boycotts and campaigns against it. Disco's message of pleasure in an integrated dancing community was also derided as shallow, compared to the complexities of art rock, the poetry of the singer-songwriters, or the "authentic" masculine posturing of the rock bands. Disco music's emphasis on a pounding beat was mocked as clichéd and mindless, in part because it suggested a formula that led to many imitations and novelties, such as *Hooked on Classics* (1981). But the music was most important initially to marginalized people – black, gay, female, working-class – for whom disco pleasure was a realization of utopian hopes for communal harmony and bodily pleasure; later, huge worldwide audiences, constituting the most diverse fan base since early rock and roll, also found disco compelling. Although it is often thought to have disappeared or gone underground in the 1980s, disco lived on, under assumed names, in the popular "dance music" of subsequent decades.

At the other extreme from disco was punk, a music which distrusted polished performances, rejected utopian fantasies, and discouraged any but the crudest dancing. Punks celebrated amateurism and anti-commerciality, in part as a reaction against the growth in power and organization of the music industry. Punk music was deliberately noisy, often featuring screamed vocals and songs that were stripped down to the bare minimum of a couple of raucously pounded chords. Instrumental virtuosity was discouraged, since it was seen as glib, false, and a contradiction of punk's egalitarian ethos. The immediate roots of this style were in the artful apocalyptic cynicism of Lou Reed (born 1942) and the Velvet Underground in 1960s, and in Patti Smith's harsh blend of poetry and music; the Ramones and Iggy Pop were among the first American punk rockers.

The English punk scene was created by younger, angrier, more working-class musicians and audiences. Malcolm McLaren created and managed the Sex Pistols, making them the most infamous of punk bands; their first single was called *Anarchy in the U.K.* (1976), and their second, *God Save the Queen* (1977), managed to hit number one on the charts even though its airplay was banned in England. The Sex Pistols claimed to be disrupting not only the fatuous complacency of corporate-dominated rock music, but the rest of the social contract as well. The Clash offered a much more articulate and focused, and no less intense, political critique in *London Calling* (1979), which earned them a US following, and *Sandinista!* (1980). Because punk rejected so many of the conventions of rock, women were enabled to participate more fully in guitar-oriented rock than ever before; Poly Styrene, leader of the band X-Ray Spex, and Siouxsie Sioux, of Siouxsie and the Banshees, are notable examples.

Other bands sprang up, using a similar combination of signifiers: calculatedly crude music accompanied by ripped clothes and shaved heads to draw attention to their alienation and hostility. Punk eventually split into the hard core style of Black Flag, the Dead Kennedys, X, and the Plasmatics, on the one hand, and the New Wave bands that adopted some part of punk's pose but cooled the music with synthesizers and ironic lyrics, on the other: the Cars, Devo, Blondie, the B-52s, and the Talking Heads. Just as Sly and the Family Stone had done earlier, in some of their band line-ups the Talking Heads made an important statement with each appearance simply by being integrated by race and gender, and in the

1980s the group drew increasingly on contemporary black, African, and Caribbean rhythms.

Some of the most successful artists of the 1960s sustained their popularity throughout the 1970s; indeed, Bob Dylan, the Rolling Stones, and the Grateful Dead all maintained a devoted following into the 1990s. Yet the death of Elvis Presley and the murder of John Lennon at the turn of the decade seemed to signal a break with the past. In various ways, 1970s music responded to the frustration of many of the dreams of the 1960s. An economic slump, the perception of chronic social problems, and distrust of government appear to have been addressed most directly by punk and heavy metal, but the new gender identities and communal ideals valorized by disco and other styles should be acknowledged as politically significant as well.

The 1980s

Technological developments shaped the music of the 1980s: affordable synthesizers and drum machines enabled musicians to produce nearly any imaginable sound; inexpensive sampling technology allowed hip hop and dance music producers to build new songs out of fragments of old ones; sequencing programs made the computer a musical instrument and brought virtually any combination of sounds under the control of one musician; satellite technology achieved global exposure for many musicians. Cassettes had individualized and democratized musical reception worldwide; the spread of cassette technology cut American music's share of the world market to one third, only half of what it had been in the 1970s. Digital Compact Discs, introduced in 1983, brought higher sound quality in a playback-only format, boosting music industry profits because they sold for higher prices yet cost no more than cassettes to produce.

MTV began broadcasting music videos on cable television in 1981, after conducting more audience research than any previous television channel had undertaken. Music television helped the careers of stars who could unite a huge audience, such as Bruce Springsteen, Michael Jackson (born 1958), Prince, and Madonna (born 1958). Initially, the cost of video production made it more difficult and expensive for unknown bands to achieve exposure, but later many groups found it easier to gain attention through MTV than through radio, where formats were often stricter. Music videos emerged as a multimedia, collaborative art form, sometimes expanding beyond the confines of the three-minute pop song and experimenting with special effects, fast cuts, unusual camera angles, and non-narrative forms. The new emphasis on spectacularity in popular music helped heavy metal's rise to unprecedented popularity in the 1980s, since metal's performing styles and stage shows had long emphasized visual spectacle. It also assisted a second British Invasion of catchy pop bands like Duran Duran, early in the decade.

Separated from Motown and eventually from his brothers, Michael Jackson made his first solo album (*Off the Wall*) in 1979 and promptly sold seven million copies of it, but *Thriller* (1982) broke all previous records by selling over forty million copies worldwide. Jackson's dynamic dancing and alternately cooing and gritty vocals, supported by Quincy Jones's compelling production and a cameo solo by virtuoso heavy metal guitarist Eddie Van Halen, united an enormous pop audience, forced MTV to alter its programming policies, and revived a slumping record industry. Since one tremendously popular album is much more profitable than several smaller sellers, *Thriller* also encouraged the industry to concentrate its resources on a reduced pool of bankable talent.

As Jackson was desegregating MTV, Prince was helping to overcome the institutionalized racism of AOR radio with *Little Red Corvette*, a tune white rock stations' listeners wouldn't let them ignore. Prince's biggest album was *Purple Rain*, released in 1984 along with a film of the same name. Songs like *Let's Go Crazy* and *Darling Nikki* evoked desire and abandon as few had done since Little Richard and Jimi Hendrix, and *When Doves Cry* displayed an androgynous vulnerability backed by music that broke all of the rules yet worked. Prince would remain one of the most musically innovative musicians of the decade, and his compelling grooves often underpinned radical explorations of gender identity.

Although MTV had done much to reinforce sexism and objectification, some of the most popular musicians of the 1980s were women, such as Tina Turner, Madonna, Pat Benatar, Cyndi Lauper, Joan Jett, and Chrissie Hynde, who projected unabashedly sexual and powerful images. Madonna became the most famous musician in the world (with the possible exception of Michael Jackson) and the most successful woman in music history by skillfully evoking, inflecting, and exploiting the tensions implicit in a variety of stereotypes and images of women. The video for Madonna's *Like a Prayer* (1989) drew both praise and blame for its critique of racism, its bold (for some viewers) enactment of an inter-racial kiss, and its linkage of the ecstatic community of a gospel choir with Catholic traditions of sacred eroticism. Whitney Houston, though a first-rate singer, was much more affirmative, sticking mostly to conventionally themed songs about romance; as an actress and model, she was ideal for the MTV-influenced pop world. Dolly Parton crossed over from the country charts in 1981 with her song *9 to 5*, a mildly Marxist analysis of the exploitation of office workers, infused with the joyous solidarity of a gospel choir.

Although country music continued to incorporate aspects of rock and pop, a traditional revival overtook the genre in the early 1980s, evident in the bluegrass impact on Ricky Skaggs and the influences of honky tonk, western swing, and rockabilly on such artists as George Strait (born 1952), Randy Travis, Dwight Yoakam, and Reba McEntire (born 1954). The release of the movie *Urban Cowboy* in 1980 sparked a temporary craze for "Western" styles of music, dancing, and fashions. Successful 1970s singers like Conway Twitty, Merle Haggard, Dolly Parton, George Jones, Waylon Jennings, and especially Willie Nelson topped the charts in the 1980s as well. Alabama, the Statler Brothers, and Oak Ridge Boys brought group harmonies and gospel influences to the fore.

The singer-songwriter tradition continued with Billy Joel and Paul Simon. The latter's *Graceland* (1986) featured the exciting, new (to America) sounds of black South African musicians, but stirred up controversy because Simon, in order to make the album, flouted a cultural boycott intended to protest South African apartheid; moreover, Simon's African collaborators were credited with few songwriting royalties for their music. Yet the album arguably did much to increase empathy for black South Africans among US audiences; its production and reception exemplify the complexity of cultural interactions. So did Bruce Springsteen's *Born in the U.S.A.* (1984): the song's celebratory music led both presidential candidates to use it in their campaigns, despite lyrics that indicted American leaders for the racism and senselessness of the Vietnam War.

Dance music continued to be popular, as Janet Jackson became a major star and singer-choreographer Paula Abdul had a string of hits. New Edition, Guy, and Bobby Brown revived the smooth sound of the soul singers and male vocal groups, mixing it with hip hop rhythms and thus defining a new genre, "new jack swing." Other successful singles artists of the decade included black pop singer Lionel Richie and white soul singers George Michael and Michael Bolton. U2's *The Joshua Tree* (1987) evoked yearning and hope with Bono's passionate vocals set over the processed polyrhythms of their guitarist, The Edge. R.E.M. moved from cult to broad popularity over the decade, building on a country/folk sound with post-punk energy and oblique lyrics.

A trend of mega-events began in 1985, as rock charity concerts Band Aid, USA for Africa, and Live Aid directed great attention to a variety of social causes. The *Sun City* album, recorded by a diverse range of musicians under the name "Artists United Against Apartheid," dramatized the facts about repressive South African racism for a broad audience. Live Aid was reportedly the largest single event in human history, witnessed by 1.6 billion people, yet it was criticized for depoliticizing famine (there is enough food to feed the world, so why exactly do some people have too much and others too little?) even as it politicized music in the name of humanity. Such events were certainly less participatory, less anti-authoritarian, and less anti-commercial than the festivals of the 1960s. Moreover, they also helped the music industry develop new markets. In fact, exploitation of world markets had become necessary for the further growth of the major record companies. Five multinational corporations now controlled two thirds of the world music market; yet only one of those companies was American-owned, marking a shift away from any simple model of cultural imperialism. 1985 also saw the formation of the Parents' Music Resource Center (PMRC) by Tipper Gore (wife of then-Senator Albert Gore, Jr.), Susan Baker (wife of then-Treasury Secretary James A. Baker), and several other wives of powerful government figures. The Center's conjugal connections enabled it to launch effective censorship campaigns and prompt Senate hearings on what they called "porn rock." The PMRC critiques centered on lyrics that were judged deviant or dangerous. Although no evidence of such danger was ever produced, their campaign for "voluntary" labeling of "offensive" records caused some major retail chain stores to refuse to stock recordings by certain artists, making their music unavailable in some areas. The music targeted by the PMRC mostly belonged to the two most influential and successful genres of the decade, heavy metal and rap.

The 1980s saw the transformation of heavy metal from the music of a subculture into one of the dominant genres of American music. A new wave of British heavy metal hit at the turn of the decade, with shorter, catchier songs, more sophisticated production techniques, and higher technical standards. Bands like Iron Maiden, Def Leppard, and Mötorhead played very different styles of music, but they all were experienced as a tide of renewal for heavy metal. Around 1983–1984, Mötley Crüe and Ratt spearheaded a revival of "glam" metal androgyny, where male appropriation of makeup and other signs of female spectacularity transgressed gender codes, enabled further male rebellion, and invited cross-gender

identification with metal's power. Metal guitarists' appropriation of techniques, values, and pedagogy accelerated throughout the 1980s, making
stunning displays of instrumental virtuosity routine at even the performances of local, unsigned bands. Southern California emerged as the
new center of heavy metal music as bands from other parts of the country –
among them Poison, and Guns N' Roses – flocked to Los Angeles in hopes
of getting signed to a major label contract.

Def Leppard's *Pyromania* (1983) brought the band stardom and led the
metal boom of the following year: in 1983, heavy metal records accounted
for only 8 percent of all recordings sold in the United States, but one year
later, that share had increased to 20 percent. Bon Jovi's *Slippery When Wet*
(1986) helped to broaden heavy metal's popularity by fusing the intensity
and heaviness of metal with the romantic sincerity of pop and the constructed "authenticity" of rock, helping to create a huge new gender-bal-
anced audience. Bon Jovi's success not only reshaped metal's musical
discourse and sparked imitations and extensions; it also gained metal substantial radio airplay for the first time. In December 1986, MTV increased
the amount of heavy metal it programmed by putting more metal videos
into their regular rotation and initiating a special program called *Head-
bangers' Ball*, which soon became the channel's most popular show with
1.3 million viewers each week. For the rest of the decade, bands like White-
snake, Bon Jovi, Poison, Mötley Crüe, and Ozzy Osbourne usually
accounted for at least half of the top twenty albums on the charts.

Fragmentation accompanied the expansion of the metal scene during
the 1980s, however. Genres proliferated as fans, magazine writers, and
record marketers began referring to thrash metal, commercial metal, lite
metal, power metal, American metal, black (Satanic) metal, white (Christian) metal, death metal, speed metal, and glam metal. The thrash metal
style, with its increased speed, growled vocals, heavy distortion, complex
song structures, and precise ensemble performances originated in the San
Francisco bay area early in the decade with groups such as Metallica, Slayer,
Testament, Exodus, Megadeth, and Possessed. The musicians who created
thrash were influenced by both heavy metal and punk, although metal had
differed greatly from punk in its emphasis on virtuosity and control.
Metallica's *Master of Puppets* (1986) became thrash metal's first platinum
album and by the early 1990s thrash metal would successfully challenge
the mainstream of metal and redefine it: Metallica and a few other bands
were able to headline arena concerts and appear regularly on MTV,
although radio play remained incommensurate with their popularity.

Much of this music articulated alienation from a corrupt world in its lyrics, and enacted collective survival in its intricate and precise ensemble work. Living Colour, an all-African American rock band, merged Led Zeppelin-style drums and guitar riffs with thrash- and free-jazz-influenced guitar solos and funky rhythms; one of their songs went so far in its suspicion of the power of media images as to implicate Joseph Stalin and Mahatma Gandhi alike in the *Cult of Personality* (1988).

Rap music developed along with break dancing and graffiti as a part of the hip hop culture of the Bronx in the 1970s. At dances and block parties, disc jockeys spun records on dual turntables, as was done in discos, creating seamless segues from tune to tune. But hip hop DJs also began to overlay bits of one record while another was playing, inventing practices of decontextualizing and then recontextualizing fragments of the musical past that continued to be at the center of hip hop composition when more sophisticated sampling technology became available. Hip hop composers recycled funky predecessors like James Brown and George Clinton, building history and collective memory into their new tracks. DJs started using the turntable as a percussion instrument rather than a simple means of playback, as they "scratched" the stylus in the groove in polyrhythmic improvisation. Meanwhile, rappers delivered boasts, critiques, warnings, exhortations, and other messages in intricate lyrics that were rhythmically declaimed rather than sung. At the same time that hip hop musicians were asserting individuality, they were also evoking collective identity through the history sedimented in their samples and rhymes. Although many listeners initially found it disorienting and non-musical, rap was heir to a long tradition of black rhetorical practices, creatively using new technologies but displaying intimate connections with traditions of preaching and toasting.

Recording companies were slow to pick up on this local style. The first rap record was the Sugarhill Gang's *Rapper's Delight* (1979), but many Americans were introduced to the genre by the first white rap hit, *Rapture* (1981), a surreal song with a popular video by the New Wave band Blondie. With *The Message* (1982), Grandmaster Flash (born 1958) and the Furious Five gave notice of rap's potential for cogent social critique. L.L. Cool J and Kool Moe Dee were among the best of the boasting rappers, conducting cutting contests with arrogance, complex word play, and compelling rhythms. Run-D.M.C. drew broader attention to hip hop culture in 1986 with their remake of Aerosmith's *Walk This Way*, which crossed over to the pop charts. Queen Latifah (born 1970), Salt-n-Pepa, and MC Lyte proved that they could rap as hard as the men as they became strong advocates for the concerns of black women and opened avenues for public dialogue about gender relations. At the end of the decade, "gangsta" rappers like Ice Cube (born 1969), N.W.A., and Ice-T (born 1958) generated tremendous controversy with their violent rapping about lives damaged by racism and poverty. Public Enemy, driven by the rhetorical virtuosity of rapper Chuck D. (born 1960), offered a highly articulate version of social criticism in the age of deindustrialization and increased the popularity of black nationalism among young African Americans. The group's production team, the Bomb Squad, used complicated sampling techniques to assemble intensely noisy, dissonant, polyrhythmic music. Despite their militancy, Public Enemy's audience was half white; complex affinities across racial lines meant that rap actually became more Afrocentric as it gained mainstream acceptance.

Although critics often lumped together heavy metal and rap, typing them as noisy and deviant, rap celebrated vocal virtuosity and technological artifice while metal prized instrumental virtuosity and live group performance. Both styles were anything but homogenous; each offered a wide range of sensibilities and themes. Their conventions were developed by mostly separated communities, although both were embraced and adopted by diverse audiences all over the world. They attracted censorship because of the power and credibility of their representations and critiques of the worlds their fans inhabited. Both genres, like many other kinds of music that were accessible through live performance, music television, and records, hosted important discussions and competing presentations of gender, race, social hierarchy, violence, and community. Musicians and fans of the 1980s proved that even in an era of increasing domination of the music business by a handful of multinational corporations, musical experience, however mediated, could be rich and diverse.

The 1990s

While 1980s styles of rap and pop balladry continued to flourish in the following decade, two new musical developments marked the early and middle years of the 1990s: the commercial breakthrough of country music and the emergence of "alternative" music. Technological and commercial developments had less impact than had been the case in the 1980s; CD sales overtook those of cassettes early in the 1990s, and sampling and sequencing techniques remained important. The copyright codes were amended in 1995 to stymie those who would freely upload and download music through the Internet. Adoption of SOUNDSCAN point-of-sale reports in 1991 brought greater accuracy to the *Billboard* charts and other measures of retail sales; as a result, rap and country suddenly appeared to be more popular than had been thought.

Corporate control of recording, promotion, retailing, and broadcasting increased throughout the 1980s and 1990s, and not without strife: 1994 found George Michael, Metallica, and The Artist (formerly known as Prince) locked in legal battle with their record companies. Still, if record companies seemed to be quicker than ever to exploit trends, their concentration on revenue generation tended to distance them from the creative process, permitting popular musicians considerable artistic autonomy. While media conglomerates increasingly sought "synergy" through mergers that allowed them to use music as a means to sell other products, and record labels offered record-breaking contracts to a handful of bankable stars – Janet Jackson, Maria Carey, Mötley Crüe, the Rolling Stones, Prince, Madonna, Michael Jackson, Aerosmith – audiences bought music that was increasingly diverse. "World music" became an important marketing category and radio format, and a number of smaller record labels weakened the dominance of the big six multinationals, which controlled 93 percent of the US market in 1990 but had only 81 percent six years later. Audiences also remained diverse: although popular music is usually perceived as youth-driven, adults over twenty bought 76 percent of all recordings in 1992. The success of soundtrack albums in the 1990s exemplified the integration of various facets of the entertainment business: of the five number one songs of 1991–1995, four had appeared in feature films. But even the best-selling music was far from homogeneous; although debates over authenticity and "selling out" have remained popular among fans and critics, failure to understand that commercial success is not incompatible with creativity "leads to the tendency to lionize artists when they are least successful and to dismiss them precisely at the moment of their greatest impact" (Garofalo 1997, p. 446).

What is alternative music? The *Spin Alternative Record Guide* points to fragmentation, bohemia, and a "neurotic discomfort over massified and commodified culture" (Weisbard 1995, p. viii), but its alphabetical listings subvert such coherence: the first slot is given to the pop group Abba, and its "Top 100 Alternative Albums" includes music by U2, Ornette Coleman, Prince, Chic, and Madonna. "Alternative" is usually defined more narrowly as an outgrowth of 1980s post-punk and college radio scenes, brought to fruition by Seattle's Sub Pop label in the late 1980s and made mainstream in 1991 by Nirvana's album *Nevermind*. Previously, "alternative" had meant "unmarketable" to industry insiders; until around 1987, when the major labels recognized college radio as a marketing tool, R.E.M. was the only really successful crossover. Nirvana's unexpected success – Geffen initially shipped only 50,000 copies of an album that would eventually sell more than ten million – completed the genre realignment that had accelerated when Guns N' Roses blurred the boundaries of heavy metal at the turn of the decade. The result was initially called "grunge," around which coalesced the idea of mainstream alternativity, with groups such as Offspring, Soundgarden, Green Day, and Stone Temple Pilots crossing over into the big time. Grunge combined influences from heavy metal, hard-core, and college radio alternative, bringing together the audiences for those genres. A related development was the creation of all-female "riot grrrl" bands, such as Bikini Kill, Bratmobile, 7 Year Bitch, L7, Babes in Toyland, and, most famously, Hole, led by Courtney Love. As with grunge, their performances were less musically virtuosic and spectacular than heavy metal, but they retained metal's sense of alienation and rebellion. The mass popularity of alternative had the effect of confusing cultural categories of mainstream and margin: with Pearl Jam outselling Michael Jackson, the question arose – alternative to what?

Alternative music is often linked to a cynical "Generation X," disillusioned heirs of the Baby Boomers. But cultural disaffection can be an entirely reasonable response to social conditions, particularly downward mobility. One year after graduation, 40 percent of the college class of 1990 was unemployed or working at a job that did not require a degree. The median age of first-time home owners rose from twenty-seven in the early 1980s to thirty-five in 1991. The decline in real wages, an ongoing trend since 1973, persisted, as did the rise in service sector employment. To many young people, the failure of the American Dream's twin tenets – "work hard and you will succeed," and "our children will have it better" – was blatant. That themes of alienation would find voice in their music should not be surprising.

Cynicism, merged with an intense sense of loss and desire, characterized a whole range of alternative music. R.E.M. continued the often wistful, indecisive, melancholy style they had pioneered, with songs such as *Losing My Religion* (1991) relying upon poetic ambiguities and directionless minor chords. In their breakthrough song *Smells Like Teen Spirit* (1991), Nirvana forcefully presented contradictory diffidence, bitter humor, and rage, bringing grunge to the mainstream. The pain in the voice of singer Kurt Cobain (1967–1994) soared over raw, repeated guitar chords to model a fragmented personality barely holding on; ambivalence about the group's commercial success was a factor in Cobain's suicide.

Similarly gritty vocals and muscular guitar helped Pearl Jam address the problems of constructing a viable identity in a declining world; *Jeremy* (1991) spoke directly to the consequences of parental neglect and abuse. Polly Jean Harvey's iconoclastic feminism built on her edgy voice and guitar playing; on *Ecstasy* (1993), she plays "bottleneck" slide guitar, quivering and swooping to support the extreme hunger, risk, and abandon invoked by the lyrics. Trent Reznor, recording as Nine Inch Nails, mixed raw guitar and synthesizer patterns influenced by industrial music to arrive at the dystopic vistas of his breakthrough album, *The Downward Spiral* (1994). Beck's melange of musical styles supported his ironic commentary on the consumerism that undercuts sincerity, stability, and community; his anthemic *Loser* alternates surreal, associative lyrical images with a *Hey Jude*-like chorus that good-naturedly locates Beck himself as a part of that same flawed world.

The Lollapalooza festival of 1991 brought together a wide range of styles united by their sense of transgression and their production of controversy. Its organizer, Perry Farrell of Jane's Addiction, included postpunk artists such as Henry Rollins, the Butthole Surfers, and Siouxsie and the Banshees, but also the black funk-metal group Living Colour, the industrial synthesis of Nine Inch Nails, and rapper Ice T's thrash band, Body Count. Lollapalooza crossed lines of race, class, and gender more than any previous tour, and overt political messages and the presence of leftist organizations at the festival created a sense of being "alternative" that was more pointed than the common use of that term as a marketing category.

The most surprising commercial breakthrough of the decade was that of country music: in 1992, 40 percent of the top twenty-five albums were by country artists, with Garth Brooks, unrelated duo Brooks and Dunn, Allan Jackson, and 1980s stars Reba McEntire, George Strait, and Alabama leading the way. A craze for country line dancing helped create new audiences for the genre, as did the fact that it presented an alternative to the aggressive sounds of rap and heavy metal, which seemed to dominate popular music at the turn of the decade. A new generation of sexy female singers complemented the tight-jeaned male "hat acts," though past stars such as Patsy Cline sold steadily, too. Martina McBride pushed the limits of popular feminism with her hit song *Independence Day* (1991), which celebrated a woman's escape from her abusive husband by means of burning down their house. Much of this music combined honky-tonk subject matter, bolstered by touches of traditional fiddle and steel guitar, with guitar (sometimes distorted) and drum sounds that helped the music cross over to a broader pop audience. Country remained the genre that was closest to Tin Pan Alley production methods: most hit songs were written by professional songwriters, pitched by demo singers to established stars, and recorded by professional studio musicians (usually in Nashville).

Garth Brooks (born 1962) achieved extraordinary success with his agile, sincere voice and strong songs on topics ranging from the joys and pains of love to raucous celebrations of working-class community, such as *Friends in Low Places* (1990) and *American Honky-Tonk Bar Association* (1993). The latter song, with its resentment of welfare recipients, seemed to confirm a host of reactionary redneck stereotypes even as it evoked bar-room camaraderie. Yet *We Shall Be Free* (1992), a song inspired by the verdict of Rodney King's police brutality case, denounced racism, homophobia, religious bigotry, and rule by the rich, appealing for free speech, equality, and environmental restoration. It became Brooks's most controversial song, but he refused to back away from the principles it articulated. At one point Brooks had four albums in the overall Top 20; by the middle of the decade, country had become the nation's most popular radio format and Brooks vied with Led Zeppelin for second greatest album sales of all time (after the Beatles).

Michael Jackson continued to be one of the world's most popular performers. His *Black or White* (1991) music video featured his dynamic singing and dancing framed by appropriations of rap, metal, and other cultural "hooks," but it provoked considerable controversy on account of its representations of cultural identities and violence. The song's individualistic anti-racism was illustrated by Jackson's performances with a variety of "ethnic" (African, Thai, Native American, East Indian, and Cossack) dancers, although the reduction of others to dancing stereotypes and Jackson's lack of interaction with most of them made for ambiguous results, despite the brilliance of his performances. The most effective portion was arguably the innovative "morphing" scene, where digital technology enabled diverse faces to blend into one another, undercutting the essentialism of appearance upon which racism depends. A concluding segment showing Jackson in a nihilistic rage was cut after protests.

The hard-core gangsta rap of Ice Cube, Ice-T, 2 Pac (Tupac Shakur), Snoop Doggy Dogg, and Dr. Dre also provoked controversy, with defenders arguing that such music is "reality rap" that documents real life, while others objected to the misogyny and violence in its lyrics and posturing. Historian Robin D. G. Kelley (1994) has analyzed the contradictions of black youth who protest their criminalization by the police and media by adopting the pose of criminals, and he also points to profane and violent ancestors such as the now-canonized Jelly Roll Morton to support the argument that rappers are unfairly typed as unprecedented deviants. Kelley and others would direct our attention to the complexities of a genre that is often demonized as shallow and monolithic and to real sources of violence and oppression – one seventh of white children live below the poverty line, whereas half of black children do; 12 percent of drug users are black, but 43 percent of drug felony convictions are of black offenders and 78 percent of prison time for such convictions is served by black people; black youth unemployment has quadrupled since 1965 while white youth unemployment has remained static. Gangsta rap cannot be fairly analyzed or evaluated without taking into account the unfair conditions to which it responds.

The large white male audiences for gangsta rap have sometimes been explained in terms of exoticism or dismissed as inconsequential to the genre, but rappers such as Ice-T (born 1958) deliberately strive to reach that segment of the public. The cover of his *Home Invasion* album (1993) depicts not only a violent act of breaking and entering but also a white youth listening to Ice Cube, reading Malcolm X, and wearing an African medallion, exemplifying the power – and to many, the danger – of black artists becoming white youth's culture heroes. This same threat appeared with what was perhaps the decade's most controversial song, *Cop Killer* (1992), recorded by the thrash band led by Ice-T, Body Count. The murders of Tupac Shakur in 1996 and the Notorious B. I. G. in 1997 dramatized the high stakes of what Tupac called "Thug Life" and robbed hip hop of two of its pre-eminent and distinctive artists. The latter rapped across bar lines like a bebopper, extending phrases with extra rhyming fragments; Tupac's precise, percussive vocals addressed a great range of topics and presented a strong yet vulnerable persona. Los Angeles's multicultural climate nurtured a great range of hip hop voices, from Mexican-American rapper Kid Frost to mixed-ethnicity group Cypress Hill, showing that the more nationalist rap became, the more marginalized groups discovered its value for working through issues of identity and community. If there is much to criticize about gangsta rap, there is also much under-appreciated artistry.

The "neo-doowop" of male groups Boyz II Men, Jodeci, and Color Me

Badd, and the female group En Vogue revived sensuous vocal harmony yet
again. The individual vocal pyrotechnics of Mariah Carey, Celine Dion,
and Whitney Houston animated songs of love and desire; Houston's
recording of *I Will Always Love You* (1993), a song written by Dolly Parton,
became the all-time best-selling single by a solo artist. The male equivalent
was Bryan Adams, whose *(Everything I Do) I Do It For You* was the most
popular song of 1991, proving that gruff but sensitive masculinity retained
its appeal for many listeners. Some of Houston's hits, and some by Paula
Abdul, Madonna, Toni Braxton, and others, owed a great deal to the compelling production of Kenneth "Babyface" Edmonds. Sexy and assertive
singing and rapping made TLC the best-selling female group of all time. A
delicate voice and searing honesty about gender relations won Tori Amos
many fans. The most popular music of the 1990s also came from 1980s
bands such as U2 and Metallica and earlier groups such as Fleetwood Mac,
the Rolling Stones, and even Kiss, whose members restored their 1970s
makeup and had the most successful concert tour of 1996. In 1997, Lilith
Fair's all-female line-up crossed genre lines and surprised promoters and
critics by becoming one of the year's biggest-grossing tours.

The decade also saw a tremendous revival of dance music, some of which
took place outside or at the margins of the music industry without regis-
tering on the usual measures of popularity and success. For example, all-
night "raves" – dances held outside of established venues – sometimes
attracted huge crowds with only word-of-mouth publicity. Dance music
genres proliferated through the 1980s and 1990s, from disco's descen-
dants "house" and "acid house" to faster "techno," New Agey "ambient,"
and darker "ilbient." Much of this music lacked conventional lyrics, traditional instruments, and musicians. DJs became star performers, admired
for their skills in matching beats, cutting, mixing, and managing a crowd's
affect and energy. "Jungle," soon renamed "drum and bass," featured
complex, virtuosic snare drum and hi-hat patterns that function separately
from the languid bass lines. The drum parts are typically made up of individual hits that are laboriously sampled and assembled, forming a nuanced
racket poised between regimental drumming and a Max Roach improvisation; Goldie was the first musician in this style to achieve much renown. By
the middle of the decade, groups such as Prodigy, the Chemical Brothers,
and Crystal Method brought sample-based dance styles to a larger audience.

Such dance music seems only tenuously related to the R&B of the 1940s
or the rock and roll of the 1950s, as do the rhythmic innovations of hip hop,

which calls into question the narrative that has been sketched. But despite their diversity, all of the musical styles considered here have participated in a shared history of dialogue with one another and response to linked social worlds, just as histories inevitably respond to the strengths, gaps, and emphases of previous writings. Because so many people identify with and invest in popular music, this chapter may seem more partial and tendentious than others; certainly, no previous studies of popular music, even lengthy books, have escaped such criticism. All perspectives are partial and all stories falsify, and the goal of this chapter has been to furnish an overview that would stimulate thought and enable understanding rather than to offer the illusion of objective, encyclopedic comprehension.

At the end of the century, popular music is the United States's second biggest net export (after aerospace products). The identities and pleasures offered by American musicians circulate globally, outpacing the music production of any other country; yet the United States's share of the world market is projected to shrink to only 20 percent by the year 2000, reminding us of the larger context within which popular musics travel and interact. Musical styles do more than reflect and preserve the cultural histories of particular social groups; popular music is one of the means people have of trying on new identities, of making contact with people and experiences which are otherwise kept separate from them. The history of rock and roll is thus a history of the experiences and values that groups have shared with one another, as well as a history which reflects the structures of power that position groups unequally. That is why the pleasures of rock and roll are of historical importance.

14

Ragtime and early jazz

JEFFREY MAGEE

Never min', for the time
Comin' mighty soon,
When the best like the rest
Gwine a-be singin' coon.
WILL MARION COOK,
Darktown Is Out Tonight

These astonishing lines from a song written in 1898 may be read as a harbinger of key developments in twentieth-century American music. Behind the mask of racist, stereotyped black dialect that marked the popular genre known as *coon song*, the black composer Will Marion Cook (1869–1944) makes a sly and powerful assertion: that African American music would become a universal musical language, that everyone would soon be "singin' coon." At least two things made it possible for Cook to imagine that scenario. First, a new generation of African Americans, born in freedom, reached maturity in the 1890s, allowing for the unprecedented blossoming of black secular music styles. Second, the same decade witnessed the emergence of a business culture that created a "cult of the new" (Leach 1993, p. 3). New merchandising techniques stoked consumer desire for novel items produced in bulk, and among the hot new commercial products was black music on published sheets and, later, sound recordings. Between 1890 and 1930, then, the rise and spread of ragtime and jazz held out the promise of realizing Cook's prediction.

Ragtime in American culture

The poetic diction that Cook adopted in *Darktown Is Out Tonight* and other songs – spiked with the derogatory word "coon" for African American – was common currency in ragtime songs dealing with black subjects at the turn of the century. Such language reveals how popular song could reflect

[388]

and reinforce social values. For it is a peculiar paradox of American culture that in the same decade that ragtime crossed racial boundaries and captivated white Americans, a net of segregation laws – the so-called Jim Crow laws – tightened around African Americans in the South, restricting their opportunities in education, work, and the simple tasks and pleasures of daily living. At the same time, lynchings became a common feature of life in the South, creating a climate in which black leader Booker T. Washington could wryly remark that "the American Negro's future seems brighter today because his present condition is about as bad as it well could be" (quoted in DeVeaux and Kenney 1992, p. 12). Black citizens were systematically, sometimes violently, being denied entrance into the social and political mainstream, just as black music was entering the musical mainstream with electrifying results. As in the minstrel song before it, the distorted diction of the coon song was one way white Americans could keep African Americans at arm's length while confronting the exhilarating, newly pervasive influence of black music and culture. And as Cook's song suggested, that influence was irrevocable.

There was already ample evidence to support the claim by the time Cook wrote it. In the 1890s, ragtime emerged from an aurally transmitted regional music developed by itinerant black pianists in the South and Midwest and entered the American musical mainstream through the mass production of sheet music. Many Americans first heard the new style in 1893 at a major national event, the World's Columbian Exposition in Chicago. But the words "rag" or "ragtime," used as musical terms, did not appear in print until 1896. The next year, publishers began issuing piano compositions with "rag" in their titles, most notably W. H. Krell's *Mississippi Rag*, the first rag ever published, and Tom Turpin's *Harlem Rag*, the first published rag by a black composer. By the end of the century, Scott Joplin, the composer who would become the acknowledged master of piano ragtime, had published his most famous composition, *Maple Leaf Rag*.

The naming and printing of ragtime in the latter 1890s marks a crucial stage in the transformation of the music and made possible its broad impact on American culture. On one hand, as Scott Joplin once wrote, "There has been ragtime in America ever since the Negro race has been here" (Berlin 1980, p. 23). The syncopated patterns that distinguish ragtime have their roots in African musical practices that came to America through the slave trade. On the other hand, there is a sense in which ragtime did not really exist until it was named and marketed as such. The music that most Americans recognized as ragtime was the outgrowth of "a process that superimposed European forms on the rich and shimmering foundation of African beliefs and practices" (Floyd 1995, p. 85). In that blending of cultural styles, ragtime became a fully American phenomenon in the 1890s.

The phenomenon was both musical and social. As a musical idiom, ragtime's most distinctive and electrifying trait is syncopation, the combination of a steady pulse and a melodic rhythm that tugs and pushes against that pulse. As was noted in chapter 7, published examples of syncopation abound before the advent of ragtime – in spirituals, minstrel songs, marches, and dance music – but the frequency, concentration, and audacity of syncopated rhythms in ragtime made the music sound so unique as to constitute a new style. A sense of ragtime's bracing impact may be gleaned from its critics, who railed at the music for its "unnatural rhythms" and "excessive use of . . . syncopation." As one writer put it, ragtime was "syncopation gone mad" (quoted in Berlin 1980, pp. 43–44).

Ragtime, then, was more than a musical style: it was a social phenomenon, even a battleground where many believed fundamental values were at stake. Notions that ragtime was "unnatural," "excessive," or "mad" imply social and moral values of rational moderation. Such values comprised the legacy of American Victorianism, to which ragtime was widely perceived as a direct threat. Ragtime, it was claimed, had the power "to lower moral standards." It was an "evil music" to which one could become "addicted" as to alcohol. Some noted ragtime's thriving presence in brothels and saloons in order to stress its degenerate effects. Not surprisingly, the moral condemnations sometimes carried racial overtones. One writer considered ragtime to be "symbolic of the primitive morality . . . of the negro type." In a racist echo of Will Marion Cook's prediction, the same writer worried that "America is falling prey to the collective soul of the negro." Meanwhile, others heard ragtime as a fresh, vital, "powerfully stimulating" music that reflected the distinctive character of America and the new century. In a widely discussed article of 1915, one writer claimed that ragtime voiced the distinctive "jerk and rattle" of urban America and that it embodied "the one true American music" (all quotations in Berlin 1980, pp. 43–51 passim). Whether or not ragtime deserved that exclusive status, its sweeping impact could not be ignored. From its emergence in the 1890s through the first two decades of the twentieth century, the new style could be heard throughout the world.

Ragtime songs

Although piano music became the focus of a ragtime revival in the 1970s – and has since remained the central repertory of ragtime – in its heyday, ragtime was above all a thriving branch of Tin Pan Alley. Even before the turn of the century, ragtime was rendering passé the ballad and waltz, the stock in trade of early Tin Pan Alley. A leading popular song publisher recalled that the shift occurred between 1893 and 1898, when "the ballad and waltz types gradually yielded . . . to the allurements of ragtime" (Witmark and Goldberg 1939, p. 113). By late 1898, ragtime was sparking Broadway, and ragtime songs were freely interpolated into revues and musical comedies (Bordman 1992, p. 161). For two decades spanning the late 1890s to the late 1910s, thousands of songs were published in the name or style of ragtime, or both.

Composers of ragtime songs tended to adopt a single syncopated rhythm and reiterate it against a sturdy beat supplied by the piano's left hand. The most familiar syncopated rhythm in the early years of ragtime song was a short-long-short figure followed by two even long notes, sometimes called the *cakewalk figure*, and notated as

$$\flat\!J \quad \flat\!|\; J\,J \quad \text{or} \quad \flat\,\flat \quad \flat \quad \flat\,\flat$$

Some of the most popular songs of the era feature this rhythm prominently, including Cook's *Darktown Is Out Tonight*, Kerry Mills's *At a Georgia Campmeeting* (1897), Joseph E. Howard's *Hello Ma Baby* (1899), Hughie Cannon's *Bill Bailey, Won't You Please Come Home?* (1902), and Bob Cole, James W. Johnson and J. Rosamond Johnson's *Under the Bamboo Tree* (1902); all of those songs feature or suggest black protagonists. The cakewalk figure also enlivened popular songs whose lyrics were not racially marked, including Howard's *Good Bye, My Lady Love* (1904) and George M. Cohan's *Give My Regards to Broadway* (1904).

Ragtime songs told a variety of stories and delivered a variety of messages. In the first few years of their popularity they tended to be linked to black imagery and dialect in the coon song. Among the most popular – and infamous – syncopated coon songs of the early period was *May Irwin's 'Bully Song'* (1896), by Charles Trevathan. Trevathan's lyrics invoke all the favored racist imagery of coon songs, describing an urban black bully who wields a razor and steals watermelons. The invigorating melody made the *Bully Song* a hit in the late 1890s, especially when sung by vaudeville headliner May Irwin, a white singer who ranked among the best-known "coon shouters" of the period for her special ability to deliver such songs. In this case, her performance was so compelling that her name became part of the song title.

While Trevathan was a newspaperman who scored a single hit, Kerry Mills (1869–1948) enjoyed longer success as a purveyor of ragtime songs. Mills, in fact, is a key figure in the genre's early history. Like many other turn-of-the-century popular music entrepreneurs, he recognized that publishers, not songwriters, stood to make the most money from a successful song, so while he continued to write music and lyrics, he opened a publishing house under his given name, F. A. Mills. As a publisher, Mills specialized in the cakewalk, and his publications helped to establish syncopated music as a formidable force in American music. The cakewalk had originally been a type of African American dance characterized by high-strutting couples moving in a circle; the exaggerated steps are believed to have their origins in the dances of slaves mocking the "high manners of the white folks in the 'big house,'" as one witness later described it (Stearns and Stearns 1968, p. 22). Music for cakewalking bore a strong resemblance to the march: both types comprised multistrain instrumental pieces in 2/4 time. Unlike marches, however, cakewalking music was laced with syncopation. Mills's instrumental *At a Georgia Campmeeting* (1897) embodies all the traits of cakewalk music of the period. Thanks largely to that composition, Mills became one of the best-known ragtime composers in the early 1900s, as closely linked to the idiom as Scott Joplin. The piece enjoyed considerable popularity in performances and recordings by bands, most notably John Philip Sousa's, which played it on several international tours between 1900 and 1905 and thereby helped to popularize ragtime abroad. In order to make the piece as widely appealing as possible, Mills added words to it. The lyrics describe a lively African American religious meeting that culminates in a cakewalk: the religious celebration of the older generation gives way to the secular dancing of the children. Behind its demeaning images of "foolish coons," the song dramatizes a key transformation in African American culture: the rise of secular forms of expression that challenged the traditional religious practices at the core of ante-bellum black culture.

Mills's linkage of cakewalking and youth speaks to a larger theme associating ragtime and a modern sensibility. That echoes through other songs of the period, most notably *Hello Ma Baby*. The song's protagonist courts his "ragtime gal" by telephone, thereby linking a communication device and a musical style that were both coming into fashion at the turn of the century. The mild dialect lyrics suggest black characters but also serve to make the lyrics sound as current as the song's musical style and subject. Indeed, it was in the ragtime era when terms of endearment like "honey" and "baby" became commonplace in popular song, and when, in general, the tone of American song lyrics shifted to the slangy vernacular.

While many Americans were excited by the new ragtime music and its colloquial lyrics, a few black musicians strove to redirect the style into more cultivated realms. Reacting against what they perceived to be the vulgar and demeaning stereotypes of coon songs, the black songwriting team of Bob Cole (1863–1911), James Weldon Johnson (1871–1938), and J. Rosamond Johnson (1873–1954) composed *Under the Bamboo Tree* (1902), a delicate love song about a romance between a "dusky maid" and a Zulu king. Set in the land of "Matabooloo," the song avoids the familiar ground of the coon song by placing its characters in a distant, exotic locale and by offering an alternative, invented African dialect ("If you lak-a-me lak I lak-a-you . . .") in place of conventional coon-song diction. The verse adopts a swaying habanera rhythm, further distancing the song from the domain of African American ragtime. The chorus features a cyclic chord progression over the cakewalk figure. The slow tempo, poignant harmonies, and dreamy musical mood, however, serve to disguise the rhythmic cliché. As a ballad depicting sincere love between characters of "dusky hue," the song is a brilliant reinvention of ragtime and the coon song.

Efforts to broaden ragtime's appeal continued, and songwriters and publishers realized that the way to reach the largest audience was to strip the ragtime song of its crude language and its racial associations. One such song was *Alexander's Ragtime Band* (1911), by Irving Berlin (1888–1989). The song brought Berlin phenomenal commercial success and international fame as the "Ragtime King." Berlin's song is about ragtime, and it aims to evoke the excitement of ragtime, but it has only a touch of ragtime's defining musical trait, syncopation. Nevertheless, contemporaries heard in Berlin's short, bustling phrases, powerful bass line, and the exhortation to "Come on and hear Alexander's Ragtime Band" the qualities of ragtime that excited them (Hamm 1997, p. 106). Berlin's role in the history of ragtime, exaggerated in the ragtime era, later became unduly neglected. His more than two hundred songs dating from the period between 1907 and 1915 reveal a consistent and imaginative engagement with the style (see Hamm 1994, pp. xli–xliii). Indeed, through sheer productivity and reiteration, Berlin did more than any other composer to inject the language and spirit of ragtime into the discourse of American popular song.

People associated Berlin with ragtime not only because of the rhythmic liveliness of his music but also because of the slang and topicality of his lyrics. In *The International Rag* (1913), published just before the outbreak of World War I, ragtime loosens up Old World formalities as it becomes a catalytic unifying force around the world. The refrain declares that "London dropped its dignity, So has France and Germany . . . Italian opera singers have learned to snap their fingers, The world goes 'round to the sound of the International Rag." In other songs, ragtime stokes the love affairs of ethnic immigrants. In *Yiddle on Your Fiddle Play Some Ragtime* (1909) a traditional Jewish wedding provides the scene where music inspires young Sadie to "jump up" and "shout" for Yiddle to play more ragtime. She endearingly refers to him as "mine choc'late baby," implying that Yiddle's electrifying performance qualifies as true African American ragtime. In *Sweet Marie, Make-a Rag-a-time Dance Wid Me* (1910), co-written with Ted Snyder, the protagonist Tony believes that his beloved Marie will requite his love if only he can get her to dance ragtime. For these Italian immigrants, ragtime has become the language of courtship, as Tony pleads (in the pseudo-Italian dialect typical of such songs), "If you love-a Tony nice-a fine, Make-a noise-a like-a rag-a time." Berlin, himself an immigrant of Russian-Jewish parentage, found in ragtime the ideal musical passport.

Although *Alexander's Ragtime Band* ranks as his biggest early hit, it was the publication of *That Mysterious Rag* a few months later in 1911 that marks a "critical turning point" for Berlin (Hamm 1994, p. xliii). In that song, Berlin suppresses all ethnic markers in the lyrics and offers a protagonist for whom ragtime itself is as compelling – even obsessive – as a love affair. From then on, none of Berlin's ragtime songs ever again suggests a black protagonist (Hamm 1994, p. xliii). Moreover, around the same time, Berlin began favoring the word "syncopated" over "ragtime." The coincidence of the song's publication and the terminological shift suggests what Berlin was up to: the deracination of ragtime, the transformation of an African American musical idiom into a musical language that anyone could speak. In his songs, ragtime becomes the medium through which an ethnically diverse population can be united, Americanized, and modernized. Berlin's early songs, then, do nothing less than tell a story about ragtime, a story about its cultural importance, its audience, and its function in American life. There could be no better elaboration of Will Marion Cook's notion of black music as a universal and unifying force.

Joplin, Stark, and "classic ragtime"

Before ragtime songs began emanating from New York, the hub of the popular song industry, a strong tradition of piano ragtime had grown in the Midwest, where most of the important composers of piano ragtime were born or had flourished for many years. Chief among these composers were those who gathered around the town of Sedalia, Missouri, later known as the "Cradle of Ragtime," where the white publisher John Stark (1841–1927) established his business before moving it to St. Louis (and later to New York). These ragtime composers were inspired by the presence in Sedalia of Scott Joplin (1868–1917), the undisputed leader of ragtime composers – the "King of Ragtime," as he was hailed several years before Irving Berlin won a similar title. Together, Joplin, James Scott (1886–1938), and Joseph Lamb (1887–1960), comprise what is generally regarded as the "big three" of piano ragtime composition.

The term "classic ragtime" is often used to distinguish the artistic achievements of Joplin, Scott, and Lamb, and a few others from the ragtime songs and piano novelties published on Tin Pan Alley. For many aficionados and historians of ragtime, the phrase acts as a terminological gatekeeper, separating "true" ragtime – the great, canonic piano works – from the supposed hack work of songwriters. That was certainly the aim of John Stark, who coined the term in the early 1900s in the hope of elevating his own publications above the rags issued by his competitors. The term began, then, as a marketing device and later entered the parlance of historians to designate music whose artistic quality supposedly transcended the marketplace.

Classic ragtime, however, comprises just a small subset of the myriad ragtime piano works that came out in the first two decades of the twentieth century, reminding us that Stark's position in the ragtime marketplace was precarious. Many composers wrote piano rags whose flash and tunefulness brought them to Tin Pan Alley, where they could make a bigger splash than Stark's publications ever could. Among the most popular of such pieces was *Wild Cherries* (1908), by Ted Snyder, a composer and Tin Pan Alley publisher. Like many rags in this style, it has a sequential right-hand pattern which feels good under the fingers. The piece enjoyed additional popularity after it was transformed into a song with words by Irving Berlin, whom Snyder employed as a staff songwriter and who would soon become Snyder's partner in publishing. Tin Pan Alley rag composers employed many stock musical figures, and one of the most common is a device known as *secondary ragtime*, an unsyncopated rhythm in which patterns of three eighth or sixteenth notes are repeated against ragtime's familiar alternating bass. This pattern appears in three big ragtime hits of the early 1900s: Charles L. Johnson's *Dill Pickles* (1906), George Botsford's *Grizzly Bear Rag* (1910), and Lyons & Josco's *Spaghetti Rag* (1910). Such pieces comprised the world of ragtime as many pianists knew it. As one ragtime pianist active around 1909–1914 put it, "I don't recall hearing any rags by Lamb or Scott [or] Joplin, aside from the *Maple Leaf Rag* . . . for the most part it was rags by [Percy] Wenrich, [Mike] Bernard, Snyder, and others" – names all but forgotten decades later (quotation cited in Berlin 1980, p. 75).

By claiming a classic pedigree for piano ragtime that his firm published, Stark paved ragtime's path to the parlor, the crucible of popular music throughout the nineteenth century. It happens that Stark's claim was backed up by the high quality of the works he chose to publish. But in order to entice sheet-music buyers to bring ragtime publications into their homes, Stark and a few other publishers who shared his aims had to create a package that would attract consumers to the musical quality within. Stark, for example, called his company the "House of Classic Rags," and his advertisements linked those rags to European masterpieces. One 1915 ad claimed that his publications "have lifted ragtime from its low estate and lined it up with Beethoven and Bach" (quoted in Berlin 1994, p. 185). Stark's point was not so much to invite a comparison between a Joplin rag and a Beethoven sonata as to suggest that ragtime composers could produce works of enduring value, and that such works belonged in the homes of cultivated men and women.

The titles and covers of Stark's and other publishers' rags reinforced the aura of cultural elitism. Many ragtime piano pieces borrowed their titles from the names of trees and flowers, imparting a sheen of gentility to a music widely believed to be crude and boisterous. Horticultural and arboreal imagery is especially prevalent in the titles of rags by Scott Joplin, as in *Maple Leaf Rag* (1899), *Sun Flower Slow Drag* (composed with Scott Hayden, 1901), *Weeping Willow* (1903), *The Chrysanthemum* (1904), *Gladiolus Rag* (1907), and *Fig Leaf Rag* (1908). These titles create an inviting link between ragtime music and things that enhance the beauty and comfort of a home. Other titles more generally conferred a spirit of class and high style, as in Joplin's *Elite Syncopations* (1902), James Scott's *Grace and Beauty* (1909) and Joseph Lamb's *Champagne Rag* (1910). Subtitles also lent an air of sophistication: Joplin's *Chrysanthemum* (1904) has the dignified subtitle *An*

Afro-American Intermezzo; Scott's *Modesty Rag* (1920) carries the immodest designation *A Classic*; and Lamb's *American Beauty* (1913) is dubbed *A Rag of Class*.

Classic ragtime cover art often complemented the imagery and tone of the titles. Sheet-music cover art – "designed to catch the busy consumer's eye and sell him the product" – counts among the merchandising techniques developed in the increasingly savvy business climate of the 1890s (Schafer and Riedel 1973, p. 161). Early ragtime covers, such as that for *At a Georgia Campmeeting*, often featured racist, cartoonish images of African Americans and their ways of life, providing a visual analog to the dialect lyrics and stereotyped images of the coon song. But with Stark's efforts to place his rags in the "parlors of culture," covers began to offer strikingly different images. The cover of *American Beauty* features a bouquet of roses. *Elite Syncopations* shows a white couple dressed for an outing and perched on two measures of a musical staff, while at the barline between them sits a cupid figure with cymbals. Many covers of classic rags display a fashionably dressed – even elaborately gowned – woman, suggesting the clientele that ragtime publishers aspired to serve. The five *Pastime Rags* (1913–1920) of Artie Matthews, for example, all feature an image of a young white woman in a long white dress playing a grand piano. Here, the combination of title and cover art sends a clear message: ragtime has become a pleasant diversion – a "pastime" – for young ladies. If such a notion has anything in common with the messages of Irving Berlin's songs, it is the larger theme that ragtime had the cultural power to transcend its racial and social roots. Ragtime cover art provides a window into the conflicting meanings with which the music was invested during its heyday. On one hand, listeners reveled in its suggestiveness, its racy and racial explicitness. On the other hand, they could enjoy ragtime's exuberance while discarding its associations with African American culture and with the disreputable clientele that gathered in the public venues where ragtime was played.

By promoting his notion of "classic ragtime" Stark trod a fine line. He wanted his publications to appeal to cultivated sensibilities, but by appealing to them he risked narrowing the potential consumer interest in his musical product. Stark's strategy worked, for although he never reached the mass market of the major Tin Pan Alley publishers, he could proudly proclaim that his publications were "both classic and popular" (Berlin 1994, p. 184). The works of Scott Joplin fueled the boldness of that claim. Joplin had begun to make his mark on the ragtime world two decades earlier. Born somewhere in northeastern Texas, Joplin grew up in the border town of Texarkana. Knowledge about Joplin's youth is patchy, but we do know that a German immigrant named Julius Weiss became Joplin's teacher and instilled in him an appreciation of European art music. As a young man, Joplin also performed in a minstrel troupe. Such experiences drew Joplin to music as both a higher calling and a form of entertainment.

Joplin, according to John Stark's son, was a "rather mediocre pianist" who "composed 'on paper' rather than 'at the piano' as all the real ragtime virtuosos did" (quoted in Berlin 1994, p. 103). He wrote his first works after moving to Sedalia in the mid-1890s, and they comprise a little survey of period parlor music: two songs, two piano marches, and a piano waltz. His first ragtime compositions appeared in 1899, including his most popular and enduring work, *Maple Leaf Rag*. Over the next two decades he composed some four dozen ragtime piano pieces, which confirmed his position as the premier ragtime composer of his day. During this period he continued to write songs and several extended works, including the ragtime opera *Treemonisha*.

Maple Leaf Rag uniquely embodied John Stark's ideals of artistic quality and commercial success. The piece far outsold every other rag in Stark's catalog. It also became a repertory staple for itinerant pianists, a model for other composers, and a paradigm whose formal structure Joplin would adopt in later rags. By all measures, *Maple Leaf* is the central work of classic ragtime.

Joplin's peers held *Maple Leaf Rag* in high regard, judging from the testimony of prominent pianists who performed it and the evidence of composers who imitated it. J. Russel Robinson singled out *Maple Leaf* as "one of the tunes I played a lot" on tour in the South around 1908 (Berlin 1994, p. 56). James P. Johnson, recalling the "popular stuff" he played in New York in 1912, mentioned *Maple Leaf Rag* as a piece that "everybody knew" by then (Davin, in Hasse 1985, p. 172). And Ferdinand "Jelly Roll" Morton named the piece among a handful that were "quite prominent in 1917" as far west as Los Angeles (Lomax 1993, p. 197). All three of these men, it should be noted, were key figures in early jazz. Indeed, *Maple Leaf* survived the ragtime era and became a jazz standard, enjoying many recordings by small groups and big bands. As for composers, the impact of *Maple Leaf Rag* extends from subtle influence on such major figures as James Scott (*Great Scott Rag*, last strain) and Joseph Lamb (*Sensation*, first strain) to "blatant and clumsy plagiarisms" by lesser composers (Berlin 1994, pp. 67–69).

Maple Leaf Rag set the mold for most of Joplin's later pieces. It has four distinctive sixteen-measure strains (A, B, C, and D), each repeated, with a modulation to the subdominant in the third strain:

Strains:	A	A	B	B	A	C	C	D	D
Key:	A♭					D♭		A♭	

The formal and tonal plan bears a striking relationship to the march, and Joplin signals that link by designating "Tempo di Marcia" at the beginning and "Trio" at the third (C) strain. The A strain's recurrence after B, rounding off the first half of the piece, reveals the crucial difference between ragtime and march form. Another typical formal feature, a four-measure introduction, is missing, and its absence is one reason *Maple Leaf* stands out from most other rags and marches. Indeed, *Maple Leaf Rag* seems to begin *in medias res*, as if throwing open a door upon a lively dance.

Almost all writings on ragtime treat *Maple Leaf Rag* as a key work in classic ragtime, and they often focus on its compositional craft. Another important quality of *Maple Leaf Rag* is less apparent to the ear and the eye, but it helps explain why so many pianists liked it: the unique kinetic thrills it offers to the accomplished player, most notably the motoric surge of the first four measures and the way in which the opening five-note figure (and later motivic variations) naturally brings out its own syncopation with octaves off the beat. Although *Maple Leaf Rag* was later arranged for all manner of small and large bands, it remains a pianistic work above all.

Whatever the inherent appeal of Joplin's scores, ragtime pianists did not play from sheet music. When J. Russell Robinson, James P. Johnson, and Jelly Roll Morton said that they frequently performed *Maple Leaf Rag*, they probably never played exactly what Joplin wrote. Nevertheless, in a set of pedagogical exercises called *School of Ragtime* (1908), Joplin writes that although the music is "rather difficult to play," he expects "that each note will be played as written" (Joplin 1981, p. 286). These twin values – virtuosity and note-perfect performance – reflect Joplin's classical training as well as his collaboration with John Stark in the larger mission of enticing cultivated amateurs to play what he calls "real ragtime of the higher class" (Joplin 1981, p. 284).

With that phrase Joplin had his own works in mind, for "higher class" ragtime was what he strove to put on paper. Given Joplin's enduring reputation as a composer of ragtime, what stands out in hindsight about his works is a startling variety in mood, style, and form that defies generic boundaries. A few pieces can serve to illustrate his range.

Despite the eupeptic mood of *Maple Leaf* and later works such as *The Easy*

Winners (1901), *Elite Syncopations* (1902), and *The Entertainer* (1902), Joplin's style puts pressure on the familiar notion of ragtime as a brisk, happy musical idiom. What comes through in many works is a refined sophistication tinged with melancholy, a mood saved from sentimentality by its strong rhythmic impulse. The first strains of *Eugenia* (1905), *Rose Leaf Rag* (1907), and *Solace* (1909), for example, feature elegant, chromatic melodies with a hesitation effect created by tied syncopation at the middle (or end) of the measure. In *Pine Apple Rag* (1908), the spirited first two strains relent to a surprisingly gentle trio whose final strain begins with an ethereal flat-sixth chord (C♭ major), a harmony that Joplin used in a variety of contexts. Joplin aimed to ensure that pianists would savor such passages by printing an insistent direction on most of his rags published from 1905 onward: "Note: Do not play this piece fast. It is never right to play 'Ragtime' fast."

Moderate tempos and quiet moods represent just two ways that Joplin stretched the boundaries of ragtime's expressive potential. A few pieces show him working out a hybrid style in which ragtime conventions work together with those of another idiom or form. The poignantly chromatic themes of *Solace*, for example, are accompanied not by ragtime's familiar alternating bass, but by a gently rocking habanera rhythm, which accounts for the piece's subtitle, *A Mexican Serenade*. In *Euphonic Sounds* (1909) and *Magnetic Rag* (1914) ragtime's conventional left-hand pattern is deployed as just one of many possibilities that include legato scalar figures, syncopated chords, and phrases in unison with the right hand. In those two later works Joplin also explores alternatives to ragtime's conventional forms. *Euphonic Sounds* amounts to a meditative rondo (in "Slow March time") in the form AABBACCA. *Magnetic Rag*, in contrast, features a progressive form rounded off by the first strain's return at the end: AABBC-CDDA. Joplin's parlor refinement of ragtime comes through most strongly in his three ragtime waltzes, most notably *Bethena*, subtitled *A Concert Waltz* (1905). This extended, five-strain piece stands out for its affecting melodies, a feature that Joplin stresses by indicating "cantabile" no less than four times in the sheet music. What happens to syncopation in waltz time? *Bethena*'s main theme is built from the simple cakewalk rhythm, minus that rhythm's last note.

While Joplin was unquestionably the leading composer of ragtime piano music, at least three others carved out an original niche within the sphere of Joplin's profound influence: James Scott, Joseph Lamb, and Artie Matthews. Among them, James Scott emerged from Joplin's shadow most spectacularly. Growing up in Neosho, Missouri, Scott spent his youth and much of his adulthood in the southern Midwest, the most fertile ground for piano ragtime. He moved to Carthage, Missouri, as a teenager, and it was there, in a black community with a "powerful drive toward middle-class respectability," that Scott established himself as a professional musician (DeVeaux and Kenney 1992, p. 2). Locally, Scott performed as both a ragtime and classical pianist. His career began to blossom in 1906 after he formed an association with John Stark, who became Scott's principal publisher.

Joplin's presence comes through generally in Scott's dual emphasis on pianistic virtuosity and thematic unity among strains. Unlike Joplin, however, Scott tended to favor consistency over variety in the realms of rhythm, harmony, and form (see DeVeaux and Kenney 1992, pp. 37–48). Rhythmically, he liked to develop variations on a few basic patterns of tied syncopation. Harmonically, his music is firmly rooted in tonic and dominant, with piquancy added by occasional diminished chords and chromatic harmonies familiar from parlor piano music; the flat-sixth chords so loved by Joplin – as in *Maple Leaf*'s first strain and *Pine Apple Rag*'s final strain – are foreign to Scott's harmonic language. In form, Scott favored the *Maple Leaf* model, but he sometimes concluded his works with a return to the B strain rather than a new D strain. Two of Scott's thirty rags may serve to illustrate his style, both its indebtedness to Joplin's model and its independent spirit. *Frog Legs Rag* (1906) was the first of Scott's pieces to be published by Stark and has been described as his "finest Joplinesque composition" (DeVeaux and Kenney 1992, p. 34). Its athletic difficulty exceeds even *Maple Leaf Rag*, and its thematic economy creates an impression of compositional unity and control. *Grace and Beauty* (1909) shows Scott finding his own voice, with its graceful arpeggios, hairpin dynamic markings, and chromatic voice-leading, all of which lend aptness to the title and the subtitle, *A Classy Rag*.

With Scott, Joseph Lamb shared the classic ragtime values of virtuosity, musical sophistication, and notated composition. He also enjoyed the support of John Stark, whose "House of Classic Rags" brought out many of his works. And his compositions, too, reflect the deep influence of Scott Joplin. Unlike Scott and other composers in Joplin's orbit, however, Lamb spent most of his life in New Jersey and New York, and he was white. He knew he stood in the racial minority among ragtime players and composers, but he nevertheless felt at home with the style. He preferred "the harder kind" of rags, and when he first encountered *Maple Leaf Rag* in

1904, it "hit me good and proper" (quoted in Hasse 1985, p. 244). Lamb was perhaps the purest of the ragtime classicists, in that for him – unlike Joplin, who had begun his career as an itinerant pianist and only later began composing music – ragtime was first and foremost a written style.

Lamb's style is more muted and genteel than Joplin's or Scott's. The opening strain of *American Beauty* (1913) features tall, arching phrases, chromatic harmony, and gently cascading arpeggios. *Patricia Rag* (1916) reveals a strong affinity to *American Beauty* while it explores another of Lamb's stylistic trademarks: chords enriched by the sixth and seventh degrees of the scale. These intervals add poignancy to Lamb's harmonic language and link it to parlor music of the era. *Ragtime Nightingale* (1915) remains one of Lamb's most haunting pieces. The left hand's c minor arpeggio in the introduction and first strain recalls a similar figure – in the same hand, key, and position – in Chopin's "Revolutionary" Etude. The link to Chopin is apt, for like the works of the great Romantic piano composers, Lamb's refined, sometimes introspective, style invites a performer to use rubato, a quality that removes his work far from ragtime's dance-like pulse.

Artie Matthews (1888–1958) grew up in Illinois and moved to St. Louis as a young man. There, he too began a fruitful association with John Stark, who published Matthews's five *Pastime Rags* (1913–1920), a unique and important contribution to the ragtime literature. These works feature a startling variety of rhythm, texture, and idiomatic piano writing. In addition to the conventional boom-chick bass, they offer many other left-hand patterns, including rolled octaves in the "grandioso" final strain of no. 1, scales and arpeggios in nos. 2 and 3, the habanera rhythm in nos. 3 and 5, and fast runs in no. 4. No. 4 is the most startling of the group, with its dissonant tone clusters in the right hand. Matthews's injunction "Don't Fake" – printed on nos. 1, 2, and 4 – echoes Joplin's insistence on playing the notes as written.

The history of ragtime is partly a history of its writing. "Classic ragtime" of the kind composed by Joplin, Scott, Lamb, and Matthews connotes a substyle that came to stand for the whole world of ragtime after the revival of interest in the music began in the 1950s with the publication of *They All Played Ragtime*, by Rudi Blesh and Harriet Janis. Blesh and Janis derided most of the music written in the name of ragtime in order to save a few masterpieces and composers. "The real story of ragtime," they wrote with the bracing urgency of their rediscovery, "is not that of Tin Pan Alley and its million-dollar hits, of hacks and copyists, of song hucksters. The real story of ragtime is that of a song that came from the people and then got lost" (quoted in Hamm 1995, p. 11). Building on the perspective of Blesh and Janis, a second wave of revival in the 1970s focused on Joplin and brought fresh performances by classically trained musicians to sound recordings and film. Joplin's *The Entertainer* became a Top 40 hit in 1974 after appearing in the Academy Award-winning film *The Sting*, reinforcing the popular appeal and enduring quality that Joplin and Stark had sought. The ragtime revivals, however, had the effect of solidifying a "modernist narrative," which depended on the strict dichotomy between commerce and artistry that Blesh and Janis had built (Hamm 1995, p. 11). In 1980, however, Edward Berlin's *Ragtime: A Musical and Cultural History* replaced that narrative with a more flexible and holistic approach that embraces the products of Tin Pan Alley along with the sophisticated piano music published by Stark. That broader perspective allows us to see more clearly the profound and pervasive impact of ragtime in American music and culture.

Toward jazz

Like ragtime, jazz had long roots in African American oral tradition before reaching the broader American public. And like ragtime, once jazz entered the marketplace, its sounds and meanings became diffused and contradictory. The term *jazz* encompassed everything from Louis Armstrong's blues-drenched solos and the sultry, murky sounds of Duke Ellington at the Cotton Club to George Gershwin's concert piece *Rhapsody in Blue* and Al Jolson's rendition of Irving Berlin's *Blue Skies* in a landmark film, *The Jazz Singer*. Jazz inspired musical and social debate: it was interpreted as both threatening and exciting. As John Philip Sousa put it, jazz "excited the baser instincts," echoing earlier condemnations of ragtime, which Sousa himself had helped to make popular. Irving Berlin, however, heard in jazz "the rhythmic beat of our everyday lives." As with ragtime a generation earlier, both sides of the controversy recognized that jazz, for better or worse, was an expression of contemporary life (Ogren 1989). These similarities between ragtime and jazz suggest a larger theme: that African American musical styles present each generation with social and musical challenges that must be negotiated and absorbed because they seem to confront individual and collective identity. By 1917, the year of Joplin's death, American culture had absorbed ragtime. Now it was presented with a fresh challenge by a new generation of musicians and new media.

Jazz emerged from a complex of cultural forces, including a massive population shift, the rise of social dancing, and the development of sound recording (Hennessey 1994). The Great Migration of African Americans from the rural South to the urban North had begun in the 1890s and it intensified after the advent of World War I. By 1920, Chicago and New York boasted large urban black populations, providing an audience hungry for music and other cultural activities suitable to their new lives in the city. Meanwhile, jazz electrified many young urban whites who longed for an alternative to the lingering Victorianism of their parents' genera-tion. F. Scott Fitzgerald captured the new sensibility in his *Tales of the Jazz Age* (1922).

The nature of social dancing itself had undergone a transformation. Before 1913, social dancing had a formal character "closely regulated by the ties of church, school, community, and family" (Hennessey 1994, p. 31). And for many years, dance halls, sometimes adjoined to saloons and houses of prostitution, had been thriving in working-class neighborhoods and in African American communities, and so they carried dubious associations for middle- and upper-class whites. That attitude began to change when Vernon and Irene Castle, a professional ballroom dance team, refined and stylized dance styles that were already popular among the working classes and many African Americans. Beginning in 1913, the Castles performed in restaurants, on Broadway, and in silent film, showing Americans that full-body "animal dances" like the grizzly bear and the fox trot could be done in a stylish, elegant manner.

The new interest in social dancing altered perceptions of the commer-cial potential of sound recording. Before 1914, sound recordings of music tended to feature opera excerpts marketed for the small elite who owned a phonograph. Vaudeville performers also made recordings as by-products of their stage careers. Now, however, a market had opened up for dance music, offering the exciting prospect of dancing at home to the same music that accompanied the Castles and their imitators. Through the 1920s, dance records usually carried on their labels some version of the phrase "Fox Trot – For Dancing."

The Great Migration, social dancing, and dance records form the back-ground from which James Reese Europe (1880–1919) emerged as a key figure who helped bring jazz and dance music into the cultural main-stream. Born in Mobile, Alabama, Europe moved with his family to Wash-ington, D.C.; then, as a young man, he went on to New York City to launch a musical career. Like Will Marion Cook and other African American musi-cians in New York in the early 1900s, Europe gravitated to the thriving

black musical theatre scene. In 1914, he began serving as the musical director for Vernon and Irene Castle. Europe wrote *Castle Walk* and *Castle House
Rag* for the couple, and the Castles developed the fox trot as Europe's
"Society Orchestra" played W. C. Handy's *The Memphis Blues* (Stearns and
Stearns 1968, pp. 97–98). Europe's 1919 recording of *Memphis Blues* gives
us a glimpse of his style through the cracks of early acoustic recording. It
features relentless drive highlighted by muscular syncopation, roaring
trombone smears, growling trumpet tones, and a startling trombone
break toward the end that stands up to the hottest breaks of the 1920s. In
an article he wrote just before his untimely death, Europe attempted to
"explain jazz." He described his musicians' "peculiar" use of mutes,
flutter tonguing, strong accents, and their efforts to "embroider their
parts" (Southern 1983, p. 239). Europe stressed these points because he
noticed that his white audiences admired them. But Europe's ensembles
were always expert readers as well: Eubie Blake called them "reading
sharks." Beyond his music-making, Europe exerted a profound effect on
jazz in the 1920s by establishing the Clef Club in 1910, a union of black
musicians in New York. Thanks to his stature as a bandleader and an organizer, Europe created a newly professional climate for black musicians in
New York, getting them the best jobs in hotels, restaurants, and ballrooms.

In 1917, as James Reese Europe led a black regimental band to France to
play and fight in the war, a small combo of white musicians who called
themselves the Original Dixieland Jazz Band made an impressive splash on
recordings and at Reisenweber's Restaurant in New York. The five
members of the ODJB hailed from New Orleans. Their performances and
recordings featured torrid tempos and a quasi-improvised polyphony
meant to suggest the style of jazz played in their home city. Their repertory
became widely adopted by jazz musicians in the 1920s and 1930s and later
became the foundation for the "Dixieland" revival in the 1940s and
beyond. The jazz standards *Clarinet Marmalade* and *Tiger Rag*, for example,
were recorded by the ODJB and published in sheet music that credits
members of the band as composers (although they were probably adaptations of pieces they had heard in New Orleans). The ODJB also sparked the
formation of other small combos of white musicians, such as the New
Orleans Rhythm Kings, the Original Memphis Five, the Louisiana Five,
Earl Fuller's Famous Jazz Band, and Ladd's Black Aces. These groups
tended to play a loud, jerky, kinetic ragtime spiced by sound effects, or
"hokum," such as the animal imitations in the ODJB's popular recording

of *Livery Stable Blues* (a.k.a. *Barnyard Blues*). Despite the occasional tune with "blues" in its title, the ODJB did not play with blues effects or intonation, which distinguished them significantly from black ensembles such as King Oliver's Creole Jazz Band. The ODJB also played an important role in constructing the popular image of jazzmen as "natural" musicians who improvised but did not read music. The band's leader and spokesman Nick LaRocca, for example, proudly claimed that the ODJB had to search for a long time before finding a pianist who could not read music. While the ODJB did not play from music sheets, their recordings make it clear that they – like many small "improvising" combos, white and black alike – carefully worked out their performances, because recurring strains tend to be almost precisely repeated.

Piano music represents a third development that links ragtime and jazz. In the 1910s a group of pianists in New York City cultivated an extension of the ragtime tradition in a piano style that came to be known as *stride*. Stride preserved the general roles of hands, with a steady beat in the left hand usually articulated by alternating bass patterns, and a variety of rhythmic patterns in the right hand that worked with and against the pulse. Stride differed from ragtime in developing a larger arsenal of left-hand patterns, including tenths – whether simultaneous, rolled, or backward (Taylor 1993, p. 16) – instead of octaves, walking bass lines, and an irregular alternation of bass note and chord. In stride, the right hand tends to favor rhythmically active figuration, often developed sequentially, more than the melodic approach of ragtime (Schuller 1968; Taylor 1993, p. 17). Also unlike ragtime, stride incorporated the twelve-bar blues into its harmonic language. And it was a more virtuoso style than ragtime, played at lightening-fast tempos. Stride players also seem to have pursued improvisation more regularly than ragtime players: recordings by Scott Joplin and Eubie Blake reveal little improvisation, where recordings by James P. Johnson and Fats Waller include considerable improvisation. (Machlin 1985; Schuller 1968, p. 214; Taylor 1993, pp. 14–15). The *locus classicus* of stride, and the test piece for any aspiring pianist, was James P. Johnson's *Carolina Shout* (1918). Though Johnson and stride style are closely linked, Johnson himself did not use the term in an important interview, preferring to describe his style as "orchestral piano" (Taylor 1993, p. 14). Stride pianists were larger-than-life figures, and they cultivated their special aura not only through virtuosity at the keyboard, but through a careful attention to their dress, demeanor, and overall appearance in public. Pianist Willie "the Lion" Smith called it "attitude." According to

Smith, "a piano player who put on a good show was said to have a sharp 'attitude.'" And "attitude" came out through sartorial style, general carriage and mien, a "signature chord" with which to begin, and original, strong piano ideas. "Attitude" not only allowed a pianist to compete with his peers, it also allowed him "to compete for the ladies" (Smith and George 1964, pp. 52–53).

The orchestral ragtime of James Reese Europe, the small-combo style of the Original Dixieland Jazz Band, and stride piano style of James P. Johnson represent three important developments in what is often regarded as the "transitional" decade when jazz "evolved" from ragtime. The notion of an evolution, however, implies a streamlined development that homogenizes a complex process. In the 1920s, few musicians or listeners really understood the difference. That confusion may have inspired Gunther Schuller's notion that jazz did not so much evolve *from* ragtime as *within* ragtime (Schuller, in Hasse 1985, p. 86). Though still based on an evolutionary paradigm, Schuller's interpretation nevertheless has the advantage of echoing popular perceptions and the experience of musicians active in the 1910s and early 1920s. In this period, writers often used "ragtime" and "jazz" as synonyms (Berlin 1980, pp. 15–16). Irving Berlin, the "Ragtime King" just a decade earlier, could be described in the popular press of the early 1920s as a "jazz composer" (Bergreen 1990, p. 258). One prominent critic could argue in 1924 that jazz was "still ragtime in essence" (Seldes 1957, p. 83). Some musicians held similar views. The white composer-pianist J. Russel Robinson, for example, recognized his recordings with the ODJB as a kind of ragtime (Gushee 1994, p. 2). Although the black clarinetist Sidney Bechet has gone down in history as one of the great early jazz musicians, he did not even believe in the word *jazz*, he said, because he considered it superfluous – a word adopted by whites to describe ragtime (Bechet 1960, p. 3).

Jazz from New Orleans

Bechet came from New Orleans, a city that holds a special place in jazz history and legend. In 1890, before the massive northern migration began and before large numbers of Europeans immigrated to New York, New Orleans had the most heterogeneous urban population in the United States. Caribbean, Spanish, French, African, and Anglo peoples cohabited there in a hybrid ethnic stew. The city's music was as diverse as its population, from the blues brought in from outlying rural areas to French and

Italian operas performed in the opera houses, which had been the pride of nineteenth-century New Orleans. In interviews at the Library of Congress toward the end of his life, the great New Orleans jazzman Ferdinand "Jelly Roll" Morton repeatedly stressed the variety of music he heard and played there (Lomax 1993). The ethnic and musical diversity of New Orleans shows that jazz grew from a cultural synthesis, a fact that got obscured in later accounts that idealized the folk purity of New Orleans jazz (Blesh 1946; Ramsey and Smith 1939).

Around 1895, New Orleans dance musicians began to shift their repertories away from imported European dance styles in favor of the homegrown two-step, which by the turn of the century had become "the dance to which ragtime was played" (Gushee 1994, p. 19). Meanwhile, brass and reed instruments were increasingly favored over strings. Moreover, some black bands, as one eyewitness put it, "often repeated the same selection, but never played it the same way twice" (quoted in Gushee 1994, p. 20). By 1900, a notable "generation gap" existed "between the older musicians, who would not tolerate playing by ear or deviating from the notes as written, and the young turks" who not only tolerated it but thrived on it (Gushee 1994, p. 15). In New Orleans, the dichotomy of readers and "ear" musicians had racial and geographical dimensions as well: the downtown Creoles of color boasted more trained readers and the uptown black community tended to have more musicians who could play by ear.

The most notable band of reading musicians was led by John Robichaux (1886–1939). Robichaux, a Creole of color, was a trained violinist who led a smooth society orchestra for dancing. In contrast, the black cornet player Buddy Bolden (1877–1931), though older than Robichaux, emerged as a catalytic figure in the newer style, with his powerful tone, rhythmic vitality, and soulful blues playing. By 1905, as the leader of a six-piece band, Bolden had become a celebrity, luring listeners away from Robichaux, against whom Bolden's band was sometimes in direct competition in adjacent venues. But Bolden's rise to fame was followed by a sharp fall: by 1907, Bolden was a destitute alcoholic who was becoming increasingly erratic and violent, and he was admitted to the mental institution where he spent the rest of his life.

The story of Bolden's spectacular rise and fall accumulated a mythical aura that turned Bolden into the first tragic hero of jazz (Marquis 1978). But Bolden and his group were part of a larger phenomenon. By the turn of the century, the repertory (music for the two-step), instrumentation (wind and brass dominated), and playing style (improvisational) that are now commonly associated with jazz had emerged, and a variety of circumstantial but compelling arguments for the shift survive in the city of New Orleans. The legend of New Orleans as the "cradle of jazz" – and of Buddy Bolden its leading figure – tends to simplify a complex story, but the city and the man undoubtedly nurtured the music.

Yet the role of New Orleans in jazz history must be modified in two important ways. First, historians have amassed significant evidence of parallel developments in the *territories*, a term encompassing a variety of cities and towns in the Midwest and South. The structure of black musical life in these areas was in many ways similar to that of New Orleans (Hennessey 1994). Second, New Orleans figures prominently in the history of jazz not so much for what musicians did there, as for what they did after leaving. And those who left tended to belong to a younger generation of musicians with greater professional ambitions than their older counterparts. Joseph "King" Oliver (1885–1938), Ferdinand "Jelly Roll" Morton (1890–1941), and Louis Armstrong (1901–1971) all hailed from New Orleans, but they made their mark in the cabarets and record studios of Chicago and New York. That their recordings might document a "pure" New Orleans style has been questioned by jazz historians focusing on the ways in which migration and commerce affected the music (Hennessey 1994; Kenney 1993; Peretti 1992).

The phrase "New Orleans style" sometimes refers to the music of Oliver, Morton, Armstrong, and their contemporaries. The term has the effect of homogenizing a striking diversity of musical styles, but its common ground remains soulful blues playing and a fluent improvisational approach in both solo and ensemble performance. These are precisely the qualities that reveal jazz developing "within" ragtime. From ragtime, jazz borrowed multistrain forms and a repertory of pieces, such as *Maple Leaf Rag*, *Tiger Rag*, and *Clarinet Marmalade*. Like ragtime, too, jazz relied on the exciting tension created by a steady, explicit pulse anchoring a free, rhythmically vital melodic line. Unlike ragtime, however, jazz incorporated the blues – blue notes, blues form, and blues intonation. And unlike ragtime, where strains might be repeated with minimal alteration, in jazz, variation became the norm: a repeated strain was never played exactly the same way twice.

These key differences account for Jelly Roll Morton's extravagant claim that he was the "inventor" of jazz. For it was Morton, more than any other early musician, who brought the blues elements and strain variation into the structure of ragtime and thereby helped to define the new idiom. A

New Orleans Creole, Morton grew up immersed in the musical gumbo of his home city. His music and career help to focus all of the overlap and contradiction and rich variety of ragtime, blues, and early jazz. As long as an inventor is recognized not so much as a solitary genius but as a catalytic force pulling together disparate materials already at hand into a unique form, then Morton's self-appraisal sounds less farfetched than it might seem.

Morton's *Original Jelly Roll Blues* has the qualities that made his music unique. It was one of Morton's earliest compositions, judging by his own claim to have written it in 1905. Published a decade later, it has been described as "probably the first published jazz composition – as distinct from ragtime or popular music" (Dapogny 1982, p. 293). It earns that distinction by virtue of its structural combination of ragtime and blues forms, and by its use of that form as the basis for a series of variations. Both strains are built on the twelve-bar blues, and there is a modulation to the subdominant for the second strain, suggesting the usual key progression of marches and ragtime. (In the 1915 publication, "Trio" appears at the beginning of the second strain, thus reinforcing the ragtime/march connection.) What is innovative and forward-looking about Morton's composition is that it uses each strain as the basis for variation. This is one key to understanding its distinctiveness as a *jazz* composition as opposed to a blues or ragtime piece. Whether playing the piece as a piano solo or with his band, Morton's recordings reveal that he conceived the first strain as the basis for *composed* variations, and the second strain as the basis for *improvised* variations.

King Porter Stomp, which Morton similarly claimed to have written as early as 1905, also reveals jazz within ragtime. It has a more conventional multistrain ragtime form, but the last strain, marked "Stomp," features a series of variations (composed out in the 1924 publication, but improvised in Morton's many piano recordings of it). The final section climaxes with a repeated right-hand syncopated figure that accents the blue third. The piece, adapted for big bands, became a standard in the Swing Era. With his seven-piece group, the Red Hot Peppers, Morton made a series of recordings from 1926 to 1928 that came to be regarded as classics of early jazz. *Black Bottom Stomp* reveals Morton at his finest. Like other Morton pieces, it represents Morton's synthesis of ragtime, blues, and jazz. It is built from sixteen- and twenty-measure strains like ragtime; it features the soulful playing of musicians steeped in the blues idiom; and it has the spirit of exuberant spontaneity that is the hallmark of many New Orleans musicians. That spontaneity, however, was tightly controlled by the band-leader-composer. As one of Morton's sidemen, drummer Baby Dodds, has written, "Jelly didn't leave much leeway for the individual musician. You did what Jelly Roll wanted you to do, no more and no less" (Dodds and Gara 1992, p. 74).

In contrast to Morton, King Oliver allowed for more freedom. Trumpeter Rex Stewart noted that when the recordings of King Oliver's Creole Jazz Band began appearing in Harlem record stores in 1923, they captured the imaginations of young New York musicians like himself (Stewart 1991, p. 72). Here was a new sound, looser, free-wheeling, and more soulful than the prevailing dance music in New York. The Creole Jazz Band was "a musical whole greater than the sum of its parts" (Schuller 1968, p. 10). Its members took occasional solos, but the band became so influential because of its ability to play together in what has come to be called collective improvisation. The "front line" players, including Oliver and Louis Armstrong on cornet, Johnny Dodds on clarinet, and Honore Dutrey or Kid Ory on trombone, meshed together very well, and with their intuitive understanding of each other, they were able to weave semi-improvised lines together in a joyous three- or four-part texture that made harmonic sense while each part had its own linear integrity.

The Creole Jazz Band played a varied repertory, including blues tunes, popular songs, and old marches and rags. *Snake Rag* opens with a brief introduction featuring a descending chromatic scale (the "snake" of the title) played by Oliver and Armstong in harmony. In fact, almost every strain in the piece features this duo-break, which Armstrong recalled as a special attraction of Oliver's band when it played in Chicago at the Lincoln Gardens (Gottlieb 1996, pp. 23 and 25). The "break" – a brief moment when the rhythm section ceased so that one or two musicians could burst out of the texture and play a brief solo – brought unpredictable excitement to a style whose primary texture was full-ensemble collective improvisation. In *Dippermouth Blues*, co-written by Oliver and Armstong, the Creole Jazz Band created a piece that became one of the earliest standards conceived within the jazz tradition. Under its original title, and in its revision for larger band by Don Redman under the title *Sugar Foot Stomp*, the piece was widely known and re-recorded by many bands throughout the 1920s and 1930s. Its vocal break – "Oh play that thing!" – became a fixture of later versions. And Oliver's three-chorus solo, with its "wa-wa" effects created by his artful, expressive use of a mute, was copied note-for-note by other trumpet players through the 1930s.

Whereas Morton channeled improvised jazz into compositions, and Oliver developed collective improvisation, Louis Armstrong helped transform jazz into a soloist's art. His early career traces an arc that merits the hackneyed phrase "meteoric rise." In his late teens Armstrong secured a good job playing in Fate Marable's riverboat orchestra on the Mississippi. Playing with Marable was like going to school, for it was there that Armstrong learned to read music, and to play the varied repertory that his professional life would demand. In 1922, Armstrong was summoned to Chicago to play with his mentor and idol King Oliver. As Oliver's sideman, Armstrong's chief role was to fit into the spirit of collective music-making that Oliver and his New Orleans colleagues had mastered. In Oliver's band Armstrong met the woman who would soon become his first wife, pianist Lillian Hardin, and she played a key role in stoking his professional ambition. So when Fletcher Henderson invited Armstrong to join his band in New York in 1924, Armstrong went. Henderson's band offered a different experience for Armstrong, demanding more music reading, rehearsal, and regularly featuring the young trumpet player as the band's solo star. Though he only stayed for a year, Armstrong made a strong and lasting impact on the New York music world. He returned to Chicago in late 1925 and began making records with a small group of New Orleans musicians under the name Louis Armstrong and his Hot Five (or Hot Seven). The fifty-odd "Hot Fives" and "Hot Sevens" of 1925–1928 have gone down as landmarks in the history of jazz. In the late 1920s, Armstrong went back to New York and made more recordings under his own name with large dance orchestras. By this time, Louis Armstrong was both a celebrity and the most towering figure in jazz.

Armstrong's solo art, already evident in his work with Henderson, emerges in full glory on the recordings he made as a bandleader. *S.O.L. Blues* (1927) is a slow, earthy blues featuring Armstrong in his dual role as singer and trumpet soloist. Armstrong's playful vocal chorus reveals his alternately coarse and sweet singing style and his spontaneous twists on a song's lyrics. The trumpet solo shows off Armstrong's powerful reinterpretation of a familiar blues pattern that trumpeters had adopted for several years: a series of phrases that tumble down from the same high note. (An earlier example can be heard in Thomas Morris's solo on *Lonesome Journey Blues*, recorded in 1923 by Thomas Morris's Past Jazz Masters.) In contrast, *Savoy Blues* (1927) is a medium-tempo blues featuring a light, graceful solo by Armstrong. The earthy, "gutbucket blues" style has vanished here in favor of a easy, relaxed stylization. In *Hotter Than That* (1927), Armstrong displays his ability to "scat," another dimension of his unique vocal style, in which a string of syllables comprise a quasi-instrumental solo. For a listener looking for content and meaning in singing, this scat style of singing sounds like nonsense. But a scat singer like Armstrong commands a huge vocabulary of syllables, or "vocables," and puts them together for pure sonic pleasure instead of lexical meaning. Like many jazz anecdotes, the story of how Armstrong began scatting stresses spontaneity and accident. The story – spread by Armstrong himself – goes that Armstrong began scatting because he dropped the lyric sheet and forgot the words to the song he was singing. In fact, scat is a virtuoso, practiced art, much more difficult to do well than singing words off a sheet.

In the late 1920s, Armstrong made records in which he is the featured musician virtually from beginning to end – presenting the melody with his trumpet, singing the words, then playing a solo over the song's chord progression, as in *Ain't Misbehavin'* and *I Can't Give You Anything But Love*. When he began fronting large orchestras in the late 1920s and early 1930s, Armstrong also began playing more popular songs, and some commentators believe that this move reveals Armstrong making commercial compromises to his art (Collier 1986, p. 68). The apparent indiscriminacy of his choices in instrumentation and repertory, however, is part of his creative genius (Williams 1983, p. 58). The notion that Armstrong somehow should have been more selective imposes European-derived criteria of taste on a practice rooted in African American signifying. Commentary on musical signifying places primary value on how musicians rework, comment upon, and parody given material rather than on how and why they select the material itself (Floyd 1995, p. 7). Throughout his career, Armstrong remained a master of signifying.

New York, 1920

That African American musicians such as Morton, Oliver, and Armstrong could make so many records in the 1920s represents a decisive change in the music industry. Before 1920, black musicians were recorded infrequently; no market was believed to exist for the records. But the advent of Mamie Smith (1883–1946) and the "blues craze" changed that. In August 1920 Smith recorded a tune called *Crazy Blues*, written by black songwriter Perry Bradford. The record sold so well that the white men who headed the record companies and publishing houses, at first reluctant to record and publish black music, realized that a large market of black consumers craved music composed and performed by black artists. By 1921, the record companies were actively courting what was then known as "race" talent, and countless black female singers – including Bessie Smith, Clara Smith, Trixie Smith (none of whom are related to Mamie or to each other), Ethel Waters, Alberta Hunter, and Ida Cox – found their way to New York recording studios. Black musicians had made records before 1920, of course, but the success of Mamie Smith's disc effected a shift in the marketplace. From now on, "race records" were seen as commercially promising products.

Bessie Smith (1894–1937) embodied the strong, tough persona that came to be associated with the female blues singers of this era. Her powerful voice, soulful intensity, and direct personal style earned her the title "Empress of the Blues." In addition to making records, like many black singers she toured the country on the vaudeville circuit of the Theater Owners Booking Agency; thus the format and style in which Smith and other female singers performed has been dubbed the "vaudeville blues." Singing to the accompaniment of jazz musicians, Smith delivered searing performances of popular standards, like *Alexander's Ragtime Band*, and Tin Pan Alley blues songs such as *Down Hearted Blues* (her first successful record, in 1923) and *St. Louis Blues*, recorded in 1925 with Louis Armstrong. Smith had a sure command of blue notes – the lowered third and seventh tones of the scale – and she was able to evoke a powerfully expressive style by singing pitches that actually lay between notes on the scale, as in the underlined syllables in the phrase "Feelin' tomor<u>row</u> like I <u>feel</u> today" in *St. Louis Blues*. In this style, the singer and lead instrument engaged in call and response, and Armstrong fills the role with phrases that seem to commiserate with the singer's plight.

In August 1920, the same month that Mamie Smith made her *Crazy Blues* disc, Paul Whiteman's Orchestra made its first recordings. Whiteman (1890–1967) stood at the opposite end of the jazz and popular music spectrum from the blues, yet he too played a key role in defining 1920s jazz. As a classically trained violinist with symphonic experience, Whiteman brought solid musicianship, leadership ability, and marketing savvy to New York in 1920. His record of *Whispering* and *Japanese Sandman* is estimated to have sold well over a million copies in 1921 alone. In the last chorus of *Whispering*, Whiteman's lead instruments take off on their own, the trumpet playing a raggy rendition of the melody and the trombone injecting several jaunty phrases between those of the trumpet. This was Whiteman's way of injecting jazz flavor into his dance arrangements.

Many other white dance orchestras developed this style, including the more boisterous California Ramblers and groups led by Vincent Lopez and Sam Lanin. Throughout the 1920s, Whiteman continued to play elaborate arrangements of popular material and his approach came to be known as "symphonic jazz." Symphonic jazz, "crammed with contrasting incident" (Harrison 1976, p. 192), depends on expert ensemble playing over improvised solos. The scores feature startling shifts of instrumental color, texture, and key. The tour de force of symphonic jazz in the 1920s was aptly titled *Whiteman Stomp* (1927). Whiteman's success with this style helped to establish the large, ten- to twelve-piece dance orchestra as an important medium for popular music and to establish Whiteman in the popular imagination as the chief purveyor of jazz, winning him the title "King of Jazz."

Early black swing: Henderson and Ellington

The summer of 1920 marked the arrival of another musician who would play a key role in shaping 1920s jazz: Fletcher Henderson (1897–1952). Coming to New York from his native Georgia after graduating from Atlanta University, Henderson was in a prime position to absorb and develop the impact of race records and jazz-inflected dance music. By 1923, Henderson stood at the center of the blues craze, serving as piano accompanist to dozens of black singers. In fact, he played on more of Bessie Smith's records than any other pianist. Also in 1923, Henderson began making recordings with a small band under his own name. The band played a varied repertory of Tin Pan Alley and Broadway songs, blues, and hot jazz numbers. The ensemble quickly emerged from the record studios and began performing at the Roseland Ballroom, a popular midtown Manhattan dance hall in an area dominated by white orchestras. It was a unique opportunity and remarkable achievement for a black band of the period. Wearing tuxedos, playing behind music stands, and billed under the dignified title of "Fletcher Henderson and His Orchestra" in a choice New York night spot, Henderson's band was celebrated in the black press for rising above the primitive stereotype that adhered to many African American musicians. An important article in a seminal anthology of black writing, *The New Negro* (1925), named Henderson among several bandleaders who were trying to "lift and divert [jazz] into nobler channels" (Rogers, in Locke 1925, p. 224). This and other writings of the mid-1920s praise Henderson's work in a similar manner, and none of them mention the band's star soloist at this time, Louis Armstrong. Later, for all the same reasons, Henderson's early work earned him the dubious moniker "the Paul Whiteman of the Race," by one influential jazz critic (Panassié 1960, p. 198).

The New York pedigree of Henderson's contribution to 1920s jazz comes through in the variegated colors of the band's arrangements by Don Redman. Redman would take a current popular song, and subject its melody to a series of variations that often got tossed around among the various soloists and sections of the band. He wrote tricky introductions, kaleidoscopic shifts of instrumentation, and surprising modulations. Sudden shifts of style and tone also mark Redman's arrangements, and may be thought of as part of his vocabulary of playful experimentation. One famous example is his arrangement of the Armstrong-Oliver tune *Dippermouth Blues*, which got retitled *Sugar Foot Stomp* when Redman adapted it for Henderson's band (1925). In Redman's arrangement, the joyous collective improvisational passages that conclude Oliver's recordings are interpolated with smooth, homophonic chords, a kind of New York-style "symphonic" interlude between the traditional polyphony associated with Oliver's brand of New Orleans jazz. Other Henderson recordings also revel in stark juxtapositions of style and texture, as in *Copenhagen* (1924), *T.N.T.* (1925), *Rocky Mountain Blues* (1927), and *Variety Stomp* (1927). In this context, the band's great improvising soloists such as Armstrong, Coleman Hawkins, Jimmy Harrison, and Buster Bailey – often singled out as leaving the most important legacy of Henderson's early work – become potent weapons in an arranger's stylistic arsenal. Stylistic juxtapositions between solo and ensemble passages are often noted by critics and historians as faults of Henderson's recordings, yet discontinuity was precisely the point in New York jazz of the 1920s, described variously by historians as a time of "restless curiosity" and "intense experimentation" (Porter and Ullman 1993, p. 74; Schuller 1989, p. 845).

Reflecting on the 1920s, Edward Kennedy "Duke" Ellington (1899–1974) recalled that "When I first formed a big band in New York, [Henderson's] was the one I wanted mine to sound like" (Ellington 1973, p. 419). Ellington first made his mark in New York as the leader of a band named The Washingtonians, after the home city of its leader and some of its members. Like Henderson, Ellington played a varied repertory in a variety of styles required by dance music. A 1924 recording of *Choo Choo* demonstrates Ellington's effort to "sound like" early Henderson, with its restless orchestration and train effects. Another important early influence on Ellington was Will Marion Cook. By the 1920s, Cook had earned an imposing seniority among the new generation of black musicians. Ellington called him "Dad" (Ellington 1973, pp. 95–97). Ellington truly came into his own at Harlem's famed Cotton Club, where he began performing in late 1927. The Cotton Club featured exotic floor shows that fired Ellington's imagination. The shows often included jungle scenes that appealed to white audiences' taste for the forbidden, sexually charged atmosphere that was stereotypically linked to black culture. Ellington composed original pieces appropriate to the dancing. His most distinctive work came to be described as "jungle style," characterized by minor keys, murky low-register orchestration, slithery chromatic melodies, and "growl" effects. All these features can be heard in *The Mooche* (1928). The features were already in place, however, by 1926, when Ellington first recorded *East St. Louis Toodle-oo*, which featured Ellington's "growl" trumpet specialist, Bubber Miley, and which is regarded as Ellington's "highest compositional achievement from the early years" (Tucker 1991, p. 248). Two other notable Ellington originals from his early years were *Black and Tan Fantasy* (1927), with its sultry, sinuous saxophone melody, and *Black Beauty* (1928), an evocative tribute to the dancer Florence Mills, who had died the previous year. All of these recordings and others enjoyed serious attention from one of America's earliest jazz critics, R. D. Darrell, writing for the *Phonograph Monthly Review* (Tucker 1993, pp. 33–40).

By 1930, Henderson and Ellington stood out as the leaders of the emerging swing style – hot music played by big bands. Though widely known through performances on record, on radio, and in ballrooms, they did not yet command a broad national following for the new music. As with Irving Berlin and ragtime, and Paul Whiteman and early jazz, it would take a savvy, hard-working, and enormously talented white musician to capture and channel a black style into a medium that a broad swath of Americans enjoyed. In 1930, Benny Goodman, twenty-one, was a hot young freelance clarinetist in New York, playing in various bands as a sideman and performing in the pit orchestra of the Gershwin musicals *Strike Up the Band* and *Girl Crazy*. Soon, he would form his own band and, with arrangements by Fletcher Henderson, take swing to a larger audience.

15

Jazz from 1930 to 1960

DAVID JOYNER

The beginning of the twentieth century marked the first true infiltration of African American music into popular culture. Through the medium of sheet music, piano ragtime won the general public over to lively syncopated music in duple meter. It was arguably the first "youth music," embraced by young people of the day and a cause for concern to their parents. A generation later, the African American music that came to be called "jazz" emerged from New Orleans and was proliferated primarily in the commercial music centers of Chicago and New York. The Great Depression that began in 1929 threatened to bring an end to jazz, but it reemerged in the 1930s more popular than ever and sporting a new name – "swing."

Benny Goodman (1909–1986) is the figure who most readily comes to mind when marking the beginning of the "Swing Era." He gave the popularization of swing jazz big bands its momentum; but he was not a stylistic originator, anymore than Scott Joplin originated ragtime or W. C. Handy originated the blues. Goodman culminated a long process that changed the context, format, and very nature of jazz. The "King of Swing" built his empire on a foundation laid by a number of innovative black and white musicians from across the United States.

More than any other entity, the Casa Loma Orchestra convinced Goodman to form his own band. The group began life as the Orange Blossoms, part of the Detroit network of bands overseen by Jean Goldkette. (This network also included McKinney's Cotton Pickers, the band that hired arranger Don Redman away from Fletcher Henderson in 1927.) In 1929, the band reorganized as the Casa Loma Orchestra, named for a Toronto nightclub. The group prided itself on well-rehearsed, precision playing mandated by the demanding arrangements of their banjoist Gene Gifford. *Casa Loma Stomp*, *San Sue Strut*, and *Wild Goose Chase* are typical of the orchestra's successful formula. Rather than subscribing to the crooning "sweet" style that dominated most white dance bands in the late 1920s

– though they did balance their repertory with moody ballads such as their theme song *Smoke Rings* – the Casa Lomans played tight, driving, riff-based melodies over a crisply articulated two-beat feel. This formula appealed to the young college-age crowd, who broke attendance records at the band's ballroom performances. The band did not swing in the manner of later bands like Goodman and Basie; in fact, many thought that the band was rigid and sterile, and did not swing by anyone's standards. However, they were envied by other bands for both their popular success and their musicianship, and they proved that a white band playing hot jazz was a viable commercial concept.

The Casa Loma Orchestra was a major influence and inspiration for the white swing bands of the 1930s. Along with the Fletcher Henderson band of New York, the Kansas City band of Bennie Moten was a major force in the development of the Swing Era's black big bands. Moten and other "territory bands" of the American Southwest existed in relative obscurity, far from the recording and publishing centers of New York, Chicago, and Los Angeles. The region had its own strong local music traditions, particularly ragtime, boogie-woogie, and the blues. Southwest musicians were exposed to jazz firsthand as New Orleans musicians passed through on their way to Chicago or California. They were also exposed to the innovations of the Fletcher Henderson Orchestra through Henderson's national radio broadcasts from the Roseland Ballroom in Manhattan, but the riff-dominated blues style made famous by Moten and his successor Count Basie became the approach most associated with Kansas City jazz.

The mature Kansas City style developed rather quickly, beginning in 1930. Moten's recordings from 1929 and 1930 demonstrate a heavy, unswinging beat that continues to draw upon midwestern ragtime, two-beat commercial dance music, and urban blues. Yet, by the time of Moten's legendary 1932 recordings made at Victor's studio in Camden, New Jersey, a marvelous transformation had taken place. The transformation began with the acquisition of the best talent from other territory bands that had suffered from erratic work and neglect by recording companies. Chief among these was Walter Page's Blue Devils from Oklahoma City, a band as endowed in talent and concept as it was unfortunate in business. During its life from 1926 to 1929, the Blue Devils employed altoist Buster Smith, arranger/trombonist/guitarist Eddie Durham, trumpeter Oran "Hot Lips" Page, singer Jimmy Rushing, and pianist Bill "Count" Basie. With the exception of Buster Smith, Moten eventually drafted all these artists, including bassist Walter Page himself. Arrangers Eddie Durham and Eddie

Barefield, who also played alto sax in the band, set about changing the Moten band's concept, forged by the swinging drive of the superlative rhythm section and the roster of great soloists. This was a positive move because of the number of Henderson-cloned bands competing in a diminishing Depression-era marketplace.

The 1932 Victor recordings must have proven a revelation to jazz listeners of the day. The extensive use of riffs rather than tuneful melodies was shared with the Henderson and Casa Loma bands but, as presented by the Moten band, the riff patterns take on a rhythmic urgency, formal development, and suggestion of collective spontaneity unmatched by the other bands. Another point of general stylistic evolution indicated in the Moten recordings relates to changes in the rhythm section instrumentation and approach. The banjo and the tuba (or bass or baritone sax), the darlings of 1920s bands and pre-microphone recordings, were replaced by the guitar and string bass. (It is noteworthy that Walter Page was fluent on string bass, tuba, and sax, as demonstrated in the 1929 recording of *Squabblin'* by the Blue Devils.) This led to a lighter, more connected beat, with the guitar and bass playing successive quarter-note strokes rather than a two-beat rhythm. The drum set now included the hi-hat or "sock cymbal." Whereas the drummer had previously played only intermittently in 1920s ensembles, the hi-hat now sounded a steady pattern descended from snare press rolls and choked cymbal rhythms that emphasized the second and fourth beats of the 4/4 measure. Combined with a constant quarter-note thumping on the bass drum, the drum set underpinned the percussive attack of the rhythm section stringed instruments.

Another revelation of the Moten recordings is the two-fisted virtuoso piano style of Count Basie (1904–1984). From the first recordings of Basie's own orchestra in 1936, we hear a sparse, modest, economical piano style that typecast him for the remainder of his career but, with Moten four years earlier, we hear a healthy striding left-hand two-beat and chattering right-hand figurations executed at break-neck tempos, particularly on *Toby* and *Prince of Wales*. Basie's early style reflects that of his mentor, Thomas "Fats" Waller, part of a coterie of New York black pianists who played an indigenous style known as "Harlem stride piano," for Basie was not originally from the Southwest but from Red Bank, New Jersey.

Fats Waller (1904–1943) established himself as a pianist and songwriter in the 1920s. He occasionally appeared on Fletcher Henderson recordings as pianist and composed *Henderson Stomp* and *Whiteman Stomp* (in collaboration with Don Redman) for the band. In 1929, he recorded the first of his influential solo piano showpieces, including *A Handful of Keys*, *Numb Fumbling*, and *Smashing Thirds*. Waller added little stylistically to what his mentor James P. Johnson had set forth, but his flawless execution and higher exposure as a popular entertainer made his influence more far-reaching. A different perspective on jazz piano was offered by Earl Hines (1903–1983), a Pittsburgh-born pianist and bandleader who held court primarily in Chicago throughout the 1920s and 1930s. Compared to the delicate, highly embroidered right-hand figurations of the Harlem stride players, Hines utilized a more terse, powerful texture dominated by octaves. He also diminished the relentless "oom-pah" rhythm of the left hand that created tantalizing ambiguities in the beat, instead planting the seeds of a sparse combo approach to piano that allowed the bass and drums to assume the duty of stating the constant pulse. Hines, as both a pianist and bandleader, had a particularly deep impact on musicians of the South-west with his broadcasts from the Grand Terrace Ballroom in Chicago from 1928 until its closing in 1939. His piano style can be heard in western swing pianists such as Al Strickland and Moon Mullican, and his "trumpet style" blended with Harlem stride in the playing of Art Tatum and Teddy Wilson.

Art Tatum (1910–1956) and Teddy Wilson (1912–1986) drew from the same influences – Fats Waller, Earl Hines, art music piano repertory, even each other – but evolved in two distinct directions. They first met in Tatum's home town of Toledo, Ohio in 1931, jammed together on occasion, then worked their way to New York to pursue their separate careers. Tatum was first and foremost a solo pianist. Taking the Harlem stride concept of "orchestral piano" a couple of steps further, he played with a dense texture comprised of sheer volume of notes as well as (for jazz) unprecedented harmonic complexity. Tatum possessed prodigious technique, unobtainable by most jazz pianists, including Wilson, but he made a greater impact on the development of jazz through his harmonic innovations. Jazz harmonic vocabulary in the early 1930s was basically triadic with flat-sevenths and an occasional ninth for effect. Tatum drew from the same Debussy/Ravel influence as Bix Beiderbecke, Duke Ellington, and Ferde Grofé, then used these harmonic devices in such a verbose manner as to make all future jazz musicians much more chord-conscious. This would finally manifest itself in the bebop style of the 1940s.

Teddy Wilson, by contrast, tended to remain harmonically simple. Where Tatum had more of a solo concept and often trounced other musicians in an ensemble situation, Wilson was a team player, possessing a lighter texture, rhythmic stability, poised energy, and a sensitive accompanimental prowess. These qualities captured the attention of John Hammond (1918–1987) who began producing small group sessions that promoted Wilson to group leader and in-demand accompanist by 1935, resulting in historic recordings with singer Billie Holiday. Hammond and Wilson also made history by the latter's inclusion in Benny Goodman's trio and quartet, not only creating some of the most sublime small group jazz of the 1930s but effectively breaking down the color barrier in public performances.

Benny Goodman and Fletcher Henderson

Some historians have dismissed Benny Goodman and his producer John Hammond as another case of white opportunism and exploitation of a black musical form. On the contrary, Hammond sought a way to bring black jazz from its social confines into the open spaces of mass popular culture, using Goodman as the conduit. Countless jazz musicians, both white and black, benefited from Hammond's efforts, though the white aggregations inevitably overshadowed their black constituency in popularity.

John Hammond grew up in great wealth, descended from the Vander-bilt family on his mother's side, but he spent his life pursuing his two great passions – jazz and fighting racism. After a brief career as a political journalist, he became a talent scout for English Columbia and Parlophone, and was a regular writer for *Gramophone* and *Melody Maker*. Hammond was a champion of the Fletcher Henderson band and produced sessions for his band and various assemblages of its sidemen. He wanted Benny Goodman to be his next recording venture, but it would take some artful persuading.

Though there was still a sizable market for jazz in Britain, the United States, including Benny Goodman, had largely given up on it by the early 1930s. Having grown up in Chicago, Benny Goodman befriended estab-lished black clarinetists Jimmie Noone and Buster Bailey. On occasion, he played jazz with middle-class white youths in Chicago such as Jimmy McPartland and Bud Freeman; but while they considered jazz more of a cause and lifestyle than a means of livelihood, Goodman was more con-cerned with providing for his impoverished family. During the Depres-sion, he resigned himself to the profitable but dreary business of studio work and playing in sweet dance orchestras.

Then in 1933, Hammond suddenly became Goodman's musical conscience. He reawakened Goodman's love for jazz and an enthusiasm
toward his potential as a creative artist and musical leader. The success of
the Casa Loma band and a promising new band founded by the Dorsey
brothers, Jimmy and Tommy, convinced Goodman to start his own band.
Hammond helped him get his first big job premiering at Billy Rose's Music
Hall in New York. After that stint met an abrupt end, Hammond procured
a twenty-six week engagement on the NBC radio program *Let's Dance*.
With little time to compile a library of new arrangements, Hammond con-
tacted Fletcher Henderson to help out. It was a fortuitous event for all
parties.

In 1934, Henderson was at the peak of his arranging powers and the ebb
of his business career. After Don Redman's departure in 1927, the band
lost its musical direction, exacerbated by Henderson's diminishing leadership acumen. By 1930, however, the band was again making positive
strides, led by their new arranger and alto man Benny Carter. As with other
bands around this time, Henderson adopted the string bass, capably
played by John Kirby, and the newly defined 4/4 beat. Additionally, the
rhythmic figures of the band against that 4/4 became more syncopated and
relaxed. They also employed riff-oriented "head" arrangements, another
new trend of the early 1930s. Henderson began taking a more active role in
arranging for his band; some of his best work includes reworkings of *Sugar
Foot Stomp*, a big band version of King Oliver's *Dippermouth Blues* arranged
by Redman and recorded in 1925, and *King Porter Stomp*, a Jelly Roll
Morton composition first recorded by Henderson in 1928. Fletcher and
his brother Horace also produced new compositions such as *Big John's
Special*, *Wrappin' It Up*, and *Down South Camp Meeting*. Unfortunately, Henderson's lack of leadership and business skills, increasing competition, and
restless sidemen overwhelmed the musical advances of the band. Even
with Hammond's faithful support, it fell apart in 1934.

At this point, Goodman needed music and Henderson needed a band.
Goodman immediately acquired the existing Henderson music and then,
with a budget for new arrangements, hired Fletcher to provide them,
mostly swing arrangements of popular songs. It took some time to find an
enthusiastic audience. A road tour from New York to the Palomar Ballroom
in Los Angeles was peppered with mishaps and hostile crowds, but, in the
end, the band met with phenomenal success. It was the teenagers who
embraced the excitement and brashness of Goodman and Henderson's

music, music that seemed new to them but was actually the product of "a dozen years of experimentation, development and gradual perfection of a style of big band arranging that was to give him [Goodman] the identity he needed" (Firestone 1993, p. 115).

It is a common practice to compare performances of Henderson arrangements by the Henderson and Goodman bands. One observation, usually made disparagingly, is that the Goodman band played with more precision and therefore less inspiration than Henderson (Schuller 1989, p. 10). The accusation of being mechanical, unemotional, and lacking in swing was also applied to the Casa Loma band, to Tommy Dorsey, Glenn Miller, perhaps Jimmie Lunceford, and every other band that distinguished itself by meticulous ensemble playing. True, Goodman drilled his band mercilessly in rehearsals to achieve "more accurate intonation, more carefully articulated phrasing, cleaner section work and a better blending of the overall ensemble" (Firestone 1993, p. 115). It is also true that Goodman could not boast of as many excellent soloists as Henderson, but to impose the view that Goodman's (or Dorsey's, Miller's, or the Casa Loma's) ensemble precision equates with emotional sterility is not altogether fair.

The increase in Goodman's recording and live appearances required more arrangements than Fletcher Henderson was able to produce by himself. To help with the load, Goodman hired, among others, Earl Hines's arranger Jimmy Mundy. Mundy's arrangements were much flashier and riff-oriented than Henderson's. Goodman's young audience came to prefer these charts, to the chagrin of John Hammond, who had precise and vehement opinions in his jazz tastes. In general, success was exacting a toll on the band's artistry, catering to the public with fast "killer-dillers" and uninspired pop song vocal features. The center of attention seemed to be drummer Gene Krupa, whose exciting visual presentation and frequent overplaying detracted from the band's musicality. Goodman's own sense of musicianship increasingly troubled him so that, by around 1939, he sought stimulus and direction of more musical than commercial substance. He found it in two ambitious young arrangers, Eddie Sauter and Mel Powell, and in increasing involvement with art music. As World War II and the American Federation of Musicians' recording ban set in, the heyday of Goodman and the Swing Era began to wane, but 1940 left Goodman in good artistic standing. The "King of Swing" had gathered the forces of a number of black and white jazz artists and made the public believe again, if only for a few years, in jazz.

Jimmie Lunceford and Count Basie

One of the great black bands of the Swing Era also known for its demanding arrangements and brilliant execution was that of Jimmie Lunceford (1902–1947). "Lunceford was an exceedingly well-trained, partly classically oriented musician who valued discipline and structured organization – and rehearsing" (Schuller 1989, p. 202). The band was also known for its lively staging and antics, an attribute we can only glimpse in rare film footage.

Lunceford's was an arranger's band, the first writers being pianist Edwin Wilcox and altoist Willie Smith. Early recordings were a stylistic hodge-podge of ragtime, blues, and Whiteman sweet style. The band's first hits were *White Heat* and *Jazznocracy* (1933) by white composer and arranger Will Hudson, brought to the band by Irving Mills, who had booked the band into the Cotton Club after Duke Ellington. These charts were hard-driving and riff-oriented, similar to the music of the Casa Loma band and unlike the earlier Wilcox/Smith style or the soon-to-come Sy Oliver style that characterized the majority of Lunceford's music. Oliver established the character of the band during his tenure from 1934 to 1936. He was definitely inspired by Duke Ellington but had established his own style with Zach White's band in Cincinnati. His arrangements show a penchant for transitions, breaks, modulations, chromatic passages, unusual orchestra combinations, a full-bodied ensemble sound, and, above all, a laid-back behind-the-beat feel over a two-beat rhythm that was irresistible for dance.

Eddie Durham came in from Bennie Moten and Earl Hines and by 1937 went with Count Basie, though he still contributed charts from time to time, such as *Running a Temperature* and *Lunceford Special*. Gerald Wilson replaced Sy Oliver as trumpeter and arranger. His *Yard Dog Mazurka* was lifted and became Stan Kenton's *Intermission Riff*. The band began to fail when Willie Smith, trumpeter Snooky Young, and Gerald Wilson left in 1940 and it died with Lunceford in 1947.

The Count Basie band was formed from the remnants of the Bennie Moten orchestra. It was "discovered" by John Hammond, who heard a radio broadcast from Kansas City's Reno Club in the spring of 1936. Hammond immediately sought the band out to sign it to his Columbia label, but Decca, who had recently arrived from England, beat him to the punch. Hammond eventually contracted the band for Columbia in 1939. Unlike the New York bands, the Basie band had a stronger, more seasoned blues base to its style. They de-emphasized complex arrangements in favor of simple, repetitive "riffs" that had more rhythmic than melodic quality. There was also a heavy emphasis on improvisation, creating an intimate small group jam session atmosphere within a big band context.

The outstanding feature of the Basie band may very well have been the rhythm section of Basie, guitarist Freddie Green, bassist Walter Page, and drummer "Papa" Jo Jones. Labeled by former Basie trumpeter Harry "Sweets" Edison as "the All-American rhythm section," the quartet of players centered the feel around Green's disciplined quarter-note pulse, freeing Basie from keeping the beat on the piano and allowing him to play a more sparse, interplaying style. Jo Jones kept a more subtle beat and featured intricate patterns for his hi-hat cymbal that added a lilt to the overall rhythmic feel.

The recording debut of the Count Basie band in 1936 was also the recording debut of its tenor saxophonist, Lester Young (1909–1959). Young's ascension was indicative of the prominence of the tenor sax soloist in the 1930s. By the latter half of the decade, "tenor battles" between Young and other Basie tenor men were a standard format of the band's arrangements. Ben Webster, a veteran of the Bennie Moten and Fletcher Henderson bands, became the first tenor soloist for the Duke Ellington orchestra. The 1930s culminated with the influential recording of *Body and Soul* by Coleman Hawkins, the patriarch of the instrument.

Hawkins (1904–1969) began playing the tenor at the age of nine, and joined Fletcher Henderson's band in 1923 while still a teenager. For the next decade he was one of the star soloists in the band and the standard by which all other tenor saxophonists were judged. From 1934 to 1939, Hawkins worked in Europe, honing his sound and style. Soon after he returned to the United States, he recorded his two-chorus improvisation of *Body and Soul*. Its double-time ballad feel, implications of extended harmonies, and technical display were a catalyst for the bebop style of the 1940s; but it also possessed enough tunefulness and expressivity to appeal to the popular audience and remain on jukeboxes well into the 1950s. By the late 1930s, Hawkins's sound was deep and robust, laden with a prominent vibrato. His improvisational approach increasingly became shaped by the extended jazz harmony pioneered by Art Tatum and others. Hawkins's style was a resilient one that remained vital well into the 1960s.

Lester Young became the second voice for tenor saxophonists, diametrically opposed to Hawkins's sound and approach, but equally influential.

Young based his instrumental approach on the sweeter, more reserved character of Frank Trumbauer, a C-melody saxophone player who worked with Bix Beiderbecke. Young's distinctive timbre cost him his job with the Fletcher Henderson band because he did not sound like Hawkins. He rejoined Count Basie's band and made his first recordings in 1936, including the often-imitated performances on *Lady Be Good* and *Shoeshine Boy*. His light, wispy sound and emotionally poised musical personality spawned a host of imitators. His smooth lines and forays into irregular phrasing were inspiration for the melodic style of bebop. His 1939 recording of *Lester Leaps In* rivaled Hawkins's *Body and Soul* recording of the same year in its influence on the young players who would mature in the 1940s.

Women in jazz during the 1930s and 1940s

Until recently, comparatively few women have been acknowledged in the jazz community. Jazz historian Linda Dahl, in her book *Stormy Weather*, lists several sociological and business factors that kept women out of jazz. There were the perceived "masculine" virtues of aggressive self-confidence, displaying powerful technical prowess, absence from home life, and working in unsavory environments. Male jazz musicians resented the increased economic competition, particularly black men. Dahl states that black women competing with black men ". . . at times came to represent both symbolic and concrete proof of the male's abilities in a culture that denigrated his manhood" (Dahl 1984, p. x).

Aside from the social and occupational roles relegated to women by the culture of the day, it is also notable that certain musical instruments were gender specific. For instance, it was a long-held belief that it was effeminate for males to play the piano. Jelly Roll Morton initially resisted taking up the piano because ". . . the piano was known in our circle as an instrument for a lady, this confirmed me in my idea that if I played the piano I would be misunderstood. I didn't want to be called a sissy. I wanted to marry and raise a family and be known as a man among men when I became of age" (Lomax 1993, p. 6). It was just as frowned upon for a young woman to play the trumpet or the drums. Therefore, many of the early female stars in jazz history were either pianists or singers.

Lillian Hardin Armstrong (1898–1971), pianist and composer, entered the canon of great jazz musicians through her involvement with King Oliver's Creole Jazz Band in the early 1920s and through her compositions and performances with her husband Louis Armstrong. Before her were countless women ragtime pianists and composers whose work has only recently been discovered and appreciated.

The next great woman pianist, composer, and arranger was Mary Lou Williams (1910–1981). She began her career in 1929 with Andy Kirk's Twelve Clouds of Joy, a Southwest territory band that rivaled Bennie Moten, Count Basie, and Jay McShann. She was not only the band's premiere soloist, but a writer of swinging arrangements that occasionally exhibited the orchestrational inventiveness of Duke Ellington. She left the Kirk band in the 1940s and became the informal teacher of many young bebop musicians, including Bud Powell and Thelonious Monk. Her own piano style evolved and she was soon exhibiting the same modern characteristics as her protégés. Her compositions became equally explorative, culminating in her *Zodiac Suite* from 1945. Like her constituent Duke Ellington, she spent her latter years composing sacred works.

Connee Boswell (1907–1976) was also a fine arranger. She and her two sisters had a great deal of formal training and all played a number of instruments. Between 1931 and 1935, the Boswell sisters formed an influential vocal trio with witty, inventive arrangements by Connee. The Boswell Sisters redefined jazz vocal harmony from rhythmically stiff barbershop style to an intricate jazz trumpet section approach. The instrumental accompaniment was equally intricate and often featured multiple changes of tempo. Connee went on as a solo singer after the demise of the trio, influencing a number of future jazz singers, most notably Ella Fitzgerald.

The genre of jazz singing was the most matriarchal. Though there were important male jazz singers such as Louis Armstrong, Jack Teagarden, and Bing Crosby they were far outnumbered by the women. The impetus was, no doubt, the numerous vaudeville blues singers of the 1920s (Mamie Smith, Trixie Smith, Bessie Smith, Clara Smith, et al.). In the 1930s, female singers proliferated in the swing big bands, though they were rarely taken seriously. Considered by the instrumentalists as "canaries" or "chirpers," their role was to look pretty and sing the song relatively straight. Yet despite the often tepid relationship with the band, the singers grew from their contact with the other members of the band, learning to adapt the intricacies of style, repertory, and improvisation to the voice. Very few singers worth their salt matured musically without the big band experience. Whatever malignment they suffered from the sidemen was compensated by their ultimate popularity. Due to circumstances such as the American Federation of Musicians' recording ban in the early 1940s, which did not affect singers, and the meteoric rise of Frank Sinatra, the big band singers ultimately became more famous than the bands that accompanied them.

The singer who commanded the greatest respect from her instrumental peers was Billie Holiday (1915-1959). She was discovered by John Hammond in 1933 and began recording under the leadership of Benny Goodman and Teddy Wilson. Though she possessed a meager voice, she assimilated the styles of Louis Armstrong, Bessie Smith, and Ethel Waters into a light, swinging style replete with creative phrasing and reshaping of the original melodies. In 1938, she teamed up with tenor saxophonist Lester Young, creating one of the great duos in jazz history – others include Bix Beiderbecke and Frank Trumbauer, Clifford Brown and Sonny Rollins, or Gerry Mulligan and Chet Baker.

Much of Billie Holiday's best work was done in intimate small group settings rather than with big bands or orchestras. While the 1930s is historically tagged as the era of the big bands, there was considerable small group activity. Almost all of the big bands had small groups within their ranks, such as Benny Goodman's trio, quartet, and sextet, Artie Shaw's Gramercy Five, Tommy Dorsey's Clambake Seven, or Woody Herman's Woodchoppers. Particularly important was the small group activity on New York's 52nd Street that would nurture the rise of the bebop style of the 1940s. The context of jazz combos also suited the budding jukebox record industry.

Jukeboxes were widely accepted in black clubs and, consequently, led to the increased recording of black jazz artists. The records were made cheaply and informally, usually comprising popular songs intended to promote sheet music sales and the black artists who rarely got radio exposure. Red Allen and Coleman Hawkins made a series of remarkable recordings in 1933, which were followed by other casually produced sessions by John Hammond and Milt Gabler of Commodore Records. Another staple in small group recording was The Chocolate Dandies, not a real band but a working name for various assemblages of musicians between 1928 and 1933. The greatest benefactor of the jukebox system was Harlem stride pianist Fats Waller. Already well established as a pianist and songwriter, he was signed as "Fats Waller and His Rhythm" in 1934 and embarked on a lucrative career as a celebrity comedian and singer on a par with Louis Armstrong. He subsequently got his own national radio program and made numerous film appearances (Priestley 1991, pp. 57-59).

Duke Ellington

Throughout the 1930s, Duke Ellington (1899–1974) continued to expand his orchestra in size and stylistic scope. It would seem that most bands of the time evolved along similar lines, descended in some way from the concepts of the Fletcher Henderson or Bennie Moten bands. Duke Ellington, like Thelonious Monk a generation later, was part of these contemporary developments but was in many ways apart from them – even above them.

In 1931, Ellington's orchestra finished its long, fruitful incubation period at Harlem's Cotton Club. In that context, Ellington stabilized his personnel and had the opportunity to write massive amounts of inventive and daring compositions. He would spend the 1930s negotiating his two musical worlds: the emerging swing music craze and his own blossoming realization of an ambitious jazz classicism. Indeed, two of his early 1930s works are indicative of these two pursuits. *It Don't Mean a Thing if It Ain't Got That Swing* not only became a huge hit in 1932, but employed the term "swing" at least two years before it came into popular use as a designation for a style of popular music. A year earlier, Ellington broke the three- to four-minute time limit for jazz pieces imposed by the 78 r.p.m. disc with his *Creole Rhapsody*.

Two Ellington works from 1935 were also of extended length: *Symphony in Black* was nine minutes long and *Reminiscing in Tempo* stretched to thirteen minutes. *Reminiscing in Tempo* stands out from other longer Ellington works in that it shows perhaps the finest formal and developmental control he ever exercised. He avoided his usual lengthening strategies of a multi-thematic single piece, a multi-movement suite of short songs, or the extension of an otherwise short piece through improvisation. *Reminiscing* is restricted to one main theme, a secondary theme, a couple of transitional passages, and a four-chord vamp. Ellington casts the theme in a variety of keys, registers, harmonic contexts, and instrumentations. He drew heavily upon his intimate knowledge of the unique tonal quality of his individual bandmembers for his developmental decisions. He did not, however, draw upon their improvisational input, using only prescribed solos (Schuller 1989, pp. 76–78). Ellington continued his assault on the regularity of the four-measure phrase in *Reminiscing*, creating twenty- and thirty-measure structures subdivided into groups of ten, fourteen, and eighteen measures. These phrasing irregularities give an effect of seamlessness and offer a balance of the predictable and the unpredictable in the unfolding of the piece.

In the latter half of the 1930s, Ellington experienced significant changes in the personnel of his band. He dismissed his first bassist, Wellman Braud, and for a time carried two bassists. They were eventually supplanted by young Jimmy Blanton, who contributed most in revolutionizing the concept and possibilities of the jazz bass, bringing it to prominence as a solo instrument. Veteran jazzman Ben Webster became Ellington's first tenor saxophone star.

The recording sessions from the spring of 1940 exhibit Ellington at the top of his compositional form, producing a series of works ranging from swinging dance numbers to dramatic concert miniatures. He culminated some of his older concepts – such as the plunger trumpet work of Cootie Williams and the three-trombone choir comprised of Lawrence Brown, Joe "Tricky Sam" Nanton, and Juan Tizol – and combined them with the innovative sound and technique of cornetist Rex Stewart, Webster, and Blanton. *Concerto for Cootie*, *Harlem Air Shaft*, *Cottontail*, and his blues masterpiece *Ko-Ko* were all recorded in 1940.

The transition to bebop

Just as the larger public came to know and accept swing music, jazz was already in transition to a newer, more eclectic style. Pianist Art Tatum and tenor saxophonist Coleman Hawkins forged new paths in the harmonic approach to jazz. Hawkins's main tenor rival, Lester Young, developed new concepts of phrasing. Trumpeter Roy Eldridge (1911–1989) extended both the range and speed of the trumpet, building on the technical innovations begun by Louis Armstrong a generation earlier. Texas guitarist Charlie Christian (1916–1942) popularized the use of the amplified electric guitar, elevating the role of the guitar from a soft, delicate rhythm instrument to a powerful front-line instrument capable of soloing over the volume of a whole band. Drummers Jo Jones (1911–1985) and Kenny Clarke (1914–1985) shifted the constant swing rhythmic pattern from the hi-hat or "sock" cymbal to the suspended, or "ride," cymbal, creating a lighter pulse.

With the onset of World War II, several factors impacted on American music and the music business. Rationing of gasoline and shellac reduced the ability of bands to travel and for record companies to produce discs in large quantities. Entertainment taxes and the shortage of male dancers curtailed dance hall business. There were disputes between the American Federations of Musicians and the recording industry and between the American Society of Composers, Authors, and Publishers and the

National Association of Broadcasters. Bands and band members who were
not drafted into military service came off the road and clustered into the
great urban centers, particularly New York City. For practical as well as
artistic reasons, most jazz ensembles working on the new music were small
combos comprised of two horns, piano, bass, and drums. This format
allowed for more casual performances and the ability to "jam," to improvise more without the constraints of a formal arrangement.

   The modern small group activity was centered at Minton's Playhouse in
Harlem and a cluster of clubs on Manhattan's 52nd Street. In these settings, older swing masters met with the new rising stars. Dr. Billy Taylor, a
New York pianist from this era, referred to the music as "pre-bop," a
transitional style that still drew heavily from the swing style but was
showing signs of modernity as the young artists began to coalesce their
innovations and assert themselves stylistically. An excellent example of the
transition from the older guard to the new is the relationship between Roy
Eldridge and John Birks "Dizzy" Gillespie (1917–1993). Eldridge drew
his inspiration from cornetist Rex Stewart, who had himself taken his style
from both Louis Armstrong and Bix Beiderbecke. However, Eldridge also
based his style on the harmonically innovative and running eighth-note
laden improvisations of saxophonist Coleman Hawkins. In early recordings of Gillespie, we hear the strong influence of Eldridge in his playing. In
fact, his first major employment in New York was as Eldridge's replacement in the Teddy Hill band.

   Gillespie first formed his innovations in his writing. It was sometime
later before he successfully and completely integrated his mature style into
his solo improvisations. *Pickin' the Cabbage* (Cab Calloway band, 1940),
Down Under (Woody Herman, 1942), *A Night in Tunisia* (Boyd Raeburn,
1944), and *Woody 'n You* (Coleman Hawkins, 1944) show musical devices
that were to pervade bebop. The sound of the tritone interval was paramount: as a melodic interval, as a root movement in a harmonic progression, as an alternate dominant chord function, and as a color tone in a
chordal sonority. Melodic lines outline more extended tertian chord tones,
such as the eleventh, thirteenth, raised or lowered fifths or ninths. The harmonic rhythm was faster. By 1944, Gillespie had established himself on
52nd Street as a bandleader, composer, soloist, and celebrity, and he was
successfully executing the new concepts in his improvised solos.

   Alto saxophonist Charlie Parker (1920–1955) developed along similar
lines in Kansas City. He drew from the older swing masters, particularly
Lester Young and local alto saxophonist Buster "Prof" Smith. He devel-

oped the ability to sustain long strings of eighth notes at rapid tempos. He favored popular songs with difficult chord progressions as his vehicles for improvisation, particularly the formidable *Cherokee*, by Ray Noble. It became a speciality number for him; there are several extant recordings of his *Cherokee* improvisations dating back to 1942 and culminating with his monumental recording of *Ko-Ko* for Savoy in 1945. As with Dizzy Gillespie, we can hear in this progression of style the gradual discarding of swing style phrasing for a newer, personal approach. Among Parker's unique contributions to bebop is the irregular phrasing he employed. His composition *Relaxin' at Camarillo* (1947) employs off-beat accents and hemiola to obscure the underlying 4/4 meter. His improvisation on *Klacktoveedsedsteene* (1947) displaces the four-measure phrasing and the melodic outlining of the underlying harmony by two beats.

Parker permanently settled in New York in 1944 and, soon thereafter, teamed up with Dizzy Gillespie. Parker and Gillespie became a stylistic binary weapon, mapping the course for much of the New York jazz scene. The later 1940s was an era of extreme standardization. The previous decade saw jazz styles that were more idiomatic to the instruments on which they were played but, after the dawn of the bop era, trombonists, guitarists, bassists, and pianists all attempted to adapt the melodic and harmonic approach of Parker and Gillespie. Gillespie's influence was disseminated as much by his teaching as by his performing. With adequate keyboard skills and an affable, open personality, Gillespie was able and willing to pass along the theory behind the music to emerging young musicians as well as the old guard interested in updating their approach. Parker was more aloof, teaching more by example.

Thelonious Monk (1917–1982) was also one of the founding fathers of the bebop style, but soon took his own unique direction, much as Duke Ellington had done within the context of swing big bands. Like Ellington, he was much more of a composer and musical colorist than many of his peers. In contrast to the typical phrasing of Parker and Gillespie, Monk composed and improvised around small, organic motifs and long silences. Instead of employing the rich, tertian harmonic figurations of other bebop pianists, he stripped his chords down to bare, sometimes abrasive, pairs of notes. Rather than using a fleet, smooth technique aspired to by other bop musicians, Monk adopted a deliberate awkwardness that suited the idiosyncratic phrasing of his compositions.

Monk had an approach to improvisation that stood apart from his bop peers. At a time when improvisers cherished creating busy new melodies to the chord progression – "blowing over the changes" – Monk harkened the philosophy of another great colorist/composer in jazz history, Jelly Roll Morton, who said "Never discard the melody" (Lomax 1993, p. 63). His solos were often elaborate paraphrases of his prescribed melodies, maintaining a consistency of musical character throughout the performance. Though this approach was the one he preferred for his own improvising, he did not require it of the other musicians in his group. Two of his tenor saxophonists, Johnny Griffin and John Coltrane, both used dense flurries of notes in their solos. Coltrane, in fact, entered his so-called "sheets of sound" period while with Monk and during his subsequent return to the Miles Davis band. Vibraphonist Milt Jackson was another 52nd Street bebop-style improviser who made many early and important recordings with Monk. By all indications, Monk not only tolerated but enjoyed the dichotomy between his motivic/thematic improvisational approach and the episodic change-running of his sidemen.

In the 1940s, Monk proved too ahead of his time. Some musicians and critics felt he was a musical hoax, eccentric and lacking in technique. Though he made some significant recordings for the Blue Note label in the late 1940s and early 1950s, the acclaim due him would have to wait for his Riverside recordings in the latter half of the 1950s. A much more influential figure among bop pianists was Bud Powell (1924–1964). Grounded in thorough classical piano training, Powell played with quick, sure technique, successfully translating the language of Parker and Gillespie's horn phrasing to the piano. Within the piano tradition, he consolidated the lighter texture of Earl Hines, Teddy Wilson, Billy Kyle, and Nat Cole, the "locked-hands" technique of Milt Buckner, and the speed and harmonic richness of Art Tatum. On top of that, he was probably the only convincing replicator of the elusive Thelonious Monk style. Like Monk, he began recording for Blue Note in the late 1940s and continued into the next decade. Unfortunately, Powell was plagued with mental illness, causing intermittent lapses in both the quality and quantity of his recorded output.

Dizzy Gillespie was also responsible for reinjecting Latin rhythms into jazz. A key ingredient in early jazz, the "Spanish tinge," as Jelly Roll Morton called it, had been eradicated by and large through the swing years. Gillespie got his first introduction to Latin music from trumpeter Mario Bauza, with whom he played in the Teddy Hill band. Soon afterward, he played in a Latin band led by Alberto Socarras which, to everyone's benefit, "Latinized" jazz and "Americanized" Socarras's style. Hints of Latin rhythm were revealed in the early Gillespie compositions *Woody 'n You* and *A Night in Tunisia*. In 1945, Gillespie formed a big band to bring the streamlined bop concept to that genre and, by 1947, sought to add a conga player and a Latin approach to the band. Chano Pozo (1915–1948) was a Cuban drummer working in New York. With Gillespie and his arranger, Gil Fuller, Pozo conceived *Manteca*, and composed *Cubano Be* with Gillespie and arranger George Russell. His stunning solo work and duet *montunos* with Gillespie started a trend of bongos, congas, and Latin rhythms in jazz and popular orchestras of the day.

Big bands in the bebop era

During and after the war years, existing big bands and newly formed ensembles began experimenting with less commercial, more artistic approaches. They not only sought to integrate the musical language of the 52nd Street scene, but to reawaken an interest in the incorporation of modern Western art music. There were several reasons for this tendency. The "big band era" of the 1930s was waning. The players and writers grew tired of the constraints of format, style, and tempo inherent in the big band model. An increasing number of young, ambitious, well-schooled musicians took up jazz, enamored with the language of Western art music modernists such as Stravinsky, Bartók, and Schoenberg. They saw jazz and classical music similarly as art, so they combined them, hoping for a music that was thoughtful, well-crafted, and original. Above all else the jazz community had a genuine need to create and perform *art* music, to disassociate their music from crass commercialism, its function merely as dance music, and to rescue both musical traditions from stasis by dismantling public stereotypes and expectations, leaving the way open for uninhibited musical exploration. As Stan Kenton told jazz writer Nat Hentoff:

> Jazz for a long time was mixed up with pop music. Now, as it has always been in Europe, jazz is being differentiated from pop music as well as classical music. The modernists deserve the credit for proving that jazz doesn't have to be danced to . . . As a matter of fact, I don't think jazz was meant to continue as dance music. People got the idea just because it was confused with pop music . . . Jazz has to develop; it can't always remain functional dance music.

> (Hentoff 1952, p. 6)

Kenton's statement is symptomatic of the psyche that distinguishes jazz from almost every other genre of music. It is constantly struggling to establish its image along the continuum from popular music to art music. Whereas blues, rhythm and blues, country, and rock have never had a problem being associated with popular music and the music business, jazz – particularly during and after World War II – became self-conscious of its popular music heritage. Jazz artists increasingly sought to distance their music from popular expectations, to achieve the status of "art music" without sacrificing the inherent musical characteristics of jazz.

One of the early big bands to make the transition from swing to bop was Woody Herman's. "The Band That Played the Blues" was formed in 1936 by former members of the Isham Jones band and had a major hit with *Woodchopper's Ball* in 1939. Herman (1913–1987) began looking for a new sound, inspired by the rich tonal palette of Duke Ellington's band and the burgeoning bebop style as it was being developed by Dizzy Gillespie. Herman, in fact, commissioned two compositions from Gillespie. It was around 1944, however, that he assembled his "First Herd," a group of exuberant, hard-driving players that combined the riffing blues of the Kansas City tradition and the bop style that was just maturing. Like most of the big bands that hoped to survive in the post-war era, Herman was able to combine artistic exploration and popular appeal. They had a huge following and a commercially sponsored radio show. The chief engineers of the First Herd sound were pianist Ralph Burns and trumpeter Neal Hefti. (In the 1950s, Hefti would be the arranger who shaped the "New Testament" Count Basie band.)

Along with appealing to the masses, the Herman band also won the admiration of no less than Igor Stravinsky. Herman in turn commissioned Stravinsky to compose *Ebony Concerto*, which was premiered at Carnegie Hall in 1946. Met with tepid reviews, particularly from the jazz press, *Ebony Concerto* was emblematic of the bewilderment felt by both classical music and jazz zealots as jazz artists explored the possibilities of a jazz/classical fusion.

Pianist Claude Thornhill (1909–1965) formed his big band in the early 1940s and soon arrived at a unique sound that won him *Down Beat* readers' poll awards in both the "sweet" and "hot" band categories. He augmented the traditional big band instrumentation with two French horns and tuba. The reed section was sometimes expanded to as many as seven clarinets. His orchestrations and sound concept for the individual musicians created a soft, pastel tonal color, closer to the sound of a wind ensemble than a jazz band. The Thornhill band began its inclusion of bebop concepts when arranger Gil Evans (1912–1988) came over from the Skinnay Ennis orchestra. Evans's arrangements ran the gamut from the lush *La Paloma* to furious renditions of bebop standards *Yardbird Suite*, *Anthropology*, and *Donna Lee*.

By the late 1940s, Gil Evans's apartment near 52nd Street became a conservatory, a musical think tank for young writers, including Thornhill members John Carisi (1922–1992) and Gerry Mulligan (1927–1996). From this environment came a rehearsal band of six wind instruments and three rhythm instruments, a writers' workshop seeking to develop a smaller version of the Thornhill sound. The personnel of the group was a cross-section of 52nd Street musicians, headed by trumpeter Miles Davis. The "Birth of the Cool" band, as it would be dubbed in later years, was virtually ignored through its short existence. The dozen or so recordings made for the Capitol label did not really catch on until they were reissued as a single LP in the early 1950s.

The "cool" concept the Birth of the Cool band supposedly spawned actually reaches back to the musical approach of Bix Beiderbecke (1903–1931). In contrast to the "hot" style of Louis Armstrong, Beiderbecke fostered a softer timbre, an elegant and less flamboyant musical personality, and a penchant for modernism that included integration of modern Western art music. Beiderbecke's understated swing and intimate, yet virile, ballad style was reflected in the playing of his saxophonist colleague Frank Trumbauer. Trumbauer, particularly through his recording of *Singin' the Blues* with Beiderbecke, became the model for swing saxophonist Lester Young. Beiderbecke's and Young's softer sound approach was imitated by bebop players such as saxophonists Wardell Gray, Allen Eager, Lee Konitz, and Warne Marsh. The "soft" or "cool" sound in bop came to be represented not only by the timbre of the instruments, but also in the phrasing of melodic lines, the combinations of unusual instruments used in the orchestrations, and the complex, rich harmonic vocabulary that created textural density and softness rather than dissonance (Hodeir 1956, pp. 116–139).

A modernist approach was also to be found on the West Coast; its chief proponent was the Stan Kenton orchestra of Los Angeles, the most unique and longest lasting emblem of classical–jazz confluence. Like Duke Ellington, Woody Herman, and Claude Thornhill, Stan Kenton (1911–1979) knew how to balance making commercial hits against artistic pursuits, using the former to subsidize the latter. What set him apart was his ability to sell his artistic wares to the general public. Even at his most uncompromising, he filled concert halls with people, making it fashionable to be a discriminating listener to esoteric music.

Kenton evokes extremes of opinion, either worshipful devotion or scathing criticism and hatred. Everyone will agree that subtlety is lost on the Kenton style. Both he and his orchestra were large, imposing figures. His ten-man brass section (before you include the occasional section of French horns or mellophoniums) delved into the extremes of range and volume. The music was often pretentious, pompous, and overdone. Kenton believed in the adage that it was better to be hated than unnoticed. There was the perennial accusation that his band did not swing. But, as Kenton arranger Pete Rugolo stated, "... it wasn't suppose to swing. Stan was trying to do a different kind of music ... It did have a beat here and there, but it didn't always have to go 4/4. And a lot of it didn't have any beat at all. They were concert pieces with a jazz sound" (Friedwald 1991).

The writers Kenton used were as far removed from the New York modernist scene as was he. Pete Rugolo (born 1915) studied with Darius Milhaud at Mills College in Oakland, California (as did Dave Brubeck and Cal Tjader). Bill Russo (born 1928) was a Chicagoan who studied with Lennie Tristano. Bill Holman studied at the Westlake College of Music in Los Angeles. Robert Graettinger (1923–1957), another Westlake student who studied extensively with studio arranger Russell Garcia, was the most enigmatic of Kenton's composers. He epitomized the intensity of Kenton's commitment to modernism – with or without deference to jazz style – in his 1948 (rev. 1951) composition *City of Glass*.

Kenton dubbed his music "progressive jazz," a tongue-in-cheek working title that stuck because no-one could come up with anything better. Pete Rugolo recalled, "It caused a whole new thing in music. It was the first time anyone wrote music that sounded very modern, like Stravinsky and Bartók ... Bernstein ... (and) Milhaud, whom I studied with. Nobody had that kind of sound before in jazz or big band music. I wrote 5/4 bars, 3/4 bars, 1/4 bars" (Daryll 1992).

Capitol Records was an important patron and documentor of the cool bop and jazz/classical style. Kenton was a staple artist for Capitol. In New York, the label recorded the Evans/Davis nine-piece Birth of the Cool band. During this same period, 1949 to 1950, Capitol also recorded a combo overseen by pianist Lennie Tristano (1919–1978). Tristano came to New York from Chicago in 1945, already established as a maverick stylist, a technical and intellectual genius, and one of the first formal jazz pedagogues. His band included his prize students: alto saxophonist Lee Konitz, tenor saxophonist Warne Marsh, and guitarist Billy Bauer. While an admirer of Dizzy Gillespie and Charlie Parker, Tristano was disgusted with the large number of their imitators. He and his bandmates created light, energetic, rhythmically elusive and tonally daring compositions and improvisations quite unlike anything Parker, Gillespie, or Monk had conceived. In fact, the Tristano group did the first recorded experiments in so-called "free jazz" during their 1949–1950 Capitol sessions.

The 1950s

The decade of the 1920s was more or less defined by the New Orleans and Chicago jazz styles, the 1930s by swing music, and the 1940s by bebop; but jazz of the 1950s comprised myriad styles with labels such as hard bop, cool bop, funky, third stream, modal, and free. This marked a new and remarkable phase in jazz, indicative of its artistic growth. The coexisting substyles reflected the ethnic, geographic, and aesthetic diversity of their practitioners, and led to much debate over the essence and ownership of jazz.

The 1950s began with conflicts over the mainstream bebop style born of Dizzy Gillespie and Charlie Parker and the white-dominated cool style. To some, it would appear that white musicians had once again tried their hand at an essentially African American music and eclipsed the black artists in popularity and financial success. The "cool" sound was defined by soft instrumental timbres, smoother phrasing, a noticeable absence of blues essence, and an almost transparent rhythm section pulse. While not lacking in energy or intellect, the cool sound was palatable and unimposing on listeners, giving them the option of meditating deeply on the music or relegating it to innocuous background music. It became particularly popular among the bohemian college crowd, so much so that one jazz group, the Dave Brubeck Quartet, began actively courting university program boards for concert bookings on campuses. Their following grew by leaps and bounds, culminating in best-selling records for the Columbia label.

Jazz histories have commonly used the terms "cool jazz" and "West Coast jazz" interchangeably. This may lead one to believe that the cool sound began in California. Conversely, it is been held by some that migrating New York cool schoolers, such as Lee Konitz and Gerry Mulligan, brought the cool style with them to the West. In fact, the cool approach developed on both coasts at the same time; only later did they cross-fertilize styles and artists. The West Coast cool was developed primarily by members and former members of the Stan Kenton orchestra such as

Lennie Niehaus and Shorty Rogers. It is only coincidental that Kenton's own propensity for modernism was realized when bebop was just coming to full flower in New York. Bebop was an addendum to a notion Kenton had been holding since the 1930s. Indeed, the most dangerous aspect of Kenton to the jazz mainstream of the 1940s was that he rendered eastern bebop almost irrelevant. It is not that Kenton was naive of bop or rejected it. His sidemen included Lee Konitz, Gerry Mulligan, Stan Getz, and Gil Evans – some of the most important figures of the New York "cool school." There was tenor saxophonist Vido Musso, veteran of the Benny Goodman band. But Kenton also had some of the most formidable bop stylists from the West Coast, particularly alto saxophonists Charlie Mariano and Art Pepper, trombonist Frank Rosolino, and drummer Shelly Manne.

Hard bop

Back in New York, efforts were being made by the black bop artists to reclaim the strong beat, extroversion, and African American elements of jazz. It is therefore no coincidence that the "hard bop" style of the 1950s was dominated by drummers: Kenny Clarke, Max Roach, Art Blakey (1919-1990), and "Philly" Joe Jones (1923-1985). All of these men brought the assertive beat back to jazz and, in their various ways, made the drum set as much an interactive and conversational instrument as it was a mere timekeeper. As early as the late 1930s, Kenny Clarke had lightened the basic pulse of swing by moving it to the ride cymbal, reserving the snare and bass drum for occasional accents, or "bombs." Max Roach was the first true polyrhythmic drummer, developing complex rhythmic interaction between his four limbs. Art Blakey's timekeeping was characterized by a crushing hi-hat on the second and fourth beats of the measure. Philly Joe Jones also played with a strong, authoritative style that may have reflected his rhythm and blues roots.

Rhythm and blues had an interesting relationship to jazz. It developed in the 1940s, partly derived from the simple, blues-based "riffing" style of the Kansas City swing bands. As bebop developed and jazz became more instrumentally abstract and inaccessible, the jazz audience split into three factions. Some accepted bebop and continued to support it. White audiences who rejected bop embraced a revival of older New Orleans and Chicago jazz styles, played either by young, white bands or by older black musicians who had played the music in its heyday. Blacks who rejected bop went with rhythm and blues, giving rise to stars like Louis Jordan

(1908–1975) and Lionel Hampton (born 1909). R&B was a necessary evil and an irritant in the eyes of some young black jazz musicians, many of whom began their careers in R&B bands, artistically shackled until their big break came to move full-time into jazz playing. R&B was something to be eventually transcended.

Nevertheless, rhythm and blues was a kindred music that came from the same primordial musical soup as jazz. It continued to be a strong essence and exerted influence on the hard boppers, however sophisticated and above it all they might have felt. The hard boppers' reinjection of earthy, bluesy elements into jazz was in some cases the reclamation of the African American tradition the cool approach had diminished; however, some hard bop artists integrated the strong beat, tunefulness, and earthy character of blues and black gospel music for its own intrinsic musical charm, with no particular cultural agenda in mind. Key among these artists was Horace Silver (born 1929). Silver was not a product of the blues tradition of the South, but a Connecticut native whose father had immigrated from the Portuguese Cape Verdean Islands, situated off the coast of Senegal. Like so many youngsters of his generation, he was fascinated by the exciting performances of the Jimmie Lunceford orchestra, the raw energy and emotion of Chicago rhythm and blues artists like Muddy Waters and Howlin' Wolf, and the exoticism and rhythmic momentum of Latin music. He combined these styles with bebop and brought this personal approach to New York in the early 1950s. In cooperation with drummer Art Blakey, trumpeter Miles Davis and others, he introduced the "funky" style that successfully negotiated between the popular audience and the jazz artistic community. His label, Blue Note, quickly embraced the upbeat, churchy, melodic style as a formula for its other jazz artists as record sales soared. A token "funky" hit single was expected from future Blue Note recordings, yielding classics such as Bobby Timmons's *Moanin'* (with Art Blakey and the Jazz Messengers), Lee Morgan's *Sidewinder* and *Cornbread*, and Herbie Hancock's *Watermelon Man*. Once again, jazz found itself in an ambiguous position between art and commerce.

"Third stream"

The blending of Latin, blues, and hard bop proved to be an aesthetically valid and commercially appealing venture. A stylistic hybridization that would prove much more problematic and controversial was the continued and intensified confluence of jazz and Western art music. The two central figures of this effort were Gunther Schuller (born 1925) and John Lewis (born 1920), leader of the Modern Jazz Quartet. Gunther Schuller, son of a New York Philharmonic violinist, was a child prodigy, developing into a formidable French horn player while still a teenager. From his earliest days, however, he had an interest in jazz, and much of his activity outside the Metropolitan Opera orchestra involved New York's 52nd Street, epicenter of the jazz scene. Observation turned to participation in late 1949 and early 1950 when Schuller became involved in the Birth of the Cool band.

Schuller divided his attention between his two musical worlds: composition in the manner of Schoenberg and Webern, and jazz composition. He was not trying to consciously legitimize or improve jazz by combining it with art music, but was seeking ways to expand its possibilities. The ongoing problem with jazz, as far as the classical world was concerned, was its limitation to short, cyclic forms, such as the twelve-bar blues form or the AABA thirty-two-measure popular song form. Both Schuller and Lewis felt that employing techniques of longer thematic development and multiple contrasting themes or sections within a composition would take jazz to the next logical step in its evolution and, consequently, resolve a significant shortcoming, as the classical music community saw it. John Lewis told journalist Nat Hentoff,

> the audience for our work can be widened if we strengthen our work with structure . . . I do not think, however, that the sections in this structured jazz – both the improvised and written sections – should take on too much complexity. The total effect must be within the mind's ability to appreciate through the ear. Also, the music will have to swing.
>
> (Goldberg 1965, p. 124)

Unfortunately, the music often did not swing. Use of traditionally non-jazz instruments played by non-jazz players often robbed performances of this confluent music of any swing. Another major problem was the dictatorial nature of the ambitiously written prescribed music on the improvising soloist. Forms were too long and complex to elicit any real freedom of improvisation, which was certainly by this time the ideal in jazz performance practice.

One of the most visible occasions for this stylistic experiment was the 1957 Brandeis University Festival of Creative Arts in Waltham, Massachusetts. For this occasion, Schuller was able to commission six works from colleagues in both the jazz and classical communities, including Charles Mingus, George Russell, Milton Babbitt, John Lewis, and himself. In a lecture, Schuller referred to this confluent music as a "third stream," fed by the two streams of jazz and European art music traditions. However sincere the efforts, the aesthetic and cultural differences between the two original streams were too great, and third stream music convinced few people in any camp.

Miles Davis

Miles Davis (1926–1990) played a major role in every jazz sub-style since the establishment of bebop. Upon his arrival in New York from St. Louis in 1945, he began performing with Charlie Parker. Within three years, he was an established leader and stylist in the New York jazz community. In 1949, Davis explored the cool style by fronting the Birth of the Cool nonet. In his 1954 recording of Richard Carpenter's *Walkin'* for the Prestige label, he explored both the funky style of hard bop (Horace Silver was, in fact, the pianist on the session) and the new recorded performance format of the long-play record.

In the early 1950s, neither Davis's style nor the personnel of his band were settled. He was battling heroin addiction and still standing in the long stylistic shadow of Dizzy Gillespie. By mid-decade, however, he was free of his addiction, had established a stable quintet of masterful players, and found a way to pursue the hard bop style on his own terms. It was a group that flourished in its contradictions: the hard-driving rhythm of drummer Philly Joe Jones versus the modest piano approach of Red Garland (1923–1984), or the powerful tone and muscular phrasing of tenor saxophonist John Coltrane compared to the fragile sound and spacious phrasing of Davis. This first great Miles Davis quintet is best represented in a series of recordings made during a marathon session for Prestige in 1955.

By 1956, Davis had officially moved over to Columbia Records, where he involved himself in yet another substyle of 1950s jazz. He participated in a "third stream" brass choir involving Gunther Schuller and bop trombonist and composer J. J. Johnson (born 1924), inspiring him to rekindle his working relationship with arranger Gil Evans. The net result was a series of albums for solo trumpet and wind orchestra. The first, *Miles Ahead*, was a series of ten pieces by different composers, arranged and edited to sound like one continuous multi-movement work. The second album, *Porgy and Bess*, resulted from the renewed popularity in 1958 of the Gershwin opera. The third album, *Sketches of Spain*, born of Davis's interest in Hispanic art music, was the least "jazzy" in style. It also demonstrated Davis's emerging interest in a modal approach to jazz.

This modal approach involved compositions with few or no chord changes and playing an appropriate mode over the key center. Bop and hard bop artists had responded to their new artistic freedom by composing short, strophic chord change cycles, averaging about sixteen measures in length. Exemplified by Eddie Vinson's *Tune Up*, Sonny Rollins's *Pent-Up House*, and epitomized by John Coltrane's *Giant Steps*, these "exercise" pieces involved chord changes as often as every two beats, played at fast tempos. Davis eventually saw this tendency as too stifling for creative improvising and sought to create a more expansive musical environment. Davis's modal playing first appeared in the soundtrack to the Louis Malle film *Ascenseur pour l'echafaud*, in the title track to the 1958 Columbia album *Milestones*, and in the 1959 *Sketches of Spain*. The most celebrated presentation of the modal concept was the album *Kind of Blue*, a variety of pieces utilizing modality and unconventional forms. Modal playing was the first cautious step toward an even freer format for improvising jazz. It would be a staple concept for John Coltrane's great quartet of the early 1960s.

Toward free jazz

As mentioned earlier, the first tentative attempts at improvising with no prescribed music, key, or form on recordings were done by Lennie Tristano's sextet in 1949 and 1950. The tracks were largely dismissed as tangential; in fact, the recording engineers erased two of the cuts, assuming they were only casual studio experiments not intended for release. In the course of the 1950s, "third stream" experiments with more atonal, free improvising took place but they made no significant impact on the jazz scene. In the last half of the decade, more compelling and high profile free jazz was produced by artists such as Charles Mingus, Ornette Coleman, Cecil Taylor, and Sun Ra.

Charles Mingus (1922–1978) grew up in Los Angeles and became one of the premier bassists in bebop, but his greater legacy was as a composer. Deeply influenced by the music of Duke Ellington, Charlie Parker, and Thelonious Monk, he also combined elements of raw folk blues and gospel music, theatre music and twentieth-century composition. His music was scantily, even haphazardly prepared for the musicians, and was performed in a semi-chaotic and always highly emotional manner reflective of Mingus's own volatile and unpredictable personality. Like Ellington's,

Mingus's music was often shaped by the unique style and character of his sidemen. The success and distinctiveness of his music is a tribute to artists like trombonist Jimmy Knepper, tenor saxophonist Booker Ervin, and Mingus's most faithful sideman, drummer Dannie Richmond. Sidemen such as Rahsaan Roland Kirk and Eric Dolphy added freer, more daring elements to Mingus's music. Mingus also wrote his share of "third stream" compositions. His *Chill of Death* and *Half-Mast Inhibition* were written in 1939 and 1940 respectively, while he was still a teenager. In 1957 he composed *Revelations* for the Brandeis Festival and *Meditations on Integration* in the early 1960s.

Ornette Coleman (born 1930) found his way into the jazz limelight through the "third stream" movement. Born and raised in Fort Worth, Texas, Coleman was a self-taught alto saxophonist who developed a highly personalized theoretical outlook on music, an approach he would eventually dub "harmolodics." While a clear definition of harmolodics is elusive, the results in Coleman's music are readily evident. His music uses no preset chord progression and little semblance of form. This necessitated the elimination of the piano from his combo's instrumentation. The bassist, devoid of chords or form, had to follow and interact with the soloist. The drummer developed a dual role of timekeeper and musical conversationalist, sensitive to the spontaneous phrasing being created by the soloist in a formless musical environment. While the nature of each instrumentalist's part may be quite conventional, tuneful, and simple, they often wandered in and out of the key center established by the composition.

Coleman formed his first group in Los Angeles and made two recordings for the Contemporary label, *Something Else!!!* and *Tomorrow Is the Question!*. Diluted by the use of a pianist and personnel from outside his primary group, the performances were seriously compromised and the public response was tepid. However, one of the bassists on the session, the Modern Jazz Quartet's Percy Heath, brought Coleman to the attention of John Lewis and, in turn, Gunther Schuller. These leading proponents of the "third stream" movement of the 1950s hailed Coleman as the new Charlie Parker and saw in him a great musical leader who would forge the next significant direction in jazz style. Coleman was signed to Atlantic Records, Lewis's and Schuller's label, and began a three-year run of innovative quartet and "third stream" recordings.

Ramblin' (*Change of the Century*, 1959) is an exemplary Ornette Coleman composition. It is a "blues," but does not follow a strict blues form. It is a simple and charming piece, pervaded with folk music elements. With a key center of D, the theme unfolds in three phrases (patterned after the three-line blues) that imply the harmonic progression I–IV–I. Coleman plays the first solo on a plastic alto saxophone. He preferred the instrument for its breathier, more human sound. He draws heavily on folk blues phrases and even includes a quotation from the folksong *Arkansas Traveler*. The underlying form is comprised of a sixteen-measure drone on the D tonality by bassist Charlie Haden, followed by a twelve-measure walking bass pattern. Haden's solo is equally folksy in character, resembling a fiddle or banjo tune. In fact, a good portion of his solo involves a rendition of *Ol' Joe Clark*.

Masterpieces like *Lonely Woman*, *Congeniality*, and *Focus on Sanity* were equally influential on the jazz community. The 1960 album *Free Jazz* was Coleman's *magnum opus* from this early Atlantic period. The group comprised two pianoless quartets, separated by stereo. The performance is delineated by several statements of brief themes that serve only to introduce each solo section. Behind each soloist, the other instrumentalists spontaneously interact with the soloist or with each other. It was a daring and groundbreaking event in the evolution of jazz.

Ornette Coleman's music was by no means universally appealing. While some hailed him as an innovative genius and the leader into a new era of jazz, others thought him a complete charlatan. Trumpeter Roy Eldridge told *Esquire* magazine in 1961, "I listened to him high and I listened to him cold sober. I even played with him. I think he's jiving, baby" (quoted in *Esquire* 1962, p. 202). Miles Davis told Joe Goldberg, "Hell, just listen to what he writes and how he plays. If you're talking psychologically, the man is all screwed up inside" (Palmer 1995). Others were more sympathetic and excited by Coleman's music. One was John Coltrane, the saxophonist who first came to prominence with Miles Davis in the mid-1950s. Upon hearing Coleman's concept, he immediately began exploring free jazz himself, even recording an album, *The Avant-Garde*, with the Coleman group.

John Coltrane

In a ten-year period, roughly 1955 through 1965, John Coltrane (1926–1967) evolved from obscure and relatively unpopular sideman to one of the most influential giants in jazz history. His combination of intensity and modesty, practicum and spirituality, virtuosity and lyricism set a new standard and gave new meaning to playing music.

Born in North Carolina, he moved to Philadelphia in 1943. He started out as a Parker-style alto player, befriending many of the local jazz artists such as Benny Golson and Jimmy and Percy Heath. He switched to tenor during a tenure with an R&B band and finally joined Miles Davis in 1955. He made his mark through the 1955 series of Prestige recordings and on the early Columbia recordings.

In 1957, Davis fired him because of his poor performance due to heroin addiction. It was a fateful year for Coltrane. His rid himself of his habit and performed with Thelonious Monk for several months. His association with Monk led him to a more personal concept in his playing, wherein he created phrases of long, furious runs that critic Ira Gitler dubbed "sheets of sound" (Gitler 1958). Coltrane also made his first recording as leader for the Prestige label in 1957. His victory over his addiction also led to a great spiritual awakening that would be musically as well as personally fruitful. In the liner notes to his 1964 album *A Love Supreme*, Coltrane proclaimed, "During the year 1957, I experienced, by the grace of God, a spiritual awakening which was to lead me to a richer, fuller, more productive life. At that time, in gratitude, I humbly asked to be given the means and privilege to make others happy through music. I feel this has been granted through his grace."

Coltrane rejoined Miles Davis in 1958, the group now expanded to a sextet including Julian "Cannonball" Adderley on alto saxophone. By 1959, Coltrane was actively exploring two lines of musical investigation. On the one hand, he followed the hard bop tendency for playing over rapidly moving progressions of chords, epitomized in his *Giant Steps*. Conversely, he participated in the modal concept that culminated in Davis's *Kind of Blue* album. This would be the approach that would shape his most distinctive works in the early sixties with his classic quartet that included drummer Elvin Jones, bassist Jimmy Garrison, and pianist McCoy Tyner.

The 1960s would be Coltrane's age of maturity and influence. He graduated from star sideman and occasional lead artist to a driving force that would affect almost all artists and all bands in jazz. He would even influence rock and fusion. From Joe Henderson to Michael Brecker and the Byrds, Coltrane's amalgam of spirituality and musicianship would pervade the decade.

16

Jazz since 1960

RONALD RADANO

Introduction

One of the most compelling portrayals of jazz develops from the theme of the downtrodden hero. According to this narrative, jazz, as an anthropomorphism of black survival – America's "living art" – endures a precarious existence, trapped within a plebeian and often hostile commercial environment. For a time, the hero narrative worked successfully to perpetuate beliefs in the music's historical and aesthetic coherence. Jazz endured, it seemed, despite the wide range of styles and practices that had emerged since its "birth" in the "cradle" of New Orleans. By the late 1950s, however, many observers had begun to suspect that something was seriously wrong with the musical body, jazz. Having taken for granted its ties to a market economy that required a constant flow of new stars, taste makers and pundits feared that jazz might soon die off unless a new figure of vision could provide a clear stylistic direction. Musical activity in a real sense had not subsided, of course. Journalistic coverage from the period shows that musicians actively performed and recorded in an array of styles, from New Orleans ensemble improvisations to gospel-inflected soul jazz, from "third stream" (a hybrid of jazz and European-based art music) to energetic extensions of bop (Lees 1960). Yet the expectations of innovation, exacerbated by market pressures, led many to believe that any lapse in discernible stylistic growth was a sure sign of a coming "death." As a matter of course, critics and audiences looked hopefully to that next "Great Man" who would build a new kind of jazz based on prior practices.

What ultimately emerged over the next two decades proved so strikingly radical that it not only reinvented traditional performance approaches, but called the very idea of "jazz" into question. With the appearance of free jazz at the turn to the 1960s and the populist-based fusion movement a decade later, creation metaphors of birth and rebirth seemed nearly obsolete. For many, the new era of "Great Men" – Ornette

Coleman (born 1930), Cecil Taylor (born 1929), John Coltrane (1926–1967), Miles Davis (1926–1990), and later, Anthony Braxton (born 1945) – were hardly committed to innovation or tradition. On the contrary, they seemed bent on "one common cause: to destroy the music that gave them birth" (Tynan 1962).

In fact, the conceptual basis for the new radicalism did grow out of ideologies and practices already existing in jazz. By the early 1950s, jazz had been touted a certified art form of democratically "free" expression. It was being championed by performers and composers of art music (André Previn, Gunther Schuller), taught on college campuses, and featured in the form of "Dixieland" at nostalgia concerts in the United States and abroad. Journalists and critics now spoke routinely of a grand, new era of artistic activity nourished by experiments in orchestration and performance that worked against the solid base of "tradition." This critical narrative of "Evolution and Essence" (Hodeir 1956), while perhaps anathema to bop sensibilities, had become increasingly accepted by younger artists who saw bop as a kind of touchstone for a new jazz artistry. Moreover, these visions of jazz as a high art were fueled by larger social patterns of change – among other things, the increased prominence of popular culture as "art"; the decline in the appeal of European-based art music – which exacerbated a leveling of cultural hierarchies once distinguishing "serious" art from pop (Radano 1993, pp. 1–27). Jazz now seemed positioned to assume a central place in a new, American-based international culture, to have finally reached the stature of a deracinated respectable art (Marek 1956).

For the newest innovators, however, jazz would make this advance neither by adhering to tried and true practices nor by recognizing the authority of tradition. Unlike earlier practitioners, who, as Martin Williams has observed, commonly adorned standard approaches by borrowing from outside the genre, the new, post-war generation of artists worked to reconfigure the standards themselves (Williams 1970). Adhering to a modernist belief in the socially progressive effects of art, they worked toward expressions that by exceeding standard practice would articulate new social realities. Indeed, the emancipation of jazz from tradition marked the inception of a kind of anti-period – the point at which a prior construct collapses against the weight of the music's own progress and invention. With each new effort to affirm the music's center, the distance from a perceived prior wholeness grew wider, to the point where even the neoclassical reaffirmations of coherence in the 1980s and 1990s would seem little more than facsimiles of a former likeness.

Modernist and vanguardist innovations
(1960–1969)

The emergence of free jazz can be credited to no single innovator, for its articulation depended on the shared complex of language and culture that defines any given artistic moment. From the beginning of its recorded documentation, revisionist approaches were as common as they were broadly determined. Some artists worked to expand bop-based performance practices by furthering compositional and rhythmic experiment – for instance, the 1955–1961 Riverside releases of Thelonious Monk (1917–1982) or by developing a thematic solo artistry (Sonny Rollins [born 1930], *Tour de Force* [1956], *The Freedom Suite* [1958]). Others explored the linear implications of bop's rapid harmonic rhythms which would ultimately undermine the music's chordal and tonal underpinnings (John Coltrane, *Giant Steps* [1959]). In the seminal modal works of Miles Davis – *Milestones* (1958); *Kind of Blue* (1959) – moreover, subdued tone colors and dynamics and a slowing of the harmonic rhythm effected a kind of classically inspired chamber sound that became increasingly influential into the 1960s. Jazz orchestra composers such as Sun Ra (1914–1993) (*Supersonic Jazz* [1956]), Gunther Schuller (born 1925) (*Jazz Abstractions* [1960], with Ornette Coleman), Gil Evans (1912–1988) (e.g. his version of George Russell's *Stratusphunk*, *Out of the Cool* [1961]), and most notably, Charles Mingus (1922–1979) (*Pithecanthropus Erectus* [1956]; *Mingus Ah Um* [1959]) pursued similar timbral experiments. Working against the background of Ellington's prior achievements, they forged new formal and performative pathways that ultimately reconceptualized big-band style.

Bringing together the extremes of improvisational and compositional experiment was the pianist Cecil Taylor, whose work best outlined the potential for a true art music / jazz hybrid. Between 1956 and 1958 Taylor had realized imaginative syntheses of jazz and modernist abstraction. As both a soloist and ensemble player, he exploited the piano's percussive and dynamic potential to advance a rhythmically explosive virtuosity highlighting brilliant juxtapositions of disparate, abstract sounds. The dramatic physicality and presence of his playing redefined modern piano-jazz artistry, while his aggressive accompaniments challenged the solo/rhythm-section hierarchy of mainstream practice, prefiguring 1960s "collective improvisation." In these latter circumstances, however, Taylor's penchant for a subtle, free-floating sense of tonality and time – vividly expressed in introductions to standards recorded on *Love for Sale*

(1959) and *Stereo Drive* (1958; re-released as *Coltrane Time* in 1962) – also magnified the ordinary playing styles of his sidemen. As a result, the performances themselves, which mixed free abstraction with tenacious commitment to melodic- and meter-based improvisation, seem now from a distance to verge on parody.

If Taylor's innovations represented a high mark of early modernist invention, the work of the Ornette Coleman Quartet – Don Cherry (1936–1995) (cornet, pocket trumpet), Charlie Haden (bass), and Billy Higgins or Ed Blackwell (drums) – identified for many the *Shape of Jazz to Come* (1959). While dismissed by many as a kind of musical joke, Coleman's initial recordings (1958–1960) and public appearances (notably, at New York's Five Spot in November 1959) gained wide approval from a new audience of artists, critics, and intellectuals who were sympathetic to the turn of jazz toward modernist abstraction. Particularly important was the support Coleman received from an elite circle of musicians and critics associated with the Lenox School of Jazz and the influential magazine, *Jazz Review*: Gunther Schuller, John Lewis, and Martin Williams. As they interpreted Coleman's genius within the historical frames of an emerging "classic-jazz" narrative, others called attention to more superficial idiosyncrasies: his laconic manner, his unusual dress, his preference for a saxophone made of white plastic. These two Colemans converged in the image of the primitive abstractionist, the "idiot savant" with a toy sax (as one recent critic named him), whose black-based innovations promised to revitalize the music's direction (C. Davis 1995).

The image of Coleman as the intuitive genius of jazz worked, of course, because so many listeners found his art appealing. This appeal may be attributed above all to the inventive ways in which he and the other group members rethought sound and performance while also maintaining approaches considered essential to jazz practice. Coleman's early band grew out of the small-group style of bop, which typically emphasized a series of solos against a fast, periodic accompaniment. While band members frequently worked from non-harmonic, marginally- or non-tonal platforms, they crafted their solos to common-time phrasing that inspired a sense of swing. Key to this rhythmic expression was bass player Charlie Haden, whose virtuosic accompaniments, like Cecil Taylor's, challenged solo/rhythm section conventions, while also maintaining a clear articulation of swing rhythm's four-beat structure. Important, too, was the work of drummer Billy Higgins (later, Ed Blackwell), who similarly introduced a new instrumental conception. His "total sound" approach sought to make use of the entire drum set, virtually at all times, while also keeping to a four-beat meter.

A similar balance of innovation and convention shows up in performances of the tunes themselves, most of which were written by Coleman. Typically, performances adhere to the song/improvisation/song formula that had oriented small-group playing since the late 1920s. Heads feature major-mode pentatonicism (which critics attributed to Coleman's Texas "folk" background) and occasionally, blues form, which give way to imaginative and often playful revisions of conventional practices. The theme of *Peace*, for example, includes an unusual segue featuring Haden playing arco bass; *Eventually* is nothing more than fast repetitions of a three-note chromatic saxophone motif played at alternating octave positions. *Poise*, on the other hand, reflects Coleman's formal training under Gunther Schuller and John Lewis at the Lenox School, as it avoids the pretentiousness that infected many "third stream" recordings. Here, each band member plays in rapid succession one of four pitches in a *Klangfarbenmelodie*, which is then restated in retrograde. The head then proceeds to a brief "folk" melody, a saxophone break, and closes with a repetition of the melody.

Coleman's solos expand on this same mix of tradition and experiment. His improvisations, together with those of Cherry, were particularly appealing to the critical audience. Most striking about Coleman's approach is the way in which he juxtaposes bop phrasing and pentatonic-based blues melodicism with fractious fits of atonal practice. Clearly Coleman had an ear for melodic turns of phrase. Yet so did he command a repertory of halting, disjunct motifs and long stretches of legato chromaticism that, at the extreme, exceeded the limits of note and scale. Frequently, Coleman worked with all of these elements, interchanging brief snatches of disparate sound with rhythmically charged pauses and gaps to shape, with a wizard's logic, remarkably cohesive performative structures. (Listen, for example, to his solos on *Focus on Sanity*, *Eventually*, and *Forerunner*.) What was construed as a kind of abstract simplicity or "primitivism" revealed above all a creative intelligence focused on recasting the controlling mechanisms of soloistic practice. Despite his misconstrued calls for "freedom," Coleman's aim seemed to be not so much a pure simplicity as much as a radically new direction in linear invention – one that might lead toward spontaneous improvisations uncontained by European dictates of note, meter, and scale. Soon Coleman would begin to challenge other jazz conventions, including single-instrument specialization (performing on violin and trumpet) and solo/accompaniment hierarchies. Notable with reference to the latter is *Beauty is a Rare Thing* (1960), where Haden and Blackwell provide a pulseless sound field against terse saxophone/trumpet improvisations.

The landmark achievement of Coleman's early oeuvre is the Atlantic recording, *Free Jazz* (1960), which outlined a new collectivist practice as it named the style of an era. In this work, Coleman amplifies convention to articulate the unconventional: a "double quartet" of standard jazz instrumentation (reeds, trumpet, bass, drums) produces a series of performance sections that turn jazz notions on end. The "head" sections collapse melody into a collection of slowly shifting clusters that prepare for improvisational sequences. While the improvisations tend to foreground a particular soloist, they typically are framed and accompanied by collective interactions that involve all four melodic instruments. The two rhythm sections perform throughout, with each assuming different tasks. Much of the time, Haden and Blackwell set the rhythmic anchor by stressing low register bass and set drumming; La Faro and Higgins, in turn, add nuance and dimension by introducing rapid eighth-note bass lines and shimmering cymbal sustains. (These roles vary significantly in an extended rhythm-section duet toward the end.) Together the ensembles produce a kind of multidimensional collision of sonic impulses that collapse conventional distinctions between harmony, melody, and rhythm. Coleman likened this musical practice to abstract expressionist painting (a point underscored by the photograph of Jackson Pollock's *White Light* inside the album cover), affirming Don Heckman's epithet for free music as "action jazz" (Heckman 1967). Later Coleman would name this blurring of harmonic and melodic distinctions "harmolodics" (Litweiler 1992; Robinson 1988).

Whether the result of market forces, critical promotion, or sheer artistic brilliance, Coleman's influence was undeniable. In the space of two years, he had supplied to jazz a new vigor, yet an ironically "anti-jazz" one that fueled the exploration of approaches departing from conventions of improvisational practice. Established performers such as Max Roach (born 1924) had already produced imaginative revisions of jazz on recordings, notably the "African" percussion sections and alterations of twelve-bar blues form on *All Africa* (*Freedom Now Suite*, 1960). By 1961, however (*Percussion Bitter Sweet*), he was also specifying conceptual alternatives: refiguring harmonic changes as "sound clusters" and rethinking rhythmic constraints that, he hoped, would give to jazz greater "freedom" (Guryan 1961). Cecil Taylor, as already observed, had also followed an independent line of development. Yet he too seemed to rethink his artistic direction against the background of *Free Jazz*. With the help of Sunny Murray (and later, Andrew Cyrille), who introduced a multidimensional form of drumming unconstrained by ostinato and meter-based conventions, Taylor realized a radically new form of creative expression. In this work, notably, the session released as Gil Evans's *Into the Hot* (1961) and another under his own name, *Unit Structures* (1966), he began borrowing directly from the tone-color and textural experiments of recent art music, to the point of removing from the "jazz sound" nearly all semblance of tonal-melodic convention. Even John Coltrane, who, with Sonny Rollins and Miles Davis, represented the premier artists of "modern jazz," openly paid tribute to Coleman's creativity. His album, *The Avant-Garde John Coltrane* (1960), featured Coleman's music as well as his sidemen.

By the time of *Live at the Village Vanguard* (1961) and *Impressions* (1961–1963), Coltrane had envisioned a personal non-harmonic approach that eventually set the standard for an early 1960s New York "free sound." Working with a regular quartet that included pianist McCoy Tyner, bass player Jimmy Garrison, and drummer Elvin Jones, he (and briefly with collaborator Eric Dolphy, during 1961 through 1963) introduced a new kind of performance style, characterized by a fiery intensity and feverish tempos that brought propulsive bop rhythm and changes to a nearly static blur. Crucial to sustaining Coltrane's virtuosic extended solos were the tightly woven collaborations of the rhythm section. Together they created an oscillating, multi-textured sound field that at once encouraged performative dynamism and affirmed tonal ground. From this base, Coltrane advanced a powerful and highly influential "modal" style that featured remnants of harmonically grounded scalar formulas cut loose from an informing chordal sequence and loud, plaintive sustains that evoked black vernacular singing. The juxtaposition and development of these various components had a powerful, compelling effect on listeners for whom the Coltrane Quartet represented the height of the new jazz and Coltrane himself its most influential figure. By 1965, Coltrane's ensemble playing had reached a radical extreme, in which dense webs of multiple percussion appeared against several melodic instruments. The versions of collective playing documented on *Ascension* (1965) and other albums marked a high point of achievement that, in popularity, overshadowed the seminal work of Coleman's *Free Jazz*.

Working parallel to these major initiatives, many New York musicians forged their own approaches, some by establishing a personal voice in a recognized style, others by charting new and often strikingly original directions. Among the chief innovators were pianist Paul Bley (born 1932), whose ensemble recordings for Bernard Stollman's influential ESP label re-affirmed the post-bop atonality associated with Taylor and Coleman; and the New York Contemporary Five (Archie Shepp, Don Cherry, John Tchicai, Don Moore, and J. C. Moses), who similarly worked within the most familiar frames of free practice. Moreover, the saxophonist Albert Ayler (1936–1970) pursued a more iconoclastic direction. He expanded on Coleman's challenges to pitch, motif, and scale in virtuoso solos built on stretches of fluctuating line and sound. Ayler's recordings, *Spiritual Unity* (1964), *New York Ear and Eye Control* (1964), and *Bells* (1965) also recorded on ESP, are among the monuments of the early free movement. Still others, notably Giuseppi Logan (born 1935), chose a more conceptually radical line of experiment by moving against jazz music's most basic stylistic assumptions. Logan's album, *Giuseppi Logan Quartet* (1965), features non-Western instruments, untempered scales, and unconventional performance practices that frequently preclude four-beat swing rhythm. In the composition *Dance of Satan* and, at moments, in *Dialogue*, these elements effect a kind of anti-virtuosity that contradicts the performance expectations of modern jazz. By playing down technical display, Logan seems to critique a European-centered virtuosity that had redirected jazz away from its "folk" origins.

Even this brief look at the new "freedom" in jazz shows that musicians had not, in contrast to the claims of many observers, simply forsaken standards. Indeed, the very best of them worked creatively to refashion what "standards" might mean. By going beyond the strictures of tonal convention, they, like their cohorts in other modernist arts, sought to express creatively new social and psychological realities that were at once liberative and critical of a "common sense" world view. As atonal improvisers, moreover, they brought vernacular "freedom" directly into the act of creation, and by so doing, merged powers of folk authenticity and high, civilized art. "Free improvisation" unrestricted by European-based musical constraints ironically became aligned with folk practices of the African American tradition. What was the height of urban modernist abstraction also signified – in the "folk" allusions of Coleman and Ayler, and in the New Orleans background associated with collective improvisation – the musical essence of black performance. For these artists, free, collective improvisations revealed the source of a vernacular musicality, celebrating the ideal of black racial authenticity while also speaking affirmatively to the multiracial intersections that typified early free music-making. These signs would be captured most dramatically in the late recordings of Coltrane (1965 through 1967), whose ecumenical, "spiritual" image became a symbol of civil rights and cultural uplift for politically progressive, integrated audiences (McMichael 1996).

Given free music's obvious connections to modernism, integration, and progressive politics, it is ironic that by 1965 it would be portrayed as a creative force opposing such ideals. Most commonly (and even in many sympathetic portraits) jazz abstraction would be figured as a kind of primitive noise, reinforcing parallel public depictions of black-male bestiality. What had announced a new moment in jazz music's creative invention – for many, it was the most strikingly original musical expression of the mid-twentieth century – was now likened to a racialized and irrational "anti-jazz." Significantly, the associations between free jazz and racial threat grew correspondingly with the rise of black activism. By the mid-1960s, several jazz performances took place in support of political initiatives, although in many cases musicians saw these forums merely as opportunities to work. Nonetheless, white fears of African American voting rights, mass protest, and black power seemed to motivate new public interpretations of free practices, as a once cerebral art was refashioned in the image of "black rage." In some ways, this idea of threat, while affirming enduring stereotypes of the dangerous black male, worked to the musicians' advantage. It lent a drama and power that performers such as Archie Shepp and critics such as Amiri Baraka and Frank Kofsky could exploit to counter the escalating appeal of rock. If these exploitations were self-serving, they nonetheless reflected a deep belief that free jazz could, with greater visibility, secure a broad following. That the spokespersons of the most intellectually ambitious expression of jazz to date could blame its decline solely on the lack of institutional representation speaks not only to the idealism of 1960s politics, but once again to the precarious position of jazz in American culture.

*

Not all free jazz musicians looked to white-controlled institutions to publicize and support their art. The group organized in Chicago as the Association for the Advancement of Creative Musicians (AACM) launched an independent, grassroots initiative in the image of black-community and -religious groups operating in the city's South Side. As a collective, the AACM worked to organize a stable forum for the presentation and promotion of a variety of black improvised musics. Eschewing the high-culture aesthetics and hierarchical structures of modernist institutions, it voiced a radical political challenge consistent with notions of the avant garde: the AACM presented as an institution a collective critique of the white-run power structures that typically regulated the performance and promotion of African American creativity. Such radical political notions, in turn, took musical form in the abstract art of the AACM's leading progenitors, who followed in the wake of New York free players and local innovators, including Sun Ra. (Sun Ra's Arkestra was based in Chicago until 1960.) Unlike the style of the New Yorkers, however, whose performances extended from the bop orientations of Coleman and Coltrane, AACM musicians typically practiced a less regulated "collective" improvisation that was also frequently situated within composed, multi-sectional contexts. Both aspects affirmed the communalist Afrocentricity of many members, for whom "black art" was at once community based and comparable to the highest forms of European-based expression.

The AACM's most influential initiatives grew out of the technical and compositional approaches of the (aptly named) Experimental Band, a rehearsal group created around 1963 by one of the Association's founding members, Muhal Richard Abrams (born 1930). As part of the AACM program, the band provided a forum for members to test their most recent compositions and improvisations. The first AACM recordings, released on Delmark (originally a blues label) and Chuck Nessa's Nessa Records (1966 through 1968) document these experiments. Performances on Abrams's *Levels and Degrees of Light* (1967), for example, highlight multi-sectional forms based on metered and non-metered temporal schemes and rich expanses of multi-colored timbral invention. The improvisations featured on the Anthony Braxton Trio's *Three Compositions of New Jazz* (1968) foreground a non-tonal, non-harmonic "collage" approach in which the musicians ironically seem to resist interaction. Especially noteworthy among the early AACM recordings are the releases by the Roscoe Mitchell Art Ensemble (later, the Art Ensemble of Chicago), *Sound* (1966) and *Congliptious* (1968). As Mitchell (born 1940) explains, on these recordings "the musicians are free to make any sound they think will do, any sound that they hear at a particular time. That could be like somebody who felt like stomping on the floor . . . Well, he would stomp on the floor" (Martin 1967, p. 21). The results reveal a striking willingness to create, quite simply, sound in time, unrestricted by the regulating forces typically associated with Western music. These performance practices reveal aesthetic sympathies with "new music" improvisers working under the influence of

John Cage and post-war jazz, with whom some AACM members (Braxton, Joseph Jarman) would associate. Yet the emancipation of jazz improvisation from the norms of Western practice reflected above all a political aim to create a conspicuously "racial art" that affirmed the social realities of black difference.

Fusion: a radical populism? (1970–1975)

In response to the increasingly arcane brand of musical modernism associated with the jazz avant garde, many musicians began to turn to performance practices that proved more accessible to mass audiences. Typically, this move toward the popular has been portrayed as "selling out," since "the popular" by this time referred mainly to rock styles, which lacked the rhythmic and harmonic complexities associated with jazz. Yet one can also read this turn as a reaffirmation of jazz music's traditional place at the center of American artistic culture, recast through the ideology of 1960s egalitarianism. By reaching beyond the music's conventional limits, musicians (and their supporting institutions) hoped to win back an audience that had been displaced by the free movement. While sympathetic to free music's willingness to challenge even the most basic aesthetic tenets, the new generation of musicians sought to satisfy those aims while also working within accessible musical conventions. If free jazz could take jazz beyond the musical norms of common time and swing, then so could "jazz-rock" – or as it would later be named, "fusion" – follow an equally radical direction that also appealed to a wide listenership. As a result of this increased appeal, fusion would ultimately grow into a veritable international style that featured American, European, and Latin-American artists coming together in a new world musical practice. The first expressions of the fusion movement may best be construed as a radical, multicultural populism extending from the free movement that reflected jazz music's global presence as it also signaled its emancipation from American performative dominance. By turning to the popular to voice a progressive artistry, jazz gained a new, rock-oriented audience whose presence seemed only to exacerbate fears of the music's decline.

The initial expressions of fusion appeared from 1966 to 1968, when a radical ethos of social idealism overwhelmed cities and campuses in mass, political demonstrations. Unlike prior jazz movements which were typically forged by African American artists, the fusion movement, from the start, consisted of a multiracial complex of musicians centered in, yet by no means limited to, the United States. From San Francisco to New York to London to Prague, a new community of performers, some with multiple backgrounds in free jazz, art music, and rock, began creating early versions of fusion hybridities. The Flock (with violinist Jerry Goodman), the New York-based Free Spirits (with Bob Moses, Lenny White, and guitarist Larry Coryell), and the California-based group, The Fourth Way (with Mike Nock, Michael White, Ron McLure, and Eddie Marshall) – it was fusion's answer to "third stream" – were among the first fusion bands working in the United States. British musicians such as guitarists John McLaughlin and Eric Clapton, and bass player Jack Bruce explored similar linkages, forging kinships that were subsequently obscured by differences in community affiliation. McLaughlin worked mainly in jazz, developing with baritone saxophonist John Surman and drummer Tony Oxley a powerful mix of post-bop, free and composed styles and practices. Yet his virtuoso playing on *Extrapolation* (1969) and on Larry Coryell's *Spaces* (1970) – with Czech bass player Miroslav Vitous and the Panamanian-American funk-jazz drummer Billy Cobham – drew considerable attention from an emerging fusion audience. Clapton and Bruce, on the other hand, remained committed to rock, ultimately forming the group Cream. On the live performances recorded as *Wheels of Fire* (1968), they produced a brand of blues-based collective improvisation that shared strong affinities with modal and atonal free jazz. The early work of other rock-based musicians and bands, including composer-guitarists Jimi Hendrix and Frank Zappa, the Velvet Underground, and from Britain, King Crimson, Soft Machine, and Yes, similarly brought to rock an experimental edge inspired by free-jazz and contemporary art music practices.

Crucial to the artistic success of fusion was the participation of one of the foremost authorities in jazz, Miles Davis. After John Coltrane's tragic death in 1967, the jazz community returned almost in reflex to the tired formula of musical demise as publicists looked searchingly for an innovator to announce its next beginning.[1] In Davis they found someone who already enjoyed a conspicuous place in the historical narrative for his role in shaping two major stylistic trends. After forging the "Birth of the Cool" and "modal" advances of the late 1940s and 1950s, Davis now seemed to be pursuing yet another artistic direction that took turns variously as a kind of hybrid of acid rock, atonal composition, and jazz.

---

1. A seeming parody of this formula appears as trumpeter Lester Bowie's unaccompanied solo, *Jazz Death?*. A recording of the performance is included on Roscoe Mitchell's album, *Congliptious* (1968).

Some observers were already skeptical about Davis's new approaches to rhythm and texture when they appeared on the albums, *Filles de Kiliminjaro* (1968) and *In a Silent Way* (1969). With *Bitches Brew* (1969), he amplified those transgressions with compelling artistic results to produce one of the landmark recordings of the fusion era. On this album, not only is swing gone; so too is the progressive linearity and rhythmic/melodic development fundamental to the jazz character. Indeed, Davis seemed to be working purposively to remove the four-beat walking bass that accommodates jazz phrasing in order to give birth to a dynamic stasis reminiscent of Coltrane's *Ascension*. Stylistically, however, this approach seemed also to conjure up repertories outside of jazz, namely the thick-textured sound masses of avant-garde art music composers Krysztof Penderecki and György Ligeti. Having broken from the developmental concerns of traditional jazz, Davis was encouraging musicians (and listeners) to focus on textural immediacies, to work collectively with brief, unrelated fragments against a constant web of animated percussive sound. On the title track of *Bitches Brew*, for example, complexity develops less from formal design (an alternation of free meter and ostinato sections) than from variations of timbral effect as swatches of funk and atonal abstraction rise and fall within a kind of melodic-percussive shimmer. The instrumental doublings and triplings, which once again recall early free masterpieces, amplify the power and effect of this fluctuating melodic rhythm.

For a generation of musicians who came of age under the spell of free jazz, new music, and rock, Miles Davis's innovations marked an exciting new standard. Like Coleman before him, Davis had combined the old and the new. Yet whereas Coleman's "tradition" supplied a grounding in swing practice, Davis's inspired a new, static rhythmic conception that radically recast jazz music's dance-based "blues" character. As performed by Miles Davis's band, fusion offered a new kind of improvisational freedom informed equally by free music's aversion to performative constraint and, ironically, rock music's vernacular-based metrical and rhythmic simplicity. In a strange sonic syncretism, abstract, atonal sounds acquired primordial energy from a funk-based rhythmic intensity that many listeners associated with the primitive and tribal. Davis's titles – *Pharaoh's Dance*, *Miles Runs the Voodoo Down* – and album covers – depicting natural African energies – reinforced this association. And with the release of *On the Corner* (1972), the imagination of the primal unfolded as a fascinating mix of overtly articulated funk-blues energy projecting the new site of vernacular authenticity: the inner-city black ghetto. Rather than merely affirming vernacular authenticity, however, Davis's funk abstractions provided a means of critiquing the purportedly interactive nature of jazz. Citing the influences of the post-World War II avant garde (for instance Karlheinz Stockhausen), Davis suggested that his work from the period challenged the collective processes central to jazz improvisation. For example, in some instances he would advise his band to avoid responding to his solos or even one another and simply chart a rhythmic/textural course.

The success of *Bitches Brew* inspired the formation of several new fusion bands, many of which were headed by former members of Davis's seminal group. Typically, these groups drew from the timbral richness observed on Davis's recordings, while also relying on conventions more easily accessible to rock audiences. John McLaughlin and Billy Cobham, for example, refashioned the Davis sound within the frames of lead-guitar/set-drumming virtuosity associated with blues-based British rock. As the Mahavishnu Orchestra (with Jerry Goodman, Irish bass player Rick Laird, and Czech electric pianist Jan Hammer) they employed unconventional instrumentation (violin, moog synthesizer, double-necked electric guitar), compound meters, and Indian-based modes and ostinatos to effect an alluring rock-based synthesis of "international sound." (The Asian allusions can be attributed to McLaughlin's devotion to the Indian spiritual leader, Sri Chimnoy.) Former Davis sideman Chick Corea (born 1941), created with Return to Forever – which in name celebrated his own conversion to Scientology – a similarly exotic style more or less modeled on McLaughlin's formula. Other Davis alumni, notably Tony Williams (as leader of Lifetime from 1969), Jack DeJohnette (several groups, including Compost from 1971) and Herbie Hancock (born 1940) also performed and recorded fusion. Of these, particularly noteworthy was Hancock, whose funk-jazz album, *Head Hunters* (1973), drew broad commercial attention. The album featured the popular hit, *Chameleon*, as well as Hancock's classic, *Watermelon Man*, recast in a Central African "jungle style" (based on an ethnographic recording of Ba-Benzélé Pygmies) as if to parody the Sambo reference in its title (Feld 1996). Such references to African "roots" authenticities appeared around the time of the "Soul Makossa" fad, which was introduced in the United States in 1973 by the Cameroonian fusion saxophonist, Manu Dibango (Dibango 1994).

Perhaps most important of the early fusion bands, finally, was Weather Report, a multiracial, multinational ensemble that featured three Davis alumni, saxophonist Wayne Shorter and the Czech musicians Josef

Zawinul (electric piano) and Miroslav Vitous (double bass). (The band also included drummer Eric Gravatt and Brazilian percussionists Airto Moreira and – replacing Moreira in 1971 – Dom Um Romao.) Initially, Weather Report pursued a radical kind of experimental fusion. This soon gave way to a compelling, frequently funk-based style reminiscent of Davis's band. The latter approach was especially successful in establishing propulsive continuities supporting extended solo improvisations. The group's innovations were articulated with particular skill and expressive power on its first albums, released between 1971 and 1973: *Weather Report*, *I Sing the Body Electric* (a musical tribute to Walt Whitman), and *Sweet Nighter*.

The broad appeal of Weather Report soon set the stage for other foreign performers, notably Jan Garbarek, Eberhard Weber, Flora Purim, and violinists Michael Urbaniak and Jean-Luc Ponty, whose presence in the mid-1970s helped to widen American conceptions of jazz and the jazz musician. As a genre, however, fusion by this time had become increasingly formalized, having been cast as a somewhat complicated version of flashy, guitar rock. The most commercially successful groups moved decidedly away from fusion's prior radicalism and toward a tonally based, romantic lushness rich with "new age" inflections. In the 1980s, the significance of fusion was revived as a precursor to an escalating hybridization of style, genre, and form. In the social context of "jazz," this was perhaps most strikingly realized by Ornette Coleman, whose ventures into various musical intersections – with, among others, Pat Metheny in 1986 and Jerry Garcia in 1988 – underscored unspoken free/jazz-rock affinities.

Crisis and critique (1975–1980)

In the wake of fusion, jazz seemed more like a fission whose trajectories moved in every direction at once. After fifteen years of radical experiment, stylists no longer ascribed to any single approach or set of standards. Now the term "jazz" could refer to virtually any form of improvised music, from night-club torch songs to rock-based jams, from free-energy spontaneity to Dixieland nostalgia. Even improvisation, which was once thought to be the music's core feature, provided little determination against the background of "third stream" artists, Supersax arrangements, and repertory-ensemble performances of swing transcriptions. Moreover, when improvisation did appear, it could take forms of great abstraction and complexity, yet without the merest hint of formal, harmonic, or rhythmic convention (thirty-two-measure song form, chord changes, swing, etc.). If jazz no longer referred to an essential musical quality, neither did it specify a particular community of listeners or tradition of learning. Indeed, "jazz" appeared in a variety of circumstances. Clubs and concert halls served as conventional forums, of course. But performances could also be heard in the garages of suburban teens and in weddings and proms performed by white-collar executives as an avocational sideline. If Charlie Parker had once epitomized the jazz artist, who could explain the new incarnations of this post-jazz "fusion" era, not to mention Miles Davis, Parker's friend and colleague, who had forsaken bop, cool, and the hipster image to appear before rock-oriented audiences clad in ostentatious, high fashion? Jazz style, jazz practice, and the jazz life now seemed like everything at once. In its diversity it expressed an absence: the many dimensions of jazz revealed "unity" to be a phantom.

What salvaged jazz for some was an enduring faith in the idea of tradition. "Tradition" once again would emerge as the operative word, even though "jazz music" now conveyed strikingly different, even oppositional versions of the past. For Keith Jarrett (born 1945), "tradition" reflected his experiences as a bop pianist and member of Davis's fusion bands (between 1969 and 1971), together with the repertory of romantic piano music which he now blended into an appealing solo virtuosity. For Warren Vaché, Scott Hamilton, and Loren Schoenberg, "tradition" referred to a legacy reaching back beyond the recent past, to the historical performances of swing, which were now being resurrected as "jazz classics." For post-nationalist Afrocentrists such as the Art Ensemble of Chicago, moreover, "tradition" referred to a trans-historical legacy of racially defined invention, which it celebrated in post-free collective abstractions of "Great Black Music, Ancient to the Future." And for still others, "tradition" referred not so much to a style as to a place: the new down-home of New York's downtown lofts, which in the mid-1970s represented the primal ground of urban creative origin.

Whither the jazz tradition? Many of those in the music business seemed convinced it was something still close at hand, confusing image with ethos to evince, in Ralph Ellison's phrase, "The Golden Age, Time Past" (Ellison 1972). Remaining committed to outmoded concepts of Great Men and organic stylistic development, producers and publicists came to believe that they had found such a figure in a former AACM composer/saxophonist now based in Paris, who, while denying a jazz affiliation, nevertheless was performing and recording some of the most adventurous experimental improvisations since early free jazz. To be sure, Anthony Braxton made for a peculiar kind of hero, though one perhaps fitting the weird paradoxes of the postmodern moment. He offers an interesting case study of the new patterns emerging at a time when jazz certainties effectively unravel.

With coaching from his producers at Arista Records, Braxton presented those aspects of a multifaceted creativity that would satisfy appeals for a return to "true" jazz practice. He did so by employing the improvisational formulas of the early Coleman quartet, in which compositionally inventive head themes set the basis for a series of hard-swinging atonal solos. Typically, Braxton's small-group works relied on an array of imaginative styles and techniques: quirky march themes and forms, angular and complex rhythmic accompaniments, and compositional approaches that reflected his studies of serialism and the repetitive music popularly called "minimalism." Braxton's solos, moreover, revealed similar affinities, particularly in the virtuosic application of highly disjunct, atonal motifs reminiscent of the "pointillistic" style commonly associated with serialism and the work of Eric Dolphy. What made Braxton's playing ultimately so appealing, however, was the way in which he combined these arcane gestures with a fiery virtuosity indebted to the styles of early free jazz. In his recorded performances (for example, *Composition 23B*, the lead track of his premier Arista album, *New York Fall 1974*) one can discern reflections of Coleman's mercurial chromaticism and Coltrane's full-textured, propulsive power, cast in an exacting rhythmic style.

For a time (1975 through 1979), Braxton gave hope that jazz had once again found its bearings in a broad synthesis of post-World War II styles. In order to sell this position, journalists called attention to the more transgressive sides of Braxton's art and personality as a way of creating a "controversy" that ironically placed difference on the margins. While openly acknowledging the artistic strength of his improvisations, they commonly focused their discussions on his "intellectual" vocabulary, his serious manner, his preference for conventional dress (deemed unconventional for a jazz musician), and his proclivity for using number/letter groupings and geometric shapes as titles of his works. This attention helped to enhance Braxton's commercial appeal, to the point where he could devote attention to experimental projects that would ultimately challenge his jazz reputation. On *Creative Orchestra Music 1976* and *Montreux/Berlin Concerts* (1976–1977), for example, he presented a new side to his creative output, featuring collective improvisations and atonal works for big band that harkened back to his days with the AACM. His Arista recordings from 1977 to 1980 represented the most arcane side of his artistry, including works for multiple orchestras (*For Four Orchestras*, 1978), unaccompanied saxophone (*Alto Saxophone Improvisations 1979*), and piano duet (*Composition No. 95*, 1980). These appeared together with his continuing work on European labels, which documented a deep commitment to experimental practices.

When observed beyond the constraints of the most exploitative journalistic categories, Braxton's artistry can be recognized as an impressive body of creative experiment, one that brings together two of the most important trajectories of post-World War II American music. In intent, this work extends the Adornian ideal of vanguardist artistry: Braxton has explained that his art seeks to outline musically his own projections of a new social order in which prior orthodoxies give way to a reinvigorated ritualized world culture. In the context of jazz, however, such idealism could only falter, since Braxton's reputation permitted nothing more than the appearance of radical non-conformity; the art itself was meant to reinforce conventional listening expectations. Once Braxton's music had transgressed this jazz category, his appeal quickly declined, leading to the cancellation of his contract with a major American record label.

Braxton's rise and fall from grace is telling, for it reveals the extent to which the jazz idea had come to depend on formulas of mediation and representation. Braxton's leadership was not something naturally occurring; it was constituted by taste makers and institutions that recorded, marketed, and publicized a new trend. What Braxton's fate revealed above all was the emptiness of the Great Man formula after the revolutions of the 1960s and early 1970s. For Braxton could fill the bill of tradition maker only when one observed the entirety of his art through a distorting lens, one that removed from the picture all that transgressed the characterization of the mainstream. Braxton's reputation, then, tells much about how far jazz had departed from its supposed roots. If Braxton identified the new ethos of jazz, then its prospects of reclaiming a discernible mainstream or center appeared to be hopeless.

Imagined traditions (since 1980)

In an effort to reverse this decentering process, many critics and musicians gave increasing emphasis to events that affirmed the vitality of jazz before free and fusion. "The music has to start swinging again," asserted David

Murray, a leading figure of free music's second generation. "People don't want music they have to suffer through – Ronald Reagan's got them suffering enough already" (F. Davis 1986, p. 42). Murray's prescription for the future did not deny the power and effect of recent innovation. His work with Oliver Lake, Hamiett Bluiett, and Julius Hemphill as the World Saxophone Quartet spoke directly to the influence of Braxton and free, as it paid tribute to the timbral experiments of the Ellington Orchestra. What Murray and many other free players sought was a way of re-visioning the past through forms that affirmed jazz music's multidimensional artistry. To be sure, one can discern in the expressions of many artists in the 1980s an effort to build on the vanguardist ethos of the free movement and its extensions. In the works themselves, however, artistic advancement frequently appeared as a vivid pastiche of styles and practices, from free atonality to four-beat swing. Stuart Nicholson calls this a moment of "consolidation," the point at which jazz moves toward "a more egalitarian climate where styles from every era of the music at last found peaceful co-existence" (Nicholson 1990, p. 1). Yet while many artists seemed more willing to embrace the past and to consider acceptable a range of musical possibilities, the assertions of renewed coherence belied once again the striking *uncertainty* of jazz as a category – an uncertainty that caused considerable consternation among the music's spokespersons and advocates.

A review of events suggests that the principal continuity in late-century jazz has been the state of convulsiveness that traces through since the late 1950s. Indeed, jazz now seemed best observed as a kind of flutter of tenuous projections associated with the postmodern moment. Differences were no longer limited to variations in style; they now outlined more profound disparities in aesthetic conception and cultural affiliation that occasioned multiplex views of jazz as such. As jazz continued to change internally and formally, so did it take on new appearances through the heightened visibility of women instrumentalists (Jane Ira Bloom, Terri Lyne Carrington), foreign musicians (Zakir Hussain, Sergei Kuryokhin), and established performers trained in European art music composition – notably, pianist Anthony Davis (born 1951), composer of the opera *X: The Life and Times of Malcolm X* (1984) – who embraced not assimilationist views, but practices that affirmed their own sense of individuality and difference. In this way, they extended the radical challenges of free, fusion, and cultural critique as they undermined familiar jazz stereotypes based on gender, race, and nationality. Even distinguished players seemed no

longer to locate stable ground. While stalwarts such as Johnny Griffin and
Art Blakey continued to fashion a powerful form of post-bop, others, from
Sonny Rollins to Herbie Hancock to Wayne Shorter, unsettled that certainty by pursuing styles reflecting fusion's prominence. Add to this the
nostalgic film celebrations of jazz as racialized tragedy – *Bird, 'Round Midnight, Let's Get Lost* – and the "reality" of jazz seemed little more than a dis-
cursive artifice: a social embodiment of the dynamism and shimmer of
late-century postmodern art.

It is certainly true that some young players, having been raised on jazz
records, radio, and school lab bands, fashioned compelling reinterpreta-
tions of historical repertories. It is also true that musicians beyond David
Murray, from John Carter to Henry Threadgill, looked searchingly to the
past out of a desire to move jazz forward. Together they presented a new
kind of art that revealed greater attention to the details of historical styles
and practices than jazz players had ever before. Yet jazz has also undergone
a radical reconceptualization *as a consequence* of the social developments
that inspired this looking back. The formation of a historical sensibility
emerges precisely when jazz becomes established within an international
culture of mass mediation and commodity capitalism; its "history" accu-
mulates as a collage of historical images more so than as a return to the past
as such. For now "jazz" must also make room for a variety of expressions
that have little to do with the dominant historical projection. "Jazz" now
includes:

> *Artists* such as Don Byron, the African American clarinetist whose
> background in free practices has helped to radicalize Jewish Klezmer
> orthodoxy; and George Lewis, a virtuoso free trombonist and associate
> of France's IRCAM, well-known in art music circles for his arcane
> computer experiments.
>
> *Performances*, whether live or recorded, that extend the trajectory of
> fusion's internationalism in hybrids of "acid jazz" (the British group,
> Us3) and hip hop (Billy Bang, et al., *Hip Hop be bop*, 1993), noise rock
> (Last Exit), and "world beat" (Rabih Abou-Khalil).
>
> *Communities* in Moscow, Jakarta, Havana, Lagos, and Belgrade for whom
> the idea of "African American artistry" seems but an abstraction
> perpetuated by mass communications networks and global markets.

If jazz is now *In the Tradition*, to quote the title of Arthur Blythe's aggressively marketed album of 1979, so has it become a trans-national matrix of
signifying sound that continually revises and redefines "tradition" in
striking ways. By the 1980s, "tradition" had come to refer to a veritable

cacophony of trans-migrational styles, conceptions, and subcultures, all related in their common claim of an equally multiple past named "jazz."

*

It is within the complex of global musical production that we can locate the multiple responses to this past named "jazz." In the 1990s, "jazz" serves as a rhetorical figure assigned to any number of contemporary constructs that are situated within a fluctuating genre category. In mass American markets, however, "jazz" typically defines one site among many: the seemingly stable trajectory of neoclassicism. Epitomized by the work of trumpeter Wynton Marsalis (born 1961), neoclassical jazz is commonly observed as a kind of resolution of an inexorable process of innovation, one linking an early-century New Orleans origin to Marsalis as new-born New Orleans incarnate. In this way, neoclassicism succeeds in projecting a simulation of continuity as a way of overcoming and ultimately erasing the discontinuity which is our lot.

As a trumpeter, Marsalis's talents are undeniable. He is among the best of a new generation of improvisers who approach the post-bop, tonal repertory as a kind of golden-age training ground for practical advancement. Like many of his colleagues, Marsalis himself developed his proficiency as a member of the Art Blakey Group, which served as the unofficial school of neo-bop performance. Marsalis's first small-group recordings, *Wynton Marsalis* (1981), *Think of One* (1982), and *Black Codes (from the Underground)* (1985) reflected this background. They featured a virtuoso musicianship grounded in an advanced tonal-harmonic style and rhythmic sensibility associated with the 1950s post-bop era. In technique and style, moreover, Marsalis and his cohorts have worked from the same high standards, turning away from free and fusion, and toward a mainstream of song forms from *Cherokee* to *Giant Steps*. Marsalis's influence – both as a small-group leader and, more recently, as artistic director of Lincoln Center's jazz program – has brought wide acclaim to the neo-bop movement, fueled by a marketing community that remains invested in the rhetoric of continuity and coherence.

What makes this "return to tradition" seem like plain common sense is the power of the critical narratives that represent it. Whereas a truly democratic depiction of practices appearing under the umbrella of "jazz" would surely reveal greater complexity, most major media portraits have overwhelmingly favored the image of the neo-bop innovator situated against the background of mid-century mainstream innovation. In the name of reaffirming tradition, these representations repress history in all of its variety. They give particularly short shrift to the range of creativity from 1960 to 1980, a twenty-year period seemingly blanked out of the historical vision. Musically, it is as if jazz history had leaped from a mid-1950s high artistry to a point three decades later, when those same mainstream practices were reinstated as a neoclassical movement. Such perspectives, while commonplace, contradict good historical judgment that recognizes musical formation as something inextricably linked to the social circumstances that constitute it.

It is therefore ironic that the idea of jazz neoclassicism could not have emerged without the precedents of free and fusion. This relationship involves something more than a conservative response to a radical transgression. While history's path is always potentially various and contingent, the particular course that led to a neoclassical jazz movement shows clear indebtedness to prior initiatives toward a racialized high black art as well as to a populist innovation accessible to a middle-class, educated audience. Neoclassical jazz continues the idea of great black music spearheaded by the jazz avant garde and the black arts movement, just as it mirrors fusion's accessibility to a general, educated listenership. Indeed, fusion's appeal helped to recover a lost jazz audience whose adolescent love of Davis, McLaughlin, and Weather Report has been rekindled by the same performers now attracting a new youth following. If neoclassical initiatives affirm a historical continuity, it is a postmodern one crafted out of the same mythologies of pastness and location that inform Afrocentric imaginations of Africa and the fusions of global sound marketed as world beat. It is for this reason that many committed radical artists seeking to reclaim a modernist certainty in jazz contend that the neoclassical turn is yet another popular, commercial movement that ultimately contradicts jazz's time-honored commitment to progress and innovation.

Marsalis's appeal is particularly fascinating because it reinforces the idea of a post-1960 "anti-jazz" continuity while also marking a profound aesthetic and stylistic shift. As a major figure, he joins an odd group of vigorously marketed "innovators" from Coleman to Davis to Braxton who give voice to institutional hopes of what the new "jazz" might be. Like Coleman and Braxton, Marsalis assumes the role of the hero who enters into conflict and controversy. Yet whereas Coleman's conflict fulfilled conventional modernist ideas of the visionary in a sea of stasis and convention, and Braxton's image at least affirmed progressive sensibilities while diverting attention from the more transgressive sides of his repertory, Marsalis's message suggests a paradox: it responds to the dynamic uncertainty of the postmodern by enacting "progress" through retrenchment. Moreover, Coleman, and to some extent Braxton, reinforce modern sensibilities by distinguishing their own artistic integrity from a more dominant, corrupting outer world. Portrayals of Marsalis, on the other hand – particularly those during the first years of his popularity – invert this logic by claiming that his obvious centrality in the American market identifies a marginal position. In this way, jazz neoclassicism parallels contemporary projections of "alternative" popular music, in which sameness – for example, identification with a broad music television audience – determines difference. So, too, does it resemble dominant conservative social movements that claim to work against the encroaching threats of political correctness, multiculturalism, etc. That "jazz," a living, progressive art, could now serve to articulate these same resistances in progress's name testifies to the maddening instability of aesthetic meaning in late-twentieth-century public culture.

17

Tonal traditions in art music from
1920 to 1960

LARRY STARR

It seems a virtually inevitable development that the creative explosions taking place in the realms of American jazz, popular, and theatrical music following World War I would find a parallel in the sphere of American art music. It also follows that much of the new art music would draw direct or indirect inspiration from those exciting and novel developments in the vernacular areas. Sometimes this took the form of direct stylistic mimicry or evocation, and other times it came across more subtly as an attempt to emulate, in art music terms, the sense of an original, energetic American identity that characterized the best of the new vernacular musics.

The prosperous United States of the 1920s proved an ideal environment for a flourishing of concert music. There was a significantly wide bourgeois audience, interested in "culture" and with money to spend, and a striking growth in upper-class financial support for art music performing organizations, concert series, and individual efforts and events – offered through personal, charitable, and corporate sources. The emergence of the United States as a world presence in the aftermath of World War I was an equally important stimulus to creativity in the art music sphere. American composers became abruptly aware of the inspiration and challenge presented to them by developments in European modernism, at the same time that they sought to establish a new and distinctive identity for American music, an identity that would speak both to their native audiences and to the world.

A significant, perhaps even tragic, paradox underlies the history of American art music during this period, however, and it is the fact that the music and example of Charles Ives remained basically unknown. For in Ives the generation of composers born in the years surrounding the turn of the century had a model for the "new" American composer. Ives's work provided its own highly original parallel to European modernism at the same time that it established an unequivocally national identity, largely through the employment of American vernacular materials as sources of inspiration and stylistic reference. Yet Ives himself might have argued that the succeeding generation was stronger for having to invent its own models.

Two representative figures: Gershwin and Copland

In the period under discussion, George Gershwin (1898–1937) and Aaron Copland (1900–1990) were the most widely celebrated examples, nationally and internationally, of the modern American art music composer. Each in his very different way forged relationships between American vernacular musics and the concert hall, and each developed his own, emphatically twentieth-century musical style demonstrating expansions of melodic, harmonic, and rhythmic vocabulary analogous to those present in contemporaneous European art music. For both of them, it is the "tonal" composers of early European modernism – such as Debussy and Stravinsky – whose works furnish the obvious analogies (and at least in Copland's case, the conscious influences), rather than the "atonal" Second Viennese School. It is important to realize, however, that for virtually all American composers of this generation "tonality" and "atonality" were not central theoretical and stylistic issues, as they were for many European composers at the time; Americans, of course, had no long-standing native tradition of tonal art music to react toward or against. The music of Gershwin, Copland, and many of their distinguished contemporaries is *incidentally* "tonal" by virtue of the character of its basic material – vernacularly derived or otherwise – rather than as a consequence of adherence to any preordained philosophical tenets. Perhaps therefore the title of this chapter, although it readily identifies a particular group of composers, focuses inordinate attention on a non-essential issue, and tends to obscure both compelling differences among the members of this group and compelling diversities within the outputs of its individual members. (In his later career, Copland did turn to serialism for a few works, without abandoning tonal writing in others. Although Gershwin in his too-brief career did no such thing, he did profess to know and admire the music of Schoenberg, Berg, and Webern.)

There are some surprising similarities between Gershwin and Copland. Both were Brooklyn-born children of immigrant Russian-Jewish parents, and both came from "non-musical" families. Their successful careers thus present versions of one American dream, that of the totally self-made, first-generation American professional. Both started the study of music with neighborhood piano teachers, rapidly outgrowing them, but it is after this that the careers diverge. Gershwin turned to the practical "school" of popular music song-plugging in Tin Pan Alley, while Copland headed abroad for formal training as an art music composer with Nadia Boulanger in Paris. Divergences were laid out here which resonate in various ways throughout the entire history of American music in the twentieth century: practical experience *versus* formal training; popular music *versus* art music; immersion in American life and culture *versus* study abroad, with its accompanying issues of nationalism *versus* cosmopolitanism and the whole question of the need or desirability of international (actually, European) "validation" for American artists. (Curiously, while many American composers went to study in Europe during this broad period, few seem to have been *directly* influenced to a significant degree by those European émigrées – including Rachmaninov, Milhaud, Hindemith, and even Schoenberg and Stravinsky – who resided in America. This issue, particularly in relation to Schoenberg, is discussed further in chapter 18.)

Gershwin, trained first-hand in American vernacular music, sought out the genres and forms of the concert hall to expand his range and visibility as an American composer. Copland, arriving back in his native land after three years' immersion in European art music, sought out the sounds and styles of American vernacular music as the appropriate source material for one who wished to proclaim himself an *American* composer. The styles and timbres of 1920s jazz bands and theatre orchestras loom large both in Gershwin's *Rhapsody in Blue* (1924) and in Copland's *Music for the Theatre* (1925), the former's first concert work and the latter's first "American" work, respectively. Each composer followed his initial success of this type by composing a piano concerto, Gershwin's Concerto in F appearing in 1925, Copland's Concerto for Piano and Orchestra the following year; in these works, the jazz influence is particularly marked. As both composers were active in New York, where the premieres of all four works took place, it is curious that they appear to have taken minimal notice of one another (Copland and Perlis 1984, p. 130). Copland's writings refer at some length to virtually every major composer among his contemporaries except Gershwin (Copland 1968). Was there an unstated rivalry in these early years, or – more likely – did Copland, along with so many formally trained composers who came after him, simply not know what to make of Gershwin? Gershwin's silence is more understandable, as he wrote and said little about most other composers, although some occasional recorded remarks

suggest what is apparent in his music: that he knew more about the larger
world of culture than he often let on, that he absorbed ideas and influences
from everywhere, and that he was capable of learning whatever and whenever he liked from the music of others.

Gershwin's concert music

When he received the commission to write a piano concerto in 1925,
Gershwin quipped that he would have to go get some books to find out
what the form of a concerto was (Jablonski 1987, p. 98). The remark
confirms the ingenuous brashness of this confident auto-didact, but it also
reveals why many in the art music world were not prepared to take him
seriously. Gershwin's concerto does have a standard three-movement
arrangement, but within the individual movements it is formally quite
original in its layout of themes and harmonic centers, a characteristic it
shares with the earlier *Rhapsody in Blue* and the later *An American in Paris*
(1928). It is entirely too easy to mistake such originality for lack of formal
control, just as it is all too easy to claim that Gershwin simply utilized
popular tunes as his melodic material in these works. In fact, beginning
with the *Rhapsody*, Gershwin wrote instrumentally conceived, often asymmetrical themes with complex harmonic implications – frequently involving blue notes – for his concert works, and spun his distinctive forms out of
their unusual potential. Ironically, the one time that Gershwin did use a
standard popular tune as the basis for a concert work, he used it to generate
a composition with a very traditional form: the *Variations on* [his own] *"I
Got Rhythm"* (1934) clearly reveals its creator's formal mastery and
imagination.

   After establishing his reputation in America, Gershwin did go abroad.
His experiences in Paris, memorialized in the tone poem bearing that
city's name, were rather different from those of the younger Copland.
Gershwin arrived to find himself famous, and although he announced his
interest in studying with some master musicians, these luminaries
informed him that they had nothing to teach him. In yet another version of
the "Europeans understand and appreciate our American artists much
better than we do" saga, both Ravel and Boulanger told Gershwin that,
since he was already so skilled at utilizing his unique combination of
talents, nothing could be gained by his studying with them (Jablonski
1987, pp. 154–158).

   As befits a composer frequently immersed in the daily immediacy of the popular music business, Gershwin wrote concert music that seems to stem directly from spontaneous experience. The score of *An American in Paris* incorporates music written for a specific set of taxi horns that its composer found in Paris and bought for himself; when composing *Porgy and Bess* in 1934 Gershwin spent a summer on Folly Island outside Charleston, South Carolina, so that he could immerse himself in the culture of the nearby community of Gullah African Americans, the people who inspired DuBose Heyward's libretto for the opera. (In contrast, Copland frequently demonstrated a traditional artist's detachment from his material. To employ another Paris example, it was in that city that Copland, who by his own admission "knew nothing about the Wild West" [Copland and Perlis 1984, p. 279], familiarized himself with cowboy songs and wrote *Billy the Kid* in 1938.)

Everything in Gershwin's career up to 1934 seems to have played a part in readying him to write his masterpiece *Porgy and Bess*. It was in this "American folk opera" (Gershwin's own subtitle for the work, which appears in the published piano-vocal score) that he was able to synthesize everything he had learned about popular song and musical theatre with everything he had learned about the composition of extended concert works. From a certain point of view, all of Gershwin's concert music – and one could extend this observation to his musical style itself – is about the synthesis of diverse elements, and over the course of his career he continued to pose himself larger and more complex problems of synthesis. Even within the standardized forms and relatively restrained style of his popular songs, for example, one may see the progressively increasing sophistication that characterizes Gershwin's employment of blue notes and their integration into a harmonic style built upon an expanded common-practice tonality. *Rhapsody in Blue* takes this harmonic and structural challenge onto a much broader field of play, while forging a link between the characteristic sounds and playing styles of a dance band and the characteristic gestures and scope of a Romantic art music rhapsody. By the time of *An American in Paris*, Gershwin is creating links among a wide variety of popular music and art music styles (the work evokes the blues and the Charleston – at one memorable point, simultaneously – along with some modernist urban sounds and reminiscences of French impressionism) in a work that is both significantly longer and structurally tighter than the *Rhapsody*. *Porgy*'s subtitle of "American folk opera" itself indicates the range and complexity of the synthesis Gershwin sought, and achieved, in his last completed work of concert music.

The music of *Porgy and Bess* runs a gamut from evocations of solo gospel-style singing (*Oh, Doctor Jesus*) and choral spirituals (*Clara, Clara*) to complex modernistic fugal passages (the crap-game fight in Act I, scene 1 – heard again in III, 1) and a modally inflected, harmonically complex aria with a middle section that rhythmically recalls Stravinsky (*Buzzard Song*). Along the way are heard evocations of polyrhythmic African drumming (opening of Act II, scene 2) and a prayer for six voices in *ad libitum* rhythm with an indeterminate alignment of the parts (beginning and ending of Act II, scene 4). Tin Pan Alley song forms also occur: to help evoke Tin Pan Alley itself in Sporting Life's jazz-tinged *There's a Boat Dat's Leavin' Soon for New York* and – in a remarkable transmutation – to help shape Serena's supremely operatic lament for her dead husband, *My Man's Gone Now*. With all this, there are no specific musical quotations in this most prodigious of American theatre works, and it is Gershwin's control over the full range of his own style that keeps its extraordinary richness from ultimately overwhelming its coherence.

In its dramatic aspects as well, the opera is utterly *sui generis*. It is, strictly speaking, neither tragedy nor comedy, while it has strong elements of both. The work certainly can be seen as the story of a community, but of the opera's major characters only one (Serena) remains in Catfish Row when the final curtain falls. Much ink has been spilled over the issues of race and possible stereotyping in *Porgy*; yet a knowledge of Gershwin's complete work will yield, as a knowledge of excerpts or truncated versions cannot, an appreciation of how complex its leading characters are. Arguably, the only truly stereotyped parts in the opera are those of the *white* southerners, whose distance from the intricate and expressive world of the black characters is emblematized by the fact that they are not even permitted by Gershwin to sing, but only to speak.

Copland's career and importance

What Gershwin might have accomplished beyond the achievement of *Porgy and Bess* must remain the subject of speculation; what is beyond question is the gravity of the loss to American music that his premature death represents. In an intriguing quirk of history, Gershwin's place as the best-known living American composer of art music was quickly filled after his death by none other than Copland. This is especially remarkable because, in the period between Copland's 1926 Concerto for Piano and Orchestra and the group of populist works on specifically American themes, beginning with *El salón México* (1933–1936), that solidified his reputation with the concert-going public, his compositional stance was essentially that of an austere modernist writing in an abstract, cosmopolitan style. It stands as Copland's great achievement that he was able to wield his always economical, meticulously coherent conception of style into the service of an exceptionally diverse variety of material over the course of his career. If Gershwin's art is that of continual, broadening synthesis, Copland's is that of constant redirection and reinvention of compositional vision. While there is no single piece of Copland's to compare with *Porgy and Bess*, it is nevertheless true that, work by work, Copland amassed an oeuvre surpassed in scope and variety only by that of Ives.

Copland's central importance as a composer rests upon two factors. From a technical standpoint, his work provides the most obvious and direct link between a twentieth-century American style and the styles of European modernism. From an expressive standpoint, he established representative and enduring musical portrayals of both rural and urban America – capturing aspects of the nation's past and present, celebrating both majestic open spaces and crowded cities, always with lurking suggestions of distance and edginess. What results is as eloquent an artistic statement on the twentieth-century human condition as may be found anywhere in American music.

Copland's fluency with the Franco-Russian strains of modernist style is already evident in the ballet score *Grohg* (1922–1925; arranged in part as *Dance Symphony*, 1930) and the Symphony for Organ and Orchestra (1924; originally composed for performance by Boulanger as soloist). Elements found in these and other scores from this period that remained hallmarks of the composer's style throughout his career include: concise, pitch-centric melodic ideas freely incorporating modal and chromatic inflections; an emphasis on rhythmic invention and variety that frequently finds expression through complex and changing meters; and a versatile and virtuosic use of the wind, brass, and percussion sections of the orchestra. Copland's great initial discovery was that these modernist elements were extremely compatible with jazz-derived ideas, and could be used in the service of a music that readily evoked the vernacular flavors of urban twentieth-century America. (Copland of course was neither alone in this discovery, nor the first to make it; works by Debussy, Stravinsky, Milhaud, and others clearly demonstrate the influence and appeal of American vernacular styles to European modernists. But Copland's explorations of the intersections between modernism and the contemporary American vernacular probed much deeper than those of any European composer, and certainly were central to his process of self-definition as an artist.) Beginning in the mid-1930s, Copland stretched his imagination still further, and found that the essentials and the integrity of his stylistic approach could be retained even when he utilized diatonic, rhythmically plain folk-based or folk-like material to evoke a more rural American landscape.

The alchemy of Copland's most famous scores, like those of Gershwin, is elusive; in the case of both, over-familiarity and the omnipresence of inferior imitations risk deafening us to their authentic magic. Echoes of Copland's music for the ballet *Billy the Kid* resound in the movies and on television whenever the "wide open spaces" are evoked: unadorned octaves and fifths for the sense of uncluttered landscape, solo wind instruments for the sense of sparse population and loneliness, widely spaced orchestral sonorities for the sense of expanse, and of course the hints of cowboy song for "authenticity." But what imitation can boast the economy of *Billy*'s opening music, *The Open Prairie*, or the overall formal and expressive balance of the entire ballet that makes the same prairie music seem at once so revelatory and so inevitable when it returns at the end? Copland's treatment of folk and folk-like material in *Billy* reflects both compositional subtlety and complexity of aesthetic stance. The section *Street in a Frontier Town* presents fragments and juxtapositions of tunes in a manner that conveys their interrelatedness, while spiking them with occasional dissonances and rhythmic "irregularities" that – far from seeming mere modernist mannerisms – help measure the distance in time and space between the composer and his Old West subject matter. Later, in *Card Game at Night*, the modal phrases recalling cowboy song are heard over an undulating, polyrhythmic, constantly mutating accompaniment, suggesting both shifting sands and the poignant inevitability of change and loss.

Analogous observations are relevant to other Copland scores from this period. In his most famous work, the ballet *Appalachian Spring* (1943–1944), the extreme diatonicism takes the twentieth-century listener to a distant American past at the same time that it captures something of the stark asceticism of the Shaker community; by the time the sole quoted tune *Simple Gifts* is heard, its scalewise material seems to arise naturally out of its surrounding musical environment. The unresolved leading-tone over the tonic note at the conclusion of this ballet score is a characteristic touch, epitomizing the unfathomable and unresolvable distance separating creator, and audience, from the subject matter, but also expressing the universal hope for new beginnings, futures, unseen horizons. As an instance of Copland's urban landscape painting, one could cite the chamber orchestra work *Quiet City* (1939–1940, from music originally written for Irwin Shaw's play). Here, the solo trumpet sounding jittery, tentative repeated notes – that eventually flower into expansive and expressive lines, only to fall back into repetitive fragments – offers a telling portrayal of personal isolation in the heart of a modern city environment.

Between his jazz-influenced scores of the mid-1920s and the Americanist works of the period just cited, Copland produced a series of pieces representing what he called his "difficult" side (Copland 1968, p. 160). These compositions, including most prominently the trio *Vitebsk* (1929), *Piano Variations* (1930), *Short Symphony* (1932–1933), and *Statements for Orchestra* (1932–1935), secured his reputation as a leading contemporary figure among composers and cognoscenti nationally and internationally. Yet even today most of these works are infrequently heard and recorded – not only in comparison to the famous Copland scores that followed, but in comparison to much European modernist music. They share this fate with many significant later works that show Copland's more abstract side, such as the Piano Sonata (1939–1941), the Quartet for Piano and Strings (1950), *Piano Fantasy* (1952–1957), the Nonet for solo strings (1960), and others. As long as superficial criteria of dissonance level and degree of rhythmic complexity are regarded as aesthetic determinants, the notion that there are two Coplands (a notion that the composer himself, reluctantly or not, endorsed – see Copland 1968, pp. 161–164, and p. 168) will prevail and will unfortunately block too many members of both general and specialized audiences from a true, full appreciation of this composer's contributions. In fact, while the variety of works attests to the breadth and richness of Copland's range, the "difficult" works are – especially now – not all that "difficult" and are not really that dissimilar to many of the more traditionally accessible ones, just as the more popular works are replete with links to modernism and reveal aesthetic complexities that place them readily on a par with this century's most impressive and important music. *Vitebsk* is as permeated by the intervals and emotional character of its borrowed Jewish folk melody as is *Billy the Kid* by the technical and expressive nature of its borrowed American tunes. *Piano Variations* is as doggedly focused on its secundal harmonic language as *Appalachian Spring* is on thirds and triads, yet within the musical world of each is the implicit acknowledgment of a larger universe: triads occasionally occur in *Variations*, seeming in this context like brittle touches of sarcastic sweetness, while polychordal dissonances are not unknown in *Appalachian Spring*, where they serve to enrich immeasurably the work's stylistic and aesthetic frames of reference. In his Quartet for Piano and Strings, Copland undertook a significant exploration of serialism, yet his treatment of an eleven-tone series was sufficiently flexible to allow an extended passage of tonal character so obvious that he endowed it with a five-flat key signature.

There are occasional Copland works that utilize within themselves a larger-than-usual stylistic range, serving somewhat as demonstrations of the composer's overall sweep. Two from the immediate post-World War II period may be mentioned: the Third Symphony (1944–1946) and *Twelve Poems of Emily Dickinson* for voice and piano (1949–1950). The former, Copland's largest work for orchestra, ranges from the leisurely diatonic string music of its opening, which seems to bask in the afterglow of *Appalachian Spring*, to the overwhelmingly intense, if still diatonic, brass and percussion dialogue of *Fanfare for the Common Man*, a 1942 work incorporated into the beginning of the last movement. Along the way, the third movement begins and ends with highly chromatic string music of very ambiguous tonality, that nevertheless derives from material in the first movement. Copland's Dickinson settings run a gamut from the opening delicate diatonicism of *Nature, the Gentlest Mother* to the ninth- and cluster-laden language of the immediately following *There Came a Wind like a Bugle*, embracing much that lies stylistically in between the two. Although Copland's vocal output is small, this song cycle must rank among his most singular and important achievements, as he rose to the formidable challenge posed by Dickinson's verse and produced a work of both impressive unity and remarkable stylistic variety.

These two examples notwithstanding – and others might perhaps be cited – it is difficult to furnish any succinct summary of Copland's position in twentieth-century American art music, a fact which in itself may be a key to understanding his contribution. Unlike Gershwin, who (like Ives) gives the impression of having poured as much of himself as possible into each major work, even to the point of enthusiastic overflow, Copland tended for the most part to set carefully focused, refined, discrete goals for each of his compositions. As a result, one cannot begin to know Copland without investigating a substantial proportion of the entire oeuvre. Each of his individual works, while complete and perfect in itself, also illuminates and enlarges the others, and the underlying vastness of the composer's vision is revealed only by a panoramic view of his entire creative field.

Copland's influence on other American composers is inestimable. There were many, both older and younger, who followed his path to Paris to study with Boulanger and went on to achieve considerable distinction, among them Walter Piston (1894–1976), Virgil Thomson (1896–1989), Roy Harris (1898–1979), Elliott Carter (born 1908) and David Diamond (born 1915). There is, however, no Copland "school." Although he certainly furnished the model for an internationally recognized, universally respected, American, *modern*, art music composer, Copland's personal fusion of a highly focused, lapidary technique with an apparently unlimited range of compositional interests was uniquely his own, and his distinguished creative colleagues paid him appropriate homage by honoring and emulating his distinction without attempting directly to imitate him.

Gershwin was a much more problematic, and an even more elusive, model for American art music composers than Copland, but one renowned composer obviously influenced by both Copland and Gershwin was Leonard Bernstein (1918–1990), whose work is discussed in chapters 12 and 20. Like Copland, Bernstein investigated the American vernacular from the standpoint of a formally trained classical musician; but Bernstein resembled Gershwin more than Copland in the extent and thoroughness of his immersion in American musical theatre and popular song.

The case of William Grant Still

There were an extraordinary number of American composers of modern, tonal concert music who came to prominence in the period between the World Wars. But an equally extraordinary historical development ensued: in the years following World War II only Gershwin and Copland from this group seemed to remain securely in the repertory, while the others found their careers in a state of gradual or sudden eclipse. (The one, partial exception to this is Samuel Barber, who will receive attention shortly.) No composer plummeted from authentic prominence to an eclipse more total than that endured by William Grant Still (1895–1978). This is particularly ironic, insofar as Still is a composer whose career and oeuvre offer many obvious parallels to those of Gershwin and Copland.

Like Gershwin, Still had a substantial career in commercial popular music. He played in dance and theatre orchestras – including that of the Blake–Sissle show *Shuffle Along* – and did a great deal of arranging for W. C. Handy, Paul Whiteman, and many others. Like Copland, he also undertook considerable formal study of art music, at Oberlin College Conservatory and privately with Chadwick and Varèse. (Having lessons within a period of a few years from both a celebrated elder of American late-Romantic music and a radical French emigrant nearly thirty years younger must have been a remarkable experience for Still, to say the least.) The Varèse connection offered modernist credentials to Still, which he affirmed in the style of early chamber orchestra works like *Black Bottom* (1922) and *From the Land of Dreams* (1924). Following this, he attempted to integrate jazz elements with art music idioms in the four songs of *Levee Land* (1925). The parallels here to the early career of Copland are readily drawn, and the noteworthy reception accorded *Levee Land* by critics had doubtless to some extent been prepared by the very recent premiere of Copland's own *Music for the Theatre*, and by the already prominent reputation of Gershwin's scarcely-older *Rhapsody in Blue*. Unlike Copland, Still turned away ideologically from modernism at this point, although much of his substantial subsequent output nevertheless bears the unmistakable imprint of early twentieth-century harmonic and orchestrational practices. The synthesis of jazz- and folk-flavored material with such practices, which is typical of Still's mature approach to composition and which associates him inevitably with Gershwin and with the populist works of Copland, may clearly be heard in his initially most celebrated – and to this day most famous – work, *Afro-American Symphony* (1930).

In certain respects, Still's reach as a composer seems to exceed even that of Copland or Gershwin. In terms of the evocation or actual utilization of vernacular material, Still ranges beyond source material from the United States and beyond the better-known Latin-American types (also used by Copland) to encompass various Native American sources, from both North and South America, and African material; the *Folk Suite # 1* (1962) even contains two "Hebraic" songs, along with Brazilian and African American melodies. Still was reportedly fond of pointing out that he inherited from his parents Scotch, Irish, Negro, Spanish, and American Indian bloodlines (Still 1995, p. iii), and he embraced a tolerant diversity in his life as well as his music. In terms of the scope and ambition of his musical output, Still's oeuvre includes no fewer than nine substantial operas, four ballets, five symphonies, a body of descriptive music for orchestra, much choral and chamber music, and a long list of pieces for solo voice and piano – an achievement that can be set beside that of any major composer of this century.

The pity is that the overwhelming majority of this music, both ambitious pieces and unassuming ones, lies presently unknown. Many important Still works remain in manuscript; others, although published, are not readily available even in libraries. Contemporary performances and recordings of Still's music are entirely too uncommon. Unless and until this music begins to be known and played on a significant scale, one really cannot venture an estimation of the relationship between Still's enormous attempted reach and his actual grasp. Above all, Still aspired to be known as an opera composer, but not one of his many efforts in this genre has ever achieved currency in performance or been recorded.

That Still's music merits a careful re-evaluation is a case readily made by a look at a few of the better-known works. These reveal the hand of a composer with a wide and effective stylistic palette and a highly refined sensitivity to vocal and instrumental color. *Three Visions* (1936) for piano, and *Songs of Separation* (1949), a cycle for solo voice and piano, serve well as illustrations.

The central movement of *Three Visions* is the leisurely and lovely *Summerland*, one of Still's own favorite compositions and one of his most frequently heard pieces; he made a number of arrangements of it for various instrumental groups. It projects a style of gently jazz-nudged impressionism in its harmonies and in its use of keyboard register and chord voicings. While *Summerland* is appealing in any of its incarnations, it is by far most effective in its original context – where it creates striking relationships with the movements that enclose it: the gruff opening *Dark Horsemen*, that reveals Still's lingering connections with European modernism in its kinship with Prokofiev and Bartók at their most aggressive, and the concluding *Radiant Pinnacle*, which summarizes and reconciles the stylistic contrast presented by the two other pieces. The breadth of style found in *Three Visions* is also seen in other Still piano works, such as *Seven Traceries* (1939), *Bells* (1944), and *Preludes* (1962). *Songs of Separation*, settings of five texts by five black poets, is a further testament to the composer's wide stylistic range, and reveals a gift for conciseness. These varied poetic and musical reflections on love gone wrong leave one curious about what riches might lie within Still's huge and unknown opera output.

The current status of Still's reputation must be considered initially in the broader context of the post-1945 decline in the general status of twentieth-century tonal art music, a decline that also impacted the reputations of Piston, Thomson, Harris, Howard Hanson (1896–1981), William Schuman (1910–1992), and many others. What accounts for the "fall from grace" of this large body of diverse and distinguished music, music that was initially welcomed and celebrated in many quarters as a significant part of what seemed a virtual American Renaissance in the arts between the World Wars? Historians can offer only conjectural answers, but some compelling possibilities may be suggested.

First, account must be taken of the cultural environment in America following World War II. Although the war had been won, the toll taken on Americans had been overwhelming. The heady optimism of the booming 1920s, which at least for some had been successfully transformed into a positive sense of common political and social purpose – in combating first the national economic depression of the 1930s and then the Axis powers in the war itself – no longer seemed a viable outlook. The country as a whole turned inward, seeking to reestablish domestic tranquillity on all levels of social and political organization. A widespread cultural conservatism was a natural result of this, bringing a consequent loss of involvement with contemporary – and even the older modern – art on the part of many in the American audience. Post-war Americans certainly craved culture, but it was the established, sanctioned culture of the "classics." This was the great era of "music appreciation," in which the appreciation of twentieth-century music played a small role, that of American music a smaller role yet (Horowitz 1987).

Then, the arts themselves turned inward after the war, perhaps in response to this altered cultural environment, perhaps as their own reaction to the horrors of the war and the resulting sense that prior aesthetic styles and stances might no longer be meaningful or relevant. In any case, there arose in America, as in Europe, a new musical avant garde involved chiefly with serialism, experimentation, and novel electronic media. To this group the music and concerns of the immediately preceding generation of American tonal composers must have seemed as far removed from their own interests as were those of the nineteenth-century European Romantics. Milton Babbitt (born 1916) was widely accepted as a representative figure for this new group of artists, composers who seemed virtually to disdain the notion of attracting any kind of broad general audience for their compositions (Babbitt 1958), but whose ideas dominated academic and intellectual life and stimulated much critical discussion (see chapter 18). The ascendance of this group in turn accelerated the marginalization of the older group of tonal composers within the culture at large. Marginalized along with them was the stance of empathy and tolerance for a wide diversity of musical styles, a stance epitomized perfectly by the public writings and discourse of Copland and represented also by others of his generation and outlook, such as Hanson and Thomson.

The young are often a highly receptive group for the new and nearly-new in music. But the post-war generation of "baby boomers" had their *own* brand-new music in rock and roll, with which any and all art music had to compete for time, attention, and above all affection. Given this development, the splintered condition of contemporary American art music itself, and the prevailingly conservative cultural landscape, the eclipse of composers such as Still and his colleagues may appear more understandable, if no less unfortunate.

In Still's case, the additional, volatile factor of race must perforce be factored into the equation. To a certain extent, the early recognition accorded Still was surely connected to the facts that he was the *first* black American to have a symphony played by a major orchestra (when the Rochester Philharmonic Orchestra under Hanson premiered *Afro-American Symphony* in 1931), the *first* black American to have an opera produced by a major opera company (when, early in 1949, the New York City Opera premiered *Troubled Island*, composed in 1941 to a libretto by Langston Hughes), the *first* black American to conduct an important orchestra (the Los Angeles Philharmonic in 1936, in a performance of his own works), and so on. Contrariwise, Still's gentlemanly approach to issues of race relations and his rejection of ethno-centered politics (Still 1995, pp. 75–79) doubtless have contributed to his perceived irrelevance in certain cultural circles from the highly politicized 1960s on to the present day. But Still's contribution to American music seems too significant to remain mired in racial – or cultural – politics. In this case, an old-fashioned objective look at the *musical* achievement stands paradoxically as an imperative mandate for future scholarship. With the aid of such scholarship, we may eventually learn to view Still's music through other than narrowly mandated lenses, as we seem finally to be learning to do with a work like Gershwin's *Porgy and Bess*.

Vocal music: Barber, Menotti, Thomson

Samuel Barber (1910–1981), while younger than any of the composers discussed thus far, was famous by the end of the 1930s. Conductor Arturo Toscanini, a conservative icon for "great" music, became an early advocate for Barber's work, assuring repertory status for the composer's *Adagio for Strings* (1936) and *[First] Essay for Orchestra* (1937) when he premiered them both at an NBC Symphony Orchestra concert in 1938. To this day, the *Adagio*, an arrangement for string orchestra of the second movement of Barber's String Quartet (1936), remains the composer's most celebrated piece; it is also one of the best-known and most frequently played works by any American composer. Its basic characteristics remained hallmarks of Barber's style throughout his career: long, lyrical melodic lines; pitch structures that take as their point of departure diatonic scales and chord relationships; and flexibility of meter.

His characteristic lyricism, along with a great sensitivity to the nuances and accentuation of poetic texts, made Barber a master of vocal music. (He was also a trained singer.) The support his works received from such renowned divas as Eleanor Steber and Leontyne Price helped secure Barber a continuing presence on vocal concert and recital programs. Among twentieth-century art song composers, probably only Poulenc is as popular as Barber among both student and professional singers; the two composers share a conservatism of style that often borders on a kind of Romanticism. Barber's temperamental kinship with European Romanticism clearly sets him apart from the other American tonal composers previously discussed; native vernacular music, for the most part, made a negligible impact on his style. It is characteristic that, in choosing his texts for musical setting, Barber tended to favor British and European poets over American sources.

If Barber seems an exception to many of the trends noted so far in this chapter, care must nevertheless be taken not to pigeonhole or underestimate his contribution on this basis. Two of his most justifiably acclaimed works, *Knoxville: Summer of 1915*, for high voice and orchestra (1947), and *Hermit Songs*, for voice and piano (1952–1953), represent atypical Barber projects to some degree. *Knoxville*, commissioned and premiered by Eleanor Steber, is an ambitious setting of an unconventional American text describing an American scene. Barber's response to James Agee's complex, asymmetrical prose (which incorporates a brief fragment of free-verse poetry) arguably constitutes his most remarkable and sustained vocal composition. Agee's reminiscence is that of an adult using deliberately unusual vocabulary and grammatical structures in an attempt to capture his childhood world of feelings and sounds. Barber's setting ranges from a child's diatonic sing-song, evoking both the motion of rocking chairs on porches in the summer evening and the innocence of childhood itself, to intense aria-like passages that portray the adult's consciousness of transience and mortality. The result is an uncategorizable, uncannily affecting verbal–musical synthesis that conveys the intricate and ambiguous ways in which the child's and the adult's perceptual worlds are bound up in one another. *Knoxville* is a lullaby sung by an adult to the child that she once was. Now frequently recorded, it is starting to become well known to the wide public it deserves.

Hermit Songs, premiered and often performed by Leontyne Price, is an unconventional and diverse cycle based on ten texts translated from medieval Irish manuscripts. The texts themselves range from brief, virtually offhand fragments (*Promiscuity*) to intense religious meditations (*The Crucifixion*). The musical settings display a correspondingly wide variety of musical styles and keyboard textures. Several of the songs last less than a minute, but the cycle builds to a substantial and impassioned conclusion with *The Desire for Hermitage*, which in effect throws a conceptually unifying backlight over all the preceding songs.

The lyrical and dramatic talent that is evidenced in Barber's songs, along with his affinity for the heritage of European Romanticism, were poised to make opera composition a potential strength for this composer. Unfortunately, Barber proved no more successful in founding a school of American opera than any of his contemporaries. His *Vanessa* (1956–1957), premiered at the Metropolitan Opera in 1958, does not appear to have entered the repertory despite initial critical approval and audience acceptance, while his Shakespearean opera *Antony and Cleopatra* (1966), written to inaugurate the Metropolitan Opera's new house in Lincoln Center, proved unsuccessful from the outset. With the single, remarkable exception of Gershwin, America's premier songwriters of the twentieth century either did not attempt opera at all – like Ives – or achieved noble failures with the genre – like Schubert. (This leaves aside the very legitimate issue of whether the Broadway musical does not in fact represent America's distinctive, authentic – and successful – native form of opera.)

In the case of *Vanessa*, Barber's not-particularly-American opera, set "in a northern country," falls victim to the same problems that haunt Copland's nearly contemporaneous pastoral opera of the American prairie, *The Tender Land* (1952–1955). Both, while boasting some splendid solo and ensemble set pieces, are relatively static dramatically, exploring the internal psychology of their characters rather than the impact of large-scale or intense stage events. It could also be claimed that the major characters in both, whether Barber's Vanessa and Erika or Copland's Laurie, are not so much developing personalities as representatives of established emotional and psychological conditions – conditions that cannot truly evolve, but can only fulfill their preordained destinies in a manner that seems inevitable but not truly dramatic.

One composer who did produce a group of operas that for a while achieved significant critical and audience recognition was the Italian-American Gian Carlo Menotti (born 1911), who was Barber's partner, as well as his librettist for *Vanessa*. Menotti's artistic temperament is, if anything, even closer to European late-Romanticism than that of Barber. But Menotti's (probably instinctive) choice of Puccini as a model for his dramatic and musical approach in works like *The Medium* (1946), *The Consul* (1950), and *The Saint of Bleecker Street* (1954) helped assure that these operas would be found both gripping and accessible by a mid-century American public.

Except for the Christmas perennial *Amahl and the Night Visitors* (1951), originally written for television, Menotti's work seems to be falling out of the repertory as the twentieth century draws to a close. Yet it is arguably unwise to let a group of clearly stageworthy, and initially successful, American operas fade into obscurity without a careful second look – especially given the relatively small number of twentieth-century American operas that have proven to be stageworthy and successful at all.

In a special category altogether are the two Virgil Thomson operas composed to librettos by Gertrude Stein, *Four Saints in Three Acts* (1927–1933) and *The Mother of Us All* (1947). These are hardly repertory items, but the challenges they pose to traditional conceptions of opera render that unsurprising, and the affection and esteem in which they are held by many connoisseurs of American music makes them important to the history of this period. The earlier work concerns rather more than four Spanish saints (in *four* acts, with two prologues); the later one concerns Susan B. Anthony and the women's suffrage movement in America; and beyond that it is difficult to state clearly what these operas are "about." Stein's librettos present a paradox that would be expected only by readers of her other works: composed largely of everyday words arranged in what appear to be straightforward grammatical structures, they rarely make conventional "sense" and present constant contradictions. Thomson found a valid musical analogy and support for Stein's texts in a deliberately homely diatonic style – clearly related to that of American hymnody – which incorporated, without apparent warning, unexpected modulations and occasional elements of "modern" dissonance and rhythmic dislocation.

In their reliance on highly restricted, often repetitive, verbal and musical materials, and in their lack of engagement with traditional notions of drama, plot, character development, musical development, and indeed with linearity in general, these works prefigure aspects of postmodernism in interesting ways and could even be viewed as conceptual antecedents to the operas of Philip Glass (born 1937). But it would be a mistake to see the operas as works utterly without precedent. They certainly owe more than a little to the prevailing aesthetics of post-World War I France. Both Thomson and Stein were admirers of Satie's *Socrate*, and both were living in Paris when Stravinsky's "opera-oratorio" *Oedipus Rex* was premiered there in 1927; such works presented significant challenges to conventional notions of musical drama (and, in the case of the Stravinsky, staging).

From the music of the operas, one would deduce correctly that Thomson was essentially a lyrical composer and, despite the considerable extent and variety of his total output, something of a miniaturist. The dozens of musical "portraits" written throughout his career (mainly for solo piano, but also for solo violin, chamber groups, and even orchestra) are indicative – embracing a variety of stylistic approaches, they could conceivably stand as his single most representative body of work. Like Barber, Thomson also favored vocal music, and composed much for solo voice and for chorus; the appropriate setting of English texts remained one of his lifelong concerns (Thomson 1989). But Thomson differed significantly from Barber in his rejection of anything suggesting Romantic style. The epic gesture, or anything that smacks of the grandiose, is thus utterly foreign to Thomson's aesthetic. (And it is this that differentiates him most clearly from his close contemporary, and good friend, Copland.)

Like Copland, Thomson was also an articulate and important writer. As music critic of the *New York Herald-Tribune* from 1940 to 1954, he made a substantial contribution to the still-slender shelf of significant journalism in the field; his taste was wide-ranging and honed with an admirable disdain for pretense and showmanship. Yet there remains a major blemish on his critical record, consisting of the condescension with which he treated two giants of American music whose musical (and personal) styles differed greatly from his own – Gershwin and Ives (Thomson 1935; Thomson 1971, pp. 22–30).

American symphonists: Hanson, Piston, Harris

As a genre, the American symphony fared much better than American opera in the period under discussion. Many important composers were drawn repeatedly to the symphony – among them Henry Cowell, Paul Creston, David Diamond, Alan Hovhaness, Peter Mennin, Vincent Persichetti, and William Schuman – and produced highly distinctive and well-regarded series of works. Among the many symphonies were several, by different composers, that became individually recognized as representatively American: for instance, Hanson's Symphony No. 2 (*Romantic*), Harris's Third, and Copland's Third.

Although Copland's symphonies are all remarkable works, they are insufficient in number and too individual in style and intent to comprise anything like a symphonic cycle; one does not think of Copland primarily when discussing American symphonists. The composers of whom one does think tend to be those who have acquired relatively standardized textbook-type classifications and characterizations over the years: Hanson, the conservative latter-day Romantic, indebted principally to European models; Piston, the academic neoclassicist, an internationalist; Harris, the rugged American individualist. Although such labels have their reasons for being, they end up inevitably oversimplifying and distorting complex, diverse careers and complex, diverse oeuvres. What follows is a brief consideration of these three American symphonists – others could just as reasonably have been chosen – in order to demonstrate that they are representative of their generation only, but crucially, insofar as their textbook labels and reputations fail utterly to do them justice.

With his Symphony No. 1, Op. 21 (*Nordic*, 1922), Hanson certainly established with one stroke his mastery of late Romantic symphonic style. While early twentieth-century European symphonists like Rachmaninov and Sibelius are the obvious points of reference for Hanson here, Americanists could also readily link this work – in style, spirit, and the titular reference to overseas inspiration – to Amy Beach's *Gaelic Symphony* of 1894–1896 (see chapter 9). With the following Symphony No. 2, Op. 30 (*Romantic*, 1930), Hanson acknowledged the roots of his aesthetic stance at the same time that he began to move beyond the confines of the late-nineteenth-century tonal system that still governed the language of its predecessor. In Symphony No. 2, while triads still serve as ultimate goals, motion is organized by local and long-range chromatic progressions in both melody and harmony, with a free handling of dissonance and lengthy periods of tonal irresolution. Hanson's "Romantic" gift for lyrical melody keeps this all very accessible, while local and large-scale cyclic repetitions maintain a clear sense of formal process.

If Hanson's evolution as a composer had ceased with his second symphony, the traditional, limiting characterizations of him might be justified; in fact, he wrote a total of seven symphonies, the last – *A Sea Symphony*, with choral settings of Whitman texts – as late as 1977. In the later symphonies, as in his other contemporaneous works, Hanson apparently attempted a rapprochement with aspects of modernism congenial to him, without ever abandoning his personal aesthetic. By the time of the Symphony No. 6 (1967), the composer had forged an individual kind of twentieth-century Romanticism; those familiar only with the first two symphonies might well have difficulty recognizing the Hanson of this work. While the music is still melodic and accessible, and the orchestral textures often lush, the structures and gestures of the nineteenth-century symphony have been discarded completely. Instead, there are six brief movements in rhapsodic forms with alternating, contrasting expressive and rhythmic characteristics. The motivic linking is subtle rather than overt, the endings of movements are often understated and epigrammatic, and the pitch language is replete with twentieth-century characteristics and pleasantly unpredictable in its direction. The closest stylistic analogies – and one feels these only at points, because Hanson seems so essentially himself in this work – are Copland, the French impressionists, and the Soviet symphonists. Above all, the breadth of style Hanson achieves here – a quintessentially American characteristic – is admirable.

Hanson also brought this wide stylistic frame of reference to his career as a conductor, serving as an advocate throughout his life for American music in all its multiple manifestations. Hanson's logical empathy for the work of Still makes his work on that composer's behalf no less praiseworthy; on the other hand, Hanson's embrace could extend to a work as far from his own predilections as Ives's *Three Places in New England*, of which Hanson conducted an early and, to this day, widely admired recorded performance. Howard Hanson is surely much more than our "conservative, latter-day Romantic" musician.

The stylistic language of Walter Piston evolved over the course of his eight symphonies as much as that of Hanson did. Piston came to the symphony late, and was past fifty when his Symphony No. 2 (1943) gained him renown by winning the New York Music Critics' Circle Award for 1944. This work, whose deep seriousness may well reflect its wartime origin, demonstrates characteristics that came to be regarded as definitive of Piston's style: concise diatonic themes with clear phrase structures, well suited for extensive harmonic and rhythmic development; crisp, uncluttered orchestration that emphasizes individual sections of strings and solo winds; a sure and relatively conventional sense of form. These characteristics, combined with the lack of obvious stylistic Americanisms, clearly account for Piston's "neoclassical" label and for his reputation as an "academic" composer. Yet these classifications seem unduly restrictive even for describing the Symphony No. 2 alone. They surely don't reflect adequately the unswerving and personal lyricism that informs the central, long Adagio movement of this work, a movement that articulates a restrained, yet undeniable, ethos of "Romanticism."

In Piston's Symphony No. 5 (1954), the "definitive" style traits of the Second Symphony are clearly heard only in the brief concluding movement – the composer now using diatonicism in particular as a goal, rather than as a point of departure. The preceding two movements present a highly chromatic melodic language, coupled with relatively dissonant harmony and an atmosphere of tonal uncertainty. In the Adagio (second) movement, the opening idea in fact immediately presents all twelve chromatic pitches, and this material persists as a source of accompanying figuration for other, more obviously pitch-centered, ideas. The final movement moves toward resolution by alternating clearly diatonic melodies and consonant harmonies with reminiscences of the earlier chromaticism and dissonance, eventually effecting a convincing peroration in a pure white-note passage that cadences on C.

While Piston's last two symphonies (No. 7, 1960; No. 8, 1965) build upon the stylistic tendencies of Symphony No. 5, in many passages pushing the concept of tonality virtually to the breaking point, the composer's Symphony No. 6 (1955) strikes a balance between his earlier and later harmonic languages. Each of the work's four movements takes diatonicism and pitch-centeredness as its point of departure and as its goal, but each strays well into some novel harmonic territory and, unusually for Piston, there are also passages demonstrating an adventurous approach to orchestration. The striking second movement, a scherzo, exhibits both aspects of novelty, with its scurrying *pianissimo* chromatic lines and percussive pizzicato seconds in the muted strings, and its elaborate use of the percussion section throughout. This is followed by a more conventional type of Piston movement: a long, slow, lyrical meditation. As a whole, the work asserts its kinship with long-standing symphonic traditions in its strong sense of harmonic movement overall from minor to major, with A being the central pitch. It also demonstrates extensively – as do all the Piston symphonies discussed – the limitations of the textbook view of this composer.

Roy Harris had the good fortune to compose a work, his Third Symphony (1939), that quickly became a repertory piece, if only for a relatively brief period of time. However, he paid a substantial price for this. The work became so identified with him that its success eclipsed interest in his other compositions, both earlier and later. Harris's *Symphony 1933* (1933; actually Symphony No. 1) was initially very well received, and was the first American symphony to be commercially recorded (by the Boston Symphony Orchestra under Koussevitzky, for Columbia in 1934); but it effectively vanished from sight once the Third Symphony had made its mark. The immediately following symphonies – and there were three of them composed between 1940 and 1944 – proved unable to fulfill expectations created by the premature "classic" status so quickly accorded the Third. (Whether this is because they are all noticeably different from the Third, and from each other – the Fourth is a work with chorus, the *Folksong Symphony* – or for other reasons, it is difficult to conjecture.) Then when the Third Symphony lost favor, along with so much other tonal American art music of its time, the consequent decline in Harris's reputation was precipitous. At present writing, the Third Symphony remains a standard textbook piece, if no longer a standard repertory piece, while the great bulk of Harris's huge output, encompassing all major genres and performance media other than opera, remains essentially unknown and even unpublished. The parallel with Still is obvious.

Harris's outstanding achievement in the Third Symphony was to create a work immediately identified and celebrated as "American," without either quoting or directly evoking pre-existing American musical materials, genres, or styles, and without relying on any programmatic adjuncts. In effect, the work provided a purely musical metaphor for American-ness. It did so by presenting an unusual synthesis of stylistic elements, a synthesis that was also recognized as Harris's personal trademark. The essential ingredient in the synthesis is melody, and the work opens with a long solo line given to the cellos. This melody is based on the plainest diatonic materials, and the most straightforward rhythmic values and configurations, yet these elements do not behave in any conventionally simple manner. Regularity of phrase structure and systematic repetition are studiously avoided, as the melody spins itself out to great and unpredictable lengths, very gradually incorporating non-diatonic tones and entering into textures involving both chordal accompaniment and elements of counterpoint. While the vertical elements tend also to be simple triads and intervals of perfect fourths and fifths, neither their progressions nor their combinations with tones of the melody are conventional or predictable. Out of these materials, Harris weaves a through-composed single-movement structure of remarkable originality, conviction, and coherence; by the end of its eighteen-minute span the listener has been taken through an uninterrupted sequence of textures and tempos that together carry the full weight of many a larger symphony. The synthesis of very basic, plain-spoken, melodic, harmonic, and rhythmic materials into a highly individual musical speech articulating asymmetrical, unprecedented, and fantastically expansive forms is as surely and essentially American as anything in our musical heritage.

That Harris can no more be typecast stylistically than any other composer discussed in this chapter is quickly established by a brief look at his Symphony No. 6 (*Gettysburg*, 1944). This time, the composer himself identified the American inspiration for his work – and then wrote music significantly different from that of his Third Symphony. Here, Harris uses the traditional four-movement arrangement, but with an unusual, inverted tempo sequence: all of the movements are moderate or slow in tempo except for the fast-moving second. This establishes a prevailing somberness of tone appropriate for this wartime work, written in the midst of one war and recalling another. While some of the melodic and formal aspects of this symphony are analogous to those of the Third, particularly in the intense and sustained third movement, nothing in the earlier work prepares us for the violent and bitter second movement, which recalls and parodies American march music with sounds and textures that link Harris to the more aggressive manifestations of modernism. Throughout, the Symphony No. 6 demonstrates a higher degree of dissonance than the Third Symphony, and the treatment of orchestral sonority, especially in the opening movement with its evocations of bells, shows a new inventiveness on the part of the composer.

*

The composers discussed in this chapter will have to serve, however problematically, as representatives for many worthy others whose accomplishments are analogous or comparable. Among these would be such diverse figures as Marion Bauer, William Bergsma, Ernest Bloch, John Alden Carpenter, Norman Dello Joio, Daniel Gregory Mason, Colin McPhee, Douglas Moore, Quincy Porter, and Randall Thompson. The American career of Mexican composer Carlos Chávez, and the early tonal pieces of Roger Sessions, Elliott Carter, and Lukas Foss could be placed in this discussion as well. Until much, much more of this work becomes readily available and sympathetically performed, there will be significant lacunae in the history, understanding, and appreciation of American

music. A large potential audience has been deprived not only of the opportunity to know and enjoy a body of important work, but of the opportunity to gain a greater general familiarity and comfort with
twentieth-century styles through exposure to some of the more accessible
practitioners. As a result, all twentieth-century composers, including the
avant garde, suffer from the consequences of this music's neglect. Perhaps
the accelerating interest in neo-Romanticism as the century draws to its
close will create a receptive climate for another look, and many more
listens, to audience-gratifying music from earlier in the century.

18

Serialism and complexity

STEPHEN PELES

In the fall of 1961 regular readers of the *New York Times* would have encountered a pair of brief articles published a day apart which, while unexceptional individually, are striking, at least in retrospect, in their
juxtaposition. Thursday, September 7 of that year saw the publication of a
short review (Salzman 1961) of a concert sponsored by the Fromm Music
Foundation. Presented the previous evening at the Metropolitan Museum
of Art under the aegis of the International Musicological Society, which
was holding its eighth congress at Columbia University from September 5
to September 12 (with ancillary events at Yale and Princeton Universities
and at the Library of Congress in Washington, D.C. [LaRue 1962]), the
concert offered only three works. Of these the first two – *Vision and Prayer*
for soprano and synthesized accompaniment, by Milton Babbitt (born
1916), and the Double Concerto, by Elliott Carter (born 1908) – were
world premieres, both commissioned by the Fromm Foundation. The
third – the Concerto for Violin, Cello, Ten Winds and Percussion by Leon
Kirchner (born 1919) – was a New York premiere.

The following day the *New York Times* printed an unattributed piece
(anon. 1961) announcing details of the New York Philharmonic's new subscription season that was doubtless read with greater anticipation by the
majority of readers. According to the article, Leonard Bernstein would
frame the season with two special "cycles," the "Gallic Approach" and the
"Teutonic Approach," occupying the first and last six weeks respectively
of the orchestra's calendar. The French cycle featured not only the works of
French composers but also works of "French influenced American
composers," and similarly for the German cycle. Mentioned on the French
side of the ledger were works by Berlioz, Debussy, Fauré, Honegger, Messiaen, Milhaud, Poulenc, Ravel, Roussel, Saint-Saëns, and Satie; also
included in the series according to the article would be premieres of works
by Walter Piston and David Diamond, along with pieces by Roy Harris,
Aaron Copland, Virgil Thomson, and Leo Smit. The "Teutonic approach"

was represented by Bach, Haydn, Mahler, Beethoven, Brahms, Walling-ford Riegger, Nielsen, and, perhaps incongruously, Ives. It was also announced that Nadia Boulanger would appear mid-season, presenting programs whose content was unspecified but deemed related to the Gallic cycle since "the distinguished French musician has served as a mentor for many American composers."

What is interesting about the juxtaposition of these two articles is not that they are odd in any sense. Quite the contrary: it is the typicality, in 1961, of the events they report, the extent to which taken together they are emblematic of a deeply divided musical culture, and the way in which the details of the events bear unmistakable vestigial traces of the half century of unprecedented historical change that engendered that division. That a prominent American conductor of Bernstein's generation would, in 1961, view the American music of this century as most usefully packaged for public consumption in terms of a French–German dichotomy is as telling an indication of the legacy of those changes as is the absence on either of the Philharmonic's nationally inspired cycles of any works by the three composers represented at the Fromm Foundation concert. Sketching the broad outlines of that legacy, and the music, musicians, and institutions involved, is the principal task of this chapter. For now it is necessary only to give some indication of certain consequences of the division between the American atonalists (as I shall call them) and established musical institutions of earlier generations, and to consider briefly some characteristics common to the music and intellectual commitments of the composers involved.

By 1961 the atonalists, like other composers of avowedly "advanced" music, had established what can only be regarded as an alternative institutional infrastructure for the support of their work – a situation clearly reflected in the two articles cited above, and one that would have been almost unimaginable at the turn of the century. By the 1970s, the tensions between many of these composers and the old guard were such that each viewed the other with indifference, and often with undisguised hostility. In economic terms these composers had of necessity come to rely rather little on the support of the general concert-going public, but instead on a frequently fragile combination of academic and foundation support. The academy was more likely to be represented by a university or college than a conservatory (though here as elsewhere there are notable exceptions); the foundations were apt to have been established precisely with the purpose of supporting new music of a sort not supported by traditional institutions like the Philharmonic. Virtually none of the alternative institutions in question were entirely the domain of the atonalists, of course – atonal composers shared office space and competed for foundation support with colleagues whose sympathies lay elsewhere – but it is the case that by the 1960s they were dependent upon those institutions, especially the university, to a greater degree than many composers of more conservative persuasions.

Of the music itself, the three works presented at the Fromm concert provide as good a sample as one might wish of the great diversity of musical sensibilities represented by the American atonalists of this generation. It is, perhaps, less immediately obvious what the three composers involved had in common. All were old enough to have lived through World War II but too young for its predecessor to have been more than a childhood memory, if that; all were university educated, and all held university appointments in 1961 (Babbitt had been on Princeton's faculty since 1948, Carter on Yale's since 1960, and Kirchner had just been appointed to Harvard's). Most importantly, all wrote music that was, in some fashion, "atonal" in ways more easily attributable to European influences of the first half of this century than to the relatively indigenous work of the American "experimental" school of the same period. Thus all were indebted, though in varying degrees and in very different ways, to the music of Arnold Schoenberg (1874–1956), despite the fact that only Kirchner, the youngest, had actually studied with him, having earned his BA from UCLA in 1940, when Schoenberg was at the midpoint of his eight-year tenure at that university.

Not insignificantly, theirs was a generation that had witnessed the heyday of non-representational visual art, and some no doubt saw a plausible parallel between the liberation of the visual artist from the necessity of referring to a world external to the art work and the liberation of the composer from the necessity of relating tones to a tonic; of the group in question many saw in Schoenberg's music suggestions, at least, of the kinds of music one might aspire to once liberated. It was also a generation nurtured on the literary works of writers like James Joyce, whose texts are not merely instances of language but are deeply, and even self-consciously, concerned with language itself. Indeed, if there was a single idea motivating this otherwise diverse group it might best be described as a "Joycean" orientation toward their work: as the reader of *Finnegans Wake* (whose very title carries a double meaning) learns, "every word will be bound over to carry three score and ten toptypsical readings throughout the book". To the extent that "complexity" was a concern to such composers, it was similarly less a matter of sheer number of notes per unit time than the number of meaningful relations that might be conferred upon an event through careful control of its context. (That many of the composers in this group – Babbitt in particular – were involved in the early dissemination in the United States of the tonal theories of Heinrich Schenker is thus less surprising than it might seem.) As a group, most shared certain central historical assumptions since most to some extent saw the music – especially the tonal music – of the European art music tradition as establishing important standards for craftsmanship, intellectual responsibility, and seriousness of purpose. At the same time that very tradition was understood as demanding a degree of originality that precluded the possibility of aspiring to those standards through a simple imitation of the music of the past. The best composers of the past were thus understood as contributing to the tradition not only great works but also, in various ways, to the enrichment of the musical language itself by investing it with new and hitherto unimagined possibilities. Of the numerous European modernists, Schoenberg, for many, most closely approximated to this ideal. It is this musical indebtedness, however indirect, to Schoenberg's atonal and twelve-tone music that provides the often tenuous link between composers of otherwise divergent musical and intellectual temperaments needed to warrant their consideration here. It must be stressed, however, that not only does that indebtedness vary widely in both degree and kind (since there was no consensus among atonal composers regarding even the proper characterization of those technical aspects of Schoenberg's music that each saw as most important), but also that it is, in some respect, nearly universal. Roger Sessions (1896–1985) stated the problem quite clearly in 1944 when he observed that "no younger composer writes quite the same music as he would have written had Schoenberg's music not existed" (Sessions 1979, p. 353). Nor does the indebtedness in question preclude the importance to some atonalists of other influences, often wholly foreign to Schoenberg's. Nonetheless, I shall endeavor to focus chiefly on those composers for whom that indebtedness seems more or less central to their mature work, straying from that principle only in cases where it is necessary to acknowledge composers of considerable stature or influence whose work straddles several of the available categories and fits neatly into none.

Early reception and dissemination

It is impossible to understand the complex reception history of the music of the Second Viennese School in America without a sense of the cultural milieu of those American composers who came of age in the years before Schoenberg's arrival in 1933. The second decade of the century witnessed a dramatic shift in the way American universities, music departments included, oriented themselves with respect to European educational institutions. Throughout the nineteenth century it was customary for Americans who wished to pursue their studies further upon completion of college to do so in Europe, and the country of choice for such advanced work, particularly in the humanities and social sciences, was Germany (Geiger 1986, p. 4). Composers who made the pilgrimage to the Continent were following a path well-worn by their academically better established colleagues from history and philosophy departments who went to absorb what they could of the ambiance of *Neuhumanismus* and of the most recent developments in *Philologie* before returning home to pursue academic careers. This German influence was reflected in the standard music curriculum in America with its emphasis on the repertory of the Austro-German tradition, and German and Austrian orchestras defined the performance standards to which most American musicians aspired. Amongst composers who were also important educators it should suffice to say that Chadwick, MacDowell, and Parker all underwent the final stages of their education in Germany (see chapters 8 and 9).

By the turn of the century the situation had begun to change, if not initially for the average musician at least for the composer. The works of Debussy and Ravel shifted public attention to Paris – by comparison Germany and Austria had begun to look musically moribund, and the musical innovations in those countries presented a far less coherent picture to the outsider. Professionally, Stravinsky's Parisian successes in the 1910s, and the prominence of *Les Six* in the 1920s, left no doubt that Paris had become the most promising springboard to a successful career, and that France, not Austria or Germany, set the standards by which American composers would be judged. Technically, the innovations of the French were much more easily understood, and were so understood at the time, as extensions to the existing tonal language than as attempts to replace it; such works were more amenable to superficial imitation than the comparatively cryptic and largely undocumented work of the Viennese. By the time America entered World War I, French-influenced and French-trained composers had been installed in important positions in some of the most prestigious music departments in the country, most notably Edward Burlingame Hill (1872–1960; a student of Widor, and a competent impressionist of a symphonic bent) at Harvard. The tradition of Parisian study that became so conspicuous from the 1920s on, with Boulanger as the chief attraction – a tradition that did not disappear until after World War II – was actually established in the years before World War I made it temporarily impossible to pursue.

Moreover, this musical sea change was contemporaneous with a shift in national popular opinion: around the turn of the century, the American public's long-standing pro-German attitude began to disappear. For the first time in living memory Germany began to look like a potential enemy, and by 1917 had became one in a war of unprecedented scope and brutality. While considerations of space preclude the possibility of treating the consequences of the war on the reception of new European music of the period in the detail they require, it must be understood that the effects of the war reverberated throughout American society for years to come. In the future, German-speaking immigrants could no longer take for granted a welcome in America – even refugees were apt to be viewed with suspicion. Some states went so far as to outlaw entirely the teaching of German, and while those statutes were ultimately struck down by the Supreme Court in 1923 the language was never to regain the prominence it had enjoyed in American education in the latter half of the nineteenth century; nor were the products of German culture ever again viewed with the unmitigated admiration they had previously inspired.

Numerous musical, political, and cultural cross-currents thus collectively made the first quarter of this century a less than auspicious time for the introduction to America of the music of the Second Viennese School. To this chaotic mix must be added some mention of the anti-intellectual streak characteristic of much American populism which, though not yet in the 1910s quite the major public influence it was to become in the 1920s and 1930s, nonetheless mitigated further against public acceptance of music that was not only unabashedly Austro-German root and branch but reputed to be "cerebral." Hence, while Schoenberg's name was certainly familiar to musicians by the time he arrived in America, his music – especially the most recent – was still little known and less understood, even by the best intentioned of his fellow composers. Henry Cowell (1897–1965) –

who long enjoyed good relations with Schoenberg and had even been invited to address one of Schoenberg's classes in Berlin – was an enthusiastic if not well-informed supporter, and offered assistance insofar as he was able by encouraging performances, supporting the publication of works of the Viennese in *New Music*, and pointing potential students in Schoenberg's direction; nonetheless his public statements about the music suggest greater admiration than understanding.

Attitudes toward Schoenberg's work thus evolved in an environment notable for the near absence of the work itself, and were largely the product of two decades of heated polemics in which friend and foe alike were more or less equally ignorant of the musical facts of the matter, and were more often than not responding to other parties in the debate than to the music itself. That the majority opinion to emerge in such a climate was largely negative is no surprise, and, as Carter has lamented, that "attitude persisted to the very end of Schoenberg's life in this country and succeeded in restricting his influence to a much smaller circle than he deserved" (Carter 1971, p. 220).

Though Schoenberg's music was little known in America – performances of his work were confined mostly to major cities on either coast and remained infrequent throughout this period – this did not prevent him from acquiring a public reputation. The American popular press, reflecting the conservative musical interests of its readership, still had its eyes turned toward Europe, and for the most part viewed with alarm the musical innovations taking place on the continent. James Huneker, reporting for the *New York Times* on the December 1912 Berlin performances of *Pierrot lunaire*, did not disguise his distaste for the Viennese. "I fear and dislike the music of Arnold Schoenberg," he wrote; "[t]he aura of Arnold Schoenberg is, for me, the aura of original depravity, of subtle ugliness, of basest egoism, of hatred and contempt, of cruelty, and of the mystic grandiose," adding that "[i]f such music-making is ever to become accepted then I long for Death the Releaser" (Huneker 1913). Nor did *Pierrot* fare better with the *New York Times* when it finally received its American premiere in 1923 under the auspices of Varèse's International Composers Guild. Conservative critic Richard Aldrich described the work as "a variedly rhythmical and dynamic succession of disagreeable and unmusical noise" (Aldrich 1923a), and its supporters as "strangely uncritical persons," who judge works by a single principle: "[t]he worse they sound the better they are said to be" (Aldrich 1923b).

The situation was only modestly better in the few specialist publications aimed more exclusively at musicians. Even sympathizers like Cowell cheerfully contributed their share of misinformation, as witness Cowell's mystifying characterization of Schoenberg's procedure as a process applied to a "twelve-tone scale," which "[b]y an ingenious method of geometric diagram he is able to discover every possible variation of the themes" (Cowell 1930, p. 41). Paul Stefan, reporting for *Modern Music* on performances in 1924 of *Erwartung* (in Prague) and *Die glückliche Hand* (in Vienna) said, unhelpfully, of the former that Schoenberg "bases this great tonal structure purely on sound effects," and, inaccurately, of Schoenberg's then most recent work that it "rests, both horizontally and vertically, entirely on a formation of fourths" (Stefan, 1925, p. 13). *Modern Music* was a convenient forum for Schoenberg's opponents, too. Alfredo Casella, in a report from Italy prompted by a series of recent performances of *Pierrot*, while expressing "profound admiration of both the musician and the man" nonetheless concluded that "his art is so alien to our temperament that the chasm [between Schoenberg and the listener] can never be bridged" (Casella 1924, pp. 8–9). Adoph Weissman's article "Race and Modernity," prominently the first essay in the first issue of *Modern Music*, was even uglier in tone and implication than reports in the popular press: "the dialectic sharpness which transformed this former Wagnerian [Schoenberg] into the reformer of music, rests on Jewish race feeling . . . His contempt for all that is consonant would of necessity lead to sterility. The German impulse must not be diluted into a paper music" (Weissmann 1924, p. 5).

Apart from the extravagance of the rhetoric on both sides, what was remarkable about this debate was the failure of all parties, whether critics writing for public newspapers or composers writing for other composers through the presumably better-informed channels of professional communication like *Modern Music*, to adduce any purely musical evidence in support of their position. This mattered more in Schoenberg's case than it might have in others, since owing to the infrequency of performances readers had no shared experience of the music to which writers could refer. With the exception of early songs and piano pieces, scores were difficult to obtain and expensive when they could be found, and even by the time of Schoenberg's arrival in 1933 virtually no recordings were available. A 1934 issue of *Modern Music* offered what was described as a "list of all available recordings of living composers, save those of pronouncedly conservative tendencies" (Kolodin 1934, p. 134). Only two works of Schoenberg are mentioned – *Gurrelieder* and *Verklärte Nacht*, both early works predating

Schoenberg's turn to atonality – and no music at all of Berg or Webern was available.

Lack of exposure to the music and the spread of misinformation regarding its technical bases are two different matters, however, and while the former problem was beyond Schoenberg's control some measure of responsibility for the latter must be laid at his doorstep. For a variety of reasons Schoenberg was reluctant to reveal technical details of his methods; in some respects he was simply unable to do so. Schoenberg's own pronouncements regarding his pre-twelve-tone atonal works made it clear that while he never doubted their musical "correctness" he nonetheless felt that neither he nor anyone else could offer an adequate theoretical account of those works. In the case of the twelve-tone works, his sketches paint a clear picture of a composer who worked largely by trial and error, not wholly understanding the general principles involved in even some of his most characteristic procedures and thus forced to reinvent aspects of the system with each piece. It is doubtful, for example, that Schoenberg ever fully understood that the property of hexachordal inversional combinatoriality – a property exploited by virtually all of his twelve-tone works after the late 1920s – is solely dependent upon the content of the hexachords, whose internal ordering is irrelevant. Moreover, Schoenberg's system did not assume its final form until 1929, so his earlier pronouncements on the subject, if not premature, must be understood as progress reports, often inadequate, on a system whose ultimate form could not be foreseen by its author, and which had not yet developed what were to become its most important technical features. His few published accounts of the twelve-tone system were late in coming and almost invariably aimed at a rather general audience whom he assumed, correctly no doubt, would find his work less puzzling if offered a means of associating it with the more familiar music of the tonal era. This circumstance naturally led him to emphasize the thematic and motivic side of his compositional practice to the exclusion of the wholly independent technical details of the system itself, even insofar as he understood them. To be sure, there was no element of deception in this, since in historical terms the system, however much it ultimately evolved into something entirely independent of its tonal ancestry, did have its origins in Schoenberg's traditional motivic technique, and Schoenberg was deeply concerned to establish himself as legitimate heir to the tradition of Bach, Mozart, Beethoven, and Brahms. But his silence on technical matters left a vacuum, quickly filled by misinformed speculation.

Contributing to the problem is the nature of the system itself, which dictates little if anything regarding its musical realization. The definition of "serialism" given in the *New Grove Dictionary of Music and Musicians* makes the point: a "method of composition in which a fixed permutation, or series, of elements is referential (i.e. the handling of those elements in the composition is governed, to some extent and in some manner, by the series)" (Griffiths 1980, p. 162). If this seems vague – "extent," "manner," and even "elements" are left undefined – it is no vaguer than it need be to accommodate its infinite number of possible interpretations. Babbitt's characterization of the sense in which the twelve-tone system is indeed a system, namely that it consists of a well-defined set of "elements, relations between, and operations upon them" (Babbitt 1946, p. viii), is more succinct yet, indicating clearly that principles of interpretation, strictly independent of the system itself, are entirely a matter of individual choice.

Full recognition of the ramifications of this could scarcely occur until Schoenberg's work was sufficiently well known by composers that they could begin to pry apart his particular use of the system from the system itself, and consider more fully the far-reaching implications of the latter. This task did not begin to bear significant fruit until after World War II; thus, to the few Americans in the late 1920s and early 1930s who adopted what they understood as twelve-tone technique, it was often simply an *ad hoc* application of traditional contrapuntal procedures to a subject that happened to contain all twelve pitch classes. To others it was merely an ostinato of a more or less abstract sort; and to most just another procedure to be added to the modern composer's tool chest along with polytonality, "advanced" chords of diverse sorts, "synthetic" scales, quartal harmony, and the whole panoply of unrelated techniques of largely local significance that happened to be in the air at the time.

In such a climate the influence of the Viennese was often more apparent than real; numerous composers experimented with the abandonment of tonality, but what they adopted in its place rarely approximated the techniques of the Viennese (much less the attendant aesthetic). John Cage (1912–1992) and Lou Harrison (born 1917), for example, each experimented with rhythmic devices arguably "serial" – Cage in his early percussion pieces based on arithmetical series, and Harrison in such gamelan-inspired works as the *Threnody for Carlos Chávez* (1978), with its multi-layered rhythmic series deployed simultaneously over different time spans – and each expressed admiration of one sort or another for Schoenberg; but in neither case does the music have much in common with that of the Viennese (except, perhaps, with certain of Berg's numerological conceits). Adolph Weiss (1891–1971), the first American to study with Schoenberg in Berlin in 1925–1926, embraced techniques somewhat more closely related to Schoenberg's, though predating by several years Schoenberg's final codification of his own method. Wallingford Riegger (1885–1961) – one of the few atonalists to play a role in Cowell's Pan American Association of Composers – adopted the system in the early 1930s in works such as the *Three Canons* for woodwinds (1931), and perhaps best typifies those Americans who treated the system largely thematically, in Riegger's case in a texture often reminiscent of Baroque polyphony. As Riegger's example indicates, the question of a composer's grasp of the technical bases of a system is independent of the question of the value of the compositions produced, of course, since misreadings of Schoenberg's method in the 1920s and 1930s were as apt to be fruitful as otherwise. Among later composers George Perle (born 1915), for example, candidly admits that his own idiosyncratic formulation of the system – one of considerable sophistication that has proved productive for Perle and his students – was the product of just such a "misunderstanding" of Schoenberg's method (Perle 1977, p. ix), which Perle attempted to infer from his initial encounter, in 1937, with the score to Berg's *Lyric Suite*. In later years Perle was to become prominent as a theorist, and his book *Serial Composition and Atonality*, published in 1962, was the first to draw a distinction between the twelve-tone system as a system, and Schoenberg's personal practice (Perle 1962).

However much personal history may have contributed to the fact that Perle's first glance at the *Lyric Suite* did not occur until he was twenty-two, or that his book did not appear until 1962, it is also symptomatic of the degree to which Schoenberg remained a somewhat marginal figure in American musical life from the time of his arrival until after World War II. When Schoenberg arrived in 1933 – no longer a young man, without funds, and already suffering from the health problems that would plague him for the rest of his life, circumstances that would hinder his involvement in public life – he did not arrive alone. He was part of a wave of European refugees that began in the late 1920s and diminished only when Axis domination of the Continent made further emigration almost impossible. By the end of 1940 a host of other composers had also immigrated, effectively shifting the musical center of gravity from Europe to America and inevitably shifting attention away from Schoenberg. But the war years

were only the last of a series of blows that by the mid-1930s had already relegated Schoenberg and his few American disciples to relative obscurity.
The prevailing neoclassicism of the 1920s had found powerful allies in conductors such as Koussevitzky, who for many years used his position with
the Boston Symphony Orchestra to champion the works of the Franco-
Russian school, of which Stravinsky was of course the most powerful
representative. Koussevitzky also promoted the Stravinsky-inspired
neo-classical works of Copland and other members of the increasingly
influential League of Composers. Most were students of Nadia Boulanger,
who had herself been a regular visitor to America since 1924 and was fully
resident during the period 1940–1946. Unsympathetic at the time to the
Second Viennese School, Boulanger contributed to the establishment of
Stravinsky as the dominant European figure on the American scene and to
the establishment of her students as his legitimate successors. Koussevitzky, as Bernstein's mentor, was to bequeath to the next generation of
major American conductors a tradition of support for such music.

Impelled by the Depression, by the early 1930s the musical language of
1920s neoclassicism had been drafted into the service of a musical populism inspired by an explicitly nationalistic concern – by no means necessarily associated with political conservatism, quite often its opposite – to
create "American" art. That concern became embodied in official public
policy with the establishment of the Works Progress Administration in
1935, and the result was a folkloristic music that not only became the dominant influence for years to come but that also managed to infiltrate mainstream musical culture to an extent hitherto unknown. Its influence would
only increase with America's entry into the war in 1941. Such an environment was almost as uncongenial to Cowell's circle as it was to Schoenberg,
though it is doubtful whether either was, by this time, as strongly inclined
to support the other as each might have been in the 1920s. By the middle of
the 1930s it had become apparent that what Schoenberg's work had in
common with that of the American ultramodernists was mostly what each
was not – tonal – and that his earlier expressionist works were every bit as
alien to the "machine music" aesthetic of the 1910s and early 1920s as were
the twelve-tone works to the dominant populist aesthetic of the 1930s. As
Perle put it, "[b]y the time of Berg's death on Christmas Eve, 1935, the
Second Vienna School was largely written off as having had its day" (Perle
1990, p. 5). A revival of interest in Schoenberg's music would have to wait
until the end of the war.

The post-war twelve-tone school

The resurgence of interest in Schoenberg's music from the 1950s on was due in part to the influence of Roger Sessions, an admirer of Schoenberg's work though deeply distrustful of his (or any other) system. Sessions's own adoption of twelve-tone procedures beginning with the Violin Sonata (1953) was late in coming and the product of so gradual an evolution as to be scarcely noticeable on the surface of his works. The new procedures were wholly subordinated to an already mature technique that had always been chromatic, vigorously linear, and developmental in character, owing little to the Franco-Russian school (with the exception of his earliest works such as the incidental music to *The Black Maskers* [1923], in which the influences of Stravinsky and Sessions's teacher Ernest Bloch are evident). By the mid-1930s densely intertwined networks of motivic associations had come to contribute at least as much to continuity and progression in his music as any vestigial traces of traditional tonal structure, and his subsequent employment of twelve-tone sets represented more an intensification of existing tendencies than anything else. Perhaps one of the last American composers whose musical thought found its most congenial expression in works for orchestra (including eight symphonies), Sessions was also highly regarded as a teacher; it was to Sessions that Babbitt went to study in the late 1930s, and whom Babbitt followed to Princeton, to be appointed to the faculty in 1938.

Babbitt's appointment set the stage for the establishment of a department that was to become an important center for the study of the works of the Second Viennese School and for the compositional extension of its techniques, though the war would delay that development for several years. In the late 1940s, however, Babbitt produced a number of works including the *Three Compositions* for piano (1947) and the *Composition* for four instruments (1948) which embodied the early results of his generalization of Schoenberg's system (particularly combinatoriality and derivation) and began its extension to rhythm as well as pitch. In 1955 he published the first of a highly influential series of articles detailing his research (Babbitt 1955), thereby making the fundamentals of the system available to a far wider range of composers than before, and without bias toward any particular stylistic persuasion in its compositional interpretation.

The same article served notice of a deepening split between the growing

American twelve-tone school and the Darmstadt composers, and Babbitt couched his critique of Euro-serialism in no uncertain terms:

> Mathematics – or, more correctly, arithmetic – is used, not as a means of characterizing or discovering general systematic, pre-compositional relationships, but as a compositional device, resulting in the most literal sort of "programme music," whose course is determined by a numerical, rather than a narrative or descriptive, "programme." The alleged "total organization" is achieved by applying dissimilar, essentially unrelated criteria of organization to each of the components, criteria often derived from outside the system, so that – for example – the rhythm is independent of and thus separable from the pitch structure; this is understood to involve "polyphony" of components, though polyphony is customarily understood to involve, among many other things, a principle of organized simultaneity, while here the mere fact of simultaneity is termed "polyphony"... Finally, the music of the past – and virtually all of that of the present, as well – is repudiated for what it is not, rather than examined – if not celebrated – for what it is.
>
> (Babbitt 1955, p. 55)

Richard Toop's article on the earliest serial works of the Darmstadt school (Toop 1974) gives a good account of the sort of procedures to which Babbitt objected. An additional point of contention, touched upon by Babbitt in his article, involved the profoundly different historical perspectives characteristic of the Americans and Europeans. It is doubtful whether even the most committed American twelve-tone composer would have agreed with Boulez's contention that "all composition other than twelve-tone is useless ... the tone-row is an historical necessity" (Boulez 1952, p. 21). While some no doubt felt that the system was a *natural* or *logical* outgrowth of the tonal system, most stopped shy of Boulez's Hegelian claim of the system's historical *necessity*, if only because the Americans were inclined to see their formalization of the system as an effort to determine what was possible, not what was necessary, and were disinclined to use it to generate pieces in either an arbitrary or purely algorithmic fashion.

These radically different orientations toward history in general and the twelve-tone system in particular were symptoms of a cultural divide as deep as that which separated Schoenberg from Americans of his generation, and was exaggerated by the participants' different experiences of the war. Americans, by and large, emerged from World War II convinced that their values and institutions had been vindicated by the conflict, while Europeans, even the victors, were apt to see the war as a failure of theirs. Many Euro-serialists were thus eager to purge their music of anything associated with the immediately pre-war past, not only the ethos of musical Romanticism but also the entire tonal system upon which it had relied. It was symptomatic of the Europeans' attitude that many Euro-serialists, beginning with Messiaen who was more a catalyst than a participant in the movement, sought historical precedents for their work not in the music of the tonal era but in Renaissance and medieval polyphony. And it was symptomatic of the American atonalists' attitude that many found the Euro-serialists' motivations puzzling and even irrational, a diagnosis confirmed in the minds of most by the rapidity with which the ideas of John Cage and his New York School associates were adopted by Darmstadt composers after 1958.

The dispute grew over the years. The inaugural issue of *Perspectives of New Music* included, along with contributions from Babbitt, Stockhausen, and others, an article by a practicing physicist taking to task *Die Reihe* for its pseudo-scientific language and "mystical belief in numerology as the fundamental basis for music" (Backus 1962, p. 171). (*Perspectives* was founded with Fromm Foundation support in 1962 by Benjamin Boretz [born 1934], a Princeton graduate, and Arthur Berger [born 1912]; since 1982 it has been edited by another Babbitt student John Rahn [born 1944]. *Perspectives* became an important vehicle for the dissemination of the theoretical work of the atonalists.) In the late 1960s the quarrel spilled over into the popular press when the *New York Times* published an interview with Boulez in which he launched what the interviewer described as "a virtuoso attack on various facets of U.S. music" (Peyser 1969). Boulez's assault ranged from the general – "They have no-one in America as good as Hans Werner Henze, and that is not setting your sights very high" – to the particular – "The idea of electronics as the big future of music is just an American trick of fashion." He made a point of the Americans' dependence upon the university: "European music is not connected with the university. There is no ivory castle for us. But here, university people and practical musicians ignore each other ... The university situation is incestuous. It is one big marriage in which the progeny deteriorates, like the progeny of old and noble families ... This endlessly, hopelessly academic work reminds me of the [Paris] Conservatoire."

There was in Boulez's attack something to offend everyone, and to say that it was both ill-timed (less than two months later it was announced that

Boulez had been appointed music director of the New York Philharmonic, a post he held from 1971 to 1977) and antagonistic is to trifle with words. To the atonalists the comparison with the Conservatoire bespoke a measure of misunderstanding regarding the importance of the university to progressive music in America. It was, after all, the university that provided the American atonalist with a livelihood, an audience (if a small one), and some semblance of a community of shared interest and expertise. Boulez's student experiences at the Conservatoire left him justifiably hostile toward academic training as he had experienced it, but the comparison between the Conservatoire, undoubtedly one of the more reactionary musical institutions in Europe at the time, and the American university, perhaps America's most progressive institution, was scarcely apt.

Not that there weren't problems in the university. In later years, Sessions complained that "[t]he Princeton musicologists thought of the music department as their private domain, and composers should be second-class citizens" (Olmstead 1987, p. 167). There were tensions at Columbia as well: when the *Musical Quarterly* under the editorship of Columbia's Paul Henry Lang published a special issue devoted to selected papers from the Fromm Foundation-sponsored Princeton Seminar in Advanced Musical Studies, Lang prefaced the issue with a ten-page editorial attacking serialism, neoclassicism, electronic music in general, and sundry manifestations of music purportedly "manipulated with the aid of electronics, stop watch, and slide rule." In passing, he characterized Stravinsky's turn to serial technique as an "abject surrender," and issued a "special warning" to the reader regarding Babbitt's allegedly "mathematical" contribution to the volume (Lang 1960).

Nevertheless, by this time the university atonalists were sufficiently secure in their position to withstand attacks from either inside or outside the academy, however much these may have contributed to the broader public's unsympathetic reception of their work. By 1970 Princeton had assembled the group of composers with which it was to be associated in years to come, and all were well-disposed toward the music of the Second Viennese School, though all responded to its influence in notably different ways. Sessions's student Edward T. Cone (born 1917) had been on the faculty since 1947. He was joined in 1958 by Babbitt student James K. Randall (born 1929), whose work in the 1960s, along with that of Godfrey Winham (1934–1975; appointed in 1965), contributed to the development of computer synthesis. Claudio Spies (born 1925) and Peter Westergaard (born 1931), both Harvard graduates who arrived in 1970 and

1968 respectively, brought special expertise in the music of Stravinsky (in Spies's case) and Webern (in Westergaard's). Paul Lansky (born 1944), a student of Perle who assisted in the formalization and extension of Perle's system, joined the staff in 1969. In recent years he has become an influential figure in digital synthesis.

Similar changes were taking place at other universities, and at the same time important developments in patterns of institutional support contributed to the spread of the atonalists' work. Chief among these were the establishment of new performing groups largely populated by young performers capable of meeting the demands of this increasingly difficult music; the founding of a number of small but professional publishing houses explicitly committed to increasing the availability of scores; the growing willingness of a few record companies to record the music; and the increasingly active role played by atonalists both in already established composers' organizations and in the creation of new ones.

The Contemporary Chamber Ensemble, founded in 1960 by Arthur Weisberg, was one of the first of the new ensembles. A Rockefeller Foundation grant made possible a three-year residency for the group at Rutgers University, and in the late 1960s the ensemble began a series of recordings of contemporary music for Nonesuch. In 1962 the Group for Contemporary Music was founded at Columbia University by composer and pianist Charles Wuorinen (born 1938), composer and flutist Harvey Sollberger (born 1938), and cellist Joel Krosnick. The Group was one of the first of a new generation of ensembles, often directed by composers who were themselves expert performers and who were young enough to have absorbed the work of the atonalists in the course of their training. Fueled by a favorable national economy together with a nationwide expansion of the educational system prompted by post-war population growth, similar ensembles emerged across the country, sometimes with support from institutions like the Rockefeller Foundation, and often at state universities such as those of Iowa, Illinois, Michigan, Pennsylvania, and the State University of New York (SUNY) at Buffalo among many others. While few had the commitment to the atonalists characteristic of the Group for Contemporary Music, they nonetheless gradually broadened the performance opportunities available and furthered the development of the movement.

A prolific composer, Wuorinen was an important presence on the New York scene, and an outspoken advocate of the twelve-tone composers in their disputes with the Euro-serialists and others. His music of this period gives a good indication of the diversity of technical devices available to atonalists by the early 1960s, combining as it did Wuorinen's adaptation of Babbitt's time-point system with pitch orderings frequently derived from Stravinsky's rotational procedures. This resulted in a non-aggregate-based surface often characterized by a degree of pitch-class centricity, owing to the unequal multiplicities of occurrence of the component pitch classes. It shares that latter characteristic with much of the later work of Stefan Wolpe (1902–1972), where such centrality often manifests as literal registral symmetry. A German-born composer who emigrated to America in 1938 and settled in New York in 1957, Wolpe's Dada-inspired aesthetic set him apart from his American colleagues, though it did not appear to diminish their respect for such ambitious works as *Enactments* for three pianos (1950–1953); in many senses he was a uniquely European voice on the American scene. Influential as much for his teaching as his music, his numerous students included Ralph Shapey (born 1921) – whose work shows the influences of both Schoenberg and Varèse – and Morton Feldman (who is discussed in chapter 19).

New York remained the center of much atonalist activity even after the movement had established important beachheads elsewhere in the country. It was there that two small but important publishers of atonalist work were established in the late 1940s, in each case by a European immigrant. Oboist Josef Marx (1913–1978), who also served for a time as the Group's general manager, founded McGinnis & Marx in 1945: the company was to become an important publisher of the works of Wolpe, Wuorinen, Sollberger, Mario Davidovsky (born 1934), and others. Boelke-Bomart, founded in 1948 by Austrian refugee Walter Boelke, developed a smaller but more focused catalog under the editorship of Jacque-Louis Monod (born 1927) – a French-born composer and student of Leibowitz – including works by Babbitt, Kirchner, Schoenberg, Spies, and Webern. New York, moreover, was home to the Columbia-Princeton Electronic Music Center, established in 1959 with assistance from the Rockefeller Foundation. The Center became an important resource for many atonalists who were characteristically attracted to the electronic medium not for its ability to produce new sounds but by the promise of more precise control of those dimensions relevant to the structures of their work, most particularly rhythm. The Center was the birthplace of numerous important pieces including Babbitt's *Philomel* (1964) and Wuorinen's Pulitzer Prize-winning *Time's Encomium* (1969), the latter commissioned by Nonesuch Records. Of the many composers associated with the Center, Mario Davidovsky perhaps did most to establish a distinctive "uptown" sound in the 1960s and 1970s, especially through his rarely serial but always atonal works for performers and tape – a genre he did much to establish – and his influence as a teacher.

Indeed, by the mid-1960s the spread of atonalism had become not only broad but so varied in its individual manifestations that distinguishable regional "schools" became evident. The department at Brandeis, for example, contributed to the development of a "Boston sound" through the works of Arthur Berger, Seymour Shifrin (1926–1979), and Martin Boykan (born 1931), composers of music variously twelve-tone and atonal but otherwise of such notably different inclinations as to render further generalization meaningless. The same could be said of most composers who wrote atonal music of one sort or another from the mid-1960s on, since by that time the practice had become sufficiently uncontroversial, at least in the university, that developing composers felt increasingly free to blend aspects of atonality with whatever else happened to interest them. The great diversity of such interests can be observed in the works of such university trained composers as Rolv Yttrehus (born 1926), Charles Whittenberg (1927–1984), Richard Swift (born 1927), Donald Martino (born 1931), and Robert Morris (born 1943). Yttrehus's work reflects his studies with Sessions, and is perhaps the most Schoenbergian of the four, though his frequent use of a cantus firmus suggests a Stravinskyan influence as well. Whittenberg discovered the works of the Second Viennese School mid-career and destroyed his earlier work; his subsequent twelve-tone music combined combinatorial arrays and rotation with a surface whose rhythms reflected the influence of Stravinsky and whose phraseology that of Varèse. Swift's work has incorporated elements as disparate as improvisation and all-partition arrays of the sort pioneered by Babbitt. Martino's music is instantly recognizable for its skillful combination of aggregate-based arrays with a surface rhetoric whose roots lie in late Romanticism; his Pulitzer Prize-winning *Notturno* (1973) is a typical (and influential) example. And in Morris's music it is not unknown for sophisticated array structures to underlie a surface reflective of his interest in non-Western music. When the American Society of University Composers was founded in 1966 by Boretz, Martino, Randall, Spies, Henry Weinberg (born 1931), Westergaard, and Wuorinen – all of whom had either studied at Princeton, taught there, or both – it was perhaps symptomatic of the missionary zeal of the time; that by 1977 it boasted more than five hundred members across the country who were by no means all or even mostly twelve-tone composers (though many had adopted one or more aspects of the technique) is a measure both of the movement's success and the extent to which it had become absorbed into an increasingly ecumenical university landscape.

During the same period the gradual adoption of serial techniques by Stravinsky in the *Cantata* (1952) and later works smoothed the path somewhat for those older and already established composers whose earlier neoclassicism had been so strongly influenced by the music of Stravinsky's middle period. Aaron Copland (1900–1990) was perhaps the most famous of these. In many respects he was typical of those composers who dabbled in aspects of serialism but for whom the technique never assumed the importance or achieved the sophistication that it did in the works of composers for whom one or another version of the system was central. *Connotations* for orchestra (1962) is perhaps the best known of Copland's serial works, though it seems likely he will be better remembered for his earlier neoclassical pieces. Though rarely strictly twelve-tone, of the composers of that generation who were associated early on with neoclassicism but later developed a personal atonal language characteristic of all their later works, Elliott Carter stands apart as reflecting most directly the influences of the two cultures from which American atonality evolved. It is impossible, that is, to conceive of the trichordal structure of the Piano Concerto (1965) or the registrally ordered twelve-tone sets of *Night Fantasies* for piano (1980) without reference to the Second Viennese School, and equally impossible to conceive of the elaborate polyrhythmic structures that span entire pieces such as the Double Concerto (1961) without reference to the American experimentalists.

Indeed, more than any other composer of his generation Carter's career and work parallels the evolution of American music in this century and synthesizes (rather more seamlessly than most) the numerous influences that gave direction to that evolution. His early personal association with Ives encouraged what would become a lifelong preoccupation with polyrhythmic structures. This interest would later lead to his study of rhythm in non-Western music – the results of which inform the works of the late 1940s and early 1950s, such as the Sonata for Cello and Piano (1948) and the Sonata for Flute, Oboe, Cello and Harpsichord (1952) – and introduced him to the works of the avant garde of the 1920s at a younger age than many of his contemporaries. In many ways more conservative than Ives and the American experimentalists, Carter's deep respect for European art music counterbalanced the early iconoclastic influence of the Americans without, however, excluding entirely the influence of certain of their techniques. Harvard educated, Carter's studies continued in Europe when in 1932 he went to France to work with Boulanger, and his music of the mid-1930s, such as the music for the ballet *Pocahontas* (1936), reflects the Stravinsky-inspired harmonic language of the time (not to mention the typically American theme of the ballet), as well as Carter's increasing familiarity with the music of Copland and Sessions. His interest in the music of the Second Viennese School no doubt motivated his long and systematic study of relations within and between subsets of the aggregate that would serve as the basis of his harmonic language.

By the early 1960s all the chief components of his mature technique were in place, as evidenced by works such as the String Quartet No. 2 (1959) and the Double Concerto. The course taken by his later music reveals a progressive intensification of trends and characteristics already present in works of that time. These include a general concern for polyphonic independence, not just of individual instrumental parts but of discrete instrumental groups within the ensemble as a whole which become invested with their own characteristic material and ways of behaving and thus give the impression of relatively independent but simultaneous strata. The overarching polyrhythms characteristic of Carter's mature work can be understood as one manifestation of this interest. Relatedly, there is a tendency to project the identity of individual parts and strata "programmatically" by imbuing each with distinct "dramatic" personalities; and a proclivity toward exhaustive use of all collections of a particular cardinality. Typical works include *A Symphony of Three Orchestras* (1976) – typical also in that, like many of Carter's pieces, it was inspired by a literary work, in this case Hart Crane's poem "The Bridge" – and the Violin Concerto (1990).

Carter's position has always been unique among the atonalists, however, and in large measure he has stood above the fray, celebrated both in Europe and America and less bound by either temperament or circumstance to the exigencies of academic life. For the rest, in a period of declining economic growth and an uncertain national commitment to higher education in general, it must be considered an open question whether atonality will survive as the intellectually and musically vibrant force it was, as it jostles for attention along with the numerous other options open to the young composer in the musically pluralistic university environment it did much to help create.

19

Avant-garde and experimental music
___

DAVID NICHOLLS

Although the terms "avant-garde" and "experimental" are often used to categorize radical composers and their works, it has been noted that "'avant garde' remains more a slogan than a definition" (Griffiths 1980, p. 743) and that "'experimental music' is ill-defined and the concept it is used to describe is vague" (Rockwell 1986, p. 91). (In fairness to Rockwell, he does also stress the "bolder, more individualistic [and] eccentric" aspects of experimentalism, which suggest an "untrammeled willingness to probe the very limits of music" [p. 91].) But equally problematically, there is no clear demarcation line between the composers and repertories to which the terms are usually applied, or between the territory supposedly described by *combining* the two terms and that inhabited by other species of contemporary composer. Thus Ruth Crawford (Seeger) (1901–1953) and George Crumb (born 1929) might be thought of as either avant garde or experimental, while Steve Reich (born 1936) and Philip Glass (born 1937) have – over a twenty-five year period – moved imperceptibly from the experimental fringe to the postmodern mainstream, without having compromised their work to any substantive degree.

These problems of definition are at least partly attributable to two linked paradoxes. First, almost all forms of radicalism will, as a function of time, progressively degenerate into normality and acceptability: today's novelty can easily become tomorrow's cliché. Second (and more important), radicalism does not exist *per se*, but rather is a function of difference when measured against contemporaneous norms. Thus, in the context of twentieth-century musical modernism, it can push the boundaries of acceptance not only forward (into "advanced" territory), but also backward (into apparent conservatism) and outward (into the exploration of musics other than those of the Eurocentric art music tradition). These three shades of radicalism might be termed prospective, retrospective, and extraspective.

None of this, however, is of much help in determining what avant-garde

music and experimental music actually *are*. Thus the present chapter proceeds from the assumption that, at any given time, both exist at the forefront of contemporary music thought and practice (and are therefore *de
facto* likely to disturb rather than reassure, challenge rather than comfort);
and that what distinguishes them is the extent to which they take the Eurocentric art music tradition as a reference point. Thus, very generally, avant-
garde music can be viewed as occupying an extreme position within the
tradition, while experimental music lies outside it. The distinction may
appear slight, but when applied to such areas as institutional support,
"official" recognition, and financial reward, the avant garde's links with
tradition – however tenuous – can carry enormous weight.

Before World War II

Although the compositional roots of Charles Ives (1874–1954) lie to a
considerable extent in the European Romantic tradition (see chapter 9), he
also "deserves pride of place as one of the first composers of experimental
music" (Burkholder 1990, p. 50). In general terms, Ives's experimentalism
manifests itself in two ways. First, he wrote a number of overtly experimental pieces, in which he tried out particular compositional techniques
including extreme chromaticism, tone clusters, polytonality, polyrhythm,
polymetre, polytempo, stratification, and spatial separation. The pieces
containing these experiments range from psalm settings and other quasi-
religious works (mainly dating from the 1890s on) through to secular
instrumental pieces (mostly written after 1905). Noteworthy examples of
the former include *Psalm 24* and the second of the *Three Harvest Home
Chorales*; and of the latter *From the Steeples and the Mountains*, *The
Unanswered Question*, and *In re con moto et al.* Second, Ives wrote music in an
unprecedentedly wide range of styles, from the popular through to the
recherché. Equally (if not more) importantly, he sought to integrate these
varied styles into a pluralistic whole, most successfully in such "late"
works as the Second String Quartet, Piano Sonata No. 2 (*Concord, Mass.,
1840–1860*), and Fourth Symphony.

Despite the apparently early dates of many of Ives's innovations – as well
as the precursorial mantle placed on him by Henry Cowell (1897–1965)
and others – the fact remains, however, that the vast majority of Ives's
works only received their first performances many years after their
composition. Furthermore, Ives revised many of his pieces before their
premieres, which has led, in recent years, to a robust debate revolving

around issues of deliberate deception and historical precedence.[1] Thus public awareness of Ives's music – dating initially from the 1920s, and at least partly resulting from his private publication and distribution of the "Concord" Sonata and *114 Songs* – was contiguous with that afforded to a later generation of radical composers, including Cowell, Crawford, and Carl Ruggles (1876–1971).

In the first quarter of the twentieth century, then, most musical radicalism on the East Coast of America was actually centered on the activities of such recent European immigrants as Leo Ornstein (born 1894), E. Robert Schmitz (1889–1949), and Edgard Varèse (1883–1965). In the 1910s, Russian-born Ornstein shocked audiences (and inspired Cowell) with his chamber music, including the infamous *Wild Men's Dance* Op. 13 No. 2 (*c.* 1915). Both Schmitz and Varèse hailed from France; and both founded organizations which promoted the cause of modern music. The latter's International Composers' Guild (operative 1921–1927) gave performances of works by such contemporary European and American composers as Berg, Cowell, Hindemith, Colin McPhee (1900–1964), Ruggles, Schoenberg, and Webern. Varèse's own compositions from this period – notably *Amériques* (?1918–1921), *Hyperprism* (1922–1923), *Intégrales* (1924–1925) and *Arcana* (1925–1927) – excited much interest and exerted much influence through their striking timbres and use of percussion. Schmitz's Pro-Musica Society (founded in New York in 1920, as the Franco-American Musical Society) was less adventurous in its programming, but among its many promotions over a twelve-year period were the first performances of Ives's *Three Quarter-tone Pieces* in 1925 and the first two movements of the Fourth Symphony in 1927. These activities can be seen as part of an emerging modernist movement, almost exclusively prospective in spirit and celebrating the generally positivist mood of the times. Another example is the early work of George Antheil (1900–1959) which includes the *Airplane Sonata* (1921) and the *Ballet mécanique* (1923–1925). Somewhat paradoxically, though, Antheil's reputation was made – and his most advanced pieces first performed – in Europe, where he received strong support from Ezra Pound, among others.

On America's West Coast, meanwhile, there had been complementary developments. In the fall of 1914, Henry Cowell had begun a series of weekly meetings with the then Chair of Music at Berkeley, Charles Seeger

---

1. As noted in chapter 9, the "standard" datings of Ives's works are given in *AmeriGrove*; the controversy surrounding those dates is summarized in Burkholder 1995, pp. 9–11.

(1886–1979), at which issues in contemporary music were discussed. By the time of the first meeting, Cowell had composed over a hundred pieces in a plethora of styles. In distinct contrast to the Eurocentric East Coast radicals – who were all to some extent indebted to Stravinsky and other European modernists – Cowell was fully aware of ". . . the rich variety of oriental musical cultures that existed in the San Francisco Bay area [and had grown] up hearing more Chinese, Japanese, and Indian classical music than he did Western music" (Saylor 1986, p. 520). What he lacked, though, was a (contemporary Western) context within which to develop his ideas; this Seeger provided. The next five years might be likened to a research program, in which Cowell and Seeger explored the intellectual limits of music at that time. The results included the first draft of Cowell's important book, *New Musical Resources* (published in revised form in 1930) and a number of increasingly radical compositions, including the String Quartet No. 1 (April 1916), the *Quartet Romantic* (September 1917) and the *Quartet Euphometric* (September 1919).

These three works all show the influence of Seeger's theory of dissonant counterpoint, in which dissonance (initially of pitch, though ultimately of all other parameters as well) rather than consonance was the norm. Through Cowell, other composers – including Ruggles and John J. Becker (1886–1961) – were introduced to its disciplines, as is shown, for instance, in Ruggles's *Portals* (1925) and his *magnum opus*, *Sun-treader* (1926–1931). Cowell's music, however, continued to be written in a wide variety of idioms, as a selection of his piano works demonstrates. *Fabric* (September 1920) adheres to the norms of dissonant counterpoint; *Dynamic Motion* (November 1916) and *Antinomy* (December 1917) are astonishing for the violence of their tone cluster dissonance; *The Tides of Manaunaun* (July 1917) also features clusters, but in accompaniment of a modal, folk-like melody; both *The Aeolian Harp* (c. 1923) and *The Banshee* (February 1925) employ the strings of the piano, but to quite different (programmatic and timbral) ends: the former is sweet and tonal, the latter an evocation of the wailing spirits of Gaelic folklore.

John Cage (1912–1992) once described Cowell as "the open sesame for new music in America" (Cage 1961, p. 71). In 1925 Cowell became a board member of Varèse's (East Coast) International Composers' Guild and founded his own (West Coast) New Music Society. Following the demise of the ICG, Cowell in effect ran its successor – the Pan American Association of Composers (operative 1928–1934) – during Varèse's long sojourn in France (1928–1933). Thus, until 1936, Cowell presided over the most important period in American musical radicalism's first wave. The concerts of the New Music Society and PAAC were seminal in bringing new pieces to public attention, in places as far apart as San Francisco, New York, Havana, Paris and Budapest. Founded in 1927, Cowell's journal *New Music Quarterly* provided a unique outlet for contemporary scores. And, like the concerts and the periodical, Cowell's 1933 symposium *American Composers on American Music* championed all those who stood consciously apart from the Eurocentric mainstream, including Ives (who provided Cowell with extensive financial backing for several of these enterprises), Crawford, Ruggles, Wallingford Riegger (1885–1961), and Dane Rudhyar (1895–1985). The range of music that benefited from these various initiatives was impressive. The PAAC tackled the Eurocentric establishment on its home ground, promoting concerts on the East Coast of America and in Europe. That given in Paris on June 6, 1931, was typical: conducted by Nicolas Slonimsky (1894–1995), it included Cowell's *Synchrony* (1930), Ives's *First Orchestral Set* (in its new chamber orchestra version), Ruggles's *Men and Mountains*, and pieces by Amadeo Roldán (1900–1939) and Adolph Weiss (1891–1971). The New Music Society and *New Music Quarterly* were more catholic in their tastes, though still rather biased toward American radical composers. Thus while new European compositions were tolerated, the names encountered most often are those of Cowell and his closest confederates – Becker, Carlos Chávez (1899–1978), Crawford, Ives, Riegger, Rudhyar, Ruggles, and Varèse – as well as such less celebrated talents as Ray Green (1908–1997) and William Russell (1905–1992).

The radical optimism of the period following World War I found its antithesis, however, in the legacy of pessimism and unemployment bequeathed by the Wall Street Crash. Although opportunities for performance and publication appear – if anything – to have increased during these years, many composers began to question the relevance of their earlier, ultra-modern, aesthetic beliefs. It is significant, for instance, that Varèse completed no new pieces during the decade bounded by *Density 21.5* for solo flute (1936) and the unpublished, speculative, *Etude pour Espace* (1947). Ruth Crawford – whose brilliant essays at the farthest reaches of dissonant counterpoint include the String Quartet (1931) and the Three Songs (1930–1932) – dallied with political texts, in the *Two Ricercari* (1932–1933), before becoming involved in folk music. Her polemical views were shared with other members of the left-wing Composers' Collective of New York, including Copland and Charles Seeger. Cowell, too, was active in the Collective for a time; but the principal feature of his work from the late 1920s onward is an increasing preoccupation with trans-ethnic matters. His earlier music – like that of Charles Griffes (1884–1920) and Henry Eichheim (1870–1942) – had already shown a more-than-casual interest in other cultures. Cowell did not, at this stage, match the wander-lust of either McPhee or Eichheim; but the Depression years certainly coincided with a deliberate attempt to engage at an intellectual level with the principles of non-Western musics. Thus from the late 1920s, Cowell regularly taught a course on "Music of the Peoples of the World," while he spent 1931–1932 in Berlin, studying comparative musicology, Indian music and Javanese music. He subsequently followed his own advice – given in the article "Towards Neo-Primitivism" (Cowell 1933b) – by drawing on "those materials common to the music of all the peoples of the world [and building] a new music particularly related to our own century." The result was a series of distinctly transethnic pieces, including *Ostinato Pianissimo* (1934), the *United Quartet* (1936), and *Pulse* (1939). To the lay observer, these and other developments in Cowell's work of the mid- to late 1930s might have seemed regressive; but in fact they played an impor-tant part in setting the agenda for the second great wave of American musical radicalism.

From the 1940s to the 1960s

The predominant thrust in avant-garde and experimental music until the mid-1930s had been assuredly prospective; but from that point on it became increasingly balanced by retrospective and extraspective tenden-cies. Cowell's compositions during the last twenty-five years of his life continued, in part, to employ advanced techniques. These include tone clusters – for instance in the *Trio in Nine Short Movements* (1965) – and exam-ples of the variable forms first encountered in the *Mosaic Quartet* (1935) and the lost *Sarabande* (1937). But the majority of his music after 1940 was stimulated by traditions other than those of his own time and/or place, transethnic influences being joined by those of earlier music and of vernacular music. Among his works are a series of Hymn and Fuguing Tunes (1943–1964); *Saturday Night at the Firehouse* (1948); *Persian Set* (1956–1957); Symphony No. 13 (*Madras*) (1956–1958); and two concertos for koto and orchestra (1961–1962; January 1965).

Cowell's inclusivity of approach set an important example to younger composers and – in some cases – had a direct influence on their work. At the more overtly experimental end of the spectrum, extreme rhythmic complexity was spiced with jazz by Conlon Nancarrow (1912–1997), whose mature output is indebted to Cowell's suggestion that intricate rhythms "could easily be cut on a player-piano roll" (Cowell 1930, p. 65). In the mid-1930s, Cage and Lou Harrison (born 1917) studied with both Cowell and Schoenberg, which led to an unusual combination in their work of (traditional) discipline with (radical) freedom. Thus contrapuntal pieces were succeeded by works for percussion and for altered piano. The percussion music of Cage and Harrison – mainly written in the late 1930s and early 1940s – reflects a general proclivity for such resources at this time: important earlier examples include Varèse's *Ionisation* (1931), Cowell's *Ostinato Pianissimo*, and pieces by several Latin American composers. Harrison's tack piano (in which thumb tacks are pushed into the hammers) and Cage's prepared piano (in which mutes of various kinds are applied to the strings) are conceptually beholden to Cowell's string piano. Such timbral innovations can be viewed as part of the broader radical trends – notably the move toward transethnicism – described above. But they also precipitated a loosening of the traditional Western bonds between notation, execution, and perception: because the notation of music for percussion or altered piano cannot be intrinsically linked with a consistent (recognizable) timbral result, the score begins to become indeterminate of its performance. Equally, intonational issues come to the fore.

At this stage, Cage's radicalism was almost exclusively prospective: his 1937 lecture–manifesto "The Future of Music: Credo" is a typically bold statement of intent, in many ways prophetic of his later work (Cage 1961, pp. 3–6). Thus, in response to the perceived need for "methods of writing music . . . which are free from the concept of a fundamental tone," from the *First Construction (in Metal)* (1939) until the early 1950s, Cage contained his timbral innovations within a formal apparatus which – through its basis in duration – was able to encompass both sound (whether pitched or unpitched) and silence. (It should be noted, however, that this so-called "square-root form" is clearly derived from Cowell's earlier formal experiments, as typified in the *United Quartet* and *Pulse*.) Square-root form proved to be an extremely flexible resource. Cage was able to utilize it when writing for instruments both conventional and unconventional; it also made possible collaborative work: the percussion quartet *Double Music* (1941) was written jointly with Harrison. More importantly, Cage could adapt it to his changing aesthetic needs. His studies with Cowell notwithstanding, Cage's dependence on the prepared piano during the 1940s might be as attributable to his poverty as to its transethnic timbres. Equally, his involvement with Indian and other mystical philosophies was, at first, as much therapeutic as cross-cultural in intent. But the discovery of *The Gospel of Sri Ramakrishna* "led him to further immerse himself in Eastern thought," notably that of Ananda K. Coomaraswamy and – ultimately – Zen Buddhism (Pritchett 1993, pp. 36–37). As a result, Cage was encouraged in the pursuit of an unusual quarry: "giving up control so that sounds can be sounds" (Cage 1961, p. 72). In the *Sonatas and Interludes* (1946–1948) Cage's taste – in the guise of "considered improvisation" (Cage 1961, p. 19) – played an important part in determining the progression of musical events; in subsequent works, however, such decisions were increasingly devolved to impersonal processes. Thus in the *String Quartet in Four Parts* (1949–1950) the musical material is restricted to a gamut of thirty-three sonorities, while in the first two movements of the *Concerto for Prepared Piano and Chamber Orchestra* (1950–1951) the sounds are contained on grid-shaped charts, about which Cage "made moves . . . of a 'thematic nature' but . . . with an 'athematic' result" (Nattiez 1993, p. 92). In the final movement of the concerto – and most remarkably in the *Music of Changes* (1951) – however, the moves were determined not by Cage but by chance, through a process derived from that used to consult the ancient Chinese book of oracles, the *I Ching*.

In January, 1950, Cage had written to the French composer Pierre Boulez that "The great trouble with our life here is the absence of an intellectual life. No one has an idea" (Nattiez 1993, p. 50). Yet within a year, his situation had changed dramatically, as a result of his meeting the other members of the so-called New York School – Morton Feldman (1926–1987), David Tudor (1926–1996) and Christian Wolff (born 1934). (The remaining member of the group – Earle Brown [born 1926] – joined in 1952.) Cage discovered the *I Ching* – which would become his most important compositional tool – through Wolff, whose father had recently published an English translation of the work. For the next few years, the mutual interaction of the group led to a quantum leap forward in musical radicalism and a questioning of the most fundamental tenets of Western art music. Although their individual methods and techniques were inevitably quite different, the principal feature that linked them was identified by Cowell, who – prior to a concert of works by Brown, Cage, Feldman, and Wolff – suggested that "here were four composers who were getting rid of glue. That is: Where people had felt the necessity to stick sounds together to make a continuity, [they] felt the opposite necessity to get rid of the glue so that sounds would be themselves" (Cage 1961, p. 71).

The most obvious manifestation of the new glue-less music was its visual aspect, Feldman being the first of the group to experiment with graphic notation. Although graphic devices are occasionally found in the works of Ives and Cowell, the score of *Projection 1* for solo cello (probably composed in late December, 1950) is unprecedented. The music is written on three systems, marked ◊ (harmonic), P (pizzicato) and A (arco); within each system, relative duration and relative pitch range (high, medium, low) are indicated quadrangularly. The appearance of the score is akin to that of some abstract paintings; indeed, Feldman is reported to have sometimes "hung" his compositions while working on them (Patterson 1994, p. 72). Earle Brown's collection of pieces entitled *Folio* (1952–1953) contains a number of innovative notational devices. The most radical is found in *December 1952*, the score of which consists of a single sheet of card, approximately A3-sized, on which are drawn thirty lines and rectangles of different thicknesses and lengths. The sheet may be placed on any of its four sides, and thus may be read in four ways. However, in later pieces Brown drew back somewhat from this extreme position. In *Available Forms I* (1961) and *Available Forms II* (1962) relatively conventional notation is combined with a Calder-like structural mobility, the order in which the various musical events are performed being decided by the conductor(s). A similar degree of flexibility characterizes much of Wolff's work from the late 1950s onward.

Following the composition of *Music of Changes*, Cage came to realize that the adoption of chance freed him of the need for either square-root form or traditional notation. Consequently, 1952 proved to be a remarkable year, in which existing practices and new possibilities jostled for attention: the post-Feldman graphs of *Imaginary Landscape No. 5* and *Music for Carillon No. 1* are contiguous with the notational normality of *Waiting* and *For MC and DT*, while in two further works, Cage leapt into the musical unknown. *Water Music* inaugurates a series of pieces – including *Variations IV* (1963), *HPSCHD* (1967–1969), *Roaratorio* (1979), and the *Europeras* (1985–1991) – in which the needs of music and theatre collide in often unexpected ways; *4′33″* opened up for the first time in Western music history the possibility of unintentional sounds being considered as important as intentional (composed) sounds. During the remainder of the 1950s, Cage employed an impressive variety of chance-based compositional tools in order to fulfill further his earlier-mentioned aim of "giving up control so that sounds can be sounds." As well as the *I Ching*, these tools included the use of templates of various kinds, and the identification and highlighting of imperfections in the manuscript paper. One particularly radical result of Cage's new approach to composition was that many of the works composed after 1951 could be performed either separately or simultaneously. Perhaps the most remarkable product of this period is the *Concert for Piano and Orchestra* (1957–1958), in effect a compendium of his compositional practices. It contains an astonishing selection of notations, for a pianist and thirteen other instrumentalists, all of whom have an unprecedented degree of control over what (and how) they perform.

Despite the wildly experimental nature of many of the New York School's innovations, however, they were taken surprisingly seriously by the European avant garde. In mid-1951, Boulez had written that he and Cage were at "the same stage of research" (Nattiez 1993, p. 97). Subsequently, many of the new ideas which characterized the work of Cage, Brown, and Feldman during this period were adopted and adapted by their European contemporaries – witness, for instance, the notational styles of *Circles* (1960) and *Sequenza III* (1966) by Luciano Berio and the mobile form of *Momente* (1961–1969) by Karlheinz Stockhausen. However, it should also be noted that Cage and Brown, in particular, had enormous respect for Boulez, and that Cage and Tudor were responsible for promoting – among other European works – the first American performances of Boulez's Second Piano Sonata (1947–1948) and Stockhausen's *Klavierstück XI* (1956). Indeed, it is possible to argue that despite their many disagreements, the New York School and their European avant-garde colleagues actually shared quite similar aesthetic goals, which were resolutely prospective in nature.

That Cowell and Harrison were not significantly involved in this international avant-garde activity is noteworthy, for by the mid-1950s their aesthetic values were markedly different from those of Cage and his colleagues. Following his return to the West Coast in 1953, Harrison increasingly followed Cowell's lead in exploring the more retrospective and extraspective facets of radicalism. During the 1930s and 1940s, Harrison had already studied world musics and written for percussion and altered piano; and as a result of reading the first (1949) edition of *Genesis of a Music* by Harry Partch (1901–1974) he also became interested in tuning systems and instrument building. These various tendencies coalesced from the late 1950s onward: two early products are the *Concerto in Slendro* (1961) and the *Pacifika Rondo* (1963). The latter work is scored for a chamber orchestra of Eastern and Western instruments; the former – for solo violin, celesta, two tack pianos and two percussionists – may be played in either equal temperament, or in the two Javanese modes specified in the score.

Harry Partch – who, like Cowell and Harrison, had a rather unconventional musical background – had in effect abandoned Eurocentric art music traditions some thirty years previously. His early rejection of Western intonation and performance practice led to his development of a new intonational system, the building of instruments capable of performing in that system, and the creation of an all-embracing aesthetic viewpoint he termed corporeality. His work shows an unusually wide frame of cultural reference, including Chinese poetry, hitch-hiker inscriptions and Greek tragedy, in *17 Lyrics of Li Po* (1930–1933), *Barstow* (1941) and *Oedipus* (1951) respectively. In the triumphant synthesis of such late pieces as *Delusion of the Fury* (1965–1966) Partch juxtaposes Japanese Noh with Ethiopian folklore; the set consists only of his amazing instruments – including kitharas, adapted guitars, and a variety of tuned idiophones – while the performers are required to play, sing and act, mainly from memory. However, the price Partch paid for such extraspective independence was enormous: he received little institutional support, and even at the height of his creative achievement, in 1966, could write bitterly to Harrison that "I went to the social security offices yesterday, and learned that the $538.20 check from the U.S. Treasurer is valid. It is my reward for having endured this society for 65 years" (Garland 1987, p. 60).

Since the 1960s

The extent to which prospective radicalism had become moderated by retrospective and extraspective tendencies may be gauged by briefly examining a selection of Cage's music from the early 1960s onward. *Variations IV* (1963) is designated as being "for any number of players, any sounds or combinations of sounds produced by any means, with or without other activities." The work is thus superficially (and outrageously) prospective in its specification not of substance (i.e. musical material) but rather of a means by which the spatial sources of such substance may be determined. As such, it is the embodiment of Charles Seeger's ultimate aim for dissonant counterpoint – complete heterophony. Seeger's concept had been of "a polyphony in which there is no relation between the parts except mere proximity in time–space, beginning and ending, within hearing of each other, at more or less the same time" (Cowell 1933a, p. 111). Significantly, though, Seeger's subsequent concession – that "Heterophony may be accidental, as, for instance, a radio-reception of Beethoven's 'Eroica' intruded upon by a phonograph record of a Javanese gamelan" – immediately introduces the possibility (if not the inevitability) of retrospective and extraspective elements being part of such a phenomenon. In practice, therefore, Cage's own recorded performance of *Variations IV* made extensive use not only of the amplified "ambient" sounds (of street, audience and radio) liberated by *4′ 33″*, but also extant discs of a wide variety of musics.

One of Cage's chief inspirations for *HPSCHD* (1967–1969) was the music of Mozart; *Cheap Imitation* (1969) paraphrases Satie (albeit in unusual circumstances); *Apartment House 1776* (1976), *Some of "The Harmony of Maine" (Supply Belcher)* (1978), and *Hymns and Variations* (1979) draw on earlier American musics; the source of the series of *Europeras* is revealed eponymously. In his use of such resources, Cage demonstrates a retrospective vulnerability shared with many other radical composers – Ives, for instance, had evoked both his own and his father's pasts through musical quotation, while Cowell had from his teens onward imitated and alluded to earlier styles. Since the early 1960s, however, such tendencies have become increasingly common and, consequently, the distinctions between retrospective radicalism, traditional conservatism and – latterly – postmodernism have blurred accordingly (see chapter 20). The third movement of the *Sinfonia* (1968–1969) by Berio – who was resident in America from 1963 to 1972 – is often cited as a prime example of the polystylism which may result, but there are many other contemporaneous instances, both European and American, including Stockhausen's *Hymnen* (1965–1967; 1969) and the *Baroque Variations* (1967) by Lukas Foss (born 1922).

Further examples of retrospective and, especially, extraspective radicalism during this period are found in the works of many composers, including Pauline Oliveros (born 1932), Henry Brant (born 1913) and Lou Harrison. Oliveros has increasingly sought to explore "the relationship of the work to its larger social context" (Taylor 1993, p. 388) – for instance in *Horse Sings from Cloud* (1975) and *Rose Moon* (?1978) – and has accordingly often invoked the musics and aesthetic practices of other cultures. Brant's penchant has been for the spatial distribution of large forces. *Meteor Farm* (1981) – like *Variations IV*, a comprehensive example of Seeger's complete heterophony – utilizes an orchestra, brass groups, percussion groups, a jazz orchestra, solo and choral voices, a Javanese gamelan, a West African drumming ensemble, and a trio of South Indian instruments. Brant's musical materials and compositional methods are equally diffuse. Harrison, meanwhile, has consolidated his position as the doyen of extraspective radicalism. Since the early 1970s he has written extensively for Javanese gamelan and pioneered the building of, and composition for, American gamelan. He has continued to explore intonational systems other than equal temperament and has produced a number of highly successful transethnic works. For instance, in the Piano Concerto with Selected Orchestra (1983–1985) the solo instrument is tuned to Harrison's favorite Kirnberger No. 2 well-temperament and the orchestral instruments follow suit, as far as is possible. Of the work's four movements, the first, third and fourth all show some Javanese influence; the second, however, is titled *Stampede* and exuberantly combines Latin influences with Cowellian tone clusters. More recently, Harrison has accomplished a further rapprochement – between transethnicism, Rugglesian dissonant counterpoint, and other influences – in the polystylistic Symphony No. 4 (*Last Symphony*) (1988–1990).

The best-known incidence of extrospective and retrospective radicalism since 1960, however, is found in the work of such composers as La Monte Young (born 1935), Terry Riley (born 1935), Steve Reich (born 1936), and Philip Glass (born 1937). The origins of so-called minimal music are complex, but center around a hybridization of elements from the Eurocentric, radical, jazz, and popular traditions. Thus Young – who has been described as "the grandfather of [minimalism]" (Rockwell 1985, p. 113) – already included very long held notes in such early serial pieces as *For Brass* (1957) and the Trio for Strings (1958). After a brief period of ultra-Cagean prospective radicalism, Young has since 1962 concerned himself with the issues of just intonation, drones, and improvisation. Young's long-toned atonal music led to Riley's long-toned consonant music, including the String Quartet (1960). Subsequently, Riley's combination of repeated melodic phrases and constant pulse – archetypically in *In C* (1964) – provided minimalism with its most recognizable trademarks; these, along with the use of drones, are clearly related to the performance practices of the Indian subcontinent. Reich's initial (prospective) experiments with tape phasing – in *It's Gonna Rain* (1965) and *Come Out* (1966) – were succeeded by instrumental works, including *Piano Phase* (1967), which echoed Riley's enthusiasm for consonance and pulse. Subsequently, Reich has supplemented his technique through the study of Ghanaian drumming, Balinese gamelan, and Hebrew cantillation. Glass, meanwhile, in his

earlier minimalist work combined Indian additive and subtractive rhythmic procedures with traditional Eurocentric scales and arpeggios. Even
more so than his colleagues, he used amplification and electric keyboards
in a conscious allusion to contemporary popular music practice.

As Glass has noted, "[by 1967] I would say there were roughly thirty
composers working in a very similar style"; among those he names are Phill
Niblock (born 1933), Frederic Rzewski (born 1938), Tom Johnson (born
1939), Terry Jennings (1940–1981), and Meredith Monk (born 1943)
(Strickland 1991, p. 113). However, it is the music of Young, Riley, Reich
and Glass himself that has tended to monopolize scholarly and media
attention. Of the four, Reich and particularly Glass might be considered to
have abandoned radicalism since the mid-1970s (see chapter 20) but Riley
and Young have remained true to their original precepts. Riley's album
Shri Camel (1976; released 1980) consists of four solo improvisations, made
using a specially adapted electronic organ in just intonation with an elaborate digital delay system. The music is cast in two basic layers – a background of interweaving, pulse-like ostinato patterns, and a foreground of
freer, ornate, melodies. Young's self-confessed fanaticism has resulted in
his overall concept of the Dream House – "in which the composition,
performance, production . . . and performance space are integrated into
a single artistic experience" (Farneth 1986, p. 580) – and such visionary
meta-compositions as *The Tortoise, His Dreams and Journeys* (1964–) and
The Well-Tuned Piano (1964–).

Despite the predominance of retrospective and extraspective tendencies, however, prospective radicalism apparently remained a potent force
in contemporary music. By 1988, Conlon Nancarrow's series of studies for
player piano(s) – commenced in the late 1940s – totaled around fifty. Some
degree of their complexity may be gleaned from the (relatively mild)
subtitle of no. 27 – "Canon – 5%/6%/8%/11%." The music of Brown,
Feldman, and Wolff continued to challenge convention in various ways.
Feldman's late works made extensive use of repetition and were often of
epic proportions: *Three Voices* (1982) lasts ninety minutes, and *For Philip
Guston* (1984) four hours. Wolff's pieces, meanwhile, became increasingly
indeterminate in nature. The 1960s and early 1970s were an important
period for radicalism in all its guises and many composers disseminated
their work through specialized journals, including *Source – Music of the
Avant Garde*. Composers also took advantage of a new generation of performers, both virtuoso and – sometimes – unskilled, in groups as different
as ONCE, Fluxus, Musica Elettronica Viva, and Speculum Musicae.

The experience of prospective radicalism after 1960 is best summarized in the music of George Crumb and John Cage. Crumb works very much at the (avant-garde) edge of tradition, his compositions often stretching notational, instrumental, and technical resources to their limits. Several scores – including *Eleven Echoes of Autumn, 1965* (1966) and *Star-Child* (1977) – include circular notations somewhat paradoxically reminiscent of Medieval and Renaissance manuscripts. *Black Angels* for string quartet (1970) is one of many pieces in which the instruments are amplified. Its performers are also required to vocalize and to play maracas, tam-tams, and water-tuned crystal goblets. In *Vox Balaenae* (1971) and *Lux Aeterna* (1971) the players wear masks; as elsewhere in Crumb's catalog, extended performance techniques are utilized. At all times, however, the aural (and dramatic) results of these demands are wholly imagined. With Cage, there is if anything a greater expectation of performers' virtuosity, as is evinced by the unusually determinate *Etudes Australes* for piano (1974–1975) and *Freeman Etudes* for violin (1977–1980; 1989–1990). In the majority of his works, though, indeterminacy is assured via a plethora of graphic and other experimental means, including uncontrollable instruments – the plants and conch shells of *Child of Tree* (1975) and *Inlets* (1977) respectively – and (fixed or flexible) time brackets. Examples of the latter include *Thirty Pieces for Five Orchestras* (1981) and the extended series of "number" pieces that commences with *Two* (1987).

After roughly a century of extreme radical activity in music, however – both in America and elsewhere in the Western world – one might be forgiven for wondering whether further development is possible. The musical universe has been expanded to the point where it contains (to paraphrase the score of Cage's *Variations IV*) "any [or no] sounds or combinations of sounds produced by any [or no] means . . . [and performed by] any number of [or no] players." There can be no boundaries – and therefore no forefront – in a universe as limitless as that predicated by *Variations IV*. Thus the conventional view of radicalism – based solely on prospective expansion, and roughly analogous to cosmology's big bang theory – fails sufficiently to explain the realities of the contemporary musical situation in which we find ourselves. A more plausible explanation – which can take into account the effects not only of prospection, but also of retrospection and extraspection – lies rather in an analogy with cosmology's steady state hypothesis, where "new" material is created not intrinsically, but rather through the infinite hybridic recombinations of existing material. We used to move forward; after *Variations IV* we can only go round and round.

Thus even the most attractive, or striking, new works – for instance those of Stephen Scott (born 1944), Peter Garland (born 1952), John Zorn (born 1953), or Gregory Walker (born 1961) – must inevitably be allusive rather than elusive, referential (and reverential) rather than radical. Scott, in his further development of the altered piano, and Garland, in his often lyrical writing for piano and/or percussion, show the continuing influence of Cowell, Cage and Harrison, among others. Zorn's music is "wildly syncretic . . . a typical Zorn piece may move from Brahms . . . to pneumatic drills to cartoon music to post-Ornette sax within half a minute" (Strickland 1991, p. 125). Walker's *Dream N. the Hood* (1993) meanwhile, has been described by its composer as the first rap symphony, and combines elements of hip hop with extended orchestral resources.

In Woody Allen's 1977 film *Annie Hall*, the schoolboy Alvy Singer explains to a psychiatrist why he no longer sees any point in doing his homework: "The universe is expanding . . . Well, the universe is everything, and if it's expanding, someday it will break apart and that will be the end of everything." Has our musical universe broken apart, or rather stopped moving altogether? Is Morton Feldman's view of Cage's work – that he "stepped aside to such a degree that we really see the end of the world, the end of art" (Feldman 1985, p. 92) – accurate? Have we truly reached "the end of everything"? Not even musical cosmologists can answer such questions with certainty; but what is clear is that the limitless musical universe of Cage's *Variations IV* lies very close to the postmodernity which other composers, from quite different traditions, currently espouse. The British composer Robin Holloway could hardly be considered a fellow-traveler with Cage: yet in 1989 his own perspective was that "Modernism is everyone's immediate past: and any remoter past can only be reached through it. Meanwhile, we have the present: infinite possibility, dislocated like a wrecked mosaic that has been incorrectly restored" (Holloway 1989, p. 66).

The contemporary musical situation in which we find ourselves need not be viewed quite so pessimistically as this, though. An alternative is simply to try and accept it: as Lou Harrison once remarked in another context "don't underrate hybrid musics BECAUSE THAT'S ALL THERE IS" (quoted in Von Gunden 1995, p. 201). And there may even yet be two areas of American music in which prospective radicalism continues to play an important part (although it is significant that both areas involve interaction with other universes, one real but parallel, the other coextensive but synthetic). The first (and less convincing) exists where music is joined with one or more of the other arts, not conventionally (as in opera, ballet, etc.) but rather more idiosyncratically (as in music theatre, performance art, etc.). Although many precedents existed, the post-1950 collaborations of John Cage and Merce Cunningham (born 1919) had enormous influence. Events like the *Black Mountain College untitled event* (1952) stressed the potential independence of simultaneously occurring aspects of a performance; Cage's *Water Music* (1952) allowed music and theatre to collide in unexpected ways; *0′00″* (1962) did for action what *4′33″* had done for sound; and almost all of Cage's scores for Cunningham's dances were conceived without reference to the choreography (and vice versa). This lead was followed avidly during the 1960s, particularly by those associated with groups such as Fluxus and ONCE. For example, La Monte Young's *Piano Piece for David Tudor #1* (1960) opens with the instruction "Bring a bale of hay and a bucket of water onto the stage for the piano to eat and drink"; in *Solo for Violin Viola Cello or Contrabass* (1962) by George Brecht (born ?1926) the performer polishes, rather than plays, his instrument; *Kittyhawk* (1964) by Robert Ashley (born 1930) combines music, movement, and theatre in an early condemnation of the oppression of women. Since 1970, such multi-media theatricality has become increasingly common: examples include Glass's collaboration with Robert Wilson, *Einstein on the Beach* (1976); *United States* (1983) by Laurie Anderson (born 1947); Ashley's *Perfect Lives (Private Parts)* (1977–1983) and *Atalanta (Acts of God)* (1982); Steve Reich's *The Cave* (1993); the work of Meredith Monk, including the quasi-operatic *Atlas* (1988–1991); and Pauline Oliveros's *Nzinga the Queen-King* (1993).

The second (and more promising) area of continuing radicalism is electroacoustic music. Radical composers have, since the early years of the century, enthusiastically explored the possible uses of electrical means, both pure and in combination with acoustic resources. By 1922, Varèse was already calling for "an instrument that will give us a continuous sound at any pitch. The composer and the electrician will have to labor together to get it" (quoted in Ouellette 1968, p. 76). Typical early examples of such instruments include the theremin, developed by Russian inventor Lev Termen who was resident in America during 1927–1938; and the rhythmicon, built in the early 1930s by Termen to a design by Cowell. Cage followed Varèse in advocating "a music produced through the aid of electrical instruments" (Cage 1961, p. 3): among other works, the *Imaginary Landscape No. 1* (1939) has parts for frequency discs, played on two variable-speed turntables, while *Credo in Us* (1942) and *Imaginary Landscape No. 4* (1951) utilize radios.

Since World War II a succession of major technical advances – notably the development of magnetic tape, synthesizers, and computers – have resulted in greatly increased musical possibilities. Pioneering tape pieces – including those of Varèse, Vladimir Ussachevsky (1911–1990), Otto Luening (1900–1996), Cage, and Brown – were followed by the creation of important electronic music studios at universities throughout America. Synthesizers – "integrated and self-contained system[s] for the production of electronic music" (Schrader 1986, p. 31) – facilitated the composition of influential works by Milton Babbitt (born 1916), Morton Subotnick (born 1933), Jon Appleton (born 1939), and others. Computers, both analog and digital, have been used as versatile and multifarious compositional tools by such composers as Lejaren Hiller (1924–1994), John Chowning (born 1934), and Roger Reynolds (born 1934). However, it might be noted that many electroacoustic compositions have tended to concentrate on technical, rather than musical, matters; and, conversely, that electroacoustic composers have been as prone as their acoustic colleagues to the temptations of retrospection and extraspection. Only if electroacoustic music becomes the truly sonic art imagined by Varèse – as perhaps in the vast soundscape of *Metropolis San Francisco* (1985–1986) by Charles Amirkhanian (born 1945) or the abstract, non-referential synthesis of *nscor* (1980–1986) by Curtis Roads (born 1951) – will it be able legitimately to claim the inheritance of prospective radicalism.

20

Tonal traditions in art music
since 1960

JONATHAN W. BERNARD

If the history of American music in the twentieth century can be said to have imparted at least one clear lesson, it is that tonality has proved to be a far more durable and resilient force than many, at least among the more progressively minded, would ever have predicted at the century's beginning. Indeed, although there is still an identifiable musical avant garde, and although prominent figures in modernism's second (post-World War II) wave, such as Milton Babbitt and Elliott Carter, are still making their voices heard, it is *tonality* in all its many varieties that seems poised to set the tone, as it were, for the concert music of AD 2000 and beyond. Among those performers and audiences with at least some interest in recently composed music, it is tonal music especially during the last two decades that has garnered the lion's share of attention. Elderly composers who grew up neoclassical and never wavered; middle-aged composers who started off as atonalists or dodecaphonists only to repent later on; and younger composers for whom a nontonal idiom was never really a viable or seriously considered option – all are enjoying exposure in performances and recordings as never before.

Why has this happened? And why now? For all its history as a melting pot, open to new influences of every sort, America has, paradoxically, always had a deeply conservative streak. And this conservatism is nowhere more evident than in its attitude toward the arts. As has often been pointed out, the first Caucasian arrivals in the territories that eventually became the United States, as well as the many succeeding waves of immigrants over the next several centuries, brought what "culture" they had from their former, European homelands. This meant that that culture, and the artifacts that constituted it, perforce served the function of preserving a memory of national origin that was at least as important as any purely aesthetic function they might have had. Thus a colonial mentality about the arts persisted long after political independence, and it tended to discourage the fostering of indigenous artistic traditions – especially, it might be argued, musical traditions, which depend so crucially upon the infra-structure of performance. The home-grown in music was suspect, regarded as no better than second-rate; the authentic product came from Europe – and this was as true of performers and teachers as it was of new works. When the principal orchestras of some American cities, after 1900, at length began to rival those of Europe in quality, this development could be attributed, quite accurately, to the fact that these orchestras were largely made up of immigrant musicians, possessed of the best European training. And everyone knows that not until the New York Philharmonic appointed Leonard Bernstein its director in 1958 did a native-born American lead a major American symphony orchestra.

America's slow progress toward learning to stand on its own two feet, musically speaking, also meant that its developing musical consciousness was modeled on an idea of European culture that was never quite up-to-date. The radical changes in the compositional landscape from *c.* 1910 on never made it into the American mix even to the limited extent that they became part of the scene in Europe; a firmly nineteenth-century ideal of programming became, and remained, the norm here. Advocates of a more modern outlook, whether native-born "experimentalists" like Henry Cowell or immigrants like Edgard Varèse, barely made a dent in this steadily ossifying tradition. When new music from abroad did find favor with American concert audiences, it was almost invariably of a markedly conservative flavor, such as the symphonies Dmitri Shostakovich wrote after his chastisement by Stalin. Europe provided other assistance in this direction as well. The first American pupils of Nadia Boulanger, in the early 1920s, were attracted by her reputation as an effective pedagogue with progressive tastes; by the 1930s, however, Boulanger had turned her back on the "old-fashioned modernism" of Berg and Bartók and had begun to hold up the neoclassicism of Stravinsky – particularly the Stravin-sky of such works as *Perséphone* – as an ideal. A whole generation of Ameri-can composition students followed suit. Another conservative European pedagogue with enormous influence in the United States was the émigré Paul Hindemith (1895–1963), who beginning in 1940 taught at the Yale University School of Music for more than a decade. Also not to be over-looked is Serge Koussevitzky (1874–1951), who assumed the directorship of the Boston Symphony in 1924 and who throughout the 1930s and 1940s played a good deal of (mostly conservative) American music in an effort to establish, as he put it, the equivalent of the Russian Five in this country.

In part, of course, it was precisely because progressive musical activity operated only at the fringes of America's cultural life that its institutions were open to this kind of conservative influence in the first place. Some of the more modernistically inclined émigré musicians among those fleeing the chaos of Europe in the 1930s, such as Bartók and Ernst Krenek, had a much more difficult time than Hindemith did in gaining a livelihood in America. Others with a modern viewpoint to offer apparently responded to the American cultural climate by pulling in their horns – most notably Schoenberg, who settled in Los Angeles, far from the major American cultural centers, and who refused to include instruction in the twelve-tone method in the courses he taught at universities there (see chapter 18).

After World War II, musical modernism appeared to gain a new lease on life. Somewhat in parallel with events in Europe, dodecaphony and serialism emerged at the forefront of progressive musical thinking, quickly seizing the imaginations of many composers as more and more became known about Schoenberg's method and the further developments to which it was being subjected by Messiaen and the Darmstadt composers (in Europe) and by Babbitt, Krenek, George Perle, and others (in the United States). Stravinsky's seemingly miraculous conversion to the twelve-tone method, accomplished in stages over a period of half a dozen years following Schoenberg's death in 1951, did much to cement the reputation of dodecaphony among American composers and other musicians. Yet there were significant differences from the European situation as well. For present purposes, the most important of these was the continued, if somewhat subdued, presence of an American neoclassical tradition. Although such native-born composers as Samuel Barber, Aaron Copland, David Diamond, Howard Hanson, Roy Harris, Vincent Persichetti, Walter Piston, and William Schuman hardly wrote in a uniform style (Copland even made limited use of dodecaphony for a time), all of them continued, in one way or another, as tonalists throughout the heyday of serialism (see chapter 17). Their music was somewhat marginalized after 1945, but it was far from totally ignored and continued in some cases to be programmed and recorded. No one familiar with the heterodox tendencies of American culture could have been surprised by this. Furthermore, it should be noted that as the 1950s drew to a close the serialists and the neoclassicists were hardly the only groups competing for attention on the American musical scene: a new, quite radical avant garde, in some ways an outgrowth of the earlier "experimental" movement, had sprung up in New York (John Cage and his associates); composers like Varèse, Stefan Wolpe, and Elliott Carter offered other, extremely different alternatives;

there was fresh activity on the West Coast, by then well on its way to defining itself independently, and along lines markedly different from those of the East. By the early 1960s, in fact, the serialists had begun to look rather established, even a little staid by comparison to the latest metamorphoses of the avant garde, such as Fluxus and the beginnings of minimalism.

In short, without a single clear successor to neoclassicism, and with the failure of post-war nontonal music to win any wide enthusiasm by the early 1960s among performers, critics, or audiences, the way was opened for the conservative tendencies of American musical culture to reassert themselves, in the form of what might best be called a second wave of *neotonality*.[1] But, as usual with American music, this development signaled the adoption of no single new point of view; rather, over the past thirty-five years or so we have been made aware, as listeners, of the truly vast number of different ways it is possible for new music to be tonal. Composers have employed "functional tonality" in a more or less common-practice sense; they have also resorted to "tonality by assertion" or pitch centrism. There has been quotation of actual pieces from the past, as well as the quotation of the styles of specific composers from the past and allusion to period styles (Baroque, Classic, Romantic, etc.). Neotonality has also embraced *modality*, including white-note diatonicism and other, more exotic forms such as octatonicism. Tonality as manifested in the minimalist and post-minimalist styles has played a very large role. And, certainly, tonalities even further outside the mainstream of Western art music as traditionally construed, such as those of various ethnic musics and those borrowed from the popular styles of folk, jazz, and rock, have become part of the picture too. In this chapter, all of these possibilities and many of their possible permutations will be covered. They turn out, in practice, to be distributed across several categories of composers, each category distinguished by a certain kind of response to the tonal imperative.

The old guard

Besides the senior group of neoclassical composers enumerated above, all of whom did their principal work before 1960, there are five Americans particularly worth singling out, four of them still living at the time of writing, whose tonal roots are well anchored in the earlier part of the

1. Eric Salzman's term *neotonality*, less style-specific than *neoclassicism*, is often more appropriate (Salzman 1974). The term "tonality by assertion," used later, is also from this source.

century yet who have continued, more or less unperturbed, to make significant contributions in the latter part without allowing the post-war rise of dodecaphony or the various avant-garde upheavals to have much of an impact on their style. They are Leonard Bernstein, Ned Rorem, Dominick Argento, Lou Harrison, and Alan Hovhaness.

Leonard Bernstein (1918–1990) was always the most glamorously visible of this group, mainly because by 1960 he was much more readily recognizable to perhaps millions of Americans as the conductor of the New York Philharmonic (and television's first classical-music star) than as a composer. And if they had heard any of his music at all, they were much more likely to know his score to the musical *West Side Story* (1957) or his music for the film *On the Waterfront* (1954) than any of the considerable body of other works he had written by then. To make such observations is certainly not to gainsay his impact as a composer, which has been quite considerable. Bernstein did aspire ardently to success as a "serious" composer, as two symphonies and the Serenade for Solo Violin, Strings, Harp, and Percussion (1954) attest, even if the rest of his output up to 1960 was, essentially, music for the theatre, such as ballet scores, musicals, and the one-act opera *Trouble in Tahiti* (1952).

Nevertheless, it is true that success in making the "big statement" mostly eluded Bernstein throughout his life (Schiff 1993). The frankly embarrassing Symphony No. 3, *Kaddish* (1963), with its overwrought narration, is a case in point. In the *Mass* (1971), Bernstein fared somewhat better, having figured out how to use music-theatrical devices to lend some sorely needed ironic distance from the utter seriousness of the message (essentially, loss of faith under the stresses and strains of the modern world). Still, despite the many genuinely beautiful and affecting passages, the constant changes of style from one number to the next begin eventually to seem quite affected, even self-indulgent – as does the fact that the Celebrant, central to the *Mass*, is all too obviously a stand-in for Bernstein himself; the laying bare of the soul which the audience must witness comes across as a rather narcissistic exercise. Bernstein's proclivity for massive heterogeneity is both his blessing and his curse: when it works, it is truly exciting (and, of course, is a large part of what makes his music distinctively American); when it doesn't work, it seems simply like overstimulation. Here is Bernstein's own description of some of the elements in his Concerto for Orchestra (*Jubilee Games*) (1986–1989):

> The first movement, "Free-Style Events," is musical athletics, with cheers and all. It is also charades, anagrams, and children's "counting-out"

games. But mainly it is celebratory, therefore spontaneous, therefore aleatoric, ranging from structured improvisation to totally free orchestral invention "in situ"... The "Diaspora Dances" of the third movement are "free-style" only in a socio-cultural, geo-Judaic sense, and hence necessarily eclectic in style, their musical connotations ranging from the Middle East back to Central European ghettos and forward again to a New-Yorkish kind of jazz music.

(Quoted in Gottlieb 1991)

The facts of Bernstein's compositional history, as well as some of what he has written about it, suggest that his problems with the big statement are in part bound up with a crisis that he went through as a composer during the 1960s. Bernstein was granted an unprecedented sabbatical in 1964–1965 from his duties with the New York Philharmonic, specifically to allow him time to compose. He later gave an amusing account, in verse, of the way in which he had spent his time, musing "Over the fads of Dada and Chance, / The serial strictures, the dearth of romance," and listening to "Pieces for nattering, clucking sopranos / With squadrons of vibraphones, fleets of pianos..." – all of which led to the *Chichester Psalms* (1965): "These psalms are a simple and modest affair, / Tonal and tuneful and somewhat square, / ... / My youngest child, old-fashioned and sweet. / And he stands on his own two tonal feet" (Bernstein 1982, p. 237). Bernstein's realization that he was meant to remain a tonal composer also led to some very public proselytizing for tonality: "How does the wild thought strike you that *all* music is ultimately and basically tonal, even when it's nontonal?" he asked an audience at Harvard University in 1973. Bernstein made the claim, in all seriousness, that any piece employing twelve tones, even a serial piece, is "haunted" by a "sense of tonality" that is conspicuous in its absence but also somehow implied by the "natural harmonic series" that gave rise to "the same old twelve tones employed by everyone else" (Bernstein 1976, pp. 291, 289). The reasoning may be somewhat muddled, but the final point is clear enough: while a system employing, for instance, thirteen notes might be capable of true atonality, *twelve*, inextricably bound up as it is with the history of tonal Western music, can't manage such a feat.

If the *Chichester Psalms* amounted to a reaffirmation of faith on Bernstein's part in the ultimate "rightness" of tonality, they were also, perhaps, intended as a declaration that, when it came to compositional scale, less from then on would be more. If so, Bernstein did not entirely manage to keep his promise – he would be periodically afflicted with a kind of elephantiasis of conception right up to the end of his career (as in the Concerto for Orchestra) – but he did succeed in striking a happy medium in certain extended works of his later years, notably *Songfest* (1977) and *Arias and Barcarolles* (1988). These works eschew the big statement in favor of programs of songlike, independent units – analogous, in a way, to the "numbers" of a musical, except that there is no plot. Here the eclecticism works; Bernstein even came to terms with the twelve-tone row, giving it the kind of specialized roles for which he apparently deemed it especially appropriate, expressing disorientation or frustration.

Another older American whose career testifies to the enduring power of song is Ned Rorem (born 1923), whose works in this genre have become staples of voice recitals everywhere. It is an orientation that was settled fairly early on, by the testimony of Rorem's diaries. At the advanced age of twenty-eight, he wrote:

> If I am a significant American composer it is because I've never tried to be New. To reiterate: it's more pertinent to be Better than to be Different. American composers have the most dazzling techniques today; but they all have "masterpiece complexes" and write only symphonies. I believe I shall be ever more tempted to write just songs (the forgotten art) with as few notes as possible.

> (Rorem 1983, p. 15)

These were not only songs "with as few notes as possible," but also, often, in the simplest tonal idioms imaginable. Later on, Rorem sometimes expressed a certain bemusement at his reputation as a composer primarily of songs. In truth, however, this reputation is justified, for the ability to write splendidly concise songs has been a fixed feature of Rorem's compositional profile, something to which he has always been able to return from more extended (and, usually, more chromatic) excursions – and, in the final analysis, it seems to be what he does best. It is also true that after 1960, even the shorter songs often exhibit a looser conception of tonality, in which the sense of key is very much in flux – almost in a "pantonal" way. Sometimes, tonality in these works seems mainly a matter of having a certain amount of consonance, maintaining a certain proportion of sonorities familiar from older practice. Rorem's style overall has remained readily recognizable from the "golden age" of American neoclassicism, with strong overtones of middle-period Stravinsky.

The value placed on his songs, however, should not be taken as an invitation to ignore entirely Rorem's efforts in larger, sometimes wholly instrumental forms. Notable among these are his opera *Miss Julie* (1965; rev.

1979); *Air Music* (1974), which won him the Pulitzer Prize in 1976 and is more chromatic than most of the rest of his output, even verging on atonality at times though never quite taking the plunge; and the more recent Violin Concerto (1984), which reaffirms Rorem's affection for traditional conceptions of form and for an unambiguous sense of tonality.

Significant contributions to late-twentieth-century vocal music have come as well from Dominick Argento (born 1927), whose reputation is based more on operas than on songs. One is tempted to predict that Argento will end up being the last American to make a serious attempt at success in this form, after generations of frustration among his countrymen at their collective inability to gain even a toehold in the rigidly, almost exclusively nineteenth-century European repertory of the major American opera houses. *Postcard from Morocco* (1971) is probably the best known of Argento's operas, which is not saying a great deal; as a stage production, it may lack broad appeal owing to its somewhat strange and static plot. This has to do with a motley assortment of travelers stranded at a railroad station, all of whom proclaim public identities apparently not supported by whatever it is they are carrying in their luggage, which they refuse to open to anyone else's inspection. The sole individual who is tricked into revealing that his suitcase is, after all, empty is left behind when the train finally does show up. The employment of distinctively different tonal idioms to characterize each of the travelers in turn is dazzlingly virtuosic; the ensemble writing is startlingly original; and the final aria of the abandoned traveler, in which it seems to be revealed that despite his empty suitcase he is in fact what he says he is, is oddly moving.

One other work of Argento's particularly worth mentioning is his *From the Diary of Virginia Woolf* (1974), awarded the Pulitzer in 1975. This song cycle is definitely conceived in a Schumannesque manner, from the overarching structure down to some of the individual sounds. (Argento himself has acknowledged a certain modeling upon *Frauenliebe und Leben*.) Its tonal language overall, however, is very much the composer's own. Sometimes its tonality is quite explicit, as in *Parents*, in an E major that quickly grows out into chromatic territory without losing its essential focus, maintained by a frequently restated motif; or in *Rome*, a c minor tango. Elsewhere, pitch centricity is often encountered, for example in the B♭ of the opening song, returned to at the very end of the cycle, and also a kind of tonality by implication, in that many familiar harmonies, both individually and in some of their progressions, are recognizable from common practice even if not always used *in toto* that way. By some accounts, the *Diary* is a twelve-tone work, but in just what sense is difficult to establish empirically. Argento's study with Luigi Dallapiccola, that Italian twelve-tone composer who often arranged his rows to mimic tonal practice, may of course be counted as a relevant influence in this connection.

In contrast to Rorem, Argento, and Bernstein a good deal of the time, the vastly prolific Lou Harrison (born 1917) has worked largely in the domain of instrumental music. At one time (the 1940s) classifiable as an experimentalist, thanks to his study with Cowell and his association with John Cage, Harrison can now be regarded as a solid citizen of tonality, with the qualifier "West Coast style" owing to his abiding interest in other musics of the Pacific Rim. One might accurately say that as the definition of American tonal music has gradually diversified over the past several decades, its sphere has expanded to include Harrison. Harrison himself has done little to publicize or popularize his work since effectively declaring his independence from eastern cultural centers some forty years ago by moving to a rural location south of San Francisco and rarely, until very recently, venturing forth.

Having beaten a path to his door, in the persons of Dennis Russell Davies, Michael Tilson Thomas, and other latter-day champions, the world has discovered that Harrison's style has altered hardly at all since his self-imposed withdrawal. Although his knowledge of the musical practices of various Asian countries has continued to grow, the formal structures which serve to convey his Asian-inflected melodies and rhythms have remained thoroughly Western, and rather old-fashioned at that. This stylistic stasis, it must be admitted, is entirely appropriate for a composer as deeply involved as is Harrison with Asian musical traditions, some of which have remained essentially unchanged for millennia and are in fact dependent upon eternal verities for their very meaning. Harrison himself has made this lack of change in his style more obvious by continually returning to earlier pieces to revise them ever so slightly, and by composing works like his *Suite for Symphonic Strings*, actually dated "1960–1936" to emphasize its retrospective character.

To listen to Harrison's recent music is to be struck anew by his powers of rhythmic invention as applied within a rather limited frame; it is also to be reminded that his first passion, during that early experimental period, was percussion music. His powers of melodic invention impress too, again for that manifest ability to do so much with such limited means. In its always transparently tone-centered – essentially *modal* – style, the music bubbles along happily and extrovertedly. It is not hard to understand why

Harrison's music has won such an affectionate response from present-day audiences: it is exotic and familiar at the same time. The recent fascination among the concert-going and record-buying public with ethnic musics, which Harrison brings to his work in eclectic profusion with alternative tunings and actual non-Western instruments, is one side of this appeal. (Harrison has even written a work, the String Quartet Set [1978–1979], in which he pays the quartet the peculiar homage of writing for it as if an out-sider to the Western tradition – certainly a different sort of ethnic exer-cise!) The other, familiar and "accessible" side of Harrison's appeal is the textural and formal simplicity of his pieces. There is, for instance, hardly any counterpoint in the usual Western sense – generally only parallel inter-vals, or a melodic part with a drone or with a bass that simply doubles important pitches in the melody. By the same token, harmonic complexity is effectively proscribed. In projecting such structures, which often have a kind of natural, "artless" quality to them, Harrison seems to be following his own generalizations about musics of the world, the majority of which, he claims, consist of melody with some sort of rhythmic accompaniment, and are essentially an amateur endeavor. At its best, the narrowness of rhythmic and melodic focus in his music exerts a certain hypnotic charm; but after a while the impression of constant repetition can become some-what wearying. Some of Harrison's adapted devices, one feels, may work well in Asian musical contexts, but not so well in Western.

Finally among the old guard there is Alan Hovhaness (born 1911), without mention of whom no account of twentieth-century tonal music would be complete. Like Harrison immensely prolific (perhaps even more so: by 1983, he had already reached his Symphony No. 50, Op. 360), and like him primarily an instrumental composer, Hovhaness is also like his near-contemporary in exhibiting stylistic conceptions that were formed long ago and that, owing to renewed popularity, have persisted in the public ear right up to the present. Hovhaness as composer also seems, at first glance, to resemble Harrison in his fascination with non-Western musics and in his interest in melding Western and Eastern traditions: "I admire the giant melody of the Himalayan Mountains, seventh-century Armenian religious music, classical music of South India, orchestra music of Tang Dynasty China around 700 AD, opera-oratorios of Handel," he wrote in explanation of his Symphony No. 4, Op. 165 (1958) (Hovhaness undated). (Hovhaness is in fact of half-Armenian heritage, though he was born in Somerville, Massachusetts.)

A sampling of his music, however, suggests that his study of Asian musical traditions has been neither as deep nor as prolonged as that of Harrison. This indicates a larger fault in Hovhaness's work, which, however sincere its expressive intent, is enormously problematic from the point of view of technique. Recently unveiled pieces not only show no change of style or technique; they are actually *less* effective expressively than many of his earlier efforts, such as the Symphony No. 2, Op. 132 (*Mysterious Mountain*, 1955) or the Symphony No. 9, Op. 180 (*Saint Vartan*, 1964). The somewhat austere grandeur of such works now seems either to have stagnated or to have become buried under layers of schmaltz. It isn't just that melodies are nearly wholly confined to varieties of diatonic scales, ascending and descending, with an occasional augmented second to provide an exotic inflection; or that, aside from unaccented passing tones, the only dissonances are coloristic (bells and so forth). A truly corny sensibility now seems to have entered the picture: in the recent works the content is insipid, the pacing almost leaden. The Symphony No. 50 (*Mount St. Helens*) is unabashedly programmatic in intent, and as a series of nature pictures is not greatly different, from an aesthetic standpoint, from Ferde Grofé's *Grand Canyon Suite* (1931), although it is definitely not as entertaining. But it would make terrific background music for a documentary film on the 1980 eruption of Mount St. Helens.

Hovhaness could be called the Grandma Moses of contemporary American music if such a remark were not easily construed as an insult to folk art. There is, of course, nothing wrong with folk art – or folk music; but to make a kind of ersatz folk music with the enormous apparatus of a modern symphony orchestra and pretend that it is akin to Handel (say) is only to sow a great deal of confusion concerning what, exactly, art music is all about. It is deplorable that modern American concert audiences – whose powers of discernment are already rapidly eroding owing to the near-disappearance of public education in the arts in the United States – are being fed (by those who ought to know better) what amounts to pap disguised as adult nourishment.

Converts

An important aspect of the recent history of American art music is the change in orientation of some of its most significantly talented composers: composers who began their careers as "post-tonalists" or experimentalists and who gradually adopted more tonal, if not always more conservative, idioms. These individuals, mostly born in the 1930s, present a composite

profile as diverse as that of the old guard, but as a group they are remarkably unanimous in their desire to reestablish a basis for their compositional
practice in tonality under one interpretation or another.

George Rochberg (born 1918), the senior member of this group, is old
enough to have had a neoclassical period (in the 1940s) before embracing
the twelve-tone method in the mid-1950s – this development perhaps a
result of his contact with Dallapiccola. An essay written around that time
praises Schoenberg to the skies, at the expense of Webern (Rochberg
1984a, pp. 29–45). By the early 1960s, however, he had begun to find
Webern and Varèse more to his liking as models – and then, in 1964, came a
personal tragedy which seemed to catalyze into action the doubts he had
begun to experience about his life as a "modernist" composer, a feeling
that "the radical avant-garde of recent years has proved to be bankrupt," as
he put it in a later essay (Rochberg 1984a, p. 239). This resulted at first in
works like the *Music for the Magic Theater* (1965), in which quotations from
pieces in all kinds of styles, from all kinds of eras, are to be found throughout the three "Acts"; the central Act II contains the largest quotation (by
far) of all, the Adagio movement from Mozart's Divertimento K. 287.
Here, as the note heading Act II states, " . . . the past haunts us with its nostalgic beauty . . . and calls to us from the deeps of inner spaces of heart and
mind . . ." Rochberg has not quoted Mozart absolutely verbatim; registral
changes such as putting the first violin part up an octave throughout seem
intended to make this music of the past sound somewhat unearthly, "as
though it were coming from a great distance" (Rochberg 1972, pp. 45, 6).
Within the next few years, Rochberg passed from this kind of collage
approach to the composition of works with whole movements in older
styles, retaining however the idea of symmetry around a center devoted to
mysterious or "inner" expression. *Electrikaleidoscope* (1972) is evidently
the first of these, with its definitely Stravinskyan first and last (fifth) movements; its second and fourth movements in a "blues-rock" style (with the
traditional Western-classical instruments amplified) that must have
sounded hackneyed and rather square even then; and a central movement
in a kind of generic late-eighteenth/early-nineteenth-century slow-move-
ment style, itself symmetrical in that it contains a central interlude in a
contrasting (later nineteenth-century) style.

Rochberg's works in this kind of deliberately emulative construction
have drawn a good deal of criticism, and perhaps none more so than his
String Quartet No. 3 (1972). The composer has been called a "progressive"
(Reise 1980/1981), a "master forger" (Block 1982/1983), a *"pasticheur"*

(Porter 1987), and a "revivalist" (Kramer 1984, who actually liked the Third Quartet but not the philosophy that spawned it – and not the next three quartets Rochberg wrote, which are entirely in tonal styles of one sort or another). In the Third Quartet, the design is basically symmetrical, but not perfectly so: while two movements in a tone-centric Bartókian style frame the central, third movement – an A major Adagio that very strongly evokes late Beethoven, with an occasional admixture of late Brahms – the final, fifth movement does not immediately return to the acerbic atonality of the opening; before that happens, the quasi-Bartók of the fourth movement is continued for a bit, then is broken off in favor of a long, essentially Mahlerian passage. When the motif of the opening at length appears, it is more in the nature of a recollection than actual recurrence, quickly giving way to a final passage in which some elements of the foregoing movements seem to be reconciled. It is in reconciliation, in fact, that Rochberg has in the long run proved to be most interested; the juxtaposition of styles traditionally viewed as disparate, already at the time of the Third Quartet, was intended in that direction: "Far from seeing tonality and atonality as opposite 'styles,' I viewed them as significant aspects of an enlarged language of musical expression with branching subdivisions of what I like to call 'dialects' . . ." (Rochberg 1984a, p. 239). In more recent works, such as the String Quartet No. 7 (1979), all evidence of overt stylistic emulation has vanished, replaced by a synthetic tonal/atonal style that sounds more like transitional Schoenberg than anything else.

Collage and overt emulation of older styles, especially those of late Romantic repertory, are certainly at the heart of the music that David Del Tredici (born 1937) has been writing for the last three decades. His earlier compositions – such as *I Hear an Army* (1964) and *Syzygy* (1966), both on texts of James Joyce – had a decidedly modernist, nontonal sound to them; soon thereafter, however, Del Tredici's literary attentions turned to Lewis Carroll, and so began a lengthy transition to a very different musical style. At first, the Alice stories were fairly tangential – and so was tonality: *Pop-Pourri* (1968) had a wildly heterogeneous batch of materials (including a bit of Carroll) but, aside from the prominent use of a Bach chorale (*Es ist genug*), was not particularly tonal in orientation. Del Tredici has said that initially he had trouble conceiving of a proper setting for Carroll's texts, since they did not seem to go well with a style, like his, that up until the late 1960s had made abundant use of dissonance unconnected to any tonal hierarchy. This may explain the somewhat "experimental" character of *Pop-Pourri*, which is also evident in *An Alice Symphony* (1969; rev. 1976). In this work, Del Tredici makes much more extensive use of Carroll, but the style remains quite modern, with its elements of collage (including explicitly tonal material), Ivesian overlaps, bitonality, and the violently contrasting materials that are juxtaposed to reflect the parallel texts (Carroll's and the one Carroll was parodying) in *Speak Roughly / Speak Gently*. There are even some plausibly *post*-modern elements, specifically the sound of an orchestra tuning up, written out in the score quite precisely and complete with the referential oboe A, that opens (and closes) the work, momentarily disorienting the listener who will wonder when, exactly, the piece has begun. In a very broad sense, that oboe A could be considered the pitch center of the work: the first movement, for instance, is based both harmonically and melodically upon a stack of perfect fifths, G–D–A–E–B, branching out from the initial tuning (open violin strings plus B), a complex of which A 440 is the exact center.

The symmetrical nature of this structure, in both its dimensions, is actually a continuation of the "mechanistic" ideas by means of which, by his own account, Del Tredici worked himself out of his first compositional crisis and wrote *Syzygy*. And, eventually, it gave him some crucial ideas about how to use tonality. In *Vintage Alice* (1972), the "found" tonal elements were *Twinkle, Twinkle, Little Star*, to go with the Carroll poem ("Twinkle, twinkle, little bat . . .") that parodies the well-known nursery rhyme; and *God Save the Queen*, to signify the Queen of Hearts: " . . . I would use the one theme very, very slowly, then the other four times as fast. I would put them in three different keys at once; I was using tonality, but the effect was rather fractured. I certainly wasn't tonal in the Bach-Beethoven-Brahms sense. But I was beginning to get a feel for tonal materials. I was subjecting tonality to all of my *Syzygy* machines" (Dufallo 1989, p. 161).

By the time of *Final Alice* (1976), Del Tredici's tonal technique had developed into a far less ambivalent attitude toward common-practice materials; one has only to compare the setting of the Mock Turtle's verses, "You told me you had been to her . . . ," in this work to the treatment they received in *An Alice Symphony*. However, the "fractured" character of earlier usages still survives in the establishment and incessant repetition of one big theme, always recognizable throughout its many changes of harmonization, orchestration, and speed of presentation, rhythmic alterations, and so on. The monothematic content (a little reminiscent of the famous waltz from Richard Strauss's *Der Rosenkavalier* in the way it begins), conveyed in unabashedly late-Romantic language with a very big orchestra, eventually sounds monomaniacal, a little crazy. This happens at least in part because although all of the Alice pieces from *Final Alice* onward make use of the tonal language in a familiarly structured way – thus are, more or less, tonal pieces – they also, at the same time, *comment upon* tonality. Del Tredici did this in order to parallel the way in which the texts that Carroll was parodying can be seen as commentary upon Carroll's own texts:

> [I] was trying to integrate into the Alice tales the true story of Lewis Carroll, the man, and his infatuation with Alice Pleasance Liddell . . . many of the nonsense texts were actually disguised versions or parodies of poems by other authors. And these other poems always concerned unrequited love – even, in one, the unrequited love of a man for a girl named Alice . . . Now it was not so much the Carrollian nonsense – a camouflage – which fascinated me, but rather what he had *not* said, the poems Carroll had in effect suppressed . . .
>
> (Dufallo 1989, p. 163)

This "intertextuality" had begun in *An Alice Symphony*, but it was only in *Final Alice* that the idea of portraying "the real feelings of Carroll the man" emerged. It explains, I believe, the elements in Del Tredici's settings that remind us of our true location late in the twentieth century: the occasional harmony that is not quite faithful to the late-Romantic style; the use of aleatory as a kind of super-upbeat, inducing a chaotic frenzy that dissipates upon resolution into triadic tonality; the passing occurrences of twelve-tone rows to represent disorienting events (Alice drinking the potion that makes her grow); and so forth. It also explains those aspects of Del Tredici's music that seem excessive or histrionic: an amplified soprano shouting or screaming Carroll's or others' words over a turbulent whirl of sound from the orchestra; or the "development" of the main, F major tune in *Haddocks' Eyes* (1985), which sounds like a patter song from Gilbert and Sullivan gone absolutely insane. Such features greatly disturbed certain critics, such as Andrew Porter, who apparently took them as a failure of expression (Porter 1989); but in fact they make perfect sense in terms of the composer's aims. Del Tredici's text settings are almost never naturalistic; listening to *In Memory of a Summer Day* (1980), for instance, in the absence of a score one must run to get one's copy of *Through the Looking Glass* in order to understand the words. This is precisely because the music is about "what Carroll had *not* said" – a form of inner expression. Arguments will continue, of course, about the defensibility of reducing the Alice texts to coded expressions of longing from a shy, lovesick Oxford don, and giving them such a single-minded, obsessive character in these settings.

While neither Rochberg nor Del Tredici has shown much inclination to follow Bernstein's or Argento's lead in making use of popular idioms in art music contexts, others among the "converted" have found this a particularly fruitful area. Prominent among them is William Bolcom (born 1938), whose conversance with American popular music of the earlier part of this century has strongly formed his mature output. Like other composers in this group, Bolcom found his way to tonality through collage: his earlier works, such as *Black Host* (1967) and *Frescoes* (1971), are wild excursions into stylistic juxtaposition and outright conflict. In the former, the simultaneous presence of a hymn-tune from the *Geneva Psalter* and a lengthy allusion to older American popular music is particularly jarring (Albright 1971). In *Frescoes*, the conceptual germ is the pitting of two triads, C major and e♭ minor, against one another. Bolcom comments: "Many composers, after years of trying to reject tonality, are now re-espousing it in one form or another, often using it in different ways from the classical masters" (Bolcom 1974). *Commedia, for (Almost) Eighteenth-Century Orchestra* (1971) tends of course in the classical direction, though there is plenty of grating dissonance interrupting the passages of more-or-less authentic eighteenth-century writing: "The influence is the *commedia dell'arte* – the stock stage characters tossed against each other in a variety of situations, often comic but . . . not without a dark side" (Bolcom 1976). It bears comparison to Rochberg's *Music for the Magic Theater*, if only to show that the artistic intentions are ultimately quite different. Some of the hallucinatory character of Rochberg's second movement, though, with its octave-too-high violin, shows up in Bolcom's lines for E♭ clarinet in a kind of manic *saltarello* style.

The song cycle *Open House* (1975), seven poems of Theodore Roethke set for tenor and chamber orchestra, showed more clearly what Bolcom's later development would be like. The composer himself called it "eclectic, invoking styles that range from Bach to Gershwin," and continued: "Perhaps a few years ago I would have fought to avoid all these associations; today I welcome them. I sense the need to re-integrate the past with the present, to treat the musical language more like spoken language: as a constantly evolving creature always taking on new flesh and bone, yet retaining its most ancient elements" (Bolcom 1976).

Bolcom's more recent works still show this eclectic sensibility, but the eclecticism is now more controlled – by an acceptance of the hegemony of tonality. There is little sense any longer of opposition of tonal and non-tonal; dissonance, when it occurs, suspends explicit tonal orientation in a fashion not so very different from that of the nineteenth century – although Bolcom, given what he has said in connection with his *Twelve New Etudes* (1977–1986), might disagree: "I now embark on a stylistic and harmonic synthesis no longer involved with any local style – that of a fusion of tonality *into* non-centered sound (often miscalled 'atonal'), as a planet in space draws gravity toward itself [*sic*]. Within this spatial (yet tonal) universe one can attempt to calibrate one's distance from a strong tonal center with greater accuracy" (Bolcom 1988). The second and sixth of the *Twelve New Etudes* are particularly interesting in respect of this characterization. In any case, the synthesis is not completely seamless, for elements of popular music still turn up at unpredictable points. One might mention the Joe Venuti-style passages in the Violin Concerto in D (1984), including liberal use of ragtime and rhythm and blues; or the fox trot-style treatment of quotations from Wagner's *Prelude and Liebestod* in Bolcom's Fifth Symphony (1990). Such episodes, however, are less incongruous than they might have been in the context of Bolcom's earlier style because *everything*, essentially, is an allusion to some older style. Though it is all done with great finesse and musicality, one can't help but feel uneasy in the presence of so many sounds that have been heard before, if never in these particular combinations.

Parenthetically at this point, it is worth mentioning that while the borrowing of popular musics in present-day art music is nothing new in America, the crossover efforts of some "classically" trained composers into pop has been complemented by some crossing over in the other direction: Chick Corea (born 1941), Keith Jarrett (born 1945), and Anthony Davis (born 1951), all well known as jazz composers, have written for ensembles usually associated with art music. These compositions are difficult to classify, which illustrates a kind of corollary to the diversification of contemporary musical activity: varieties of music are springing up that respect none of the old stylistic boundaries. The work of performance artist Laurie Anderson (born 1947), comprising approximately equal parts pop and avant garde, is another example of this trend. And then there is Frank Zappa (1940–1993), best known for his work in rock but with serious aspirations, in part realized, to write for orchestras and smaller acoustic concert ensembles, as well as combinations of orchestral forces and amplified instrumentation. All of this is in some sense "tonal American music since 1960" as well.

Another convert to tonality is John Harbison (born 1938) who has also made use of popular idioms, though to much lesser extent than William

Bolcom, as seems appropriate for a composer whose musical approach is a good deal more introspective. For Harbison, too, tonality is a more complicated issue, in the sense that he has handled it in so many different ways in his music since the mid-1970s. His earlier works, such as *Confinement* (1965), were spiky and modernist – a quality that has never been completely superseded but was definitely showing some signs of mitigation by the time of *The Flower-Fed Buffaloes* (1976). This work, a cantata for chorus, solo baritone, and piano, is very consciously (almost self-consciously) "American" in its outlook; especially with its chorus, it has the manner of Americana by composers of one or two generations back and seems to acquire an aura of tonality around its edges through these associations. There is also a lot of ostinato in several of the movements, which has a way of asserting a certain pitch-centric foundation. The Piano Concerto (1978) takes a different tack, moving ever closer to explicit tonality as it progresses, at the end of the last movement emerging in a thoroughly tonal-cadential way on a major triad. In a later work for large forces, the Concerto for Double Brass Choir and Orchestra (1989–1990), Harbison is quite explicit about pitch centricity, describing it in terms of conflict and resolution: in the first movement, the fourth G–D rubs dissonantly against the fourth F♯–C♯, resolved in favor of a G tonality in the last movement.

Among Harbison's works for chamber ensembles, particularly worthy of mention is the strikingly original and elegant *November 19, 1828* (1988), a piano quartet named after Schubert's death date. The title of the first movement – *Introduction: Schubert crosses into the next world* – is accompanied by Harbison's description of it: "Schubert begins his journey haunted by sounds which are not his music, but pertain to his music in disturbing ways" (Harbison 1992). This should tell us clearly enough that his piece "asserts Schubert's relevance to the present rather than any nostalgia for the past" and lends a useful perspective on the nature of Harbison's attraction to tonality. For other converts previously discussed, of course, tonality is a good deal more than an exercise in nostalgia – but nostalgia does play a role nevertheless. Harbison is much more unambiguously forward-looking. In the "hall of mirrors" of the second movement, "everything is played back immediately upside down," a musical device unfamiliar to Schubert in real life. And Harbison's continuations of the rondo fragment of 1816 and the fugue subject by Sechter (S–C–H–U–B–E–R–T), in the third and fourth movements respectively, are by no means attempts to duplicate Schubert's style: they partake of tonality as practiced at the time, of course, but also go far beyond these bounds. The same sort of "progressive" approach to tonality is to be found in the Piano Quintet (1981). Harbison never simply imitates (though with this ensemble it would have been tempting to imitate Brahms); listening to this work, one could almost imagine that twentieth-century American music had continued developing along German-influenced lines flowing out of Brahms through Zemlinsky and Schreker – *almost* as though Schoenberg had never existed.

It would be hard to find a twentieth-century work designed according to more scrupulously "modern" principles than *Diaphonia Intervallum* (1965) by Joseph Schwantner (born 1943). The title means, according to the composer, "dissonant interval," in this case the major seventh, "the building-block interval of the piece" (Schwantner 1978). Schwantner still favored an atonal language by 1973, the year *In Aeternum (Consortium IV)* was written, but by this time ostinatos and sustained pitches abound, and it is obvious that some sort of stylistic change is in the works. A piece for amplified piano, winds, and percussion . . . *and the mountains rising nowhere* (1975), is solidly built on B, with many ostinatos and a tightly constrained repertory of gestures. This extremely splashy and "colorful" piece also makes use of the kind of exotica that have been hallmarks of Schwantner's compositions ever since, such as tuned water glasses (played with a bow), humming on drone pitches by ensemble members, and so forth. *Sparrows* (1979) is even more obviously tonal, with its substantially triadic harmonic language and cyclic progressions such as the one found in measures 83–136, starting and ending on the "root" F♯ and alternating descending major thirds and minor seconds sequentially in the bass. This work also makes more explicit references to music of the past than Schwantner's previous works, with its Renaissance band and a passage reminiscent of Baroque style near the end.

Two other composers who are also converts to tonality – in quite different senses from the five previously discussed, and also from each other – deserve at least brief mention here. Frederic Rzewski (born 1938) was a musical radical at the start of his career, which included, among other activities, membership in the Rome-based Musica Elettronica Viva. Works like the minimalist *Les Moutons de Panurge* (1969) and *Coming Together* (1972), though still quite radical, also reveal a growing interest in tonal materials; this emerges more clearly in his solo piano pieces of the 1970s built on the progressively elaborate recomposition of pre-existing melodies. *Variations on "No place to go but Around"* (1973) was the first of these; it was followed by perhaps his most spectacular essay in the genre, the "Diabelli"-length *The People United Will Never Be Defeated!* (1975), a set of thirty-six variations on a Chilean folksong. In this work, the process of variation slowly transforms the initial, diatonic material, taking it in several stages through chromaticism to an atonal treatment and back again (Wason 1988). A further development of such ideas, divorced from the seriatim structure of a standard variation set, can be detected in the four *North American Ballads* (1978–1979), where the treatment of the familiar tunes, drifting in and out of more complicated and chromatic passages, will inevitably remind the listener at first of Ives. But the method, in reality, is very different: the tune is not suddenly eclipsed, as so often happens in Ives, but is very slowly obscured by accretion (or brought to light by the reverse process) – and even once it has completely disappeared there persists the sense of the tune permeating the texture in a kind of atomized form. *Which Side Are You On?*, the second ballad, is a good example of this technique, with the tune's head motif used to the point of saturation in many overlapping different transpositions at different speeds. Rzewski's rhythm is also very different from Ives's, with a strong underlying pulse that may reflect the composer's improvisational background as well as his experience with minimalism. Also notable are the Four Pieces for Piano (1977), where highly inventive use is made of the "tonal-transparent/atonal-opaque" dichotomy, moving back and forth in ever-changing ways, some of them reflecting a considerable familiarity with jazz harmonic practice.

The most unusual take on tonality among all the composers in this group probably belongs to Fred Lerdahl (born 1943). His career began in the 1960s with several chamber works – including, most notably, *Wake* (1967–1968), for soprano and chamber ensemble – in what he now refers to as his "post-Schoenbergian atonal/romantic" style (Lerdahl 1990). Another work for soprano and chamber ensemble, *Eros* (1975), showed a significant turning toward tonality in its strict use of variation form (twenty-one variations, each twenty measures long; every third variation canonic in emulation of the "Goldberg Variations") and a substantial revision in pitch organization, in that hierarchical ideas now controlled the deployment and subsequent elaboration of the harmonic structure. Soon thereafter came a compositional development that seems in some ways to have been definitive for Lerdahl: in his First String Quartet (1978), the tonal hierarchy controls the temporal dimension as well, as a continuous variation process begins with the bare minimum of tonality-defining information, which then is progressively composed out in fourteen subsequent sections, each roughly half again as long as its predecessor.

(Lerdahl has employed similar structures in more recent pieces, and with particular brilliance in his *Fantasy Etudes* of 1985.) Ideas of this sort obviously owe something to the Austrian theorist Heinrich Schenker (1868–1935), whose positing of "structural levels" in eighteenth- and nineteenth-century music has spawned an entire school of thought in American universities since World War II, and also to work in the theory and analysis of tonal music, modeled on Chomsky's ideas of "generative grammar," that Lerdahl undertook in the 1970s in collaboration with a linguist – work that led eventually to a book-length study (Lerdahl and Jackendoff 1983). In a sense, then, Lerdahl's turn toward tonality was *anti*-Romantic, in decided contrast to Rochberg, Del Tredici, and Schwantner, and even to Harbison and Rzewski for whom the change signaled no particular attraction to or antipathy toward Romanticism. It also reflects a consciously intellectual attitude toward musical materials and style that is common in the academy, though it doesn't always produce music that is as convincing and memorable as Lerdahl's.

Minimalism goes tonal

The avant-garde movement that came to be known as minimalism, after a number of other labels ("trance," "systems," "solid-state") failed to stick, in its early years either exhibited an indifference to tonality or occasionally appropriated it for radically different purposes than anything preceding it, as in the landmark work *In C* (1964) by Terry Riley (born 1935) (see chapter 19). This was true right through the first flush of popularity that minimalism enjoyed in New York in the late 1960s, where Steve Reich (born 1936) and Philip Glass (born 1937) were by then working, when a new kind of "mainstream" audience began to produce sellout crowds, if usually in small venues. Riley never truly joined this scene, returning to the West Coast after a few years in New York and pursuing his own idiosyncratic vision, which has gained a larger audience in recent years as the result of some very fruitful collaborations with the Kronos Quartet. *Salome Dances for Peace* (1985–1986), for example, which was written for the Kronos, like many of his pieces gives the impression of a mosaic of tonalities, none dominating for very long; often, these pitch-centric sections are marked by the modal quality of Indian music that has fascinated Riley throughout his career.

Meanwhile, Reich and Glass moved independently, and in quite different ways, toward tonality in the sense of a more explicitly harmonic basis. For Reich, the watershed piece was *Music for Eighteen Musicians*

(1976), in which an eleven-chord succession, stated with, for Reich at the time, unaccustomed rapidity at the outset, gives way to eleven sections each based on one of the chords. This is still minimal music, in that it reflects a response to serial (visual) art, and also in terms of its repetitive devices which induce change over extended periods of time (Bernard 1995); however, it is also diatonic, sectionalized, and somewhat hierarchical – features which might be taken to outweigh the lack of strong pitch centricity in giving the music a specifically tonal identity. This trend is continued in works like *Music for a Large Ensemble* (1978) and *Variations for Winds, Strings, and Keyboards* (1980), where one can detect process *per se* being pushed into the background, leaving the sections of a predetermined form to be simply filled up. It is probably not a coincidence that at this same time Reich began to write pieces for ensembles other than the one he had founded and directed; the shift in technique into something a little less radical may have made it possible for others to play his music without his close supervision and control.

Reich's new-found harmonic technique was sufficiently powerful, in fact, to allow him a kind of vacation from minimalism: in *Tehillim* (1981), he was prepared to handle the new challenge of text-setting in terms of his already greatly changed ideas about form. At the same time, the constant pulse of minimalism was retained, as were the repetition and permutation (applied to individual sections). Form called even greater attention to itself, in its overriding symmetrical design, in *The Desert Music* (1982–1984), a work which also saw further emphasis on harmonic succession and the relative ambiguity or clarity of tonalities. By *Different Trains* (1988), and continuing in *The Cave* (1993) and *City Life* (1995), the widening dichotomy of process and result, always implicit in Reich's minimalism despite the composer's earlier protestations to the contrary (Reich 1974), was becoming very obvious in that while the rhythm and intonation of recorded snippets of human voices controlled the melodic dimension, the harmony was independently arrived at.

For Glass, whose path turned in the direction of large staged works (called "operas" for lack of a better term) rather than the large concert works to which Reich gravitated, the experience of *Einstein on the Beach* (1975–1976) led him, as he has recounted (Glass 1987), into previously unsuspected realms of harmonic possibilities. Mostly, these turned out to be short successions of chords, used as repeating modules to which the device of additive rhythm was applied to vary their proportions and total duration in ever-changing patterns. The successions themselves, though usually made up primarily, or exclusively, of triads, rarely sounded like common-practice harmonic progressions (aside from the reliable presence of an unambiguous tonic), owing to a quirky application of chromaticism and an utter disregard for canonical principles of voice leading.

In *Satyagraha* (1980), such patterns were wedded explicitly to chaconne-like cycles, although the result hardly bore much resemblance to Bach. Instead, the chord successions began to take on some of the stock features of pop music progressions – a development perhaps unsurprising, considering that from the beginning Glass's music, with its extremely simple components, pounding pulse, and amplified instrumentation featuring the electric organ, among all the products of minimalism was destined to appeal the most readily to an audience raised on rock and roll. Within the past dozen years, in fact, Glass has made some more explicit moves in the direction of crossover, in a collaboration with several well-known pop lyricists (*Songs from Liquid Days*, 1985) and two symphonies based on themes by pop composers David Bowie and Brian Eno (*Low*, 1992; *Heroes*, 1996). Meanwhile, his more recent music-theatrical works, such as *Akhnaten* (1983) and *La Belle et la Bête* (1994) – the last a technological *tour de force*, painstakingly worked out to synchronize exactly with Cocteau's film as a substitute sound track – apply the same harmonic and rhythmic methods worked out in his earlier operas, with some largely superficial alterations to suggest, say, ancient Egypt (many parallel fifths), or France at some indeterminate date in the past (whole-tone scales and augmented triads).

Unlike Reich and Glass, John Adams (born 1947) came to minimalism second hand, without the formative influence of minimalist visual art that resonates so vividly in the two older composers' music. Adams merely heard minimalist music, liked it, and sought to apply some of its devices to his own work. In this effort he has been smashingly successful – and, having made the external facts of the style very much his own, has proved able to strike out in new directions. For Adams, minimalism was always fundamentally allied with harmony, as he shows in the early solo piano piece *Phrygian Gates* (1977), where sections based on Lydian and Phrygian scales alternate in a readily perceivable pattern, connected by what are effectively common-tone modulations that sound very little like anything in common-practice tonality. Similar practices obtain in the string septet *Shaker Loops* (1978). The minimalist pulse is almost always present throughout these pieces, but in both there are sections where it is not, confirming the status of minimalism for Adams as a consciously assumed, pre-existent style with certain attributes that may be independently adopted or not, or combined with other styles. Listening to Adams's next several pieces, one is struck by the moments of resemblance, often occurring in rapid alternation, to Glass's and Reich's music. Also clear is a steady progression, through *Harmonium* (1980–1981), *Grand Piano Music* (1982), *Light over Water* (1983), *Harmonielehre* (1985), and *The Chairman Dances* (1985), toward dilution of the minimalist style with other materials and procedures: progressions hardly at all found in Reich's or Glass's music, such as root motions by a fifth (even V–I cadences); building to climaxes in a manner more typical of tonal music long before minimalism. By the time of *Short Ride in a Fast Machine* (1986), in fact, one could say that Adams had made the pulse and repeating patterns of minimalism a kind of motor for a substantially redesigned vehicle, one which burned a different kind of fuel and followed very different structural routes from those of older minimalist models. Aside from the motoric aspect, minimalism has left its mark on Adams principally in the confidence to write in elongated, sometimes greatly elongated, forms. This is certainly noticeable in his first opera, *Nixon in China* (1987). To an extent, it is also noticeable in his second opera, *The Death of Klinghoffer* (1989–1991), although by this time Adams has stopped stretching out single harmonies to quite the degree that he had been previously. In Adams's most recent works, especially the Chamber Symphony (1992) and the Violin Concerto (1993), minimalist traits (except for the constant pulse) have been gradually vanishing, while tonal plans, as if in compensation, have gained something in complexity; also notable is an appreciable increase in *contrapuntal* complexity, the origins of which seem to date back to the ensembles in *Nixon in China*. And even the pulse has now been put in the service of traditional forms, such as the repeating bass of the chaconne and the *moto perpetuo* of the toccata in the second and third movements respectively of the Violin Concerto.

If Adams's most recent music could be said to qualify as "post-minimalist," the work of Michael Torke (born 1961) has belonged in that category from the start. Torke has if anything gone one better than Glass in his attempts to make of the minimalist style a commercially viable product. His music is slick and accessible, colorfully orchestrated, minimalist in the sense of projecting extremely restricted harmonic materials in nervously inventive rhythms. Its uniform tempo (not always explicitly pulsed) makes it eminently danceable, as some notable collaborations with Peter Martins have demonstrated. So far in his career, Torke seems best able to handle work or movement durations on the shorter side; without the large frames afforded by Glass's additive processes, for example, the longer pieces can begin to seem directionless after a while. Torke's music, with its facile appropriation of diatonic harmony in its most elementary form, makes ideal pops-concert fare, suitable for the short attention spans that usually prevail at such events; pieces like *Bright Blue Music* (1985) – nine minutes of nothing much besides tonic and dominant in D major – and *Javelin* (1994) spring readily to mind. A hearing of several of his works in chronological succession well bears out the analogy he has drawn, in a recent interview, between his compositional process and factory production (Ryang 1996). It would be a mistake to confuse such aims with the more serious ones of his predecessors in the minimalist line – or to take at face value, for example, the gloss on Wittgenstein that supposedly explains the eternally repeated V–I progressions of pieces like *Bright Blue Music* and *Ash* (1989) (Kennicott 1991). Torke is talented and intelligent, but he also comes across as extremely cynical.

New and newer Romantics

The Horizons festival of new music sponsored by the New York Philharmonic in June 1983 came with a title dreamt up by festival director Jacob Druckman: "Since 1968, a New Romanticism?". Whether or not the term "Romantic" accurately described all of the music programmed on that occasion – perhaps The New Romanticism should be called, as has been suggested, The New Synthesis or Tonal Reformation (Kendall 1987) – the question posed in that title was already very much in the air throughout the American musical world, and is now answerable in the affirmative, with many of the contemporary composers most often played by American orchestras these days identifiable, in different ways and to greater or lesser degrees, as "Romantics." In this section, we survey the work of several currently active (or, at least, influential) composers of this ilk, in two groups: those who emerged as significant figures in the 1980s or slightly earlier, and those whose careers have brought them their first sustained attention in the 1990s.

John Corigliano (born 1938) was one of the first in the former category to attract serious notice. His Clarinet Concerto (1977) showed that it was not necessary to display overtly tonal tendencies in order to write Romantic music. This tremendously virtuosic work is written in a generally dissonant idiom, but in the insistently exaggerated and extroverted gestures, with every stupendous climax followed by another even more stupendous,

one finds a distinctly over-the-top quality certainly not foreign to Romanticism but hardly necessary in such abundance, either. This quality is
something that has not dissipated in Corigliano's music over the years,
although he has become noticeably more conservative as a harmonist, at
least, as one can see from comparing the Concerto to his more recent Symphony No. 1 (1988–1989). This work, whose first movement bears the title
Apologue: Of Rage and Remembrance, honors those who have died of AIDS,
and it certainly does wear its emotions on its sleeve, as it were – perhaps too
much so, for the composer's wholly justifiable anger and bitterness have
been taken as sufficient motivation for the terrible, grinding climaxes with
which this piece is punctuated; in strictly musical terms (by which, ultimately, any piece, regardless of its subject matter, must live or die), they
often feel unearned. Even more conservative is his opera *The Ghosts of Ver-
sailles* (1991), largely an exercise in eighteenth-century pastiche.

Joan Tower (born 1938) is certainly not a tonal composer in the sense of
using a lot of triads or exhibiting a penchant for allusion to older styles.
"Tonal" is, however, a plausible descriptor for her music, owing to the
presence of pitch centers of varying explicitness and also to the extensive
use of octatonic materials. Already in the 1970s, Tower's tonal predilections were clearly in formation. The first movement of *Breakfast Rhythms I
and II* (1974), for instance, is a hexachord piece, but the hexachords in
question alternately combine with, overlap, and exclude one another in
ways that have nothing to do with the twelve-tone method; the two movements center on B and G♯ respectively. The critical acclaim Tower received
in the 1980s came principally from two substantial works for orchestra,
Sequoia (1981) and *Silver Ladders* (1986), both written in an energetic and
exuberant style that communicates in a quite straightforward manner.
Sequoia is firmly fixed on G at the beginning, in the middle, and at the end;
in between, the pitch center migrates. Composing out this structure,
Tower displays a definite predilection for octatonic structures, which
branch out from the migrating center at its various locations – hence, presumably, the ramified metaphor of the title. *Silver Ladders* is even more
explicitly octatonic, with a rising motif in alternating whole and half steps
that governs much of the piece.

Ellen Taaffe Zwilich (born 1939) might conceivably have been placed in
the section on "Converts", except that her atonal period does not appear to
have lasted very long, confined essentially to the few years after her study
with Elliott Carter and Roger Sessions. Already by the time of her
Chamber Symphony (1979) she was moving toward a more open-textured,

less densely chromatic style; also audible in this work is a definite favoring of octatonic pitch collections. *Passages* (1981) displays clear tendencies to tonal centering in some of its movements, tendencies which become even stronger in the Symphony No. 1 (1982). Zwilich's prefatory note to this score, a 1983 Pulitzer Prize winner, mentions a preference for the "organic" approach to form, "an interest in the elaboration of large-scale works from the initial material," and for "modern principles of continuous variation." These Schoenbergian concerns are combined with "older (but still immensely satisfying) principles, such as melodic and pitch recurrence ..." (Zwilich 1983). Significant in this connection, surely, is the palpable emphasis on A at the end of the first and last movements. This piece in particular shows a good deal of affection for Sessions's ideas of symphonic form; there are also strong overtones of the twentieth-century tonal Russian school (Prokofiev and Shostakovich), which come more clearly to the fore in the Symphony No. 2, *Cello* (1985). This is also a much more deliberately tonal work, combining strong and frequently recurring pitch centers with strikingly dissonant harmonies.

Among Zwilich's other pieces, worthy of mention is the *Prologue and Variations* (1983), which bears the motto D–E♭–C–B, the well-known musical signature of Shostakovich,[2] and also, not incidentally, an octatonic set, subsequently transposed to many different pitch levels. As in Zwilich's symphonies, there are many Shostakovichian references, and the same kind of "extended tonality" prevails here as in those works (and in Shostakovich's). Also notable is the Concerto Grosso (1985), based on Handel's Violin Sonata in D in a very interesting way. The five-movement arch form will inevitably remind the listener of Rochberg's Third Quartet, but the design is actually Rochberg inside out, in that the explicitly tonal (common-practice) material is confined to the outer movements, made up of quotations from the Handel piece with offshooting, newly composed material. The inner movements, by contrast, are tonal in other ways; a progression of "keys," plausible in the eighteenth-century sense yet also roughly retrograded from the middle (third) movement to the end, unites the whole. The result offers a closer correspondence to the spirit of Harbison's Schubert piece than to anything of Rochberg's.

Listening to the music of Stephen Albert (1941–1992), one becomes aware very quickly of how large Romanticism – by whatever name –

2. The motto abbreviates Shostakovich's name as "DSch" and interprets these letters according to the German musical alphabet: "S" = Es = E♭; "H" = B (♮). See Shostakovich's String Quartet No. 8 for an extensive exemplification of this motto.

loomed in his work. Under the circumstances, it is somewhat ironic that so many of the pieces he wrote during his brief career were settings (literally sung or not) of James Joyce, a name practically synonymous with modernism. Yet Joyce's words seem to have stirred Albert with particular emotional force. All of these pieces are in a sense interconnected, beginning with *To Wake the Dead* (1977–1978), a setting of rearranged fragments from *Finnegans Wake*; not only in their Joycean associations, but also in their motivic content. This interconnection is quite explicit in the case of Albert's symphony, *RiverRun* (1983–1984), the Pulitzer winner for 1985, and *TreeStone* (1984), composed more or less simultaneously. In the second movement of *TreeStone*, Albert has amplified the constant juxtaposition of various disparate material already found in *Finnegans Wake* by extracting certain passages related to the Tristan myth and setting them with musical juxtapositions such as "a dirge-like march, a children's music-box ditty and rowdy pub music" (Smith 1989), a procedure that greatly resembles that of the third movement of *RiverRun*. Albert's tonal language in general is quite original, which does not prevent the listener from being reminded now and then of neoclassical Stravinsky. Particularly striking in this regard is *Into Eclipse* (1981), which takes as its text Ted Hughes's adaptation of Seneca's *Oedipus*. Many of the sounds in this setting are reminiscent of Stravinsky's *Oedipus Rex* (1927), although the "objective" Stravinskyan affect has been heavily romanticized. Albert finds other uses for the past in his Violin Concerto, *In Concordiam* (1986; rev. 1988), which is very deliberately based on sonata form; and in *Flower of the Mountain* (1985), a setting of the end of Molly Bloom's soliloquy that concludes *Ulysses*, which is, like the "dirge-like march" of his earlier Joyce pieces, highly Mahlerian in its sound and sensibility.

As for the younger Romantics, they are an even more conservative group, by and large, than their senior colleagues. Richard Danielpour (born 1956), in fact, seems to have become more so as time has passed, a judgment that comparison of two piano works, *Psalms* (1985) and *The Enchanted Garden* (1992), will bear out. Danielpour himself describes his music as "contextually [as opposed to "hierarchically"] tonal," and harmonically rather than polyphonically oriented, which seems a fairly accurate assessment (Humphrey 1992). Having studied with Peter Mennin and Vincent Persichetti, he has taken up their general aesthetic stance (as well as some specific lessons from both in rhythm and harmony respectively). One really could not ask for a better demonstration of the persistence of the American neotonal school. Danielpour's piano music sounds quite French, with large debts to Messiaen and (at more removes) Debussy; his technical accomplishments (including orchestration) are formidable; but the music, like a powerful, shiny new car, has a certain impersonality about it. The Symphony No. 3 for soprano and orchestra, *Journey without Distance* (1989), tries very hard, perhaps too hard, to be an uplifting experience. But the text, which has to do with psychological healing, has little to recommend it from either a musical or a literary standpoint, and the result is, unfortunately, quite trivial.

The names of fellow Minnesotans Stephen Paulus (born 1949) and Libby Larsen (born 1950) seem destined always to be linked in discussions of recent American music. This is mainly due to the somewhat parallel paths of their careers: both students of Argento at the University of Minnesota, at the same time; both recently (and simultaneously) composers-in-residence with the Minnesota Orchestra. Paulus, like his teacher, is evidently drawn especially to writing for the voice: during the years 1979–1985 he wrote three operas, and he is well positioned to succeed Rorem as the American composer most devoted to the genre of art song. His cycles *All My Pretty Ones* (1983) and *Bittersuite* (1987) are engagingly modest affairs, demonstrating a good ear for text; the settings tend to be sparse, with triadic sonorities at important articulative moments, and are otherwise also in a readily identifiable neoclassic-American-pandiatonic style. Among his instrumental works, the movements of the *Symphony in Three Movements* (1985) bear the Romantic titles *Unrestrained*, *Impassioned*, and *Volatile* – and Romantic the music is, but nonetheless definitely in a restrained way. The middle, slow movement is suffused with Shostakovichian overtones as well as a lot of octatonic melodic material. There is nothing here that offends, but nothing that really stands out, either: it is pale, slightly anonymous music. Larsen's work has a little more verve: her *Symphony: Water Music* (1985), for instance, quotes fragments of Handel's *Water Music* throughout the first movement, but the piece as a whole has nothing to do with allusion or pastiche and stands perfectly well on its own: buoyant, lively, and consistently interesting. *Collage: Boogie* (1988) is lighter fare, highly entertaining and not at all demanding, the sort of curtain-raiser that many younger American composers have felt compelled to produce if they want to hear anything at all of theirs played by large orchestras. Also like much else that is being written by Americans these days, young and old, it rather rambunctiously expresses an affection for popular idioms, shared as well by the music of the last three composers to be treated in this section.

Although for many contemporary Americans the use of jazz, rock, or other popular musics has been a form of dabbling, indulged in for the sake of its novelty appeal, for Michael Daugherty (born 1954) popular idioms are his bread and butter, essentially inseparable from the themes or icons of mass culture that he takes as his subject material. Daugherty is very much the wise guy among the young neoconservatives; his music is lurid and cartoonish, fitted out with garish orchestrations that rival the Las Vegas Strip in their lack of subtlety. Daugherty's harmonic technique consists generally of sitting on one or two sonorities, usually quite tonal-sounding, thereby indirectly exploiting the achievements of minimalism. There is something breathtakingly brash about his whole project – but also something disturbing when issues usually considered serious, such as the abuses of power perpetrated by a certain erstwhile Director of the FBI, are played for laughs, as in *Sing Sing: J. Edgar Hoover* (1992). Mostly, the jokes just go on for too long, as in *Desi* (1990), which purports to be about Desi Arnaz, Lucille Ball's bongo-playing husband in the old TV sitcom *I Love Lucy*. The conga dance beat is repeated insistently and, eventually, frenetically, but the piece is otherwise devoid of content. In the *Metropolis Symphony* (1993), derived thematically from the Superman comics, the last movement (*Red Cape Tango*) juxtaposes a tango-like ostinato with the "Dies irae" melody à la Berlioz – and that's pretty much it for thirteen minutes. Some of what Daugherty does is undeniably funny, but whether it will remain so for very long is certainly a question.

A better balance between pop and art is achieved by Aaron Jay Kernis (born 1960), whose music has been much played and recorded during the last ten years. Kernis brought an already formidable technique to his first attempts at integration of pop elements into art-song contexts, in *America(n) (Day) Dreams* (1987), a setting of some wonderfully nutty poems by May Swenson. When Swenson, at the end of the second poem used in Kernis's cycle, quotes the title line from the pop song by Herman's Hermits, *There's a Kind of Hush All Over the World* (1967), the singer is not given that tune to sing, but something else while the piano, softly, plays the chord changes from the Hermits song in somewhat disguised form. Some of the pieces that delve more extensively into pop styles are rather light and forgettable, such as the guitar quintet *100 Greatest Dance Hits* (1993); others, such as *New Era Dance* (1992), a kind of "street-scene" piece with many popular idioms juxtaposed and tangled up with one another, are a little more interesting. It is true, however, that Kernis's lengthier works are of a more serious tone, and here popular elements make their appearance only fleetingly, if at all. Kernis's tonal style is a curious (though convincing) synthesis of impressionism, minimalism, the occasional Bernsteinian mixed meters, octatonicism (his early *Nocturne* [1983] is based purely on the octatonic scale on F), and a kind of Romantic chromaticism in an American neoclassical vein that owes quite a lot to Samuel Barber. (See, for example, the third movement of *Symphony in Waves* [1989], with its slow ascents, stretched over many minutes, that are so reminiscent of Barber's *Adagio for Strings*.) "I want everything to be included in music," Kernis has said, "and for every possible emotion to be elicited actively by the passionate use of these elements" (Swed 1992) – sentiments which are clearly Romantic and that have led him into some much darker-hued territory of late, as the English horn concerto *Colored Field* (1994) and the piano quartet *Still Movement with Hymn* (1993) attest. It remains to be seen whether Kernis's subsequent development will involve pop in any way at all.

Such a question seems to have been definitively answered, in a very different way, in the case of the career of Christopher Rouse (born 1949), whose great love for very loud rock music has been widely acknowledged. Rarely, however, is there any such thing as an explicit "rock beat" in his work; such devices are reserved for special purposes, such as *Bonham* (1988), a tribute to the late Led Zeppelin drummer, John Bonham – and even here, although the rock drummer soloist is in a sense central to the piece, the other percussionists involved take the soloist's quotation of Bonham's riff from Led Zeppelin's *When the Levee Breaks* (1971) and transform it in ways that owe little if anything to straight-ahead rock practice. It is rather the omnipresence of percussion in some of Rouse's works in fairly simple, "driving" ways that indebts his music to rock. In effect, this amounts to a *textural* use of percussion that is mirrored in the way other choirs of the orchestra are used as well, as in *Gorgon* (1984). In such works, harmony and line are secondary considerations.

Especially since the Symphony No. 1 (1986), Rouse's musical style has seemed almost schizophrenic, consisting of harsh, crashingly loud and monolithic sonorities on the one hand, bleak, soft music on the other, with hardly anything between these extremes. In the Violoncello Concerto (1992), this vast contrast divides the two movements one from the other. From the motivic or the harmonic point of view, everything is kept very simple; structure is based on statement and recurrence of readily recognizable elements. Tonality is mainly a matter of assertion of pitch centers, in which ostinato and other forms of repetition play a big part. Rouse is also

moderately fond of quotation and allusion: the Symphony No. 1 makes
use, as Zwilich has done, of the Shostakovich signature motto; very near
the end of his Trombone Concerto (1991), a Pulitzer winner in 1993, the
main theme of the *Credo* from Bernstein's *Kaddish* Symphony is quoted;
Monteverdi and Schumann make their appearance near the end of the Violoncello Concerto.

*

We have, it seems, returned to the era of Bernstein and Koussevitzky, when
conservatively minded conductors control our major orchestras and, if
they play American music at all, show interest mainly in resuscitating "forgotten" old (tonal) masters, or in latching onto the latest trend, or in
arguing their case that modernism was an aberration and that the true
American music is and always was tonal. But if those who do not remember
history are condemned to repeat it, nevertheless one can say that neotonality the second time around is different from the first; the second wave of
modernism in between has vastly expanded the resources available to a
composer working in any idiom, even under the restrictions usually considered to operate if that idiom is tonal – and even though many composers
now writing tonal music, especially the young, prefer as a matter of public
relations not to acknowledge what they have learned from modernism. It
is difficult to make reliable predictions on the basis of developments that
are so recent, but one could hope that, in all respects that matter, the
expression "return to tonality" is a misnomer, that composers, audiences,
performers, and critics will eventually tire of the dwelling on the past and
other retrogressive aspects of this movement, and that the progressive elements that shine forth in some of its better products will win out in the
twenty-first century.

Bibliography and references

Individual biographical entries in *The New Grove Dictionary of American Music* – henceforth *AmeriGrove* – are not cited unless actually quoted from in the text.

Discographic references are included only where deemed appropriate by individual chapter authors.

General items

Chase, Gilbert *America's Music* 2nd edn. (New York, 1966)
    America's Music rev. 3rd edn. (Urbana, 1987)
Hamm, Charles *Music in the New World* (New York, 1983)
Hitchcock, H. Wiley *Music in the United States* 3rd edn. (Englewood Cliffs, New Jersey, 1988)
Hitchcock, H. Wiley, and Sadie, Stanley (eds.) *The New Grove Dictionary of American Music* [*AmeriGrove*] (4 vols.) (London, 1986)
Horn, David *The Literature of American Music in Books and Folk Music Collections* [*LOAM* I] (Metuchen, New Jersey, 1977)
Horn, David, with Jackson, Richard *The Literature of American Music in Books and Folk Music Collections. Supplement I* [*LOAM* II] (Metuchen, New Jersey, 1988)
Kernfeld, Barry (ed.) *The New Grove Dictionary of Jazz* (2 vols.) (London, 1988)
Krummel, D. W. *Bibliographical Handbook of American Music* (London, 1987)
Marco, Guy A. *Literature of American Music III, 1983–1992* [*LOAM* III] (Lanham, Maryland, 1996)
    Checklist of Writings on American Music 1640–1992 [index to *LOAM*] (Lanham, Maryland, 1996)
Oja, Carol J. (ed.) *American Music Recordings: A Discography of Twentieth-Century U.S. Composers* (Brooklyn, New York, 1982)
Southern, Eileen *The Music of Black Americans: A History* 2nd edn. (New York, 1983a)
Spottswood, Richard K. *Ethnic Music on Records: A Discography of Ethnic Recordings Produced in the United States, 1893–1942* (7 vols.) (Urbana, 1990)

1 American Indian musics, past and present

A Cry from the Earth: Music of the North American Indians 1979 (Folkways FA 37777)
An Anthology of North American Indian and Eskimo Music 1973 (Ethnic Folkways FE 4541)
Authentic Music of the American Indian undated (Everest 3450/3)

Baker, Theodore 1882 *Über die Musik der nordamerikanischen Wilden* (Leipzig) trans. Ann Buckley as *On the Music of the North American Indians* (New York, 1977)

Ballard, Louis 1971 *The American Indian Sings* (Santa Fe)

Black Bear, Ben, and Theisz, R. D. 1976 *Songs and Dances of the Lakota* (Rosebud, South Dakota)

Brancaleone, Francis 1989 "Edward MacDowell and Indian Motives" in *American Music* vol. 7, no. 4, pp. 359–381

Burton, Frederick 1909 *American Primitive Music, with Especial Attention to the Songs of the Ojibways* (Port Washington, New York)

Bushnell, David I. 1909 *The Choctaw of Bayou Lacomb, St. Tammany Parish, Louisiana (Bureau of American Ethnology Bulletin 48)* (Washington, D.C.)

Buttree, Julia M. 1930 *The Rhythm of the Redman in Song, Dance and Decoration* (New York)

Choctaw-Chickasaw Dance Songs 1977 (A and R Records)

Collaer, Paul 1973 (ed.) *Music of the Americas: An Illustrated Music Ethnology of the Eskimo and American Indian Peoples* (New York)

Creation's Journey: Native American Music 1994 (Smithsonian/Folkways CD SF 40410)

Culbertson, Evelyn Davis 1992 *He Heard America Singing: Arthur Farwell, Composer and Crusading Music Educator* (Metuchen, New Jersey)

Densmore, Frances 1910 *Chippewa Music* (Washington, D.C.)

  1921 *Indian Action Songs* (Boston)

  1992 [1918] *Teton Sioux Music and Culture* (Lincoln, Nebraska)

Dewdney, Selwyn 1975 *The Sacred Scrolls of the Southern Ojibway* (Toronto)

Diamond, Beverley, Cronk, M. Sam, and von Rosen, Franziska 1994 *Visions of Sound: Musical Instruments of First Nations Communities in Northeastern America* (Chicago)

Eskimo Songs from Alaska 1966 (Ethnic Folkways FE 4069)

Evans, Bessie, and Evans, May G. 1931 *American Indian Dance Steps* (New York)

Fenton, William 1950 *The Roll Call of the Iroquois Chiefs: A Study of a Mnemonic Cane from the Six Nations Reserve* (Washington, D.C.)

Fletcher, Alice C. 1884 "The 'Wawan,' or Pipe Dance of the Omahas" in *Peabody Museum Annual Reports* vol. 3, nos. 3 and 4, pp. 308–333

  1893 *A Study of Omaha Indian Music* (Cambridge, Massachusetts)

  1994 [1915] *Indian Games and Songs* (Lincoln, Nebraska)

Fletcher, Alice C., and La Flesche, Francis 1992 [1911] *The Omaha Tribe* (Lincoln, Nebraska)

Frisbie, Charlote J. 1980 (ed.) *Southwestern Indian Ritual Drama* (Albuquerque)

  1993 [1967] *Kinaaldá: A Study of the Navaho Girl's Puberty Ceremony* (Salt Lake City)

Giglio, Virginia 1994 *Southern Cheyenne Women's Songs* (Norman, Oklahoma)

Gu-Achi Fiddlers: Old Time O'odham Fiddle Music 1988 (Canyon CR-8082)

Hatton, Orin 1986 "In the Tradition: Grass Dance Musical Style and Female Powwow Singers" in *Ethnomusicology* vol. 30, pp. 197–222

Heartbeat: Voices of First Nations Women 1995 (Smithsonian/Folkways CD SF 40415)

Herndon, Marcia 1980 *Native American Music* (Darby, Pennsylvania)

Herzog, George 1928 "The Yuman Musical Style" in *Journal of American Folklore* vol. 41, no. 160, pp. 183–231

1936 "A Comparison of Pueblo and Pima Musical Styles" in *Journal of American Folklore* vol. 49, no. 194, pp. 284–417

1938 "Music in the Thinking of the American Indian" in *Peabody Bulletin* May, pp. 1–5

Heth, Charlotte 1980 (ed.) *Selected Reports in Ethnomusicology* vol. 3, no. 2 (Los Angeles)

1992 (ed.) *Native American Dance: Ceremonies and Social Traditions* (Washington, D.C.)

Howard, James, and Levine, Victoria Lindsay 1990 *Choctaw Music and Dance* (Norman, Oklahoma)

Indian Music of the Pacific Northwest Coast 1967 (Ethnic Folkways FE 4523)

Keeling, Richard 1989 (ed.) *Women in North American Indian Music: Six Essays* (Bloomington)

1992 *Cry for Luck: Sacred Song and Speech among the Yurok, Hupa, and Karok Indians of Northwestern California* (Berkeley)

Keillor, Elaine 1995 "Indigenous Music as a Compositional Source: Parallels and Contrasts in Canadian and American Music" in Timothy McGee (ed.) *Taking a Stand: Essays in Honor of John Beckwith* (Toronto) pp. 185–218

Kiowa Church Songs 1972 (Indian House IH 2506)

Koranda, Lorrine D. 1980 "Music of the Alaskan Eskimos" in Elizabeth May (ed.) *Musics of Many Cultures: An Introduction* (Berkeley)

Kurath, Gertrude P., with Garcia, Antonio 1970 *Music and Dance of the Tewa Pueblos* (Santa Fe)

La Vigna, Maria 1980 "Okushare, Music for a Winter Ceremony: The Turtle Dance Songs of San Juan Pueblo" in *Selected Reports in Ethnomusicology* vol. 3, no. 2, pp. 77–99

Lee, Dayna Bowker 1995 (ed.) *Remaining Ourselves: Music and Tribal Memory, Traditional Music in Contemporary Communities* (Oklahoma City)

Levine, Victoria Lindsay 1990 "Choctaw Indian Musical Cultures in the Twentieth Century" (unpubl. diss.; University of Illinois at Urbana-Champaign)

1993 "Musical Revitalization Among the Choctaw" in *American Music* vol. 11, no. 4, pp. 391–411

McAllester, David P. 1949 *Peyote Music* (New York)

1954 *Enemy Way Music* (Cambridge, Massachusetts)

Merriam, Alan P. 1967 *Ethnomusicology of the Flathead Indians* (New York)

Mirabal, Robert 1991 *Warriors* (Yellow Aspen Cloud Productions)

Music of New Mexico: Native American Traditions 1992 (Smithsonian/Folkways CD SF 40408)

Music of the Pueblos, Apache, and Navaho 1961 (Taylor Museum of the Colorado Springs Fine Arts Center)

Nattiez, Jean-Jacques 1983 "Some Aspects of Inuit Vocal Games" in *Ethnomusicology* vol. 27, no. 3, pp. 457–475

Nettl, Bruno 1954 *North American Indian Musical Styles* (Philadelphia)

1955 "Musical Culture of the Arapaho" in *Musical Quarterly* vol. 41, pp. 325–331

1986 "North American Indian Music in the History of Ethnomusicology" in *Musicologica Austriaca* vol. 6, pp. 227–237

1989 *Blackfoot Musical Thought: Comparative Perspectives* (Kent, Ohio)

Newcomb, Franc Johnson 1956 *A Study of Navajo Symbolism* (Cambridge, Massachusetts)

Ortega, Paul 1974 *Three Worlds* (Canyon APO-3-C)

Plains: Comanche, Cheyenne, Kiowa, Caddo, Wichita, Pawnee undated (Library of Congress AFS L39)

Powers, William K. 1990 *War Dance: Plains Indian Musical Performance* (Tucson, Arizona)

Rafinesque, Constantine S. 1954 [1833] *Walam Olum or Red Score: The Migration Legend of the Lenni Lenape or Delaware Indians* (Indianapolis)

Red Earth Singers 1978 (Indian House IH 4502)

Rhodes, Willard 1963 "North American Indian Music in Transition" in *Journal of the International Folk Music Council* vol. 15, pp. 9–14

Roberts, Helen 1936 *Musical Areas in Aboriginal North America* (New Haven)

Seton, Ernest Thompson 1917 *The Book of Woodcraft and Indian Lore* (Garden City, New York)

Songs from the Iroquois Longhouse undated (Library of Congress AFS L6)

Sousa, John Philip 1977 [1890] *National, Patriotic and Typical Airs of All Lands* (New York)

Stevenson, Robert 1973a "Written Sources for Indian Music Until 1882" in *Ethnomusicology* vol. 17, no. 1, pp. 1–40

1973b "English Sources for Indian Music Until 1882" in *Ethnomusicology* vol. 17, no. 3, pp. 399–442

1982 "The First Published Native American (American Indian) Composer" in *Inter-American Music Review* vol. 4, no. 2, pp. 79–84

Toledo, Charlie 1973 *Navajo Music Class* (Chinle, Arizona)

Vander, Judith 1988 *Songprints: The Musical Experience of Five Shoshone Women* (Urbana)

Vennum, Thomas, Jr. 1982 *The Ojibway Dance Drum: Its History and Construction* (*Smithsonian Folklife Studies*, 2) (Washington, D.C.)

Vetromile, Eugene 1866 *The Abnakis and Their History or Historical Notices on the Aborigines of Acadia* (New York)

Washo-Peyote Songs 1972 (Ethnic Folkways FE 4384)

Wovoka 1973 (Epic Records)

2 Music in America: an overview (part 1)

Ancelet, Barry Jean 1984 *The Makers of Cajun Music* (Austin)

Benjamin, Walter 1969 *Illuminations* ed. Hannah Arendt (New York)

Broyles, Michael 1992 *"Music of the Highest Class": Elitism and Populism in Antebellum Boston* (New Haven)

Burkholder, J. Peter 1995 *All Made of Tunes: Charles Ives and the Uses of Musical Borrowing* (New Haven)

Burton, Humphrey 1994 *Leonard Bernstein* (New York)

Chase, Gilbert 1966a *America's Music* 2nd edn. (New York)

1966b (ed.) *The American Composer Speaks* (Baton Rouge)

Crawford, Richard 1968 *Andrew Law, American Psalmodist* (Evanston)

Daniel, Ralph T. 1966 *The Anthem in New England Before 1800* (Evanston)

Epstein, Dena J. 1977 *Sinful Tunes and Spirituals: Black Folk Music to the Civil War* (Urbana)

Foner, Philip 1975 *American Labor Songs of the Nineteenth Century* (Urbana)

Hamm, Charles 1983 *Music in the New World* (New York)

Hofstadter, Richard 1969 *Anti-intellectualism in American Life* (New York)

Jackson, George Pullen 1933 *White Spirituals in the Southern Uplands* (Chapel Hill)

Lomax, John, and Lomax, Alan 1934 *American Ballads and Folk Songs* (New York)

Lott, Eric 1995 *Love and Theft* (New York)

McKay, David P., and Crawford, Richard 1975 *William Billings of Boston: Eighteenth-Century Composer* (Princeton)

Miller, Perry 1956 *Errand into the Wilderness* (Cambridge, Massachusetts)

Mueller, John H. 1951 *The American Symphony Orchestra* (Bloomington)

Nathan, Hans 1962 *Dan Emmett and the Rise of Early Negro Minstrelsy* (Norman, Oklahoma)

Patterson, Daniel W. 1979 *The Shaker Spiritual* (Princeton)

Pemberton, Carol A. 1985 *Lowell Mason* (Ann Arbor)

Preston, Katherine K. 1993 *Opera on the Road: Traveling Opera Troupes in the United States, 1825–60* (Urbana)

Rodnitzky, Jerome 1976 *Minstrels of the Dawn* (Chicago)

Schabas, Ezra 1989 *Theodore Thomas, America's Conductor and Builder of Orchestras, 1835–1905* (Urbana)

Schiff, David 1983 *The Music of Elliott Carter* (New York)

Scholes, Percy A. 1934 *The Puritans and Music in England and New England* (London)

Sessions, Roger 1979 *Roger Sessions on Music* (Princeton)

Shanet, Howard 1975 *Philharmonic* (Garden City, New York)

Slobin, Mark 1982 *Tenement Songs: The Popular Music of the Jewish Immigrants* (Urbana)

Smith, M. B. 1943 *The Life of Ole Bull* (Princeton)

Sonneck, Oscar 1907 *Early Concert-Life in America (1731–1800)* (Leipzig; repr. 1978, New York)

1915 *Early Opera in America* (repr. 1963, New York)

Stevenson, Robert 1966 *Protestant Church Music in America* (New York)

Upton, William Treat 1939 *Anthony Philip Heinrich* (New York)

1954 *William Henry Fry. American Journalist and Composer-Critic* (New York)

3 Secular music to 1800

American Revolutionary War Songs to Cultivate the Sensations of Freedom 1976 (Folkways NH 5279)

Anderson, Gillian B. 1978 *America Independent, or, The Temple of Minerva* (Washington, D.C.)

1987 *Music in New York during the American Revolution* (Boston)

Bailyn, Bernard 1986 *The Peopling of British North America* (New York)

Benson, Norman Arthur 1963 "The Itinerant Dancing and Music Masters of Eighteenth-Century America" (unpubl. diss.; University of Minnesota)

Bourassa-Trépanier, Juliette, and Poirier, Lucien 1990 *Répertoire des données musicales de la presse québécoise* (Québec)

Bridenbaugh, Carl 1938 *Cities in the Wilderness* (London)

Britt, Judith S. 1984 *Nothing More Agreeable: Music in George Washington's Family* (Mount Vernon, Virginia)

Camus, Raoul F. 1989 *National Tune Index: Early American Wind and Ceremonial Music 1636–1836* (New York)

1995 *Military Music of the American Revolution* (Westerville, Ohio)

Carson, Cary, Hoffman, Ronald, and Albert, Peter J. 1994 *Of Consuming Interests: The Style of Life in the Eighteenth Century* (Charlottesville, Virginia)

Corry, Mary Jane, Keller, Kate Van Winkle, and Keller, Robert 1997 *The Performing Arts in Colonial American Newspapers, 1690–1783* (New York)

Courville, Louise 1985 Liner notes to recording of *Danses & Contredanses de la Nouvelle France* (Harmonie Mundi HMB 5145)

Cripe, Helen 1974 *Thomas Jefferson and Music* (Charlottesville, Virginia)

da Silva, Owen 1954 *Mission Music of California* (Los Angeles)

Farish, Hunter Dickinson 1957 *Journal and Letters of Philip Vickers Fithian* (Charlottesville, Virginia)

Greene, Jack P. 1988 *Pursuits of Happiness: The Social Development of Early Modern British Colonies and the Formation of American Culture* (Chapel Hill)

Housewright, Wiley L. 1991 *A History of Music and Dance in Florida, 1565–1865* (Tuscaloosa, Florida)

Keller, Kate Van Winkle 1981 *Popular Secular Music in America through 1800: A Preliminary Checklist of Manuscripts in North American Collections* (Philadelphia)

1991a *"If the Company can do it!" Technique in Eighteenth-Century American Social Dance* (Sandy Hook, Connecticut)

1991b "James Alexander's Collection of Dances, New York, 1730" in Israel J. Katz (ed.) *Libraries, History, Diplomacy, and the Performing Arts: Essays in Honor of Carleton Sprague Smith* (Stuyvesant, New York) pp. 353–369

Keller, Kate Van Winkle, and Rabson, Carolyn 1980 *National Tune Index: 18th-Century Secular Music* (New York)

Koegel, John 1991 "Continuity and Change in the Musical Life of a Hispanic-American Village: Tomé, New Mexico since 1739" (unpubl. diss.; University of Cambridge)

1994 "Spanish and Mexican Dance Music in Early California" in *Ars Musica Denver* vol. 7, no. 1, pp. 31–55

Lambert, Barbara (ed.) 1980, 1985 *Music in Colonial Massachusetts 1630–1820* (2 vols.) (Boston)

Lemmon, Alfred 1993 "Te Deum Laudamus: Music in St. Louis Cathedral from 1725 to 1844" in Glenn R. Conrad (ed.) *Cross, Cozier, and Crucible* (Lafayette, Louisiana) pp. 489–504

1996 "Music and Art in Spanish Colonial Louisiana" in Gilbert Din (ed.) *The Spanish Presence in Louisiana, 1763–1803* (Lafayette, Louisiana) pp. 433–445

Leppert, Richard 1988 *Music and Image* (Cambridge, England)

Lowens, Irving 1957 *Benjamin Carr's Federal Overture (1794)* (Philadelphia)

McKendrick, Neil, Brewer, John, and Plumb, J. H. 1982 *The Birth of a Consumer Society: The Commercialization of Eighteenth-Century England* (Bloomington)

Mexican Baroque: Music from New Spain 1994 (Teldec 4509-96353-2)

Molnar, John W. 1963 "A Collection of Music in Colonial Virginia: The Ogle Inventory" in *Musical Quarterly* vol. 49, no. 2, pp. 150–162

Music of the Federal Era 1978 (New World NW 299)

Over the Hills and Far Away Being a Collection of Music from 18th-Century Annapolis 1990 (Albany H103)

Porter, Susan L. 1991 *With an Air Debonair: Musical Theatre in America, 1785–1815* (Washington, D.C.)

Russell, Craig H. 1993 "The Mexican Cathedral Music of Ignacio de Jerusalem: Lost Treasures, Royal Roads, and New Worlds" in *Revista de Musicología* vol. 16, no. 1, pp. 99–133

Sonneck, Oscar 1905 *Francis Hopkinson, the First American Poet-Composer (1737–1791) and James Lyon, Patriot, Preacher, Psalmodist (1735–1794): Two Studies in Early American Music* (repr. 1967, New York)

1907 *Early Concert-Life in America (1731–1800)* (Leipzig; repr. 1978, New York)

1915 *Early Opera in America* (repr. 1963, New York)

1964 *A Bibliography of Early Secular American Music (18th Century)* rev. and enl. by William Treat Upton (New York)

Spell, Lota M. 1927 "Music Teaching in New Mexico in the Seventeenth Century" in *New Mexico Historical Review* vol. 2, pp. 27–36

1936 *Music in Texas* (Austin)

Spiess, Lincoln B. 1964 "Benavides and Church Music in New Mexico in the Early Seventeenth Century" in *Journal of the American Musicological Society* vol. 17, pp. 144–156

Summers, William 1981 "Spanish Music in California, 1769–1840: A Reassessment" in *Report of the Twelfth Congress Berkeley 1977, International Musicological Society* (Kassel)

1987 "The Spanish Origins of California Mission Music" in *Transplanted European Music Cultures (Miscellanea Musicologica, Adelaide Studies in Musicology)* vol. 12, pp. 109–126

1997 "Opera Seria in Spanish California: An Introduction to a Newly-Identified Manuscript Source" in Malcolm Cole and John Koegel (eds.) *Music in Performance and Society: Essays in Honor of Roland Jackson* (Warren, Michigan) pp. 267–290

Talley, John Barry 1988 *Secular Music in Colonial Annapolis: The Tuesday Club 1745–56* (Urbana)

The Birth of Liberty: Music of the American Revolution 1976 (New World NW 276)

The Music Teacher of Williamsburg undated (Colonial Williamsburg WS-104)

Virga, Patricia H. 1982 *The American Opera to 1790* (Ann Arbor)

4 Sacred music to 1800

"A Land of Pure Delight": Anthems and Fuging Tunes by William Billings 1992 (Harmonia Mundi HMU 907048)

America Sings, vol. 1: The Founding Years (1620–1800) 1993 (VoxBox CDX 5080)

Bandel, Betty 1981 *Sing the Lord's Song in a Strange Land: The Life of Justin Morgan* (Rutherford, New Jersey)

Barbour, J. Murray 1972 *The Church Music of William Billings* (New York)

Becker, Laura L. 1982 "Ministers vs. Laymen: The Singing Controversy in Puritan New
    England, 1720–1740" in *The New England Quarterly* vol. 55, no. 1, pp. 79–96
Benson, Louis F. 1962 *The English Hymn: Its Development and Use in Worship* (Richmond,
    Virginia)
Billings, William 1977–1990 *The Complete Works of William Billings* ed. Hans Nathan and
    Karl Kroeger (4 vols.) (Boston)
Britton, Allen Perdue 1949 "Theoretical Introductions in American Tune-books to
    1800" (unpubl. diss.; University of Michigan)
Britton, Allen Perdue, Lowens, Irving, and Crawford, Richard 1990 *American Sacred
    Music Imprints 1698–1810: A Bibliography* (Worcester, Massachusetts)
Buechner, Alan Clark 1960 "Yankee Singing Schools and the Golden Age of Choral
    Music in New England, 1760–1800" (unpubl. diss.; Harvard University)
Bushnell, Vinson Clair 1978 "Daniel Read of New Haven (1757–1836): The Man and
    His Musical Activities" (unpubl. diss.; Harvard University)
Chase, Gilbert 1966 *America's Music* 2nd edn. (New York)
Cooke, Nym 1986 "Itinerant Yankee Singing Masters in the Eighteenth Century" in
    Peter Benes (ed.) *The Dublin Seminar for New England Folklife: Annual Proceedings
    1984* (Boston) pp. 16–36
    1990 "American Psalmodists in Contact and Collaboration, 1770–1820" (2 vols.)
        (unpubl. diss.; University of Michigan)
    1991 "William Billings in the District of Maine, 1780" in *American Music* vol. 9, no. 3,
        pp. 243–259
    1993 Unpubl. database on music in New England towns
Crawford, Richard 1975 "A Hardening of the Categories: 'Vernacular,' 'Cultivated,' and
    Reactionary in American Psalmody" in Richard Crawford, *American Studies and
    American Musicology: A Point of View and a Case in Point* (Brooklyn, New York) pp.
    16–33
    1979a "From Ritual to Art: The Transformation of Sacred Music in 18th-Century
        America" (unpubl. paper proposal; Organization of American Historians)
    1979b "A Historian's Introduction to Early American Music" in *Proceedings of the
        American Antiquarian Society* vol. 89, part 2, pp. 261–298
    1981 *Andrew Law, American Psalmodist* (New York)
    1984 (ed.) *The Core Repertory of Early American Psalmody* (Madison)
    1985 "Massachusetts Musicians and the Core Repertory of Early American
        Psalmody" in Barbara Lambert (ed.) *Music in Colonial Massachusetts 1630–1820; II:
        Music in Homes and in Churches* (Boston) pp. 583–629
    1986 "Psalmody" in *AmeriGrove* vol. 3, pp. 635–643
    1990 "'Ancient Music' and the Europeanizing of American Psalmody, 1800–1810"
        in Richard Crawford, Allen R. Lott, and Carol J. Oja (eds.) *A Celebration of
        American Music: Words and Music in Honor of H. Wiley Hitchcock* (Ann Arbor)
        pp. 225–255
    undated "Formation of Choirs" (unpubl. list)
Crawford, Richard, and Krummel, D. W. 1983 "Early American Music Printing and
    Publishing" in William L. Joyce, David D. Hall, Richard D. Brown, and John B.
    Hench (eds.) *Printing and Society in Early America* (Worcester, Massachusetts)
    pp. 186–227

Cummings, Harmon Dean 1975 "Andrew Adgate: Philadelphia Psalmodist and Music Educator" (unpubl. diss.; Eastman School of Music, University of Rochester)

Daniel, Ralph T. 1979 *The Anthem in New England before 1800* (New York)

Downey, James C. 1968 "The Music of American Revivalism" (unpubl. diss.; Tulane University)

Echols, Paul C. 1986 "Hymnody" in *AmeriGrove* vol. 2, pp. 446–455

Epstein, Dena J. 1977 *Sinful Tunes and Spirituals: Black Folk Music to the Civil War* (Urbana)

Foote, Henry Wilder 1961 *Three Centuries of American Hymnody* (Hamden, Connecticut)

Goen, Clarence C. 1962 *Revivalism and Separatism in New England, 1740–1800* (New Haven)

Goostly Psalmes: Anglo-American Psalmody, 1550–1800 1996 (Harmonia Mundi HMU 907128)

Gould, Nathaniel D. 1972 *Church Music in America* (New York)

Hitchcock, H. Wiley 1988 *Music in the United States* 3rd edn. (Englewood Cliffs, New Jersey)

Hood, George 1970 *A History of Music in New England* (New York)

Ingalls, Jeremiah 1981 *The Christian Harmony; Or, Songster's Companion* with an introduction by David Klocko (New York)

Irwin, Joyce 1978 "The Theology of 'Regular Singing'" in *The New England Quarterly* vol. 51, no. 2, pp. 176–192

Jenks, Stephen 1995 *Stephen Jenks: Collected Works* ed. David Warren Steel (Madison)

Jones, Daniel C. L. 1991 "Elias Mann (1750–1825): Massachusetts Composer, Compiler, and Singing Master" (unpubl. diss.; University of Colorado)

Kaufman, Charles H. 1981 *Music in New Jersey, 1655–1860* (Rutherford, New Jersey)

Keeling, Richard 1992 *Cry for Luck: Sacred Song and Speech among the Yurok, Hupa, and Karok Indians of Northwestern California* (Berkeley)

Klocko, David Grover 1978 "Jeremiah Ingalls's *The Christian Harmony: or, Songster's Companion* (1805)" (3 vols.) (unpubl. diss.; University of Michigan)

Kroeger, Karl 1974 (ed.) *A Moravian Music Sampler* (Winston-Salem, North Carolina)
   1976 "The Worcester Collection of Sacred Harmony and Sacred Music in America, 1786–1803" (2 vols.) (unpubl. diss.; Brown University)
   1981 "A Yankee Tunebook from the Old South: Amos Pilsbury's *The United States Sacred Harmony*" in *The Hymn* vol. 32, no. 3, pp. 154–162
   1994 *American Fuging Tunes, 1770–1820: A Descriptive Catalog* (Westport, Connecticut)
   1995– (general ed.) *Music of the New American Nation: Sacred Music from 1780 to 1820* (15 vols.) (New York and London)

Lincoln, William 1837 *History of Worcester, Massachusetts* (Worcester, Massachusetts)

Lomax, Alan 1968 *Folk Song Style and Culture* (New Brunswick, New Jersey)

Lowens, Irving 1964 *Music and Musicians in Early America* (New York)

Make a Joyful Noise: Mainstreams and Backwaters of American Psalmody, 1770–1840 1996 (New World NW 80255-2)

Marini, Stephen A. 1982 *Radical Sects of Revolutionary New England* (Cambridge, Massachusetts)
   1984 "Rehearsal for Revival: Sacred Singing and the Great Awakening in America" in *Journal of the American Academy of Religion* vol. 50, no. 1, pp. 71–91

McCorkle, Donald M. 1958 "Moravian Music in Salem" (unpubl. diss.; Indiana
    University)

McCormick, David W. 1963 "Oliver Holden, Composer and Anthologist" (unpubl.
    diss.; Union Theological Seminary)

McKay, David P., and Crawford, Richard 1975 *William Billings of Boston: Eighteenth-
    Century Composer* (Princeton)

Messiter, A. H. 1970 *A History of the Choir and Music of Trinity Church, New York* (New
    York)

Metcalf, Frank J. 1967 *American Writers and Compilers of Sacred Music* (New York)

Murray, Sterling E. 1975 "Timothy Swan and Yankee Psalmody" in *Musical Quarterly*
    vol. 61, no. 3, pp. 433–463

Nathan, Hans 1976 *William Billings: Data and Documents* (Detroit)

Nettl, Bruno 1973 *Folk and Traditional Music of the Western Continents* (Englewood Cliffs,
    New Jersey)

Osterhout, Paul Ragatz 1978 "Music in Northampton, Massachusetts to 1820"
    (unpubl. diss.; University of Michigan)

Owen, Barbara 1979 *The Organ in New England* (Raleigh, North Carolina)
    1985 "Eighteenth-Century Organs and Organ Building in New England" in Barbara
        Lambert (ed.) *Music in Colonial Massachusetts 1630–1820; II: Music in Homes and in
        Churches* (Boston) pp. 655–714

Pichierri, Louis 1960 *Music in New Hampshire, 1623–1800* (New York)

Read, Daniel 1995 *Daniel Read: Collected Works* ed. Karl Kroeger (Madison)

Silverman, Kenneth 1976 *A Cultural History of the American Revolution* (New York)

Sonneck, Oscar 1905 *Francis Hopkinson, the First American Poet-Composer (1737–1791)
    and James Lyon, Patriot, Preacher, Psalmodist (1735–1794): Two Studies in Early
    American Music* (repr. 1967, New York)

Southern, Eileen 1983 *The Music of Black Americans: A History* 2nd edn. (New York)

Steel, David Warren 1982 "Stephen Jenks (1772–1856): American Composer and
    Tunebook Compiler" (unpubl. diss.; University of Michigan)

Stevenson, Robert 1966 *Protestant Church Music in America* (New York)

Swan, Timothy 1997 *Timothy Swan: Psalmody and Secular Songs* ed. Nym Cooke
    (Madison)

Symmes, Thomas 1720 *The Reasonableness of, Regular Singing, or, Singing by Note*
    (Boston)

Temperley, Nicholas 1979 *The Music of the English Parish Church* (Cambridge, England)
    1981 "The Old Way of Singing: Its Origins and Development" in *Journal of the
        American Musicological Society* vol. 34, no. 3, pp. 511–544
    1986 "Psalms, Metrical" in *AmeriGrove* vol. 3, pp. 643–648
    1995 "Worship Music in English-Speaking North America, 1608–1820" in Timothy
        J. McGee (ed.) *Taking a Stand: Essays in Honor of John Beckwith* (Toronto) pp.
        166–184
    1997 "First Forty: The Earliest American Compositions" in *American Music* vol. 15,
        no. 1. pp. 1–25

Temperley, Nicholas, and Manns, Charles G. 1983 *Fuging Tunes in the Eighteenth Century*
    (Detroit)

The New England Harmony: A Collection of Early American Choral Music 1964 (Folkways FA 2377)

Thwing, Walter Eliot 1908 *History of the First Church in Roxbury, Massachusetts* (Boston)

Vermont Harmony 1 (Revised Edition): A Collection of Fuging Tunes, Anthems, and Secular Pieces by Vermont Composers, 1790–1810 (undated) (University of Vermont Choral Union UVCU-250)

Vermont Harmony 2: The Works of Hezekiah Moors and Jeremiah Ingalls 1976 (Philo PH 1038)

Walter, Thomas 1721 *The Grounds and Rules of Musick Explained* (Boston)

Webb, Guy Bedford 1972 "Timothy Swan: Yankee Tunesmith" (unpubl. diss.; University of Illinois at Urbana-Champaign)

Weston, Massachusetts 1901 *Town of Weston: Births, Deaths and Marriages: 1707–1850* (Boston)

Wienandt, Elwyn A., and Young, Robert H. 1970 *The Anthem in England and America* (New York and London)

Wilcox, Glenn C. 1957 "Jacob Kimball, Jr. (1761–1826): His Life and Works" (unpubl. diss.; University of Southern California)

Willhide, J. Laurence 1954 "Samuel Holyoke: American Music Educator" (unpubl. diss.; University of Southern California)

Wilson, Ruth Mack, and Keller, Kate Van Winkle 1979 *Connecticut's Music in the Revolutionary Era* (Hartford, Connecticut)

Wolfe, Richard J. 1980 *Early American Music Engraving and Printing* (Urbana)

Worst, John William 1974 "New England Psalmody, 1760–1810: Analysis of an American Idiom" (unpubl. diss.; University of Michigan)

5 African American music to 1900

Allen, William Francis, Garrison, Lucy McKim, and Ware, Charles Pickard 1983 [1971, 1867] "From *Slave Songs of the United States*" in Southern 1983a, pp. 149–174

Astley, Thomas 1968 [1745–1747] (ed.) *A New General Collection of Voyages and Travels Consisting of the most esteemed Relations which have been hitherto published in any Language. Comprehending Everything Remarkable in Its Kind in Europe, Asia, Africa, and America* (4 vols.) (London)

Bailey, Ben E. 1985 "Music in the Life of a Free Black Man of Natchez" in *The Black Perspective in Music* vol. 13, no. 1, pp. 3–12

1988 "The Red Tops: The Orchestra that Covered the Delta" in *The Black Perspective in Music* vol. 16, no. 2, pp. 177–190

Bunch, Lonnie 1988 *Black Angelenos: The Afro-American in Los Angeles, 1850–1950* (Los Angeles)

Burke, Fred 1974 [1970] *Africa* rev. edn. (Boston)

Coolen, Michael T. 1984 "Senegambian Archetypes for the American Folk Banjo" in *Western Folklore* vol. 43, no. 2, pp. 117–132

Courlander, Harold 1963 *Negro Folk Music U.S.A.* (New York)

Creel, Margaret Washington 1988 *"A Peculiar People": Slave Religion and Community-Culture Among the Gullahs* (New York)

Curtin, Philip D. 1969 *The Atlantic Slave Trade: A Census* (Madison)

Dark, Philip J.C., and Hill, Matthew 1971 "Musical Instruments on Benin Plaques" in Klaus P. Wachsmann (ed.) *Essays on Music and History in Africa* (Evanston) pp. 65–78

DjeDje, Jacqueline Cogdell 1998 "West Africa: An Introduction" in Ruth M. Stone (ed.) *Africa: The Garland Encyclopedia of World Music. Volume 1* (New York) pp. 442–470

Epstein, Dena J. 1977 *Sinful Tunes and Spirituals: Black Folk Music to the Civil War* (Urbana)

Equiano, Olaudah 1969 [1789] *The Life of Olaudah Equiano . . .* (New York)

Estes, David C. 1990 "Traditional Dances and Processions of Blacks in New Orleans as Witnessed by Antebellum Travelers" in *Louisiana Folklore Miscellany* vol. 6, no. 3, pp. 1–14

Franklin, John Hope, and Moss, Alfred A., Jr. 1994 *From Slavery to Freedom: A History of African Americans* 7th edn. (New York)

Genovese, Eugene D. 1974 [1972] *Roll, Jordan, Roll: The World the Slaves Made* (New York)

Greenberg, Joseph H. 1970 *The Languages of Africa* (Bloomington)

Hall, Gwendolyn Midlo 1992 *Africans in Colonial Louisiana: The Development of Afro-Creole Culture in the Eighteenth Century* (Baton Rouge)

Hall, Richard L. 1990 "African Religious Retentions in Florida" in Joseph E. Holloway (ed.) *Africanisms in American Culture* (Bloomington) pp. 98–147

Higgins, W. Robert 1976 "Charleston: Terminus and Entrepôt of the Colonial Slave Trade" in Martin L. Kilson and Robert I. Rotberg (eds.) *The African Diaspora: Interpretive Essays* (Cambridge, Massachusetts) pp. 114–131

High, Ronald Henry 1988 "Black Male Concert Singers of the Nineteenth Century: A Bibliographic Study" in George R. Keck, and Sherrill V. Martin (eds.) *Feel the Spirit: Studies in Nineteenth-Century Afro-American Music* (New York) pp. 117–134

Hinson, Glenn 1978 Liner notes to recording of *Eight-Hand Sets and Holy Steps: Traditional Black Music of North Carolina* (North Carolina Department of Cultural Resources Crossroad c-101)

Hirschberg, Walter 1969 "Early Historical Illustrations of West and Central African Music" in *African Music* vol. 4, no. 3, pp. 6–18

Jerde, Curtis D. 1990 "Black Music in New Orleans: A Historical Overview" in *Black Music Research Journal* vol. 10, no. 1, pp. 18–24

Jordan, Carolyne Lamar 1988 "Black Female Concert Singers of the Nineteenth Century: Nellie Brown Mitchell and Marie Selika Williams" in George R. Keck, and Sherrill V. Martin (eds.) *Feel the Spirit: Studies in Nineteenth-Century Afro-American Music* (New York) pp. 35–48

Knight, Roderic C. 1984 "Music in Africa: The Manding Contexts" in Gerard Béhague (ed.) *Performance Practice: Ethnomusicological Perspectives* (Westport, Connecticut) pp. 53–90

Kubik, Gerhard 1980 "Angola" in Stanley Sadie (ed.) *The New Grove Dictionary of Music and Musicians* (London) vol. 1, pp. 431–435

Kulikoff, Allan 1986 *Tobacco and Slaves: The Development of Southern Cultures in the Chesapeake, 1680–1800* (Chapel Hill)

Levine, Lawrence W. 1978 *Black Culture and Black Consciousness: Afro-American Folk Thought from Slavery to Freedom* (New York)

Lovejoy, Paul E. 1982 "The Volume of the Atlantic Slave Trade: A Synthesis" in *Journal of African History* vol. 23, pp. 473–501

Lovell, John, Jr. 1972 *Black Song: The Forge and the Flame. The Story of How the Afro-American Spiritual Was Hammered Out* (New York)

Mabogunje, Akin L. 1976 [1971] "The Land and Peoples of West Africa" in J. F. A. Ajayi, and Michael Crowder (eds.) *History of West Africa* 2nd edn. (London) pp. 1–32

Mason, William M., and Anderson, James 1969 "The Los Angeles Black Community 1781–1940" in Russell E. Belous (ed.) *An Exhibition of America's Black Heritage: Los Angeles County Museum of Natural History, History Division Bulletin* (Los Angeles) vol. 5, pp. 42–64

Merriam, Alan P. 1980 "Zaire" in Stanley Sadie (ed.) *The New Grove Dictionary of Music and Musicians* (London) vol. 20, pp. 621–626

Mintz, Sidney W., and Price, Richard 1976 *An Anthropological Approach to the Afro-American Past: A Caribbean Perspective* (Philadelphia)

Monts, Lester 1984 "A Reassessment of Vai Musical Instruments in the Nineteenth Century: the Koelle Account" in *Afrika und Übersee* vol. 67, pp. 219–231

Nketia, J. H. Kwabena 1971 "History and the Organization of Music in West Africa" in Klaus P. Wachsmann (ed.) *Essays on Music and History in Africa* (Evanston) pp. 3–25
    1974 *The Music of Africa* (New York)

Olmstead, Frederick Law 1976 [1856] "Negro Jodling: The Carolina Yell" in *The Black Perspective in Music* vol. 4, no. 2, pp. 140–141. Originally published in *A Journey into the Seaboard Slave States, with Remarks on Their Economy* (New York)

Raboteau, Albert J. 1978 *Slave Religion. The "Invisible Institution" in the Antebellum South* (New York)

Ramsey, Frederic 1960 *Been Here and Gone* (New Brunswick, New Jersey)

Rawick, George P. (ed.) 1977–1979 *The American Slave: A Composite Autobiography* (48 vols.) (Westport, Connecticut)

Rawley, James A. 1981 *The Transatlantic Slave Trade: A History* (New York)

Roberts, John Storm 1972 *Black Music of Two Worlds* (New York)

Sears, Ann 1988 "Keyboard Music by Nineteenth-Century Afro-American Composers" in George R. Keck, and Sherrill V. Martin (eds.) *Feel the Spirit: Studies in Nineteenth-Century Afro-American Music* (New York) pp. 135–155

Southern, Eileen 1983a *The Music of Black Americans: A History* 2nd edn. (New York)
    1983b [1971] (ed.) *Readings in Black American Music* 2nd edn. (New York)

Southern, Eileen, and Wright, Josephine 1990 *African-American Traditions in Song, Sermon, Tale, and Dance, 1600s–1920: An Annotated Bibliography of Literature, Collections and Artworks* (Westport, Connecticut)

Spencer, Jon Michael 1990 "The Hymnody of the African Methodist Episcopal Church" in *American Music* vol. 8, no. 3, pp. 274–293

Stoddard, Tom 1982 *Jazz on the Barbary Coast* (Chigwell, England)

Sullivan, Lester 1988 "Composers of Color of Nineteenth-Century New Orleans: The History Behind the Music" in *Black Music Research Journal* vol. 8, no. 1, pp. 51–82

Tracey, Andrew 1948 *Chopi Musicians: Their Music, Poetry, and Instruments* (London)
    1980 "Mozambique" in Stanley Sadie (ed.) *The New Grove Dictionary of Music and Musicians* (London) vol. 12, pp. 662–667

Vansina, Jan 1966 *Kingdoms of the Savannah: A History of Central African States Until European Occupation* (Madison)

Vass, Winifred Kellersberger 1979 *The Bantu Speaking Heritage of the United States* (Los Angeles)

Vidal, Túnjí 1977 "Traditions and History in Yoruba Music" in *Nigerian Music Review* vol. 1, pp. 66–92

Waterman, Richard 1952 "African Influence on the Music of the Americas" in Sol Tax (ed.) *Acculturation in the Americas: Proceedings and Selected Papers of the 29th International Congress of Americanists* (Chicago) pp. 207–219

Wax, Darold D. 1973 "Preferences for Slaves in Colonial America" in *The Journal of Negro History* vol. 48, no. 4, pp. 371–401

Wilson, Olly 1974 "The Significance of the Relationship Between Afro-American Music and West African Music" in *The Black Perspective in Music* vol. 2, no. 1, pp. 3–22

6 Immigrant, folk, and regional musics in the nineteenth century

Ancelet, Barry Jean 1984 *The Makers of Cajun Music* (Austin)

Babow, Irving 1954 "The Singing Societies of European Immigrants" in *Phylon* vol. 15, pp. 289–295

Bayard, Samuel P. 1982 *Dance to the Fiddle, March to the Fife: Instrumental Folk Tunes in Pennsylvania* (University Park, Pennsylvania)

Benson, Adolph B., and Hedin, Naboth 1950 *Americans from Sweden* (Philadelphia)

Bliss, P. P., and Sankey, Ira D. 1875 *Gospel Hymns and Sacred Songs* (Cincinnati and New York)

Bohlman, Philip V. 1984 "Hymnody in the Rural German-American Community of the Upper Midwest" in *The Hymn* vol. 35, pp. 158–164

Brasseaux, Carl A. 1992 *Acadian to Cajun: Transformation of a People, 1803–1877* (Jackson, Mississippi)

Breathnach, Breandan 1971 *Folk Music and Dances of Ireland* (Dublin)

Broyles, Michael 1992 *"Music of the Highest Class": Elitism and Populism in Antebellum Boston* (New Haven)

Buchanan, Annabel Morris 1938 *Folk Hymns of America* (New York)

Cobb, Buell E. 1978 *The Sacred Harp: A Tradition and Its Music* (Athens, Georgia)

Corry, Mary Jane 1983 "The Role of German Singing Societies in Nineteenth-Century America" in Edward Allen McCormick (ed.) *Germans in America: Aspects of German-American Relations in the Nineteenth Century* (New York) pp. 155–168

Crawford, Richard 1968 *Andrew Law, American Psalmodist* (Evanston)

Cusic, Don 1990 *The Sound of Light: A History of Gospel Music* (Bowling Green, Ohio)

Downer, Alan S. 1966 (ed.) *The Memoir of John Durang, American Actor, 1785–1816* (Pittsburgh)

Drummond, Robert 1908 "Early Music in Philadelphia with Special Reference to German Music" in *German-American Annals* vol. 6, pp. 157–179

Eskew, Harry 1971 "American Folk Hymnody" in *The Hymn Society of Great Britain and Ireland Bulletin* vol. 7, no. 8, pp. 142–154

Faust, Albert Bernhardt 1909 *The German Element in the United States with Special Reference to its Political, Moral, Social, and Educational Influence* (2 vols.) (New York)

Ferrero, Edward 1859 *The Art of Dancing, Historically Illustrated. To Which is Added a Few Hints on Etiquette; Also the Figures, Music and Necessary Instruction for the Performance of the Most Modern and Approved Dances* (New York)

Fornell, Martha, and Fornell, Earl W. 1957 "A Century of German Song in Texas" in *American-German Review* vol. 24, no. 1, pp. 29–31

Hamm, Charles 1979 *Yesterdays: Popular Song in America* (New York)

Hartmann, Edward G. 1967 *Americans from Wales* (Boston)

Jackson, George Pullen 1933 *White Spirituals in the Southern Uplands* (Chapel Hill)
    1937 *Spiritual Folk Songs of Early America* (New York)
    1939 *Down-East Spirituals and Others* (New York)

Laws, G. Malcolm, Jr. 1957 *American Balladry from British Broadsides* (Philadelphia)

Lengyel, Cornel 1939 (ed.) *Music of the Gold Rush Era* (*History of Music in San Francisco Series, Vol. 1: January 1939*) (New York)

Lowens, Irving 1964 *Music and Musicians in Early America* (New York)

Lyon, George W. 1980 "The Accordian in Cajun, Zydeco, and Norteno Music" in *Sing Out* vol. 82, no. 4, pp. 14–17

McCullough, Lawrence 1974 "An Historical Sketch of Traditional Irish Music in the United States" in *Folklore Forum* vol. 7, pp. 177–191

Morley, Thomas 1597 *A Plaine and Easie Introduction to Practicall Musicke* (London)

Morrow, Mary Sue 1989 "Singing and Drinking in New Orleans: The Social and Musical Functions of Nineteenth-Century German Mannerchöre" in *The Southern Quarterly* vol. 27, no. 2, pp. 5–24

Nathan, Hans 1962 *Dan Emmett and the Rise of Early Negro Minstrelsy* (Norman, Oklahoma)

Nelson, Carl L. 1963 "The Sacred Music of the Swedish Immigrants" in Iverne J. Dowie, and Ernest M. Espelie (eds.) *The Swedish Immigrant Community in Transition* (Rock Island, Illinois) pp. 51–60

O'Neill, Francis 1973 *Irish Minstrels and Musicians* (Darby, Pennsylvania)

Parades, Américo 1976 *A Texas-Mexican Cancionero: Folksongs of the Lower Border* (Chicago)

Peña, Manuel 1985 *The Texas-Mexican Conjunto: History of a Working-Class Music* (Austin)

Perrin, Phil D. 1968 "Theoretical Introductions in American Tune-Books from 1800 to 1860" (unpubl. diss.; Southern Baptist Theological Seminary)

Playford, John 1654 *An Introduction to the Skill of Musick* (London)

Randolph, Vance 1982 *Ozark Folksongs* (Urbana)

Reynolds, William Jensen 1963 *A Survey of Christian Hymnody* (New York)

Robb, John Donald 1954 *Folk Songs of New Mexico* (Albuquerque)

Roberts, John Storm 1979 *The Latin Tinge: The Impact of Latin American Music on the United States* (New York)

Sankey, Ira D. 1906 *My Life and Sacred Songs* (London)

Sharp, Cecil J., and Karpeles, Maud 1917 *The Country Dance Book* vol. 5, "The Running Set" (London)

Shepard, Leslie 1973 *The History of Street Literature: The Story of Broadside Ballads, Chapbooks, Proclamations, News-Sheets, Election Bills, Tracts, Pamphlets, Cocks, Catchpennies, and other Ephemera* (Detroit)

Snyder, Suzanne Gail 1991 "The Männerchöre Tradition in the United States: A Historical Analysis of its Contribution to American Musical Culture" (unpubl. diss.; University of Iowa)

Stevenson, Robert 1966 *Protestant Church Music in America* (New York)

Stewart, James 1995 "TuneIndex search" with Introduction (http://celtic.stanford.edu/tunesearch/html)

Taddie, Daniel 1996 "Solmization, Scale, and Key in Nineteenth-Century Tunebooks: Theory and Practice" in *American Music* vol. 14, no. 1, pp. 42–64

Temperley, Nicholas 1981 "The Old Way of Singing: Its Origins and Development" in *Journal of the American Musicological Society* vol. 34, no. 3, pp. 511–544

Thernstrom, Stephan 1980 (ed.) *Harvard Encyclopedia of American Ethnic Groups* (Cambridge, Massachusetts)

Whitfield, Irénè Thérèse 1939 *Louisiana French Folk Songs* (Baton Rouge)

Witke, Carl 1967 *The Germans in America: A Student's Guide to Localized History* (New York)

Wright, Robert L. 1975 (ed.) *Irish Emigrant Ballads and Songs* (Bowling Green, Ohio)

7 Nineteenth-century popular music

Abrahams, Roger D. 1992 *Singing the Master: The Emergence of African American Culture in the Plantation South* (New York)

After the Ball: A Treasury of Turn-of-the-Century Popular Songs 1987 (Elektra Nonesuch 79148–2)

Allen, Robert C. 1991 *Horrible Prettiness: Burlesque and American Culture* (Chapel Hill)

American Dreamer: Songs of Stephen Foster 1992 (Angel CDC 07777-54621-28)

An Evening with Henry Russell 1977 (Nonesuch H71338)

Austin, William W. 1987 *"Susanna," "Jeanie," and "The Old Folks at Home": The Songs of Stephen C. Foster from His Time to Ours* (Urbana)

Broyles, Michael 1992 *"Music of the Highest Class": Elitism and Populism in Antebellum Boston* (New Haven)

Camus, Raoul 1986 "Bands" in *AmeriGrove* vol. 1, pp. 127–137

Cockrell, Dale 1989 *Excelsior: Journals of the Hutchinson Family Singers, 1842–1846* (Stuyvesant, New York)

   1997 *Demons of Disorder: Early Blackface Minstrels and Their World* (Cambridge, England)

Crawford, Richard 1977 (ed.) *The Civil War Songbook: Complete Original Sheet Music for 37 Songs* (New York)

   1993 *The American Musical Landscape* (Berkeley)

Don't Give the Name a Bad Place: Types and Stereotypes in American Musical Theater 1870–1900 1978 (New World NW265)

Epstein, Dena J. 1973 [1871] (ed.) *Complete Catalogue of Sheet Music and Musical Works* (New York)

   1977 *Sinful Tunes and Spirituals: Black Folk Music to the Civil War* (Urbana)

Ewen, David 1977 *All the Years of American Popular Music* (Englewood Cliffs, New Jersey)

Glass, Paul, and Singer, Louis C. 1975 (ed. & arr., respectively) *Singing Soldiers: A History of the Civil War in Song* (New York)

Hamm, Charles 1979 *Yesterdays: Popular Song in America* (New York)
    1986 "Popular Music" in *AmeriGrove* vol. 3, pp. 589–610
Harwell, Richard B. 1950 *Confederate Music* (Chapel Hill)
Hazen, Robert M., and Hazen, Margaret Hindle 1987 *The Music Men: An Illustrated History of Brass Bands in America, 1800–1920* (Washington, D.C.)
Jackson, Richard 1976 (ed.) *Popular Songs of Nineteenth-Century America* (New York)
Loesser, Arthur 1954 *Men, Women, and Pianos: A Social History* (New York)
Loney, Glenn 1984 (ed.) *Musical Theatre in America: Papers and Proceedings of the Conference on the Musical Theatre in America* (Westport, Connecticut)
Lott, Eric 1993 *Love and Theft: Blackface Minstrelsy and the American Working Class* (New York)
Mahar, William J. 1988 "'Backside Albany' and Early Blackface Minstrelsy: A Contextual Study of America's First Blackface Song" in *American Music* vol. 6, no. 1, pp. 1–27
Marks, Edward B. 1934 *They All Sang: From Tony Pastor to Rudy Vallée* (New York)
Mates, Julian 1985 *America's Musical Stage: Two Hundred Years of Musical Theatre* (Westport, Connecticut)
McConachie, Bruce A. 1988 "New York Operagoing, 1825–50: Creating an Elite Social Ritual" in *American Music* vol. 6, no. 2, pp. 181–192
    1992 *Melodramatic Formations: American Theatre and Society, 1820–1870* (Iowa City)
Moore's Irish Melodies 1984 (Nonesuch 79059)
Nathan, Hans 1962 *Dan Emmett and the Rise of Early Negro Minstrelsy* (Norman, Oklahoma)
19th Century Concert and Parlor Music for Piano 1972 (Vox SVBX 5302)
Paskman, Daily, and Spaeth, Sigmund 1928 *"Gentlemen, Be Seated!": A Parade of the Old-Time Minstrels* (New York)
Popular Music in Jacksonian America 1982 (Musical Heritage Society MHS 834561)
Porter, Susan L. 1991 *With an Air Debonair: Musical Theatre in America 1785–1815* (Washington, D.C.)
Preston, Katherine K. 1993 *Opera on the Road: Traveling Opera Troupes in the United States, 1825–60* (Urbana)
Riis, Thomas L. 1989 *Just Before Jazz: Black Musical Theater in New York, 1890–1915* (Washington, D.C.)
Root, Deane L. 1981 *American Popular Stage Music 1860–1880* (Ann Arbor)
    1991 "The 'Mythtory' of Stephen C. Foster or Why His True Story Remains Untold" in *American Music Research Center Journal* vol. 1, pp. 20–36
    1994 (ed.) *Nineteenth-Century American Musical Theater* (New York)
Sanjek, Russell 1988 *American Popular Music and Its Business: The First Four Hundred Years* (New York)
Saunders, Steven, and Root, Deane L. (eds.) 1990 *The Music of Stephen C. Foster* (Washington, D.C.)
Scott, Derek 1989 *The Singing Bourgeois: Songs of the Victorian Drawing Room and Parlour* (Milton Keynes, England)
Songs by Henry Clay Work 1975 (Nonesuch H71317)
Songs by Stephen Foster 1983 (Elektra Nonesuch 79158-2)
Songs of the Civil War 1976 (New World NW202)

Spaeth, Sigmund 1948 *A History of Popular Music in America* (New York)

Spitzer, John 1994 "'Oh! Susanna': Oral Transmission and Tune Transformation" in *Journal of the American Musicological Society* vol. 47, no. 1, pp. 90–136

Tawa, Nicholas E. 1980 *Sweet Songs for Gentle Americans: The Parlor Song in America, 1790–1860* (Bowling Green, Ohio)

　1982 *A Sound of Strangers: Musical Culture, Acculturation, and the Post-Civil War Ethnic American* (Metuchen, New Jersey)

　1984 *A Music for the Millions: Antebellum Democratic Attitudes and the Birth of American Popular Music* (New York)

The Early Minstrel Show 1985 (New World NW338)

The Smithsonian Collection of American Musical Theater: Shows, Songs, and Stars 1989 (Smithsonian RD 036 A4 20483)

There's a Good Time Coming and Other Songs of the Hutchinson Family 1979 (Smithsonian N020)

Toll, Robert 1974 *Blacking Up: The Minstrel Show in Nineteenth-Century America* (New York)

Vaudeville: Songs of the Great Ladies of the Musical Stage 1976 (Nonesuch H71330)

Virga, Patricia H. 1982 *The American Opera to 1790* (Ann Arbor)

Winans, Robert B. 1984 "Early Minstrel Show Music, 1843–1852" in Glenn Loney (ed.) *Musical Theatre in America* (Westport, Connecticut) pp. 71–97

Wolfe, Richard J. 1964 *Secular Music in America, 1801–1825: A Bibliography* (New York)

Woll, Allen 1989 *Black Musical Theatre: From Coontown to Dreamgirls* (Baton Rouge)

Yerbury, Grace D. 1971 *Song in America, from Early Times to About 1850* (Metuchen, New Jersey)

8 Art music from 1800 to 1860

Ammer, Christine 1980 *Unsung. A History of Women in American Music* (Westport, Connecticut)

Block, Adrienne Fried, and Neuls-Bates, Carol 1979 *Women in American Music* (Westport, Connecticut)

Broyles, Michael 1985 "Lowell Mason on European Church Music and Transatlantic Cultural Identification: A Reconsideration" in *Journal of the American Musicological Society* vol. 38, no. 2, pp. 316–348

　1991 "Music and Class Structure in Antebellum Boston," in *Journal of the American Musicological Society* vol. 44, no. 3, pp. 451–493

　1992 *"Music of the Highest Class": Elitism and Populism in Antebellum Boston* (New Haven)

Charosh, Paul 1992 "'Popular' and 'Classical' in the Mid-Nineteenth Century" in *American Music* vol. 10, no. 2, pp. 117–135

Chase, Gilbert 1987 *America's Music* rev. 3rd edn. (Urbana)

Crawford, Richard 1993 *The American Musical Landscape* (Berkeley)

Estavan, Lawrence 1939 (ed.) *San Francisco Theatre Research. History of Opera in San Francisco*, vol. 7 in Cornel Langyel (ed.) *History of Music in San Francisco Series* (Works Progress Administration, Northern California) (San Francisco)

Graziano, John 1990 "Jullien and His *Music for the Million*" in Richard Crawford, R.

Allen Lott, and Carol J. Oja (eds.) *A Celebration of American Music. Words and Music in Honor of H. Wiley Hitchcock* (Ann Arbor) pp. 192–215

Hamm, Charles 1979 *Yesterdays: Popular Song in America* (New York)

1983 *Music in the New World* (New York)

Hart, Philip 1973 *Orpheus in the New World: The Symphony Orchestra as an American Cultural Institution* (New York)

Haugen, Einar, and Cai, Camilla 1993 *Ole Bull. Norway's Romantic Musician and Cosmopolitan Patriot* (Madison)

Johnson, H. Earle 1953 "The Germania Musical Society," in *Musical Quarterly* vol. 39, no. 1, pp. 75–93

Kmen, H. A. 1966 *Music in New Orleans* (Baton Rouge)

Lawrence, Vera 1988 *Strong on Music. The New York Music Scene in the Days of George Templeton Strong, 1836–1874. Volume 1: Resonances. 1836–1850* (Oxford)

1995 *Strong on Music. Volume 2: Reverberations. 1850–1856* (Chicago)

Lott, R. Allen 1986 "The American Concert Tours of Leopold de Meyer, Henri Herz, and Sigismond Thalberg" (2 vols.) (unpubl. diss.; City University of New York)

1990 "Bernard Ullman: Nineteenth-Century American Impresario" in Richard Crawford, R. Allen Lott, and Carol J. Oja (eds.) *A Celebration of American Music. Words and Music in Honor of H. Wiley Hitchcock* (Ann Arbor) pp. 174–191

Lowens, Irving 1964 *Music and Musicians in Early America* (New York)

Mahling, Christoph-Hellmut 1991 "Berlin: 'Music in the Air'" in Alexander Ringer (ed.) *The Early Romantic Era* (Englewood Cliffs, New Jersey) pp. 109–140

Maretzek, Max 1855, 1890 [1968] *Revelations of an Opera Manager in 19th Century America: Crotchets and Quavers and Sharps and Flats* (New York)

Martin, George 1993 *Verdi at the Golden Gate. Opera and San Francisco in the Gold Rush Years* (Berkeley)

Miller, Bonnie 1994 "Ladies' Companion, Ladies' Canon? Women Composers in American Magazines from *Godey's* to the *Ladies' Home Journal*" in Susan C. Cook, and Judy S. Tsou (eds.) *Cecilia Reclaimed. Feminist Perspectives on Gender and Music* (Madison) pp. 156–182

Morris, Richard B. 1976 *Encyclopedia of American History* (New York)

Mueller, John 1951 *The American Symphony Orchestra: A Social History of Musical Taste* (Bloomington)

Orr, N. Lee 1995 *Alfredo Barili and the Rise of Classical Music in Atlanta* (Atlanta, Georgia)

Perkins, Charles C., and Dwight, John S. 1883–1893 [1977] *History of the Handel and Haydn Society, of Boston, Massachusetts, from the Foundation of the Society through Its Seventy-fifth Season* Vol. 1 (Boston [New York])

Preston, Katherine K. 1993a *Opera on the Road: Traveling Opera Troupes in the United States, 1825–60* (Urbana)

1993b "San Francisco to Timbuctoo: The Amazing Adventures of the Lyster and Durand English Opera Company in California, 1859" (unpubl. paper read before the Sonneck Society for American Music, Pacific Grove, California)

1994 "Antebellum Concert-Giving and Opera-Singing: The Triumphant 1838–1840 American Tour by Jane Shirreff and John Wilson, British Vocal Stars" in James Heintze (ed.) *American Musical Life in Context and Practice to 1865* (New York) pp. 173–201

Ringer, Alexander 1991 "The Rise of Urban Musical Life between the Revolutions, 1789–1848" in Alexander Ringer (ed.) *The Early Romantic Era* (Englewood Cliffs, New Jersey) pp. 1–31

Ritter, Frédéric Louis 1890 [1972] *Music in America* (New York)

Sablonsky, Irving 1986 *What They Heard. Music in America, 1852–1881. From the Pages of Dwight's Journal of Music* (Baton Rouge)

Sachs, Joel 1991 "London: the Professionalization of Music" in Alexander Ringer (ed.) *The Early Romantic Era* (Englewood Cliffs, New Jersey) pp. 201–235

Shanet, Howard 1975 *Philharmonic: A History of New York's Orchestra* (New York)

Sonneck, Oscar 1915 *Early Opera in America* (repr. 1963, New York)
    1949 *Early Concert-Life in America* (New York)

Southern, Eileen 1982 *Biographical Dictionary of Afro-American and African Musicians* (Westport, Connecticut)

Starr, S. Frederick 1995 *Bamboula! The Life and Times of Louis Moreau Gottschalk* (Oxford)

Stoutamire, Albert 1972 *Music of the Old South: Colony to Confederacy* (Rutherford, New Jersey)

Tick, Judith 1983 *American Women Composers Before 1870* (Ann Arbor)

Upton, William Treat 1930 *Art-Song in America* (Boston)
    1954 *William Henry Fry. American Journalist and Composer-Critic* (New York)

Weber, William 1986 "The Rise of the Classical Repertoire in Nineteenth-Century Orchestral Concerts" in Joan Peyser (ed.) *The Orchestra. Origins and Transformations* (New York) pp. 361–386

Yerbury, Grace D. 1971 *Song in America, from Early Times to about 1850* (Metuchen, New Jersey)

Young, Percy 1980. "Chorus (i) 4: From the Mid-18th Century to the Later 19th" in Stanley Sadie (ed.) *The New Grove Dictionary of Music and Musicians* (London) vol. 4, pp. 351–356

9 Art music from 1860 to 1920

Baker, Theodore 1882 *Über die Musik der nordamerikanishcen Wilden* (Leipzig) trans. Ann Buckley as *On the Music of the North American Indians* (New York, 1977)

Block, Adrienne Fried 1983 "Why Amy Beach Succeeded as a Composer: The Early Years" in *Current Musicology* vol. 36, pp. 41–59
    1990a "Amy Beach's Music on Native American Themes" in *American Music* vol. 8, no. 2, pp. 141–166
    1990b "Dvořák, Beach, and American Music" in Richard Crawford, R. Allen Lott, and Carol J. Oja (eds.) *A Celebration of American Music. Words and Music in Honor of H. Wiley Hitchcock* (Ann Arbor) pp. 256–280

Block, Adrienne Fried, and Neuls-Bates, Carol 1979 *Women in American Music* (Westport, Connecticut)

Bomberger, E. Douglas 1991 "American Music Students in Germany" (unpubl. paper read before the American Musicological Society, Chicago)

Broyles, Michael 1992 *"Music of the Highest Class": Elitism and Populism in Antebellum Boston* (New Haven)

Burkholder, J. Peter 1995 *All Made of Tunes: Charles Ives and the Uses of Musical Borrowing* (New Haven)

C. A. 1910 "Woman – The Potent Influence in Our Musical Life" in *Musical America* vol. 12, pp. 3–4

Cooney, Denise Von Glahn 1996 "A Sense of Place: Charles Ives and 'Putnam's Camp, Redding, Connecticut'" in *American Music* vol. 14, no. 3, pp. 276–312

Crawford, Richard 1996 "Edward MacDowell: Musical Nationalism and an American Tone Poet" in *Journal of the American Musicological Society* vol. 64, no. 3, pp. 518–560

Culbertson, Evelyn Davis 1987 "Arthur Farwell's Early Efforts on Behalf of American Music, 1889–1921" in *American Music* vol. 5, no. 2, pp. 156–175

Damrosch, Walter 1923 *My Musical Life* (New York)

Davis, Ronald L. 1970 "Sopranos and Six-Guns: The Frontier Opera as Cultural Symbol" in *American West* vol. 7, pp. 10–18, 63

  1980 *A History of Music in American Life. Volume II: The Gilded Years, 1865–1920* (Huntington, New York)

Fay, Amy 1880 *Music Study in Germany* (New York)

Feder, Stuart 1992 *Charles Ives: "My Father's Song"* (New Haven)

Fletcher, Alice C. 1893 *A Study of Omaha Indian Music* (Cambridge, Massachusetts)

Foote, Arthur 1979 *Arthur Foote 1853–1937. An Autobiography* (New York)

Gilman, Lawrence 1908 *Edward MacDowell, A Study* (New York)

Gleason, Frederick Grant 1887 "American Music and Native Composers" in *American Art Journal* vol. 47, no. 18, pp. 261, 273

Glenn, George D., and Poole, Richard L. 1993 *The Opera Houses of Iowa* (Ames, Iowa)

Gottschalk, Louis Moreau 1964 *Notes of A Pianist* ed. Jeanne Behrend (New York)

Grau, Robert 1914 "Woman's Business Sense a Cause of Country's Musical Prosperity" in *Musical America* vol. 20, no. 13, pp. 13–14

Hart, Philip 1973 *Orpheus in the New World: The Symphony Orchestra as an American Cultural Institution* (New York)

Horowitz, Joseph 1994 *Wagner Nights: An American History* (Berkeley)

Howard, John Tasker 1931 *Our American Music* (New York)

Howe, M. A. DeWolfe 1939 "John Knowles Paine" in *Musical Quarterly* vol. 25, no. 3, pp. 257–267

Hughes, Adella Prentiss 1947 *Music is My Life* (Cleveland)

Hughes, Rupert 1900 *Contemporary American Composers, A Study of the Music of This Country, Its Present Conditions and Its Future, with Critical Estimates and Biographies of the Principal Living Composers and an Abundance of Portraits, Fac-Simile Musical Autographs, and Compositions* (Boston)

J. B. 1909 "Women Who Are Managing Important Undertakings" in *Musical America* vol. 9, p. 6

Jeffrey, John B. 1889 *Guide and Directory to the Opera Houses, Theatres, Public Halls, Bills Posters, Etc. of the Cities and Towns of America* 11th edn. rev. (Chicago)

Jenkins, Walter S. 1994 *The remarkable Mrs. Beach, American composer, a biographical account based on her diaries, letters, newspaper clippings, and personal reminiscences* (Warren, Michigan)

Kirkpatrick, John 1965 Preface to published score of Charles Ives Symphony No. 4 (New York)

Langford, Laura 1883 *The Mothers of Great Men and Women, and Some Wives of Great Men* (New York)

Locke, Ralph P. 1994 "Paradoxes of the Woman Music Patron in America" in *Musical Quarterly* vol. 78, no. 4, pp. 798–825

MacDowell, Edward 1912 *Critical and Historical Essays: Lectures Delivered at Columbia University* (Boston)

Martin, George 1993 *Verdi at the Golden Gate, Opera and San Francisco in the Gold Rush Years* (Berkeley)

Matthews, W. S. B. 1873 "William Foster Apthorp" in *Nation* vol. 16, pp. 115–117
    1889 *A Hundred Years of Music in America* (Chicago)

Morgan, Robert P. 1977 "Spatial Form in Ives" in H. Wiley Hitchcock, and Vivian Perlis (eds.) *An Ives Celebration* (Urbana) pp. 145–158

Mussulman, Joseph A. 1971 *Music in the Cultured Generation: A Social History of Music in America, 1870–1900* (Evanston)

Petteys, Leslie 1992 "Theodore Thomas's 'March to the Sea'" in *American Music* vol. 10, no. 2, pp. 170–182

Preston, Katherine K. 1993 *Opera on the Road: Traveling Opera Troupes in the United States, 1825–60* (Urbana)

Ritter, Frédéric Louis 1890 [1972] *Music in America* (New York)

Schabas, Ezra 1989 *Theodore Thomas, America's Conductor and Builder of Orchestras, 1835–1905* (Urbana)

Schmidt, John C. 1980 *The Life and Works of John Knowles Paine* (Ann Arbor)

Smither, Howard E. forthcoming *The Mainstream in the Nineteenth Century: Germany, England, North America, France* vol. 4 of *A History of the Oratorio* (Chapel Hill)

Starr, S. Frederick 1995 *Bamboula! The Life and Times of Louis Moreau Gottschalk* (Oxford)

Swafford, Jan 1996 *Charles Ives: A Life with Music* (New York)

Tawa, Nicholas 1991 *The Coming of Age of American Art Music, New England's Classical Romanticists* (New York)

Thomas, Theodore undated Concerts/Programs, Theodore Thomas Collection, Newberry Library, Chicago

Upton, George P. 1905 (ed.) *Theodore Thomas, A Musical Autobiography* (Chicago)

Whitesitt, Linda 1986–1990 "'The Most Potent Force' in American Music: The Role of Women's Music Clubs in American Concert Life" in Judith Long Zaimont (ed.-in-chief) *The Musical Woman* vol. 3 (Westport, Connecticut)
    1989 "The Role of Women Impresarios in American Concert Life, 1871–1933" in *American Music* vol. 7, no. 2, pp. 159–180
    1991 "Women's Support and Encouragement of Music and Musicians" in Karin Pendle (ed.) *Women and Music* (Bloomington) pp. 301–313

Yellin, Victor Fell 1990 *Chadwick, Yankee Composer* (Washington, D.C.)

10 Music in America: an overview (part 2)

See also the bibliography and references to chapter 2

Attali, Jacques 1985 *Noise* (Minneapolis)

Austin, William W. 1987 *"Susanna," "Jeannie," and "The Old Folks at Home": The Songs of Stephen C. Foster from His Time to Ours* (Urbana)

Barzun, Jacques 1956 *Music in American Life* (Garden City, New York)

Blacking, John 1995 *Music, Culture, and Experience* (Chicago)

Cage, John 1961 *Silence* (Middletown, Connecticut)

   1967 *A Year from Monday* (Middletown, Connecticut)

Chase, Gilbert 1966 (ed.) *The American Composer Speaks* (Baton Rouge)

Copland, Aaron 1968 *The New Music, 1900–1960* (New York)

Cowell, Henry 1930 *New Musical Resources* (New York; republ. 1969, New York; republ. 1996, Cambridge, England)

   1933 (ed.) *American Composers on American Music* (Palo Alto, California; republ. 1962, New York)

Culbertson, Evelyn Davis 1992 *He Heard America Singing: Arthur Farwell, Composer and Crusading Music Educator* (Metuchen, New Jersey)

Duckworth, William 1995 *Talking Music* (New York)

Dvořák, Antonín 1894 "Music in America" in *Harper's New Monthly Magazine* vol. 90, pp. 432–433

Epstein, Dena J. 1969 *Music Publishing in Chicago before 1871* (Detroit)

Frith, Simon 1978 *The Sociology of Rock* (London)

Gottschalk, Louis Moreau 1964 *Notes of a Pianist* ed. Jeanne Behrend (New York)

Hamm, Charles 1979 *Yesterdays: Popular Song in America* (New York)

Hitchcock, H. Wiley (ed.) *The Phonograph and our Musical Life* (Brooklyn, New York)

Hodeir, André 1956 *Jazz: Its Evolution and Essence* trans. David Noakes (New York)

Howard, John Tasker 1953 *Stephen Foster: America's Troubadour* (New York)

Ives, Charles 1961 *Essays before a Sonata, and Other Writings* ed. Howard Boatwright (New York)

Jones, LeRoi 1967 *Black Music* (New York)

Kirkpatrick, John 1960 *A Temporary Mimeographed Catalogue of the Music Manuscripts . . . of Charles Edward Ives* (New Haven)

Lucier, Alvin 1995 *Reflections* (Cologne)

Malone, Bill C. 1985 *Country Music, U. S. A.* (Austin)

Marcus, Greil 1975 *Mystery Train* (New York)

   1995 *The Dustbin of History* (Cambridge, Massachusetts)

Marks, Edward B. 1934 *They All Sang: From Tony Pastor to Rudy Vallée* (New York)

   1944 *They All Had Glamour* (New York)

McCarthy, Albert 1974 *Big Band Jazz* (New York)

Nettl, Bruno 1964 *Theory and Method in Ethnomusicology* (Glencoe, Illinois)

Nicholls, David 1990 *American Experimental Music, 1890–1940* (Cambridge, England)

Nyman, Michael 1974 *Experimental Music – Cage and Beyond* (London)

Pritchett, James 1993 *The Music of John Cage* (Cambridge, England)

Reich, Steve 1974 *Writings about Music* (Halifax, Nova Scotia)

Schaefer, John 1987 *New Sounds* (New York)

Schuller, Gunther 1968 *Early Jazz* (New York)

Schwartz, Elliott, and Childs, Barney 1967 (eds.) *Contemporary Composers on Contemporary Music* (New York)

Seeger, Charles 1977 *Studies in Musicology 1935–1975* (Berkeley)

Spaeth, Sigmund 1948 *A History of Popular Music in America* (New York)
Tirro, Frank 1977 *Jazz: A History* (New York)

11 Immigrant, folk, and regional musics in the twentieth century

Abrahams, Roger D. 1970 *A Singer and Her Songs* (Baton Rouge)

Abrahams, Roger D., and Foss, George 1968 *Anglo-American Folksong Style* (Englewood Cliffs, New Jersey)

Ancelet, Barry Jean 1984 *The Makers of Cajun Music* (Austin)

Appadurai, Arjun 1996 *Modernity at Large: Cultural Dimensions of Globalization* (Minneapolis)

Averill, Gage forthcoming *Four Parts, No Writing: A Social History of Barbershop Quartet Singing* (New York)

Bachmann-Geiser, Brigitte, and Bachmann, Eugen 1988 *Amische: Die Lebensweise der Amischen in Berne, Indiana* (Berne, Switzerland)

Baker, Houston A., Jr. 1984 *Blues, Ideology, and Afro-American Literature: A Vernacular Theory* (Chicago)

Bastin, Bruce 1986 *Red River Blues: The Blues Tradition in the Southeast* (Urbana)

Belden, H. M. 1973 (ed.) *Ballads and Songs Collected by the Missouri Folk-Lore Society* (Columbia, Missouri)

Blumhofer, Edith forthcoming "Fanny Crosby and Protestant Hymnody" in Bohlman and Blumhofer forthcoming

Bohlman, Philip V. 1988 *The Study of Folk Music in the Modern World* (Bloomington)
1997 "Ethnic North America" in Bruno Nettl et al. *Excursions in World Music* 2nd edn. (Upper Saddle River, New Jersey) pp. 269–308

Bohlman, Philip V., and Blumhofer, Edith forthcoming (eds.) *Music in American Religious Experience* (Chicago)

Burnim, Mellonee 1983 "Gospel Music: Review of the Literature" in *Music Educators Journal* vol. 69, no. 8, pp. 58ff.

Cantwell, Robert 1984 *Bluegrass Breakdown: The Making of the Old Southern Sound* (Urbana)
1996 *When We Were Good: The Folk Revival* (Cambridge, Massachusetts)

Case, Sue Ellen, Brett, Philip, and Foster, Susan Leigh 1995 (eds.) *Cruising the Performative: Interventions into the Representation of Ethnicity, Nationality, and Sexuality* (Bloomington)

Cooley, Timothy forthcoming "Ethnography, Tourism, and Music Culture of the Tatra Mountains: Negotiated Representations of Polish Gorale Identity" (unpubl. diss.; Brown University)

Courlander, Harold 1963 *Negro Folk Music U.S.A.* (New York)

Crawford, Richard 1993 *The American Musical Landscape* (Berkeley)

Currid, Brian 1995 "'We Are Family': House Music and Queer Performativity" in Case, Brett, and Foster 1995 pp. 165–196

Denisoff, R. Serge 1973 *Great Day Coming: Folk Music and the American Left* (Baltimore)

Erlmann, Veit 1991 *African Stars: Studies in Black South African Performance* (Chicago)

Evans, David 1982 *Big Road Blues: Tradition and Creativity in the Folk Blues* (Berkeley)

Ferris, William, and Hunt, Mary L. 1985 (eds.) *Folk Music and Modern Sound* (Jackson, Mississippi)

Georges, Robert A., and Stern, Stephen 1982 *American and Canadian Immigrant and Ethnic Folklore: An Annotated Bibliography* (New York)

Gilroy, Paul 1993 *The Black Atlantic: Modernity and Double Consciousness* (Cambridge, Massachusetts)

Glaser, Ruth 1995 *My Music Is My Flag: Puerto Rican Musicians and Their New York Communities, 1917–1940* (Berkeley)

Glassie, Henry et al. 1970 *Folksongs and Their Makers* (Bowling Green, Ohio)

Greene, Victor 1992 *A Passion for Polka: Old-Time Ethnic Music in America* (Berkeley)

Greenway, John 1953 *American Folksongs of Protest* (Philadelphia)

Harris, Michael W. 1992 *The Rise of Gospel Blues: The Music of Thomas Andrew Dorsey in the Urban Church* (New York)

Heilbut, Tony 1985 *The Gospel Sound: Good News and Bad Times* 3rd edn. (New York)

Hollinger, David A. 1995 *Postethnic America: Beyond Multiculturalism* (New York)

Ives, Edward D. 1978 *Joe Scott: Woodsman-Songmaker* (Urbana)

Jackson, Bruce 1972 *Wake Up Dead Man: Afro-American Worksongs from Texas Prisons* (Cambridge, Massachusetts)

Jackson, Irene V. 1979 *Afro-American Religious Music: A Bibliography and Catalogue of Gospel Music* (Westport, Connecticut)

Jairazbhoy, Nazir A., and DeVale, Sue Carole 1985 (eds.) *Asian Music in North America* (Los Angeles)

Kallen, Horace M. 1956 *Cultural Pluralism and the American Idea: An Essay in Social Philosophy* (Philadelphia)

Keil, Charles, Keil, Angeliki V., and Blau, Dick 1992 *Polka Happiness* (Philadelphia)

Klassen, Doreen Helen 1990 *Singing Mennonite: Low German Songs of the Mennonites* (Winnipeg)

Korson, George 1960 (ed.) *Pennsylvania Songs and Legends* (Baltimore)

Lornell, Kip 1988 *"Happy in the Service of the Lord": Afro-American Gospel Quartets in Memphis* (Urbana)

Loza, Steven 1992 *Barrio Rhythm: Mexican American Music in Los Angeles* (Urbana)

Malone, Bill C. 1979 *Southern Music / American Music* (Lexington, Kentucky)

Mazo, Margarita forthcoming "Singing as an Experience of American-Russian Molokans" in Bohlman and Blumhofer forthcoming

McCulloh, Judith 1983 (ed.) *Ethnic Recordings in America: A Neglected Heritage* (Washington, D.C.)

Miller, Terry E. 1986 *Folk Music in America: A Reference Guide* (New York)

Nettl, Bruno 1976 *Folk Music in the United States: An Introduction* 3rd edn., rev. and ed. Helen Myers (Detroit)

Nicholls, David 1996 "Transethnicism and the American Experimental Tradition" in *Musical Quarterly* vol. 80, no. 4, pp. 569–594

Odum, Howard W. 1911 "Folk-Song and Folk-Poetry as Found in the Secular Songs of the Southern Negro" in *Journal of American Folklore* vol. 24, pp. 262ff.

Oliver, Paul 1968 *Spirituals and Gospel Songs* (Milan)

O'Neill, Frances 1903 *The Music of Ireland* (Chicago)
     1913 *Irish Minstrels and Musicians* (Chicago)

Paredes, Américo 1958 *With His Pistol in His Hand: A Border Ballad and Its Hero* (Austin)

Peña, Manuel 1985 *The Texas-Mexican Conjunto: History of a Working-Class Music* (Austin)

Pietsch, Rudolf 1994 "Zu den Begriffen 'Ethnic Music' und 'Ethnic Mainstream'" in Elizabeth T. Hilscher, and Theophil Antonicek (eds.) *Vergleichend-systematische Musikwissenschaft: Beiträge zu Methode und Problematik der systematischen, ethnologischen und historischen Musikwissenschaft* (Tutzing) pp. 451–474

Proulx, E. Annie 1996 *Accordion Crimes* (New York)

Raichelson, Richard M. 1975 "Black Religious Folksong: A Study in Generic and Social Change" (unpubl. diss.; University of Pennsylvania)

Randolph, Vance 1980 [1946–1950] (ed.) *Ozark Folksongs* (4 vols.) (Columbia, Missouri)

Riddle, Ronald 1983 *Flying Dragons, Flowing Streams: Music in the Life of San Francisco's Chinese* (Westport, Connecticut)

Robb, J. D. 1954 *Hispanic Folk Songs of New Mexico* (Albuquerque)

Rosenberg, Neil V. 1993 (ed.) *Transforming Tradition: Folk Music Revivals Examined* (Urbana)

Slobin, Mark 1982 *Tenement Songs: The Popular Music of the Jewish Immigrants* (Urbana)

1993 *Subcultural Sounds: Micromusics of the West* (Hanover, New Hampshire)

Spaeth, Sigmund 1940 *Barbershop Ballads* (Englewood Cliffs, New Jersey)

Spottswood, Richard K. 1990 *Ethnic Music on Records: A Discography of Ethnic Recordings in the United States, 1893–1942* (7 vols.) (Urbana)

Titon, Jeff Todd 1977 *Early Downhome Blues: A Musical and Cultural Analysis* (Urbana)

1988 *Powerhouse for God: Speech, Chant, and Song in an Appalachian Baptist Church* (Austin)

Wagner, Christoph 1993 *Das Akkordeon: Eine wilde Karriere* (Berlin)

Whisnant, David E. 1983 *All That Is Native and Fine: The Politics and Culture in an American Region* (Chapel Hill)

White, Newman I. 1928 *American Negro Folk Songs* (Cambridge, Massachusetts)

Work, John W. 1940 *American Negro Songs and Spirituals* (New York)

Wright, Robert L. 1965 *Swedish Emigrant Ballads* (Lincoln, Nebraska)

Wright, Rochelle, and Wright, Robert L. 1983 *Danish Emigrant Ballads and Songs* (Carbondale, Illinois)

12 Popular song and popular music on stage and film

Altman, Rick 1987 *The American Film Musical* (Bloomington)

Atkins, Irene Kahn 1983 *Source Music in Motion Pictures* (Rutherford, New Jersey)

Attridge, Derek 1982 *The Rhythms of English Poetry* (London)

Babington, Bruce, and Evans, Peter Williams 1985 *Blue Skies and Silver Linings: Aspects of the Hollywood Musical* (Manchester)

Banfield, Stephen 1992 "The Ironbridge Letters" in *American Music* vol. 10, no. 1, pp. 80–88

1993 *Sondheim's Broadway Musicals* (Ann Arbor)

1996 "Sondheim and the Art That Has No Name" in Robert Lawson-Peebles (ed.) *Approaches to the American Musical* (Exeter) pp. 137–60

Barrios, Richard 1995 *A Song in the Dark: The Birth of the Musical Film* (New York)

Bergreen, Laurence 1990 *As Thousands Cheer: The Life of Irving Berlin* (New York)

Block, Geoffrey 1993 "The Broadway Canon from 'Show Boat' to 'West Side Story' and the European Operatic ideal" in *The Journal of Musicology* vol. 11, no. 4, pp. 525–544

Bordman, Gerald 1978 *American Musical Theatre: A Chronicle* (New York)

Bradley, Edwin M. 1996 *The First Hollywood Musicals: A Critical Filmography of 171 Features, 1927 through 1932* (Jefferson, North Carolina)

Briggs, George Wright, Jr. 1985 "Leroy Anderson on Broadway: Behind the Scene Accounts of the Musical 'Goldilocks'" in *American Music* vol. 3, no. 3, pp. 329–336

Citron, Stephen 1995 *The Wordsmiths: Oscar Hammerstein 2nd and Alan Jay Lerner* (New York)

Davis, Lee 1993 *Bolton and Wodehouse and Kern: The Men Who Made Musical Comedy* (New York)

Delamater, Jerome 1981 *Dance in the Hollywood Musical* (Ann Arbor)

Everett, William A. 1994 "Golden Days in Old Heidelberg: The First-act Finale of Sigmund Romberg's *The Student Prince*" in *American Music* vol. 12, no. 3, pp. 255–282

Ewen, David 1964 *The Life and Death of Tin Pan Alley: The Golden Age of American Popular Music* (New York)

    1970 *Great Men of American Popular Song* (Englewood Cliffs, New Jersey)

Fehr, Richard, and Vogel, Frederick G. 1993 *Lullabies of Hollywood: Movie Music and the Movie Musical, 1915–1992* (Jefferson, North Carolina)

Feuer, Jane 1993 *The Hollywood Musical* 2nd edn. (Basingstoke)

Forte, Allen 1995 *The American Popular Ballad of the Golden Era: 1924–1950* (Princeton)

Frye, Northrop 1957 *Anatomy of Criticism* (Princeton)

Furia, Philip 1990 *The Poets of Tin Pan Alley: A History of America's Great Lyricists* (New York)

Gammond, Peter 1991 *The Oxford Companion to Popular Music* (Oxford)

Gänzl, Kurt 1994 *The Encyclopedia of the Musical Theatre* (2 vols.) (Oxford)

Gilbert, Stephen 1995 *The Music of Gershwin* (New Haven)

Goldberg, Isaac 1930 *Tin Pan Alley: A Chronicle of the American Popular Music Racket* (New York)

Green, Stanley 1981 *Encyclopedia of the Musical Film* (New York)

Hamm, Charles 1979 *Yesterdays: Popular Song in America* (New York)

    1986 "Musical Theatre, §III. The Tin Pan Alley Era" in *AmeriGrove* vol. 3, pp. 595–601

    1994 "Irving Berlin and Early Tin Pan Alley" in *Irving Berlin: Early Songs I, 1907–1911* (Madison) pp. xv–xlix

    1995 *Putting Popular Music in its Place* (Cambridge, England)

    1997 *Irving Berlin: Songs from the Melting Pot: The Formative Years, 1907–1914* (New York)

Heskes, Irene 1984 "Music as Social History: American Yiddish Theater Music, 1882–1920" in *American Music* vol. 2, no. 4, pp. 73–87

Huron, David 1989 "Music in Advertising: An Analytical Paradigm" in *Musical Quarterly* vol. 73, no. 4, pp. 557–574

Hyland, William G. 1995 *The Song Is Ended: Songwriters and American Music, 1900–1950* (New York)

Isacoff, Stuart 1986 "Advertising, Music in" in *AmeriGrove* vol. 1, pp. 9–11

Johns, Donald 1993 "*Funnel* Tonality in American Popular Music, ca. 1900–70" in *American Music* vol. 11, no. 4, pp. 458–472

Karmen, S. 1989 *Through the Jingle Jungle* (New York)

Kreuger, Miles 1990 "Some Words About *Girl Crazy*" in liner notes booklet (Elektra Nonesuch 7559–79250–2) pp. 15–24

Lamb, Andrew 1986 "From *Pinafore* to Porter: United States – United Kingdom Interactions in Musical Theater, 1879–1929" in *American Music* vol. 4, no. 1, pp. 34–49

Larson, Steve 1993 "Dave McKenna's Performance of 'Have You Met Miss Jones?'" in *American Music* vol. 11, no. 3, pp. 283–315

Lax, Roger, and Smith, Frederick 1989 *The Great Song Thesaurus* 2nd edn. (New York)

Marks, Martin 1979–1980 "Film Music: The Material, Literature, And present State of Research" in *Notes* vol. 36, no. 2, pp. 282–325

Mattfield, Julius 1962 *Variety Music Cavalcade* rev. edn. (Englewood Cliffs, New Jersey)

McCarthy, Albert 1974 *The Dance Band Era: The Dancing Decades from Ragtime to Swing, 1910–1950* (London)

McGlinn, John 1990 "Finding the Bliss", booklet accompanying New World Records CD (80387–2), pp. 10–16

Mooney, Hughson F. 1954 "Songs, Singers and Society, 1890–1954" in *American Quarterly* vol. 6, no. 3, pp. 221–232

Murray, Albert 1970 *The Omni-Americans: New Perspectives of Black Experience and American Culture* (New York)

Music from the New York Stage: 1890–1920 1993 (4 vols.) (Pearl GEMM CDS 9050–9061)

Nye, Russel 1970 *The Unembarrassed Muse: The Popular Arts in America* (New York)

Osolsobě, Ivo 1981 "A Letter from the Other Side: To [the] *Musical Theatre in America* Conference: Wassenaar, March 23, 1981" (typescript)

Paddison, Max 1993 *Adorno's Aesthetics of Music* (Cambridge, England)

Palmer, Christopher 1990 *The Composer in Hollywood* (London)

Pessen, Edward 1985 "The Great Songwriters of Tin Pan Alley's Golden Age: A Social, Occupational, and Aesthetic Inquiry" in *American Music* vol. 3, no. 2, pp. 180–197

Riis, Thomas L. 1984 "Black Musical Theater, 1870–1930: Research Problems and Resources" in *American Music* vol. 2, no. 4, pp. 95–100

Roberts, John Storm 1979 *The Latin Tinge: The Impact of Latin American Music on the United States* (New York)

Root, Deane L. 1984 (ed.) "Music of the American Theater" issue, *American Music* vol. 2, no. 4

Shout, John, D. 1985 "The Musical Theater of Marc Blitztein" in *American Music* vol. 3, no. 4, pp. 413–428

Southern, Eileen 1983 *The Music of Black Americans: A History* 2nd edn. (New York)

Starr, Lawrence 1986 "Gershwin's 'Bess, You Is My Woman Now': The Sophistication of Subtlety of a Great Tune" in *Musical Quarterly* vol. 72, no. 4, pp. 429–448

Stempel, Larry 1992 "The Musical Play Expands" in *American Music* vol. 10, no. 2, pp. 136–169

Stubblebine, Donald J. 1996 *Broadway Sheet Music: A Comprehensive Listing, 1918–1993* (Jefferson, North Carolina)

Suskin, Steven 1992 *Show Tunes 1905–1991: The Songs, Shows and Careers of Broadway's Major Composers* 2nd edn. (New York)

Swain, Joseph 1990 *The Broadway Musical: A Critical and Musical Survey* (New York)

Tagg, Philip 1979 "Kojak – 50 Seconds of Television Music: Towards the Analysis of Affect in Popular Music" (unpubl. diss.; University of Göteborg)

Tawa, Nicholas 1990 *The Way to Tin Pan Alley: American Popular Song, 1866–1910* (New York)

Van der Merwe, Peter 1989 *Origins of the Popular Style: The Antecedents of Twentieth-Century Popular Music* (Oxford)

Van Leer, David 1987 "Putting It Together: Sondheim and the Broadway Musical" in *Raritan* vol. 7, no. 2, pp. 113–128

Wickes, E. M. 1916 *Writing the Popular Song* (Springfield, Massachusetts)

Wilder, Eric 1972 *American Popular Song: The Great Innovators, 1900–1950* (New York)

Wilk, Max 1991 *They're Playing Our Song: Conversations with America's Classic Songwriters* rev. edn. (Mount Kisco, New York)

13 The rock and roll era

Bennett, Tony, Frith, Simon, Grossberg, Lawrence, Shepherd, John, and Turner, Graeme 1993 (eds.) *Rock and Popular Music: Politics, Policies, Institutions* (New York)

Brackett, David 1995 *Interpreting Popular Music* (Cambridge, England)

Broven, John 1974 *Rhythm and Blues in New Orleans* (Gretna, Louisiana)

Buckley, Johnathan, and Ellingham, Mark 1996 (eds.) *Rock: The Rough Guide* (London)

Chapple, Steve, and Garofalo, Reebee 1977 *Rock 'n' Roll is Here to Pay* (Chicago)

Cross, Brian 1993 *It's Not About a Salary. . . . Rap, Race, and Resistance in Los Angeles* (New York)

Dawson, Jim, and Propes, Steve 1992 *What Was the First Rock 'N' Roll Record?* (Boston)

Eisen, Jonathan 1969 (ed.) *The Age of Rock: Sounds of the American Cultural Revolution* (New York)

Frith, Simon 1981 *Sound Effects: Youth, Leisure, and the Politics of Rock 'n' Roll* (New York)
1988 *Music for Pleasure: Essays in the Sociology of Pop* (New York)

Frith, Simon, and Goodwin, Andrew 1990 (eds.) *On Record: Rock, Pop, and the Written Word* (New York)

Frith, Simon, Goodwin, Andrew, and Grossberg, Lawrence 1993 (eds.) *Sound and Vision: The Music Video Reader* (New York)

Garofalo, Reebee 1992 (ed.) *Rockin' the Boat: Mass Music and Mass Movements* (Boston)
1993 "Black Popular Music: Crossing Over of Going Under?" in Bennett, Frith, Grossberg, Shepherd, and Turner 1993, pp. 231–248
1997 *Rockin' Out: Popular Music in the USA* (Needham Heights, Massachusetts)

Garr, Gillian G. 1992 *She's a Rebel: The History of Women in Rock and Roll* (Seattle)

Gillett, Charlie 1983 *The Sound of the City: The Rise of Rock and Roll* rev edn. (New York)

Goodwin, Andrew 1992 *Dancing in the Distraction Factory: Music, Television and Popular Culture* (Minneapolis)

Hamm, Charles 1979 *Yesterdays: Popular Song in America* (New York)
> 1983 *Music in the New World* (New York)
> 1986 "Rock" in *AmeriGrove* vol. 4, pp. 62–68
> 1995 *Putting Popular Music in Its Place* (Cambridge, England)

Hebdige, Dick 1979 *Subculture: The Meaning of Style* (London)

Jones, LeRoi 1963 *Blues People: Negro Music in White America* (New York)

Keil, Charles 1966 *Urban Blues* (Chicago)

Keil, Charles, and Feld, Steven 1994 *Music Grooves: Essays and Dialogues* (Chicago)

Kelley, Robin D. G. 1994 "Kickin' Reality, Kickin' Ballistics: 'Gangsta Rap' and
> Postindustrial Los Angeles" in *Race Rebels: Culture, Politics, and the Black Working
> Class* (New York) pp. 183–227

Laing, Dave 1985 *One Chord Wonders: Power and Meaning in Punk Rock* (Philadelphia)

Larkin, Colin 1995 (ed.) *The Guinness Encyclopedia of Popular Music* 2nd edn. (New York)

Lewis, Lisa A. 1990 *Gender Politics and MTV: Voicing the Difference* (Philadelphia)
> 1992 (ed.) *The Adoring Audience: Fan Culture and Popular Media* (London)

Lipsitz, George 1990 *Time Passages: Collective Memory and American Popular Culture*
> (Minneapolis)
> 1994a "'Ain't Nobody Here But Us Chickens': The Class Origins of Rock and Roll"
> in *Rainbow at Midnight: Labor and Culture in the 1940s* (Urbana) pp. 303–333
> 1994b *Dangerous Crossroads: Popular Music, Postmodernism, and the Poetics of Place*
> (London)

Longhurst, Brian 1995 *Popular Music and Society* (Cambridge, England)

Malm, Krister, and Wallis, Roger 1992 *Media Policy and Music Activity* (New York)

Malone, Bill C. 1985 *Country Music U.S.A.* rev. edn. (Austin)
> 1990 Booklet accompanying *Classic Country Music* (Smithsonian RD042)
> 1993 *Singing Cowboys and Musical Mountaineers: Southern Culture and the Roots of
> Country Music* (Athens, Georgia)

Malone, Bill C., and McCulloh, Judith 1975 (eds.) *Stars of Country Music: Uncle Dave
> Macon to Johnny Rodriguez* (Urbana)

Marcus, Greil 1969 (ed.) *Rock and Roll Will Stand* (Boston)
> 1982 *Mystery Train: Images of America in Rock 'n' Roll Music* rev. edn. (New York)

Marsh, Dave 1989 *The Heart of Rock and Soul: The 1001 Greatest Singles Ever Made* (New
> York)

Marsh, Dave et al. 1985 (eds.) *The First Rock and Roll Confidential Report: Inside the Real
> World of Rock & Roll* (New York)

Martin, Linda, and Segrave, Kerry 1988 *Anti-Rock: The Opposition to Rock 'n' Roll*
> (Hamden, Connecticut)

McClary, Susan 1991 *Feminine Endings: Music, Gender, Sexuality* (Minneapolis)

Middleton, Richard 1990 *Studying Popular Music* (Philadelphia)

Miller, Jim 1980 (ed.) *The Rolling Stone Illustrated History of Rock and Roll* rev. edn. (New
> York)

Moore, Allan F. 1993 *Rock: The Primary Text* (Philadelphia)

Murray, Charles Shaar 1989 *Crosstown Traffic: Jimi Hendrix and the Rock 'n' Roll Revolution*
> (New York)

Negus, Keith 1996 *Popular Music in Theory: An Introduction* (Hanover, New Hampshire)

Otis, Johnny 1993 *Upside Your Head! Rhythm and Blues on Central Avenue* (Hanover, New Hampshire)

Palmer, Robert 1981 *Deep Blues* (New York)
  1995 *Rock & Roll: An Unruly History* (New York)

Peterson, Richard A. 1997 *Creating Country Music: Fabricating Authenticity* (Chicago)

Pichaske, David 1979 *A Generation in Motion: Popular Music and Culture in the Sixties* (New York)

Pielke, Robert G. 1986 *You Say You Want A Revolution: Rock Music in American Culture* (Chicago)

Pratt, Ray 1990 *Rhythm and Resistance: Explorations in the Political Uses of Popular Music* (New York)

Reynolds, Simon, and Press, Joy 1995 *The Sex Revolts: Gender, Rebellion, and Rock 'n' Roll* (Cambridge, Massachusetts)

Roberts, John Storm 1979 *The Latin Tinge: The Impact of Latin American Music on the United States* (New York)

Roman, Leslie G. 1988 "Intimacy, Labor, and Class: Ideologies of Feminine Sexuality in the Punk Slam Dance" in Leslie G. Roman, and Linda K. Christian-Smith (eds.) *Becoming Feminine: The Politics of Popular Culture* (London) pp. 143–184

Rose, Tricia 1994 *Black Noise: Rap Music and Black Culture in Contemporary America* (Hanover, New Hampshire)

Ross, Andrew, and Rose, Tricia 1994 (eds.) *Microphone Fiends: Youth Music and Youth Culture* (New York)

Sanjek, Russell, and Sanjek, David 1996 *Pennies from Heaven: The American Popular Music Business in the Twentieth Century* (New York)

Sexton, Adam 1995 (ed.) *Rap on Rap: Straight-Up Talk on Hip-Hop Culture* (New York)

Shank, Barry 1994 *Dissonant Identities: The Rock 'n' Roll Scene in Austin, Texas* (Hanover, New Hampshire)

Shepherd, John, Horn, David, Laing, Dave, Oliver, Paul, Tagg, Philip, Wicke, Peter, and Wilson, Jennifer 1997 (eds.) *Popular Music Studies: A Select International Bibliography* (London)

Shuker, Roy 1994 *Understanding Popular Music* (New York)

Small, Christopher 1987 *Music of the Common Tongue: Survival and Celebration in Afro-American Music* (New York)

Solt, Andrew 1995 *The History of Rock 'n' Roll [vol. 3]: Britain Invades, America Fights Back* (Warner Home Video)

Steinberg, Susan 1995 *The History of Rock 'n' Roll [vol. 4]: Plugging In* (Warner Home Video)

Steward, Sue, and Garratt, Sheryl 1984 *Signed, Sealed, and Delivered: True Life Stories of Women in Pop* (Boston)

Street, John 1986 *Rebel Rock: The Politics of Popular Music* (New York)

Szatmary, David P. 1996 *Rockin' in Time: A Social History of Rock and Roll* 3rd edn. (Englewood Cliffs, New Jersey)

Tagg, Philip 1982 "Analyzing Popular Music: Theory, Method, and Practice" in *Popular Music* vol. 2, pp. 37–67

Tate, Greg 1992 *Flyboy in the Buttermilk: Essays on Contemporary America* (New York)

Théberge, Paul 1997 *Any Sound You Can Imagine: Making Music/Consuming Technology* (Hanover, New Hampshire)

Thornton, Sarah 1996 *Club Cultures: Music, Media, and Subcultural Capital* (Hanover, New Hampshire)

Tichi, Cecelia 1994 *High Lonesome: The American Culture of Country Music* (Chapel Hill)

Toop, David 1991 *Rap Attack 2: African Rap to Global Hip Hop* (New York)

Tucker, Bruce 1989 "'Tell Tchaikovsky the News': Postmodernism, Popular Culture, and the Emergence of Rock 'n' Roll" in *Black Music Research Journal* vol. 9, no. 2, pp. 271–295

Walser, Robert 1993 *Running with the Devil: Power, Gender, and Madness in Heavy Metal Music* (Hanover, New Hampshire)

   1995 "Rhythm, Rhyme, and Rhetoric in the Music of Public Enemy" in *Ethnomusicology* vol. 39, no. 2, pp. 193–217

Ward, Ed, Stokes, Geoffrey, and Tucker, Ken 1986 *Rock of Ages: The Rolling Stone History of Rock & Roll* (New York)

Weinstein, Deena 1991 *Heavy Metal: A Cultural Sociology* (New York)

Weisbard, Eric, with Marks, Craig 1995 (eds.) *Spin Alternative Record Guide* (New York)

West, Cornel 1988 "On Afro-American Popular Music: From Bebop to Rap" in *Prophetic Fragments* (Grand Rapids, Michigan) pp. 177–187

Whitburn, Joel 1996 *The Billboard Book of Top 40 Country Hits* (New York)

Whiteley, Sheila 1992 *The Space Between the Notes: Rock and the Counter-Culture* (New York)

Wicke, Peter 1990 *Rock Music: Culture, Aesthetics, and Sociology* (Cambridge, England)

14 Ragtime and early jazz

Armstrong, Louis 1988a *Louis Armstrong – The Hot Fives, Vol. 1* (Columbia CK 44049)

   1988b *Louis Armstrong – The Hot Fives and Hot Sevens, Vol. 2* (Columbia CK 44253)

   1989a *Louis Armstrong – The Hot Fives and Hot Sevens, Vol. 3* (Columbia CK 44422)

   1989b *Louis Armstrong and Earl Hines, Vol. 4* (Columbia CK 45142)

   1990 *Louis in New York, Vol. 5* (Columbia CK 46148)

Badger, Reid 1995 *A Life in Ragtime: A Biography of James Reese Europe* (New York)

Bechet, Sidney 1960 *Treat It Gentle* (New York)

Bergreen, Laurence 1990 *As Thousands Cheer: The Life of Irving Berlin* (New York)

Berlin, Edward A. 1980 *Ragtime: A Musical and Cultural History* (Berkeley)

   1994 *King of Ragtime: Scott Joplin and His Era* (New York)

Blesh, Rudi 1946 *Shining Trumpets: A History of Jazz* (New York)

Blesh, Rudi, and Janis, Harriet 1950 *They All Played Ragtime* (New York)

Bordman, Gerald 1992 *American Musical Theatre: A Chronicle* 2nd edn. (New York)

Bushell, Garvin, and Tucker, Mark 1988 *Jazz from the Beginning* (Ann Arbor)

Collier, James Lincoln 1986 "Louis Armstrong" in *AmeriGrove* vol. 1, pp. 67–71

Crawford, Richard 1993 *The American Musical Landscape* (Berkeley)

Dapogny, James 1982 *Ferdinand "Jelly Roll" Morton: The Collected Piano Music* (Washington, D.C.)

DeVeaux, Scott, and Kenney, William Howland 1992 *The Music of James Scott* (Washington, D.C.)

Dodds, Baby, and Gara, Larry 1992 *The Baby Dodds Story* rev. edn. (Baton Rouge)

Ellington, Duke 1973 *Music Is My Mistress* (New York)
  1991 *The OKeh Ellington* (Columbia C2K 46177)
Finson, Jon W. 1994 *The Voices That Are Gone* (New York)
Floyd, Samuel 1995 *The Power of Black Music: Interpreting its History from Africa to the United States* (New York)
Furia, Philip 1992 *The Poets of Tin Pan Alley* (New York)
Gottlieb, Robert 1996 *Reading Jazz* (New York)
Gushee, Lawrence 1994 "The Nineteenth Century Origins of Jazz" in *Black Music Research Journal* vol. 14, no. 1, pp. 1–24
Hamm, Charles 1994 (ed.) *Irving Berlin: Early Songs* (3 vols.) (Madison)
  1995 *Putting Popular Music in Its Place* (Cambridge, England)
  1997 *Irving Berlin: Songs from the Melting Pot* (New York)
Harrison, Max 1976 *A Jazz Retrospect* (New York)
Hasse, John Edward 1985 *Ragtime: Its History, Composers, and Music* (New York)
Henderson, Fletcher 1994 *A Study in Frustration: The Fletcher Henderson Story* (Columbia 57596)
Hennessey, Thomas J. 1994 *From Jazz to Swing* (Detroit)
Joplin, Scott 1981 *Scott Joplin, the Complete Piano Works*, ed. Vera Brodsky Lawrence (New York)
Kenney, William Howland 1993 *Chicago Jazz* (New York)
Leach, William 1993 *Land of Desire* (New York)
Locke, Alain 1925 *The New Negro* (New York)
Lomax, Alan 1993 [1950] *Mister Jelly Roll: The Fortunes of Jelly Roll Morton, New Orleans Creole and "Inventor of Jazz"* (New York)
Machlin, Paul 1985 *Stride: The Music of Fats Waller* (Boston)
Marquis, Donald 1978 *In Search of Buddy Bolden* (Baton Rouge)
Morton, Jelly Roll 1990 *The Jelly Roll Morton Centennial: His Complete Victor Recordings* (Bluebird 2361-2-RB-A/CB)
Ogren, Kathy 1989 *The Jazz Revolution* (New York)
Panassié, Hugues 1960 *The Real Jazz* rev. edn. (New York)
Peretti, Burton 1992 *The Creation of Jazz* (Urbana)
Porter, Lewis, and Ullman, Michael 1993 *Jazz: From Its Origins to the Present* (Englewood Cliffs, New Jersey)
Ramsey, Frederick, Jr., and Smith, Charles Edward 1939 *Jazzmen* (New York)
Schafer, William J., and Riedel, Johannes 1973 *The Art of Ragtime* (Baton Rouge)
Schuller, Gunther 1968 *Early Jazz* (New York)
  1989 *The Swing Era: The Development of Jazz 1930–1945* (New York)
Seldes, Gilbert 1957 *The Seven Lively Arts* rev. edn. (New York)
Smith, Willie "the Lion," and Hoefer, George 1964 *Music on My Mind* (New York)
Smithsonian Collection of Big Band Jazz 1983 (Smithsonian DMM 6-0610)
Smithsonian Collection of Classic Jazz 1987 (Smithsonian RD 033 A5 19477)
Southern, Eileen 1983 [1971] (ed.) *Readings in Black American Music* 2nd edn. (New York)
Stearns, Marshall, and Stearns, Jean 1968 *Jazz Dance* (New York)
Stewart, Rex 1991 *Boy Meets Horn* (Ann Arbor)
Taylor, Jeffrey James 1993 *Earl Hines and Black Jazz Piano in Chicago, 1923–28* (Ann Arbor)

Tucker, Mark 1991 *Ellington, The Early Years* (Urbana)

    1993 *The Duke Ellington Reader* (New York)

Williams, Martin 1983 *The Jazz Tradition* rev. edn. (New York)

Witmark, Isadore, and Goldberg, Isaac 1939 [1976] *The Story of the House of Witmark* (New York)

15 Jazz from 1930 to 1960

Chambers, Jack 1985 *Milestones: The Music and Times of Miles Davis* (New York)

Coleman, Ornette 1993 *Beauty Is a Rare Thing: The Complete Atlantic Recordings* (Rhino Atlantic Jazz R2 71410)

Coltrane, John 1959 *Giant Steps* (Atlantic 1311)

    1964 *A Love Supreme* (Impulse MCA 5660)

Dahl, Linda 1984 *Stormy Weather: The Music and Lives of a Century of Jazzwomen* (New York)

Daryll, Ted 1992 Liner notes to recording of *Retrospective* (Capitol 7777973502)

Davis, Miles 1957 *Miles Ahead* (Columbia CK 40784)

    1958 *Porgy and Bess* (Columbia CK 40647)

    1959 *Kind of Blue* (Columbia PC 8163)

    1959 *Sketches of Spain* (Columbia PC 8271)

    1989 *Birth of the Cool* (Capitol Jazz CDP 7 92862 2)

DeVeaux, Scott 1988 "Bebop and the Recording Industry: The 1942 AFM Recording Ban Reconsidered" in *Journal of the American Musicological Society* vol. 41, no. 1, pp. 126–165

Ellington, Duke 1976 *Duke Ellington: An Explosion of Genius 1938–1940* (Smithsonian P6 15079 R 018)

    1991 *Reminiscing in Tempo* (Columbia CK 48654)

Esquire's World of Jazz 1962 Commentary by James Poling (New York)

Firestone, Ross 1993 *Swing, Swing, Swing: The Life and Times of Benny Goodman* (New York)

Friedwald, Will 1991 Liner notes to recording of Stan Kenton *The Complete Capitol Recordings of the Holman and Russo Charts* (Mosaic MD4–136)

Gillespie, Dizzy 1976 *Dizzy Gillespie: Development of an American Artist* (Smithsonian R 004 P 13454–5)

Gitler, Ira 1958 Liner notes to recording of John Coltrane *Soul Trane* (Prestige 7142)

Goldberg, Joe 1965 *Jazz Masters of the 50s* (New York)

Goodman, Benny 1950 *Benny Goodman at Carnegie Hall* (Columbia G2K-40244)

Hammond, John, with Townsend, Irving 1977 *John Hammond on Record* (New York)

Hawkins, Coleman 1980 *Allen and Hawkins* (Smithsonian R 022)

Henderson, Fletcher 1994 *A Study in Frustration: The Fletcher Henderson Story* (Columbia 57596)

Hentoff, Nat 1952 "Jazz Isn't Meant to Continue as Dance Music, Says Kenton" in *Down Beat* (August 27) p. 6

Hines, Earl (undated) *57 Varieties* (Sony/CBS 63364)

Hodeir, André 1956 *Jazz: Its Evolution and Essence* trans. David Noakes (New York)

Kenton, Stan *City of Glass: Stan Kenton Plays Bob Graettinger* (Capitol Jazz
      7243 8 32084 2 5)
Lomax, Alan 1993 [1950] *Mister Jelly Roll: The Fortunes of Jelly Roll Morton, New Orleans
      Creole and "Inventor of Jazz"* (New York)
Mingus, Charles 1992 *Let My Children Hear Music* (Columbia CK 48910)
Moten, Bennie (undated) *Kansas City Style: Count Basie* (RCA AFM1-5180)
Owens, Thomas 1995 *Bebop* (New York)
Palmer, Robert 1995 Liner notes to recording of *Beauty Is a Rare Thing* (Atlantic Jazz
      R2 71410)
Pearson, Nathan 1987 *Goin' to Kansas City* (Urbana)
Placksin, Sally 1990 *American Women in Jazz: 1900 to the Present* (New York)
Porter, Lewis, and Ullman, Michael 1993 *Jazz: From Its Origins to the Present* (New York)
Priestley, Brian 1991 *Jazz On Record: A History* (New York)
Sales, Grover 1984 *Jazz: America's Classical Music* (New York)
Schuller, Gunther 1968 *Early Jazz* (New York)
      1989 *The Swing Era: The Development of Jazz 1930-1945* (New York)
Smithsonian Collection of Classic Jazz 1987 (Smithsonian RD 033 A5 19477)
Sweet and Low Blues: Big Bands and Territory Bands in the 1920s 1977 (New World NW256)
Tatum, Art undated *Piano Starts Here* (Columbia CS 9655)
Thomas, J. C. 1977 *Chasin' the Trane* (New York)
Waller, Fats 1991 *The Fats Waller Piano Solos: Turn on the Heat* (Bluebird 2482-2-RB)
Wilson, Teddy 1973 *Teddy Wilson and His All-Stars* (Columbia KG 31617)

16 Jazz since 1960

Abrams, Muhal Richard 1967 *Levels and Degrees of Light* (Delmark DS413)
Art Ensemble of Chicago (see Mitchell, Roscoe)
Ayler, Albert 1964 *New York Ear and Eye Control* (ESP 1016)
Bou-Khalil, Rabih 1992 *Blue Camel* (Enja ENJ-7053 2)
Braxton, Anthony 1974 *New York Fall 1974* (Arista AL4032)
Byron, Don 1992 *Tuskegee Experiments* (Elektra Nonesuch 79280-2)
Coleman, Ornette 1959 *The Shape of Jazz to Come* (Atlantic 1317)
      1960 *Free Jazz* (Atlantic 1364)
Coltrane, John 1965 *Ascension* (Impulse A95)
Conroy, Frank 1995 "The New Jazz Age" in *New York Times Magazine* (June 25)
      pp. 27-33
Davis, Anthony 1989 *X: The Life and Times of Malcolm X. An Opera in Three Acts*
      (Gramavision R2-79470)
Davis, Clive 1995 "No Room Today for Specialists" in *The [London] Times* (June 28) p. 38
Davis, Francis 1986 *In the Moment: Jazz in the 1980s* (New York)
Davis, Miles 1969 *Bitches Brew* (Columbia J2C 40577)
Dibango, Manu 1994 *Three Kilos of Coffee: An Autobiography* (in collaboration with
      Danielle Rouard) trans. Beth G. Raps (Chicago)
Ellison, Ralph 1972 "The Golden Age, Time Past" in *Shadow and Act* (New York)
      pp. 199-212

Feld, Steven 1996 "Pygmy Pop. A Genealogy of Schizophonic Mimesis" in *Yearbook for Traditional Music* vol. 28, pp. 1–35

Guryan, Margo 1961 Liner notes to recording of Max Roach *Percussion Bitter Sweet* (Impulse AS-8)

Heckman, Don 1967 "New Jazz" in *Down Beat* (February 9) pp. 24–25

Hodeir, André 1956 *Jazz: Its Evolution and Essence* trans. David Noakes (New York)

Jones, LeRoi 1967 *Black Music* (New York)

Jost, Ekkehard 1974 *Free Jazz* (Graz, Austria)

Lees, Gene 1960 "Report on Chicago" in *Down Beat* (February 18) pp. 18–21

Litweiler, John 1992 *Ornette Coleman: A Harmolodic Life* (New York)

Logan, Giuseppe 1964 *Giuseppi Logan Quartet* (ESP 1007)

Mahavishnu Orchestra 1971 *Inner Mounting Flame* (Columbia KC31067)

Marek, Georg 1956 "From the Dive to the Dean, Jazz becomes Respectable" in *Good Housekeeping* (June) pp. 120–124

Marsalis, Wynton 1982 *Think of One* (Columbia EC38641)

Martin, Terry 1967 "Blowing out in Chicago: Roscoe Mitchell" in *Down Beat* (April 6) pp. 20–21

McMichael, Robert K. 1996 "Consuming Jazz: Black Music and Whiteness" (unpubl. diss.; Brown University)

Mingus, Charles 1963 *The Black Saint and the Sinner Lady* (Impulse 35)

Mitchell, Roscoe Sextet 1966 *Sound* (Delmark DS-408)

Monson, Ingrid 1996 *Saying Something: Jazz Improvisation and Interaction* (Chicago)

Nicholson, Stuart 1990 *Jazz. The 1980s Resurgence* (New York)

Radano, Ronald M. 1993 *New Musical Figurations: Anthony Braxton's Cultural Critique* (Chicago)

Robinson, J. Bradford 1988 "Free Jazz" in Barry Kernfeld (ed.) *The New Grove Dictionary of Jazz* (London) vol. 1, pp. 404–405

Roach, Max 1960 *We Insist! Freedom Now Suite* (Candid 8002)

Sun Ra 1976 *Live at Montreux* (Inner City 1039)

Taylor, Cecil 1966 *Unit Structures* (Blue Note BLP4237)

Tomlinson, Gary 1991 "Cultural Dialogics and Jazz: A White Historian Signifies" in *Black Music Research Journal* vol. 11, no. 2, pp. 229–264

Tynan, John 1962 "Record Reviews" in *Down Beat* (June 18) p. 28

Weather Report 1972 *I Sing the Body Electric* (Columbia KC31352)

Williams, Martin 1970 *The Jazz Tradition* (New York)

Wilmer, Valerie 1977 *As Serious as Your Life: The Story of the New Jazz* (London)

17 Tonal traditions in art music from 1920 to 1960

Alpert, Hollis 1990 *The Life and Times of Porgy and Bess: The Story of an American Classic* (New York)

Ardoin, John 1985 *The Stages of Menotti* (Garden City, New York)

Arvey, Verna 1984 *In One Lifetime* (Fayetteville, Arkansas)

Babbitt, Milton 1958 "Who Cares if You Listen?" in *High Fidelity* vol. 8, no. 2, pp. 38–40, 126–127, repr. in Gilbert Chase (ed.) *The American Composer Speaks* (Baton Rouge, 1966) pp. 235–244

Benser, Caroline C. 1991 *Randall Thompson: A Bio-Bibliography* (New York)

Berger, Arthur 1953 *Aaron Copland* (New York)

Broder, Nathan 1954 *Samuel Barber* (New York)

Bumgardner, Thomas A. 1986 *Norman Dello Joio* (Boston)

Butterworth, Neil 1985 *The Music of Aaron Copland* (London)

Copland, Aaron 1952 *Music and Imagination* (Cambridge, Massachusetts)
 1960 *Copland on Music* (New York)
 1968 *The New Music 1900–1960* (New York)

Copland, Aaron, and Perlis, Vivian 1984 *Copland: 1900 Through 1942* (New York)
 1989 *Copland: Since 1943* (New York)

Crawford, Richard 1979 "Gershwin's Reputation: A Note on *Porgy and Bess*" in *Musical Quarterly* vol. 65, no. 2, pp. 257–264

Floyd, Samuel A., Jr. 1990 (ed.) *Black Music in the Harlem Renaissance: A Collection of Essays* (Westport, Connecticut)

Gilbert, Steven E. 1995 *The Music of Gershwin* (New Haven)

Grieb, Lyndal 1974 *The Operas of Gian Carlo Menotti, 1937–1972: A Selective Bibliography* (Metuchen, New Jersey)

Gruen, John 1978 *Menotti: A Biography* (New York)

Hamm, Charles 1987 "The Theater Guild Production of *Porgy and Bess*" in *Journal of the American Musicological Society* vol. 40, no. 3, pp. 495–532

Hennessee, Don A. 1985 *Samuel Barber: A Bio-Bibliography* (Westport, Connecticut)

Heyman, Barbara B. 1992 *Samuel Barber: The Composer and His Music* (New York)

Hoover, Kathleen, and Cage, John 1959 *Virgil Thomson: His Life and Music* (New York)

Horowitz, Joseph 1987 *Understanding Toscanini: How He Became an American Culture-God and Helped Create a New Audience for Old Music* (New York)

Jablonski, Edward 1987 *Gershwin* (New York)

Kimberling, Victoria J. 1987 *David Diamond: A Bio-Bibliography* (Metuchen, New Jersey)

Kushner, David 1988 *Ernest Bloch: A Guide to Research* (New York)

Meckna, Michael 1986 *Virgil Thomson: A Bio-Bibliography* (Westport, Connecticut)

O'Connor, Joan 1994 *John Alden Carpenter: A Bio-Bibliography* (Westport, Connecticut)

Oja, Carol J. 1990 *Colin McPhee: Composer in Two Worlds* (Washington, D.C.)
 1992 "'New Music' and the 'New Negro': The Background of William Grant Still's *Afro-American Symphony*" in *Black Music Research Journal* vol. 12, no. 2, pp. 145–169
 1994 "Gershwin and American Modernists of the 1920s" in *Musical Quarterly* vol. 78, no. 4, pp. 646–668

Patterson, Donald L., and Patterson, Janet L. 1988 *Vincent Persichetti: A Bio-Bibliography* (New York)

Perone, James E. 1993 *Howard Hanson: A Bio-Bibliography* (Westport, Connecticut)

Pollack, Howard 1981 *Walter Piston* (Ann Arbor)
 1995 *Skyscraper Lullaby: The Life and Music of John Alden Carpenter* (Washington, D.C.)

Rosenberg, Deena 1991 *Fascinating Rhythm: The Collaboration of George and Ira Gershwin* (New York)

Rouse, Christopher 1980 *William Schuman Documentary: Biographical Essay, Catalogue of Works, Discography, and Bibliography* (New York)

Schreiber, Flora R., and Persichetti, Vincent 1954 *William Schuman* (New York)

Shirley, Wayne D. 1974 *"Porgy and Bess"* in *The Quarterly Journal of the Library of Congress* vol. 31, no. 2, pp. 97–107

Skowronski, JoAnn 1985 *Aaron Copland: A Bio-Bibliography* (Westport, Connecticut)

Slomski, Monica J. 1994 *Paul Creston: A Bio-Bibliography* (Westport, Connecticut)

Smith, Julia F. 1955 *Aaron Copland: His Work and Contribution to American Music* (New York)

Starr, Lawrence [Larry] 1981 "Copland's Style" in *Perspectives of New Music* vol. 19, nos. 1 & 2, pp. 68–89

1984 "Toward a Reevaluation of Gershwin's *Porgy and Bess*" in *American Music* vol. 2, no. 2, pp. 25–37

Stehman, Dan 1984 *Roy Harris: An American Musical Pioneer* (Boston)

1991 *Roy Harris: A Bio-Bibliography* (New York)

Still, Judith A. 1995 (ed.) *William Grant Still and the Fusion of Cultures in American Music* 2nd edn. (Flagstaff, Arizona)

Still, Judith A., Dabrishus, Michael J., and Quin, Carolyn L. 1996 *William Grant Still: A Bio-Bibliography* (Westport, Connecticut)

Thomson, Virgil 1935 "George Gershwin" in *Modern Music* vol. 13, no. 1, pp. 13–19

1966 *Virgil Thomson* (New York)

1971 *American Music Since 1910* (New York)

1981 *A Virgil Thomson Reader* (New York)

1989 *Music with Words: A Composer's View* (New Haven)

Tommasini, Anthony C. 1985 *Virgil Thomson's Musical Portraits* (New York)

Westergaard, Peter 1968 "Conversation with Walter Piston" in *Perspectives of New Music* vol. 7, no. 1, pp. 3–17, repr. in Benjamin Boretz, and Edward T. Cone (eds.) 1971 *Perspectives on American Composers* (New York) pp. 156–170

Wittke, Paul 1996 "Vignettes of his Life and Times" in *Virgil Thomson Centennial Catalogue* [The Virgil Thomson Foundation, U.S.A.] pp. 1–48

18 Serialism and complexity

anon. 1961 "2 Cycles Listed by Philharmonic: Bernstein to Lead 'Gallic and Teutonic Approach'" in *New York Times* (September 8) p. 36

Aldrich, Richard 1923a "The New York Symphony" in *New York Times* (February 5) p. 18

1923b "Some Judgments on New Music" in *New York Times* (February 11) sec. 7, p. 3

Babbitt, Milton 1946 "The Function of Set Structure in the Twelve-Tone System" (unpubl. diss.; Princeton University)

1955 "Some Aspects of Twelve-Tone Composition" in *The Score and I.M.A. Magazine* vol. 12, pp. 53–61

Backus, John 1962 "Die Reihe: A Scientific Evaluation" in *Perspectives of New Music* vol. 1, no. 1, pp. 160–171

Boulez, Pierre 1952 "Schönberg is Dead" in *The Score* no. 6, pp. 18–22

Carter, Elliott 1971 "Expressionism and American Music" in Benjamin Boretz and Edward T. Cone (eds.) *Perspectives on American Composers* (New York) pp. 217–229

1996 *Elliott Carter: Collected Essays and Lectures, 1937–1995* ed. Jonathan W. Bernard (Rochester)

Casella, Alfredo 1924 "Schoenberg in Italy" in *Modern Music* vol. 1, no. 1, pp. 7–10

Cowell, Henry 1930 *New Musical Resources* (New York; republ. 1969, New York; republ. 1996, Cambridge, England)

Geiger, Roger L. 1986 *To Advance Knowledge: The Growth of American Research Universities, 1900–1940* (Oxford)

Griffiths, Paul 1980 "Serialism" in Stanley Sadie (ed.) *The New Grove Dictionary of Music and Musicians* (London) vol. 17, pp. 162–169

Huneker, James 1913 "Schoenberg, Musical Anarchist Who Has Upset Music" in *New York Times* (January 19) sec. 5, p. 9

Kolodin, Irving 1934 "American Composers and the Phonograph" in *Modern Music* vol. 11, no. 3, pp. 128–137

Lang, Paul Henry 1960 "Editorial" in *Musical Quarterly* vol. 46, no. 2, pp. 145–154

LaRue, Jan 1962 (ed.) *Report of the Eighth Congress: New York 1961* (2 vols.) (Basle)

Mead, Andrew 1994 *An Introduction to the Music of Milton Babbitt* (Princeton)

Olmstead, Andrea 1985 *Roger Sessions and his Music* (Ann Arbor)

1987 *Conversations with Roger Sessions* (Boston)

Perle, George 1962 *Serial Composition and Atonality: An Introduction to the Music of Schoenberg, Berg, and Webern* (Berkeley)

1977 *Twelve-Tone Tonality* (Berkeley)

1990 *The Listening Composer* (Berkeley)

Peyser, Joan 1969 "A Fighter From Way Back" in *New York Times* (March 9) sec. 2, p. 19

Salzman, Eric 1961 "Music: Three Distinguished Works" in *New York Times* (September 7) p. 41

Schiff, David 1983 *The Music of Elliott Carter* (London)

Sessions, Roger 1979 "Schoenberg in the United States" in Edward T. Cone (ed.) *Roger Sessions on Music: Collected Essays* (Princeton) pp. 353–369

Stefan, Paul 1925 "Schoenberg's Operas" in *Modern Music* vol. 2, no. 1, pp. 12–15

Toop, Richard 1974 "Messiaen/Goeyvaerts, Fano/Stockhausen, Boulez" in *Perspectives of New Music* vol. 11, no. 1, pp. 141–169

Weissman, Adolph 1924 "Race and Modernity" in *Modern Music* vol. 1, no. 1, pp. 3–6

19 Avant-garde and experimental music

Burkholder, J. Peter 1985 *Charles Ives: The Ideas Behind the Music* (New Haven)

1990 "Charles Ives the Avant-Gardist, Charles Ives the Traditionalist" in Klaus Wolfgang Niemölle (ed.) *Bericht über das Internationale Symposion "Charles Ives und die amerikanische Musiktradition bis zur Gegenwart" Köln 1988 (Kölner Beiträge zur Musikforschung* vol. 164) (Regensburg) pp. 37–51

1995 *All Made of Tunes: Charles Ives and the Uses of Musical Borrowing* (New Haven)

Cage, John 1961 *Silence* (Middletown, Connecticut)

1967 *A Year from Monday* (Middletown, Connecticut)

1981 *For the Birds* (London)

Cowell, Henry 1930 *New Musical Resources* (New York; republ. 1969, New York; republ. 1996, Cambridge, England)

1933a (ed.) *American Composers on American Music* (Palo Alto, California; republ. 1962, New York)

1933b "Towards Neo-Primitivism" in *Modern Music* vol. 10, no. 3, pp. 149–153

Cowell, Henry, and Cowell, Sidney 1955 *Charles Ives and his Music* (New York)

DeLio, Thomas 1984 *Circumscribing the Open Universe* (Lanham, Maryland)

1996 (ed.) *The Music of Morton Feldman* (New York)

Duckworth, William 1995 *Talking Music* (New York)

Farneth, David 1986 "La Monte Young" in *AmeriGrove* vol. 4, pp. 579–581

Feder, Stuart 1992 *Charles Ives: "My Father's Song"* (New Haven)

Feldman, Morton 1985 *Essays* ed. Walter Zimmermann (Kerpen)

Gagne, Cole 1993 *Soundpieces 2: Interviews with American Composers* (Metuchen, New Jersey)

Gagne, Cole, and Caras, Tracy 1982 *Soundpieces: Interviews with American Composers* (Metuchen, New Jersey)

Gann, Kyle 1993 "La Monte Young's *The Well-Tuned Piano*" in *Perspectives of New Music* vol. 31, no. 3, pp. 134–162

1995 *The Music of Conlon Nancarrow* (Cambridge, England)

Garland, Peter 1982 *Americas: Essays on American Music and Culture* (Santa Fe)

1987 (ed.) *A Lou Harrison Reader* (Santa Fe)

1991 *In Search of Silvestre Revueltas: Essays 1978–1990* (Santa Fe)

Gillespie, Don 1986 (ed.) *George Crumb: Profile of a Composer* (New York)

Glass, Philip 1987 *Music by Philip Glass* ed. Robert T. Jones (New York)

Goldberg, RoseLee 1988 *Performance Art: From Futurism to the Present* (London)

Griffiths, Paul 1980 "Avant garde" in Stanley Sadie (ed.) *The New Grove Dictionary of Music and Musicians* (London) vol. 1, pp. 742–743

1981 *Cage* (Oxford)

Harley, Maria Anna 1997 "An American in Space: Henry Brant's 'Spatial Music'" in *American Music* vol. 15, no. 1, pp. 70–92

Hitchcock, H. Wiley 1977 *Ives* (London)

Holloway, Robin 1989 "Modernism and After in Music" in *The Cambridge Review* vol. 110, pp. 60–66

Ives, Charles 1972 *Memos* ed. John Kirkpatrick (New York)

James, Richard S. 1987 "ONCE: Microcosm of the 1960s Musical and Multimedia Avant-Garde" in *American Music* vol. 5, no. 4, pp. 359–390

Kostelanetz, Richard 1971 (ed.) *John Cage* (London)

1988 (ed.) *Conversing with Cage* (New York)

1992 "A Conversation, in Eleven-Minus-One Parts, with Lou Harrison about Music/Theater" in *Musical Quarterly* vol. 76, no. 3, pp. 383–409

Lichtenwanger, William 1986 *The Music of Henry Cowell: A Descriptive Catalog* (Brooklyn, New York)

Manion, Martha L. 1982 *Writings about Henry Cowell: An Annotated Bibliography* (Brooklyn, New York)

Mead, Rita H. 1978 *Henry Cowell's New Music, 1925–1936* (Ann Arbor)

Mertens, Wim 1983 *American Minimal Music* (London)

Nattiez, Jean-Jacques 1993 (ed.) *The Boulez–Cage Correspondence* (Cambridge, England)

Nicholls, David 1990 *American Experimental Music, 1890–1940* (Cambridge, England)

1996 "Transethnicism and the American Experimental Tradition" in *Musical Quarterly* vol. 80, no. 4, pp. 569–594

1997 (ed.) *The Whole World of Music: A Henry Cowell Symposium* (Amsterdam)

Nyman, Michael 1974 *Experimental Music – Cage and Beyond* (London)

Ouellette, Fernand 1968 *Edgard Varèse* (New York)

Partch, Harry 1974 *Genesis of a Music* (New York)

1991 *Bitter Music* ed. Thomas McGeary (Urbana)

Patterson, David 1994 "Cage and Beyond: An Annotated Interview with Christian Wolff" in *Perspectives of New Music* vol. 32, no. 2, pp. 54–87

Perlis, Vivian 1986 "Pro-Musica Society" in *AmeriGrove* vol. 3, pp. 633–634

Pescatello, Ann M. 1992 *Charles Seeger: A Life in American Music* (Pittsburgh)

Pritchett, James 1993 *The Music of John Cage* (Cambridge, England)

Reich, Steve 1974 *Writings about Music* (Halifax, Nova Scotia)

Rockwell, John 1985 *All American Music* (London)

1986 "Experimental music" in *AmeriGrove* vol. 2, pp. 91–95

Saylor, Bruce 1977 *The Writings of Henry Cowell: A Descriptive Bibliography* (Brooklyn, New York)

1986 "Henry Cowell" in *AmeriGrove* vol. 1, pp. 520–529

Schrader, Barry 1986 "Electroacoustic music" in *AmeriGrove* vol. 2, pp. 30–35

Schwartz, K. Robert 1996 *Minimalists* (London)

Seeger, Charles 1940 "Henry Cowell" in *Magazine of Art* vol. 33, no. 5, pp. 288–289, 322–323

1994 *Studies in Musicology II: 1929–1979* ed. Ann M. Pescatello (Berkeley)

Straus, Joseph N. 1995 *The Music of Ruth Crawford Seeger* (Cambridge, England)

Strickland, Edward 1991 *American Composers – Dialogues on Contemporary Music* (Bloomington)

1993 *Minimalism: Origins* (Bloomington)

Taylor, Timothy D. 1993 "The Gendered Construction of the Musical Self: The Music of Pauline Oliveros" in *Musical Quarterly* vol. 77, no. 3, pp. 385–396

Tick, Judith 1997 *Ruth Crawford Seeger – A Composer's Search for American Music* (New York)

Varèse, Louise 1972 *Varèse–A Looking-Glass Diary* (New York)

Von Gunden, Heidi 1983 *The Music of Pauline Oliveros* (Metuchen, New Jersey)

1995 *The Music of Lou Harrison* (Metuchen, New Jersey)

Ziffrin, Marilyn 1994 *Carl Ruggles: Composer, Painter, and Storyteller* (Urbana)

Zimmermann, Walter 1976 *Desert Plants: Conversations with Twenty-three American Musicians* (Vancouver)

20 Tonal traditions in art music since 1960

Albright, William 1971 Liner notes to recording of William Bolcom *Black Host* (Nonesuch H-71260)

Bernard, Jonathan W. 1995 "Theory, Analysis, and the 'Problem' of Minimal Music" in
　　Elizabeth W. Marvin, and Richard Hermann (eds.) *Concert Music, Rock, and Jazz
　　since 1945: Essays and Analytical Studies* (Rochester) pp. 259–284
Bernstein, Leonard 1976 *The Unanswered Question* (Norton Lectures, 1973) (Cambridge,
　　Massachusetts)
　　1982 *Findings* (New York)
Block, Steven 1982/1983 "George Rochberg: Progressive or Master Forger?" in
　　Perspectives of New Music vol. 21, pp. 407–409
Bolcom, William 1974 Liner notes to recording of *Frescoes* (Nonesuch H71297)
　　1976 Liner notes to recording of *Commedia* and *Open House* (Nonesuch H-71324)
　　1988 Liner notes to recording of *Twelve New Etudes* (New World NW354-2)
Duckworth, William 1995 *Talking Music* (New York)
Dufallo, Richard 1989 "David Del Tredici" in *Trackings: Composers Speak with Richard
　　Dufallo* (New York and Oxford) pp. 157–170
Glass, Philip 1987 *Music by Philip Glass* ed. Robert T. Jones (New York)
Gottlieb, Jack 1991 Liner notes to recording of Leonard Bernstein Concerto for
　　Orchestra (*Jubilee Games*) (Deutsche Grammophon 429-231-2)
Harbison, John 1992 Published score of *November 19, 1828* (New York)
Hovhaness, Alan undated Liner notes to recording of Symphony No. 4 (Mercury MG-
　　50366)
Humphrey, Mary Lou 1992 Conversation with Richard Danielpour in liner notes to
　　recording of *Urban Dances* and other works (Koch 3-7100-2H1)
Kendall, Christopher 1987 Conversation with Stephen Albert in liner notes to
　　recording of *Flower of the Mountain* and *Into Eclipse* (Elektra Nonesuch 9-79153-2)
Kennicott, Philip 1991 Liner notes to recording of *Michael Torke's Color Music* (Argo 433
　　071-2)
Kramer, Jonathan D. 1984 "Can Modernism Survive George Rochberg?" in *Critical
　　Inquiry* vol. 11, pp. 341–354
Lerdahl, Fred 1990 Liner notes to recording of *Wake* and other works (CRI CD-580)
Lerdahl, Fred, and Jackendoff, Ray 1983 *A Generative Theory of Tonal Music* (Cambridge,
　　Massachusetts)
Porter, Andrew 1987 "Tumult of Mighty Harmonies" in *Musical Events: A Chronicle,
　　1980–83* (New York) pp. 464–470
　　1989 "Child Mabel" in *Musical Events: A Chronicle, 1983–86* (New York) pp. 496–501
Reich, Steve 1974 *Writings about Music* (Halifax, Nova Scotia)
Reise, Jay 1980/1981 "Rochberg the Progressive" in *Perspectives of New Music* vol. 19,
　　pp. 395–407
Rochberg, George 1972 Published score of *Music for the Magic Theater: For a Chamber
　　Ensemble of Fifteen Players* (Bryn Mawr, Pennsylvania)
　　1984a "Tradition and Twelve-Tone Music" [1955] and "On the Third String
　　Quartet" [1974] in William Bolcom (ed.) *The Aesthetics of Survival: A Composer's
　　View of Twentieth-Century Music* (Ann Arbor) pp. 29–45 and 239–242 respectively
　　1984b "Can the Arts Survive Modernism?" in *Critical Inquiry* vol. 11, pp. 317–340
Rorem, Ned 1983 *The Paris and New York Diaries of Ned Rorem, 1951–1961* (San
　　Francisco)

Ryang, Michelle 1996 Conversation with Michael Torke in liner notes to recording of
 Javelin and other works (Argo 452 101-2)

Salzman, Eric 1974 *Twentieth-Century Music: An Introduction* 2nd edn. (Englewood Cliffs,
 New Jersey)

Schiff, David 1993 "Re-Hearing Bernstein" in *The Atlantic Monthly* vol. 271, no. 6, pp.
 55-76

Schwantner, Joseph 1978 Published score of *Diaphonia Intervallum* (New York)

Smith, Steven C. 1989 Liner notes to recording of Stephen Albert *TreeStone* (Delos DE-
 3059)

Strickland, Edward 1991 *American Composers: Dialogues on Contemporary Music*
 (Bloomington)

Swed, Mark 1992 Liner notes to recording of Aaron Jay Kernis *Symphony in Waves* and
 String Quartet (*musica celestis*) (Argo 436 287-2)

Wason, Robert W. 1988 "Tonality and Atonality in Frederic Rzewski's *The People United
 Will Never Be Defeated*" in *Perspectives of New Music* vol. 26, no. 1, pp. 108-143

Zwilich, Ellen Taaffe 1983 Published score of Symphony No. 1 (*Three Movements for
 Orchestra*) (Newton Centre, Massachusetts)

Index